MW01697529

Pursuing

Perfect Service

Using a Practical Approach to Lean Six Sigma to Improve the Customer Experience and Reduce Costs in Service Industries

Rob Ptacek and Jaideep Motwani, Ph.D.

ISBN 978-1-4507-6633-3

07 06 05 04 03 5 4 3 2 1

MCS Media, Inc.
888 Ridge Road
Chelsea, MI 48118
United States of America
Telephone 734-475-4301
E-mail: info@theleanstore.com

Cover concept and art direction: William Callaghan
Page design: Janice McKinley
Content edit: Emma Tinsley

Library of Congress Cataloging-in-Publication Data

This publication is designed to provide the most up-to-date, accurate, and authoritative information for the improvement of administrative processes and practices. It is sold with the understanding that neither the authors, editors, nor the publisher are engaged in providing legal, accounting, or other professional service. If legal advice or other expert assistance is required, the services of a competent professional consultant should be sought.

Message

This book is dedicated to the growing legions of service organizations, providers, and people serving in service industries around the world. As the global economy evolves, the service sector will provide fertile ground for leaders and workers in all facets of service to reduce waste by using a systematic approach to continuous improvement. This book is for those who wish to lead the change to improved service delivery, and is intended to provide a foundation and process to facilitate such improvement in pursuit of "perfect service."

Table of Contents

Part Two. Beginning the Lean Sigma for Service Excellence Journey

Chapter 3 - Understanding the Lean Sigma for Service Excellence Journey

Part Three. Deploying the Lean Sigma for Service Excellence Improvement Process

Chapter 4 - Define Phase

Chapter 5 - Measure Phase

Chapter 6 - Analyze Phase

Part Four. Putting It All Together to Achieve and Sustain Lean Sigma for Service Excellence

Chapter 9 - Sustainability (or Becoming Green)

Chapter 10 - Transformation Case Study

Appendix

Publisher's Message

We are excited to present this book defining a simple, step-by-step approach to applying the tools and concepts of Lean within the Six Sigma methodology to the Service Sector. We struggled with highlighting "perfection" in the title when we ourselves are humbled by errors and waste in our own processes. In the end, we agreed that we will always be in pursuit of perfection and believe all Lean Sigma organizations are.

We have witnessed great success of Lean and Six Sigma methods and tools in the manufacturing sector and believe that these methods and tools can be directly translated to great success for service organizations. We sincerely hope that service organizations in areas such as government, education, security, contract services, entertainment, event planning, hospitality, lodging, food service, healthcare, financial and professional services, retail, construction, and any other service find value in this approach. We believe that leaders and managers who desire to remain in business and drive profitable growth in the 21st century will use this book as the basis for business improvement and transformation. This book will assist organization executives, human resource managers, training managers, continuous improvement coordinators, team leaders, managers, and client contact level service providers to improve service flow and customer satisfaction, while increasing productivity and improving the bottom-line.

We would like to thank the authors of the numerous outstanding books that have already been written on this topic of Lean, Six Sigma, and Lean Sigma. Even though the Lean Sigma tools and the structured methodology discussed in these publications are similar, we believe our focus on case reviews and real-world applications makes our book unique from the others. In this book, we discuss in detail and review numerous actual examples from service organizations that the authors have personally assisted in their improvement efforts. In addition, we also present a comprehensive and detailed start-to-finish case that illustrates a step-by-step process for a service organization's transformation from a traditional service organization to a Lean Sigma service organization. Throughout the book, we have provided straight-forward listings and extensive examples of Lean Sigma methods, tools, and steps to facilitate service organizations in the proper selection and use or application of each Lean Sigma tool or method.

Service providers are faced with literally thousands of transactions and client interactions a day, and must quickly and effectively identify client needs and expectations, determine how to best satisfy their needs, and how to do so at the lowest possible cost. *Pursuing Perfect Service* provides insight into the real-life challenges faced day-to-day by all types of service providers. Chapters 1 - 3 provide a solid foundation upon which Lean Sigma concepts, methods, and tools can be applied in the service sector. Chapters 4 - 9 provide a step-by-step guide for Lean Sigma tool application in the service environments. Chapter 10 details a step-by-step approach for total organizational Lean Sigma transformation.

This book can be used as a full Lean Sigma transformation guide or simply a tool application reference source for implementing a form of continuous improvement. Chapter summaries, worksheets, actual work-related examples, and case reviews are used to assist readers in improving the customer experience and service flows for their organization.

We intentionally designed several distinctive features into this book to enable readers to find applicable examples and tools that fit their particular need, and make the best, most effective use of the information. The distinctive features are:

- Non-technical "jargon" and applicability to all service sectors
- Simple, straightforward approach to applying Lean Sigma methods and tools
- Total system and results focused approach
- Extensive use of examples and case reviews from various service industries
- Simple Lean Sigma tools definitions and applications
- Case reviews and real life applications
- Readiness Guides and Assessments to check for understanding and readiness to move forward
- Comprehensive real-world Lean Sigma organizational transformation case study review
- Detailed Lean Sigma for Service Excellent Assessment and Gap Analysis

Leveraging the great success of the Lean Sigma approach from manufacturing sectors, and now, after extensive work with service organizations, we are certain that the Lean Sigma methods and tools apply equally as well in service environments. Research supports this assertion, as many service organizations are currently using Lean Sigma techniques. There is no "status quo" in today's fast-paced world. Don't fall behind. Begin your Lean Sigma journey today by studying and applying the tools, methods, and practices contained in *Pursuing Perfect Service*!

Don Tapping

Note to Black Belts and Lean Senseis

This book bridges the gap between a highly quantitative analysis of a process that requires extensive training (i.e., a Black Belt certification level) and a more simplified approach that can be used and understood by the masses. The goal of this book is to make the methods and tools of Six Sigma and Lean accessible to more people and take a common sense approach to problem solving and continuous improvement. *Pursuing Perfect Service* is intended to be used by Black Belts, Lean Senseis, Continuous Improvement Specialists, managers and supervisors of departments and work groups, and improvement team members, etc. in their efforts to improve the overall service experience within their organization.

There are over 100 different types of tools, including charts, graphs, various types of worksheets available in the continuous improvement "bag." In *Pursuing Perfect Service* we have taken the 50+ most common tools that have been used over the years by these two authors and are presenting them in a standard way in which the information can be used to assist you in your improvement activities.

Author's Bios

Rob Ptacek
President and CEO, Competitive Edge Training and Consulting
Partner, Global Lean Institute, LLC

Mr. Ptacek is a Partner in the Global Lean Institute and President and CEO of Competitive Edge Training and Consulting, a firm specializing in leader and organizational development, and Lean Enterprise transformations. He is an Approved Scanlon Leadership Network Consultant. Mr. Ptacek holds a BS in Metallurgical Engineering from Michigan Technological University, Houghton, MI (USA), and a Masters of Management from Aquinas College, Grand Rapids, MI (USA).

Mr. Ptacek is an adjunct instructor of Management Principles, Manufacturing Strategy, and Total Quality Management, and has instructed at Grand Valley State University, Aquinas College, Davenport University, and currently instructs in the Lean Champion Certification program at Grand Rapids Community College. Mr. Ptacek has an extensive client list and has provided Lean and Leadership training and consulting in North America, Asia, and Europe.

Mr. Ptacek has held leadership positions in Quality, Sales, and Operations Management, and has over 25 years of practical experience implementing continuous improvements in a variety of industries. He speaks on leadership and continuous improvement topics for several industry associations including the Precision Metal Forming Association (PMA), Society of Manufacturing Engineering (SME), American Society for Quality (ASQ), American Mold Builders Association (AMBA), and the Scanlon Leadership Network (SLN).

Mr. Ptacek's email address is ptacek@i2k.com.

Jaideep Motwani, Ph.D.
Chairperson and Professor of Management
Seidman College of Business
Grand Valley State University

Dr. Jaideep Motwani is Chair and Professor of Management at the Seidman College of Business, Grand Valley State University since 2000. He is also the E. Seidman Endowed Chair of Management. He received his Ph.D. in Operations Management from University of North Texas. He has co-authored a book entitled "Classics in Operations Management," and published more than 150 articles in prestigious journals. The majority of Dr. Motwani's publications are in the area of total quality management, customer service, service strategy, managing for results, and creativity and innovation, among others.

Dr. Motwani serves as an Editor for two international journals and is on the Editorial Board of 12 prestigious national and international journals. He has taught and conducted research seminars in major universities in Canada, China, Costa Rica, Hong Kong, India, France, Germany, Thailand, and the United Kingdom. He also serves as a global consultant and trainer for a number of organizations in the Unites States, India, Europe, and Middle East. Some of his recent clients include: Herman Miller, Nokia, and Oliver Products, among others.

In 2004, Dr. Motwani was ranked among the Top 1% Researcher in the field of Technology Management by the International Association of Management of Technology (IAMOT). He also appears in several *Who's Who in the World* publications annually and is the recipient of the Michigan Outstanding Educator's Award granted by the Governor of Michigan. Dr. Motwani has taught and conducted seminars in the area of healthcare and hospitality management at major universities around the world and serves as a global consultant and trainer for a number of professional service organizations.

Dr. Motwani's email address is motwanij@gvsu.edu.

Who Is It For?

This book is designed for organizations striving for a systematic way to improve their customer-focused services and processes. Service organizations differ from manufactures in that they must consider more rapid customization and adaptation of products and services to their client's desires. Customer satisfaction is determined by those features of the service that the client recognizes as beneficial, e.g. timeliness, courtesy, consistency, accessibility, completeness, clarity, value, fair price, etc. In all of these features, managing customer expectations may involve meeting a customer's physical needs (i.e., supplies, equipment, transportation, etc) as well as their technological needs (instant information and accessibility). This book will assist organization executives, human resource managers, training managers, continuous improvement coordinators, team leaders, managers, and client contact level service providers to improve overall service flow and customer satisfaction on all levels, while increasing productivity and improving the bottom-line.

The business leaders, who are guiding organizations to new levels of service in flat or growing markets require a straight-forward and systematic approach to leading the improvement process. Throughout this book, we discuss how a Lean Sigma methodology can help an organization achieve a new level of service and lead this change. Organizations struggling to be more competitive must continually improve the value of the service for the client or customer as well as increase value to its shareholders. *Pursing Perfect Service* will assist in that process.

Reading this book will provide an insight into the challenges faced day-in and day-out by all types of service providers. Examples and case studies are examined in a variety of service industries. The book provides the reasoning why and how the methods for continuous improvement can become a way of life within an organization. This book was formatted with chapter summaries, worksheets, actual work-related examples and case studies to assist you in improving the customer experience for your service organization.

Finally, service organization leaders in government, education, security, contract services, entertainment, event planning, hospitality, lodging, food service, healthcare, financial and professional services, retail, and construction who desire to be competitive in the 21st century will use this book as the basis for business improvement and transformation.

What Is Inside?

Pursuing Perfect Service is a comprehensive and detailed set of instructions on how to implement Lean and Six Sigma tools and concepts in a variety of environments. It will provide the solid foundation upon which Lean Sigma tools can be applied in any service organization. Service providers are continually processing daily requests and must know how to identify client needs and expectations, how to best satisfy their needs, and how to do so at the lowest possible cost. This book is a step-by-step guide for implementing continuous improvement while creating a solid foundation upon which to build a service excellence culture. *Pursuing Perfect Service* also provides insights and examples on how Information Technology can be used to improve data and information flow to enhance the overall client experience, while ensuring organizational profitability.

This book has been arranged into four distinct parts. To transform an organization from a traditional service provider to a Lean Sigma for Service Excellence provider, it is recommended that the book be followed in order, from Part One to Part Four. However, it may be useful to review Chapter 10, Transformation Case Study, as it chronicles one company's journey using this approach or methodology. The four parts are:

Part One. Setting the Foundation for Lean Sigma for Service Excellence. This part is comprised of two chapters. In chapter one, the readers will be provided with an overview of service organizations and why it is critical for them to achieve excellence. This will be followed by a discussion, in chapter two, of how an organization can achieve excellence by applying the Lean Sigma methodology. Explaining the basic tools and concepts of Lean and Six Sigma, understanding how behavior and change must occur, and determining what measurements and outcomes are critical, will set the foundation for the Lean Sigma journey.

Part Two. Beginning the Lean Sigma for Service Excellence Journey. This part is comprised of one chapter that focuses on the four enablers of Lean Sigma and the steps required to build a solid foundation. In order for the Lean Sigma initiative to be successful, all four enablers need to be actively present within an organization.

Part Three. Deploying the Lean Sigma for Service Excellence Improvement Process. This part is comprised of five chapters and demonstrates through detailed explanation of the tools, as well as case study examples, how the Six Sigma's DMAIC (Define - Measure - Analyze - Improve - Control) methodology can be applied in service industries. Creating processes that allow customer expectations and services to be free of waste will create business success. This will entail obtaining a detailed analysis of current processes, creating standards, and balancing workloads evenly to meet each and every customer demand. This is the heart of Lean Sigma and will take the most time to implement.

Part Four. Putting it All Together to Achieve and Sustain Lean Sigma for Service Excellence. This part is comprised of two chapters. The first chapter provides definition and guidance for becoming a sustainable organization. Sustainability is defined in terms of global impact in environmental, economic, and social areas. A plan to reduce environmental impact is often called "becoming green." True sustainability goes beyond just environmental impact and also considers economic and social areas. This chapter defines the Triple Bottom Line for sustainability and also details some basic tools for becoming green. The second chapter details an organizational transformation of a traditional service provider to a Lean Sigma for Service Excellence organization. The case provides valuable insights into how Lean Sigma transformations take place from an initial assessment, through project selection and tool implementation, to a complete organizational Lean Sigma transformation. The case chronicles the trials and tribulations an organization may face during their transformation journey and can be used to help readers navigate their own Lean Sigma transformation.

Distinctive Features of this Book

The distinctive features of the book are as follows:

Tools focused – Throughout the book basic and advanced tools are discussed that can be adopted by service organizations. For each tool there is a brief discussion, a service-related example, at times step-by-step instructions, and many times an example of that tool demonstrated in the end-of-the-chapter case study. It is expected that this will provide you with enough relevant content to tackle 80% of your issues and problems within your service organization.

Note: To make the Lean Sigma tools accessible to more people, many of these forms, charts, etc. were developed in Microsoft Excel. Detailed steps for creating many of the forms, maps, and charts can be found in *The Lean Desktop and Networking Pocket Guide XL* and *iLean* (available at amazon.com and theleanstore.com). Also, for many of the topics discussed throughout this book there are numerous books and information available via the Internet for additional information.

Case Studies – Throughout the book, real-world short case studies are presented to show readers how Lean Sigma tools were successfully applied by various types of service organizations. These case studies have been modified to demonstrate the application of the tools as well as provide confidentiality to the contributing organizations. Each case study presented at the end of each of the main five chapters will accentuate that chapter's DMAIC Phase.

Chapter Readiness Guides – There is a 20-question Readiness Guide at the end of each chapter. The purpose of the assessment is two-fold: first, it should be used to find out the extent the tools and techniques discussed in the chapter are currently being *applied* at the respondent's organization, and second, it should be used to gauge the comfort level of the respondent's *knowledge and understanding* of the concepts and tools in the chapter. For implementation purposes we recommend completing the individual chapter Readiness Guide before moving on to the next chapter or phase.

Comprehensive Case Study - In chapter 10, a comprehensive real-world case study is provided that documents an organization's transformation from a traditional service provider to a Lean Sigma service provider. This case study highlights the high level road map, tools, and steps that any service organization can follow to achieve excellence.

Lean Sigma for Service Excellence Assessment and Gap Analysis - In addition to the Readiness Guides at the end of each chapter, we also provide and recommend that the readers conduct an initial comprehensive Lean Sigma for Service Excellence Assessment and Gap Analysis that is discussed in Chapter 3 (with the complete Assessment provided in the Appendix). This Assessment will assist a team in specific functional areas that Lean Sigma tools may assist the organization. There is also a suggested course of action for any lower scoring areas. We strongly encourage you to complete this assessment prior to any Lean Sigma project.

Non-Technical - This book is designed to be non-technical in nature. Though we use, illustrate, and recommend the application of quantitative techniques for Lean Sigma application, we strongly believe that the systematic, practical approach using Lean tools with the D-M-A-I-C methodology can be implemented with minimal training and resources.

Tool Applications - There are many Lean Sigma tools described in this book; however the list is not all inclusive. New ways of applying the tools are developing every day and continual learning and investigation is encouraged.

Lean Sigma Tool Preview

The following tools are listed alphabetically. Each tool will be thoroughly explained in the forthcoming chapters of the book.

5 Whys
5S
Action Item Log
Brainstorming
Cause and Effect (or Fishbone) Diagrams
Check Sheets
Constraint or Bottleneck Analysis
Cross-Training
Demand Analysis and Takt Time
Effective Meetings
Employee Balance Charts
Force Field Analysis
Frequency Charts
Histogram, Ogive Chart, and Cumulative Frequency
Impact Maps
Interrelationship Diagrams
Issues and Opportunities Log
Key Metric Data Profiles
Layered Process Audits
Mass Customization
Measurement System Analysis
Mistake Proofing
Pareto and Pie Charts
Performance Management
Plan-Do-Check-Act (PDCA)
Process
Problem Solving – Corrective and Preventative Actions
Process Capability
Process or Work Area Layout
Project Charter
Project Management
Project Planner
Quality Function Deployment
Quick Changeover (QCO)
Radar Charts
Rapid Improvement Events
Run Charts
Scatter Plots
Service Flow
Standard Work
Standard Work for Leaders
Statistical Process Control (SPC)
Supplier-Input-Process-Output-Customer
Team Charter
Teaming
Total Productive Maintenance (TPM)
Value Stream and Process Maps
Value-Added versus Non Value-Added Analysis
Visual Controls
Visual Management
Voice of the Customer

Final Comments Before You Begin

As you progress through the reading of this book, keep in mind that each project you encounter will use a variety of Lean and Six Sigma tools. Rarely, if ever, will any one project require every tool listed in this book.

We have presented these tools in the logical sequence of the DMAIC phases; however, use this as only a guide. It is acknowledged that many of the tools discussed in one phase can also be used in another phase. For example, a Run Chart can be used in the Measure Phase as well as the Control Phase; Brainstorming and the Fishbone can be used in just about every phase. Focus on the objective for that phase. As your familiarity and experience increases, so will your ability to select the more appropriate tools.

Pursuing Perfect Service

Part One.
Setting the Foundation for Lean Sigma for Service Excellence

Chapter 1

Understanding Service

The New Economic Landscape

Chapter Overview

The service sector of the global economy is growing at an extraordinary rate. According to The Bureau of Economic Analysis (2010), the service sector accounted for 79% of the U.S. GDP, up substantially from the 1980s. This trend is expected to continue. A recent study conducted by the Bureau of Labor Statistics projected employment in the service sector to increase by 13% in comparison to the manufacturing sector which is expected to decline by 3%. Today, more than three out of every four jobs (75%) is in the service sector and this number is projected to increase. The above statistics clearly emphasize the importance and growth of the service sector and the need for implementing innovative approaches for achieving excellence.

In today's competitive market, customers' expectations from the service organizations are continually on the rise and service organizations have no choice but to provide innovative and better services in order to be competitive. In this chapter we will provide the readers with an overview of the service sector and discuss how service organizations can achieve a higher level of excellence.

Service and Service Quality

***Service** is generally defined as work performed for someone else's benefit or pleasure.* This can be a landscaping company mowing the grass for other businesses, a law firm drafting and filing a last will and testament, a financial institute providing a loan to a home buyer, or a clown performing at a child's birthday party. In its broadest sense, all types of businesses provide some type of "service" to their clients whether they consider themselves in the service sector or not. Even traditional manufacturing organizations typically have a Customer Service Department. In this light it is important for every organization to understand the services they provide to their client, the client's expectations, and how they can continuously improve and provide better services.

Service quality differs from product quality in that service specifications and requirements are not typically as clearly defined or articulated by the customer. In fact, it is quite common for customers of the same service business to have completely different expectations and requirements. Service businesses must therefore define their own service quality parameters, measures, and specifications based on specific customer needs and then communicate these to their clients (i.e., customers) in an effort to achieve a high level of customer satisfaction. In that endeavor, service providers need to consider rapid identification and customization or adaptation to the client's desires.

Quality in general is often confused with product or service features. For example, a person may consider a Hilton hotel to be a higher quality than a Motel 6. These two lodging providers each provide similar base services, yet the Hilton may offer additional features (room service, fitness center, pool and sauna, valet services, etc.) along with overnight accommodations. They each have specifications and requirements designed for different target markets or customers. They each can provide quality facilities and services to meet their client's needs.

Features such as swimming pools, fitness rooms, dining rooms, office services, etc. are considered additional features, not improved quality. A guest wanting only an inexpensive, clean, and safe place to sleep for the night may be perfectly satisfied, and even delighted, with a high quality room at a Motel 6. Each provider may have equally high quality in the services and features they provide.

Service Deliverables

Service deliverables themselves can be complex and subjective. They can be characterized by the following general parameters:

Service Deliverables Parameters

- Integrity – Making and honoring commitments, deadlines and expectations
- Timeliness – Delivery of service in a reasonable time frame
- Courtesy – Being respectful and courteous in service or information delivery
- Consistency – Having similar results meeting each service transaction
- Predictability - Meeting normal expectations in a predictable fashion
- Accessibility – Being accessible to the client when they need to meet or communicate

- Completeness – Resolving issues and providing services as agreed upon
- Clarity – Providing clear and unambiguous service, instruction, or information and defining expectations and outcomes clearly
- Value – Providing a fair and reasonable service deliverable for the fees incurred
- Accuracy – Providing accurate information and results or outcomes
- Cleanliness – Providing clean facilities or equipment for client use and interaction
- Enjoyment realized – How a service or transaction makes a person feel

In identifying and defining client specifications, and requirements, service organizations should consider these parameters, and make sure that they are appropriately satisfied.

Classification of Service Organizations

Service organizations fall under the following major categories based on the primary service they provide. Some of these categories may overlap, when service organizations flow from one form of service delivery to the next. The following table defines several major service categories discussed throughout this book:

Service Category	Examples
Advice	Doctors, marketing organizations, financial advisors, law firms, technology help lines, Web support lines, and consulting organizations
Entertainment	Casinos, musicians, comedians, actors, and other entertainers
Government Services	Services provided by the federal, state, and local branches of the government
Hospitality, Food and Lodging	Hotels, restaurants, bars, resorts, and guide services
Information Transfer or Processing	News organizations, associations, internal business functions, and Web-based organizations
Maintenance and Repair Services	Auto repair and maintenance shops, small engine repair, office machine repair, lawn care, snow removal, and facility services
Medical Services	Healthcare centers, hospitals, radiology labs, and out-patient services
Organization and Customer Support	Internal and external customer service departments or functions in manufacturing firms
Personal Services	Hair salons, security, spas, etc.
Professional Services	Tax preparers, attorneys, Web designers, and insurance providers
Retail Sales	Department and clothing stores, including online sales
Training and Education	Colleges and universities, other schools, and training firms
Use of Consumable	Power companies, water and sewage providers, phone companies, etc.
Use of Equipment or Facilities	Golf courses, amusement parks, equipment rental organizations, Web servers and hosts

Many organizations fit into several categories of service, for example:

- DisneyWorld, would be in Entertainment (shows and amusement rides), Hospitality, Food & Lodging (Contemporary Hotel and others on site), Maintenance and Repair Services (ensure rides are safe to standards), etc.
- Norwegian Cruise would be in Entertainment (shows, casinos, kids activities, musicians), Food and Lodging (restaurants, bars, hotels), Personal Services (massages, spa), and Maintenance and Repair Services (air conditioning, swimming pools, exercise equipment).
- Marriott Resorts would be in Entertainment (shows, casinos, kids activities, musicians), Advice (conceirge services for setting tours, places to eat, travel tips), Food and Lodging (restaurants, bars, hotels), Retail Sales (clothing, swimming accessories, food) Personal Services (massages, spa), and Maintenance and Repair (air conditioning, swimming pools, exercise equipment).
- Mayo Clinic (hospitals) would be in Advice and Medical Services (treatment, medication), Food and Lodging (cafeteria, hospital rooms), Personal Services (massages, spa, physical therapy), and Maintenance and Repair (scanners, radiology equipment).
- Crown Jewel Salon and Spa would be in Advice (treatment, haircut), Personal Services (massages, manicure, pedicure), and Entertainment (music, magazines)
- Edward Jones Financial would be in Advice and Professional Services (investment counseling, banking, trusts, retirement management, etc.)
- Microsoft would be in Information Transfer or Processing (support web-site maintenance, help lines, software applications) and Retail Sales (products, support, etc.)
- Ernst & Young would be in Advice and Professional Services (financial management, online help, consulting, accounting services, etc.)

Some service deliverables or outcomes are more objective or measureable than others. For example, the performance of an automobile after repair can easily be measured while the enjoyment from attending a concert is subjective, or more difficult to measure. The illustration on the top of the next page plots the ability to objectively measure the service outcome of various industries, against the type or focus of the service provided.

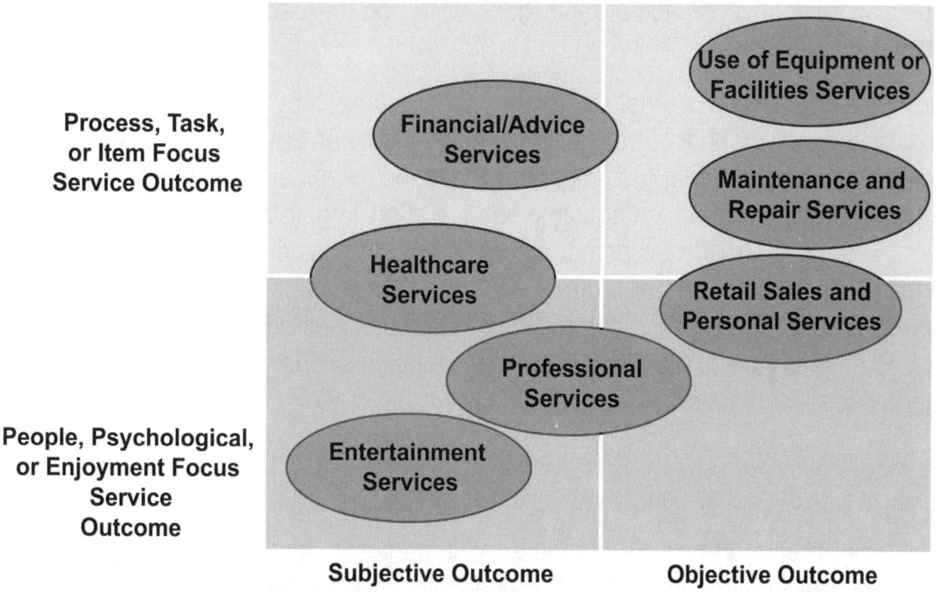

Many service transactions shift fluidly during the service delivery process. An example might be a communication between a customer and a bank teller while processing a deposit. The deposit being entered accurately is clearly measurable, yet the "feeling" that the customer has during the process may not be as easily measured. In fact, one customer may desire a friendly and talkative experience, while the next customer does not value any chit-chat. The teller may behave the same for each of these customers, and will get good reviews from one, and poor reviews from the other. Herein lies one of the keys to developing service excellence - understanding the customer's need.

Another way to look at service organizations and offerings is to review their common attributes. Even though there are enormous varieties in offerings and methods of delivering services, service organizations share several common attributes. Service organizations typically have the following attributes:

- Direct customer contact and sales
- Primary benefit subjective to measure, as it is typically not a physical product
- The output or deliverable is created and delivered on demand
- Output is not storable or transferable
- Timing and speed are critical

We can also categorize service organizations based on the following three general classifications:

Service Delivered to an External Customer is characterized by a high level of customer interaction and total number of transactions completed by an organization. Organizations providing services to external customers may have to face extreme competitive pressures and may be engaged in marketing campaigns in effort to gain additional clients. In this category, a service provider or person interacts with the customer directly and typically performs a task or physical deliverable. Delivered services usually have more tangible outcomes than service process completions. Organizations compete on quality of outcomes. Examples include fast food restaurants, bank tellers, lawn maintenance services, laundry services, and the like.

Service Process Used by an External Customer are similar in that they typically face extreme competition, yet are different in that the service provider may also have to educate their potential clients on how to use the service process. Many of these organizations are using the power of the internet to improve their process delivery and options, by having customers complete the ordering process, or data entry rather than direct interaction between a service worker and a customer. Service processes typically have less tangible outcomes than delivered services. Organizations compete on speed and simplicity of the process. Examples include automated teller machines (ATM's), self check-in monitors for airlines, self check-outs at retail stores, vending machines, and all other service types where where customers use a process directly without "direct" person-to-person interaction.

Service Process Internal to an Organization typically faces less competitive pressures because they have been established by the organization to serve the organization. However, they too must educate their users regarding the features and use of their internal service processes. Examples include human resources, Information Technology (IT), counseling, internal supply rooms, or janitorial services within an organization.

Why Service Excellence?

Service organizations today face consumer and fiscal pressure like never before in history. The modern consumer is well-educated and informed and expects quick, accurate, and superior value in their transactions and interactions. Service organizations, unlike manufacturing organizations, deliver a different type of product. In manufacturing, product quality can be directly measured by product specifications versus actual performance. For service organizations, quality is measured in less direct ways such as customer satisfaction surveys, customer pleasure or enjoyment, timeliness, accuracy of information, completeness, perceived value, and the like.

Implementing improvements through the methodology presented in this book will assist service organizations to quantify the total customer satisfaction experience and provide a systematic improvement plan to improve the overall customer experience and value. This will not only develop positive relationships with customers and clients and reduce employee stress, but it will also lead to business growth through an increase in repeat and new customers desiring your services.

There is clear evidence that Lean Sigma has been applied with great success in customer service, finance, billing, accounting, quoting, and IT departments in all types of industries. The basic concepts, tools, and practices of Lean Sigma applies to all organizations!

For example, the following processes are critical to customers and need to be standardized, streamlined, and made as efficient and effective as possible:

- Providing an estimate or quote
- Entering a customer order
- Generating an invoice
- Creating an engineering drawing
- Completing a surgical or medical procedure such as an X-ray or MRI
- Filling out a medical insurance form
- Filing an insurance claim
- Applying for a mortgage
- Depositing a check at your local bank
- Opening a savings account
- Checking into a hotel
- Repairing an automobile
- Washing soiled laundry
- Providing legal documents
- Providing massage or physical therapy
- Conducting a blood pressure check or blood sample draw

Most service excellence techniques provide tools and concepts to eliminate process variations that can cause waste and cost over-runs in the above processes. The following are examples of how Lean Sigma principles have helped service organizations become more efficient:

- A customer check-in process that usually takes 8 minutes to complete and tends to frustrate exhausted travelers can now be done in seconds
- A credit or coupon that requires two people for approvals (and takes days) can be done by one person in minutes
- A security inspection and clearance for an overseas cargo container that takes two days can be done in minutes
- A patient being moved into or out of a surgical procedure which may take up to an hour can be done in less than thirty minutes
- An insurance claim that takes two-three days for settlement can be completed in just a few hours
- A mortgage application that takes five days to process can be processed in less than eight hours

The most important point to understand about Lean Sigma is that it has proven to be effective in every business application. Throughout the book we provide and illustrate how service organizations can apply Lean Sigma tools and principles to enhance their service performance. These tools and practices have been compiled from years of research and on-the-job experiences. We strongly believe that the practical and hands-on approach used in writing these chapters will help you to obtain instant process improvements and results.

Chapter Summary

This brief overview of service organizations is meant to illustrate the similarities and differences between service organizations and traditional manufacturing organizations. Defining the similarities and differences in service processes, deliverables, outcomes, and measurements can provide a deeper understanding of how service organizations provide and measure value. Most importantly, this chapter is intended to allow readers to understand how their organization can benefit from a Lean Sigma approach for continuous improvement.

Lean Sigma for Service Excellence Applications

The following observations may assist in understanding how to apply the concepts and tools contained in this chapter:

- Communicate to employees the concepts and categories of service and service quality.
- Document and communicate your organizations service parameters, deliverables, and measurements.
- Continue to read and learn about service excellence from other sources (books, Webinars, conferences, blogs, benchmarking, etc.).
- Focus on the customer and their expressed and non-expressed needs.
- Continue to learn and apply service excellence tools and practices.
- Establish ways to align and measure performance and quality.

Understanding Service Readiness Guide

The following Understanding Service Readiness Guide allows you to ensure there is application of the chapter's content before proceeding to apply the Lean Sigma tools and concepts in the next chapter. If you score less than 70%, consider working on the lower scoring areas before moving on.

Understanding Service Readiness Guide	
Use the following 5-level Likert item scale to rank each of the statements: **1 = Strongly Disagree** **2 = Disagree** **3 = Neither Agree nor Disagree** **4 = Agree** **5 = Strongly Agree**	
	Score
1. Quality is well-defined in my organization.	
2. Our definition of quality is customer driven.	
3. My organization has clearly defined quality parameters.	
4. My organization has clearly defined quality measures.	
5. My organization clearly communicates with its customers.	
6. My organization adapts well with customer needs.	
7. My organizations does a good job of quantifying the total customer satisfaction experience.	
8. My organization has a systematic improvement plan to improve overall customer experience and value.	
9. My organization does a good job of standardizing and steamlining individual tasks or processes.	
10. My organization does a good job of communicating to employees the concepts and categories of "service."	
11. My organization does a good job of documenting and communicating service deliverables.	
12. My organization is continuously involved in benchmarking and improving.	
13. My organization does a good job of focusing on the customer and their expressed and non-expressed needs.	
14. My organization is truly a learning organization.	
15. My organization is focused on continuous improvement.	
16. My organization is process-focused.	
17. My organization is people-focused.	
18. My organization would benefit from applying Lean Sigma tools, processes, and strategies.	
19. I feel comfortable applying Lean Sigma tools, processes, and strategies.	
20. I believe my organization should utilize and apply the concepts and tools discussed in this chapter.	
Total Score	

Chapter 2

Understanding Lean Sigma

A New Way to Look at Things

Chapter Overview

The Toyota Production System, waste elimination, and process or continuous improvement are all used synonymously with Lean Sigma methods throughout the world. This chapter will briefly explain the overriding theme or philosophical approach upon which the tools and concepts of Lean are integrated within a Six Sigma methodology and statistical approach.

What is Lean, Six Sigma, and Lean Sigma?

Lean is a way of thinking that can fairly easily be applied to every type of organization, whether manufacturing or service. ***Lean** is a never-ending, systematic approach for identifying and eliminating waste, and improving flow for a process.* The entire focus of Lean is customer-driven and it is the customer who determines the value and the amount they are willing to pay for the service.

Six Sigma is a statistical term. Sigma (σ) defines the variation or "spread" of a process. Six Sigma defines how much of the total process falls inside the normal process variation. ***Six Sigma**, as a business tool, is a structured, quantitative, five phase approach to continuous improvement and problem solving.* The five phases are: Define - Measure - Analyze - Improve - Control and are commonly referred to as the D-M-A-I-C Phases. Each of these Phases will be explained in detail in Chapters 4 - 8.

The term Sigma refers to the number of standard deviations that are away from the mean in a bell-shaped normal distribution curve, as shown below:

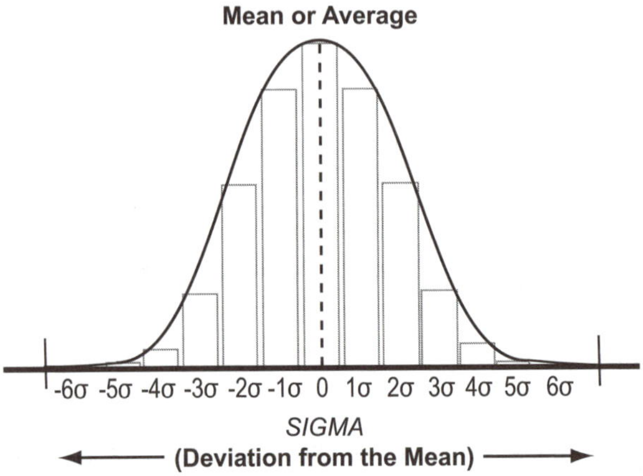

The goal of Six Sigma is to eliminate defects and minimize variability. In statistical terms, if a service organization achieves Six Sigma level of performance, 99.99966% of its customers are satisfied as they are receiving services that are defect-free and meet their expectations. In a service industry, 6 sigma, can be viewed as 3.4 defects or errors per million opportunities. For example, based on the 2010 year volumes, if the United States Postal Service was running a 4 sigma operation, it would be allowed to lose ~2000 articles of mail per hour; however, if it was operating under 6 sigma, the acceptable error rate would be ~1.1 per hour. If a telephone company was operating under 4 sigma, a phone customer would encounter a phone difficulty for up to 9 minutes per week, while under 6 sigma, the same customer would only encounter a phone problem for 2.6 minutes each decade.

The table below summarizes the sigma level and error rate per million opportunities.

Process Capability or Sigma Level	Defects (or Errors) Per Million Opportunities (DPMO)	Percent Acceptable
6 σ	3.4	99.99966%
5 σ	233	99.9767%
4 σ	6,210	99.379%
3 σ	66,807	93.32%
2 σ	308,538	69.15%
1 σ	691,462	30.9%

The method in which to calculate a Sigma level is discussed in Chapter 5 - Key Metric Data Profiles.

Six Sigma forces organizations to pursue perfection by asking if 99% acceptability is good enough. If 99% acceptability is good enough, consider the following:

99% Good (3.8 Sigma)	99.99966% Good (6 Sigma)
20,000 lost articles of mail per hour (based on 2,000,000/hr)	Seven lost articles per hour
Unsafe drinking water for almost 15 minutes each day	One unsafe minute every seven months
5,000 incorrect surgical operations per week	1.7 incorrect operations per week
Two short or long landings daily at an airport with 200 flights/day	One short or long landing every five years
2,000,000 wrong drug prescriptions each year	680 wrong prescriptions per year
No electricity for almost seven hours each month	One hour without electricity every 34 years

The following Sigma Level Versus Defects chart highlights the sigma levels for three broad categories of organizations:

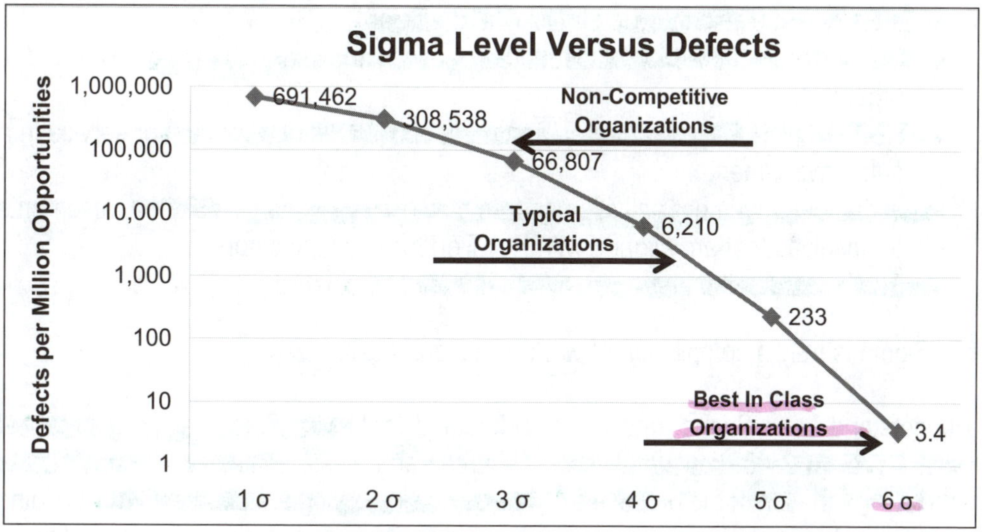

***Lean Sigma** is the combination of the customer-focused efforts of Lean and waste elimination with the quantitative D-M-A-I-C methodology of Six Sigma.* Lean Sigma can be, and is for many organizations, a very powerful improvement technique. It systematically blends the best of the above two approaches to eliminate all waste (i.e., non value-added activities) and variation from processes. This in turn, lowers the cost and improves the quality of the process. The continued focus on the elimination of waste should be a daily, hourly, or minute-by-minute review. Lean Sigma is designed to use people and resources wisely to satisfy customer needs. With that thought in mind, work elements or job duties may need to be modified to accommodate a waste-free Lean Sigma environment. This will allow companies to remain globally competitive, develop a cross-trained workforce, and establish a safe workplace while pleasing the customer.

Lean Sigma tools are used to:

- Improve customer satisfaction and the total customer experience
- Identify and eliminate waste quickly and efficiently
- Increase communication and speed of services and information at all levels of the organization
- Reduce costs, improve quality, and meet obligations of a product or service in a safe environment
- Initiate improvement activities and empower employees to make improvements themselves that are aligned with Key Performance Indicators
- Track and monitor improvements to ensure sustainability

Lean Sigma is truly a compilation of world-class practices.

To understand Lean Sigma, one must understand that Lean Sigma is, in its broadest sense, a philosophy of conservation of resources and waste elimination. Six Sigma is for reducing variation in the process and Lean is for improving the process flow. Building on this Lean Sigma philosophy are Lean Sigma principles, concepts, methods, and tools. These are the building blocks of a structured and supported approach to a total Lean Sigma transformation. Lean Sigma principles must be built on a basic understanding of a Lean Sigma philosophy. Many organizations have forgone a basic understanding of Lean Sigma philosophy and tried to build a Lean Sigma organization on a weak foundation, only to be disappointed with their results. It truly pays to start with and build on a strong foundation of a Lean Sigma philosophy and principles.

Conceptually, these building blocks are illustrated in the diagram below. Starting with a strong foundation of Lean Sigma Philosophies and Lean Sigma Principles, these can be used to support an organization utilizing Lean and Sigma Concepts and Tools in providing the Methods to Delight Customers and (obtain) Profitable Growth.

* **Not all inclusive of Lean Sigma tools**

Lean Sigma Philosophies and Principles

The overriding theme for a solid foundation rests with understanding and practicing Lean Sigma Philosophies. The philosophies of a continuous (relentless) elimination of waste and non-value added activities in everything we do and the conservation of all resources, at every level of operation are key to a successful Lean Sigma transformation of any kind. Additionally, Lean Sigma philosophy calls for the simplification of all tasks and efforts to eliminate waste and variation from processes and improve flow. Absolute perfection is seen as the goal. Very few organizations embrace Lean Sigma Philosophies at this level. Toyota Motor Company has been practicing Lean (Sigma) for over 70 years, and due to their quality problems and brief diversion from the basic principles and practices (of Lean Sigma) in 2010, still need to improve!

Lean Sigma Principles must also be present for Lean Sigma transformations. Lean Sigma Principles provide the unchanging, solid foundation to build and improve upon. The three key Lean Sigma Principles, supported by Lean Sigma Philosophies, are:

1. Focus on Customers and Value Streams – Focus on the entire process, from the customer pull or demand to demand fulfillment and customer satisfaction. Focus on how materials and information flow through a process..
2. Continuous Improvement in Processes and Results – Do not focus only on the results or bottom-line. Instead, focus on processes that deliver consistent, waste-free results.
3. Employee Involvement – Organization leaders must make it safe for people to make improvements and suggestions.

Lean Concepts

There are basically three reasons why Lean can be used with confidence. First of all, the training requirements and implementation time for Lean are minimal. Basic concepts of Lean can be taught very quickly and improvements can be implemented the same day. For example, when an individual understands that some of their daily activities are non value-added or waste activities (such as excess time spent walking, waiting, and moving), immediate changes can be made to improve the process. Waste reduction will become automatic for people as they become aware of waste. Improvements are continuously made at all stages of work. Often, the completion of one Lean or Rapid Improvement Event stimulates the participants to think of other areas for improvement.

Secondly, Lean's application in an organization is broad. Attempts are made to eliminate waste in all areas. With Six Sigma, projects are more narrowly focused and are highly recommended to have a direct correlation to strategic priorities and the bottom-line. There are tools, such as 5S, that can get everyone engaged and in the right mind set for applications of Lean. 5S is a workplace organization program that assists to improve efficiencies by having information, work (electronic and paper-based), supplies, or equipment for areas or processes, electronic files and folders in the right place with minimal effort to retrieve.

The third reason is that improvements made while utilizing Lean concepts can positively impact other areas of the organization as well as the bottom-line. Customers are more satisfied with the decreased wait times, reduction of duplicate documentation, and fewer errors or mix-ups. This elimination of waste impacts the bottom-line by decreasing the number of required resources to complete the same amount of work. Employees are empowered to change work they are directly involved in, making their work more effective (less waste) and more rewarding.

The following are several Lean, as well as Six Sigma, concepts that will drive a Lean Sigma transformation. It is essential that people at all levels understand these over-riding concepts to facilitate a smooth and effective Lean Sigma transformation. These concepts are explored further throughout this book. The fundamental Lean concepts that comprise the pillar of Lean Concepts are:

- Value and Waste
- Quality First
- Speak with Data and Facts
- Total Employee Involvement
- Seek Perfection
- Plan-Do-Check-Act (scientific process)
- Flow
- Waste Elimination
- Customer Focus
- Performance Measures

Six Sigma Concepts

There are several Six Sigma concepts that will drive a Lean Sigma transformation. At the heart of Six Sigma is the Define-Measure-Analyze-Improve-Control (DMAIC) methodology and its statistical analysis for problem solving. Following each of these steps will ensure the improvement project is completed in an orderly manner as well as ensure it is sustained. It is essential that people at different levels be trained in and understand these Sigma concepts to facilitate a smooth and effective Lean Sigma transformation. These concepts are explored further throughout this book. The fundamental Six Sigma concepts that comprise the pillar of Lean Concepts are:

- Scientific Method
- Statistical Methods
- Focus on Variation
- Proven Methodology
- Common Goal of Six Sigma
- D-M-A-I-C
- Quantitative Analysis
- Look for Hidden Wastes
- Voice of the Customer
- Zero Defects

One of the main over-riding themes between Lean and Six Sigma Concepts is the goal of identifying and eliminating waste. The following twelve wastes will be explored in detail and examples of those wastes will be provided.

The Twelve Forms of Waste - The Dirty Dozen

The various wastes can fall into twelve categories. The twelve categories of waste are:

1. Overproduction
2. Inventory or Work In Process (WIP)
3. Waiting or Delays
4. Motion
5. Transport
6. Defects or Errors
7. Overprocessing
8. Skills and Knowledge
9. Unevenness
10. Overburden
11. Environmental
12. Social

Lean Sigma tools and concepts assist employees in identifying and eliminating the twelve types of waste. It is critical that employees have a fundamental knowledge and understanding of waste in order to identify and eliminate it. The purpose of Lean Sigma practices is to identify, analyze, and eliminate all sources of process inefficiency (i.e., elimination of waste). This elimination of waste should be subject to a daily, hourly, or minute-by-minute scrutiny.

The following is a Pie Chart representing the twelve wastes and their relationship to value-added activities.

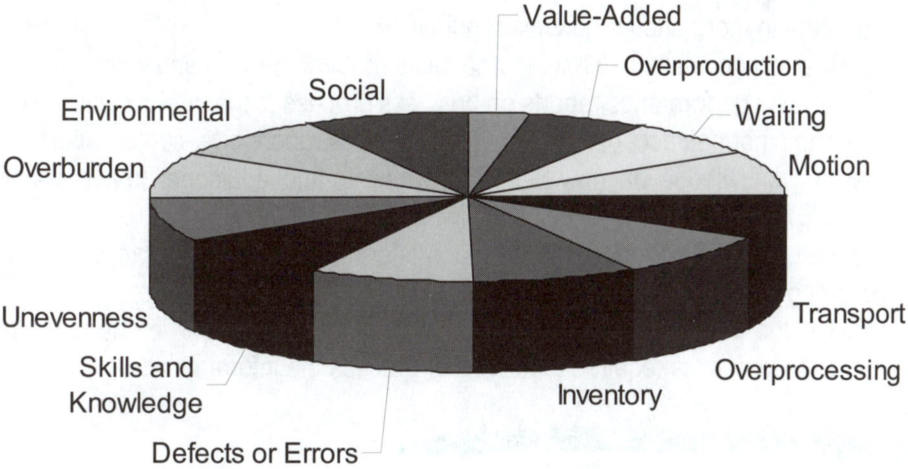

1. The Waste of Overproduction

Producing some type of work prior to it being required is waste of overproduction. Providing a service above and beyond what is needed is also considered overproduction. Overproduction is when too much of something is made or served. This is the greatest of all the wastes. Overproduction of work or services can cause other wastes. For example, by preparing extra copies of a report, you are using extra paper, extra time to handle the reports, and extra motion and transportation to dispose of the reports, and so on.

The following are some examples of this waste, along with references to the Lean Sigma tools that would assist in its elimination.

Examples of overproduction waste are:

- Emailing, faxing the same document multiple times
- Entering repetitive information on multiple documents
- Attending or conducting ineffective meetings
- Producing reports that are not used, or providing additional fields for reporting that are not viewed or used by anyone
- Producing regular reports that the user does not need to view unless an 'exception' occurs
- Performing more analysis than is required
- Unclear expectations of what information is required by who and when
- Generating performance reports on business processes that are currently operating within normal, acceptable limits (e.g., debtors report, cost-center report)
- Lacking knowledge on how-to-use or where-to-find additional features in MS Word/Excel designed to significantly increase productivity
- Sending completed reports or too much information to the next process without knowing when, or exactly what, is needed
- Having too many services, options, or selections in the user interface (or program) than what is required to access or process the information

Typical tools to reduce overproduction waste are:

- Demand Analysis (Takt time)
- Pitch
- Work Standards
- Service Flow

2. The Waste of Waiting (or Delays)

Waiting for anything (people, signatures, information, etc.) is waste. This waste of waiting is "low hanging fruit" which is easy to reach and ripe for the taking. We often do not think of paper sitting in an In-basket or an unread email as waste. However, when looking for the item (document or email), how many times do we mull through that In-basket or the Inbox folder to try to find it? How many times do you actually touch something before it is completed? It is the finish it, file it, or throw it away system that can help eliminate this waste of waiting.

The following are some examples of this waste, along with references to the Lean Sigma tools that would assist in its elimination.

Examples of waiting waste are:

- Requiring excessive signatures or approvals
- Having no priority level for someone to complete a work assignment
- Delaying in obtaining feedback/approvals/decisions from peers or higher-level management
- Lacking Key Performance Indicators (KPIs) or 'performance dashboards' to highlight exceptions/notifications/deviations and enable timely corrective actions
- Delaying responding to emails within a certain time period (e.g., 24 hours)
- Delaying in starting the next process step because a previous step operates as a batch-and-queue process, causing printer (machine) output delays
- Delaying in getting information from another department, customer, or system report
- Using ineffective methodologies of software development which requires extra steps in processing information due to no user input into the user interface

Typical tools to reduce waiting waste are:

- Value Stream (or Process) Mapping
- 5S
- Pitch
- Mass Customization
- Runners
- Visual Controls
- Service Flow
- Standard Work

3. The Waste of Motion

Any movement of people, paper, and/or electronic exchanges that does not add value is waste. This waste is created by poor office layout or design, faulty or outdated office equipment, supply inaccessibility, and movement of information or data that does not add value. The waste of motion is insidious and is hidden in office procedures that have not been reviewed for continuous improvement initiatives. Regardless of the industry, motion waste may appear as someone who is looking "busy" but not adding value to the work or service. Lean Sigma tools will assist to identify, reduce, and/or eliminate this waste.

The following are some examples of this waste, along with references to the Lean Sigma tools that would assist in its elimination.

Examples of motion waste are:

- Searching for electronic files
- Searching for all types documents in file cabinets and file folders
- Hand-carrying paper to another process
- Having cross-departmental resource commitments without proper communications
- Using excessive email distribution lists, along with any and all attachments
- Using an excessive number of transaction screens to support decision-making
- Presenting data that is not easy-to-read or not 'user friendly' to support decision-making
- Sending event notifications that do not provide all the details, or do not allow a user to take action without going to another screen/interface for further information
- Selecting additional keystrokes and fields to retrieve information
- Not using default 'speed keys' that can help operate multiple Desktop screens faster

Typical tools to reduce motion waste are:

- Standard Work
- Process or Work Area Layout
- 5S
- Effective Meetings
- Service Flow
- Employee Balance Chart

4. The Waste of Transport

Transport waste is the excess movement of materials, documents, information, etc. within an organization. Excess transport affects the time of delivery of any work. Even with the Internet and email readily available, too often, or not often enough, documents (i.e., files) that provide little or no value are moved downstream regardless of need. Reducing or eliminating excess transport waste is important. Locating all work in sequential process operations and as physically close together as possible will help eliminate or reduce this waste. Transport between processes that cannot be eliminated should be automated as much as possible. Ask questions such as: "Is the office layout optimal?," "Is the release and request for work automated?," and "Is IT aware of the problem and can they help?"

The following are some examples of this waste, along with references to the Lean Sigma tools that would assist in its elimination.

Examples of transport waste are:

- Delivering unneeded documents
- Filing same work documents in different locations (e.g., keeping hardcopy while also having it available electronically)
- Over-addressing e-mail distribution lists
- Hand-carrying paper to another process
- Reviewing customer information from another process before it is sent downstream
- Filing/saving documents that will never be used again
- Moving data from one system to another
- Updating customer records in different systems
- Sending and/or requesting unnecessary data to/from the customer (e.g., if you have a self-serve order-entry web portal and still must contact the customer for information)

Typical tools to reduce transport waste are:

- 5S
- Value Stream (or Process) Mapping
- Just-In-Time
- Visual Controls
- Employee Balance Chart
- Service Flow
- Standard Work

5. The Waste of Overprocessing

Putting more effort into the work than what is by internal or external customers is waste. Excessive processing does not add value for the customer and the customer will not pay for it. This is one of the most difficult wastes to uncover. Some questions to ask to assist in the identification of this waste are: "What are the most basic processes required to meet the customer needs?" or "Is there a clear understanding of the customer's needs?"

The following are some examples of this waste, along with references to the Lean Sigma tools that would assist in its elimination.

Examples of overprocessing waste are:

- Duplicating reports or information or providing more detailed information than is requested
- Entering same data in different systems
- Sharing information ineffectively
- Constantly revising documents
- Attending or conducing ineffective meetings
- Processing excessive emails to highlight issues or actions requiring attention
- Using Excel spreadsheets to retain or analyze information 'outside' of the core IT system
- Entering data into multiple systems and/or 'stand-alone' spreadsheets for reporting purposes
- Over-resourcing a process to meet the 'peak demand' rather than investigating work leveling opportunities
- Over-checking an email Inbox for new messages
- Lacking a system to manage incoming emails, causing emails to be read and re-read (again at a later date) before responding

Typical tools to reduce overprocessing waste are:

- Visual Controls
- Standard Work
- Voice of the Customer (VOC)
- Mistake Proofing
- Mass Customization
- SIPOC Analysis

6. The Waste of Inventory

Excessive piles of paperwork, computer files, supplies, and time spent searching for documents is waste. They all take up space or require someone's time. If a document is waiting for additional information (i.e., signature, review, approval, etc.) and there is a change, then the time the document has been waiting is waste. There are basically two types of inventory waste related to administrative areas: 1) office supplies and 2) time.

The following are some examples of this waste, along with references to the Lean Sigma tools that would assist in its elimination.

Examples of inventory waste are:

- Requiring excessive signatures or approvals
- Awaiting task completion by others
- Having to sort through obsolete files
- Using obsolete office equipment
- Not having sufficient training of back-ups
- Purchasing excessive office supplies
- Filing unfinished service requests never to be used again
- Keeping multiple copies of reports
- Keeping unused 'required fields' in reports/documents/templates that will not be used in company reports
- Using excessive icons on the Desktop
- Creating excessive document revisions rather than overwriting previous copy
- Keeping excessive 'un-read' emails in your Inbox

Typical tools to reduce inventory waste are:

- 5S
- Standard Work
- Service Flow
- Value Stream (or Process) Mapping
- Pull Systems and Kanbans
- Pitch

7. The Waste of Defects or Errors

Defect waste refers to all processing required in creating a defect and the additional work required to correct a defect or error. Defects and errors (either internal or external) result in additional processing that will add no value to the product or service. It takes less time to do work correctly the first time than the time it would take to do it over. Rework or correction of work is waste and adds more cost to any product or service for which the customer will not pay. This waste can reduce profits significantly.

The following are some examples of this waste, along with references to the Lean Sigma tools that would assist in its elimination.

Examples of defect waste are:

- Having data entry errors
- Forwarding incomplete documentation
- Losing files or records
- Providing incorrect information on documents
- Returning forms/applications due to incomplete data
- Having discrepancies in data content because they are stored in different systems (e.g., customer master database)
- Submitting wrong/inaccurate data
- Creating a document that requires extensive correction by colleagues
- Handling a report numerous times
- Having no integrated IT systems (e.g., the sales order system is not integrated with the inventory management system)
- Missing information due to poorly specified information requirements or features

Typical tools to reduce defect waste are:

- 5S
- Standard Work
- Voice of the Customer (VOC)
- Quality Function Deployment (QFD)
- Visual Controls
- Mistake Proofing
- Problem Solving
- Statistical Process Control (SPC)

8. The Waste of People's Skills or Knowledge

The underutilization of people is a result of not placing people where they can (and will) use their knowledge, skills, and abilities to the fullest in providing value-added work and services. An effective performance management system will reduce this waste significantly. Use company policies and procedures to effectively place people where they will most benefit the organization. The employees performing the work tasks know the work the best. It is a waste of their knowledge not to listen to them and involve them in improvement initiatives.

The following are some examples of this waste, along with references to the Lean Sigma tools that would assist in its elimination.

Examples of people's skills and knowledge waste are:

- Not involving employees in improvement ideas and teams
- Lacking balanced work within the department or work group
- Having high absenteeism and turnover
- Having an inadequate performance management system
- Hiring someone with inadequate skills
- Assigning employees two jobs due to understaffing
- Providing no cross-training when people are sitting 'idle' due to bottleneck in upstream process

Typical tools to reduce people's skills and knowledge waste are:

- 5S
- Standard Work
- Rapid Improvement Events
- Teaming
- Service Flow
- Employee Balance Chart
- Voice of the Customer (VOC)
- Effective Meetings

9. The Waste of Unevenness

Lack of a consistent flow of inputs/information/scheduled work from upstream processes causes many of the other types of waste previously mentioned. The waste of unevenness creates fluctuations in workload and unbalanced service delivery. This waste directly impacts customers and can cause frustration for employees.

The following are some examples of this waste, along with references to the Lean Sigma tools that would assist in its elimination.

Examples of unevenness waste are:

- Having incomplete information ahead of time to meet month-end deadlines, thus causing overtime
- Scheduling all work to be completed at the end of the month and not during the month at even intervals
- Having no leveling of work within the department or work group
- Having poor office standards/processes causing difficulty in finding documents/reports when staff member is on annual leave (vacation)
- Lacking performance standards (or clearly defined work parameters) from the downstream process (i.e., customer)

Typical tools to reduce unevenness waste are:

- Value Stream Mapping
- Standard Work
- Mass Customization
- Service Flow
- Employee Balance Chart
- Pull Systems and Kanbans

10. The Waste of Overburden

Overburdening or overloading is when the capacity of the process is not known and/or is not adequately scheduled. This typically causes other wastes to occur. Overburden must be handled as a separate waste as it can be identified easily during the value mapping process and is often expressed in terms of capacities of equipment or people. Usually this waste causes a great sense of frustration, anger, and job dissatisfaction on the part of the employee. This most likely would have a negative impact on the customer as well.

The following are some examples of this waste, along with references to the Lean Sigma tools that would assist in its elimination.

Examples of overburden waste are:

- Having people "cover" for others while they are away without adequate training
- Being awarded a new contract for services but not having the additional man-hour capacity
- Knowing demand will increase for a brief period of time but not making available additional resources

Typical tools to reduce overburden waste are:

- Service Flow
- Standard Work
- Statistical Process Control (SPC)
- Performance Measurements
- Employee Balance Chart
- Visual Controls

11. Environmental Waste

As service organizations become more sustainable or "Green," they have to make extra efforts to protect the environmental resources as they are becoming very scarce. Any waste that is generated by a service organization that negatively impacts the environment, whether it is solid or liquid, is classified as environmental waste.

Examples of environmental waste are:

- Providing no process to recycle paper and plastic products, batteries, computers, etc.
- Using the utilization of power with machines and equipment without regard
- Providing no process on water usage conservation

Typical tools to reduce environmental waste are:

- Standard Work
- Resource Treasure Hunt
- Triple Bottom Line (TBL) Measures
- Value Stream (or Process) Mapping with Environmental Symbols
- 5S
- Sustainability or Green Metrics
- Rapid Improvement Events
- Waste Walk

12. Social Waste

Social waste is another category of waste that service organizations need to acknowledge if they wish to become more sustainable. The term social waste is broad and includes areas such as poverty, discrimination, malpractices, health and injuries, nutrition, literacy and education, and also waste on account of social media networking.

Examples of social waste are:

- ❖ Socializing excessively in person, via phone/texting/emailing or visiting social networking sites
- ❖ Advertising products on social networking sites that are not read by target customers
- ❖ Having fraud, theft, and abuse occurring
- ❖ Discriminating against an employee or prospective new hire for any reason as defined legally

Typical tools to reduce social waste are:

- ❖ Performance Measurements
- ❖ Employee Balance Chart
- ❖ Triple Bottom Line (TBL) Measures
- ❖ Teaming
- ❖ Standard Work
- ❖ Service Flow
- ❖ Standard Work for Leaders
- ❖ Effective Meetings

To summarize and create the basic understanding of waste, consider the following leading questions.

Leading Waste Questions:

1. How can I communicate these wastes throughout the organization?
2. What are some of the obvious wastes (low-hanging fruit)?
3. What can be done to immediately improve customer satisfaction?

These questions should stimulate others and promote more open communications regarding waste. Once these wastes are understood, it is advised that the project team conduct a Waste Walk to relate the wastes to their improvement project.

*A **Waste Walk** is an activity during which project team members visit a process area that is being considered for improvement, ask questions, and then identify the wastes on the current state value stream or process map.* The following (next page) Waste Walk Checklist can be used by teams or individuals to identify waste in their work environments. Simply take the form into the work environment and look for a waste or two in each of the "Dirty Dozen" waste categories. This exercise develops a deeper understanding of waste and may provide a starting point for an initial project. At a minimum, the results will stimulate discussion, learning, and waste observation.

The Waste Walk accomplishes the following:

- Ensures everyone is aligned to the physical location of the processes being analyzed
- Ensures process workers are engaged in the improvement event
- Allows for all process workers to provide input
- Allows for open communications about the team's project
- Allows for discussions about the process to clear up any questions

To conduct a Waste Walk consider the following:

1. Communicate to the employees working in the prospective areas/processes/departments when you will be bringing the group through and explain your purpose using the elevator speech. *An **elevator speech** is a brief, comprehensive verbal overview on the purpose and related activities regarding the product, process, or service being examined.*
2. Assign one person in each group to take notes. Use the following Waste Walk Checklist as a guide.
3. Ensure the team has thought of questions to ask, including: What are the issues affecting your work? What could be improved? Do you help out when things get busy? If not, why? Do you know when you are behind schedule? Do you know when the work you provide is needed downstream (to the next process)?
4. Do not cause any disruption to the process. (e.g., If a Waste Walk is to be conducted through, for example, an Emergency Department in a hospital, schedule the walk during their least busy time.)
5. If the group is larger than 5, break into smaller groups.
6. Start with the most downstream process and work upstream.
7. Thank the person(s) (and departmental manager/supervisor) for their time.

Once the Waste Walk has been completed and the information is fresh in everyone's mind, convey the various wastes on a value stream or process map.

Waste Walk Checklist

Types of Waste	Waste Observations
Overproduction Producing more material or information than is needed or used.	
Skills and Knowledge Not using people's minds and getting them involved.	
Transport Moving tools and materials excessively.	
Inventory Any unncessary materal, information, etc. that resides between processes.	
Motion Any unncessary movement that does not add value.	
Defects or Errors Redoing work that had been done previously.	
Overprocessing Providing work or a service that is not part of the customer requirement.	
Waiting or Delays The delay waiting for information, materials, people, etc.	
Overburden Work that is added with no additional support or resources.	
Unevenness Work that arrives without being scheduled and in varying amounts.	
Environmental Products or activites that are not good for the planet.	
Social Communication and networking that does not add value.	

Lean Sigma Tools

Lean Sigma tools that apply in a mass production manufacturing environment also can apply to a service environment, but they might not be a direct fit. Just as one would not use a screw driver to loosen a hex-head bolt, not every Lean Sigma tool will apply to every service environment and culture. The savvy Lean Sigma practitioner will identify the key applicable Lean Sigma tools and apply them as needed. We have demonstrated this application of the Lean Sigma tools in each of the case studies as well as provided service-related examples when discussing each tool.

Combining the simple concepts and tools of Lean with the concepts and tools of Six Sigma is the following Lean Sigma Tool Application Grid (listed as they will appear in this book). This grid is not all inclusive but these are the main tools typically used in a Lean for Service Excellence transformation. These tools are found to be the most applicable to service organizations. Keep in mind that any of these tools can be used in more than one of the five phase D-M-A-I-C process.

Where the Lean Sigma Tool is Covered in the Book					
	DEFINE - Chapter 4	MEASURE - Chapter 5	ANALYZE - Chapter 6	IMPROVE - Chapter 7	CONTROL - Chapter 8
Lean Sigma Tools					
Teaming	X				
Effective Meetings	X				
Project Charter	X				
Team Charter	X				
Project Planner	X				
Action Item Log	X				
Issues and Opportunities Log	X				
Voice of the Customer		X			
Quality Function Deployment		X			
Value Stream and Process Maps		X			
Supplier-Input-Process-Output-Customer (SIPOC) Diagrams		X			
Key Metric Data Profiles		X			
Check Sheets		X			
Frequency Charts		X			
Run Charts		X			
Measurement System Analysis		X			

	DEFINE - Chapter 4	MEASURE - Chapter 5	ANALYZE - Chapter 6	IMPROVE - Chapter 7	CONTROL - Chapter 8
Lean Sigma Tools					
Value-Added versus Non Value-Added Analysis			X		
Constraint or Bottleneck Analysis			X		
Demand Analysis and Takt Time			X		
Histogram, Ogive Chart, and Cumulative Frequency			X		
Pareto and Pie Charts			X		
Cause and Effect (or Fishbone) Diagrams			X		
Brainstorming			X		
5 Whys			X		
Radar Charts			X		
Scatter Plots			X		
Process Capability			X		
Force Field Analysis			X		
Interrelationship Diagrams					
Employee Balance Charts			X		
Impact Maps			X		
Rapid Improvement Events				X	
Plan-Do-Check-Act (PDCA) Process				X	
5S				X	
Visual Controls				X	
Mistake Proofing				X	
Standard Work				X	
Process or Work Area Layout				X	
Mass Customization				X	
Service Flow				X	
Quick Changeover (QCO)				X	
Total Productive Maintenance (TPM)				X	
Cross-Training				X	
Project Management					X
Statistical Process Control (SPC)					X
Visual Management					X
Standard Work for Leaders					X
Performance Management					X
Problem Solving - Corrective and Preventative Actions					X
Layered Process Audits					X

Lean Sigma - The Best of Both Worlds

The following chart summarizes some of the unique qualities of Lean and Six Sigma. Now, with a Lean Sigma approach, an organization can have both!

Six Sigma	Lean
Longer duration to complete project	Relatively short duration for eliminating waste
Hierarchical structure for oversight	Less need for hierarchical structure and oversight
Requires extensive training for individuals to attain certification levels (e.g., Black, Green, or White Belt status)	Less extensive training for the learning, implementation, and maintenance
Projects/teams must have a management sponsor and project manager or leader	Anyone can make quick improvements with knowledge of the process - no one is working in a vacuum
Selected projects tie to strategic priorities of the organization	Goal is to eliminate all waste throughout the organization
Projects are not considered successful unless there is a positive impact to the bottom-line	Projects that eliminate non value-added activities (waste) are considered successful
Heavy reliance on statistical methods	Lean can be successful without statistics
Sophisticated problem solving approach utilizing complex tools	Practical approach to problem solving utilizing user-friendly tools
More difficult to teach, understand, implement, and maintain	Easier to teach, understand, implement, and maintain

Lean Sigma Outcomes

There is a great deal of data regarding the success of organizations completing a Lean Sigma transformation. In planning your Lean Sigma transformation, be careful not to set your expectations too low. Organizations implementing Lean Sigma can expect to realize some or all of the following:

- High organization morale, teamwork, and effort through alignment of goals and measures
- Clear communication of priorities, expectations and results through visual and statistical controls (i.e., the "right" things get done "right")
- Clean, organized, and efficient worksite with minimal waste or errors
- High quality outputs and results
- Smooth flow of work or services
- No unscheduled downtime or surprises
- Perfection with zero defects or errors
- Less inventory, delays, transportation, motion, and rework or correction
- Less costs, more profit and Return-On-Investment (ROI)
- Increased capacity and sales
- Improved Net Promoter Score (the Net Promoter Score is an indication of how many of your customers would recommend or promote your services to another person or company, and is thought to be the key indicator for service organization success.)

Chapter Summary

This Lean Sigma overview was intended to provide a general understanding of Lean Sigma and to make the connection to service environments. A solid foundation and understanding of Lean Sigma philosophies, principles, concepts, methods and tools will provide a basis for transforming an organization from a traditionally managed organization to a Lean Sigma organization.

This brief overview of Lean Sigma philosophies, principles, concepts, methods, and tools also defines the basic processes and approach used to improve processes. The challenge for service organizations will be to learn and apply the Lean Sigma methods and tools, practiced for more than 50-plus years in manufacturing environments, into their service-oriented environments.

Lean Sigma for Service Excellence Applications

These observations may assist in understanding how to apply the concepts and tools contained in this chapter:

- Communicate to employees the simple concept of waste elimination for both the physical and electronic movement of information, as well as the flow of work in a service environment.
- Continue to read and learn about Lean, Six Sigma, and Lean Sigma from other sources (books, Webinars, conferences, blogs, benchmarking, etc.).
- Keep communication lines open regarding Lean Sigma and its purpose.
- Brush up on Lean Sigma tools your organization may already use.
- Understand that Lean Sigma compliments other programs.
- Keep in mind that Lean Sigma tools and practices are from all over the world in all types of businesses.
- Attempt small employee-driven improvements first and gain ownership and success.
- Establish ways to align and measure performance.
- Build an environment which embraces learning; Lean Sigma is a learned behavior and people are the key to its success.
- Continue to engage the employees on how Lean Sigma should be used to make their work easier and reduce stress.

Understanding Lean Sigma Readiness Guide

The following Understanding Lean Sigma Readiness Guide allows you to ensure there is application of the chapter's content before proceeding to apply the Lean Sigma tools and concepts in the next chapter. If you score less than 70%, consider working on the lower scoring areas before moving on.

Understanding Lean Sigma Readiness Guide

Use the following 5-level Likert item scale to rank each of the statements:

1 = Strongly Disagree
2 = Disagree
3 = Niether Agree nor Disagree
4 = Agree
5 = Strongly Agree

	Score
1. Waste is well-defined in my organization.	
2. My organization has a good system in place for eliminating waste.	
3. My organization has a good system in place for measuring the cost associated with waste.	
4. My organization does a good job of conserving resources.	
5. My organization is customer-focused.	
6. My organization strongly believes in continuous improvement.	
7. My organization utilizes value stream or process mapping regularly.	
8. My organization has a strong emphasis on employee involvement.	
9. My organization does a good job of applying Lean Sigma concepts.	
10. My organization does a good job of applying Lean Sigma tools.	
11. My organization does a good job of applying Lean Sigma methods.	
12. My organization focuses on value-added processes.	
13. My organization understands the value of a Waste Walk.	
14. Quality is built into the organization's products and services.	
15. My organization uses objective information to evaluate process performance.	
16. My organization does a good job in understanding its customer needs.	
17. My organization does a good job in integrating Lean and Six Sigma.	
18. My organization allows time for employees to learn about Lean Sigma.	
19. My organization understands the possible outcomes of using Lean Sigma.	
20. I believe my organization should utilize and apply the concepts and tools discussed in this chapter.	
Total Score	

Case Review - Waste Walk for Arvis Car Rental

JoAnn is the manager of the airport branch of the Arvis Rental Car agency. JoAnn had recently attended a Lean Sigma for Service seminar offered at the local university and had many ideas in which to apply what was learned back at Arvis. One tool that she thought she could use immediately was the "Waste Walk" audit form. Arvis Rental Car had been meeting its quarterly performance objectives set by corporate; therefore it ran pretty well, so, there was not an immediate concern for starting with a new improvement activity.

Within a few days after JoAnn's return from the seminar small problems started to occur. Several cars had not been returned on time and the clean-up crew was wasting time in the garage with nothing to do. If the cars did not come in soon, JoAnn would not have cars for the customers scheduled to arrive that day

On top of this, JoAnn was training a new employee, Mary, at the customer service desk and there were a couple situations where the customers became frustrated and entered formal complaints. JoAnn had to intervene and fix the situations. Usually when this happened, JoAnn had to give a free upgrade of some type or lose the rental.

During one of the busiest times of the day, several special needs customers arrived, which slowed the rental process down to a crawl. Lines were out the front door and several customers walked across the parking lot to the competitor. Mary had suggested that everyone skip their normal break schedule, but JoAnn was too busy to listen to this suggestion. When another customer service representative, Michelle, left for her break, customers got even more frustrated.

To make things worse, the district manager for Arvis showed up right as JoAnn was handling the most irate and vocal complaining customer. The customer had complained that they had just flown from Detroit to Tampa in 2.5 hours and they had been in line for nearly an hour - emphasizing that this was not right! After the customer left, the district manager informed JoAnn that she better "tighten" this agency up. The district manager had a way of saying things, which may not have been the most tactful, but had left JoAnn with a feeling of enormous stress and a sense of urgency to do something.

JoAnn immediately told a key group, two customer service reps (including the new one), two cleaning crew members, and one administrative assistance that she needed them to stay late that night to work. They all agreed and made the appropriate calls to their families notifying them that they were asked to stay late. JoAnn did not make the meeting mandatory, but her leadership style had earned her the respect of her employees.

JoAnn had arranged for some pizza to be delivered at their 7:00 p.m. meeting, which she committed to lasting no more than two hours. JoAnn knew that this was not the time for the intensive training she recently experienced at the university.

As a way to focus and document their ideas JoAnn wanted to complete a "Waste Walk" with the team, and from that, create some immediate solutions to ensure the problems that they had experienced that day would not reappear. JoAnn passed out a blank form on a clipboard to each team member and asked them to jot down their thoughts as they walked through the process of a customer renting a car. The following (next page) is the completed Waste Walk Checklist form as the result of their 20-minute walk-through.

.

Waste Walk Checklist

Types of Waste	Waste Observations
Overproduction Producing more material or information than is needed or used.	Often the cleaning crew works ahead by 10 -12 cars, just to stay busy.
Skills and Knowledge Not using people's minds and getting them involved.	Listen more to ideas.
Transport Moving tools and materials excessively.	The customers have to be bussed from the terminals. The cars have to be moved to the garage for cleaning and prep.
Inventory Any unncessary material, information, etc. that resides between processes.	The cars and transport busses are the inventory. Sometimes we have too many, sometimes too few.
Motion Any unnecessary movement that does not add value.	At the service desk, we only have one printer, and each sales person has to walk to the printer for each rental contract.
Defects or Errors Redoing work that had been done previously.	Sometimes we have to re-do customer contracts if they do not like the car we gave them, or we make an error.
Overprocessing Providing work or a service that is not part of the customer requirement.	Our policy to "Talk up" customers to bigger vehicles only works about 2% of the time and we spend about 3 minutes per customer trying to get them to upgrade.
Waiting or Delays The delay waiting for information, materials, people, etc.	Our customers wait for the bus at the terminal, then they wait in line at the office, then they wait in line to exit the parking lot.
Overburden Work that is added with no additional support or resources.	During the busy periods, there are just not enough people in the office to process the customers and the clean-up crew is just standing around.
Unevenness Work that arrives without being scheduled and in varying amounts.	Work load varies greatly. The airline schedules seems to deliver the customers in big batches and our busses wait until they are full to bring customers to the office.
Environmental Products or activites that are not good for the planet.	We have a hopper of printed material that we dispose of every day.
Social Communication and networking that does not add value.	We have no policy for social networking and personal, smart/4G phone use at work, and some abuse the privilege. This irritates customers, and is not fair to all.

The Waste Walk was very revealing and the improvement ideas just seemed to flow from the team. The team spent the next 15 minutes brainstorming and documenting the following improvement ideas.

Improvement ideas generated after the "Waste Walk" were:

1. Have the entire cleaning crew clean as many cars are needed for the first 2 hours in the morning and afternoon, and then 3 of them stop and assist in the office. The cleaning crews would need some additional training, but this would help during busy times, and make things better for everyone, including the customers.
2. JoAnn needs to listen to employee ideas. Mary's idea regarding breaks would have helped tremendously and Mary would have felt better about her work.
3. Request to increase capacity by having a second bus allowing the customers to arrive at the office sooner after their flight arrives. These smaller "batches of customers" would help to smooth work loads and flow, and reduce waiting times at the terminal and office.
4. Purchase printers for each customer service position and look into an upgrade to the server speed. Contact corporate IT and investigate further.
5. Track of errors and re-dos and have a contest with a prize for the lowest team every month. The team wanted a trip to the Bahamas as a prize. However, a less extravagant award would be chosen.
6. Create signals and standards for when to try and up-sell customers with larger vehicle, pre-purchased gas option, insurance, navigation, etc. and when not to.
7. Investigate into ways to print less paper. Why do we print copies of the customer contract just to throw them away? Some of the copies were reports for JoAnn and corporate. Can they use an electronic version with an end-of-day summary? Talk to corporate and determine exactly what they need.
8. Establish a fair policy for personal cell phone use and texting.

The next 30 minutes Action Items were assigned to each team member to implement the above suggestions. Everyone seemed very positive and knew that many of these problems were just "accepted" as normal business. JoAnn thanked the team for their input and summarized the list in an email to her boss. Not all the improvement ideas could be implemented because some of them took considerable time to implement, but since all the improvements were documented they all would be addressed in the very near future. JoAnn also signed-up two of the team members for the next Lean Sigma for Service Excellence workshop. The meeting concluded at 8:45 pm, 15 minutes earlier than expected (to the delight of everyone).

JoAnn realized on her drive home that evening, the journey had begun!

Pursuing Perfect Service

Part Two.
Beginning the Lean Sigma for Service Excellence Journey

Chapter 3

Understanding the Lean Sigma for Service Excellence Journey

Every Journey Begins with the First Step

Chapter Overview

The first steps of any journey are some of the most critical ones. Getting started in the right direction, with the right resources, and for the right reasons makes the journey safer and more fruitful. It is critical that an organization understand whether they are embarking on a journey to achieve a Lean Sigma environment or simply beginning to apply Lean Sigma tools for a near-term performance improvement. This chapter examines the critical differences between basic tool applications and Lean Sigma transformations. This chapter also details the overall Lean Sigma for Service Excellence transformation journey, what is needed, and what to expect. Four organizational enablers are reviewed to help leaders ensure the key items are in place for success.

More than just communicating the need to change, a manager (or leader) must establish the pathway and commit the resources for an organization to achieve success. Leaders must identify and communicate the need to change, what to change to, and how to do it together. This chapter is designed to aid leaders and managers in completing this crucial work and begin the Lean Sigma for Service Excellence transformation journey.

Lean Sigma Transformations versus Tools Application

Many service organizations have begun using Lean Sigma tools with various levels of success. While basic Lean Sigma tools can help service organizations improve, if the implementation of tool applications is not part of a true transformation commitment, the result can be inconsistent and short-lived. The following Lean Sigma Journey Readiness flow diagram can be used to determine whether an organization is ready to commit to the Lean Sigma transformation process or only implement Lean Sigma tools:

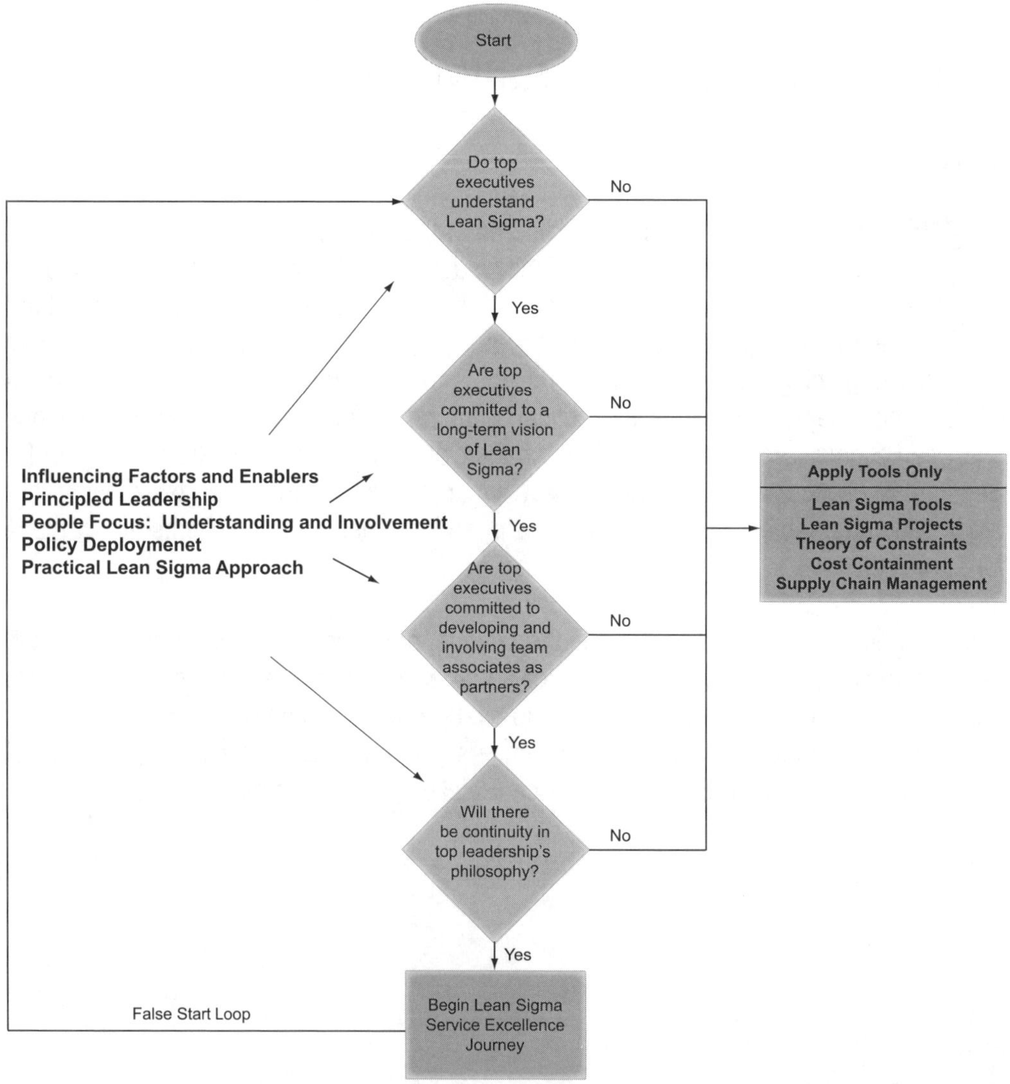

The following explains the main segments comprised of the Lean Sigma Journey Readiness flow diagram:

Do top executives understand Lean Sigma?

To execute a Lean Sigma transformation, it is critical that the top executives understand the fundamental Lean Sigma concept of waste and waste elimination, and that there is a systematic approach to leading an organization through a Lean Sigma transformation. If top executives do not understand the basics of Lean Sigma and their role, they will have difficulty properly supporting the effort, doing their standard work, and asking the right questions to ensure sustainable success. Leaders must demonstrate through their actions that they understand Lean Sigma. Failure to do this will jeopardize a true Lean Sigma transformation and/or cause an organization to engage in a "False Start."

Are executives committed to a long-term vision of Lean Sigma?

A yes to this question is critical to the success of a Lean Sigma transformation. Executives must understand that a Lean Sigma transformation is a long term commitment to how the organization is run, rather than a short term action item to be included on a list or on an individual's personal goals. Top executive commitment to a Lean Sigma vision is truly a prerequisite for a full Lean Sigma transformation. Leaders should develop a long term vision for the organization that includes Lean Sigma, and then behave in a manner that supports the vision. Failure to do this will jeopardize a true Lean Sigma transformation and or cause an organization to engage in a "False Start."

Are top executives committed to developing and involving team associates as partners?

The very foundation of Lean Sigma principles are grounded in total participation, training, and continual learning. Organizations wishing to pursue a Lean Sigma transformation must be willing to invest in training and be willing to develop worker initiative to identify and reduce wastes. This includes the commitment to tolerate and learn from mistakes made during the transformation. If mistakes are not seen as an opportunity and a responsibility to improve, organizations will have trouble with a true transformation. Leaders should demonstrate through their actions and behaviors that they are committed, engaged and working as partners in the transformation. Failure to do this consistently will jeopardize a true Lean Sigma transformation and/or cause an organization to engage in a "False Start."

Will there be continuity in top leadership's philosophy?

Many Lean Sigma transformations have been derailed due to change in leadership or a change in their philosophy regarding how to run the organization. Changing economic times is not a reason to change the long term vision for the organization. Constancy of purpose and philosophy will create a trusting environment that will support a Lean Sigma transformation. If your organization follows the trend of the month, a true Lean Sigma transformation is not for you. Leaders should work to provide a stable and consistent environment that supports Lean Sigma improvements. Failure to do this will jeopardize or slow a true Lean Sigma transformation and/or cause an organization to engage in a "False Start."

There have been many well-intentioned leaders that have started their organizations down the path of a Lean Sigma transformation, only to be disappointed with their progress and success over time. The best advice for leader's finding themselves in this situation is to look in the mirror. The reason for most transformation failures lies in the four questions previously discussed which are controlled by leadership.

Many organizations will make significant progress on their Lean Sigma journey before stagnation, plateau, diminishing returns or even back-slide or regression occurs. After the initial excitement and easy improvements are implemented, stagnation and regression is common in many transformations. The key at this point is for leadership to recommit to the transformation efforts. If a recommitment cannot be accomplished soon enough, organizations may have to start over at the beginning. This restart is termed the "False Start Loop."

If top executives cannot answers "Yes" to the transformation readiness questions in the decision boxes of the flow diagram, it is recommended that organizations pursue basic improvement tool applications only (Apply Tools Only), and not expect a full Lean Sigma cultural transformation to occur. While isolated improvement tool applications can be very beneficial for organizations, it alone will not deliver the significant rewards of a true Lean Sigma cultural transformation, which is the key to sustaining the gains.

If your organization is only ready to apply tools, you should proceed to Chapters 4 - 8 and begin a project. Project selection should come from one of the following areas:

- Key Market or Leader Needs
- Customer Mandates
- Key Organizational Performance Measures
- Governmental Regulations
- Lean Sigma Assessments

If on the other hand your organization is ready to begin the Lean Sigma journey or transformation, or wishes to learn more regarding how to get to the point where you can begin this journey, continue reading (and working) on the concepts and tools explained in this chapter.

A graphical representation of the process or steps of a Lean Sigma for Service transformation is represented in the following flow diagram:

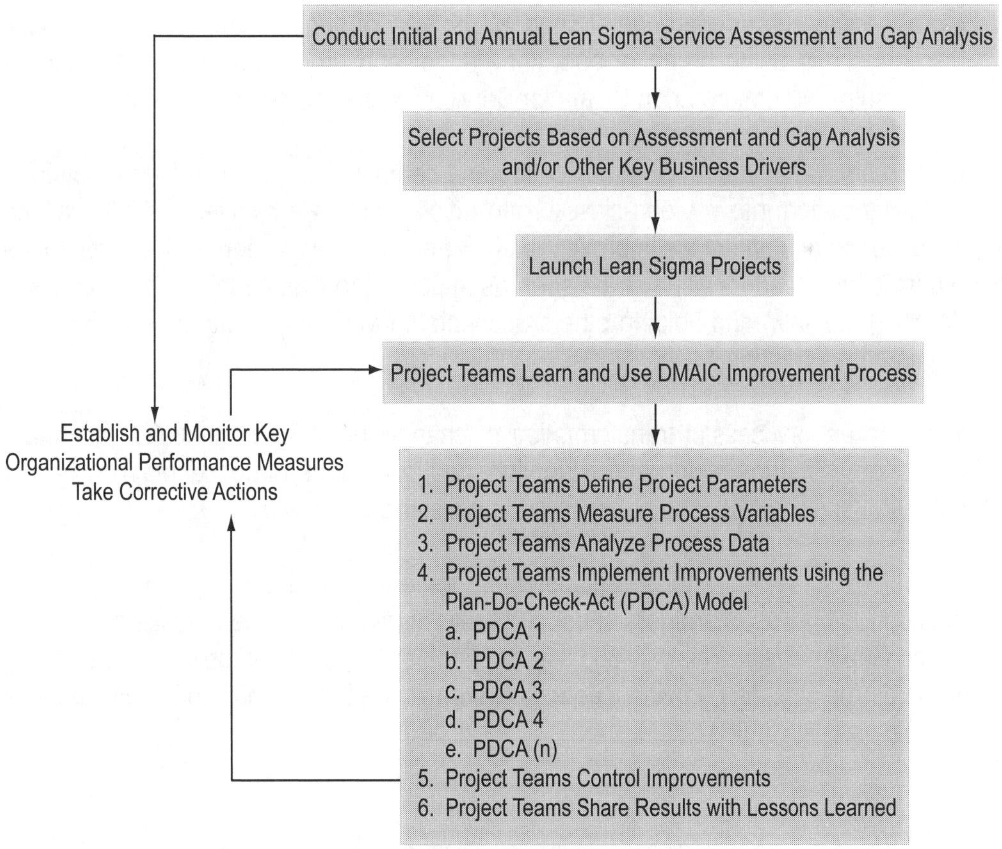

Lean Sigma for Service Excellence transformations can take anywhere from a few months to a few years. It will depend on the following:

1. The overall size of the organization. The smaller the organization, the less time it will typically take. For a large organization (500 or more employees), pilot (or beta) Lean Sigma for Service Excellence projects should be started in a department or area and then expanded to the other areas. Small organizations may also find it beneficial to start with smaller, targeted pilot projects rather than organization wide-deployment.

2. Availability of the tools and resources. This book will provide the detailed road map, forms, templates, and actual examples with which the team can use and reference as a benchmark. Other resources such as time for work sessions and implementation activities need to be planned for and committed by the organization's leadership.

3. Understanding of the benefits. Fully understanding and communicating the value of cross-training, inter-departmental sharing, the use of generalists versus specialists, discerning and using organizational knowledge, and promoting employee-manager partnerships will ensure Lean Sigma for Service Excellence success.

4. Leadership commitment. Communicating and demonstrating the resolve to transform the organization into a world-class organization bolsters employee confidence and speed to engage and make improvements. Something that is seen as important to the organization's leaders will also be seen as important to the organization's members. "Walking the Talk" and holding others accountable to do the same speeds the Lean Sigma transformation.

The keys to any successful transformation or change within an organization are management commitment, training and education, goal alignment and accountability, barrier identification and removal, and patience and persistence.

To understand an organization's readiness to pursue a Lean Sigma transformation, it is recommended that key managers conduct a Lean Sigma for Service Excellence Assessment and Gap Analysis. This will help assure alignment, open communications regarding issues and problems, and provide a perspective on where the organization needs to focus resources.

Lean Sigma for Service Excellence Assessment and Gap Analysis

Organizations can use a Lean Sigma for Service Excellence Assessment and Gap Analysis type instrument to document the current state of the entire organization or a specific department or process with regard to Lean Sigma initiatives. The assessment should be conducted at a minimum of once per year.

The Lean Sigma for Service Excellence Assessment and Gap Analysis is designed to create an understanding of what may be some improvement opportunities as well as provide a baseline to compare with future improvement initiatives (and subsequent assessments). The assessment and gap analysis can also be used to assist organizations to prioritize where to start their journey.

The assessment has the following five main categories:

1. Leadership
2. Customer Focus
3. Process Management
4. People Management
5. Information and Analysis

Each section is further broken down into statements that describe qualities for each category as well as a Bar Chart representing each statement. An example of the Customer Focus category is shown below:

Section 2 Customer Focus		Score (1-5)
Listening	My organization does a good job of listening and involving its customers.	3
Measures	Customer satisfaction measurements capture actionable information needed for improvement.	3
Benchmarking	My organization obtains and uses customer service information relative to competition and/or benchmarks.	2
Expectations	Customer satisfaction takes top priority at my organization.	5
Flexibility	My organization remains flexible to changing customer needs and expectations.	1
Equity	We practice fair and equitable business practices for our customers, shareholders, and employees.	1
Average		**2.5**

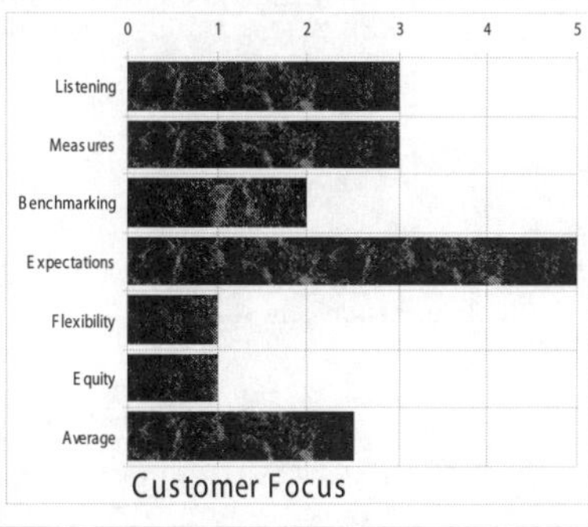

Note: The complete Lean Sigma for Service Excellence Assessment and Gap Analysis is provided in the Appendix.

Note: The Bar Charts and Radar Chart (next page) have the minimum value of "0" for readability. The responses will be 1, 2, 3, 4, or 5.

Each statement can be scored with the following five-level Likert item scale:

1 = Strongly Disagree
2 = Disagree
3 = Neither Agree nor Disagree
4 = Agree
5 = Strongly Agree

Once all the statements have been scored, the average for each category is plotted on a Bar Chart and a Radar Chart. The nature of this type of assessment is that there will always be a lowest category score or individual question score. It is suggested that brainstorming, 5 Why Analysis, Cause and Effect Diagramming, etc. be used to further investigate the lower scoring areas. With the subsequent information and discussion, specific improvement activities can be planned and implemented.

The following Bar Chart and Radar Chart show that the areas of Process Management and Leadership may be considered for initial Lean Sigma projects:

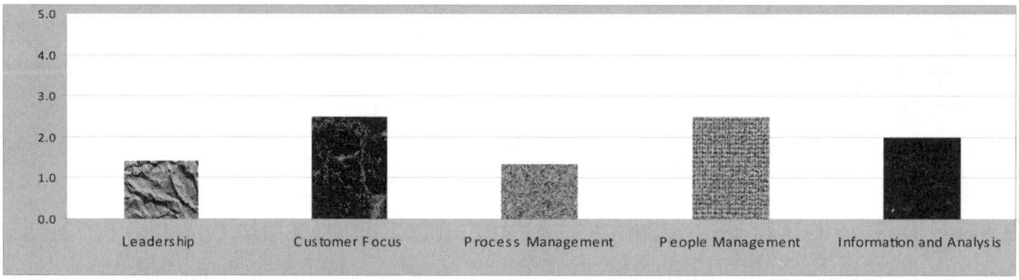

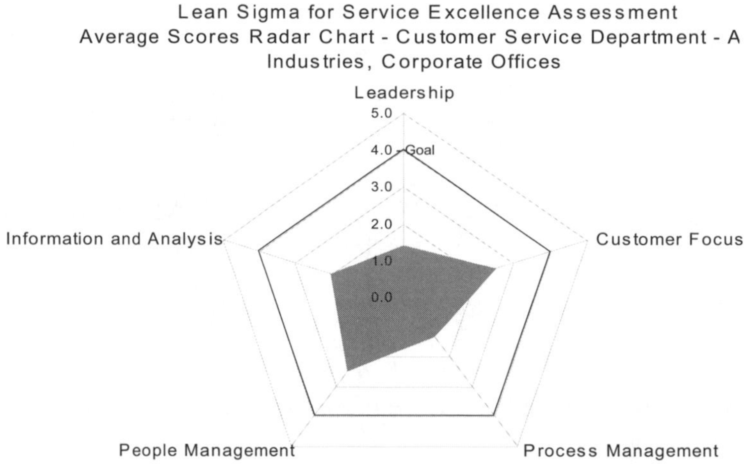

The score obtained on the assessment must be considered with other business performance (scorecard) measurements to determine where the resources of the organization will most likely have the biggest impact. There likely will be other organization factors that should also be considered.

It is recommended that a Lean Sigma for Service Excellence Assessment and Gap Analysis be completed with your organization's leadership team to stimulate discussion regarding the organizations readiness and need to begin a Lean Sigma transformation.

It is desirable for the scores in every category and for each question in any category to achieve a score of 4 (Agree) or 5 (Strongly Agree). Scores below a 4 represent a gap or opportunity for improvement and/or additional investigation or study. The Gap Analysis is completed by reviewing the scores in each category and each question versus the desired target scores. The gaps represent areas of possible improvement projects. The larger the gap, the more opportunity there is for improvement, and typically the areas of larger gaps should be addressed first.

Organizational Enablers

There are four organizational enablers that should be in place to successfully launch a Lean Sigma for Service Excellence transformation. The enablers allow an organization to engage all employees and will affect everything done during the transformation. They must always be present and understood wherever you are on the Lean Sigma journey. You will not succeed without them. Each enabler will involve understanding, educating, and involving your people. They provide the foundation on which all will rest. The proper balance of the four enablers also becomes critical during the transformation. Leaders must work to understand and adjust the balance between four enablers.

The four organizational enablers (4 P's) are:

Enabler #1 - Principled Leadership: Demonstrating Management Commitment and Effective Leadership
Enabler #2 - People Focus: Ensuring Employee Engagement
Enabler #3 - Policy Deployment: Creating Goal Alignment, Ownership, and Accountability
Enabler #4 - Practical Lean Sigma Tool Application: Using the Right Tool for the Job

The following will explain in more detail the four enablers.

Enabler #1: Principled Leadership: Demonstrating Management Commitment and Effective Leadership

In classical management study, management's role is to lead, plan, organize, and control. These four responsibilities are critically important when leading an organization through a Lean Sigma transformation. Too often these responsibilities are performed poorly or left to chance. In fact, most Lean Sigma transformation failures are due to the lack of an organization performing these key management functions. Let us examine these responsibilities further and address the special needs for Lean Sigma transformations and Service Excellence.

Leading is often misunderstood. People sometimes mistake leadership for charismatic sound bites so often heard on the six o'clock news or ESPN's popular show, SportsCenter. Their perspective of leadership is influenced and twisted by media, and sports programming. In truth, there are many effective leaders in business and industry that do not share the spotlight or receive the attention of the celebrity leaders. Effective leaders come in all styles.

Leadership has three primary functions of (1) being responsible for setting direction, (2) establishing rules and policies, and (3) motivating people to high levels of achievement. These functions are further explained as follows:

1. Leaders must define the direction for an organization. This might be done with some type of formal strategic planning process or perhaps a simple verbal instruction. For a Lean Sigma transformation, management must set the journey and direction for the organization. In Steven Covey's "7 Habits of Highly Effective People" Covey describes the difference between managers and leaders through a short story about a group of people cutting a path through a thick rain forest. While the managers are on the ground encouraging people to chop faster, the leaders are climbing the trees to determine the direction. Of course in the story, the managers are too busy managing to listen to the leaders' directions.

2. Leaders must set or establish the rules, guidelines, or standards for how an organization will function. This includes basic policies, practices, and acceptable behaviors or standards. In the best run organizations, this is often done in a participative manner with its membership. This ensures the highest level of commitment and ownership at all levels. It also tends to be self, or peer policing, in that people are committed to sound business practices and behaviors that will root out any under or non-performers. This in turn builds a healthy, motivating environment.

3. Leaders must build a motivating environment. This is best done by creating internal processes where people can motivate themselves to high levels of performance and success. This is easier said than done. The key to creating a self-motivating environment is employing many of the Lean Sigma methods and tools.

Planning is another key responsibility for management. Management must identify the steps or journey to achieve the strategy. This includes identifying and ensuring that key resources are made available to support the plan and its timing. Planning is basically establishing who, what, when, where, and how an organization will proceed. Planning at this level may also include identifying and eliminating potential barriers or roadblocks to the plan.

The next major responsibility of management is to organize to support the plan. It is not uncommon for organizations going through a Lean Sigma transformation to have to reorganize, or change roles and responsibilities during the transformation. Often large organizations create an internal Lean Sigma Champion network of personnel to support the Lean Sigma transformation. While this is not necessary in all cases, managers must look for opportunities to improve the effort through appropriate organizational changes.

The last classical responsibility of managers is to control the organization's performance. This is done through establishing organizational performance measures and monitoring them by creating an environment where people can motivate themselves to high levels of performance and success to determine next steps.

Lean Sigma transformations must be driven from the top down. Top management must make a 100% commitment to positive change and must be 100% convinced that a Lean Sigma transformation represents the best opportunity for continued or newfound success. A partnership led by top management, and developed and implemented by a motivated work force, will ensure Lean Sigma initiatives are not only implemented, but sustained.

The phrase "walk the talk" means that a leader's or manager's behavior must match his or her expressed strategy for the organization. A leader or manager must be willing to do and sacrifice at the same level that they expect from others. People quickly see where leaders do not "walk the talk" which can lead to confusion and lack of trust in an organization and subsequently foil most improvement efforts. A Lean Sigma transformation will not work without total commitment from management. A CEO reading about Lean Sigma in the Wall Street Journal on a flight coming home from vacation, and then telling his top manager that "it sounds like a good idea," does not reflect or constitute a long-term desire for continuous improvement.

Management commitment must be driven by a passion to improve. The top manager must be totally involved in the implementation of Lean Sigma. Even, if that first Lean Sigma project only involves three people, top level commitment must be present. Management commitment is:

- Committing the necessary resources to the Lean Sigma initiatives
- Being present at the first meeting
- Providing coaching and counseling to the team when needed
- Displaying interest in the team's progress by attending meetings
- Rewarding and recognizing the team's effort
- Having empathy and providing support when the team is struggling

The previous is not an exhaustive list, but it does show a general framework for how management commitment can be manifested.

In Lean Sigma Service transformations, leader's responsibilities include the following:

1. Identify, define, and communicate the need to improve: *Lean Sigma Mission*
2. Identify, define, and communicate the vision of what to improve to: *Lean Sigma Vision*
3. Identify, define, and provide leadership and resources to make the improvements: *Lean Sigma Methods and Tools*

To define and communicate the need to improve, leaders often use a Mission Statement, which can include the mission, vision, and values.

Lean Sigma Mission

Mission Statements *are a basic statement of the identity of an organization and its purpose or mission.* Organization leaders often see this as the bland, generic mission statement on a conference room wall. To a savvy Lean Sigma leader, the Mission Statement provides the opportunity to define the organization and the customers or markets they serve. It is used to define the compelling need to change and achieve excellence. Lean Sigma leaders use a Mission Statement to identify the organizations stakeholders and set priorities and, if done properly, as a rallying point for the members of the organization. It is a key to establishing a self-motivating environment, which leads to continuous process improvement and a customer-focused culture.

Many organizational leaders speak of developing "culture." The Mission Statement is the foundation document to do this. Do not skip creating or updating the current Mission Statement if you are serious about pursuing excellence. The following is an example of a service organization Mission Statement. Again, the best run organizations develop Mission Statements in a participative manner with different levels of the organization.

LEAN SIGMA MISSION STATEMENT
KLARK INTERMEDIATE SCHOOL DISTRICT

The mission of the Klark Intermediate School District (KISD) is to ensure the opportunity for all students to possess the marketable skills necessary to support success, adaptability, and lifelong learning in the changing workplace.

Purpose Statement: KISD exists to provide career and technical education that satisfies our customers' needs for career exploration, continuing education, and successful employment.

Values: Those values that we uphold are...

Accountability and Responsibility - Being depended on to fulfill professional obligations

Continuous Improvement - Learning and constantly developing to achieve our vision, values, purpose, and goals

Cooperation - Working together toward a common goal

Flexibility - Being open and adaptive to change requirements

Integrity - Acting with honest intent

Quality - Striving for excellence which results in customer satisfaction

Respect - Recognizing the worth, quality, and importance of others regardless of position and background

Trust - Placing and having confidence in others

Lean Sigma Vision

*The **vision** defines the future identity of the organization.* Visions are sometimes relegated to the conference room walls as well, and this is a missed opportunity for the Lean Sigma leader. Vision statements can help to control the behaviors of the organization. They define what the organization is trying to become. The vision can define the guidelines for behavior change and improvement.

Leaders need to initiate the vision, and then develop a shared understanding and support. This is best done through a participative development process. The vision should be sufficiently detailed and comprehensive to allow the members of the organization to "see the picture" of what they are striving to become. Too vague of a vision tends to confuse people, and does not provide enough detail to modify behavior. Too detailed a vision tends to confine an organization to over-burdensome bureaucratic behaviors.

A simple way to define a vision for an organization is to define the current state of behaviors. The following are some questions to assist in determining the acceptable behaviors for the organization's members:

- Is it acceptable to not clean up after yourself?
- Is it acceptable to show up late for meetings?
- Is it acceptable not to follow work standards?
- Are people treated fairly and equitably for their contributions?
- Is it acceptable to pass poor quality?
- Is it acceptable to scream and shout at people?
- Does the organization learn from their failures?
- Is there accountability or discipline to rules and goals?
- Do all levels receive proper training?

Then, define the new vision by defining what the organization wants to become. The following are some statements of acceptable behavior for the organization's members:

- Always clean up after yourself. Leave an area cleaner than when you arrived.
- Be on time for all meetings. Start all meetings on time.
- Follow all work standards and rules, if in doubt ask someone.
- Treat people fairly; show no favoritism.
- Do not pass on poor quality.
- Treat people with respect and dignity. Value and train on diversity.
- Develop a system to learn from failures.

Developing a vision is the responsibility of management. It is not always easy, but well worth the effort if done properly. The vision provides the framework for holding people accountable and improving the organizational culture.

In summary, management's role is to provide the plan and vision, the leadership, the organization structure, and the sustainable control process to clear the path for the Lean Sigma for Service Excellence transformation. To ensure the transformation is successful organizational enablers should be in place.

Enabler #2 - People Focus: Ensuring Employee Engagement

This enabler helps employees understand why current ways of doing business may not be good enough. As companies grow and take on more work, waste reduction must become prevalent in all aspects of the organization. Employees must recognize that every type of task has a cost associated to it. This enabler will help to effectively communicate this need for change and create a learning and action-oriented organization.

The introduction and initial implementation of Lean Sigma must first change behavior if a continuous improvement culture is to emerge. The sequencing of Lean Sigma outlined in this book will begin to establish the groundwork for change (continuous improvement through Total Employee Involvement). But change cannot be accomplished overnight. Employees must understand that positive change (i.e., Lean Sigma) will contribute to the organization's, and their personal, long-term success.

Understanding human behaviors and attitudes within an organization are critical to achieving success in any improvement initiative. This is particularly so in a service organization where employees frequently interact with the customer directly.

The Non-Lean Sigma Approach figure indicates that managers attempted to change the culture first, expecting that attitudes would change, and the desired behavior would result. Upon closer examination of Lean Sigma and the Toyota Production System models, researchers discovered a drastically different approach. They discovered that as Lean Sigma tools are introduced and used, people's behavior changed to one of identifying and eliminating abnormalities and waste. Once employees felt in control of their jobs through eliminating waste and making their jobs easier, their behavior changed to one of continuous improvement. As each employee changes his or her behavior, the culture of the entire organization begins to change radically from "catching mistakes" to "preventing mistakes." For example, in service in the early 2000s, air travelers could not check on the status of their flights or re-book onto another flight from the comfort of their home or office. When travelers arrived at the airline check-in counter they expected the airline employee to update them with detailed information. Employees in this environment many times did not have current information to share which caused an increase in stress level for both the customer and the employee. The higher level of stress was often reflected in their behavior. Even though the employees may have been told correctly how to

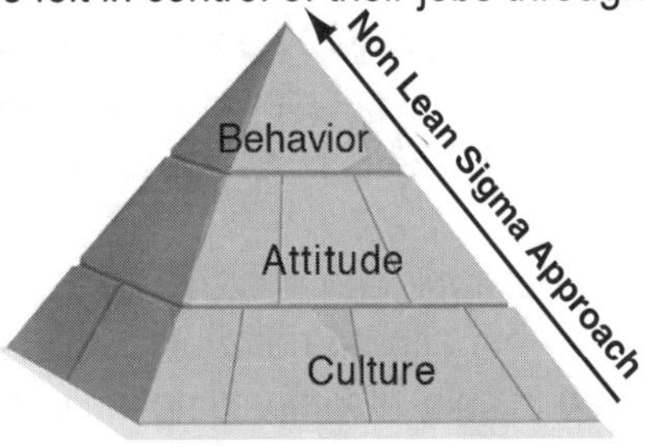

provide superior service, they could not deliver. Management's desire to shift the culture to excellence could not be realized as the behaviors drove the attitude and culture. Ten years ago, service employees were still catching mistakes after they occurred, and were hampered by wasteful practices, such as multiple approvals for making simple changes or small credits. This frustration drove their behavioral response, which drove customer satisfaction and organization culture.

The overall Lean Sigma Approach model is simple. It requires a diligent effort from both managers and employees. Established work habits are difficult to break. Training, education, discipline, dedication, determination, and communication are required to move an organization forward. Small successes will create the momentum to move from the simple behavior and attitude change to an organizational Lean Sigma culture. Today for example, organizations focused on applying continuous improvement methods and tools have created environments where employees can act to prevent problems for their customers. Creating an environment such as this leads to the correct behavior, which then leads to the desired culture. Employees that have the information and tools to identify and prevent (or resolve) issues quickly deliver superior customer service. By improving the work environment, the behavioral response changes to a positive, Lean Sigma response.

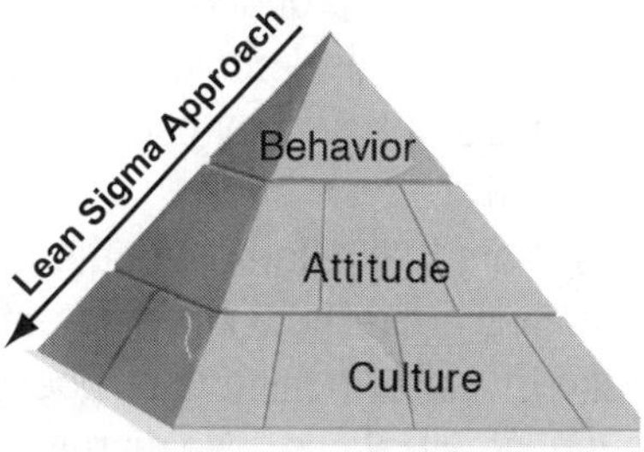

The key to implementing Lean Sigma and sustaining it is the continual, daily effort to improve. As behavior changes, you will want to initiate a reward and recognition system to acknowledge the changes that are occurring. Quick adapters to change will embrace this system. They will see the benefits immediately. Slow adapters may fight the system and hold on to old habits. Slow adapters will struggle for awhile; however, be as understanding as possible as the system will speak for itself when implementation is under way and employees start to experience the benefits. Continue to invest in employee training and development through all phases of the Lean Sigma journey to accelerate these changes. Engage people on improvement teams and expect them to be accountable and take responsibility for improvements. It is their job after all.

Reducing wastes and costs and improving the total customer satisfaction will lead to overall business growth and profitability. Growth and profitability are essential for any business to survive. Through implementing a Lean Sigma transformation, a business will survive, become stronger, and will be able to provide wage and earnings growth, and advancement in a safer, more stable work environment. But at the heart of any Lean Sigma transformation is understanding your people (i.e., specifically the generations in today's workforce).

There are four generations in the workforce today interacting on a day-to-day basis, each with different computer skills and work experiences. These differences, if not acknowledged and leveraged appropriately can give rise to frustration, clashes, and misinterpretation – all of which can contribute to a non-Lean Sigma work environment. However, utilizing each generation's positive work styles (i.e., technical and work experience skills) can also create a more creative and diverse atmosphere in which the organization can then excel and create a competitive advantage. It is imperative for managers, as well as the front-line workers, to understand these differences from both a generational and computer skills point-of-view. Working to improve communications between these generations will ultimately improve the quality of decision-making as well as improve the flow of information, products, services, etc. throughout the organization. Even though this book is a technical book, it is imperative to not underestimate the importance of people's attitudes and how they can impact work processes within an organization.

The years that differentiate the generations in today's workforce, as outlined in this section, may be defined a bit differently due to a certain set of criteria used by various organizations. Keep in mind the bigger picture of the "groups" of people as a generation; these are generalizations. We do not mean to "categorize" a certain age group in any negative way. The intent is to recognize the differences that do exist and use those differences, along with the right balance of technology, to improve an organization's communication. The following are the four working generations and some general attributes of each that exist in today's workforce (years and numbers referenced are for the United States):

The **Matures (Traditionalist, Veterans, and Silent) Generation** is the oldest generation in the workforce and these people were born between 1925 and 1945. There are approximately 63.2 million Matures in the workforce. The Matures are currently retiring or facing retirement in the next few years. This group was largely defined by their experiences in the Great Depression (1929) and in World War II (1941 – 1945).

- Value: respect for authorities, conformity, and discipline
- Key Word: loyal
- Their families are very traditional (nuclear)
- Education is typically seen as a dream
- Communicate face-to-face
- Deal with money by saving it, and when spent, paying with cash

The **Baby Boomer Generation** is the second oldest generation in the workforce, and these people were born between 1946 and 1964. There are roughly 76.8 million Baby Boomers in the workforce. The Baby Boomers are currently becoming empty nesters (i.e., having no children at home) and make up the largest segment in the workforce. These people grew up post World War II and have experienced Kennedy's Camelot years at the White House, Woodstock, and the Vietnam War.

- Value: being involved
- Key Word: optimistic
- Their family is disintegrating (divorce rates beginning to increase dramatically)
- Education is a birthright
- Communicate by phone and liked to be called at anytime
- Deal with money by buying something now and paying for it later

The **Generation Xers** are the people born between 1965 and 1980. There are roughly 52.4 million Gen Xers in the workforce. These people are buying, if they can afford it, their first homes, waiting longer to start families, and beginning to move to higher-level management positions being vacated by the Matures and Baby Boomers. These people grew up in the decade after the Cold War and during the fall of the Berlin Wall.

- Value: fun and informality
- Key Word: skepticism
- Family is noticing latchkey kids (children leaving the household)
- See education as a way to get some place in life
- Communicate with cell phones and like to be called only when at work
- Deal with money by saving, conserving, and being cautious

The **Generation Y (Millenials)** are the youngest working generation in the workforce and these people are born between 1981 and 1999. There are roughly 7.6 million Millenials in the workforce now, with many more on the way - and they do not all reside in Chicago! These people are facing independence and moving out of their parent's homes after completing college and entering the workforce while seeking further academic degrees.

- Value: confidence, extreme fun, and being social
- Key Word: realistic
- Families are typically merged
- Education is seen as an incredible expense
- Communicate using email, iPhones, and Internet
- Deal with money by earning it then spending it

The following Pie Chart summarizes the current breakdown of workers in the U.S. workforce as of 2010:

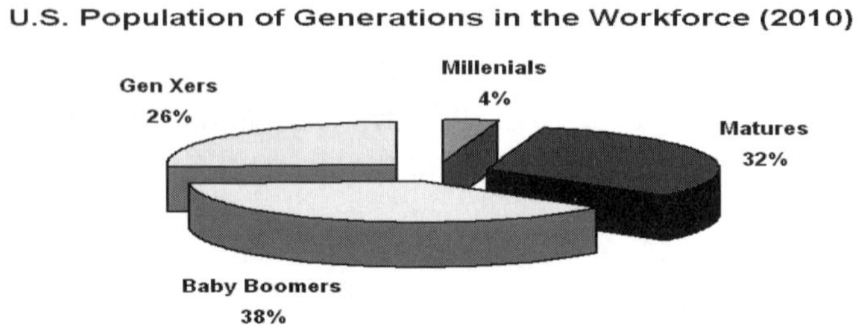

The emerging workforce born after 1999 is the "**Cyber Generation**." This group of youngsters is still in elementary and high schools yet may have a profound effect on work environments and service expectations. The potential number of workers in the Cyber Generation rival that of the Baby Boomer generation, yet their childhood influences will be quite different. The Cyber Generation will have spent their entire lives with the constant availability and bombardment of real-time news, videos, communication, social cyber interaction, and instant information and gratification. This group has watched military conflicts and world crisis unfold in real-time, and will expect the same of their business interactions and buying habits. As workers and consumers, their demands will far exceed those of any previous generation, and their respect for conformance and red tape will be intolerable. Some qualities of this generation are:

- Never lived without an internet connection
- Never lived without a cell phone with instant text or messaging
- Never lived without laptops and small micro-computing tablets
- Angry and or feel helpless when out of 4G communications
- You-Tube instant learning opportunities and Wikipedia at their finger tips
- Socially connected instantly
- Constant detailed world event news available
- Use of Facebook, Skype, cell phone, tablets, email, etc.
- Fear of loss of social contact
- Reality and social television on demand

The mix of workers in the workforce will be a continually changing dynamic, and leaders must continually adapt their strategy to achieve success.

The 10 Tips to Help Bridge the Socio – Techno Gap are as follows:

1. ***Communicate early and often.*** All generations have a need to be included in any change; however, it is acknowledged that there are times when everyone cannot be part of the team that is initiating or designing the change. If that is the case, ensure communication from the manager is done early in the process as well as provide regular updates. It is suggested that updates be provided online.

2. ***Be enlightening.*** Show how diversity can benefit a company. Be positive when it comes to generational gaps and working toward eliminating the gaps. Discuss openly what could be some additional motivators for each generation. For example, the Baby Boomer employee may want additional time-off after the completion of a large project while a Generation X employee may prefer a flex-schedule to accommodate their lifestyle. Human resources may need to be involved.

3. ***Be open.*** Share experiences and viewpoints in a safe environment. Knowing there are differences between generations is important, however, it is more important to manage these differences. When and where appropriate, have employees share work and technical experiences via the company newsletter, blog, or Intranet.

4. ***Be flexible.*** Create a work environment that all generations will like. If a Mature Generation employee likes title recognition then create an appropriate title. If a Baby Boomer wants a formal meeting, let that happen but limit the time to accommodate the Generation Y employees (Generation Y employees like short meetings). Utilize email, iPhones, and the Internet to accommodate the younger generations communication style but also have formal meetings to accommodate the Baby Boomers and Matures.

5. ***Be creative.*** Be creative in providing rewards for people. Different generational employees like different rewards, therefore, research what rewards each generation likes and accommodate accordingly. For example, the Mature and Baby Boomer Generations would most likely prefer a certificate or monogrammed company sweater than a team lunch or gift certificate.

6. ***Create learning opportunities for new software applications.*** Ensure there is available training for new applications and make it optional. If at all possible have training made available in different platforms, such as traditional classroom, online, or self-paced. Having a learning or training opportunity on multiple platforms will not single out the older generations.

7. ***Create rules and standards.*** Every generation wants to know what is expected of them as well as what is acceptable and what is not acceptable in terms of communication (i.e., all emails must be returned within 1 business day, receiving text messages or any type messages for non-emergency reasons while at work, etc.).

8. ***Create opportunities.*** Promote employee's skills within the organization as well as communicate their successes via any and all organizational bulletin boards.

9. ***Understand generational differences***. Always keep in mind that the Matures and Baby Boomer Generations value active participation and want their ideas to be heard or acknowledged. However, the Gen Xers and Millenials prefer less formal meetings and do not feel the need to have everyone's ideas heard.

10. ***Keep a balance.*** Since there exists these generations in the workforce, and as the next generation enters, try not to let one generational style dominate as that will lead to discernment and frustration on the part of the employee as well as the manager.

Understanding the generational gaps in the workplace can be a very important ingredient when implementing any of the Lean Sigma tools. Using the previous information and adjusting communications and work assignments accordingly will improve the following:

- ❖ Employee satisfaction
- ❖ Customer satisfaction
- ❖ Communication problems
- ❖ Office productivity

The following are a few examples of the types of waste that can be eliminated by understanding each generation. Use these as a springboard to discuss other ways your organization can reduce and eliminate similar types of wastes that exist.

Overproduction – Example: A Mature generation employee phoning a Generation X or Y associate that they just emailed them the information. The phone call is waste.

Transport – Example: Meeting with a colleague for lunch just to answer a simple question when an email would suffice.

Overprocessing – Example: Having everyone attend meetings when only certain people need to be present.

People Utilization – Example: Requiring everyone to receive training on a new application or functionality, whereas, some employees may learn it on-the-job.

Not adapting and adjusting your work style to these generational issues contribute to pro-higher turnover among the X-Y Generation worker and less overall productivity.

There are some overlaps with the various attributes between the generations; this is because some traits carry on for longer than one generation. For example, agreeing to hierarchy standards in companies was common in the first two generations, however, now people are becoming less interested in 'titles' and more focused on the task at hand and using people's talents given the situation, regardless of their title. Understanding these generational strengths and weaknesses in the workplace by managers and employees alike will give an organization a competitive advantage.

The following two charts summarize the generational personal and lifestyle characteristics, along with the workplace behaviors previously discussed and listed.

Workplace Behaviors				
	Matures 1925 - 1945	Baby Boomers 1946 - 1964	Gen Xers 1965 - 1980	Millenials 1981 - 1999
Work Ethic	Hard workers Dedicated to job	Workaholics Works efficiently	Eliminate the task	Whats next? Multi-taskers
Work is...	An obligation	An exciting adventure	A difficult challenge A contract	A means to an end Fulfillment
Leadership Style	Directive Command and control	Consensual Collegial	Everyone is the same Challenge others Ask why	TBD
Interactive Style	Individual	Team player Loves to have meetings	Entrepreneur	Participative
Communication	Formal Memo	In person	Direct Immediate	Email, Text Messages Voicemail
Feedback and Rewards	No news is good news Satisfaction in a job well done	Does not appreciate it Money Title recognition	Sorry to interrupt, but how am I doing? Freedom	Whenever I want it, or at the push of a button Meaningful work
Messages that motivate	Your experience is respected	You are valued and needed	Do it your own way and forget the rules	You will work with others who are bright and creative

Generational Personal and Lifestyle Characteristics				
	Matures 1925 -1945	Baby Boomers 1946 - 1964	Gen Xers 1965 - 1980	Millenials 1981 - 1999
Values	Respects authority Disciplined	Optimism Involvement	Skepticism Fun times Informality	Realistic Confidence Extreme fun Social
Family	Traditional Nuclear	Divorce Family members moving out	Latch-key kids	Merged families
Education	A dream	More plausible A right	A way to get someplace	Very expensive
Communication	One-on-one Formal memos	Touch-tone phones Call anytime	Cell phones Call at certain times	Internet iPhones, Text messages Email
Money	Save Pay cash	Buy, buy, buy and pay later	Cautious Conservative Save	Earn the money then spend

In summary, elder generations are a natural match for their younger counterparts. Older workers are rich in experience and insight, and the younger workers can benefit from their successes and challenges. Combining that with the younger generations enthusiasm and technical aptitudes, organizations can immensely benefit from this interaction in any Lean Sigma transformation.

Enabler #3 - Policy Deployment: Creating Goal Alignment, Ownership, and Accountability

Policy Deployment *is a methodology to consistently establish, align, communicate, and measure the progress of an organization in achieving their strategic objectives and mission.* It involves setting goals, assigning responsibility, and providing follow-up communications to ensure appropriate progress is being made. Specific and measureable goals, with time lines, must be established and communicated to all members of the organization. The goals must be aligned with the organizations Mission Statement and assigned to individuals and teams. As simple as it sounds, many organizations do a poor job with this key enabler.

Goals must be aligned to an organization's Mission Statement in order for the strategy to be realized. Goal conflict or misalignment within an organization erodes teamwork and impedes progress in Lean Sigma transformations. The Lean Sigma tool of Hoshin Planning is used to document, align, and cascade goals and tactical plans throughout the entire organization. Hoshin Planning, though beyond the scope and purpose of this book, is a systematic approach to planning, doing, and reviewing daily, weekly, and monthly actions and tasks to bring about the strategic vision of the organization. It is the development and monitoring of the tactical plan to achieve the strategic vision. Hoshin Planning begins with the strategic vision and through a series of systematic planning sessions, establishes and links the activities and goals of the organization to each and every individual. Further, Hoshin Planning calls for regular or standard reviews of progress toward the plan, where counter-measures can be taken as needed to ensure success. There are other methods as well and further study of Policy Deployment techniques should be considered to better establish what technique will work best for your organization.

The acronym of SMART helps leaders and managers establish goals. The acronym SMART stands for the following.

S= Specific
M= Measurable
A= Assigned
R= Realistic
T= Time-bounded

For example, a SMART goal for the receptionist in an office would be to politely greet people with a smile, direct callers and visitors to the right individual or department within 1 minute from initial contact or arrival. A SMART goal for a team member at McDonald's might be to greet each customer with a smile, and deliver the customer's order with no omissions or errors, within 2 minutes from taking the order.

Goals meeting the SMART criteria at all levels lead to an environment where people can motivate themselves to high levels of performance and achievement. Organizations that do not bother with SMART goal setting are plagued by confusion, conflict, and chronic underachievement.

It is the leader's responsibility to create a work environment where people can be inspired to achieve their full potential. Setting SMART goals, providing resources, and holding people accountable to achieve the goals are part of creating such an environment. Lean Sigma environments are exciting and engaging for people at every level of an organization. If a leader wants to improve organizational culture, then SMART goal setting and fair accountability is a solid place to start.

At the highest level, Policy Deployment is a process used to put action to the strategic plan and it provides the basis for action and organizational performance management. In its simplest form, Policy Deployment is a method used to establish goals and measurements for an individual or parts of an organization. The Policy Deployment process forces organizations to identify their vital few key measures, monitor them, and prioritize activities to optimize the use of resources.

Policy Deployment accomplishes the following:

- Provides a participative way to educate and align the organizational resources
- Provides a regular and real-time means to monitor the health of the organization
- Balances the organizations long term and short term needs
- Enables organizations to sustain the gains of Lean Sigma transformations

By aligning the organization's resources, Policy Deployment techniques provide crystal clear focus on the objectives and measures of success. It allows people to understand and "buy-into" the path of the organization.

Real-time feedback provides people within an organization of the information they need to improve and maintain performance. The Policy Deployment process allows everyone the ability to see how well the organization is performing and provides a call to action.

Service organization measures may vary significantly depending on the type of service provided. Below are several examples of service organization key performance measures. Note the similarities and differences in the following key measures:

Sales Inc.

- Customer Focus: Sales revenue, new accounts, new proposals
- Quality Focus: Customer evaluations
- Delivery Focus: Commitments met on-time
- Productivity Focus: Revenue per person
- People Focus: Turnover
- Financial Focus: Profit, Return-On-Investment (ROI)

A-1 Construction

- Customer Focus: Sales revenue, new projects, bids
- Quality Focus: Customer satisfaction, sign-offs, customer complaints, budget-to-actual performance
- Delivery Focus: On-time projects
- Productivity Focus: Revenue per person, projects per person, materials use to budget
- People Focus: Turnover, safety
- Financial Focus: Profit, ROI

Comfort Eats

- Customer Focus: Sales revenue, room fill rates, new menu items and specials
- Quality Focus: Customer surveys at tables, customer complaint and feedback, tips, reject and wrong order rate
- Delivery Focus: Drink and food delivery times
- Productivity Focus: Sales per person, table turnover rates
- People Focus: Turnover, attendance, training and advancements
- Financial Focus: Profit, ROI

Bob's Bakery

- Customer Focus: Sales revenue, new product offerings, new customers
- Quality Focus: Scrap or rejects per day
- Delivery Focus: On-time delivery to customers
- Productivity Focus: Sales per person, units per person, materials use to budget, improvement savings per person
- People Focus: Turnover, attendance, loss time injury rates, training
- Financial Focus: Profit, ROI, performance to budget

First Bank of Janesville

- Customer Focus: New accounts, new products
- Quality Focus: Customer surveys and feedback, error rate of transactions, balancing records
- Delivery Focus: Average customer wait times
- Productivity Focus: Transactions per day per person
- People Focus: Focus group discussions, turnover, training
- Financial Focus: Profit, ROI

Janesville Medical Center

- Customer Focus: Revenue, new offerings or services provided
- Quality Focus: Error rate per person and team, customer complaints, exit surveys
- Delivery Focus: Speed of service transactions, average customer wait time
- Productivity Focus: Sales revenue per employee, patients per month per person, improvement savings per person
- People Focus: Turnover, safety, training
- Financial Focus: Profit, ROI

Jeb's Job Shop

- Customer Focus: Sales revenue, new accounts, quotes
- Quality Focus: Scrap and reject rates, rework costs, quote accuracy
- Delivery Focus: On-time delivery to the customer commitments
- Productivity Focus: Sales per person, contribution margin per person
- People Focus: Turnover rate, attendance, safety, training
- Financial Focus: Profit, ROI

Janesville Power Company

- Customer Focus: Sales revenue, new clients/hook-ups, outages
- Quality Focus: Outages per month not weather related, customer surveys and feedback
- Delivery Focus: Average time to restore power after outage, days on-line at full capacity
- Productivity Focus: Sales per person, kilowatt hours supplied per person
- People Focus: Employee surveys, turnover, safety, training
- Financial Focus: Profit, ROI, performance to budget

Janesville Intermediate School District

- Customer Focus: Revenue, class offerings, teacher/counselor to student ratio
- Quality Focus: Graduation rates, standardize test scores
- Delivery Focus: Percent students graduating on-time, days open to schedule
- Productivity Focus: Student to teacher ratio, student to administration ratio
- People Focus: Turnover, training, employee surveys
- Financial Focus: Profit, ROI, performance to budget

Many of the measurements that determine the health of a business are common regardless of the organization size or type of business and many times are reviewed on a monthly basis. While this is good, it seems at times to be too late to do anything about it. It is like driving a car by looking in the rear-view mirror or getting a detailed report on your average speed for a trip, but not having a speedometer to monitor during the trip. Monthly data reporting simply cannot drive problem solving and improvement behaviors quickly enough. It is critical to review key performance measures and frequency of measurements at all levels to determine the exact method and frequency to report data. The best systems are collecting and presenting data daily and rolling data up to summarize on a monthly basis.

The steps or alignments to achieve for Policy Deployment are as follows:

1. Create the vision and mission of the organization.

   - Describes the desired future
   - Creates passion, meaning, and challenge – to inspire us
   - Creates the context for goal setting – to control us
   - Timeless, but regularly reviewed – to remind us
   - All stakeholders should see how it serves them
   - There should be visions for the company, departments, teams, and individuals

2. Establish the long-term objectives.

   - Develop a strategic plan to set the direction
   - Consider internal Strengths and Weaknesses and external Opportunities and Threats (SWOT's)
   - Complete the SWOT matching analysis to determine Leverages, Constraints, Vulnerabilities, and Problems
   - Develop high level goals and objectives to achieve the plan
   - Basic Question: "In the next 3 - 5 years, what must we accomplish?"

3. Establish the annual business goals and objectives.

   - Business fundamentals (e.g., Gross margin, turnover)
   - Annual objective – In place for a single planning cycle
   - Development objective – To put a process or system in place that is necessary but not a true objective, such as "clarify market data"

4. Develop and document target actions and goals to achieve the objectives.

   - SMART Goals for teams and individuals that support the higher level objectives
   - Specific course of action that will lead to the accomplishment of objectives
   - Supported by one or more detailed action plans
   - Essential elements of what, who, and when

5. Complete regular supportive reviews.

   - Progress is reported, help is offered, changes are made to ensure the original objectives are achieved and to improve predictability
   - Part of PDCA – "You get what you check."
   - Cascades up: team, department, organization
   - Conduct daily (15 minute) team huddles, and weekly (20 minute) team performance improvement and review sessions, where accountability, roadblocks, countermeasures, and action plans are developed, planned, and reviewed

To align the measures and goals for all levels of the organization, leaders can create direct links to measures at various levels. The following story describes how an organization links worker level actions to organizational performance.

Late one evening at the PDCA Hotel, the Site Manager, Lee, was leaving the building, and noticed a new employee mopping the floor in the laundry area. Lee stopped by to introduce himself to the new employee, Joe, and ask what his job was. Lee was shocked by Joe's answer.

Joe quickly responded that his job was to increase return on investment (ROI) for the shareholders and to improve job security. Lee commented, "It looks like you're mopping the floor, how does that improve ROI?"
Joe responded as follows, "Well, if I do my job mopping and cleaning, the housekeeping team can come in and safely get right to work. If the housekeeping team is able to get right to the work, they'll meet their productivity goals for the day. If they meet their productivity goals for the day, we'll make our schedule attainment goals. If we meet our schedule attainment goals, we'll meet our on-time goals for our customers. If we meet our on-time goals to our customers, we'll be a preferred location. If we are a preferred location, we will be able to get more customers in here. If we can get more customers in here, we'll be able to meet our sales growth goals. If we meet our sales growth goals, we'll improve our ROI for the shareholders and job security for all employees! So, my job is critically important to increase ROI and improve job security."

This commitment to and understanding of the big picture comes from linked and aligned goals, and a systematic approach to leadership and policy deployment in organizations. When leaders use a cascading goals system with key performance indicators that are linked to rewards and company success, they optimize the potential for individuals and the organization. Everyone wins.

Enabler #4 - Practical Lean Sigma Tool Application: Using the Right Tool for the Job

Not every Lean Sigma tool will apply to every organization and situation. It is critical Lean Sigma leaders to recognize this and subsequently select the appropriate Lean Sigma tool that will help eliminate waste. While some Lean Sigma tools are universal such as value stream or process mapping, 5S, or visual management, other Lean Sigma tools may simply not apply to a specific environment. For example, the concept of pitch (group or timed paced flow) may be more appropriate than takt-time (demand paced flow) for a particular service process. Since takt time in an office or service setting such as a bank may often be very small to flow the work, the bank might be better off using pitch or the adjusted takt time when determining the optimal work flow size through the value stream. Another example would be a cashier who balances his or her cash register at a pitch of twice a day rather than after each transaction.

Lean Sigma tool selection and application are more important than trying to use every tool in the Lean Sigma tool box. The objective of Lean Sigma is to eliminate waste, not to use tools. This book illustrates where each Lean Sigma tool might be appropriate to use in different areas within service organizations.

There are basic tools that are universal and can be easily be applied or implemented by every worker at every level (e.g., 5S, visual control, etc.); advanced tools typically can be used by individuals or small teams to provide solutions to performance gap problems (e.g., leveling, performance management, standard work, etc.).

The team or individual should thoroughly understand the process that is under review to determine the Lean Sigma tool to use. Do not try to randomly apply any Lean Sigma tool. With the examples and structure in this book, it should provide you with a reference point on determining when and where to use these tools.

Lean Sigma Service Excellence Journey Stages

Developing the road map for the Lean Sigma transformation is the responsibility of management. Leaders can use the mission and vision for the starting point. The mission describes the compelling need to improve, the vision defines what to improve to, and the journey employing Lean Sigma methods and tools defines how the organization will do it. At a minimum, the Lean Sigma for Service Excellence Journey Stages lays out the steps to engage the organization and what to expect in a Lean Sigma transformation. The stages are;

Stage 1 - Getting Started: Identify Needs, Train, and Launch Projects
Stage 2 - Engage Everyone with Basic Lean Sigma Tools and Support Projects
Stage 3 - Engage Improvement Teams with Advanced Lean Sigma Tools and Expand Projects
Stage 4 - Celebrate Success and Continue Efforts

Note that the stage time frames are to be used as guidelines and are not firm. In fact they tend to overlap a bit as organizations transition from one stage to the next. Continue to use the Lean Sigma for Service Excellence Assessment and Gap Analysis tool (Appendix) to monitor the organization's progress through the stages.

The following will explain in more detail the four stages:

Stage 1 - Getting Started: Identify Needs, Train, and Launch Projects
Zero to Six months

At this stage of engagement, organization leaders should be spending time investigating sources for training and increasing their own Lean Sigma knowledge. There are many sources for gaining knowledge. The tools defined in this book, as well as other books, are also available with an Internet search, however, you may have to spend considerable time going to commercial sites that are trying to sell you something. Be sure to take advantage of any Lean Sigma benchmark tours that may be available in your area and try to learn from those organizations. Look for potential trainers (i.e., consultants), if appropriate, and ensure organizational values and culture fit with whomever is chosen. If you use an outside consultant or training group, ensure they have had success in this area.

Lean Sigma measures should be examined and defined for the organization. Again, look to others that have pioneered Lean Sigma service measures. After initial Lean Sigma training has been developed, begin to implement improvement activities. Additional activities to consider are as follows:

- Obtain Lean Sigma knowledge. Train in people in business, teaming, and technical skills.
- Define customer needs and service quality parameters.
- Define a mandate and Lean Sigma vision.
- Select projects or areas of focus
- Establish Lean Sigma measures to track progress.
- Map value steams
- Begin Rapid Improvement or Kaizen Events.
- Implement Policy Deployment. Define and measure Key Performance Indicators.
- Create detailed plans for improvement.
- Identify and commit resources.

Stage 2 - Engage Everyone with Basic Lean Sigma Tools and Support Projects
Three to Nine months

At this stage of the transformation every member of the organization is getting some Lean Sigma training and being asked to engage with simple Lean Sigma tools. There should be a sense of optimism for eliminating waste. Many low cost and no cost improvements can be made with the basic Lean Sigma tools. Customers will start to notice a difference in that there is an improved level of consistency with each service encounter. Organization members will find it easier to do the right thing as standard work is employed. Problems will come to the surface and be fixed as people engage and discuss improvement ideas. Leaders should focus on the Key Performance Indicators to track Lean Sigma progress. Additional activities to consider are as follows:

- Make available Lean Sigma learning for everyone.
- Develop a growth strategy.
- Eliminate roadblocks and recommit resources.
- Encourage grass roots activities in 5S, visual management, and standard work.
- Start value stream projects based on priorities.
- Use Policy Deployment. Measure and analyze Key Performance Indicators.
- "Do" improvements.

Stage 3. Engage Improvement Teams with Advanced Lean Sigma Tools and Expand Projects

Six to Twelve months

At this stage of the transformation several groups may be making progress at several areas throughout the organization. It is likely that some areas have back-slid and will need to be readdressed. This is typical. Leaders should remain focused on the systematic approach to the Lean Sigma transformation. This stage is also the stage where many organizations begin to struggle with resource commitments. This will test the management's commitment to Lean Sigma. It is critical to stay on course at this time. Additional resources may be considered, such as dedicated personnel, training, outside consulting, and the like, but should pay back quickly.

It is also common for organizations to have to step back and revisit past stages of the transformation process. Due to attrition or turnover, training may need to be revisited or reviewed. Involve your experienced people as trainers. Continue to focus on Key Performance Indicators and drive improvement at all levels. Additional activities to consider are as follows:

- Introduce Lean Sigma to all organizational areas.
- Relate pay to proven performance.
- Find right-size tools.
- Make everything transparent.
- Reorganize to support Lean Sigma initiatives.
- Create a Lean Sigma function that has sole responsibility for the Lean Sigma transformation.
- Use Policy Deployment.
- Make and control improvements.

Stage 4. Celebrate Success and Continue Efforts

Twelve to Twenty-four months

This stage represents the home stretch. Some attributes of companies that have achieved this stage include sustainable and systematic identification and elimination of waste, organization structure around value streams rather than departments or functions, and consistent success in key customer and financial success factors. Some very high performing organizations may even be Malcolm Baldrige Quality Award winners and the Shingo Prize winners. All these companies have become more competitive due to lower cost, less wastage, better customer service, and higher market share. Continued emphasis should be placed on the Key Performance Indicators and Policy Deployment techniques. Organizations will need to develop their own internal training program that can be used internally, as well as with suppliers. Also at this stage Lean Sigma leaders should begin to shift the responsibility for developing and sustaining the Lean Sigma transformation to the organization's Lean Sigma leaders and all operational staff. By this time several people will have excelled in Lean Sigma methods and tools. These people can now be used to lead and help facilitate Lean Sigma efforts. Additional activities to consider are as follows:

- Teach Lean Sigma methods to suppliers.
- Develop global growth strategy.
- Transition from top-down to bottom-up improvement.
- Aggressively support policy deployment. Improve and control all processes by using Key Performance Indicators.
- Continue the "Plan – Do - Check - Act" improvement process at all levels.

Chapter Summary

This chapter identifies management's role and responsibilities in initiating and leading a Lean Sigma transformation. The fundamental management responsibilities of Leading, Planning, Organizing, and Controlling are discussed in relation to leading Lean Sigma transformations. The importance of organization missions and visions during a Lean Sigma transformation are also reviewed. Finally, the Lean Sigma Service Excellence Journey stages are described to provide the Lean Sigma leader a plan or structure to follow to initiate the Lean Sigma Service Excellence transformation.

Lean Sigma for Service Excellence Applications

These observations may assist in understanding how to apply the concepts and tools contained in this chapter:

- Complete a Web search for organization Mandates, Missions, and Visions. Use your findings to draft your own or enhance the current one.
- Gather a small cross-functional team to discuss the current state of acceptable behaviors. Ask the group to help define a vision of what should be the acceptable behaviors.
- Communicate the teams draft to the members of the organization. Collect their comments and feedback. Be open to their ideas and suggestions.
- Begin to define the Key Performance Measures for your organization.
- Identify some sources to begin your organization's Lean Sigma learning.
- Develop a comprehensive training program to train people in business, teaming, and technical skills.
- Investigate methods for Policy Deployment.

Understanding Lean Sigma for Service Excellence Journey Readiness Guide

The following Understanding Lean Sigma for Service Excellence Journey Readiness Guide allows you to ensure there is application of the chapter's content before proceeding to apply the Lean Sigma tools and concepts in the next chapter. If you score less than 70%, consider working on the lower scoring areas before moving on.

Understanding Lean Sigma for Service Excellence Journey Readiness Guide	
Use the following 5-level Likert item scale to rank each of the statements: **1 = Strongly Disagree** **2 = Disagree** **3 = Neither Agree nor Disagree** **4 = Agree** **5 = Strongly Agree**	
	Score
1. My organization does a good job of communicating the need to change.	
2. My organization provides adequate resources to ensure successful change.	
3. My organization does a good job of assessing gaps and baseline improvements.	
4. My organization is good at conducting benchmarking analysis to identify gaps.	
5. My organization does a good job in identifying key organizational performance measures.	
6. My organization strongly believes in continuous improvement.	
7. My organization keeps track of customer demands and changes.	
8. My organization is fully supportive of cross-training and inter-departmental sharing.	
9. The management of my organization is committed to becoming a world-class organization.	
10. The management of my organization not only "Walks the Talk" but also holds others accountable.	
11. My organization does a good job of instituting basic policies, practices, and acceptable behaviors.	
12. My organization's environment motivates people to achieve high levels of performance and success.	
13. My organization does a good job of establishing and monitoring organizational performance measures.	
14. My organization's mission statement is committed to pursuing excellence.	
15. My organization has a vision that is sufficiently detailed and comprehensive.	
16. My organization does a good job of understanding human behaviors and attitudes.	
17. My organization inspires people to achieve their full potential.	
18. My organization does a good job of applying quantitative tools for measurement and improvement.	
19. My organization would benefit from using the Lean Six Sigma processes and tools.	
20. I believe my organization should utilize and apply the concepts and tools discussed in this chapter.	
Total Score	

Case Review – Initial Assessment for MSI Services, Inc.

MSI Services, Inc. operates an online computer dating and relationship management website. They operate globally, with most of their clients being in the US. They employ a staff of web masters and computer experts to maintain their websites, as well as relationship advisors to develop web content. Their Leadership team consists of the 5 originators of the firm, as well as 4 new leaders brought in during the last year as the firm grew. The Leadership team completed the Lean Sigma for Service Excellence Assessment and Gap Analysis process with the following scores:

Summary	Average Score	Goal
Leadership	2.6	4.0
Customer Focus	3.2	4.0
Process Management	1.7	4.0
People Management	3.3	4.0
Information and Analysis	1.8	4.0

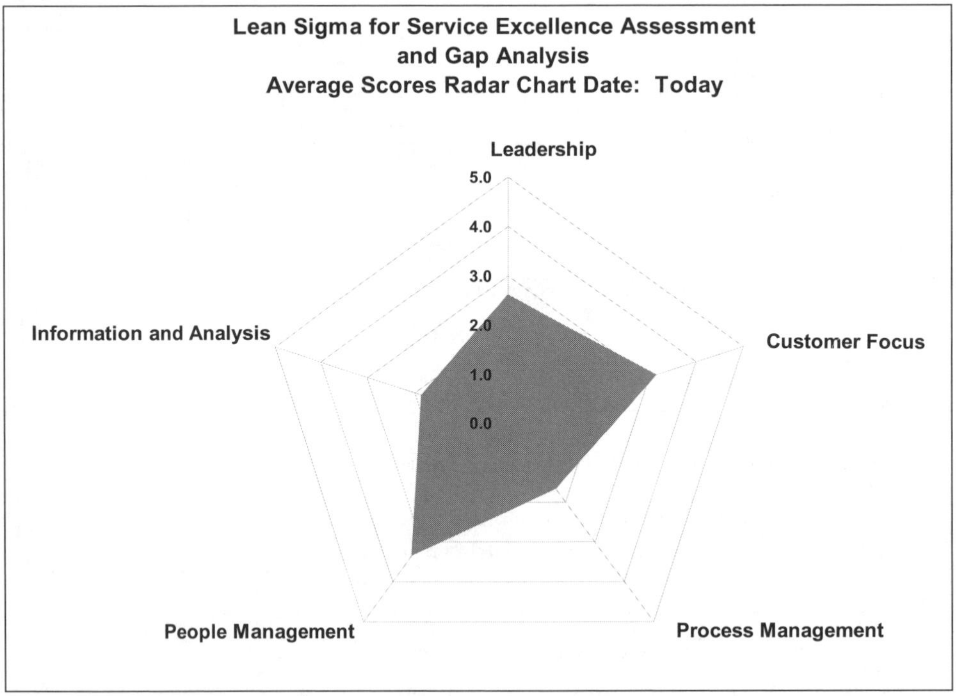

From the Radar Chart analysis, it can be seen that MSI Services have relative strengths in People Management (3.3), Customer Focus (3.2), and Leadership (2.6), while their weaknesses are in the areas of Process Management (1.7) and Information and Analysis (1.8).

Note: Typically, any indicator scoring below 3 should be addressed with an improvement plan. If no score is below 3, the areas with the lowest scores or gaps from "Ideal State" should be addressed with improvement plans. Prioritize based on the lowest score needing the most attention first. Look at the specific question scores in any category to determine the type of improvement action that is needed. Once the type of improvement has been identified, develop a Project or Team Charter to address the area.

MSI Services decided to capitalize on their people management strength and address their weaknesses by having each area team develop process maps with performance indicators for the key processes in their area. Targets or goals would be established for each process and weekly meetings would be held to review performance data. MSI Services believed that by monitoring the process data with statistical control techniques, they would improve their process and analysis focus, as well as provide improved services to their clients. The most difficult step is the first one, and this critical step by MSI Services took a commitment to process mapping, measuring and reporting data, and standard work sessions to review and act on the findings.

Over the next six months, the MSI Services teams completed several DMAIC improvement projects targeted at improving Process Management Information and Analysis. After completing the Lean Sigma projects, the leadership team completed another Lean Sigma for Service Excellence Assessment and Gap Analysis, and found that the results form the Lean Sigma projects had a positive impact on their scores. Their updated scores are:

Leadership = 2.9 (gap 1.1)
Customer Focus = 3.2 (gap 0.8)
Process Management = 2.8 (gap 1.1)
People Management = 3.1 (gap 0.9)
Information and Analysis = 3.0 (gap 1.0)

The teams next step was to initiate additional Lean Sigma projects in the Process Management area and investigate why the People Management score had declined slightly. Overall, the team felt confident that they were off to a great start with their Lean Sigma transformation.

Pursuing Perfect Service

Part Three.

Deploying the Lean Sigma for Service Excellence Improvement Process

Chapter 4

Define Phase

Achieve Alignment on What to Improve

Chapter Overview

Getting improvement projects started in the right direction can be critical to the success of the project. All too often, organizations start projects in a random manner, never really defining their intent or goals. The Define Phase of the DMAIC process helps teams get started in the right direction with the right level of support and resources. In Lean Sigma transformations, the Define Phase is used to initiate and align improvement teams and to provide teams the general direction regarding expectations, outcomes, and resources. This chapter provides an overview of the Define Phase of the DMAIC process and tools.

Define Phase Training and Alignment

A brief training needs assessment should be conducted before each DMAIC Phase. In the early stages of Lean Sigma transformations, organizations may require significant training on the improvement process and tools. As organizations advance in their transformation and become more familiar with the process and tools, less emphasis can be placed on training, and more on project implementation. Ideally, a brief refresher training of the process and tools should be conducted regardless of team make-up or how far an organization is along their Lean Sigma transformation. This will reinforce the need to practice the process and tools in every day operations and promote a Lean Sigma culture.

For the Define Phase, team members should have an understanding of the following.

- Lean Sigma overview
- Lean Sigma 12 wastes
- DMAIC improvement process
- Define Phase tool overview
- Basic project planning and management techniques

Project team alignment is usually initiated at a project kick-off session. Project Charters are used by organizational leaders to identify high level projects and are used to define the high level project objectives and expectations. The Project Charter is used by the team (or teams) to develop a detailed Team Charter or multiple Team Charters. The communication and approval of the Team Charter provides additional alignment between an organization's leaders and their improvement project teams. A simple flow diagram of this process is shown below:

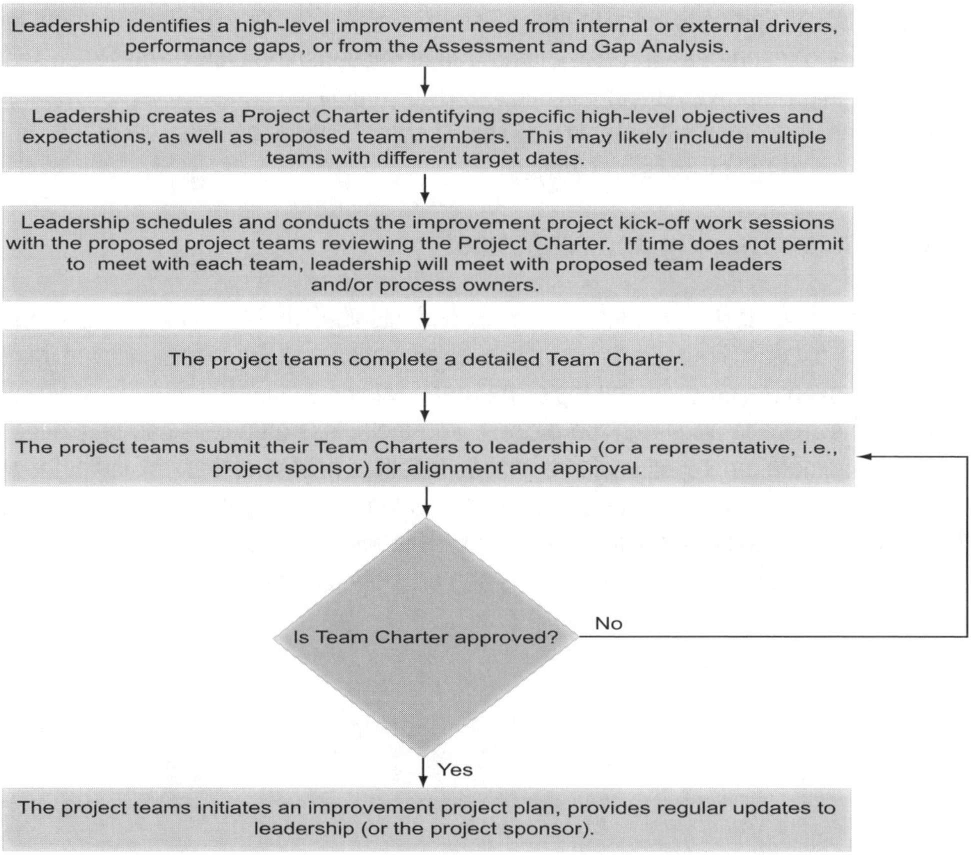

Define Phase Tools

The key Define Phase tools and their application are identified in the following table:

Phase	Lean Sigma Tool	Application Guide
DEFINE	Teaming	Teaming is a group of individuals working together for a common cause or objective. New projects will require people to meet either physically in a conference room or by remote Web-collaboration means. The basics of teaming remains the same.
	Effective Meetings	Effective meetings allow for efficient and timely organizational communication to take place, for issues to be discussed, for priorities to be set, actions planned and updated, and for decisions to be made with a group of people.
	Project Charter	The Project Charter is a high-level document used to launch or initiate an improvement team. The Project Charter is usually initiated by leadership and targeted at a major improvement need for the organization. The Project Charter identifies the project scope, high level goals, initial resources, and time frames. The Project Charter is based on Key Performance Indicators, customer mandates, competitive pressures, or a Lean Sigma for Service Excellence Assessment and Gap Analysis.
	Team Charter	The Team Charter is used to detail the specific scope and objectives for a targeted improvement area. The Team Charter also defines the expected outcomes, measures, goals, resources, and duration for the project or initiative at a more detailed level than the Project Charter. Use the Team Charter to align team members and leaders when initiating a project.
	Project Planner (PP)	The Project Planner (PP) is used to document and track the progress of a project initiative. The PP follows a basic project management format utilizing Gantt Chart tracking. Use the PP to plan, track, and report project activities and steps.
	Action Item (AI) Log	The Action Item (AI) Log documents and tracks the actions required, responsibilities, and completion dates for specific action items identified to complete projects. Actions items can come from various places, but are usually discussed and agreed to by team members at team work sessions. Teams usually review and update the AI Log at team work sessions. Use the AI Log throughout the duration of the improvement initiative.
	Issues and Opportunities (IO) Log	The Issues and Opportunities (IO) Log is used to capture opportunities, ideas, issues, roadblocks, and general "parking lot" items identified throughout the duration of the improvement project or initiative. Teams usually review the IO Log at team work sessions and determine if and when IO Log items should be moved to the AI Log for action. Some IO Log items may never make it to the AI Log. Use the IO Log throughout the duration of the improvement initiative.

Understanding the basics of teaming and effective meetings will go a long way for ensuring a successful outcome of a Lean Sigma project.

Teaming

***Teaming** is a group of individuals working together for a common cause or objective.* New projects will require people meeting together on a regular basis that may have had very little experience working with others on a formal problem or issue. These meetings may be in a conference room face-to-face, or through the use of remote communication via Web collaboration, or a combination of both. The basics of meetings remains the same.

Individuals that have been working in their departments for many years may have been doing their jobs with little input from peers, managers, and/or an internal consultant (i.e., Lean Sigma facilitator, Lean Sensei, etc.). Therefore, it is imperative that all those involved in the project learn to work together in a team atmosphere and have a positive experience if improvements are to be made and people's ideas respected. This effort does not come naturally. Everyone must understand team dynamics as well as their roles and responsibilities.

Often a group or team will be comprised of people who may struggle with group (team) participation. This may occur for some of the following reasons:

- Previous ideas were shot down or not acknowledged
- Previous ideas were acknowledged as good, but not discussed any further
- Strong managerial control precluded input from the employees
- No standard method for reaching a consensus or decision-making
- Fear of public or group speaking
- Fear of job loss by improving the process(es)
- Poor meeting facilitation

For success to occur, everyone must feel free to contribute. The use of Lean and Six Sigma tools will require adaptation and creativity - and change. People must understand the tools and have a desire to apply them in their area. The following are suggestions for how to involve everyone:

- Assign and rotate the functions of the facilitator, scribe, timekeeper, and any other functions among the team members, whenever practical
- Train and practice proper brainstorming techniques
- Communicate that the Lean Sigma project is about improving processes
- Acknowledge that improvements will involve change for everyone

Teaming for new groups occurs in several stages.

Teaming Stage 1 - Forming or Getting Started

The Forming stage of teaming involves reviewing the project, establishing team roles, determining meeting times, and ensuring the right members are on the team. This is the stage where team members experience difficulties going from working as individuals to being a contributing team member. There is excitement, anticipation, and optimism. While there is also the pride a member may feel about being chosen to be part of the team, the "flip-side" may be feelings of suspicion, fear, and anxiety of what is to come.

Additional points to consider at this initial stage are:

- Ensure roles are clearly defined and that a consensus (agreement) is achieved on all decisions
- Rotate team member roles (scribe, timekeeper, etc.)
- Conduct training activities on teaming or have team members attend a teaming workshop or seminar
- Establish team ground rules (i.e., turn cell phones/pagers off or on vibrate, be on time, etc. - with each team creating their own set of ground rules)

The team leader can remain in control by consistently using Lean Sigma Define tools, conducting effective meetings, using proper communications, and respecting team members' ideas. This stage of teaming is similar to a white water rafting trip where an experienced guide assists the team with specific duties, as well as calms fears about the unknown.

Teaming Stage 2 - Storming or Going in Circles

At this stage, the team members begin to realize the task is different and/or more difficult than they first imagined. Impatience about the lack of progress and/or inexperience on group dynamics has some team members wondering about the entire project. Also, the team may experience some of the following:

- Continuing to rely on their personal experience of team projects and resisting collaboration
- Arguing among members, even when they agree on the real issue
- Being defensive and competitive
- Additional meetings may be putting more pressure on a members regular work load.

This stage can be difficult for any team. Teams that do not understand and acknowledge the five stages - especially this stage - most likely will disband or continue to struggle in this stage without being able to move forward.

The following ideas may assist teams through this stage:

- Constantly acknowledge the five stages with the team
- Communicate to the team that disagreements are part of the teaming process
- Focus on the team's goals
- Acknowledge progress to date
- Always focus on the process, not people or their personalities
- Conduct effective meetings (next section)

In this part of the rafting trip experience, the raft is struggling down the river. Team members are learning as they go, but have a guide to help them along. People may need to change positions to better accommodate the team's mission (or prevent the raft from going in circles).

Teaming Stage 3 - Norming or Staying on Course

At this stage, team members accept the team concept. The team ground rules are being adhered to, communication is occurring without disruptions, and progress is being made toward the objective. At this stage, everyone feels that the team concept is working efficiently and effectively. Everyone is contributing in a positive way.

The team may also be doing some of the following:

- Expressing criticism constructively
- Attempting to achieve harmony by avoiding conflict
- Confiding in each other
- Exhibiting a sense of team bonding

Continued communications and acknowledgement of the team members' efforts should be done often, allowing progression to Performing (next stage) and preventing the team from falling back to the Storming stage, and therefore staying on course.

In this part of the rafting trip experience, the raft is handling the rapids; everyone is contributing and feeling some accomplishment.

Teaming Stage 4 - Performing or Full Speed Ahead

By the time this stage has been reached, the team can begin to diagnose and solve problems with relative ease. This stage includes:

- Achieving project milestones earlier than anticipated
- Team members, in a supporting role, coaching and mentoring others
- Team members requesting to help facilitate other improvement projects

Everyone on the raft at this time is doing their roles as expected. As they go through the rapids, the team is confident - as well as excited for the next set of rapids. The rafting experience would be a positive recommendation to others.

Teaming Stage 5 - Closing or Celebrating the Finish

Closure of the project team is the final stage of teaming. In this stage, the team has accomplished their goals, shared their results, and has disbanded. Closure brings mixed feelings to team members. By this time, the team members have been through a lot together and the thought of not working as a team anymore can be disappointing. However, Lean Sigma project teams are not usually designed to be together forever. An organization's reporting structure usually handles the long-term team structure. Lean Sigma improvement teams are, by nature, cross-functional and have a specific purpose and life. Additionally, there is value in establishing new teams to work on new projects. This stage includes:

- New employees becoming trained and involved
- Providing leadership the opportunity to reflect on the improvements made and thank or congratulate the team

Teaming can be a challenge the first time. Utilizing the DMAIC methodology will assist greatly in allowing the team to progress through all the stages of team development, minimizing the likelihood that some problem adversely affecting the project.

Effective Meetings

***Effective meetings** allow for efficient and timely organizational communication to take place, for issues to be discussed, for priorities to be set, and for decisions to be made with a group of people.* Conducting effective meetings does not involve trial and error. Effective meetings are an efficient use of people's time when they are gathered together working to obtain a desired result. Meetings, like any process, can be studied and improved upon.

There are four keys to effective meetings:

1. Identify clear objectives for each meeting.
2. Create and adhere to rules and guidelines (i.e., standards).
3. Ensure everyone participates and is engaged.
4. Use good time management principles.

Meetings can be one of the most powerful business tools or one of the least. Common complaints about meetings are that they:

- Accomplish nothing
- Are poorly organized
- Have everyone with their own agenda
- Last too long
- Have people who always arrive late
- Have no one in control

However, people need to meet in order to benefit from the collective knowledge and experience of the group. While many decisions can be made by phone, email, text message, or in a hallway discussion, there will be other times that people will need to meet in person or through Web conferencing and gain a consensus on an issue or problem that needs to be resolved. A more Lean way to conduct meetings with members that are distant is through video conferencing and/or document sharing and conference calls. Some common applications to share information remotely are: Google Docs, Cicso WebEx, Gbridge, GoToMeeting, NetMeeting, and Microsoft's SharedView.

Effective meetings provide a forum to make necessary decisions and solve problems without wasting people's time. If meetings are effective, then something positive will be the result. People will arrive on time, participate, offer information and ideas, and have positive attitudes. However, if meetings are not effective, people will show up late, be less likely to participate, and their attention and ideas will be less productive. To achieve effective meetings, treat them as processes, create standard rules to follow, and then adhere to those rules.

Approach conducting an effective meeting as follows:

1. Agree on a clear objective and agenda for the meeting.
2. Choose the right people for the meeting and notify everyone in advance.
3. Clarify roles and responsibilities for the meeting (i.e., champion, leader, facilitator, technical representative, scribe, timekeeper, and team member).
4. Ensure everyone adheres to meeting etiquette (being on time, turning off cell/smart phones, no text messaging during the meetings, etc.).
5. Assign a scribe to take the meeting's minutes.
6. Assign a timekeeper to ensure the times allocated for each of the topics are adhered to.
7. Evaluate the meetings and improve where needed.
8. Provide minutes to participants within 24 hours after the meeting.

The following are the definitions and activities of the various team member roles.

*The **team champion** is the person who has the authority to commit the necessary resources for the team.* The champion should "kick-off" the first meeting and then be updated regularly via copies of the Project Planner, Action Item Log, and Issues and Opportunity Log, as well as other pertinent documents that communicate how the team is progressing. Other duties of the team champion may include, but are not limited to: continually being involved and communicating often with the team leader, refereeing cross-functional resource requests by removing barriers to project success, assisting to ensure the team is aligned with strategic goals, appointing the team leader, handling issues that the team leader cannot, and providing team guidance when the team is struggling. The team champion is mainly responsible for creating the Project Charter.

*The **team leader** is responsible for the day-to-day or week-to-week running of the team.* Other duties of the team leader may include, but are not limited to: scheduling and coordinating the meeting times (agenda, and location), making change happen, providing supervisory authority, buying into to the project, suggesting additional team members, understanding team dynamics, and respecting others. The team leader also communicates directly with the team champion.

The ***facilitator*** *ensures that everyone attending the meeting stays on task and everyone participates.* The facilitator should not have any vested interest in the project, one way or another - other than ensuring the meetings are effective. These duties include, but are not limited to: keeping discussion focused on topic, intervening if multiple conversations are occurring, preventing one person from dominating, promoting interaction and participation, bringing discussions to a close, and guiding the group in accordance with the Project or Team Charter and agenda.

The ***timekeeper*** *is responsible for ensuring the scheduled times (start, stop, topics) are followed.* The timekeeper can manage the process and agenda. This frees everyone else to focus on contributing ideas. Other duties of the timekeeper may include, but are not limited to: monitoring time with respect to the agenda, notifying team when it is behind schedule, updating the team on progress to time allocated, assisting with determining appropriate time allocation for next meeting, and contributing as a team member.

The ***scribe*** *is the person who records the notes of the meeting and/or the person who captures the group's thoughts on flip charts, white boards, or the laptop that is being projected on the wall or screen, etc.* The scribe is responsible to represent the ideas of the group, without imposing his/her own interpretation on them.

The ***technical representative (tech rep)*** *is the person from IT (or someone with advanced computer application skills) who provides insights into technology tools available and/or makes the team aware of upcoming technology that may impact the team's mission.*

The ***team member*** *- the most important part of the team - is responsible for keeping an open mind, being receptive to change, and contributing their ideas in a respectful manner.*

Note: It is important that both the facilitator and scribe duties not be assigned to the same person. Many organizations may have a continuous improvement specialist (Black Belt or Lean Sensei) that can assist as the facilitator. The team leader and process owner most likely may be the same person.

When teams meet, there should be ground rules (i.e., proper etiquette) that everyone follows. These may be initially created by the team leader (i.e., process owner) prior to the first meeting and then reviewed and agreed upon by the team at the conclusion of the first meeting. These ground rules should be posted at the meeting location, distributed prior to the meeting, and/or reviewed at the beginning of each meeting session. Ground rules may include the following:

Attendance. Management should place a high priority on meeting attendance. There should be defined legitimate reasons for missing a meeting with a procedure to inform the team leader if a member cannot attend. The best way to ensure good attendance is to run effective meetings.

Timing. Meetings should begin and end on time. This avoids wasting time and makes it easier on everyone's schedule. Meetings are sometimes shorter when this rule is enforced. Each team should create specific ways to enforce this rule.

Participation. Every member can make a valuable contribution to the meeting. Emphasize the importance of speaking freely and listening attentively. If unequal participation is a problem, then the team facilitator can structure the meeting so that everyone participates through various types of structured and unstructured brainstorming techniques.

Basic Courtesies. Everyone, regardless of their level within the organization should use basic conversational courtesies. Listen to what people have to say, do not interrupt, have only one conversation at a time, and respect others. Is it okay for participants to put phones on vibrate and leave the meeting to take calls or is it expected that everyone turn their cell phones off for the duration of the meeting? This can be a major issue.

Breaks and interruptions. Decide when breaks for phone calls, text messaging, etc. are allowed, and when they are not.

Other ground rules (if appropriate). Decide on other ground rules that seem appropriate. For example, what kind of humor is acceptable? What kind of language? What is OK to talk about and what is not? Is it OK to receive and/or send text messages during the meeting?

Meetings, as stated previously, are a process like any other and should be evaluated on a regular basis. The following Effective Meeting Evaluation Worksheet can be used with your team to continuously improve your meetings:

Effective Meeting Evaluation

Directions:

1. Spend only five minutes evaluating your meetings.
2. This form is most successful when everyone's responses are shared.
3. Focus on the weak spots, applaud the high ratings.

Rating System: Use the following 5-level Likert item scale:

1 - Strongly Disagree
2 - Disagree
3 - Neither Agree nor Disagree
4 - Agree
5 - Strongly Agree

1	We stayed on the agenda.	**3.6**
2	We focused on the right things during the meeting.	**4.1**
3	We focused on the issues and did not place blame.	**4.3**
4	Time was used wisely.	**4.1**
5	Information was presented accurately and was clear.	**3.8**
6	Everyone participated.	**4.6**
7	Action Items were assigned evenly.	**4.0**
8	The pace of the meeting was appropriate.	**3.6**
9	Questions and concerns were addressed appropriately.	**3.9**
10	All ideas were explored to the extent possible given the time element.	**4.2**
	TOTAL:	**40.2**

Scoring Guidelines

45 - 50 Doing Well - Keep up the good work.
40 - 44 Doing OK - Must make more effort during meeting.
35 - 39 Not So Good - Must improve dramatically.

The following key documents, improvement teams are able to define, implement and report on their team's progress in an orderly fashion:

Project Charter

*The **Project Charter** defines the high level objectives and expectations for an improvement project team.* It is developed by organizational leaders based on internal or external needs. It is important to note that one Project Charter will require one or more teams to be launched. Each team will develop a separate Team Charter described later in this chapter.

The purpose of the Project Charter is to document:

- Reasons for undertaking the project
- Objectives and constraints of the project
- Directions concerning the solution
- Names of the main stakeholders

The three main uses of the Project Charter are to:

- Authorize the project projects can be ranked and authorized by Return on Investment (ROI)
- Serve as the primary sales document ensuring the project receives a priority
- Ensure tight scope management of the improvement

The following are examples of potential internal and external needs of an organization:

Potential internal needs may include:

- Low productivity or Lean Sigma Assessment scores
- Poor quality or schedule attainment
- Loss of key personnel or high turnover
- New or modified equipment and applications

Potential external needs may include:

- Increases or decreases in customer demand
- New market or competitor pressures or process needs
- New customers with new demands and needs

The following are examples of Project Charters from various improvement projects:

Hotel Restaurant and Bar Project Charter example:

Project Charter

Company Name:
Hotel Restaurant & Bar

Name of Team:
Lunch Wait Team

Proposed Team Members:

Peter	Viola	Prince
Lavan	Anna	

Leadership Sponsor:
Patrick

HIgh Level Objective:
Improve sales during slow business cycle (lunch time).

Why is this important to our organization?
We need additional sales revenue during slow economic period of fewer guests.

Boundary Conditions (Process Scope and Organizational Scope):
Coconut Beach Bar

Project Budget:
Less than $500.00

Expected Deliverables and Outcomes:
Higher sales receipts for the same number of visitors due to improved service and hospitality.

Goal/Target Action (this supports):

Metrics	Current Condition	Target Condition
Productivity/Cost	5 people during lunch	No change
	Receipts per day per person	15% increase in receipts per day per person
Quality	Good	Better to increase receipts
Delivery	Good	Improved to increase receipts
People	Good	More attentive to increase receipts
Customer	Happy!	Happy!
Financial	Soft	15% improvement in revenues

Projected Project Completion Date:
Improvement plan in place by May 1

Customer Service Call Center Project Charter example:

Project Charter

Company Name:
Xfinity Support Services

Name of Team:
Call Center Staff

Proposed Team Members:

Charlie	Ruben	Nicole
Amy	Kelly	Jennifer

Leadership Sponsor:
Mary Ann

HIgh Level Objective:
Reduce customer wait time.

Why is this important to our organization?
Reduce customer wait time will improve customer service scores and allow our sales team to leverage call center service to increase sales.

Boundary Conditions (Process Scope and Organizational Scope):
Call center calls

Project Budget:
$1,000.00

Expected Deliverables and Outcomes:
Reduced customer service call wait time.

Goal/Target Action (this supports):

Metrics	Current Condition	Target Condition
Productivity/Cost	6 people Current call potential per day	No change Increase call potential per day
Quality	Good	Same or better
Delivery	Current maximum wait time is no more than 4 mins. Current average wait time is 90 secs.	Reduce maximum wait time to less than 3.5 mins. Target less than 75 secs. wait time
People	Good	Good
Customer	Survey scores OK	Improved survey scores
Financial	N/A	N/A

Projected Project Completion Date:
Implemented before Feb 1, 3 months duration.

Computer Repair Services Project Charter example:

Project Charter

Company Name:
Computer Alley Repairs

Name of Team:
Repair staff technicians

Proposed Team Members:

Mack	Greg	John
Matt	Doug	Brenda

Leadership Sponsor:
Bill

HIgh Level Objective:
Reduce repeat repairs and reworks.

Why is this important to our organization?
Repeat and rework are costing us extra time and money. We need to fix things right the first time.

Boundary Conditions (Process Scope and Organizational Scope):
Computer repair department

Project Budget:
$1,000.00

Expected Deliverables and Outcomes:
Reduced repeat repairs and reworks.

Goal/Target Action (this supports):

Metrics	Current Condition	Target Condition
Productivity/Cost	6 people Capacity	No change Improved capacity per day
Quality	Poor. 20% repeat repairs and reworks	Good. Zero repeat repairs and rewworks
Delivery	Current 1 week commitment	No change
People	Good	Good
Customer	Upset	Satisfied after first visit
Financial	Average 20 hours per week overtime	Less than 10 hours per week overtime

Projected Project Completion Date:
Fix things before holiday season/year end.

Team Charter

The ***Team Charter*** *details and documents the team structure, membership, and overall objectives, measures, and resources required to be successful.* It is developed by the project team and is used to fully explore the scope and resources required to complete an improvement project. Multiple Team Charters may be derived from the Project Charter, or simply, a Project Charter can be modified to be the Team Charter, if appropriate.

After an initial kick-off session, the team is responsible to complete a Team Charter. The team may have to conduct several work sessions to complete the Team Charter with sufficient detail. Some items from the Project Charter might be direct carry-overs to the Team Charter, however most items will require a greater level of detail and study before the Team Charter will be complete. As part of the Define Phase and for clarification, the project team may develop and include a simplified flow, value stream, or process map of the targeted process without the data that will be gathered in the Measurement Phase. This will assist in communicating the exact process targeted for improvement.

One of the team leader's responsibilities is to act as a liaison between the organization's leadership or project sponsors and the team to ensure that the developing Team Charter is on target with the original intent of the improvement project. The on-going communications between the improvement project team leader and the leadership sponsor are critical to the success of the project.

Team Charter Section Overview

Project Name – This is where the team determines a common name for the team. The name may be as simple as the targeted process or as creative as the team wants to get. Examples might be "Customer Service Team," "Security Improvement," or "The High Fliers." Let the team be creative here.
Revision Date – The latest revision date.
Objective - The purpose of a Team Charter.

1. *Mission or Purpose of the Project:* Define the mission of the team. An example might be, "The mission of the process improvement team is to reduce the cycle time of the customer service process by 10% in the next 3 months."
2. *Deliverables or Expected Outcomes:* This section allows teams to elaborate on additional deliverables and outcomes. This section might include the use of visual management techniques or other specific Lean Sigma tools. A good question to consider is: "After completion of this project, what do we expect to be different?"

3. *Benefits of Expected Outcomes:* This section allows the project team to provide some quantitative and qualitative benefits of the project.
4. *Expected Approach and Activities:* This section allows the project team to define the DMAIC approach, or a different methodology for action.
5. *Time Frame: (Start Date, End Date, Major Milestones target dates)* – In this section the team should document the start and end dates of the project, as well as any key milestone dates, such as having a new service up and running by a specific date.
6. *Team Resources:* This section is where the team members and roles are defined. This section also allows teams to identify any special foreseeable resources needed such as a specific technology, software, or training. This also includes the *Team Meeting Plan* where the team defines the meeting or work session schedule. It is recommended that all teams start with a weekly meeting until it is determined that a different schedule is appropriate.
7. *Measures: (Current and Future State Targets, Consider Cost, Quality, etc.)* This is where the team will attempt to define specific measures (Key Performance Indicators or KPIs) that will lead to the achievement of the overall goal. If for example the overall goal is to "have in place an effective service scheduling system," the team should refine this goal and determine a measure that is defined "effective." Is effective 80 schedule attainments or less than 5 minutes per transaction? These measures should be specific and objective. Some projects may include measures in all areas and some will not.
8. *Key Customers and Suppliers:* This is where teams identify the key customers and their needs, key suppliers and what they supply, as well as current process inputs and outputs. At this point in the process data may not be readily available, so a shell of a process may be included without data that will be gathered in the Measure Phase of the improvement process.
9. *Assumptions:* List any key assumptions such as "No new equipment or buildings" or "No change in staff levels." Document other assumptions that are being made.
10. *Current Issues to Address or Solve:* This is where a team may identify a current issue to solve or fix. Occasionally, improvement projects are launched to attack a specific problem. If this is the case, document it here.
11. *Risks to Consider:* Brainstorm with the team potential risks of the project as defined. This could include slower than normal process time when the team is in work sessions, to risks of losing customers if the process improvements do not occur.
12. *Team Signatures:* This is where the team signs off that they are committed to the team and process. This section is intended to gain buy-in and commitment to success.

The following are examples of Team Charters from various improvement projects:

Hotel Restaurant and Bar Team Charter example:

Team Charter - Coconut Beach Bar

Team Charter **Date:** Feb 1

1. Mission or Expected Outcomes:
Improved sales during slow business cycle.

2. Deliverables or Expected Outcomes:
Higher sales receipts for the same number of visitors due to improved service and hospitality.

3. Benefits of Expected Outcomes:
We hope to improve our sales revenue during a slow time in the business cycle.

4. Expected Approach and Activities:

1. The team will meet weekly to develop and implement improvement ideas.
2. Team members will try new ways to increase revenues according to the plan.
3. Sales receipts will be measured daily to check our progress.

5. Time Frame (Start Date, End Date, and any Major Milestone Target Dates):
February 1 - May 1

6. Team Resources:

Role	Name	Comments
Champion or Sponsor	Patrick	
Team Leader	Peter	
Scribe	Lavan	
Member	Viola	
Member	Anna	
Member	Prince	

Team Meeting Plan (frequency, data storage plan, notes distribution, etc.):
The team will meet every Tuesday after their shift. Activities will be reviewed periodically by Patrick.

7. Measures (Current and Future State Targets, Consider Cost, Quality, etc.):

Category	Measure	Current State	Future State
Productivity/Cost	1. Number of people on lunch wait staff	5 people	5 people
	2. Sales dollar at lunch	$650.00 per day	$750.00 per day
Quality	No specific measure		
Delivery	No specific measure		
People	No specific measure		
Customer	No specific measure		
Financial	No specific measure		See above

8. Key Customers and Suppliers:

Customer	Outputs Used	Suppliers	Inputs Used
Guests	Service	Food service	Food and beverages
	Food and drinks	Cleaning service	Housekeeping
	Music	Bar service	Bar items
	Environment	Facilities dept	Maintenance and decorating

Hotel Restaurant and Bar Team Charter example (continued):

9. Assumptions:
1. No additional lunch wait staff.
2. No additional customers due to poor economy.
3. We need to increase the expenditure of each guest without pressuring them.

10. Current Issues to Address or Solve:
1. How can we get our current guests to spend more time at the restaurant and bar, and to spend more money.

11. Risks to Consider:
1. We do not want to become too pushy. We want our guests to feel unpressured and relaxed.

12. Team Signatures:

Call Center Team Charter example:

Team Charter - Call Center

Team Charter **Date:** Feb 1

1. Mission or Expected Outcomes:
Reduce call center customer wait time.

2. Deliverables or Expected Outcomes:
Measure reduction in call center wait time.

3. Benefits of Expected Outcomes:
Reduced customer wait time will improve customer service scores and allow our sales team to leverage call center service to increase sales.

4. Expected Approach and Activities:
1. The team will meet weekly to develop and implement improvement ideas.
2. Team members will implement improved methods to reduce customer wait times.
3. Call center customer wait times will be measured daily to check our progress.

5. Time Frame (Start Date, End Date, and any Major Milestone Target Dates):
February 1 - May 1

6. Team Resources:

Role	Name	Comments
Champion or Sponsor	Mary Ann	
Team Leader	Charlie	
Scribe	Amy	
Member	Rueben	
Member	Nicole	
Member	Jennifer	

Team Meeting Plan (frequency, data storage plan, notes distribution, etc.):
The team will meet from 1:00 pm to 2:00 pm every Wednesday in the HR Conference Room beginning February 8th (project completion by April 30th). Minutes published within 24 hours.

7. Measures (Current and Future State Targets, Consider Cost, Quality, etc.):

Category	Measure	Current State	Future State
Productivity/Cost	1. Number of people on shift	6 people	6 people
	2. Call potential/capacity	Not known	TBD
Quality	1. Call survey scores	95% approval	>95% approval
Delivery	1. Maximum wait time	4 minutes	<3.5 minutes
People	No specific measure	N/A	N/A
Customer	1. Call survey scores	Same as Quality	Same as Quality
Financial	No specific measure	N/A	N/A

Call Center Team Charter example (continued):

8. Key Customers and Suppliers:

Customer	Outputs Used	Suppliers	Inputs Used
Callers	Service accuracy, speed and completeness Attitude and friendliness Helpfulness and empathy	Tech support IT support Accounting	Technical support for products Computer and phone system support Financial information

9. Assumptions:

1. No additional call center staff.
2. No new equipment or phone system upgrades.

10. Current Issues to Address or Solve:

1. How can we reduce our customer call wait time?
2. How do we spend our time now?
3. What are the time wasters?
4. How can er shave time off our key processes?

11. Risks to Consider:

1. We do not want to become too short with our customer callers. They need to feel like we care. We want our callers to feel unpressured, relaxed, and have their problem solved.

12. Team Signatures:

Computer Repair Services Team Charter example:

Team Charter - Computer Repair Services

Team Charter **Date:** Sept 1

1. Mission or Expected Outcomes:
Reduce repeat repairs, reduce overtime, and reworks to improve customer satisfaction.

2. Deliverables or Expected Outcomes:
Reduce or eliminate repeat repairs and reworks and reduce overtime hours per week.

3. Benefits of Expected Outcomes:
Reduced repeat repairs and rewords will reduce overtime hours and improve customer satisfaction. This in turn will make us the repair center of choice for more customers.

4. Expected Approach and Activities:
1. The team will meet weekly to develop and implement improvement ideas.
2. Team members will implement improved methods to reduce customer wait times.
3. Rework repairs and overtime will be measured weekly to check our progress.

5. Time Frame (Start Date, End Date, and any Major Milestone Target Dates):
September to year end

6. Team Resources:

Role	Name	Comments
Champion or Sponsor	Dewayne	
Team Leader	Mack	
Scribe	Matt	
Member	Greg	
Member	Doug	
Member	John	

Team Meeting Plan (frequency, data storage plan, notes distribution, etc.):
The team will meet every Thursday from 12:30 to 1:00 in effort to develop plans to reduce overtime and increase first-time success with repairs. Mack will update Dewayne with weekly reports.

7. Measures (Current and Future State Targets, Consider Cost, Quality, etc.):

Category	Measure	Current State	Future State
Productivity/Cost	1. Number of people on shift	6 people	6 people
	2. Call potential/capacity	150 hours/week	TBD
	3. Average repair time	65 minutes	65 minutes
Quality	1. Reduce repeat repairs	20% repeat	<5% repeat
Delivery	1. One week lead time	1 week	1 week
People	No specific measure	N/A	N/A
Customer	1. Customer complaints	See Quality	See Quality
Financial	1. Reduce overtime expense	20 hours/week	<10 hours/week

8. Key Customers and Suppliers:

Customer	Outputs Used	Suppliers	Inputs Used
Computer owners	Repaired computers	Tech support	OEM Techical support
	Advice	Parts suppliers	Parts and supplies
	Helpfulness	Accounting	Financial information
	Wait time	Customer Service	Calls customers for approvals

Computer Repair Services Team Charter example (continued):

9. Assumptions:

1. No additional Technical staff.
2. No new equipmen.

10. Current Issues to Address or Solve:

1. How can we reduce our repair error rates?
2. How can we reduce overtime?
3. What wastes do we have during the repair process?
4. How can we shave time off our key processes?

11. Risks to Consider:

1. We do not want the repair to take too long. We should improve quality before delivery, but we need both in line to succeed.

12. Team Signatures:

Project Planner (PP)

The ***Project Planner (PP)*** *is a project planning, tracking, and management tool used by improvement teams to identify and track the main steps required to complete the improvement project.* Weekly updates are recommended to keep a team on track throughout the duration of the improvement project. To provide status and progress updates to team members and sponsors, an updated PP can be posted to the appropriate Web page or shared-drive area, or a copy can be physically placed on the area's bulletin or information board. Typically a Gantt Chart will be used to represent the PP information and the main steps listed will be obtained by reaching a consensus. *A* ***Gantt Chart*** *shows a graphical representation of project tasks, sequence, relationships, status, and time required.*

After alignment is achieved between organizational leadership or sponsor, and the improvement project team, a Project Planner can be established by the team. The Project Planner identifies major activities by deliverables and time frames for completion. It utilizes the DMAIC process flow and basic project planning and management techniques for execution. The initial PP is generated by the project team by brainstorming the steps and actions required to complete each phase of the improvement process. For the most part, the generic PP template can serve as a standard for any improvement project.

The effective use of a PP will depend of your experience with project management tools and techniques. What is important is that the team follows the DMAIC process in making the improvements.

An example of a typical PP Gantt Chart for the Computer Repair Services improvement project referenced in a previous example in this chapter is on the next page.

Project Planner - Computer Repair

Objective: Record and track the key events and milestones to complete the initiative. **Revision Date:** June 28

Project Planner (PP)
3 Month Plan

Project Planner Objective: Identify major activities by deliverable and time frame to complete.

% Complete: 0% (not started) 25% (underway) 50% (half complete) 75% (nearly done) 100% (complete)

- Medium shading or green color signifies completed implementation activities.
- Dark shading or red color signifies behind target for implementaion activities.
- Light shading or yellow color signifies on target for implementation activities.

	Define Phase	% Comp	Month 1				Month 2				Month 3			
			1	2	3	4	1	2	3	4	1	2	3	4
1	**Project Charter**	100%												
2	**Team Charter**	100%												
3	Team leader to align with Sponsor	100%												

	Measure Phase	% Comp	Month 1				Month 2				Month 3			
			1	2	3	4	1	2	3	4	1	2	3	4
1	**Baseline Data Collection and Process Mapping**	50%												
2	Material and information flow maps	50%												
3	Develop the current state map	100%												
4	Collect process flow data	50%												

	Analyze Phase	% Comp	Month 1				Month 2				Month 3			
			1	2	3	4	1	2	3	4	1	2	3	4
1	**Critical Review of Data**	0%												
2	Review current state map for process and flow	0%												
3	Review other data	0%												
4	**Identify High Potential Improvement Actions**	0%												
5	Document process and opporunities	0%												

	Improve Phase	% Comp	Month 1				Month 2				Month 3			
			1	2	3	4	1	2	3	4	1	2	3	4
1	**Develop Improvement Implementation Plan**	0%												
2	Complete a future state map	0%												
3	Develop the detailed improvement plan for PDCAs	0%												
4	**Implement Improvements**	0%												
5	TBD	0%												

	Control Phase	% Comp	Month 1				Month 2				Month 3			
			1	2	3	4	1	2	3	4	1	2	3	4
1	**Establish Measures and Audit Plan to Sustain Improvements**	0%												
2	Provide ongoing weekly scoreboard reports	0%												

Action Item (AI) Log

The ***Action Item (AI) Log*** *documents and tracks the actions required, responsibilities, and completion dates for specific action items identified to complete projects* The AI Log lists specific action items, who is responsible to complete the action item, and when the action item is due to be completed for each of the phases of the project. The AI Log can be used during regular team work sessions to follow-up on progress and to reassign resources and/or dates as necessary.

The level of detail on the AI Log is typically more detailed than the steps listed on the Project Planner (PP) (previous topic). The PP defines the major or key events, while the AI Log details who, what, when, and how the key events will be accomplished. The AI Log is used by the team leader to ensure responsibility and accountability in specific project action items.

As an improvement project progresses, items are identified and added to the AI Log. The team and team leader will establish who will complete the action item, and when it needs to be complete, and then update the AI Log. As with the Project Planner, it is recommended that weekly updates to the AI Log be documented and posted/published in a common location for on-demand access or physically posted in storyboard fashion, if applicable, in the department or area for viewing.

There are many versions of AI Logs. Typically, color-coding is used: red for items that have had no action or are behind schedule, yellow for actions in progress, and green for completed actions. This will help to obtain a quick overview of the project at-a-glance. This color-coding is a form of visual management discussed elsewhere in this book.

An example of a typical AI Log for the Computer Repair Services improvement project referenced in a previous example is on the next page.

Action Item Log - Computer Repair

Objective: Record and track actions in progress and agreements related to team activities.

Revision Date: June 28

- Medium shading or green color signifies completed implementation activities.
- Dark shading or red color signifies behind target for implementaion activities.
- Light shading or yellow color signifies on target for implementation activities.

	Action Item	Responsibility	Target Date	Percent Complete	Completed Date	Actions
1	Mack to meet with Dewayne to make sure we agree on the Team and Project Charter	Mack	15 May	100%	13 May	
2	Team to modify (add lead times) Team Charter per Dewayne's and Mack's meeting.	Team	2 Jun	100%	2 Jun	Push overtime issue.
3	Finalize Team Charter (ensure lead times are included)	Mack	1 Jun	100%	2 Jun	
4	Subteam of Greg,Doug, and Brenda to complete initial current state map.	Greg	15 Jun	100%	15 Jun	
5	Team review current state map.	Team	18 Jun	100%	18 Jun	
6	Gather additional data for current state map.	Brenda	10 Jul	50%		
7	Doug to obtain parts delivery schedule.	Doug	10 Jul	100%	28 Jun	
8	Brenda to obtain scheduling data.	Brenda	10 Jul	100%	14 Jun	
9	Greg to get standard repair times based on service part history.	Gregg	10 Jul	50%		Use estimates.
10	Matt to obtain repeat repair numbers.	Matt	10 Jul	25%		
11	Mack to obtain overtime numbers from Jerry.	Mack	10 Jul	100%	20 Jun	
12	Greg to get customer complaint history by service technician.	Greg	10 Jul	0%		IT involvement.
13	Complete current state map	Team	10 Jul	75%		Meet before 3 Jul.
14	Begin Analyze Phase.	Team	15 Jul	50%		Analyze data.
15						
16						
17						
18						
19						
20						

Issues and Opportunities (IO) Log

*The **Issues and Opportunities (IO) Log** is used to capture opportunities, ideas, issues, roadblocks, and general "parking lot" items identified throughout the duration of the improvement project or initiative.* (Parking Lot items are items that may be important to people, but are currently not in scope, or the group is not ready to address. Parking lot concept can be valuable in keeping the team on target while not losing valuable ideas that, while not on topic, may have value later.) Teams usually review the IO Log at team work sessions and determine if and when IO Log items should be moved to the AI Log for action. Some IO Log items may never make it to the AI Log. Use the IO Log throughout the duration of the improvement initiative. The Issues and Opportunity Log is updated as items are identified and may have an indirect impact on Team Charter objectives. It is common for opportunities, ideas, and issues to arise during an improvement project. The IO Log acts as a holding place for opportunities and ideas that the team is not ready to act upon. Through periodic review and discussion the team will observe that certain items from the IO Log are ready to be acted upon and subsequently move them from the IO Log to the Action Items Log and make the appropriate assignments. At the end of the project the team can review the IO Log to determine if additional actions are required or perhaps a new improvement team should be formed to address new improvement items.

The IO Log should be posted/published in a common location for on-demand access or physically posted in storyboard fashion, if applicable, in the department or area for viewing. The IO Log will stimulate additional ideas for improvement projects in the same or different areas of the organization. Leaders of organizations should regularly review all open IO Logs to identify actions required by them to minimize or eliminate roadblocks and for prospecting for future improvement projects.

Teams are encouraged to use the IO Log as a living document. That is to continually update the log with new entries as they occur.

An example of an IO Log for the Computer Repair Services improvement project referenced in previous examples in this chapter is on the next page.

Under the Category column, notice how the Log is used for several types of issues (i.e., for Opportunities (O) denoting other improvement ideas that are out of the scope of this project, Ideas (I) that are not able to be implemented yet, Roadblocks (RB) that the team is not sure what to do about, as well as other Parking Lot (PL) items that may need to addressed at a later time). Do not spend excess time determining if the IO Log item is an opportunity, idea, parking lot item, or roadblock. It is more important to capture the ideas than it is to log the category properly.

Issues and Opportunities Log - Computer Repair

Objective: Record and track Opportunities (O), Ideas (I), Roadblocks (RB), and Parking Lot (PL) items. **Revision Date:** June 28

Medium shading or green color signifies moved to Action Item Log.

	Opportunity (O), Idea (I), Roadblock (RB), or Parking Log (PL)	Category (O/I/RB/PL)	Benefit	Action Summary	Date Logged	Date Closed
1	Should Dewayne attend all sessions?	I	Dewayne would save timeband our meetings will run smoother.	Dewayne agreed to only attend montly, with weekly email updates.	10 May	14 May
2	We need a cross-check after each service repair ensure it was done right.	I	Reduce repeat errors?	Save for Improve Phase.	16 May	
3	What if we worked on a First-In First-Out schedule?	O	Reduce scheduling.	Save for Improve Phase.	25 May	
4	We need more parking space in the rear of the building.	PL	No street parking.	Out-of-scope.	25 May	25 May
5	We are too busy doing this the service work to do this DMAIC process!	RB	Necessary for business.	Continue to meet.	25 May	25 May
6	Team Charter should include lead times.	O	Reduce lead times.	Move to AI Log. (Item #3)	1 Jun	1 Jun
7	The customer compaint field is not functioning due to a virus.	RB	Accurate data.	Submit IT request.	1 Jun	1 Jun
8	We need to standardize our repair practices with standard hours.	I	Accountability.	On hold for later.	8 Jun	
9	Hire college intern to work weekends to extend service hours.	I	Increase sales.	On hold for later.	8 Jun	
12						
13						
14						
15						
16						
17						
18						
19						
20						

Chapter Summary

This chapter provides a detail overview of the Define Phase or the first stage of the DMAIC process. This is a very critical Phase because it is in this Phase that the improvement need is clearly identified and the purpose and the scope of the project is clearly articulated. Also, it is in this Phase that customer's expectations are considered and a realistic time line and cost measures are estimated and developed. The ultimate decisions made at this stage is whether the DMAIC process is really needed and if the management support for process improvement exists.

This chapter also discusses the different tools that improvement teams can use to clearly articulate the opportunity or improvement need. The creation of Project and Team Charters are the most important outputs of the Define Phase.

Lean Sigma for Service Excellence Applications

These observations may assist in understanding how to apply the concepts and tools contained in this chapter.

- Gather a small cross-functional and cross-level team to discuss the current project management and improvement techniques at your organization.
- Gather a small cross-functional and cross- level team to develop a Project or Team Charter template or enhance the one that is currently being used.
- Communicate the team's draft Team Charter to your immediate leader and seek approval to begin an improvement initiative. Be open to their influence.
- Identify additional sources such as books, reference materials, and consultants to help begin the journey.

Define Phase Readiness Guide

The following Define Phase Readiness Guide allows you to ensure there is application of the chapter's content before proceeding to apply the Lean Sigma tools and concepts in the next chapter. If you score less than 70%, consider working on the lower scoring areas before moving on.

Define Phase Readiness Guide

Use the following 5-level Likert item scale to rank each of the statements:

1 = Strongly Disagree
2 = Disagree
3 = Neither Agree nor Disagree
4 = Agree
5 = Strongly Agree

	Score
1. My organization does a good job of defining projects prior to selection.	
2. Identification of training needs is an important component of the Define Phase in my organization.	
3. Project team alignment is emphasized in the project kick-off sessions in my organization	
4. My organization uses Project Charters to create high level project objectives and expectations.	
5. Key event schedules are used in my organization to track the progress of a project or initiative.	
6. Team Charters are used in my organization to align team members and leaders.	
7. My organization utilizes simple tools like the Gantt Chart to plan and track projects.	
8. My organization utilizes the Action Item (AI) Log throughout the duration of the improvement initiative.	
9. My organization utilizes the Issues and Opportunities (IO) Log to identify opportunities throughout the project.	
10. My organization conducts structured meetings.	
11. I feel comfortable applying the DMAIC process to defining projects.	
12. I feel comfotable applying the Lean Sigma concept to launch a project.	
13. I understand the Project Charter.	
14. I feel comfortable assisting in creating the Team Charter.	
15. I feel comfortable in basic project management skills.	
16. I feel comfortable using basic tools such as a Gantt chart for creating a Project Planner (PP) and scheduling and controlling activities.	
17. I feel comfortable preparing and using the IO Log.	
18. I feel comfortable preparing and using the AI Log.	
19. I see the value in clearly defining projects using the DMAIC process and tools.	
20. I believe my organization should utilize and apply the concepts and tools discussed in this chapter.	
Total Score	

Case Review – Define Phase for CCVB Convention Center

The Centennial County Visitors Bureau (CCVB) is an organization comprised of professional planners, event organizers, and administrative support personnel that provides professional assistance in planning, organizing, and delivery of special events, such as seminars, festivals, sporting events, conferences, and other similar events in Centennial County and the surrounding area.

CCVB provides services to academic, professional, and industrial organizations and associations. They provide a full range of services depending on the needs of the group's event planner. National event planners may require extensive local organization committee support, while state and local event planners, being more familiar with the area, typically require less support.

The services provided by the CCVB vary widely. Some of the services provided are listed below.

- Conference design and planning management
- Permitting and parking
- Facilities acquisition and decoration. Examples: Tents, tables, chairs, rest rooms, signage, setup, and arrangement.
- Local transportation arrangements
- Reservations and hotel/motel bookings
- Local entertainment
- Site and venue selection
- Technology requirements, audio visual, IT support, web services
- Logistics
- Leisure time management and secondary events such as spouse/family tours, entertainment, and the like
- Marketing and advertisement
- Printing
- Speakers recruiting and selection
- Food services
- Funding and sponsorship recruitment
- Financial management and budget control
- Public relations
- Security, medical, and emergency plans
- Contingence planning for weather, cancellations, or other unforeseen events

The CCVB works with local partners and volunteer organizations to satisfy almost any request of the organization event planner. Overall, their mission is to be a full-service provider to event planners in effort to generate return events and increase commerce in the Centennial County area.

As the area was growing in popularity, partially due to the excellent services provided by the CCVB, the CCVB staff was becoming increasingly busy and stressed. As their work load increased, Maxine, the CCVB Director, was beginning to consider adding staff; however, she wanted to make sure her staff were working in the most efficient and effective way. The CCVB had recently hosted a Lean Sigma event held by the local American Society for Quality (ASQ) chapter. Maxine was invited to attend and sat through multiple sessions of Lean and Six Sigma. She was most impressed with the Lean Sigma approach, combining the best of both methodologies. So, Maxine decided to use the Lean Sigma methods and tools to improve and optimize productivity (before deciding if she really needed to hire any additional staff).

Define Phase

Before starting the improvement initiative, Maxine spoke with a local Lean Sigma service provider that had presented at the recently held ASQ conference and learned that her first step should be to document a high level Project Charter. She secured a Project Charter template from the Internet and customized it for CCVB. The CCVB Project Charter is shown on the next page.

Project Charter - CCVB

Company Name:

Centennial County Visitors Bureau (CCVB)

Proposed Team Members:

Liz	Jim	Nancy
Dave	Mary	

Leadership Sponsor:

Maxine

HIgh Level Objective:

Improve and optimize productivity.

Why is this important to our organization?

If we can improve and optimize productivity, we may be able to defer hiring additional staff. This will enable us to operate at a lower cost and provide better return to our shareholders, customers, and employees.

Boundary Conditions (Process Scope and Organizational Scope):

Consider activities from the organization's firm commitment to the area until completion of the follow-up satisfaction survey.

Project Budget:

Estimated $2,200.00

Expected Deliverables and Outcomes:

Increased productivity

Goal/Target Action (this supports):

Metrics	Current Condition	Target Condition
Cost	OK, but considering new resources	Improved with current resources
Quality	Excellent, but beginning to slip	Excellent
Delivery	On time	On time
People	Stressed	Less stressed
Customer	Satisfied	Satisfied
Financial	OK	Better

Projected Project Completion Date:

3 month project duration

Maxine's next step was to sit down with the team and begin the project. She wanted the team to take her Project Charter and develop a more detailed Team Charter for guidance. At the meeting the team members initially were concerned about the additional time they felt the project would take from their already busy schedule. Maxine explained that the group needed to make time to work on improvements, as it was an investment in their future and the future for the organization. Maxine agreed to attend the team sessions as an added resource if the team wanted her to.

As the team reviewed the Project Charter, Jim, one of Maxine's direct reports who was assigned as the team leader, noticed that there were no specific measures listed for the Goal/Target Action in regards to Metrics. Jim wondered how the team's success would be measured and expressed this to Maxine. Maxine explained that she would work with the team to develop clearer measures.

The first step for the team was to complete the Team Charter. For the most part, the team was able to take items directly from the Project Charter, however, when they got to the Goal/Target Action section they found that Jim was right; they did not currently have clear measures.

The CCVB Team Charter is shown on the next two pages.

Team Charter - CCVB

Team Charter **Revision:** 11/28

1. Mission or Expected Outcomes:

1. Improve and optimize productivity.

2. Deliverables or Expected Outcomes:

1. If we can improve and optimize productivity, we may be able to defer hiring additional staff. This will enable us to operate at a lower cost and provide better return to our stockholders, customers, and employees.
2. Improved productivity and efficiency.

3. Benefits of Expected Outcomes:

1. If we can improve and optimize productivity, we may be able to defer hiring additional staff. This will enable us to operate at a lower cost and provide better return to our stockholders, customers, and employees..

4. Expected Approach and Activities:

1. Use Lean Sigma methods and tools.
2. Conduct weekly follow-up and planning sessions.

5. Time Frame (Start Date, End Date, and any Major Milestone Target Dates):

3 month project duration

6. Team Resources:

Role	Name	Comments
Champion or Sponsor	Maxine	
Team Leader	Liz	Liz has a busy travel schedule, so we need a co-leader.
Co-Leader	Jim	
Scribe	Nancy	
Member	Dave	
Member	Mary	

Team Meeting Plan (frequency, data storage plan, notes distribution, etc.):

Nancy will take and distribute minutes within 1 business day including agreed upon action items from each work session.

7. Measures (Current and Future State Targets, Consider Cost, Quality, etc.):

Category	Measure	Current State	Future State
Productivity/Cost	To be determined	OK, but considering new resources	Improved, with current resources
Quality	To be determined	Excellent, but beginning to slip	Excellent
Delivery	To be determined	On time	On time
People	To be determined	Stressed	Less stressed
Customer	To be determined	Satisfied	Satisfied
Financial	To be determined	OK	Better

8. Key Customers and Suppliers:

Customer	Outputs Used	Suppliers	Inputs Used
National Events State Wide Events Local Events Others?		Local partners Printers Volunteers	

9. Assumptions:

1. Next year's bookings will be the same or greater than this year's bookings.

10. Current Issues to Address or Solve:

1. We need to streamline our processes so we can get more done with the current team.
2. We need to make certain activities easier to do we can get moredone with the current team.
3. We need to identify the vital key key measures and begin measuring them consistently.

11. Risks to Consider:

1. We are currently very busy and may not have the time to invest in this project to do it well, and still serve our customers.
2. Our service could suffer in the short term.

12. Team Signatures:

After the first pass of creating the Team Charter, the team focused on the Goal/Target Action Metric section. They had to have a great deal of discussion on this topic. In fact, it took nearly 1 hour to nail down clear measures that could easily be tracked and reported. The team brainstormed for key performance measures in each category. Their list of brainstorming ideas is documented in the table below:

Brainstormed Key Performance Measures			
Category	**Measure**	**Current State**	**Future Target**
Productivity / Cost *(Productivity / Cost measures should be an output divided by an input)*	1. Events per person 2. Revenue per event 3. Revenue per payroll dollar 4. Action Items completed per person 5. Action items completed per payroll dollar 6. Duration of closed action items 7. Time spent per action item	OK, but considering	Improved, with current resources
Quality	1. Event planner satisfaction 2. Event attendee satisfaction 3. Event presenter satisfaction 4. Event sponsor satisfaction 5. Event planning partner satisfaction 6. Attendance projection percent attainment	Excellent, but beginning to slip	Excellent
Delivery	1. Commitments met on-time 2. Action items schedule attainment 3. Open action items or backlog	On time	On time
People	1. Impact to the local economy 2 Hotel/motel room bookings during the event 3. Number of participating local partners or merchants 4. Relationships with event organizers	Stressed	Less stressed
Customer	1. Return events 2. Post event customer satisfaction surveys	Satisfied	Satisfied
Financial	1. Impact to the local economy 2 Hotel/motel room bookings during the event 3. Revenue generated for the CCVB	OK	Better

The next step was to determine which, if any, they were currently measuring, or could measure for baseline or current state performance. Jim took on the assignment to discuss the list with Maxine and each team member agreed to investigate the data that was currently available.

The team found that it is very difficult to track some of the key measures proposed such as "revenue per event," "impact to the local economy," and "relationships with event organizers," so some of these measures were not selected as the final key measures for this project. Measures such as "action items," however was easily measured as each person tracked their open and completed action items online. Other data such as "post-event satisfaction surveys" were collected after the conclusion of the events.

The team discovered that if they only tracked certain data, they could be led in the wrong direction. For example, if they only focused on the time spent on each action item, they might go faster, but the quality level could decline. The team concluded that they needed to balance the measurements by tracking key measures in each category. After several work sessions, Maxine and the team agreed on the following Key Performance Indicators or measures:

Productivity/Cost

- ❖ Action items per person
- ❖ Duration of closed action items
- ❖ Time spent per action item

Quality

- ❖ Post Event Satisfaction surveys

Delivery

- ❖ Action items schedule attainment
- ❖ Open action items or backlog

People

- ❖ Hotel/Motel room bookings during event
- ❖ Number of participating local partners and merchants

Customer

- ❖ Return bookings

Financial

- ❖ Revenue generated for the CCVB

The Team Charter was modified to reflect these measurements and a data collection and reporting plan was developed by the team. The data collection plan describes the key measure, who will document it at what frequency, and how it will be reported. Ideally, the key performance measures should be in a graphical format and posted or published in a scoreboard (or dashboard) type fashion.

With the project clearly defined, the team could now move to the Measure Phase of the improvement initiative.

Note: The lack of clear KPIs or performance measures is likely to be the case for many service organizations. Definable performance measures are a critical prerequisite to continuous improvement initiatives. The lack of clear measures needs to be addressed early in the improvement process. Questions to ask are "How do we measure our success in each metric category of cost or productivity, quality, delivery, people, customer, and financial categories?" and "What are the vital few measures, that if improved, will improve the overall customer satisfaction and organization performance?" It is critical to take the time to get this section documented. The improvement team may need to make several attempts to define the current state with clear measures, but the investment will pay back by providing focus and alignment for the team through the next four phases.

The team also put together the initial Project Planner worksheet and the Action Item and Issues and Opportunities Logs as identified in the following three illustrations.

Project Planner - CCVB

Objective: Record and track the key events and milestones to complete the initiative. **Revision Date:** 12/6

Project Planner (PP)
3 Month Plan

Project Planner Objective: Identify major activities by deliverable and time frame to complete.

% Complete: 0% (not started) 25% (underway) 50% (half complete) 75% (nearly done) 100% (complete)

Medium shading or green color signifies completed implementation activities.
Dark shading or red color signifies behind target for implementaion activities.
Light shading or yellow color signifies on target for implementation activities.

	Define Phase	% Comp	Month 1: 1	2	3	4	Month 2: 1	2	3	4	Month 3: 1	2	3	4
1	**Project Charter**	100%												
2	**Team Charter**	100%												
3	Team leader to align with Sponsor	100%												
	Measure Phase	**% Comp**	**Month 1: 1**	**2**	**3**	**4**	**Month 2: 1**	**2**	**3**	**4**	**Month 3: 1**	**2**	**3**	**4**
1	**Baseline Data Collection and Process Mapping**	50%												
2	Material and information flow maps	50%												
3	Develop the current state map	100%												
4	Collect process flow data	50%												
5	Collect Key Performance Indicators (KPIs)	100%												
	Analyze Phase	**% Comp**	**Month 1: 1**	**2**	**3**	**4**	**Month 2: 1**	**2**	**3**	**4**	**Month 3: 1**	**2**	**3**	**4**
1	**Critical Review of Data**	0%												
2	Review current state map for process and flow	0%												
3	Review other data	0%												
4	**Identify High Potential Improvement Actions**	0%												
5	Document process and opporunities	0%												
	Improve Phase	**% Comp**	**Month 1: 1**	**2**	**3**	**4**	**Month 2: 1**	**2**	**3**	**4**	**Month 3: 1**	**2**	**3**	**4**
1	**Develop Improvement Implementation Plan**	0%												
2	Complete a future state map	0%												
3	Develop the detailed improvement plan for PDCAs	0%												
4	**Implement Improvements**	0%												
5	TBD	0%												
	Control Phase	**% Comp**	**Month 1: 1**	**2**	**3**	**4**	**Month 2: 1**	**2**	**3**	**4**	**Month 3: 1**	**2**	**3**	**4**
1	**Establish Measures and Audit Plan to Sustain Improvements**	0%												
2	Provide ongoing weekly scoreboard reports	0%												

Action Item Log - CCVB

Objective: Record and track actions in progress and agreements related to team activities.

Revision Date: 12/6

- Medium shading or green color signifies completed implementation activities.
- Dark shading or red color signifies behind target for implementaion activities.
- Light shading or yellow color signifies on target for implementation activities.

	Action Item	Responsibility	Target Date	Percent Complete	Completed Date	Actions
1	Identify key measures.	Liz and team	6 Dec	100%	6 Dec	IO Log Item #1.
2	Set meeting schedule.	Liz	6 Dec	100%	6 Dec	Tuesdays, 1:00 - 2:30
3	Finalize Team Charter.	Team	13 Dec	50%		
4	Begin to collect data.	Team	6 Dec	50%		
5	Develop current state maps and process flows.	Team	13 Dec	25 %		
6						
7						
8						
9						
10						
11						
12						
13						
14						
15						
16						
17						
18						
19						
20						

Issues and Opportunities Log - CCVB

Objective: Record and track Opportunities (O), Ideas (I), Roadblocks (RB), and Parking Lot (PL) items. **Revision Date:** Dec 13

Medium shading or green color signifies moved to Action Item Log.

	Opportunity (O), Idea (I), Roadblock (RB), or Parking Log (PL)	Category (O/I/RB/PL)	Benefit	Action Summary	Date Logged	Date Closed
1	We need to identify key measures.	O	Key measure will drive improvement.	Team to identify key measures on Team Charter.	6 Dec	10 Dec
2	We should use our partners better.	I	If we delegate work to our partners, we have more time to service our clients.	No action at this time.	6 Dec	
3	We need to update our marketing materials.	PL	We will have current materials to send out.	No action at this time.	13 Dec	
4	We don't have time for a project.	RB	No project, no progress.	Do the project!	6 Dec	6 Dec
5						
6						
7						
8						
9						
10						
11						
12						
13						
14						
15						
16						

With the project clearly defined and some action items and opportunities in place, the team could now move to the Measure Phase of the improvement initiative.

Measure Phase

The team had to begin measurements at the Key Performance Indicator (KPI) level and the process improvement level. The KPIs are defined on the Team Charter, but since several of the measures were not currently tracked, the team needed to develop a plan for measurement and posting. The team developed a data collection plan that included the data source, how, when, and what frequency the data was to be collected, who would collect it, and what the target goal would be. The next step was to begin collecting the data. It took some time to collect enough data for analysis of trends and performance improvement opportunities.

Data collection at the process level involved developing a data collection chart of the services they provide, the frequency of the services, and the time to complete the services. The team began collecting this data as well at the process level.

Analyze Phase

To analyze the data, the team used Pareto Charts to determine where to start their improvement in effort to have the greatest positive impact. The data indicated that the most frequent activity was "Event Planner Requests." The average time to complete tasks were also analyzed with Pareto Chart techniques. The analysis indicated that the three activities that take the most time are: Volunteer Requests, On-Site Requests, and Attendance Building Requests.

The team's direction was not clear until they reviewed the total time spent per year. This analysis again indicated that the Event Planner Requests are where the team members spend most of their time annually. A further breakdown of their specific requests was discussed as a potential action item. The team needed to know more specifics regarding what requests the Event Planners were asking for.

Improve Phase

Over the following two months the team continued to work to develop a better understanding of the specific needs of Event Planners. The results varied widely and the team decided to leave the Event Planner Requests as a customized service.

The team was able to find fertile ground in the additional improvement opportunities areas. They found that many of the On-Site, Dining, Transportation, and Attendance Building Requests had many common and repetitive requirements. The team was able to work with their local partners to develop standardized responses to these requests. The team used standard work tools to develop improvements in their ability to service the Event Planners in a more efficient and effective manner.

Control Phase

To control and sustain the improvements, the CCVB team continued to track and monitor the KPIs. The KPIs were able to focus the team's efforts on improvement action items that drive improved productivity and customer satisfaction. They conducted quarterly CCVB review sessions to ensure they were aligned with their customers and Maxine's needs.

The CCVB implemented a monthly performance scoreboard to monitor these activities. Since completing the improvement project, event room bookings are up 25% and the local businesses are realizing profitable growth. The CCVB clearly exceeded their expectations for this project.

Measure Phase

Speaking with Data

Chapter Overview

It has been stated "What gets measured, gets done." and "You treasure what you measure." And, even though many organizations have some type of Key Performance Indicators (KPIs), they quite often are incomplete or the wrong ones entirely. The most common performance measures are linked to financial performance. Lean Sigma measures are different. Lean Sigma performance measures are linked first to the twelve wastes and then cascade upward to financial measures. The key to Lean Sigma performance measures is that they allow teams of people to "see the waste" and act as guides for action and improvements. This chapter outlines key factors and tools for measuring process performance in a way that identifies or "illuminates" waste. Once this waste is identified, it can be reduced or eliminated. This is a key for successful Lean Sigma transformations.

Measure Phase Training and Alignment

Lean Sigma measurements may seem a bit foreign at first to service environments, so it is even more critical that the proper level of training be conducted and understood. Many service organizations are accustomed to working with people and subjective measures, that they have all but lost their focus and understanding of objective performance measures. Some service organizations will even challenge the very premise that their service performance can be measured. "How can you measure the joy, pleasure, and fulfillment of attending a classical music concert?" However, they can be measured using exit polls, post event surveys (telephone, email, or twitter), guest comments on Facebook, noise levels at the concert (clapping, cheers), etc.. Having the proper measures and allowing them to drive improvement is a powerful and rewarding path for a service organization. Those that are still questioning "How?" should learn from those that are doing it, before it is too late!

Before beginning the Measure Phase, team members should have an understanding of the following:

- Lean Sigma
- Lean Sigma 12 wastes
- DMAIC Improvement process review
- Define Phase tool application
- Measure Phase tool overview
- Basic data collection and presentation methods and techniques

Basic data collection and presentation methods are covered in further detail in the Measure Phase Tool section of this chapter. These are key prerequisite skills to learn during this phase.

Measuring Customer Needs

One of the most critical measurements to understand is your customer's needs or market demand. For service organizations the customer's needs may change with every customer or moment-to-moment with the same customer!

The Lean Sigma Measure Phase generally begins by documenting customer's needs or market demand for the process being improved as a continuation of the Define Phase. Once need is established and quantified, processes can be designed to satisfy demand with minimal waste. Customer's needs must be quantified. The following are a few examples of customer's needs being quantified:

- Transactions per day
- Customer/client/patient satisfaction
- Guests per week
- Security searches per day
- Customer/client/patient wait times
- Attendance per event
- Market share per event

This type of information must be understood and available to improvement teams. Notice the nature of the customer demand measures. Each measurement is time-based. The time-based demand picture is fundamental to the application of Lean Sigma improvement tools. This is sometimes called the "pace of demand" or "takt time" and may vary by customer, hour, day, season, or weather!

If time-based demand information is not available, the project team will need to establish a measurement and data collection plan to capture the true demand picture. It is also useful to understand how the demand is communicated or expressed to the organization.

It may be easier initially to identify demand at a high level such as customers per last fiscal or calendar year. At this point take any customer demand data that is available. More than likely the demand picture measurements will need to be further analyzed by the improvement team.

Measure Phase Tools

The key Measure Phase tools and their application are identified in the following table:

Phase	Lean Sigma Tool	Application Guide
MEASURE	Voice of the Customer (VOC)	Use the Voice of the Customer (VOC) tool concepts to identify and document basic customer needs and expectations.
	Quality Function Deployment (QFD)	Use the Quality Function Deployment (QFD) tool when a comprehensive review, analysis, and prioritization of customer needs and expectations is needed. Often used for new product/service development.
	Value Stream and Process Maps	Use process or value stream maps to document current and future state conditions, flow, and key process Key Performance indicators (KPIs).
	Supplier-Input-Process-Output-Customer (SIPOC)	Use the SIPOC analysis to document key suppliers, inputs, outputs and customers for a process.
	Key Metric and Data Profile	Use Key Metric and Data Profiles to document data gathered during the mapping process which may include calculating a Six Sigma value, if appropriate.
	Check Sheets	Use Check Sheets to create and collect key process data.
	Frequency Charts	Use Frequency Charts to create and collect key process data.
	Run Charts	Use Run Charts to document, improve, and control key process variables over time.
	Measurement System Analysis (MSA)	Use MSA to design experiments that seek to identify the components of variation in the measurement.

By using these key tools, improvement teams are able to quantify key data for subsequent improvement opportunity analysis.

Voice of the Customer (VOC)

Voice of the Customer (VOC) *is a term used in business and Information Technology to describe the in-depth process of capturing a customer's expectations, preferences, and aversions.* The VOC tool is a process that will deliver a greater understanding of a customer's expressed and unexpressed needs. The VOC is done by conducting market research through a variety of potential methods. Customer needs then can be ranked and prioritized in effort to create an improved service process. A common tool or instrument to do this in the service industry is the customer feedback survey. Other tools intended to create a better understanding of customer desires are: focus group studies, complaint analysis, internet monitoring, or customer interviews. In each case, customer needs and priorities are documented and used for further analysis. The objectives of the VOC tool or process are to develop specific and measureable needs or specifications, provide a common language for the improvement team and input for new and innovative services.

There are basically five levels of activities in the VOC process. Teams must decide which levels will provide the best fit for the scope and duration of the project. The five levels are:

1. *Relationship tracking* - This is used when organizations need to track the quality of customer relationships over time.
2. *Interaction monitoring* - This is used when every customer interaction, from a web-based or online transaction to a call into the call center, is important. Organizations need a way to monitor how effectively they handle these customer interactions.
3. *Continuous listening* - This is used when you need to hear what customers are saying, such as listening to calls in the call center, reading blogs, reading inbound emails, and visiting appropriate customer locations (i.e., retail outlets, satellite offices, physician groups, etc).
4. *Project infusion* - This is used when new services need to be provided and insights about customers are needed. Despite the clear need for this type of effort, many companies lack a formalized approach for incorporating customer insights into projects.
5. *Periodic immersion* - This is used when employees need to understand the product and services that are being offered, but from the customer's perspective. This would involve spending a significant amount of time interacting directly with customers or working alongside frontline employees. All levels of the organization would find this of value.

Survey and question design are critical to elicit valid information. Instrument designers need to address the quality of the questions, legitimacy and accuracy of the data, as well as how useful the information is in the improvement process. The following are qualities of a desirable VOC.

Credibility - How widely accepted is the measure? Does it have a good track record of results? Is it based on a scientifically and academically rigorous methodology? Will management trust it? Is there proof that it is tied to financial results?

Reliability - Is it a consistent standard that can be applied across the customer life cycle, multiple channels, and customer situations?

Precision - Is it specific enough to provide insight? Does it use multiple related questions to deliver greater accuracy and insight?

Accuracy - Is the measurement right? Is it representative of the entire customer base or just a segment of it? Do the questions capture self-reported importance or can they derive importance based on what customers say? Does it have an acceptable margin of error and realistic sample sizes?

Actionability - Does it provide any insight into what can be done to encourage customers to be loyal, to purchase and remain a customer? Does it prioritize improvements according to biggest impacts?

Predictability - Can it project the future behaviors of the customer?

Additional points to consider when creating a Voice of the Customer survey:

- Analyze current customer satisfaction levels
- Ensure a cross-functional (or multi-disciplinary) team has input
- Determine competitor's strengths and weaknesses, if appropriate
- Use quantitative (e.g., complaint logs, etc.) and qualitative (e.g., mini-surveys, etc.) data
- Consider specific questions and wording
- Determine acceptable scoring scale
- Ensure correct sample size
- Consider sources of bias

When designing and conducting a VOC survey, expert assistance might be required.

Sample customer VOC surveys are illustrated below:

The Garden Restaurant

Customer Experience Survey:

Please rate the following areas from 1 = Poor to 5 = Excellent. Thank you!

The Lobby

Was the lobby staff friendly and did they welcome you to the restaurant?

Were you seated in a timely, efficient manner?

The Server

Was your server attentive and there when you needed him/her?

Was your server knowledgeable and able to answer your questions about our food and beverages?

How was the pace of your meal?

The Food

How would you rate the taste of your food?

Please rate the temperature of your food, hot food being piping hot.

Please rate your visit on the value for the money.

Overall, how would you rate your visit?

Would you recommend the Garden Restaurant to a close friend or relative?

The Table Area

Was your table area clean when you were seated?

What one thing did you like most about your visit?

What one thing could we do to improve your experience at The Garden Restaurant?

Thank you for your feedback! **Please come again!**

Please take a moment to tell us about your stay.

	Exceeded Expectations	Met Expectations	Did Not Meet Expectations
Reception/ Front Desk	❑	❑	❑
Housekeeping	❑	❑	❑
Room Maintenance	❑	❑	❑
Food & Beverage Outlets	❑	❑	❑
Convention & Catering	❑	❑	❑
Overall Level of Service	❑	❑	❑
Would you stay with us again?		Yes ❑	No ❑

We sincerely appreciate any written comments you have about our performance.

____

____

Name ____________________

Room # __________ E-mail __________

Date __________ Affiliation __________

By completing this comment card, you are agreeing to receive promotional information via e-mail. At no time will your information be re-distributed or sold.

Quality Function Deployment (QFD)

Qualify Function Deployment (QFD) *is a tool that takes the VOC information and turns it into specific and measurable quality requirements that can be used to design improved service processes.* QFD methods provide a systematic approach to the design of a quality process. For example, QFD takes the VOC statement such as "I want to be assisted immediately upon arrival" into specific actions such as "Greet and assist every customer within 15 seconds of their arrival."

QFD uses a comprehensive matrix system to relate VOC priorities to specific measureable characteristics and to a quality measurement and improvement plan. The first critical step in completing the QFD for a service process is to identify specific and measurable customer needs using VOC techniques. Develop a method or survey to collect information directly from the customer. Document customer needs on the QFD matrix. Once this is done, document the technical or organizational needs for the process being examined on the QFD matrix. These may be specific capabilities or target markets. Once this information is identified and documented, the customer and organization's needs can be compared on a QFD matrix. The following example (i.e., steps) will serve as a guide in creating and understanding the QFD matrix.

Step 1. The improvement project team uses previously collected VOC data or collects VOC data. The following Customer luggage priorities were identified and documented through airline gate face to face surveys, where travelers were asked to rank their top four priorities regarding luggage (i.e., a VOC survey):

Customer Priority	Customer Requirements (Voice of the Customer)
1	Do not lose my luggage.
2	Do not damage my luggage.
3	Have my luggage arrive with me.
4	Get my luggage to me within 15 minutes from when I arrive at the luggage pick up area.

Step 2. The improvement team then identifies organizational requirements for the area targeted which may include competitive pressures. The following organizational requirements were developed by a airline luggage handling improvement team:

	Organizational Requirements
1	Worker safety
2	Bags travel with passengers
3	Timely unloading and loading of aircraft
4	Minimal luggage catch-up and administrative time
5	Minimal cost of labels and label process
6	Meet security requirements

Step 3. The improvement team also identifies and documents the technical and procedural requirements for the improvement target area. The following technical (and procedural) requirements were identified or developed by an airline luggage handling improvement team:

	Technical Requirements
1	Bar coding of each bag
2	Label attached to bag, and matching bag tag to the customer
3	Label tracking to bag must match
4	Use bag storage and staging areas only as designated
5	Use current conveying systems
6	Use appropriate tarmac practices and procedures
7	Use appropriate vehicle capabilities and sizes
8	Use standard luggage routing from counter to aircraft

Step 4. The improvement team constructs the basic QFD diagram, populating the appropriate data into the diagram as follows:

QFD Air Travel Luggage Example		1	2	3	4	5	6	7	8	9		
Customer Priority	**Customer Requirements (Voice of the Customer)**	**Organizational Requirements (O)**	Worker safety	Bags with passengers	Timely unloading and loading of aircraft	Minimal luggage catch-up and administrative time	Minimal cost of labels and label process	Meet security requirements			**Current Measures**	**Competitive Measures**
1	Do not lose my luggage.											
2	Do not damage my luggage.											
3	Have my luggage arrive with me.											
4	Get my luggage to me within 15 minutes from when I arrive at the luggage pick up area.											
		Technical Requirements (X)	Bar coding	label to bag	Label tracking to bag match	Bag storage and staging areas	Conveying systems	Tarmac practices	Vehicle capabilities and sizes	Luggage routing from counter to aircraft		
		1	2	3	4	5	6	7	8	9		

Step 5. The improvement team then identifies on the QFD diagram where the Organizational and Technical Requirements impact each Customer Requirement by placing an O or X in the corresponding box. This process is expected to create dialog and learning, as well as an updated QFD. Notice how an overlap is indicated on the QFD with an O and X - "⊗" symbol. These are strong relationships and are critical areas to address and improve.

QFD Air Travel Luggage Example		1	2	3	4	5	6	7	8	9		
Customer Priority	Customer Requirements (Voice of the Customer)	Organizational Requirements (O)	Worker safety	Bags with passengers	Timely unloading and loading of aircraft	Minimal luggage catch-up and administrative time	Minimal cost of labels and label process	Meet security requirements			Current Measures	Competitive Measures
1	Do not lose my luggage.		X	⊗	X	⊗	X	X	X	X		
2	Do not damage my luggage.			X	O	⊗	X	X	X	X		
3	Have my luggage arrive with me.			O	X	O		O				
4	Get my luggage to me within 15 minutes from when I arrive at the luggage pick up area.		O		⊗	X	X	X	X	X		
		Technical Requirements (X)	Bar coding	label to bag	Label tracking to bag match	Bag storage and staging areas	Conveying systems	Tarmac practices	Vehicle capabilities and sizes	Luggage routing from counter to aircraft		
		1	2	3	4	5	6	7	8	9		

Step 6. The improvement team completes their QFD by inputting the current state performance measures, and competitive measures if they are available. It is a good idea to obtain these to ensure best in class performance will be achieved. From the process of completing the QFD, and the QFD itself, teams can begin to identify improvement actions and priorities to improve the target process.

QFD Air Travel Luggage Example		1	2	3	4	5	6	7	8	9		
Customer Priority	Customer Requirements (Voice of the Customer)	Organizational Requirements (O)	Worker safety	Bags with passengers	Timely unloading and loading of aircraft	Minimal luggage catch-up and administrative time	Minimal cost of labels and label process	Meet security requirements			Current Measures	Competitive Measures
1	Do not lose my luggage.		X	⊗	X	⊗	X	X	X	X	98.6%	98-99.9%
2	Do not damage my luggage.			X	O	⊗	X	X	X	X	99.9%	99-100%
3	Have my luggage arrive with me.			O	X	O		O			97.9%	98.99.9%
4	Get my luggage to me within 15 minutes from when I arrive at the luggage pick up area.		O		⊗	X	X	X	X	X	95.0%	96-99.9%
		Technical Requirements (X)	Bar coding	label to bag	Label tracking to bag match	Bag storage and staging areas	Conveying systems	Tarmac practices	Vehicle capabilities and sizes	Luggage routing from counter to aircraft		
		1	2	3	4	5	6	7	8	9		

To complete the QFD matrix impact analysis process, each Organizational Requirement and Technical Requirement are reviewed to determine the impact on each Customer Requirement. For example, The Organization Requirement of "Worker Safety" is reviewed against each Customer Requirement identified on the QFD matrix.

In this example, the improvement team believes there is no significant relationship between the Organizational Requirement of "Worker safety" and each of the first 3 Customer Requirements, however, they do believe that there is a significant relationship or impact between the "Worker Safety" and the 4th Customer Requirement of "Get my luggage to me within 15 minutes from when I arrive at the luggage pick up area." Luggage handlers must obey safe speed signs on the tarmac, other safety requirement such as assisted lifts for oversized luggage, and the like. The actual time required to follow safety requirements varies by flight, depending on travelers packing habits and loads. This variation may delay the luggage from getting to the pickup area within the required 15 minutes. Therefore, an "O" is placed in the intersecting box to show this relationship and potential impact on Customer Requirement. In this manner, each Organizational Requirement is reviewed to determine the potential impact on each Customer Requirement, and an "O" in the intersecting box shows that there is a potential impact in satisfying the Customer Requirement.

In a similar manner, each Technical Requirement is reviewed against each Customer Requirement. For example, the Technical Requirement of "Bar coding" is believed to impact the Customer Requirement 1 of "Do not lose my luggage," but no other, so an "X" is placed in the corresponding box. Luggage handlers are required to bar code scan each piece of luggage to ensure airline tracking ability. In this extra step, luggage may be misplaced and could become lost. Bar coding also helps reduce lost luggage by providing a positive count for all luggage on a particular plane. This is a positive impact and is shown by placing and "X" in the intersecting box.

In this particular case, the team believes that both the Organizational Requirement of "Bags with passengers" and the Technical Requirement of "Label to bag" can potentially impact the Customer Requirement of "Do not lose my luggage." This dual relationship is shown by placing both an "O" (Organizational Requirement) and an "X" (Technical Requirements) in the corresponding box. This dual marking is shown by an "⊗." The impact and relationships decisions are usually agreed through discussion by the team before moving on.

The QFD matrix helps organizations identify gaps in their processes that need to be addressed to fully satisfy their customers. Once gaps are identified, improvement actions can be implemented to close the gaps and deliver a quality product or service by focusing the various business functions toward achieving a common goal - customer satisfaction.

Value Stream and Process Maps

There are several useful mapping tools to consider for visualizing service processes. Each tool has its advantages and disadvantages. Mapping techniques are usually considered at several levels within an organization. It is best to match the mapping technique with the level of the process being examined. The two key mapping processes highlighted in the this section are value stream maps and various types of process maps. These mapping variations are covered in further detail on the following pages.

Value Stream Maps

*A **value stream map** is a visual representation of the material, work, and information flow, as well as the queue times between processes for a specific customer demand.* The value stream map is a very powerful tool and does an excellent job at highlighting the waste in a process. A current state value stream map provides this representation of how the process is currently running. A future state value stream map will show the process with the proposed improvements that are to be implemented. The future state value stream map is a road map for improvement. It is recommended that a current state value stream map be drawn on a whiteboard or on a large sheet of paper that can be hung on the wall. Post-it Notes can then represent various activities within a process. If a large sheet of paper is not available, tape multiple flip chart sheets on the wall and line them up horizontally. Number each flip chart sheet to ensure they stay organized once the event is over. If the map is drawn on a whiteboard, a photograph can be taken of the map for documentation and sharing.

Most current state value stream mapping exercises are done on paper that is posted on the wall. This means there may be waste involved if the team desires to subsequently recreate the map electronically. However, that type of waste is minimal compared to the engagement and interaction of the team members in the process. Do not underestimate the importance of this!

The Chicken and the Egg Syndrome

Do you gather data prior to the mapping exercise? Or, do you create your map and then gather data? The answer to both of these questions is yes. Most likely, you will have some data prior from the Define Phase to create the first pass of the current state value stream map, and then after reviewing it with the team, additional data will need to be collected and placed on the map. Either way, creating an accurate current state value stream map requires good data.

To have the first pass of a current state value stream map completely filled out (or populated with data) at the first team session would require:

1. Each process of the value stream map clearly identified and known
2. Activities listed under each process, accurate cycle times through reports, observations, and/or historical analysis (cycle time is the time elapsed from the beginning of a work process or request until it is completed), customer satisfaction levels, number of workers, number of shifts, uptime of equipment, quality issues, etc.
3. Overall start and stop times for each process are obtained from an appropriate sample size to establish overall lead time and queue/delay time between processes

It will not be likely that a current state value stream map will be totally completed and accurately populated with data prior to meeting with the team for the first time, however, certain parts of it can be completed and serve as a straw man for when the team meets. Either way, accurate, reliable, and the most current data should be conveyed on the map. Be careful to not place estimates of the cycle times and queue times on a value stream map. This would compromise the integrity of the improvements obtained once the future state map has been implemented.

Value stream mapping begins with creating the current state and proceeds according to the following steps:

1. Use the following icons to draw a "shell" of the current state, listing the main processes, customers, and suppliers (internal and external). Consider creating additional icons that may be appropriate to your value stream (e.g., creating a laptop icon to demonstrate interactivity with the Customer Relationship Management (CRM) system).

Dedicated Process Box - the main process, department, or area where value-added and/or non value-added work occurs

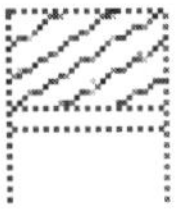

Shared Process Box - where multiple value streams all inter-relate (mail rooms, human resources, billing, admissions, lobby areas, service counters, etc.)

Attribute Area - characteristics of the process (cycle times, number of people, internal defects, delay times, etc.)

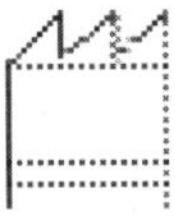

Customer or Supplier - the upstream and downstream customer or supplier, with its respective attributes

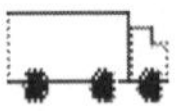

Truck Shipment - denotes the physical arrival or departure of work related to the value stream (e.g., transporting customers or goods, supplies, etc.)

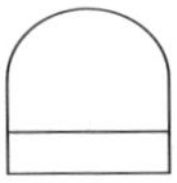

Queue (Wait) Time - the amount of time, work, people, or information that resides between two processes

Database/Internet Interaction - computer interaction (CRM, Email, Web, etc.)

Manual Information Flow - physical conveyance of work, employees, or customers between two processes within the value stream (e.g., hand carrying work to another area, transporting customers to a venue, etc.)

Electronic Information Flow - the electronic signal that communicates information from database to process or from database to database

Mail - the arrival or sending of metered mail

Folder - a single unit of work (i.e., document)

Folders - multiple units of work grouped together and moved through a common process

Go-See Scheduling - the physical viewing and collecting of information on the processes to determine work loads (e.g., customer lines getting longer, customers waiting in queue, etc.)

Push - the movement of the customer, work, or information downstream regardless of the need

Staff - the person(s) assigned to the particular process

Service Measure - the quality of customer service measure

Hassle Factor - (not to be confused with David Hasselhoff ☺) - indicates high hassle factor/frustration level for the customer or the worker

Smiley Face - indicates customer satisfaction or delight options

2. Visit the areas, beginning with the most downstream process and walk the flow in reverse order to collect the attributes (i.e., cycle times, defects, etc.) related to the value stream and, if applicable, gather actual data. Use a stopwatch (if practical) and clearly communicate to everyone in the area what you are doing and why. This may also be the time to conduct the Waste Walk (pages 36 - 37) while you are visiting the area.

3. Determine the amount of time between processes. This is the main determinant of the separation of process boxes on a value stream map. You can determine that if delays are occurring with a process more than a certain percentage (say 10% of the overall lead time), then that may warrant a separation of those processes on a value stream map. (Later, additional tools will be used to further analyze these delays within the process.)

4. Determine the quantity of work that arrives at each process (i.e., # of documents, # of customers, interruptions per hour, etc.).

5. Determine what is done with the work after the process has been completed. What is the next process? Does anything special need to be done prior to the work arriving at the next process?

6. List all the process attributes on the current state map. If there are other departmental or process attributes (i.e., cycle time of the activities, # customers seen, # rooms available, errors/defects/mistakes, etc.) specific to the process, list those as appropriate.

7. Draw all forms of communication, electronic and/or manual.

8. Total the process cycle times within the process box. This is typically the value-added time which may include some of the non value-added time due to a poor process (which can be later analyzed for waste). If delays are listed within the process attributes, then it would be acceptable to include those delays within the total process cycle time. Additional Lean Sigma tools will be used to separate and eliminate those wastes; however, many times the larger waste of time (i.e., delay) will be between the processes. There is no right or wrong method to list delays, just be consistent in your approach when mapping.

9. Compile a step graph at the bottom of the value stream map displaying the total cycle time for each process, including the queue/wait/delay times between processes.

10. The map should convey the total lead time and total queue time, along with any other key metrics (e.g., total lead time, total wait or queue time, Sigma value, etc.) that the team has found to be significant.

The following are some examples of current state value stream maps from various improvement projects:

Hotel Check-In Current State Value Stream Map

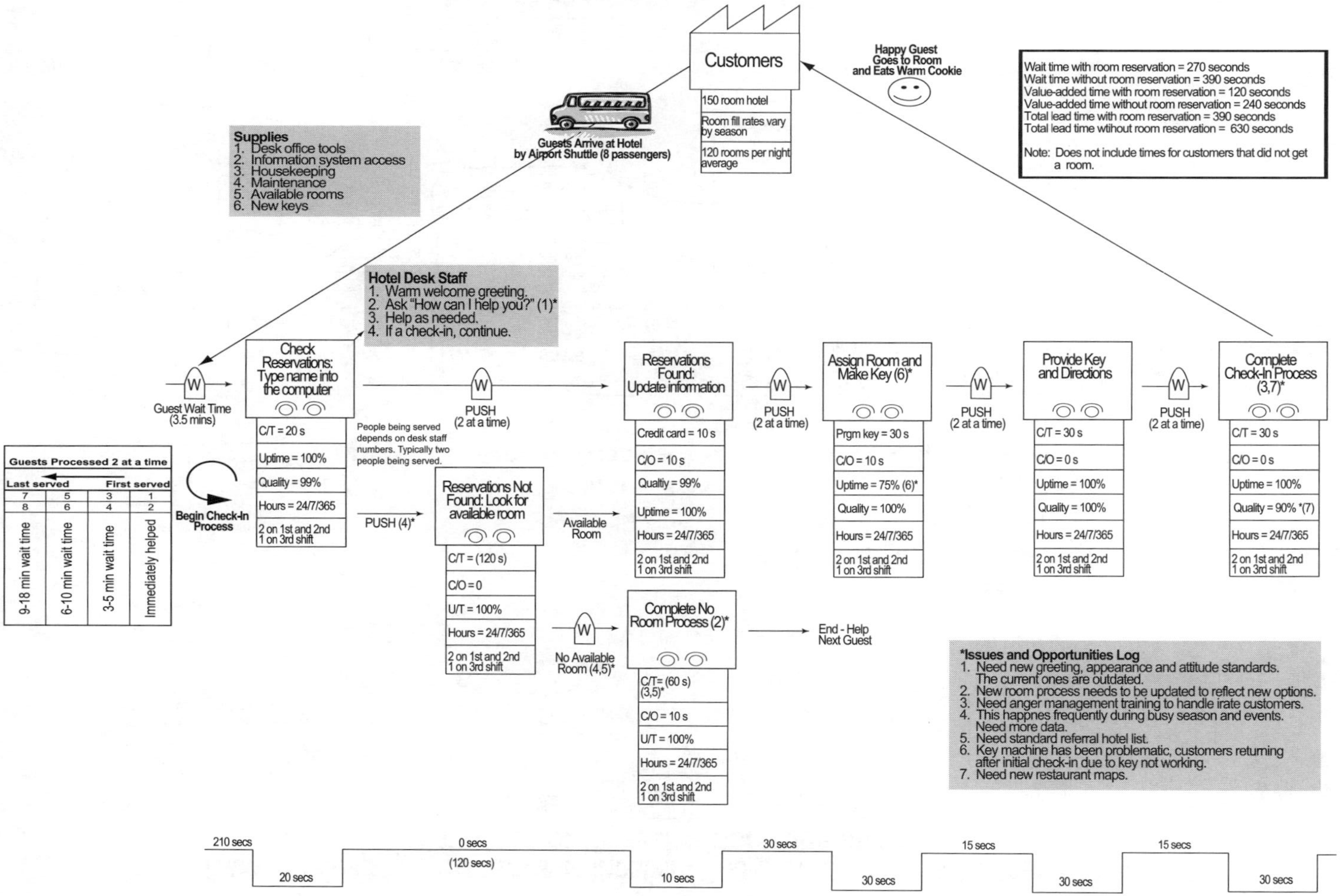

Oakview Hospital's ED Arrival to Inpatient Bed Current State Value Stream Map (comprised of three distinct value streams)

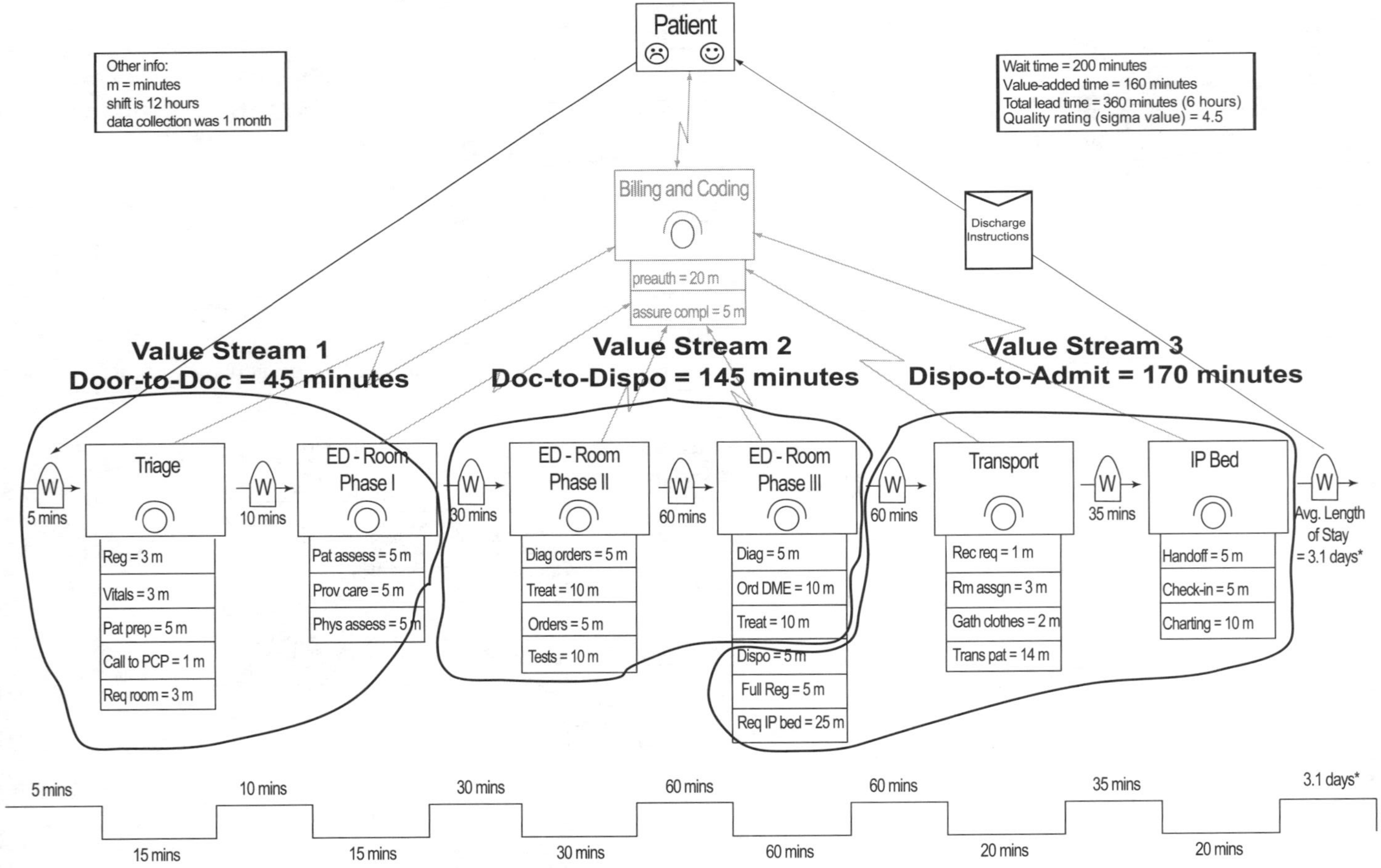

* This information is not included in the total lead time for this value stream.

Rock Band Fireside Booking to Payment Current State Value Stream Map

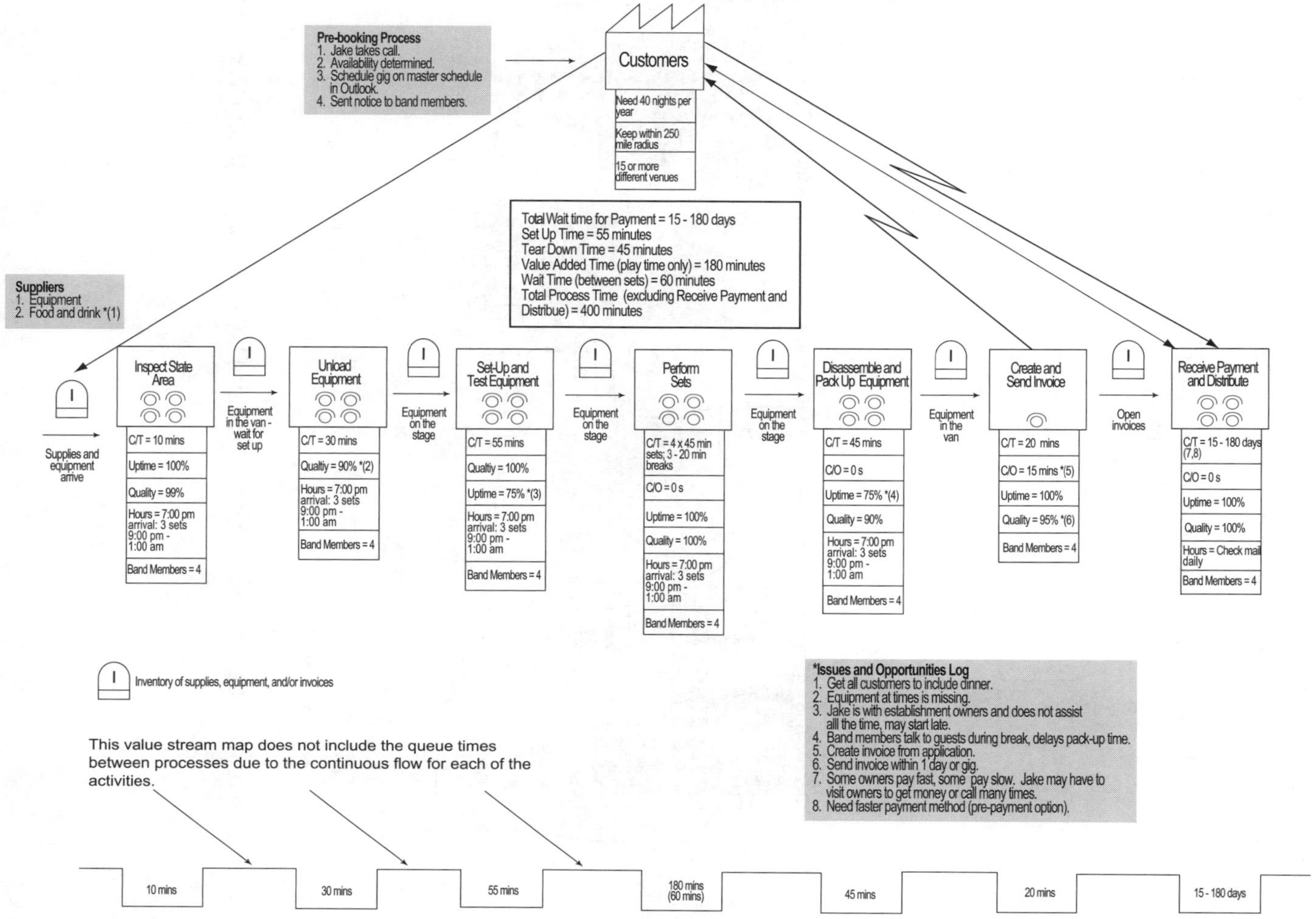

11. If a Waste Walk (pages 36 - 37) has been conducted (step 2) then use Post-It Notes to place the various wastes identified on the walk, as well as the process issues, on the current state value stream map as shown in the example below:

Oakview Hospital's ED Arrival to Inpatient Bed Current State Value Stream Map
Waste Walk Update

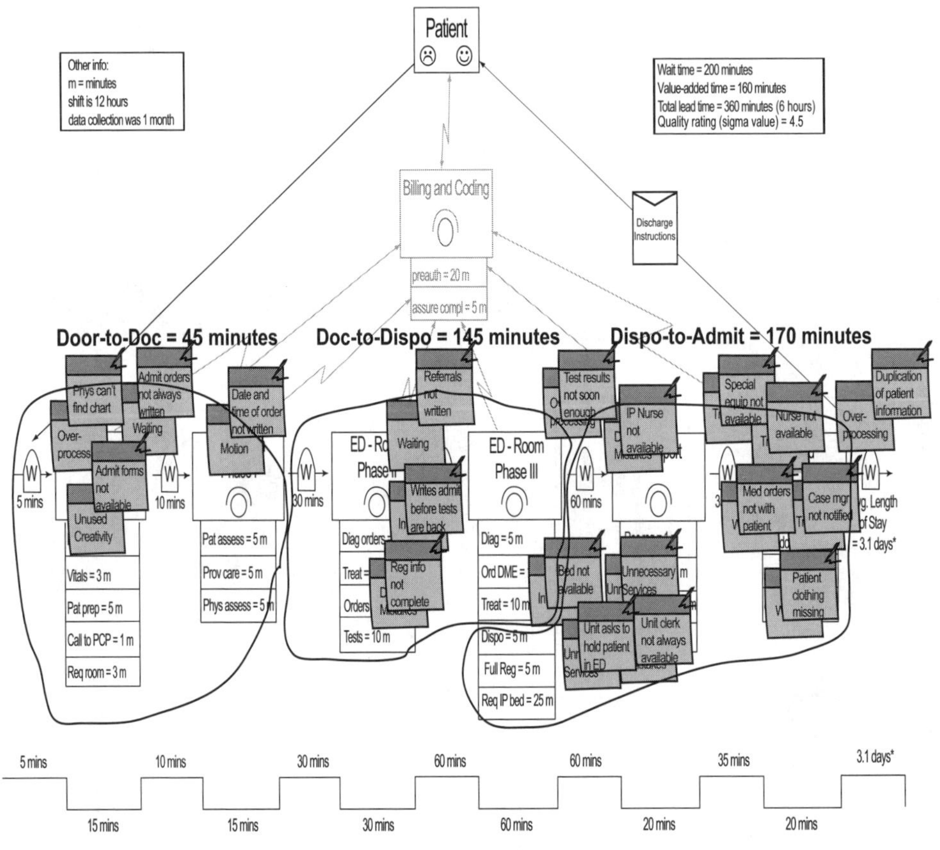

* This information is not included in the total lead time for this value stream.

Note: Ensure all ideas for improvement are listed in the Issues and Opportunities Log.

Once the current state value stream map has been created, ensure a consensus is reached by all team members regarding the representation shown on the map. If additional data is required, create action plans on the AI Log to complete the data collection required. The basis for creating a realistic future state map depends on the accuracy of information obtained and displayed on the current state map.

The future state value stream map is a visual representation of Lean tools applied to the current state value stream map. The future state value stream map is seldom implemented all at once. It is typically implemented over a period of time (i.e., six to eighteen months, or even longer depending on allocated resources). A team may work on a series of smaller improvements within a value stream, and then continue to monitor the results to ensure the improvements can be controlled and sustained over time prior to any enterprise-wide (or full value stream) roll-out.

Creating a future state value stream map begins with the current state map and proceeds according to the following steps:

1. Ensure everyone understands the various Lean Sigma tools and concepts.

2. Brainstorm and use the following icons to create a future state value stream map. Each of the following Lean Sigma tool icons will be explained in the subsequent chapters. Teams can create their own icons to identify their unique processes.

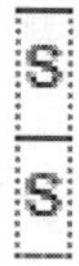

Safety Resources - temporary resources to assist work flow when there is a sudden influx of customer demand (temporary employees, volunteers, overtime, retirees, cross-training, etc.)

Buffer Resources - temporary resources to assist work flow when there are internal issues such as turnover, illness, vacation, etc. (temporary employees, volunteers, overtime, retirees, cross-training, etc.)

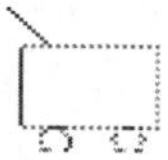

Cart - a device used to distribute work units or supplies throughout the value stream (signature/confidential papers, equipment, etc.)

Kanban (also represented as folders from current state icons) - work unit(s) or information packets for delivery to a process

Supermarket - a physical location located between two processes to hold work until it is required downstream

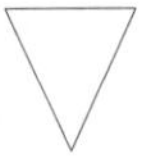

Signal Kanban - the signal used to replenish a material lot

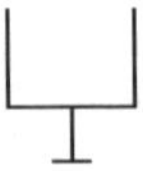

Kanban Post (or Bin) - the physical location where Kanbans Cards are placed in order to be picked up

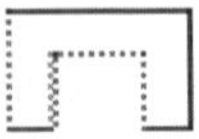

U-Shaped Work Area - the arrangement of desks, fax machines, copiers, laptops, etc. to accommodate efficient work flow

Pull - the representation of work (i.e., documents, suppliers, equipment, etc.) being requested from a downstream process

Pitch Board - the physical device used to hold work based only on volume

FIFO - a physical location located between processes to hold work (or patients) sequentially for the downstream process

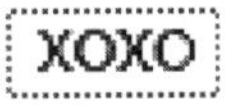

Heijunka Box - a physical device used to hold work based on volume and variety

Runner's Route - the route the runner will use to deliver and pick up work (kanbans, documents, supplies, etc.) throughout the day

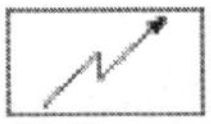

Dashboard - the physical device or location where daily goals are made visual

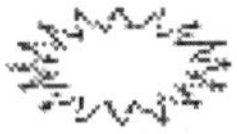

Kaizen Event (improvement activity) - a focused effort in the application of the Lean tools to a specific area of the value streams

Note: Once a current state value stream state map has been created, additional analysis of the processes can be done using additional tools in the Analyze Phase (e.g., Value-Added versus Non Value-Added Analysis). This further analysis can include a portion of or just one of the processes on the value stream map.

The overall goal of creating a current and future state value stream map is to clearly identify where waste lies, create a shared vision for improvement, and determine which Lean Sigma tools can be used for waste elimination. Future state maps will require numerous iterations as progress is made and team members learn from their implementation experiences. The future state map, similar to the Team Charter, is a living document, and will reflect all changes as they occur or are projected to occur. It has proven useful for improvement teams to draw an "ideal" future state map with no existing limitations. This is usually a radical and simplified value stream with minimal waste. From this, the team usually can obtain several ideas which they can include in their future state map over the next 6 - 18 months.

The value stream map is a great tool to use if processes are sequential and there are flow issues (i.e., delays) that need to be addressed. However, there may be times when there are just too many activities (i.e., decisions on where information or work flows presenting Yes - No type decisions) to easily present on a value stream map. If that is the case, then consider a type of process map (next section).

A value stream map is very useful if it is used within a systematic approach to Lean implementation. Share the maps by posting them on the Intranet and placing a hardcopy in the appropriate area.

A simpler approach is to take a digital photograph of the value stream maps for documentation. The digital photograph can be quickly and easily shared, and posted in a variety of software programs. Improvement teams must remember that the purpose of the mapping process is to identify waste and improvement action items. A highly polished map may only reflect the waste of overprocessesing! Do not spend too much time making "pretty" maps, as this wastes critical resources.

Two of the most widely used applications to create a value stream map are (1) MS Excel and (2) MS Visio. Both have easy-to-use features to quickly and effectively create a value stream map. You may find that Microsoft has bundled both applications into your system.

Whether to create a value stream map in Excel or Visio will be determined by several factors. These factors are driven by the limited drawing capabilities of Excel and the considerable and advanced drawing capabilities of Visio.

Factors to consider for value stream maps created in Excel:

- Requires a simple value stream map with limited number of process boxes, typically 5 - 10
- Is a single function value stream or within the same department
- Has a minimal number of data sets (e.g., cycle times, wait times, First Time Right (FTR), quality measures, etc.)
- Has a limited volume or throughput of work such as documents, orders, applications, etc.
- Is a repeatable process
- Requires a step graph that will sum up total cycle and queue times from process boxes using Excel formulas

Pro's when using Excel:

- Easy to create simple value stream maps
- Accessible/available software package on nearly all PCs
- Requires less computer knowledge to use than Visio
- Easily "groups" your autoshapes together to move them around the page
- Easy to use Excel's add, subtract, or sum features to calculate process metrics

Con's when using Excel:

- Limited number of unique autoshapes for use
- Difficult to rescale your map once created
- Generally not viewed as a sophisticated "drawing" tool and has limited capabilities
- No easy feature to use when you need to grab, move, and/or adjust the drawing
- Hard to insert objects and images from Visio into Excel
- Hard to write text onto and/or into all autoshapes

Factors to consider for value stream maps created in Visio:

- ❖ Requires a complex value stream map with 10+ process boxes
- ❖ Has complex, cross-functional and cross-boundary processes
- ❖ Has complex data sets (e.g. cycle times, wait times, First Time Right (FTR) or quality measures)
- ❖ Has a high volume throughput of work such as documents, orders, applications, high $ value, etc.
- ❖ Has numerous process owners with multiple lines of reporting
- ❖ Connects processes with a high degree of individual discretion

Pro's when using Visio:

- ❖ It is easier to create complex value stream maps
- ❖ It is very easy to rescale your map once created and add more complexity to it
- ❖ Provides for a large range of unique autoshapes for almost "any" drawing requirements
- ❖ You can easily "group" your autoshapes together to move them around the page
- ❖ Application is viewed as a sophisticated "drawing" tool with good drawing capabilities
- ❖ Has an easy to use "click, select" feature to grab, move, and/or adjust all or part of the drawing
- ❖ Easy to insert objects and images from Excel into Visio
- ❖ Easy to write text onto and/or into all autoshapes

Con's when using Visio:

- ❖ Less accessible/available software package
- ❖ Requires more computer knowledge to use than Excel
- ❖ Not available on all office PC's and other users may not be able to open your Visio .dwg file unless you save it as a PDF file

The following are the future state value stream maps from the same improvement projects as illustrated on pages 159 - 161. Note the creativity on how some items were displayed.

Hotel Check-In Future State Value Stream Map

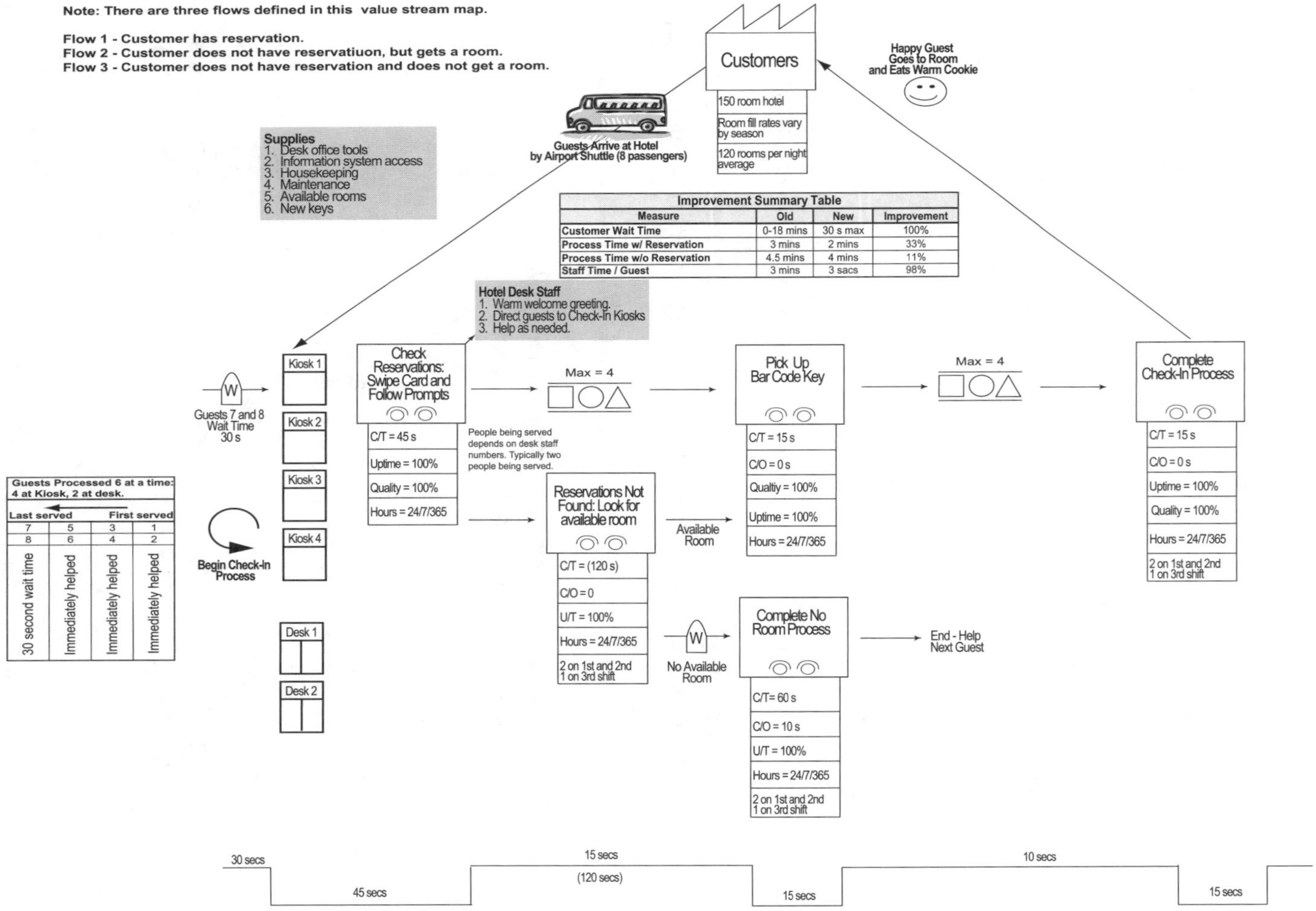

Improvement Summary Table

Measure	Old	New	Improvement
Customer Wait Time	0-18 mins	30 s max	100%
Process Time w/ Reservation	3 mins	2 mins	33%
Process Time w/o Reservation	4.5 mins	4 mins	11%
Staff Time / Guest	3 mins	3 sacs	98%

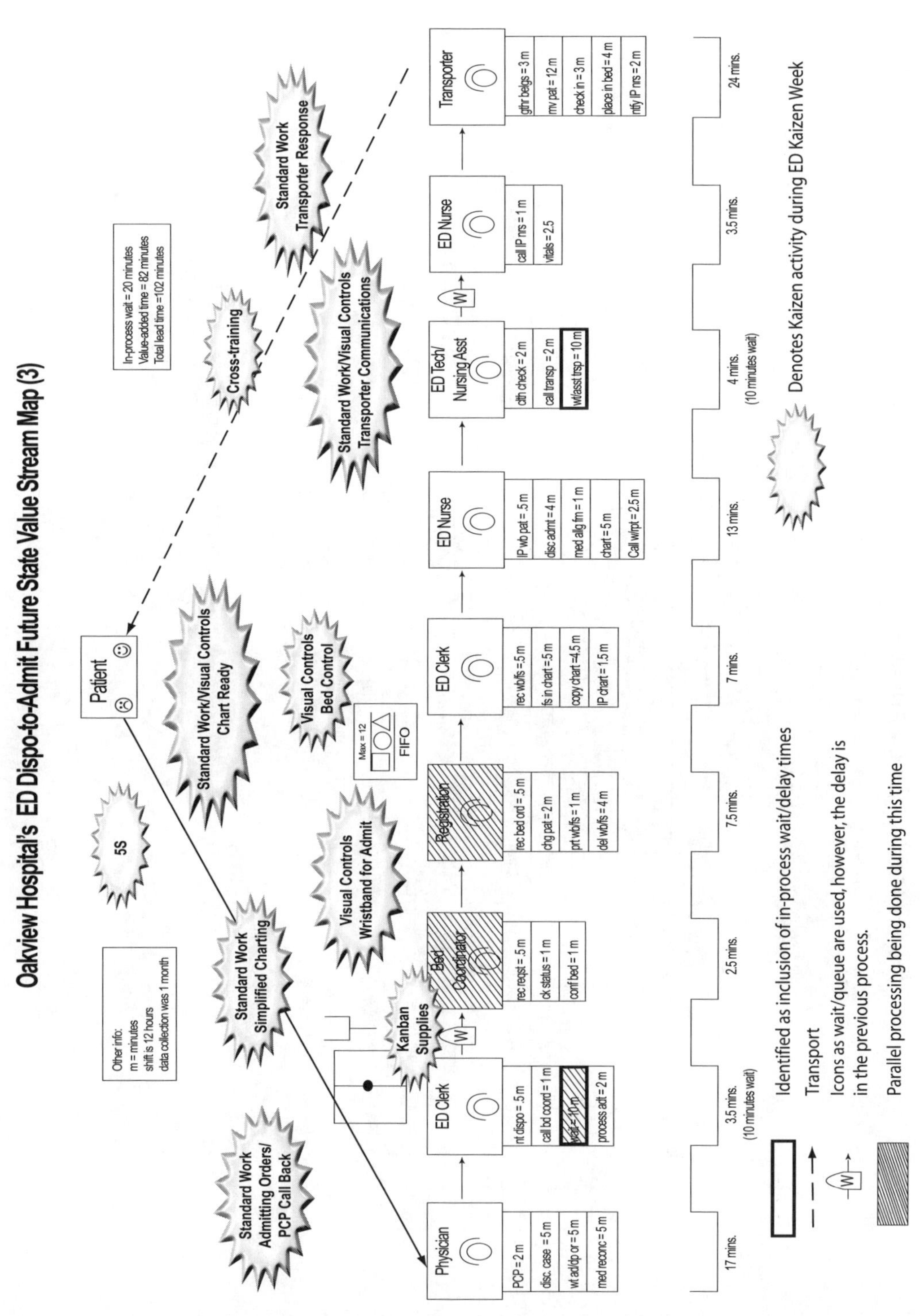
Oakview Hospital's ED Dispo-to-Admit Future State Value Stream Map (3)
Other info:
m = minutes
shift is 12 hours
data collection was 1 month
In-process wait = 20 minutes
Value-added time = 82 minutes
Total lead time =102 minutes
Patient
Standard Work Admitting Orders/ PCP Call Back
Standard Work Simplified Charting
Kanban Supplies
5S
Visual Controls Wristband for Admit
Standard Work/Visual Controls Chart Ready
Visual Controls Bed Control
Max = 12
FIFO
Cross-training
Standard Work/Visual Controls Transporter Communications
Standard Work Transporter Response
Physician
PCP = 2 m
disc. case = 5 m
wt ad/dp or = 5 m
med reconc = 5 m
ED Clerk
nt dispo = .5 m
call bd coord = 1 m
wait = 10 m
process adt = 2 m
Bed Coordinator
rec reqst = .5 m
ck status = 1 m
conf bed = 1 m
Registration
rec bed ord = .5 m
chg pat = 2 m
prt wb/fs = 1 m
del wb/fs = 4 m
ED Clerk
rec wb/fs = .5 m
fs in chart = .5 m
copy chart =4.5 m
IP chart = 1.5 m
ED Nurse
IP wb pat = .5 m
disc admt = 4 m
med allg fm = 1 m
chart = 5 m
Call w/rpt = 2.5 m
ED Tech/ Nursing Asst
dth check = 2 m
call transp = 2 m
wt/asst trsp = 10 m
ED Nurse
call IP nrs = 1 m
vitals = 2.5
Transporter
gthr belgs = 3 m
mv pat = 12 m
check in = 3 m
place in bed = 4 m
ntfy IP nrs = 2 m
17 mins.
3.5 mins. (10 minutes wait)
2.5 mins.
7.5 mins.
7 mins.
13 mins.
4 mins. (10 minutes wait)
3.5 mins.
24 mins.
Identified as inclusion of in-process wait/delay times
Transport
Icons as wait/queue are used, however, the delay is in the previous process.
Parallel processing being done during this time
Denotes Kaizen activity during ED Kaizen Week

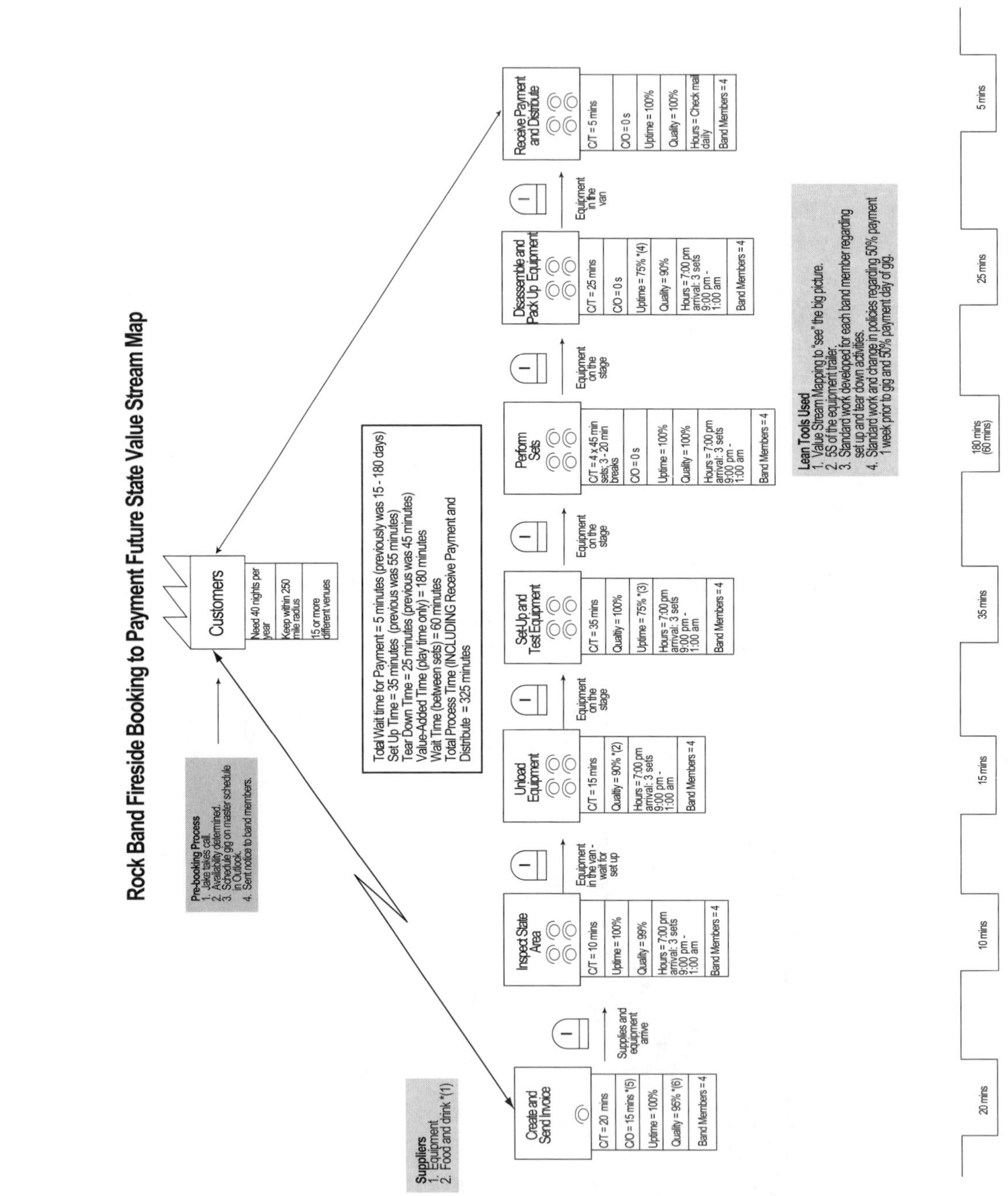
Rock Band Fireside Booking to Payment Future State Value Stream Map
Pre-booking Process
1. Jake takes call.
2. Availability determined.
3. Schedule gig on master schedule in Outlook.
4. Sent notice to band members.
Customers
Need 40 nights per year
Keep within 250 mile radius
15 or more different venues
Suppliers
1. Equipment
2. Food and drink *(1)
Total Wait time for Payment = 5 minutes (previously was 15 - 180 days)
Set Up Time = 35 minutes (previous was 55 minutes)
Tear Down Time = 25 minutes (previous was 45 minutes)
Value-Added Time (play time only) = 180 minutes
Wait Time (between sets) = 60 minutes
Total Process Time (INCLUDING Receive Payment and Distribute = 325 minutes
Create and Send Invoice
C/T = 20 mins
C/O = 15 mins *(5)
Uptime = 100%
Quality = 95% *(6)
Band Members = 4
Supplies and equipment arrive
Inspect State Area
C/T = 10 mins
Uptime = 100%
Quality = 99%
Hours = 7:00 pm arrival: 3 sets 9:00 pm - 1:00 am
Band Members = 4
Equipment in the van - wait for set up
Unload Equipment
C/T = 15 mins
Qualtiy = 90% *(2)
Hours = 7:00 pm arrival: 3 sets 9:00 pm - 1:00 am
Band Members = 4
Equipment on the stage
Set-Up and Test Equipment
C/T = 35 mins
Qualtiy = 100%
Uptime = 75% *(3)
Hours = 7:00 pm arrival: 3 sets 9:00 pm - 1:00 am
Band Members = 4
Equipment on the stage
Perform Sets
C/T = 4 x 45 min sets; 3 - 20 min breaks
C/O = 0 s
Uptime = 100%
Quality = 100%
Hours = 7:00 pm arrival: 3 sets 9:00 pm - 1:00 am
Band Members = 4
Equipment on the stage
Disassemble and Pack Up Equipment
C/T = 25 mins
C/O = 0 s
Uptime = 75% *(4)
Quality = 90%
Hours = 7:00 pm arrival: 3 sets 9:00 pm - 1:00 am
Band Members = 4
Equipment in the van
Receive Payment and Distribute
C/T = 5 mins
C/O = 0 s
Uptime = 100%
Quality = 100%
Hours = Check mail daily
Band Members = 4
Lean Tools Used
1. Value Stream Mapping to "see" the big picture.
2. 5S of the equipment trailer.
3. Standard work developed for each band member regarding set up and tear down activities.
4. Standard work and change in policies regarding 50% payment 1 week prior to gig and 50% payment day of gig.
20 mins
10 mins
15 mins
35 mins
180 mins (60 mins)
25 mins
5 mins

Process Maps

*A **process map** is a visual representation of a series of operations (tasks, activities) consisting of people, work duties, and transactions that occur in the delivery of a product or service.* There are a variety of types of process maps. Some of the main types are:

- Flowchart maps
- Macro process maps
- Micro process maps
- Deployment or Swim Lane maps
- Spaghetti maps

The key difference between process maps and value stream maps are that value stream maps contain considerably more relevant data. Process maps tend to show flow or steps in a more effective manner as they are typically less cluttered with data. Improvement teams might wish to try several mapping methods to find the best map that leads them to improvement initiatives.

When creating a process map, the project team should tackle the activity as if it were doing an investigation (find out exactly what is and is not happening in the process). Process maps use standard symbols to represent a type of operation, process, and/or set of tasks to be performed. The use of standardized symbols provides a common language for the project team to visualize problems and also allows for the process to be easier to read and understand, thus making it a viable source to see areas of waste, process variation, and/or redundancy.

There are five types of flowcharts or process maps: basic - macro, basic - micro, deployment, opportunity, and spaghetti diagram.

1. *Basic process maps (macro level)* identifies all the major steps in a process - usually no more than six steps. They are mostly used for the 30,000 foot view for management review.
2. *Basic process maps (micro level)* examines the process in detail and indicates all the steps or activities (i.e., the decision points, waiting periods, tasks that frequently must be redone (rework), and any feedback loops). This is the ground level listing of the tasks and activities.
3. *Deployment process maps* examines the process in terms of who is carrying out the steps, and is conveyed in the form of a matrix, showing the various participants and the flow of steps among these participants. These maps are helpful if the process being mapped crosses departmental boundaries.
4. *Opportunity process maps* examines the activities that comprise the process and list differences between value-added and non value-added activities.
5. *Spaghetti diagram process maps* uses a continuous line to trace the path of a part, document, person, or service that is being provided through all its phases. Spaghetti diagrams expose inefficient layouts and large distances traveled between steps. These diagrams should also display electronic information flow (emails, spreadsheets, documents, etc.).

The following symbols can be used to map your current process flow. Just as with creating a value stream map with a team, ensure the team can view it as it is being created.

Ovals are used to represent the beginning and ending points of the process.

Rectangles are used to describe an action taken or a task completed.

Diamonds contain questions that require a “Yes” or “No” decision and indicate appropriate process flow.

A partial page represents a document produced by the process.

Multi-partial pages are used to represent a report or an output with multiple documents.

An arrow represents the direction of the process flow.

A queue symbol represents a delay in the process.

Rectangles with drop shadows represent a more detailed flowchart is available.

A modified rectangle represents a standard, protocol, or Standard Operating Procedure to follow.

A triangle represents a measurement.

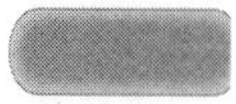
A rounded rectangle represents a meeting, conference call, or Webinar.

A circle represents where the flow continues on a different page or to another process.

Note: This is the standard set of flowchart icons. The team can create new ones if that would help to improve the visualization of the process flow.

The following are examples of each type of flowchart as well as the basic steps to follow in creating one.

Basic process map (macro level)

Approach creating this process map as follows:

1. Define the process boundaries with the beginning and ending points of the process.
2. Create no more than six boxes denoting what is occurring between the start and end points.
3. Review the map with management to ensure everyone is on the same page with this macro view of the process or work flow.
4. Create a more detailed process (micro level) or value stream map (if appropriate).

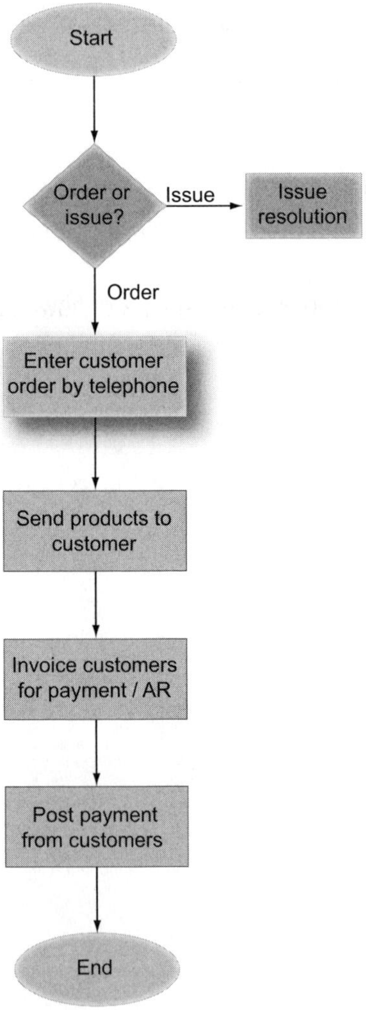

Basic process map (micro level)

Approach creating this process map as follows:

1. Identify the right people needed to develop the process map. This may require people from outside the project team for their expertise and knowledge.
2. Define the process boundaries with the beginning and ending points of the process.
3. Define the level of detail required.
4. Determine conditions and boundaries for the process flow.
5. List all the steps contained within the process flow. The project team may need to walk the process.
6. Circulate the map to other people within the process for input and/or clarification.
7. Identify areas for improvement.

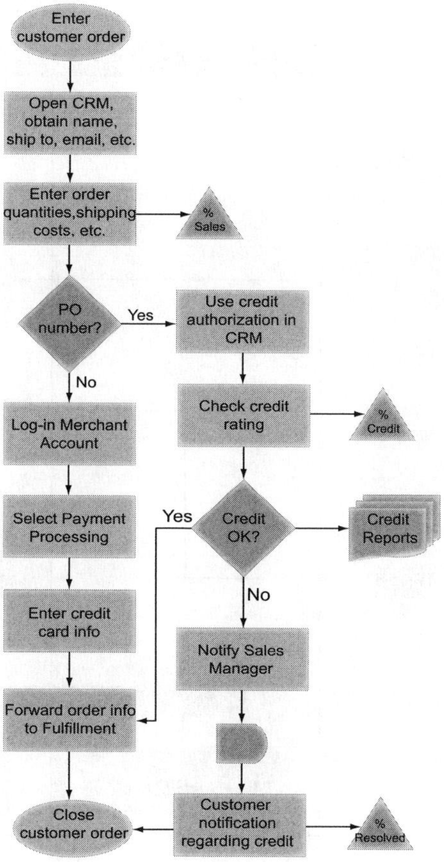

Deployment (or swim lane) process map

Approach creating this process map as follows:

1. Identify the right people needed to develop the process map.
2. Define the process boundaries with the beginning and ending points of the process.
3. List the major steps (or time element) of the process on the left side of the sheet.
4. List the responsible department (or process worker) across the top, each in a separate column.
5. List all the steps in their appropriate column and ensure they are connected by arrows.
6. Circulate the map to other people within the process for input and/or clarification (if appropriate).
7. Identify areas for improvement.

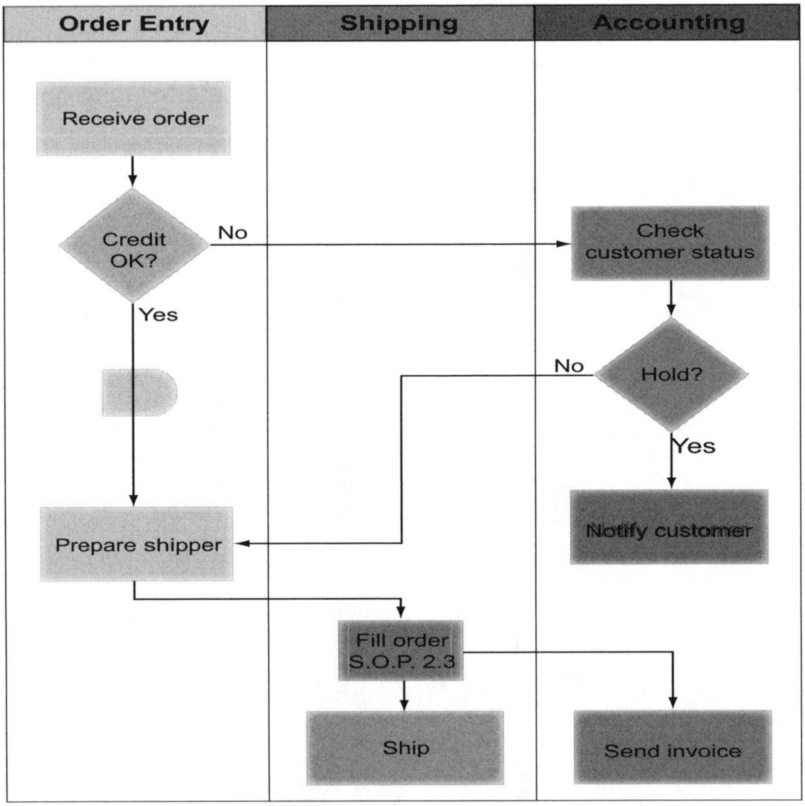

Opportunity process map

Approach creating this process map as follows:

1. Create a process map (micro level).
2. Create separate columns and label one Value-Added and the other one Non Value-Added (or Cost-Added Only).
3. List each step from the process map in either column and ensure they are connected by arrows. Expand the steps to show specific areas of concern, if needed.
4. Identify areas for improvement.

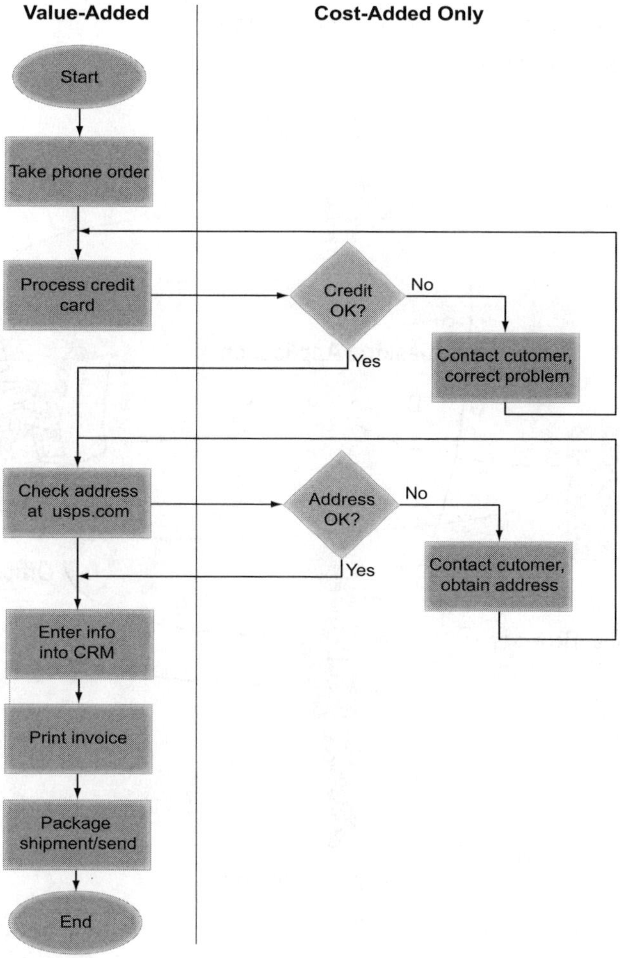

Spaghetti diagram process map

Approach creating this process map as follows:

1. Define the beginning and ending of the process.
2. Obtain an engineering drawing, create a scale representation of the physical layout of the process, or document the screen selections.
3. List each step of the process on the map (or on a separate piece of paper).
4. Label and draw each of the steps (3) sequentially as how the process flows. Connect each step with an arrow line denoting the flow.
5. Gain a consensus if the process is inefficient (i.e., too many touches or screen selections, too many hand-offs, too much travel, etc.).
6. Identify areas for improvement.

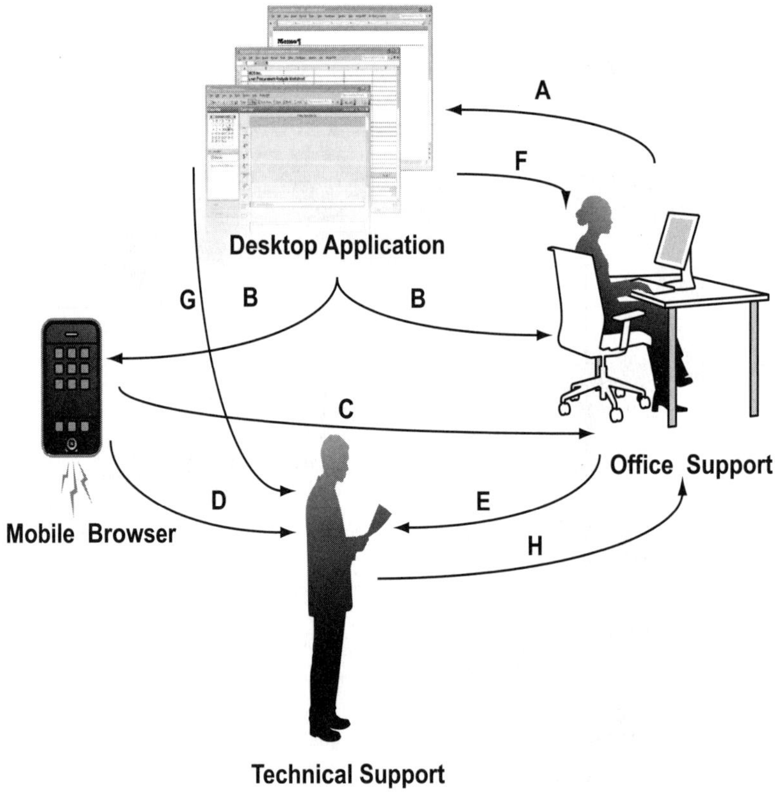

Whatever type of process map is created, use the following sequence of steps to further analyze the process being mapped:

1. Examine each process for bottlenecks, redundancy or unnecessary steps, lack of capacity, weak links, poorly-defined steps, cost-added-only steps, etc.

2. Examine each activity and decision symbol to determine if it can be streamlined or removed.

The following is a review of value stream and process mapping:

Value Stream Mapping	Process Mapping
✔ Makes the waste and source visible	✔ Makes waste visible, can show source by identifying function
✔ New icons	✔ Familiar flowchart
✔ Fairly new tool	✔ Commonly used to analyze business processes
✔ Requires repeatable sequential processes	✔ Can be done with a repetitive or non-repetitive process
✔ Customer focused driven	✔ Task/activity driven
✔ How value is created	✔ How the work flows
✔ Highlights delays between processes	✔ Highlights extraneous steps within a process

Note: There are many applications available for purchase that provide enhanced graphics and illustrations for representing data and information flow other than MS Office Excel and Visio. Some common applications available are: SmartDraw, Smooth Flowcharter, FlowBreeze, ConceptDraw, SigmaFlow, etc. Many of these allow a 30-day trial prior to purchasing.

Note: If someone desires to create the map in Visio, Microsoft Excel, or PowerPoint, etc. with the team present (not recommended), then ensure the following occurs:

- The person is very proficient in using the software or otherwise team members will get frustrated watching someone learn-as-they-go
- The map is projected on a screen so everyone can see it
- Everything: LCD, projector, software, etc. is ready prior to the mapping exercise

Supplier - Input - Process - Output - Customer (SIPOC) Diagram

*A **SIPOC Diagram** is a tool used by a team to identify all relevant elements of a process improvement project or identified value stream to help ensure all aspects of the process are taken into consideration and that no key components are missing.* The SIPOC is the ideal tool to help layout the whole business process under review for improvement and assess "what" data is required and "how-to" proceed with data collection. SIPOC is an acronym for the Suppliers (the 'S' in SIPOC) of the process, the Inputs (I) to the process, the Process (P) that is under review, the Outputs (O) of the process, and the Customers (C) that receive the process outputs. It helps to create specific objectives from a complex project that may not be well-scoped or defined and is typically employed at the Measure phase of the Six Sigma DMAIC methodology. The SIPOC Diagram provides a framework to help ensure relevant information is included in creating a process map, value stream map, or provide additional data used with in/out-of-scope tools.

The SIPOC Diagram and process to create supplements the Team Charter where key suppliers and customers are initially documented. It allows teams to collect and document more detailed data regarding the supply chain flow of materials and information. A useful way to use this tool is to create a flowchart of the process and list each Process (1) in the center, and list Suppliers (5) and Inputs (4) to the left side of the flowchart, and Outputs (3) and Customers (2) on the right side of the Process. Then identify every Customer that is connected to each Process. Then, list all conceivable Outputs from the process relative to the Customer (2). When this is complete, work backwards to the Inputs and Suppliers of the Inputs. This provides a clear vision of the entire process and allows teams to document key data in an organized format. Use the completed SIPOC to ensure the required deliverables are achieved, and for diagnosing abnormalities in the supply chain. Often new information, such as cause and effect relationship and communication gaps, can be discovered while completing the SIPOC Diagram.

Before starting the SIPOC Diagram, key questions to be asked are:

Why improve the process?
What are issues with the process?
What is out-of-scope?
Who are the suppliers and customers? What are their requirements?
What metrics do you wish to improve?
What data needs to be collected?

Note: Many times the SIPOC Diagram will be completed on a sub process within the larger-scale value stream map.

The SIPOC Diagram is designed to prompt a team to consider all relevant elements of a "process improvement" project before any data is collected, or certainly before any improvements are implemented. Once you have filled in the SIPOC Diagram, which assists to answer the key questions previously listed, it will be much easier to determine "what" data you need to collect. Using the SIPOC Diagram will provide clarity about what data is required before time and effort is allocated in collecting the data.

The following is an example of a SIPOC Diagram for laundry services:

Supplier > Input > Process > Output > Customer (SIPOC)				
Supplier 5	Input 4	Process 1	Output 3	Customer 2
1. Leased trucks, BP gas, Company employees	1. Trucks, gas, and drivers	1. Go to laundry collection site	1. At collection site	1. The customer
2. Purchased bags & labels (General Supply), Company employees	2. Bags, labels, and workers	2. Collect, bag and identify laundry pick up	2. Bagged and labeled dirty laundry	2. Internal laundry processors
3. Leased trucks, BP gas, Company employees	3. Trucks, gas, and drivers	3. Return dirty laundry to cleaning site	3. Dirty laundry at processing site	3. Internal laundry processors
4. General Supply and Company employees	4. Table, sorting bins, and workers	4. Unload and sort dirty laundry	4. Sorted dirty laundry ready to be washed	4. Internal laundry processors
5. Milnor washers, Washer Supply Detergents, Public Utilities, and Company employees	5. Washers, soap, water, electricity, heat, and workers	5. Wash dirty laundry	5. Clean and wet laundry	5. Internal laundry processors
6. Milnor Dryers, Public Utilities, and Company employees	6. Dryers, gas & workers	6. Dry clean laundry	6. Dry & clean laundry	6. Delivery drivers
7. General Supply Labels, Quality Department - Standards, Company employees	7. Labels, standards, and workers	7. Sort and prep clean and dry laundry for delivery	7. Sorted and staged clean & dry laundry	7. Delivery drivers
8. Leased trucks and company employees	8. Trucks and workers	8. Load and deliver clean and dry laundry	Returned clean and dry laundry to distribution centers	8. Clean laundry, distribution, customer
9. Wash Company, distribution site employees and cash box.	9. Clean and dry laundry, cost sheets, cash box, and workers	9. Distribute clean and dry laundry	9. Clean and dry laundry back to the customer	9. Customer

Mapping Perspectives

Maps can be drawn at a variety of levels based on project team need and intended use. A map of the universe can be used to understand the relationship of the earth to the sun, and yet this is of little use if your need is directions to a gas station. A local map (or GPS) with businesses identified would best serve this need. Unfortunately, there are no GPS equivalents for service processes! For service organizations, high level maps can be made for complete supply chains involving multiple external companies (or divisions within the same organization) and low level maps can be drawn for the specific steps or tasks to complete a single service transaction. Both maps can be useful depending on the need of the project team. Different levels of maps will illuminate different wastes and improvement opportunities.

The matrix on the next page represents the mapping alternatives identified in the previous two sections, and can be used by project teams as a guide to determine the best mapping technique to use.

The High Level (50,000 Feet) maps are used to identify how larger groups or functions of the supply chain or process chain interact. This level map is useful across multiple external upstream suppliers and downstream customers. This level map will show your organizations relationship and position in the overall supply chain and may be useful for large, multi-company examination of waste and flow improvement opportunities.

Mid-High Level (20,000 Feet) maps are used within organizations to illustrate wastes, relationships, flows, and improvement opportunities. This level map is useful to examine the department to department relationships and flows within a single location. This level map can be useful to orient new people to the overall operations of the organization.

Mid-Low Level (5,000 Feet) maps are used within departments or areas to illustrate task flow, specific processing times, wastes, and other improvement opportunities. On this level map, specific inputs and outputs can be clearly illustrated for deeper examination and improvements. This level map can be useful to orient new people to the operations and function of the department or area.

Low Level (Ground level) maps are used by project teams to document and define specific tasks, actions or movements required to complete service transactions or tasks. Specific and detailed movements can be documented and examined for improvement opportunities with this level map. This level map can also be used to document specific standard work instructions and is very useful for training new workers.

Process Level	High (50,000 Feet)	Mid-High (20,000 Feet)	Mid-Low (5,000 feet)	Low (Ground level)	Advantages and When used
Process Map Level	External Value Stream Map	Internal Value Stream Map	Department or area	Work Task	
Value Stream Map or Process Map Macro Level	X	X			Value stream or supply chain macro data and flow, clearly identifies constraints and macro flow waste and opportunities.
Deployment or Swim Lane Process Map	X	X			Macro flow with multiple companies or areas, used to address who does what, when.
Process Map Micro Level		X	X		Micro flow within an organization, department or areas, used to address who does what, when.
Supplier-Input-Process-Output-Customer (SIPOC) or Opportunity Process Map		X	X		Flow with input and output, used to understand input and output relationships.
Standard Work Chart (Chapter 7)			X	X	Process flow used to document and measure actions, tasks, and/or decision steps.
Spaghetti Diagram Process Map			X	X	Physical flow and steps used to identify waste and improvement opportunities.

Key Metric and Data Profile

*The **Key Metric and Data Profile** tool assists the team to consider and determine the key data that will need to be collected.* Basically, the Key Metric Data Profile tool is used for data collection for a process. This data will be used to further define the problem area(s) as well as provide additional information for the value stream or process map. This would also include calculating a sigma value for the process, if appropriate. A list for a Key Metric Data Profile is as follows:

- Adjustment times
- Batch sizes
- Change over times
- Customers
- Cycle times
- Delay times
- Delivery schedules
- Demand or takt time
- Down times
- Efficiency percentages
- Failure rates
- Inputs
- Lot sizes
- Maintenance times
- Mean time between failures
- On-time-delivery performance
- Number of people required
- Number of pieces of equipment
- Number of shifts
- Process times
- Quality yield
- Queue times
- Reference procedures (SOPs)
- Rework percentages
- Sigma value
- Special packaging instructions
- Suppliers
- Tools
- Total hours available
- Up times
- Value-added times
- Warm up times

Data collection is probably one of the most important functions of a team. It is confusing, at times, to the team members as they struggle with questions such as:

1. What data do I collect? From which processes in the value stream?
2. How much data do I collect? What is the sample size? What is the total population of the sample size?
3. Who will collect the data? Can we rely on a report generated from the system? Is it accurate or not?
4. Will the data be easy to collect? Do we need to make observations of an area or process to obtain actual numbers? If so, how many hours/days do we observe the process?
5. If data is not accessible and cannot be observed, can I rely on the process worker to provide accurate data?

Before those questions are answered, let us cover a few aspects of data collection, display, and the importance of using a Key Metric and Data Profile tool.

There is a fine line between collecting too much data and falling into the "analysis by paralysis" trap and not collecting enough statistically significant data to base long-term solutions and/or enterprise-wide improvements upon.

Data collection and its subsequent analysis allows for "data" or "numbers" to provide meaningful information for the Lean Sigma project. This collection of data is a crucial part of the transformation. The highest quality data must be attained through proper planning of how to gather the data to ensure stability and reliability in the collection process. Failure to properly gather data will compromise the project as well as create wasted time as staff generate additional efforts to gather the necessary data.

Steps to Good Data Collection

Use the following steps as a guide when you plan to collect data. The four steps ensure that the most accurate data will be collected using a reliable methodology.

1. Plan for data collection. This is where you would specify the goals and objectives for the data to be collected. This would include providing an overview of the process or processes and the reasoning behind the data collection (e.g., need to populate the value stream map to be able to establish a benchmark). Determine what data is to be gathered and how, the amount (time, duration) of data to be gathered, and at which processes this data will be collected.

2. Standardize how cycle times are measured. It may be a challenge to obtain exact cycle times for some of the activities within a process, but do not let that stop you - be as accurate as you can and improve from there.

3. Collect the data as defined in steps 1 and 2.

4. Analyze and present the data. This is where you determine the data's repeatability, accuracy, and stability. For example, if an area was observed and the data was skewed (distorted or biased in some way) then observations may be necessary. The team must reach consensus on the data that was collected as to its accuracy and reliability. This is not to say that the empirical data collected should give-way to the opinions of the team, however, the data or method in which the data was collected, should be reasonable as to what team members' experiences have been. When there is a thought like, "that can't be right" from team members regarding collected data, discuss it with the team and proceed back to (1). Also, present as much of the data as possible in graphical form (i.e., Bar or Pareto Chart, Scatter Diagram, etc.) when appropriate.

Note: At the first team meeting, the facilitator should be careful not to present too much historical data (i.e., trends, mediums, modes, frequency, variances, etc.). Team members can be overwhelmed if they are overburdened with numbers at an early stage. If historical data is available, then a few overall numbers may be used. Too many Six Sigma projects have failed because Black Belts were too aggressive in presenting data. As good and accurate as this data may be, it is still about getting the process worker involved. Work with the team at that first meeting to reach a consensus on which data will be most useful. Determine which type of data collection technique is appropriate for your project.

Data Display

Once data has been collected, there are many forms in which to display the data. The following guidelines should be used when presenting data:

1. Determine who the data is for and its purpose.
2. Write the message that needs to be conveyed in 1 - 2 sentences.
3. Use the right type of graph (line, bar, pie, pareto, scatter, histogram, table, etc.) using key words from (2). Teams will get better at this with practice.
4. Use a display method that will express the data and not impress (keep the graphs simple and on point).

Now let's answer those key questions listed earlier.

1. What data do I collect?

Remember that the goal is to gather data that accurately reflects the process being observed to the level of detail that is helpful in analysis. Start with the highest level that will be helpful and use the Key Metric and Data Profile tool.

2. How much data do I collect?

The amount of data to be collected should be enough to give you a good representation of the actual process. The minimum recommended number is 30 samples (Note: A sample size of 30 is recommended because of the distribution patterns of data; no matter how skewed the data may be, as the sample size grows larger, the data begins to take the shape of a normal distribution. If statistical testing is going to be included in the project, you may need to run a power and sample size test to determine exactly how many samples you need.) Collecting fewer samples may give a distorted view of the process. The number of data points for a statistically significant sample size is determined by a formula. If it is possible to collect that much data - so much the better. If not, collect as much as is reasonable but 30 should be the minimum. This will give you a valid mean (average) and standard deviation (representation of the distribution of data around the mean).

It is also important to collect data that is random in nature. That is, do not collect the first 30 customers that arrive on Monday morning or call into customer service that day. Try to collect data in a way that is representative of the time for the overall process. For example, divide each 24-hour period into 4-hour blocks, then select 1 or 2 customers from each of those time blocks, representing 4 to 8 customers a day or 28-plus customers in a week. If the first 28 customers were representative of the process and were truly random, that would be sufficient.

3. Who will collect the data?

Typically, data collection assignments are divided up between the team members, so that everyone has an equivalent "homework" assignment. When the data collection is divided up in this way, be sure everyone knows exactly what to collect and how to collect it, so that the team can do an "apples-to-apples" comparison.

Note: Using data from computer reports may look like an easy method, but it is important to find out: who put the information into the computer system, how it was collected, and if the times reflect the actual time of activity or the time the data was entered. Making an assumption about computer-based data can lead to an inaccurate perception of how the process really works.

4. Will the data be easy to collect?

Collection by computer-generated reports can be "easy" if the information can be validated as representing real-time activities in the process.

When the team is putting together their data collection plan, they should balance the ease of method with the time available for data collection. When in doubt, use the method that will give the best picture of the process, rather than an "easier" method that may yield an inaccurate perception of the process.

5. If the data is not accessible and cannot be observed, can I rely on process workers?

Process workers can assist with data collection, however, consider the following:

a. The data collection process must be very quick - for example, making a check on a checklist or writing a time down on a form. Lengthy or cumbersome data collection instructions will most likely not be followed.
b. The data collection should be for a very defined period of time - one shift, one day, one week - so that the workers are well aware of the amount of time they will have to contribute this "extra" effort.
c. The data collection process should ideally be done on a form the worker is already using. Second-best would be a checklist or form that was easy to use, but remember that the workers will have to carry it or keep it available throughout the study period.
d. The workers should be asked to participate as partners - give them the explanation of what the project is about and how it will benefit them. Ask for ideas and feedback about the data collection and incorporate them when possible. Share the information after it has been collected and plan for the recognition of those who participate.
e. Where possible, match some worker-collected data with other objective measures to evaluate validity.

Data will need to be collected before, during, and after the improvement event.

Sigma Calculation

Many organizations that are currently deploying Six Sigma require a Sigma value for their projects. However, a Lean Sigma approach may or may not require such a calculation. The following is an example of a Sigma calculation for a telemarketing organization for their order entry value stream:

Sigma Calculation Worksheet

Process Name Order Entry **Date** 2/16

No.	Action	Equations	Your Calculations
1	Name the process.		Order Entry
2	The number of units produced by the process.		1,283
3	The number of units that were error-free.		1,138
4	Compute the yield for the process.	= (Step 3) / (Step 2)	.887
5	Compute the defect rate based on Step 4.	= 1 - (Step 4)	.113
6	Determine the number of potential things that could create a defect (note: use N = 10 as a conservative number of potential defects).	= N number of Critical-To-Quality characteristics (CTQs)	10
7	Compute the defect rate per CTQ characteristic.	= (Step 5) / (Step 6)	.0113
8	Compute the Defects Per Million Opportunities (DPMO).	= (Step 7) x 1,000,000	11,300
9	Convert the DPMO (Step 8) into a Sigma value, using a Six Sigma Conversion Chart (google: six sigma conversion table).	Includes a 1.5 sigma shift for all listed values of Z	3.8
10	Draw conclusions.		Opportunity for improvement

Alternative methods to calculate the sigma level are online sigma calculators and Sigma Look-Up tables and charts based on percent defective or DPMO (Defects Per Million Opportunities). A sigma calculator can be found by completing a web search for "sigma calculator." To use most sigma calculators, enter in the observed DPMO and the calculator will provide the sigma level.

To use the sigma look up tables and graphs, simply determine the percent defective or DPMO's, then find the corresponding numbers on the following tables and graphs. For example, a Pediatrician has 20 late appointments a week out of a total of 95 total scheduled appointments. The reasons for late appointments should be analyzed and presented in a Pareto Chart for further study and improvement. To identify the sigma level of this performance indicator, first determine the DPMO through the following calculation. DPMO = [20 late appointments per week / 95 total appointments per week] * 1,000,000 = 210,526. Look up 210,526 DPMO on the following chart (lower one) to find a sigma level of ~ 2.35 sigma. Due to the nature of look up tables, the accuracy may be somewhat less than pure calculations. Ensure the level of precision matches the need.

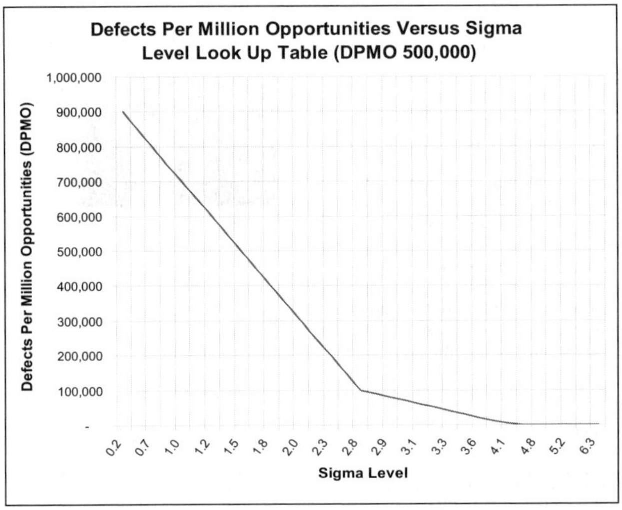

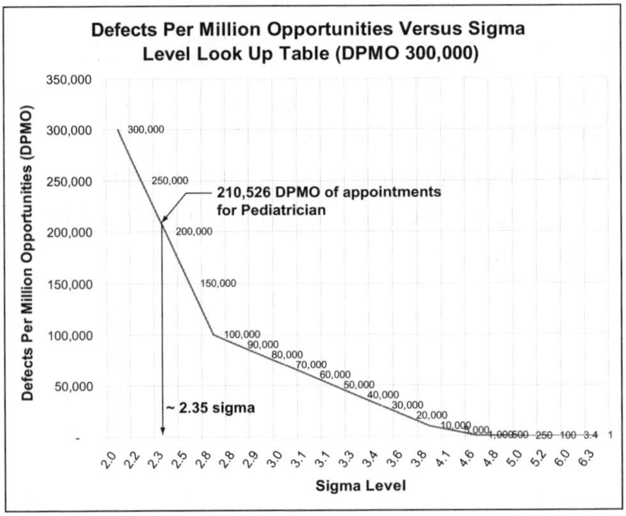

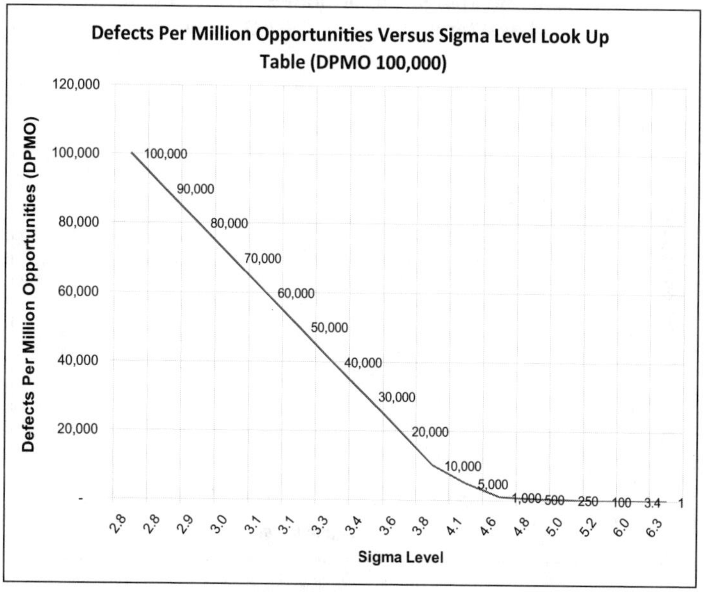
Defects Per Million Opportunities Versus Sigma Level Look Up Table (DPMO 100,000)
Defects Per Million Opportunities (DPMO)
120,000
100,000
80,000
60,000
40,000
20,000
-
100,000
90,000
80,000
70,000
60,000
50,000
40,000
30,000
20,000
10,000
5,000
1,000
500
250
100
3.4
1
2.8
2.8
2.9
3.0
3.1
3.1
3.3
3.4
3.6
3.8
4.1
4.6
4.8
5.0
5.2
6.0
6.3
Sigma Level

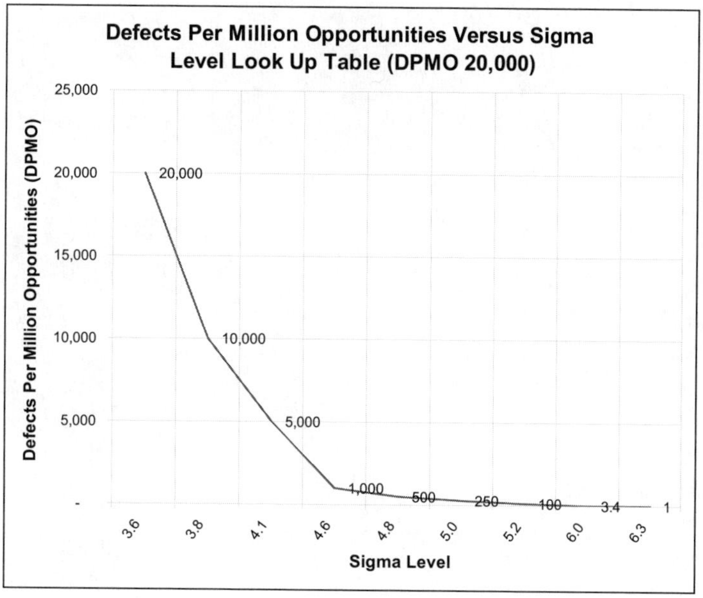
Defects Per Million Opportunities Versus Sigma Level Look Up Table (DPMO 20,000)
Defects Per Million Opportunities (DPMO)
25,000
20,000
15,000
10,000
5,000
-
20,000
10,000
5,000
1,000
500
250
100
3.4
1
3.6
3.8
4.1
4.6
4.8
5.0
5.2
6.0
6.3
Sigma Level

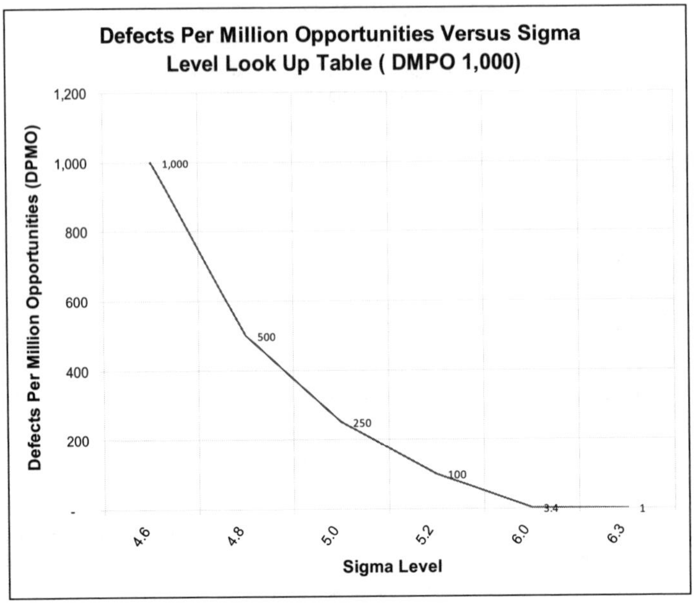

Defects Per Million Opportunities Versus Sigma Level Look Up Table (DMPO 1,000)
Defects Per Million Opportunities (DPMO)
1,200
1,000
800
600
400
200
-
1,000
500
250
100
3.4
1
4.6
4.8
5.0
5.2
6.0
6.3
Sigma Level

Check Sheets and Frequency Charts

***Check Sheets and Frequency Charts** are basic data collection tools used to collect, organize, prioritize, and analyze data.* They can be used to answer the question, "How often is an event occurring?" They help you "see" the variation in the process and are a basic yet important data collection tool to use in the Measure Phase of the improvement process.

To complete a Check Sheet simply identify the data to be collected or measured and who will measure it at what frequency. Be specific. Make sure the data definitions are clear to everyone collecting data. Then construct a simple table for data collection and begin collecting data. This will be new for many service organizations. It may take several attempts to get the right data gathered correctly. After a specified period of time, or as significant data is collected, summarize the data for analysis. Further visualization of the data using the Chart Wizard in Excel will help you "see" variations in the data. This can be done be creating a Pareto or Pie Chart. Use the Check Sheet data to better understand and update the current state or to track and ensure improvements are maintained.

An example of a Check Sheet and Frequency Chart of emails for one week for a satellite dish installer is shown below. The customer service representative simply kept track of incoming emails in a Check Sheet format and then placed the data in a simple Excel worksheet for analysis.

Emails by Type (1 week of data) Check Sheet and Frequency Chart

Call Reason	Frequency Check	Frequency
Request for Proposals	卌 卌 卌 卌 卌 卌 卌 卌	40
New Orders	卌 卌 卌 卌 卌 ///	28
Service Request	卌 卌 卌 卌 /	21
Complaints or Problem	卌 卌	10
Personal	卌 卌 卌 卌 卌 卌 //	32
Other	//	2
	Total for Week =	133

Run Charts

A ***Run Chart****, in its most simple form, is a method to display several data points over time.* Because our minds are not good at remembering patterns in data, a visual display will allow us to see the measurement(s) of an entire process over time. This will enable us to see trends over time and to make adjustments accordingly. Improvement activities must be tracked to determine their overall effectiveness. For example, if an improvement activity did not result in having an impact on eliminating a waste, then that should not be part of any long term or enterprise-wide solution.

Run Charts will allow a team to compare performance measurements before and after implementation of a solution to measure its effectiveness. Run Charts are a powerful tool in demonstrating whether the vital changes made to the current state value stream had the intended impact to the future state value stream.

The Run Chart example below is a monthly KPI Schedule Attainment Bar Graph Run Chart for a repair service organization. The notes on the Run Chart indicate assignable cause issues that contributed the organization to miss their schedule.

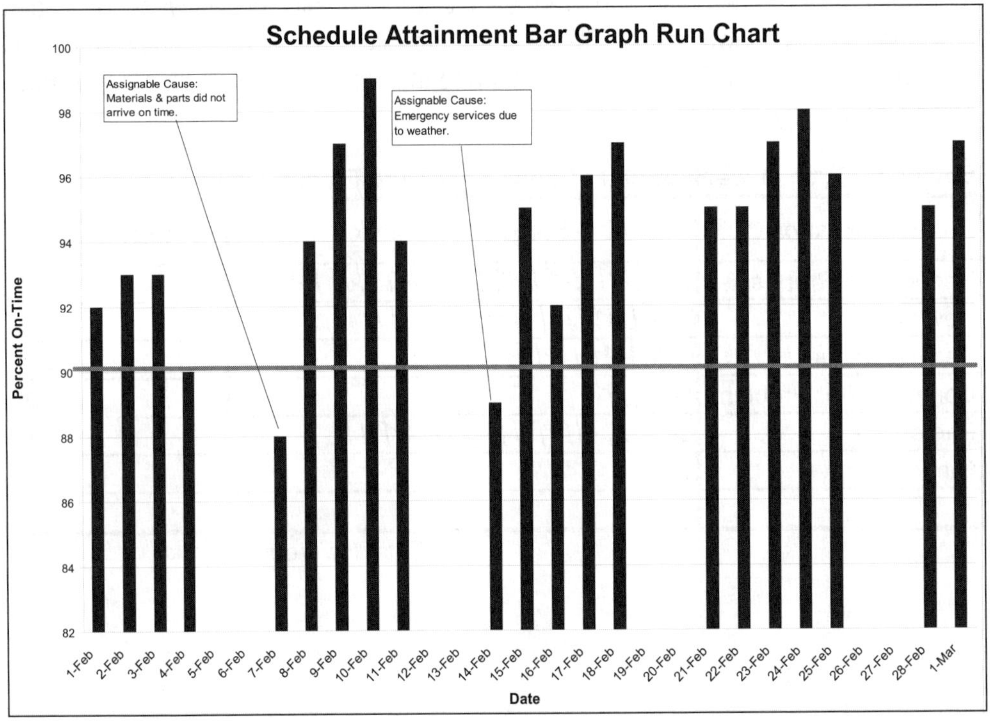

Run Charts can be Bar or Line graphs depending on preference. Both can show trends and problems. The following graph is the same data set as the previous chart, but is illustrated as a Line graph:

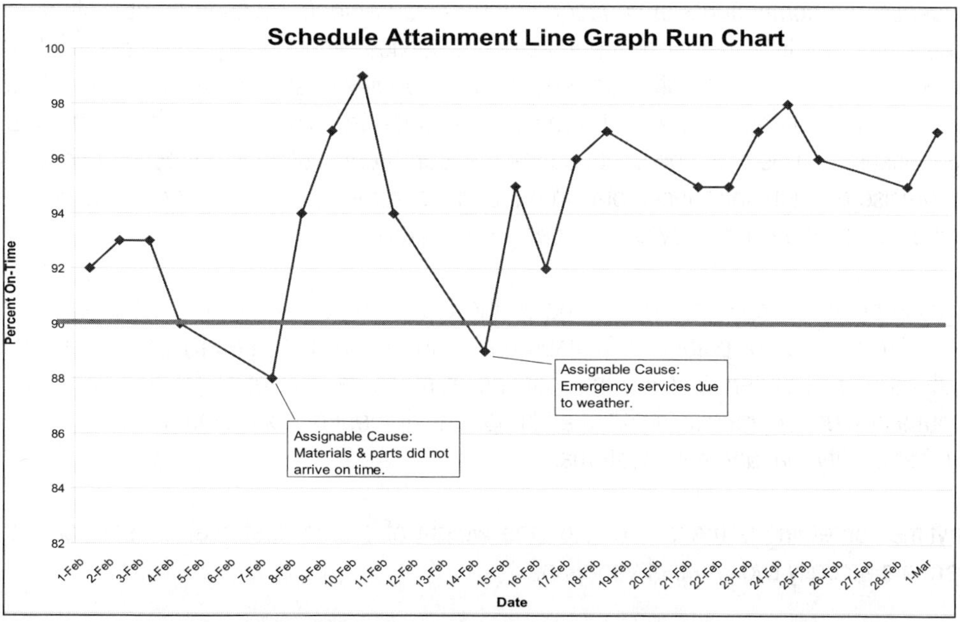

Run Charts are a powerful tool to illustrate, analyze, and monitor improvement data. Run Charts show trends and abnormalities which are caused by waste and can lead to problems, and lost sales. They show progress or regression in KPIs and are a critical, unbiased driver for on-going improvements.

Measurement System Analysis (MSA)

*A **Measurement System Analysis (MSA)** is a specially designed experiment that seeks to identify the components of variation in the measurement.* Measurement systems are used every day in a variety of manufacturing, service, and sales environments. Often measurements are made with little regard for the quality of such measurements. All too often, the measurements are not representative of the true value of the characteristic being measured. This might be because the measurement system is not accurate enough, not precise enough, introduces bias into the measurement, or is not properly being used by the service worker or service provider (or operator).

Measurement System Analysis evaluates the test method, measuring instruments, and the entire process of obtaining measurements to ensure the integrity of data used for analysis and to understand the implications of measurement error for decisions made about a product or process. MSA is an important element of Six Sigma methodology and of other quality management systems.

Anytime something is measured (e.g., the weight of a part, customer satisfaction, etc.) there are actually two types of variation:

1. The variation within the parts/process being examined (P)
2. The variation within the measurement system itself (M)

The total variation being examined (T) can be explained by a formula:

$$T = P + M$$

In a perfect world, the variation due to M (measurement system) would be zero, meaning that the only variation observed would be due to the process (P). In reality, there is often enough variation with the measurement system that true variation of the process cannot be defined. This is especially so in qualitative surveys. If this is the case, an improvement team's efforts to improve the process may only lead to frustration, as the measurement system masked the true variation of the process.

This is why MSA is so important. Improvement teams should complete MSAs to determine what part of the total variation is due to the process and how much is due to the actual measurement system.

MSA analyzes the measurement system error to equipment, operations, procedures, software, and personnel. MSA is a critical first step that should precede any data-based decision making, including Statistical Process Control, Correlation and Regression Analysis, and Design of Experiments.

A Measurement Systems Analysis considers the following:

- Selecting the correct measurement and approach
- Assessing the measuring device or instrument
- Assessing procedures and service workers and service providers
- Assessing any measurement interactions
- Calculating the measurement uncertainty of individual measurement devices and/or measurement systems

Following are general requirements of all capable measurement systems:

- Statistical stability over time
- Variability small compared to the process variability
- Variability small compared to the specification limits (tolerance)
- The resolution, or discrimination, of the measurement device must be small relative to the smaller of either the specification tolerance or the process spread (variation). As a rule of thumb, the measurement system should have resolution of at least 1/10th the smaller of either the specification tolerance or the process spread. If the resolution is not fine enough, process variability will not be recognized by the measurement system, thus blunting its effectiveness.

A measurement system can be characterized, or described, in the following five ways:

Accuracy or Location (Average Measurement Value vs. Actual Value):

1. Stability refers to the capacity of a measurement system to produce the same values over time when measuring the same sample. As with Statistical Process Control charts, stability means the absence of "Special Cause Variation," leaving only "Common Cause Variation" (random variation).
2. Bias, sometimes referred to as Accuracy, is a measure of the distance between the average value of the measurements and the "True" or "Actual" value of the sample or part. See the illustration on the next page for further explanation.

3. Linearity is a measure of the consistency of Bias over the range of the measurement device. For example, if a bathroom scale is under by 1.0 pound when measuring a 150 pound person, but is off by 5.0 pounds when measuring a 200 pound person, the scale Bias is non-linear in the sense that the degree of Bias changes over the range of use.

Precision or Variation (Spread of Measurement Values)

4. Repeatability assesses whether the *same* appraiser can measure the same part/sample multiple times with the same measurement device and get the same value.

5. Reproducibility assesses whether *different* appraisers can measure the same part/sample with the same measurement device and get the same value.

The diagram below illustrates the difference between the terms “Accuracy” and “Precision”:

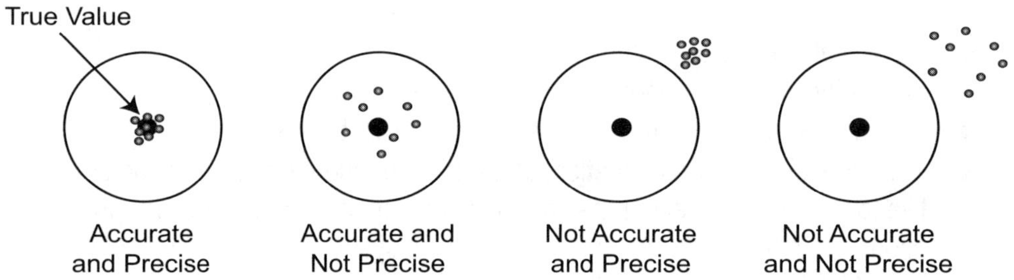

Efforts to improve measurement system quality are aimed at improving both accuracy and precision.

Factors affecting measurement systems might include:

- Equipment: measuring instrument, calibration, fixturing, etc.
- People: operators, training, education, skill, care
- Process: test method, specification
- Samples: materials, items to be tested (sometimes called "parts"), sampling plan, sample preparation, etc.
- Environment: temperature, humidity, conditioning, pre-conditioning (i.e., interview or question bias), etc.
- Management: training programs, metrology system, support of people, support of quality management system, etc.

These can be plotted in a Cause and Effect or "Fishbone" Diagram (discussed in the Analyze Phase) to help identify potential sources of measurement variation.

Common tools and techniques of Measurement Systems Analysis include:

- Calibration studies
- Fixed effect ANOVA
- Components of variance
- Attribute Gage Study
- Gage R&R
- ANOVA Gage R&R
- Destructive Testing Analysis, and others

The tool selected is usually determined by characteristics of the measurement system itself. Further study is needed beyond the scope of this book on many of these tools. Two of the most common and basic types of MSA tools are the Gage R & R study and the Attribute Gage study.

Gage R & R study is used when dealing with variable data (data we can measure like weight, distance, etc.). This stands for Gage Repeatability & Reproducibility.

Attribute Gage study is used when dealing with attribute data (pass/fail, good/bad, etc.).

When using a new measurement system for a characteristic which has not been previously measured on it, a measurement capability analysis should be performed. Measurement capability analyses are critical to the success of every measurement and ensure that future measurements will be representative of the process characteristic being measured.

The following six rules will help organizations perform good gage capability studies. These steps are fundamental to performing a meaningful study.

1. Measurements or observations should be made in a random order to ensure that any drift or changes that occur due to unknown factors will be spread randomly throughout the study.
2. The worker should be unaware of which numbered part is being checked in order to avoid any possible knowledge bias. However, the person conducting the study should know which numbered part is being checked and record the data accordingly, that is Operator A, Part 1, first trial; Operator B, Part 4, second trial, etc.
3. The readings should be estimated to the nearest number that can be obtained. If possible, readings should be made to one-half of the smallest graduation. For instance, if the smallest graduation is 0.0001, then the estimate for each reading should be rounded to the nearest 0.00005.
4. The study should be observed by a person who recognizes the importance of the caution required in conducting a reliable study.
5. The measurement procedure should be documented and all workers (operators) trained to the procedure prior to the study.
6. Each worker should use the same procedure - including all steps - to obtain the readings.

There are many on-line Gage R & R versions available for free download. Find an appropriate version and use the basic steps below to conduct a Gage R & R study.

This discussion refers to the data collection Gage R&R study that follows:

1. Determine the number of appraisers, trials, and parts, which may vary from study to study. A rule of thumb is 2-3 appraisers, 2-3 trials, and 5-10 parts - with 10 being greatly preferred. In this example, we will use 3 appraisers, 2 trials, and 10 parts.
2. Identify three appraisers who are all trained in the proper measurement procedure and identify them as Operators 1, 2, and 3.
3. Fill in the yellow blanks at the top of the form with the required background information and total specification tolerance. It may also be useful to document the gage, part, or process being studied.
4. Collect ten parts that represents the range of process variation. If the parts do not vary as much as the process, the gage error will be overstated.
5. Identify each part with a number 1-10 in such a way that the appraisers cannot see the numbers as they take the measurements.

6. Each appraiser completes their measurements and documents their results. Operator 1's two trials are recorded in columns O1-1 and 01-2. Likewise, Operator 2 has columns O2-1 and 02-2 and Operator 3 has columns 03-1 and 03-2.
7. Start with Operator 1 and measure each of the ten parts in random order. A third party should record the results of the first trial in column O1-1. Proceed to Operators 2 and 3 following the same process. Then repeat the process for additional trials.

Below is an example of the gage R & R study previously described:

Gauge Repeatability and Reproducibility

This spreadsheet is designed for up to three operators, three trials, and ten samples. Enter data ONLY in yellow shaded cells.

Number of operators	3	Upper specification limit	1
Number of trials	2	Lower specification limit	0.5
Number of samples	10		

Data	Operator 1				Operator 2				Operator 3			
	Trial				Trial				Trial			
Sample #	1	2	3	Range	1	2	3	Range	1	2	3	Range
1	0.630	0.590		0.040	0.560	0.560		0.000	0.510	0.540		0.030
2	1.000	1.000		0.000	1.040	0.960		0.080	1.050	1.010		0.040
3	0.830	0.770		0.060	0.800	0.760		0.040	0.810	0.810		0.000
4	0.860	0.940		0.080	0.820	0.780		0.040	0.810	0.810		0.000
5	0.590	0.510		0.080	0.430	0.430		0.000	0.460	0.490		0.030
6	0.980	0.980		0.000	1.000	1.040		0.040	1.040	1.000		0.040
7	0.960	0.960		0.000	0.940	0.900		0.040	0.950	0.950		0.000
8	0.860	0.830		0.030	0.720	0.740		0.020	0.810	0.810		0.000
9	0.970	0.970		0.000	0.980	0.940		0.040	1.030	1.030		0.000
10	0.640	0.720		0.080	0.560	0.520		0.040	0.840	0.810		0.030
Range average				0.037				0.034				0.017
Sample average				0.830				0.774				0.829

				Tolerance analysis
Average range	0.029	Repeatability (EV)	0.134	26.75%
X-bar range	0.056	Reproducibility (AV)	0.147	29.37%
		Repeatability and Reproducibility (R&R)	0.199	39.73%
		Control limit for individual ranges	0.096	

Note: any ranges beyond this limit may be the result of assignable causes. Identify and correct. Discard values and recompute statistics.

The version of the Gage R & R above indicates the percent of the tolerance used by the measurement device.

EV is equipment variation, AV is appraiser variation, and R&R is the combination of EV and AV. The Tolerance Analysis column indicates the percentage of the tolerance used by the EV, AV, and EV/AV combination. The rule of thumb for acceptance of a measurement system is a total Gage R&R of 30% or less of Total Variation or the Specification Tolerance. In this case the EV and AV are less than 30% of the total tolerance, however, the combination of the two are greater than 30% of the tolerance, and actions should be taken to improve the measurement systems such as increasing the tolerance or improving the measurement equipment or technique/procedure.

If the MSA shows the system is not capable (i.e., R&R > 30%), the first step to improve results is to analyze the breakdown of the error source. If the largest contributor to error is Repeatability, then the equipment must be improved. Likewise, if Reproducibility is the largest source of error, appraiser training and adherence to procedures can yield improvement.

Chapter Summary

By using these key measurement tools, improvement teams are able to document and measure the current state condition of a value stream or process to be improved. This initial measurement condition provides the basis for improvement measures and comparisons. The Measure Phase tools provide key insight into the opportunities for improvement by illuminating and highlighting waste in a process. Examples of several measurement and documentation tools were discussed in detail in this chapter.

Lean Sigma for Service Excellence Applications

These observations may assist in understanding how to apply the concepts and tools contained in this chapter:

- Form a small team and discuss how the different levels of mapping apply to your organization.
- Select a value stream and sketch a process or value stream map.
- Gather a small cross functional and cross level team and document a current state map.
- Complete a web search for value stream maps to see how others have completed this critical phase of their improvement project.
- Complete a Spaghetti Diagram for an everyday process at your organization.
- Use a current state map to identify the Dirty Dozen wastes.
- After completing a current state map, identify 3 -4 low cost improvement projects that can immediately be implemented.

Measure Phase Readiness Guide

The following Measure Phase Readiness Guide allows you to ensure there is application of the chapter's content before proceeding to apply the Lean Sigma tools and concepts in the next chapter. If you score less than 70%, consider working on the lower scoring areas before moving on.

Measure Phase Readiness Guide	
Use the following 5-level Likert item scale to rank each of the statements: **1 = Strongly Disagree** **2 = Disagree** **3 = Neither Agree nor Disagree** **4 = Agree** **5 = Strongly Agree**	
	Score
1. My organization does a good job of identiying the Key Performance Indicators (KPIs) or measures.	
2. The measurement system used in my organization is complete and accurate.	
3. Most of the measures used in my organization are linked to financial performance.	
4. My organization does a good job of measuring the twelve types of waste.	
5. My organization does a good job of measuring customer's needs.	
6. My organization effectively utilizes the QFD tool.	
7. My organization does a good job of mapping current and future state conditions and flow.	
8. My organization utilizes the SIPOC analysis to document suppliers, inputs, processes, customers, and outputs.	
9. My organization uses Check Sheets and Frequency Charts to create and collect key process data.	
10. My organization uses Run Charts to document process variability.	
11. I feel comfortable applying the DMAIC process to documenting customer needs.	
12. I feel comfortable applying the Voice of the Customer tool.	
13. I feel comfortable applying QFD.	
14. I feel comfortable using value stream and process maps to document current and future states.	
15. I feel comfortable preparing a Key Metric and Data Profile worksheet or template.	
16. I feel comfortable using the SIPOC analysis.	
17. I feel comfortable preparing and using Check Sheets and Frequency Charts.	
18. I feel comfortable preparing and using Run Charts.	
19. I see the value in using the DMAIC process and tools for measuring projects.	
20. I believe my organization should utilize and apply the concepts and tools discussed in this chapter.	
Total Score	

Case Review – Measure Phase for Klark Intermediate School District

The Klark Intermediate School District (KISD) is a regional educational service agency serving the community, student, educator, and business needs in the local area. They have two primary goals: Student Achievement and Customer Satisfaction. The Klark ISD exists to support local communities by providing learning opportunities for a wide variety of learners. The KISD has programs in the following areas:

- Vocational Learning
- General Education Diplomas
- Business Programs
- Community Learning

The staff at KISD work extensively through business, school, and community partnerships focusing on the needs of their customers. Their primary customers are students, businesses, and local school districts. Over the past year, new demands have been placed on the KISD. Reduced enrollment has led to a reduction in state funding dollars and the KISD is faced with some difficult decisions. Before layoffs and closures would be considered, their President Jim Baker insisted that they engage in a continuous improvement effort. Jim contacted a local manufacturing business owner that had been practicing Lean Sigma techniques for some ten years with great success.

Jim established a cross-functional improvement team and set up a work session with the manufacturing firm. Under the manufacture's direction, the KISD team used the DMAIC process to implement the improvements.

Define Phase

The KISD team used the Define Phase tools. The Team Charter identified the following key measures for success:

1. Customer Satisfaction: Students, businesses, and communities
2. Student Achievement: Students achieving greater than 2.0 GPA
3. Student Retention
4. Graduate Placement
5. Attendance
6. Safety

With the Team Charter, Project Planner, Actions In Progress and Opportunity Logs started, the team moved on to the Measure phase.

Measure Phase

The KISD team quickly learned that the keys for their success were not currently being measured. They agreed to divide the work amongst the 8 members on the team. The following assignments were made:

Measure	Person
Customer Satisfaction: Students, businesses, and communities	Mary, Bill, & Jack
Student Achievement: Students achieving greater than 2.0 GPA	Anna
Student Retention	Jesse
Graduate Placement	Michelle
Attendance	James
Safety	Lisa

Each person or sub team was to compile the data from the previous fiscal year. The data was stored in several different locations. Some data was buried in file cabinets; other data was contained on various spreadsheets maintained by several different people. The team scheduled the next work session and began their data search.

At the next work session the team found that much of the data was available, however customer satisfaction information had not been collected for over three years and the old data was not very well documented. The team decided to post the data they had and design a new method to quickly collect customer satisfaction data. They discussed several different ideas regarding how to gather customer satisfaction information. Some of their ideas included mail surveys, online surveys, project completion evaluations, and exit or completion interviews. The team felt that time was of the essence, so they decided to contact their top five customers directly and conduct phone interviews as their customer satisfaction data.

Mary would call the local schools that sent their students to the KISD, Bill would contact the business customers, and Jack would talk to community organization leaders who used the ISD services.

Note: This is a likely scenario for many service organizations. A great deal of data will be available, but other key data will need to be collected. Use the data collection tools to begin to collect key data. In a short time, your team should have enough data to begin to see trends and then draw conclusions. Be careful not to guess at the data. Make sure to use the appropriate data collection process to yield unbiased data. Gather data quickly to provide a "snap-shop" of the process performance.

The customer satisfaction team designed a short questionnaire to discuss with their key clients on the phone interviews and capture this information on the Voice of the Customer (VOC) tool. For the most part, everyone was willing to answer the questions, as it was done in a personal way. The following questions were asked.

1. How many students/participants used the KISD from your organization?
2. How many students/participants completed the program they started?
3. If the student/participant did not complete the program, what were the reasons?
4. Are the students/participants who completed the program able to apply their new skill or knowledge?
5. What do you see as the major positives about the services the KISD provided?
6. What do you see as the major weaknesses of the KISD programs and services?
7. Do you have any suggestions regarding how we can improve our programs and services?
8. How would you grade the programs and services of the KISD?

The raw data Check Sheets from these surveys are found below:

KISD Voice of the Customer Measurements									
Questions	**Org. 1**	**Org. 2**	**Org. 3**	**Org. 4**	**Org. 5**		**Org. 65**	**Org. 66**	**Summary**
1. How many students/participants used the KISD from your organization?	2	1	3	0	1		1	2	1.4
2. How many students/participants completed the program they started?	100%	100%	67%	0%	0%		100%	50%	60%
3. If the student/participant did not complete the program, what were the reasons?	See Notes below								
4. Are the students/participants who completed the program able to apply their new skill or knowledge?	Y	Y	N	N/A	N/A		Y	Y	
5. What do you see as the major positives about the services the KISD provided?	See Notes below								
6. What do you see as the major weaknesses of the KISD programs and services?	See Notes below								
7. Do you have any suggestions regarding how we can improve our programs and services?	See Notes below								
8. How would you grade the programs and services of the KISD?	A	C	B	C	A		C	B	C+

Questions Summaries	
3. If the student/participant did not complete the program, what were the reasons?	Frequency
Moved to another program	12
Not appropriate classes	6
Too difficult	3
Left employer	1
Transportation problems	1
5. What do you see as the major positives about the services the KISD provided?	Frequency
Service to businesses and customization	42
Practical classes	23
Location	12
Instructors	6
6. What do you see as the major weaknesses of the KISD programs and services?	Frequency
Students ability to problem solve	22
Location	18
Reputation of second class	2
7. Do you have any suggestions regarding how we can improve our programs and services?	Frequency
Focus on problem solving	18
Deliver classes at organizations	15
Get better instructors	3
Seek quality awards	2

The results of the VOC activities led to additional discussion and the development of a student survey to capture additional student customer VOC information. The student VOC data indicated additional key findings. The team put their findings together in the following Quality Function Deployment (QFD) diagram:

QFD KISD		1	2	3	4	5	6	7	8	9		
Customer Priority	Customer Requirements (Voice of the Customer)	Organization Requirements (O)	Worker safety	Good instructors	Instructors form businesses	Appropriate curriculum	Fair costs to all	Enrollment to maintain funding			Current Measures	Competitive Measures
1	Get me a good job			X	X	X					63.0%	80%
2	Get me good people with appropriate skills			X	X	X					85.0%	50%
3	Do this at a reasonable cost			X			X	X			85.0%	90%
4	Do this at a reasonable time				X	X					85.0%	90%
		Technical Requirements (X)	Specific class development	Semester delivery system	Conventional GPA system	Positive cash flow	Use of physical assets	Administration				
		1	2	3	4	5	6	7	8	9		

It took about two weeks for the other team members to compile data on the key measures. The table below summarizes the team's findings:

Measure	Measure	Conversion
Student Customer Satisfaction	C	70.0%
Business Customer Satisfaction	B +	85.0%
Community Customer Satisfaction	A -	88.5%
Student Achievement: Students achieving greater than 2.0 GPA	87	87.0%
Student Retention	79	79.0%
Graduate Placement	62	63.0%
Attendance	99.6	99.6%
Safety	100	100.0%

With much of the data collected, the team decided to document the overall process flow for the education need and delivery process. They decided not to use a formal value stream map as they believed the SIPOC Diagram relative to the process flow would allow them to better illustrate the situation where they have several customers of the same process. The following process flow and SIPOC matrix was developed as part of the Measure Phase:

Supplier > Input > Process > Output > Customer (SIPOC)					
Process Step	**Supplier** 5	**Input** 4	**Process** 1	**Output** 3	**Customer** 2
1	1. Community, businesses, and potential students 1. Surveyors	1. Multiple customer need data via market need surveys	1. Establish Market needs	1. Market needs compiled survey results	1. Community, businesses, and potential students
2	2. Administration	2. Text books, current class offerings, and research of other programs	2. Develop curriculum and class	2. Curriculum and class outlines	2. Department heads
3	3. Administration and department heads	3. Curriculum and class outlines	3. Set instructional schedule	3. Class offering schedule	3. Community, businesses, and potential students 3. Administration and department heads
4	4. Department heads	4. KISD staff & Local businesses	4. Identify & select instructor	4. Instructor selected.	4 Department heads and administration
5	5. Instructor	5. Buildings, materials, books, & students	5. Deliver instruction	5. Completed class	5. KISD administration & students, businesses, and community
6	6. Community, businesses, students, and instructors	6. Feedback card scores, and comments	6. Post deliver survey	6. Data to analyze for improvement	6. Administration, department heads, and instructors

With the process flow and many of the key measurements fully understood, the team moved on to the Analyze Phase of the DMAIC process.

Analyze Phase

Analysis of the data presented indicates that the weakest three performance measures or areas are:

Graduate Placement = 63%
Student Customer Satisfaction = 70%
Student Retention = 79%

The analysis indicated that the KISD programs for business and community customers were doing well, however their student customers were clearly not satisfied.

A brainstorming analysis using a Cause and Effect Diagram indicated that these measures could be related. Poor placement results leads to dissatisfied student customers, which leads to poor retention as students leave to other alternatives. The team then brainstormed ideas that might help improve the placement of graduates in their studied fields. The following ideas from their brainstorming session were selected for implementation:

1. Conduct career fairs with local businesses
2. Provide individual placement assistance form administrators
3. Collect additional data from local businesses regarding improved curriculum

The group used an Affinity Diagram to better organize and group the survey data.

Improve Phase

Over the following two months the team continued to work to develop and implement the selected improvement ideas. Additional interviews with local businesses indicated that stronger math and problem solving skills were needed to make their graduates more likely to be hired. As a result, the KISD contracted with a problem solving training firm to deliver a Systematic Problem Solving Seminar for all graduating students and to assist in developing a business problem solving class for future sessions.

Additionally, each graduating student was paired with a "Placement Buddy" from the staff, for assistance in interviewing skills and resume drafting. This was a burden at first, but once the staff understood that this improvement could improve their job security, they became very helpful.

Also, the KISD revived their Career Fair activities with local businesses. The first session they had a record 33 local businesses participate and shortly thereafter placed over 90% of their graduating students!

To improve employability the KISD pursued ways to involve local businesses more with curriculum development and instruction. A separate team was established to work closer with the local business community to improve employability and placement.

Control Phase

To control and sustain the improvements, the KISD began tracking placement records for each session. They began to focus their curriculum on the local business needs in effort to continue to raise placement figures. They conducted quarterly business customer needs assessments to better understand what their needs were. They then provided this information to the curriculum committee, which used the data to modify and improve the classes offered.

The KISD implemented a monthly performance score card to monitor these activities. Over the next twelve months, the KISD was able to improve to the following levels:

Graduate Placement = 83% (previously 63%)
Student Customer Satisfaction = 80% (previously 70%)
Student Retention = 85% (previously 79%)

The improvement team continues to meet monthly to monitor the performance measures and implement improvement initiatives.

Chapter 6

Analyze Phase

Making the Data Speak to Everyone

Chapter Overview

Analyzing data seems to be a lost art these days. In a world of instant messaging, multi-tasking, and instant gratification, the tendency is to jump to conclusions and give quick answers. In fact this behavior is often rewarded whether the conclusions are right or wrong. In truth, a data driven, systematic analytical approach is more fruitful and successful people already know this. Lean Sigma methods include this vital step in the process for improvement. Analytical methods, tools, and techniques allow improvement teams to review data in a systematic manner and have the data point to the next logical step. They help improvement teams discover key opportunities and determine the appropriate improvement tools to apply. In this chapter, analytical methods, techniques, and tools are reviewed in greater detail to provide improvement teams the means to succeed.

Analyze Phase Training and Alignment

Lean Sigma analytical techniques are designed to illuminate opportunities and cause and effect relationships. Analytical techniques are typically easier if the right data is collected the right way during the Measure Phase. It is recommended that training for improvement teams in analytical methods be completed concurrently with the Measure Phase training to ensure that the data measured is that which will lead to proper analysis.

Before beginning the Analyze Phase, team members should have an understanding of the following:

- Lean Sigma
- Lean Sigma 12 wastes
- DMAIC Improvement process review
- Measure Phase tool application
- Analyze Phase tool overview
- Basic data collection and presentation methods and techniques

Basic analytical and presentation methods are covered in further detail in the Analyze Phase Tools section of this chapter. These are key prerequisite skills to learn during this phase.

Analyze the Current State

Documenting and measuring the current state with objective data is the first step in the Measure Phase of the DMAIC improvement process. During the Measure Phase it is common to uncover key issues and opportunities regarding the process being studied. This discovery is actually the beginning of the Analyze Phase of the DMAIC process. Not only does the very process of gathering data lead to basic analytical findings, the right data will flow smoothly into analytical tools and methods.

When reviewing current state data, look for abnormalities, wastes, bottlenecks, and constraints that impede flow; places where the process flow is interrupted or starts and stops frequently. Look for areas of excess batching, queue/wait time, or poor quality. These disconnects are opportunities for improvement. Use the Analyze Phase tools to further analyze data to discover improvement opportunities and ideas.

Analyze Phase Tools

The key Analyze Phase tools and their application are identified in the following table.

Phase	Lean Sigma Tool	Application Guide
ANALYZE	Value-Added (VA) versus Non Value-Added (NVA) Analysis	Use VA versus NVA analysis to understand and illuminate the wastes or non value-added activities in a process.
	Constraint or Bottleneck Analysis	Use constraint or bottleneck analysis to identify the constraint or bottleneck in a process.
	Demand Analysis Plots and Takt Time	Use Demand Analysis Plots and Takt Time analysis tools to understand the pace of customer demand or pull. This in turn will identify target improvement actions and outcomes.
	Histogram, Ogive Chart, and Cumulative Frequency	Use Histograms to present data and graphically illustrate the spread of a population or sample of data.
	Pareto and Pie Charts	Use Pareto and Pie Charts to graphically illustrate and stratify critical data and to identify and align teams on the most significant areas to improve. Use layered Pareto Charts to drill down to root causes.
	Cause and Effect (or Fishbone) Diagrams	Use Cause and Effect (or Fishbone) Diagrams to graphically illustrate and align teams on possible root causes. Also use Cause and Effect Diagrams to plan required resources to accomplish an objective.
	Brainstorming	Use brainstorming to facilitate team discussion regarding next steps, causes, improvements, and other team actions.
	5 Whys	Use 5 Why analysis to methodically determine the causes of a problem.
	Radar Charts	Use Radar Charts to graphically illustrate critical data and to identify and align teams on the most significant areas to improve.
	Scatter Plots	Use Scatter Plots to understand the correlation between two variables.
	Process Capability	Use Process Capability studies to monitor a process output over time to determine if a process is capable.
	Force Field Analysis	Use Force Field analysis to understand and illustrate the forces for and against an idea, direction, strategy, or decision. Review the advantages or positives versus the disadvantages or negatives.
	Interrelationship Diagrams	Use Interelationship Diagrams to understand and illustrate the inputs and outputs and relationships of key processes or data. This tool is also useful for understanding and illustrating the causal relationships of process steps or inputs.
	Employee Balance Charts	This is a visual display in the form of a Bar Chart that represents the work elements and cycle times relative to the total value stream cycle time and takt time (or pitch).
	Impact Maps	This tool helps a team identify the solutions that will most likely have the greatest impact with the least amount of effort.

By using these key analytical tools, improvement teams are able to analyze, implement, and report on their team's progress in an orderly fashion.

Value-Added (VA) versus Non Value-Added (NVA) Analysis

*The **VA versus NVA Analysis** is used to illuminate the waste in a process.* Once the process steps are documented in the Measure Phase by a value stream or process map, VA and NVA times can be measured and placed into a simple data table to compare the value-added (VA) to non value-added (NVA) time content for a portion (one process) of the value stream or all the processes. This is a form of a time study. When conducting time studies, do not be overly concerned with whether the time is from the fastest or slowest person. Take accurate measurements and document them. If there is concern regarding the relative speed (or lack thereof) for an activity or task, simply document the concern in the Issues and Opportunities Log. The fact that there is this concern over the possible variation in times will lead to discussions and will very well lead to key process improvements.

The following is an example of a VA versus NVA Analysis table for a Customer Phone Order process, which is the first segment in a Customer Service Order to Cash value stream:

Process Step	Process Name	Type	Begin Time	Operation Time	End Time	Value-Added?	Value-Added Total
1	Answer Phone	Process	0:00:00	0:00:25	0:00:25	Yes	0:00:25
2	Ask for Customer Information	Process	0:00:25	0:00:40	0:01:05	Yes	0:01:05
3	Does Customer have Account?	Process	0:01:05	0:00:05	0:01:10	Yes	0:01:10
4	Place on Hold and Forward	Transport	0:01:10	0:01:15	0:02:25	No	0:01:10
5	Ask for Customer Information	Process	0:02:25	0:00:20	0:02:45	No	0:01:10
6	Take Information for Credit App	Process	0:02:45	0:03:45	0:06:30	Yes	0:04:55
7	Wait for Credit Approval	Delay	0:06:30	0:06:05	0:12:35	No	0:04:55
8	Approved?	Decision	0:12:35	0:00:00	0:12:35	Yes	0:04:55
9	Ask for Customer Information	Process	0:12:35	0:00:40	0:13:15	No	0:04:55
10	Does Customer have Standard Product?	Process	0:13:15	0:00:05	0:13:20	No	0:04:55
11	Determine Product Needs	Process	0:13:20	0:01:30	0:14:50	Yes	0:06:25
12	Is Product on Hand?	Process	0:14:50	0:00:15	0:15:05	No	0:06:25
13	Check System for Lead Time	Process	0:15:05	0:00:10	0:15:15	No	0:06:25
14	Quote Lead Time to Customer	Process	0:15:15	0:00:05	0:15:20	No	0:06:25
15	Is Lead Time Acceptable?	Process	0:15:20	0:00:00	0:15:20	No	0:06:25
16	Contact Operations for LT Information	Process	0:15:20	0:07:35	0:22:55	No	0:06:25
17	Is Lead Time Acceptable?	Process	0:22:55	0:00:00	0:22:55	No	0:06:25
18	Place Order	Process	0:22:55	0:01:45	0:24:40	Yes	0:08:10
19	Validate Customer Ship Info	Inspect	0:24:40	0:00:30	0:25:10	No	0:08:10
20	Thank Customer	Process	0:25:10	0:00:10	0:25:20	Yes	0:08:20

The following describes each of the headings in the VA versus NVA Analysis table:

Process Step: A number assigned for each step in the process for future reference
Process Name: A short name to describe the process
Type: An organizational descriptor for each process step (i.e., database, Excel spreadsheet, CRM, email, wait for signature, etc.)
Begin Time: The time when the process step starts
Operation Time: The actual time for the process step to be completed which should equal the difference between the Begin Time and the End Time
End Time: The time when the process step stops
Value-Added?: The categorization of the step as Value-Added (Yes) or Non Value-Added (No)
Value-Added Total: The cumulative value-added time

Note: It is helpful to color-code (e.g., green for VA and red for NVA) the column entries for more visual impact and to facilitate ease of analysis.

With the VA and NVA Analysis table completed, various charts can be constructed to illuminate the waste and identify opportunities for improvement. The VA to NVA comparison Pie, Bar, and Pareto Charts below are for the previous VA versus NVA Analysis table:

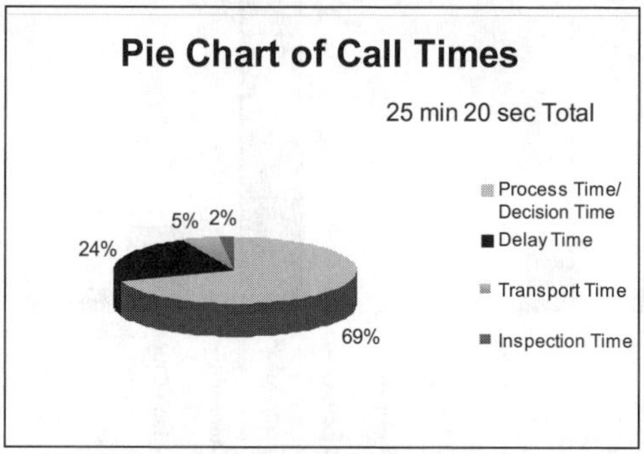

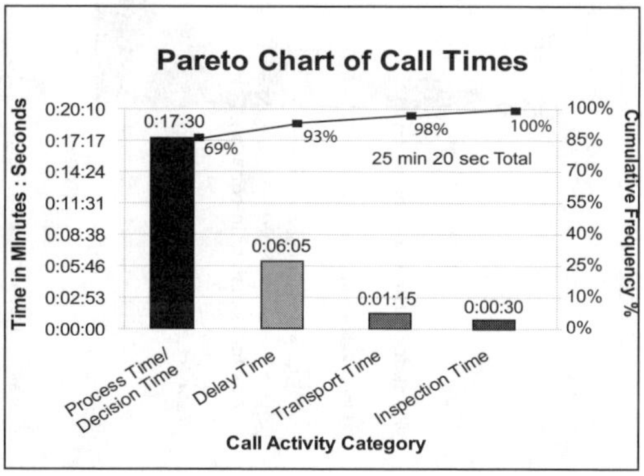

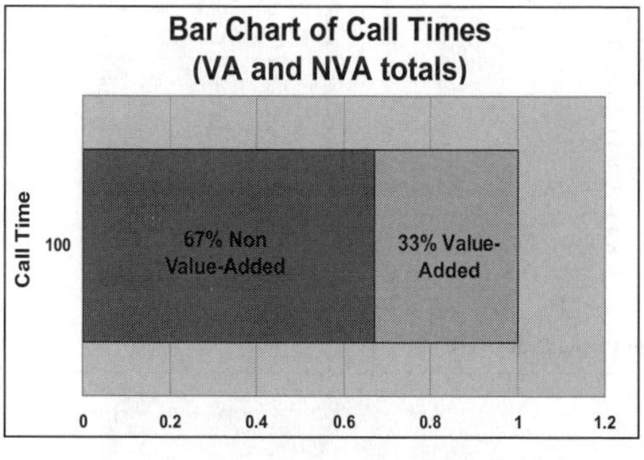

Constraint or Bottleneck Analysis

*A **Constraint or Bottleneck Analysis** is the identification of the slowest process step(s) in the product or service being provided.* It can be done in a number of ways and is commonly called the constraint or bottleneck for a process. If a VA versus NVA Analysis has been completed, the constraint is simply the slowest VA process step in the sequence. A constraint or bottleneck will usually lead to a backup, delay, or added wait time of some type. For example, the constraint for an amusement park ride is usually the ride time itself in relation to the number of seats or positions. With a fixed-ride time, the lines waiting for the ride will increase as the demand increases.

The primary constraint in the Customer Phone Order process in the previous VA versus NVA Analysis section is Step 16, "Contact Operations for LT Information," at 7 minutes 35 seconds (7:35). This can be visually presented in a simple Bar Chart of the process where the highest bar represents the slowest process or constraint.

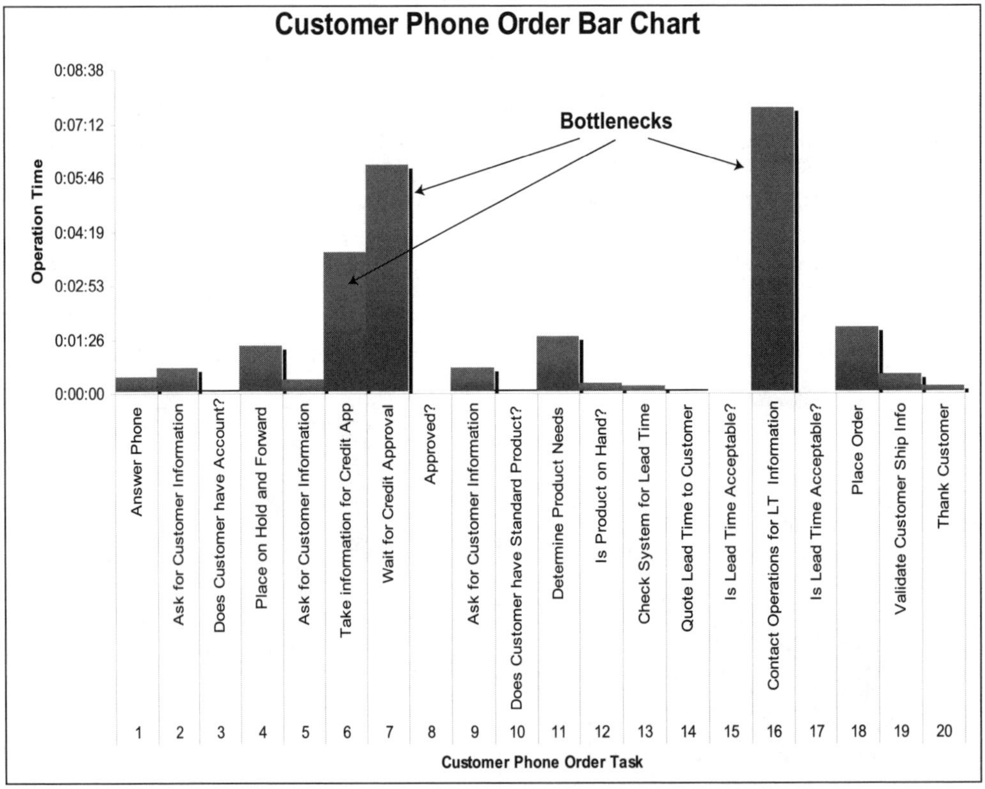

If a value stream map or flow diagram (process map) has been completed as demonstrated in the Measure Phase, the constraint can be determined again by identifying the slowest process on the map or diagram. On a value stream map it is typical for inventory or wait time to build up just before, or immediately after the constraint.

Notice the similarities and differences between the value stream map and the flow diagram on the next few pages. The value stream map groups process steps in value-added groups, while the flow diagram more closely follows the tabular data as indicated by the previous VA versus NVA Analysis table. It is common to construct both a value stream map and a flow diagram to thoroughly analyze the processes being improved upon. However, this is not always the case.

The value stream map and process flow diagram on the next four pages will assist to visually see these constraints relative to the entire process flow:

By reviewing the flow diagram or the value stream map, it can be seen that there are three basic loops in the process flow. The three process loops are as follows:

1. The Standard Product Loop is for a customer who has an account and the product is on-hand
2. The Credit Approval Loop is for the customer who needs to apply for credit and product is on-hand
3. The Lead Time Info Loop is for the customer who does not require credit approval and the product is not on-hand

Each loop has a constraint operation. For the Standard Product Loop (1) the constraint is "Place Order" (Step 18) at 105 seconds. For the Credit Approval Loop (2) the constraints are "Wait for Credit Approval" (Step 7) at 365 seconds and "Take Information for Credit App" (Step 6) at 225 seconds . For the Lead Time Info Loop (3) the constraint is "Contacting Operations for LT Information" (Step 16) at 455 seconds. By following the flow of any given order, the time for the longest operation becomes the constraint. Organizations will be best served by working on the constraints in each process loop.

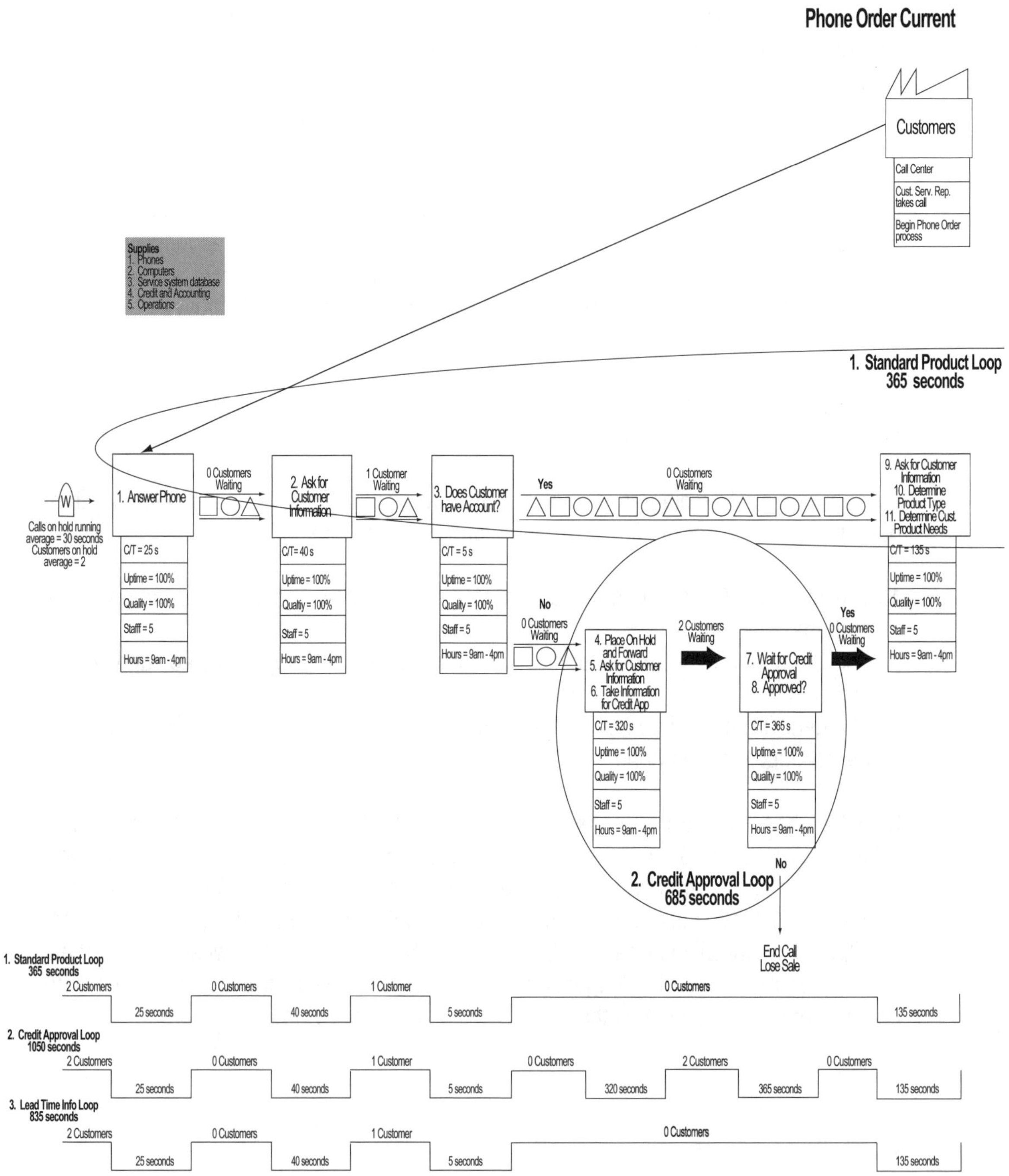
Phone Order Current
Customers
Call Center
Cust. Serv. Rep. takes call
Begin Phone Order process
Supplies
1. Phones
2. Computers
3. Service system database
4. Credit and Accounting
5. Operations
1. Standard Product Loop
365 seconds
Calls on hold running average = 30 seconds
Customers on hold average = 2
1. Answer Phone
C/T = 25 s
Uptime = 100%
Quality = 100%
Staff = 5
Hours = 9am - 4pm
0 Customers Waiting
2. Ask for Customer Information
C/T= 40 s
Uptime = 100%
Qualtiy = 100%
Staff = 5
Hours = 9am - 4pm
1 Customer Waiting
3. Does Customer have Account?
C/T = 5 s
Uptime = 100%
Quality = 100%
Staff = 5
Hours = 9am - 4pm
Yes
0 Customers Waiting
9. Ask for Customer Information
10. Determine Product Type
11. Determine Cust. Product Needs
C/T = 135 s
Uptime = 100%
Quality = 100%
Staff = 5
Hours = 9am - 4pm
No
0 Customers Waiting
4. Place On Hold and Forward
5. Ask for Customer Information
6. Take Information for Credit App
C/T = 320 s
Uptime = 100%
Quality = 100%
Staff = 5
Hours = 9am - 4pm
2 Customers Waiting
7. Wait for Credit Approval
8. Approved?
C/T = 365 s
Uptime = 100%
Quality = 100%
Staff = 5
Hours = 9am - 4pm
Yes
0 Customers Waiting
No
2. Credit Approval Loop
685 seconds
End Call
Lose Sale
1. Standard Product Loop
365 seconds
2 Customers
25 seconds
0 Customers
40 seconds
1 Customer
5 seconds
0 Customers
135 seconds
2. Credit Approval Loop
1050 seconds
2 Customers
25 seconds
0 Customers
40 seconds
1 Customer
5 seconds
0 Customers
320 seconds
2 Customers
365 seconds
0 Customers
135 seconds
3. Lead Time Info Loop
835 seconds
2 Customers
25 seconds
0 Customers
40 seconds
1 Customer
5 seconds
0 Customers
135 seconds

State Value Stream Map

Important Note:
Typical value stream maps display a queue time between processes; however, in this case it was a number of customers waiting as the queue entity. The number of customers waiting at any one time indicated how many customer service representatives were working this overall value stream. This value stream map was used as an initial constraint analysis and later was used to create a process or flow map. For advanced analysis and improvements to reduce the number of customers waiting queueing theory should be used.

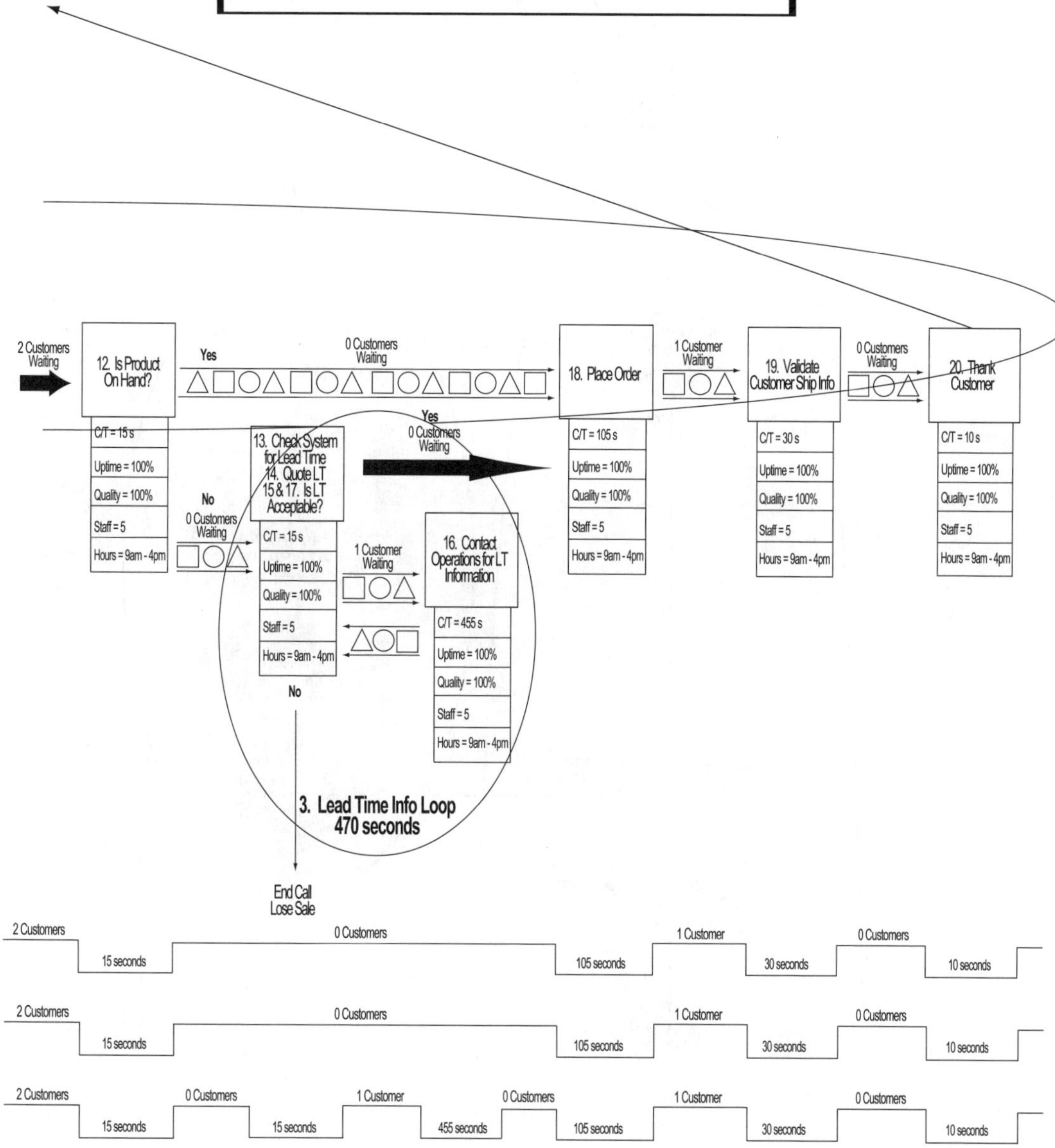

Phone Order Current

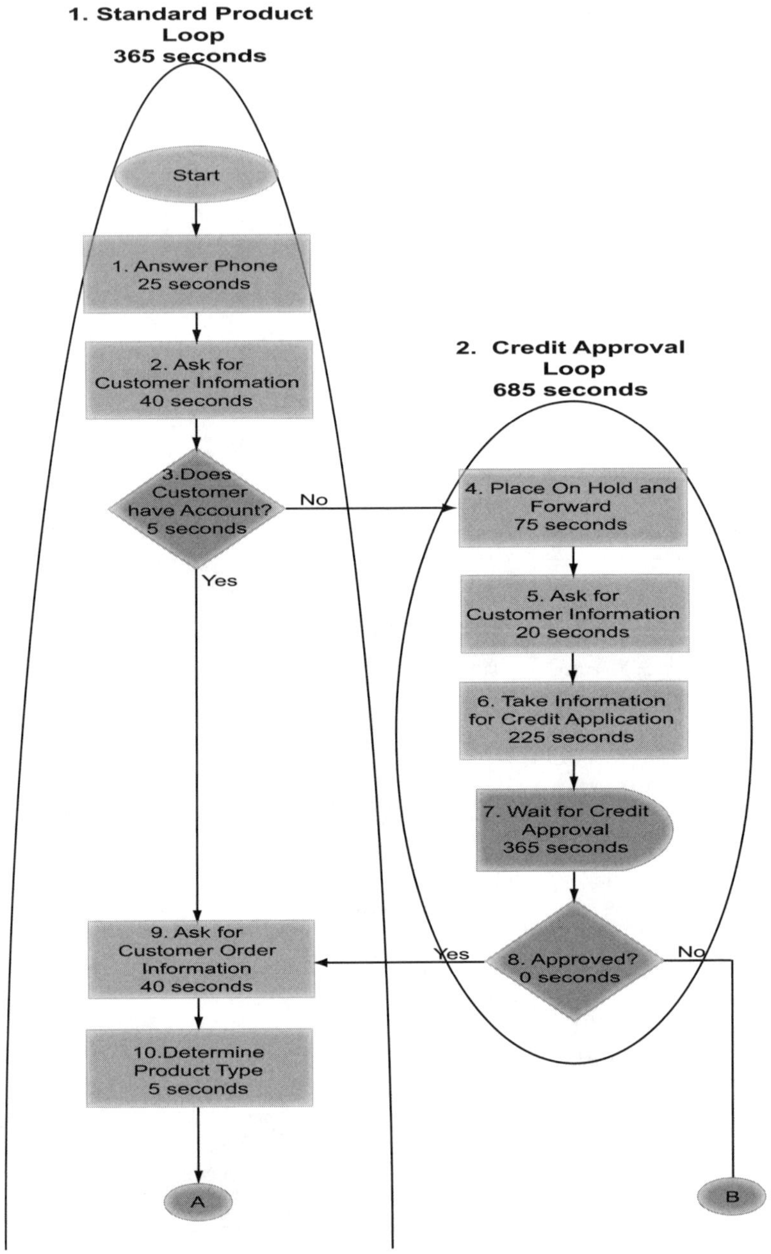

State Flow or Process Map

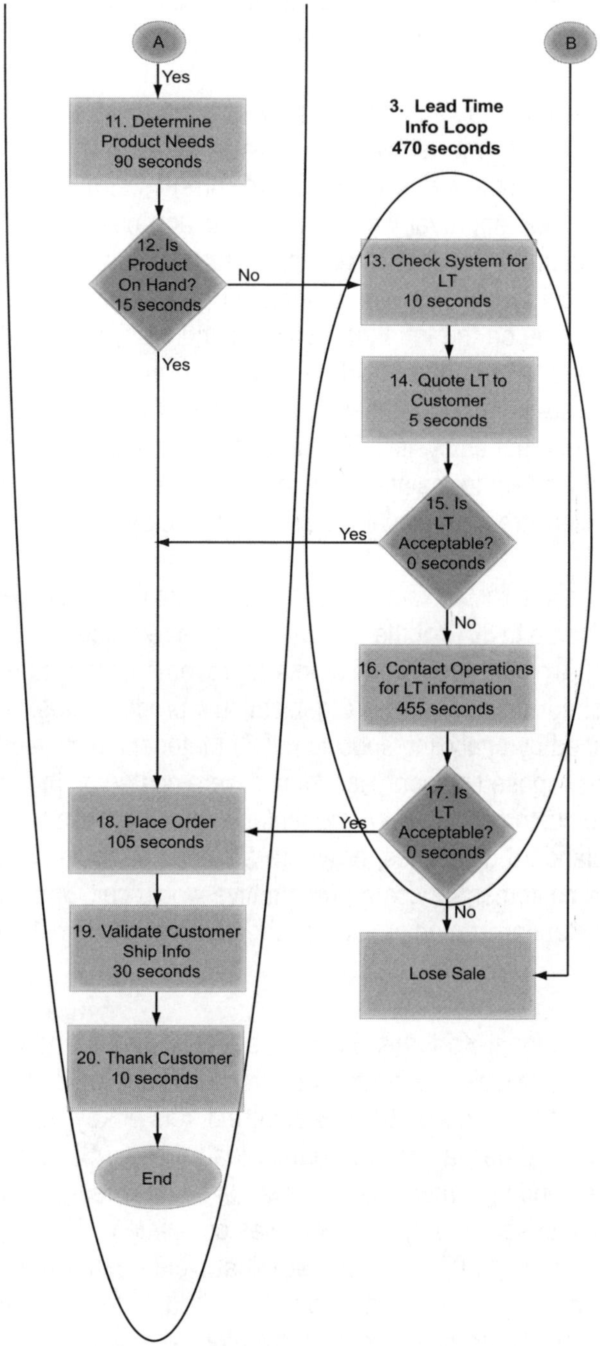

The Phone Order value stream map and flow diagram was very useful for the team that worked on this project. As a result of using these tools, the improvement team came up with the following improvement opportunities:

1. Standardize the credit approval process so that up to 90% of credit requests can be computed by the customer service representative rather than having to call the credit department. Target time reduction is 15% of current state. For this improvement idea, standards for credit approval were established and posted on the organization's intranet. As customers request credit approval, customer service representatives will collect the critical credit approval information and review the data versus the credit approval standards on the intranet. It was found that many credit approval requests met the standard criteria and could be handled in this manner. If further the request fell outside the standard requirements, the customer was then transferred to the Credit Department for further analysis. This standardization improvement project still enabled the Credit Department to maintain control of the credit approval parameters, yet have most of the actual credit approval review completed by Customer Service.

2. Standardize the special lead time request process so that customer service representative can resolve up to 80% of the special lead time requests of customers. Target time reduction is 10% of current state. For this improvement idea, standard lead time tables were established for most of the organization's product lines. Lead time standards were determined by analyzing specific Bill Of Material typical lead times and processing time. The proposed standard lead times were posted on the organization's intranet system where customer service representative could access them. For items that fell outside the standard guidelines, or where a customer could not accept the improved lead-time, the customer service representative would call Operations. This lead time improvement standardization project required Operations to establish weekly lead time guidelines.

3. Implement Pull Signal Kanbans on more standard items and standard materials, to ensure product availability. The target here is to have up to 80% of standard items in a supermarket kanban. By holding supermarkets of key raw materials, Operations could produce to order faster and reduce lead times. Simple Pull Signal Kanbans were implemented in the raw material area. In the finished goods area, an analysis of annual usage and seasonality by model was completed. The organization developed a schedule for putting pull cards in place that would better match the seasonality of product demand. By following the standard schedule for supermarket pull cards, the organization was able to minimize their inventories.

Demand Analysis Plots and Takt Time

Demand analysis techniques are used to understand the pace of customer demand. Understanding the pace of demand is critical to implementing improvement activities. When the rapidly shifting demands of service providers are well understood, predictive resource management techniques can be employed to better serve the customers. Service organizations better serving customers will grow and prosper.

The two primary methods for illustrating customer demand are Demand Analysis Plots and Takt Time.

Demand Analysis Plots

*The **Demand Analysis Plots** identify customer demand in terms of transactions or needs over a given time period.* The time period could be one day, one year, or one season depending on the type of service provided.

In the following hotel front desk visit example of a Demand Analysis Plot, it can be seen that there are three primary peaks in activity: in the morning as people are waking up and checking out, around noon when people are at lunch and have time to call, and around 4 - 5 pm when people are checking in. There is a small peak around 9 pm when people are planning their next day and asking for wake-up calls. A savvy hotel manager may choose to staff the front desk accordingly.

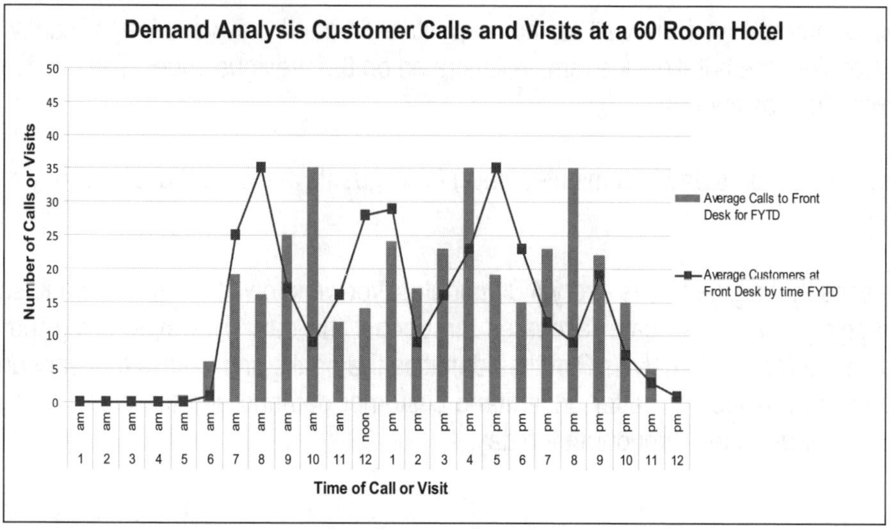

Takt Time

Takt time *on the other hand defines the pace of repetitive customer demand.* Takt time is presented in units of time and is calculated with the following equation:

Takt Time = Time available to work / Average daily demand

For an example of repetitive customer demand, consider the Transportation Security Administration (TSA) inspectors at an airport security check station. Consider the following data for a typical TSA security check station:

> Average Daily Passengers inspected/processed = 2000
> Hours of operation are 5 am – 11 pm, or 18 hours of continuous operation

Takt time for the TSA security inspection service can be determined as follows:

Takt time = (18 hours/day * 60 minutes/hr) / 2000 passengers /day = 0.54 minutes

This means that the TSA group in this example needs to process a person every .54 minutes or approximately 30 seconds. To do this, they would need to design and staff the station with the appropriate people and machines to meet the takt time. If the flights for the terminal were cut in half due to adverse weather, they could redeploy resources accordingly.

Takt time may not work as well for non-repetitive demand that varies significantly over time. Consider the hotel desk example illustrated on the previous page. The takt time for this example is as follows:

Takt time = (24 hours/day * 60 minutes/hour) / 317 guests at the front desk per day = 4.54 minutes

This means that a guest visits every 4.54 minutes, yet we know this is not true and should not be solely used to allocate resources throughout the day. However, using the data based on the Demand Analysis Plot that identifies the peaks and valleys that vary greatly during the day, helped to better understand customer demand and therefore, resources can be better allocated throughout the day.

In the Tech Support Call by Day (Demand Analysis Plot) below, it can be seen that Mondays are a peak day for calls, with Saturday being a secondary peak . It is believed that after the weekend, people have encountered issues that they require technical support with and perhaps Saturdays are when people are trying to get issues cleared on their support needs. A manager cannot staff every day to the average daily demand without causing excessive wait times during peak demand periods. Perhaps a staffing plan to historical demand is more appropriate.

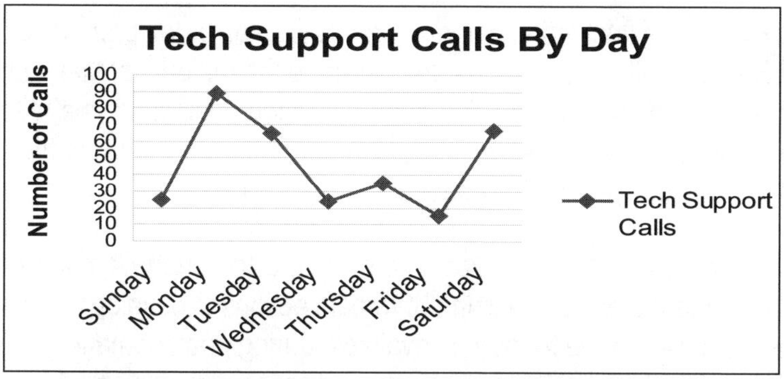

The Demand Analysis Plot for Monthly Bookings at Bahamas Villa Run Chart below indicates that the peak bookings are in March (dark gray line); however, the most days booked per month are in January and May. In January and May, there are typically two 14 day stays for total booking days of 28. In March, the duration of the stay is shorter, so even though this is the greatest booking month, it is not the greatest number of days booked per month. To an owner, the greater number of guests (bookings) means that the villa will have to be cleaned more frequently. Proper staffing to handle this demand is required.

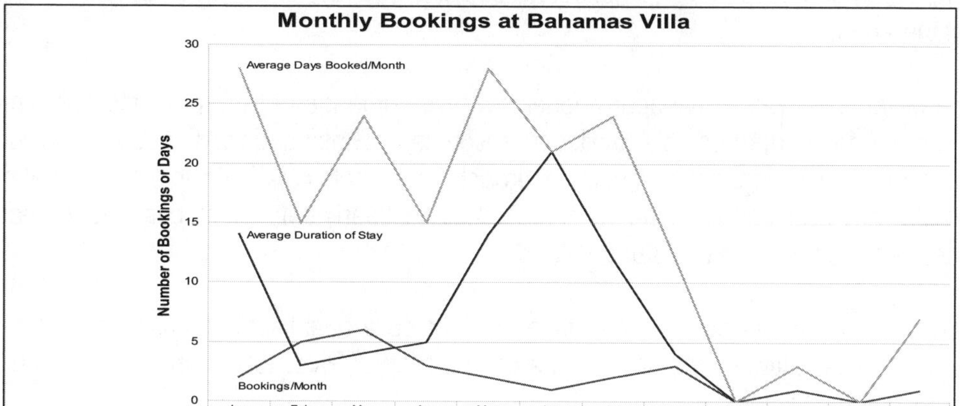

	Jan	Feb	Mar	Apr	May	Jun	Jul	Aug	Sep	Oct	Nov	Dec
Bookings/Month	2	5	6	3	2	1	2	3	0	1	0	1
Average Duration of Stay	14	3	4	5	14	21	12	4	0	3	0	7
Average Days Booked/Month	28	15	24	15	28	21	24	12	0	3	0	7

Regarding demand leveling, it may be apparent in the previous Bahamas Villa example, that the demand is based on holiday seasons and seasonal travel. In this case, as in many service environments, it will be difficult to level the demand. Service organizations must develop standard work and flexible resources to meet fluctuating or seasonal customer demand. During off peak times, vacation rentals can use steeply discounted off-season rates to try to level demand. Ski resorts often promote hiking and ski lift rides during the summer. It is difficult but they can minimize the seasonality by taking such actions

Other good examples of fluctuating demand are retail sales or tax preparation businesses in the United States. Both service industries generate the majority of their annual revenue in a two-to-three month time frame. The tax preparation business cycle revolves around the US tax deadlines, while the retail stores can generate up to 90% of their annual revenue near the end of the year holiday season.

All service organizations are well served to complete a thorough Demand Analysis, then develop and implement predictive and improvement actions to develop flexible work teams to smooth the work load of the resources available during peak demand. This can be accomplished by using additional Lean Sigma tools discussed in this chapter.

The following is another example to illustrate how takt time can be used (referenced from *The Lean Desktop and Networking Pocket Guide XL* and *iLean* books, MCS Media, Inc., 2010).

The VP of Sales for House, Inc. notified the manager of their Miami sales office that the product HOUSE5637 was not selling well from their outlet. However, this product was consistently in the top percentile of overall sales, by product, in all House outlets throughout the world.

The Miami sales office manager needed to have some idea of the products "takt time" (customer demand) to be able to allocate resources. These additional resources include discounts, advertising, different sales approach for the sales staff, etc. in meeting that demand. They decided to use the takt time formula to clearly define their customer demand in terms the employees could understand.

Takt time should be used and calculated to provide a quantifiable number to customer demand. The following example used a combination of Pivot Tables and Excel formulas to calculate takt time.

The annualized sales data (partially shown below) for the Miami store is thousands of lines long:

	A	B	C	D	E	F	G	H
1	Sales Docket	Customer No	Created on	GI Date	DelDate	Product Code	Store	Sale Qty
2	0080694609	0000117694	1/03/2007	1/03/2007	1/03/2007	HOUSE7401	Miami	2.000
3	0080694381	0000117862	1/03/2007	1/03/2007	1/03/2007	HOUSE2450	Miami	12.000
4	0080693788	0000115866	27/02/2007	28/02/2007	1/03/2007	HOUSE9450	Miami	12.000
5	0080693788	0000115866	27/02/2007	28/02/2007	1/03/2007	HOUSE9450	Miami	12.000
6	0080693789	0000109724	27/02/2007	28/02/2007	1/03/2007	HOUSE9450	Miami	24.000
7	0080693790	0000117715	27/02/2007	28/02/2007	1/03/2007	HOUSE9450	Miami	24.000
8	0080693795	0000117371	27/02/2007	28/02/2007	1/03/2007	HOUSE9450	Miami	24.000
9	0080694293	0000112513	1/03/2007	1/03/2007	1/03/2007	HOUSE7001	Miami	12.000
10	0080694377	0000115605	1/03/2007	2/03/2007	1/03/2007	HOUSE9001	Miami	12.000
11	0080693791	0000117616	27/02/2007	28/02/2007	1/03/2007	HOUSE9450	Miami	36.000
12	0080693792	0000113351	27/02/2007	28/02/2007	1/03/2007	HOUSE9450	Miami	36.000
13	0080694123	0000116012	28/02/2007	1/03/2007	1/03/2007	HOUSE5500	Miami	12.000
14	0080694123	0000116012	28/02/2007	1/03/2007	1/03/2007	HOUSE0005	Miami	12.000
15	0080694123	0000116012	28/02/2007	1/03/2007	1/03/2007	HOUSE0002	Miami	24.000
16	0080694119	0000113575	28/02/2007	1/03/2007	1/03/2007	HOUSE5020	Miami	1.000
17	0080694124	0000113886	28/02/2007	1/03/2007	1/03/2007	HOUSE8020	Miami	1.000
18	0080694140	0000117694	28/02/2007	1/03/2007	1/03/2007	HOUSE1005	Miami	4.000
19	0080694368	0000101268	1/03/2007	2/03/2007	1/03/2007	HOUSE2020	Miami	1.000
20	0080694375	0000112551	1/03/2007	2/03/2007	1/03/2007	HOUSE9005	Miami	4.000
21	0080694378	0000113409	1/03/2007	2/03/2007	1/03/2007	HOUSE8020	Miami	1.000
22	0080694379	0000010237	1/03/2007	2/03/2007	1/03/2007	HOUSE9020	Miami	1.000
23	0080694410	0000010237	1/03/2007	1/03/2007	1/03/2007	HOUSE9020	Miami	1.000
24	0080694615	0000010236	1/03/2007	1/03/2007	1/03/2007	HOUSE1020	Miami	1.000
25	0080694380	0000107064	1/03/2007	1/03/2007	2/03/2007	HOUSE1100	Miami	1.000
26	0080694825	0000116829	2/03/2007	6/03/2007	2/03/2007	HOUSE3000	Miami	1.000
27	0080694348	0000112967	1/03/2007	1/03/2007	2/03/2007	HOUSE1020	Miami	1.000
28	0080694824	0000114548	2/03/2007	7/03/2007	2/03/2007	HOUSE8005	Miami	4.000

Using the Pivot Table function in Excel, the raw data above can be summarized into something like the table shown below:

Sum of Sale Qty	
Product Code	**Total**
HOUSE5637	6896
HOUSE5214	4977
HOUSE7419	4790
HOUSE9713	4534
HOUSE2583	4300
HOUSE2541	1904
HOUSE9513	1500
HOUSE9658	1763
HOUSE4569	1462

Note: Spreadsheet analysis using the Pivot Table function in Excel, as well as other statistical software applications such as Minitab, can be very useful when large volumes of data need to be analyzed.

	A	B	C	D	E	F	G	H	I
1									
2	No. of work days = 52 weeks in the year x 5 work days, minus 7 holidays =					253	work days		
3	No. of work minutes in a year = 253 days x 7.25 hr work day x 60 minutes =					110,055	minutes		
4	No. of work minutes in a day = 7.25 hr work day x 60 minutes =					435	minutes		
5									
6									
7	Pivot 1 (last 12 mths actual sales)		Actual units sold per day (using Pivot1 data)	Average Takt Time (in minutes)		Pivot 2 (average sales, last 3 yrs)		Actual units sold per day (using Pivot2 data)	Average Takt Time (in minutes)
8	Sum of Sale Qty					Sum of Sale Qty			
9	Product Code	Total				Product Code	Total		
10	HOUSE5637	6970	27.5	16		HOUSE5637	6896	27.3	16
11	HOUSE5214	5700	22.5	19		HOUSE5214	4977	19.7	22
12	HOUSE7419	4678	18.5	24		HOUSE7419	4790	18.9	23
13	HOUSE9713	4500	17.8	24		HOUSE9713	4534	17.9	24
14	HOUSE2583	3467	13.7	32		HOUSE2583	4300	17.0	26
15	HOUSE2541	2300	9.1	48		HOUSE2541	1904	7.5	58
16	HOUSE9513	2300	9.1	48		HOUSE9513	1500	5.9	73
17	HOUSE9658	1560	6.2	71		HOUSE9658	1763	7.0	62
18	HOUSE4569	1345	5.3	82		HOUSE4569	1462	5.8	75
19	HOUSE4530	941	3.7	117		HOUSE4530	1056	4.2	104
20	HOUSE4560	934	3.7	118		HOUSE4560	890	3.5	124
21	HOUSE5438	810	3.2	136		HOUSE5438	789	3.1	139
22	HOUSE8547	789	3.1	139		HOUSE8547	755	3.0	146
23	HOUSE3652	778	3.1	141		HOUSE3652	608	2.4	181
24	HOUSE3570	629	2.5	175		HOUSE3570	598	2.4	184
25	HOUSE7458	560	2.2	197		HOUSE7458	590	2.3	187
26	HOUSE7608	490	1.9	225		HOUSE7608	505	2.0	218
27	HOUSE6901	456	1.8	241		HOUSE6901	506	2.0	218
28	HOUSE9510	345	1.4	319		HOUSE9510	358	1.4	307
29	HOUSE1452	290	1.1	380		HOUSE1452	305	1.2	361
30	HOUSE4628	267	1.1	412		HOUSE4628	290	1.1	380
31	HOUSE7531	256	1.0	430		HOUSE7531	269	1.1	409

Pivot 1 was constructed using the last 12 months of actual sales data and Pivot 2 using 3 years of sales history. Then, arithmetic formulas were used to create the "Actual units sold per day" C10 (=B10/$F$2) and H10 and "Average Takt Time" D10 (=B10/$F$2) and I10. Takt time is traditionally based on future demand, however, we have used it here on historical data, as there is little to no data available (in a retail shop-front environment) that would provide actual specific customer demand, on any given day, at an individual retail store.

As indicated by Pivot Table 1 above, both "Actual units sold per day" and "Average Takt Time" can be useful measurements. In some cases, one being more meaningful than the other. In the case of HOUSE5637 reveals that the Miami store should generally sell one unit every 16 minutes. This is meaningful for a sales person on the floor, because it tells them more information than the "27.5 units per day" figure in cell C10. So, takt time actually provides the sales person a clear idea of the customer demand. The Miami store also referred to this takt time as "predictive selling."

Note: Many times a multiple of takt time, referred to as pitch, is used to move work throughout the value stream. ***Pitch** is the adjusted takt time that "groups" work to ensure maximum work process efficiency is maintained.* For example, a canal boat ride service schedules its departures on a 1/2 hour pitch during peak hours.

Histogram, Ogive Chart, and Cumulative Frequency

Histograms *utilize measurement data and display the spread and shape of the distribution.* Histograms are simple Bar Chart representations of the range, amount, and pattern of variation for data (i.e., the population). The bars are placed together to make it easier to compare data. Histograms are a "picture" of the sample data and can provide clues as to how the process is running. An Ogive Chart is a line chart in Excel that can be constructed using cumulative frequency, cumulative relative frequency, or cumulative percentage. This can combine the Pareto analysis principle with additional visual data presentation options.

With most data sets, almost all numbers will be unique. ***Bin numbers*** *are used to represent the intervals you want the Histogram tool to use for measuring the input data.* The Histogram tool counts the number of data points between the current bin number and the adjoining higher bin, if any. A number is counted in a particular bin if it is equal to or less than the bin number, down to the last bin. All values below the first bin value are counted together, as are the values above the last bin value and must be in ascending order. If you omit the bin range, the Histogram tool creates a set of evenly distributed bins between the data's minimum and maximum values. However, because these bin intervals may have little relation to your data, or the type of analysis you are looking for, it is recommended that you create your own bins. Typically, no fewer than 5 and no more than 20 class intervals or bins should be created. Remember that a Histogram is trying to capture the shape of the distribution. Too few bins, and the shape is lost. Too many bins, and the shape is lost by the random fluctuations of the data.

In the example below the bins are defined by the Average $ per Invoice column. The frequency of those invoices meeting the bin range is defined in the Number of Invoices column.

Average $ per Invoice	Number of Invoices
$ 0-100	1
$ 100-500	3
$ 500-1000	7
$ 1000-2000	25
$ 2000-3000	68
$ 3000-4000	73
$ 4000-5000	45
$ 5000-6000	12
$ 6000-7000	3
$ 7000-8000	5
> $ 8000	1

This data is presented in a Histogram as shown below:

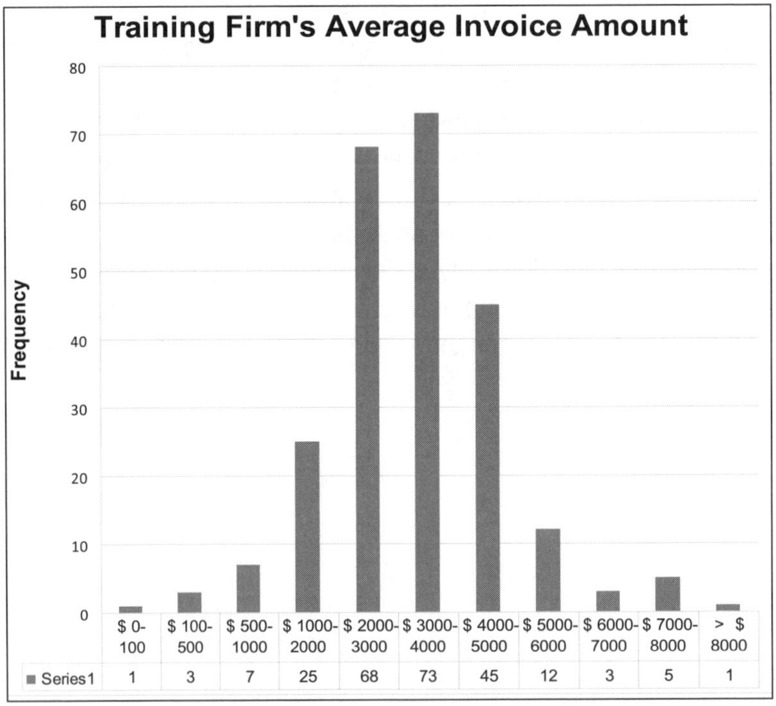

At a glance it can be seen that this sales team's Histogram indicates that the average invoice dollar amount is between $2,000 – $5,000. The sales team had a decrease in sales revenue for their area and used this information to assign additional marketing resources to target the higher-end clients (i.e., $7,000 - $8,000).

In the example shown below, the Histogram of Average Days Stay at a long-term lodging establishment below, it can be seen that there are several peaks in stay duration. This was determined to be due to vacation and work week routines.

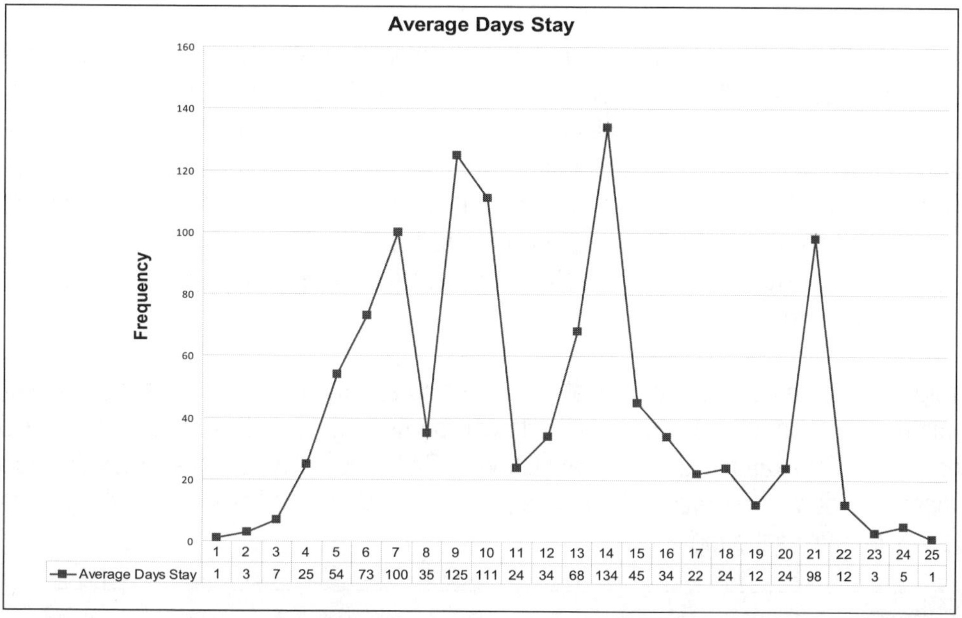

An organization can use this information for special promotional offers to encourage longer stays to increase revenue.

Note: To keep things simple, this book shows only standard normal statistics considerations. For additional study beyond standard normal data distributions, readers should consult a statistics manual or seek the advice of a Six Sigma Black Belt or Lean Sensei. Examples of non-standard normal distributions are Kurtosis, where the Histogram has longer tails than a standard normal curve, Skewness, where the Histogram has a short tail on one side or the other, or Multi-Modal effects, where the Histogram has two or more "peaks," are special circumstances that require additional statistical study and analysis. For this book, we present only standard normal curve conditions/considerations. Service organizations may encounter special distributions such as these due to shift to shift variances, multiple process flows, and/or personnel work methods differences (lack of standard work) and may need to seek assistance for interpretation and subsequent root cause analysis.

Pareto and Pie Charts

Pareto Charts

*The **Pareto Chart** is in a bar chart format that represents the Pareto principle. The **Pareto principle** states that 20% of the sources cause 80% of the problems.* For example, 80% of taxes paid are paid by 20% of all tax payers. By analyzing data with a Pareto (or Pie) Chart, improvement teams can understand what the 80% of the problems are. In the following example, it can be seen that the majority of the call time is spent in Process Time and the second greatest time spent during the call is Delay Time. To improve customer experience, improvement teams will attack the waste of Delay Time and seek to streamline the overall order Process Time.

Pareto Charts are powerful analytical tools used to stratify data and focus improvement teams on the main issues. Pareto Charts can be used to "Drill Down" to more specific information. For example, in the Pareto Chart of Call Time below, the team may decide to further break down the Process Time category in a Pareto Chart to determine the process category that takes the most time.

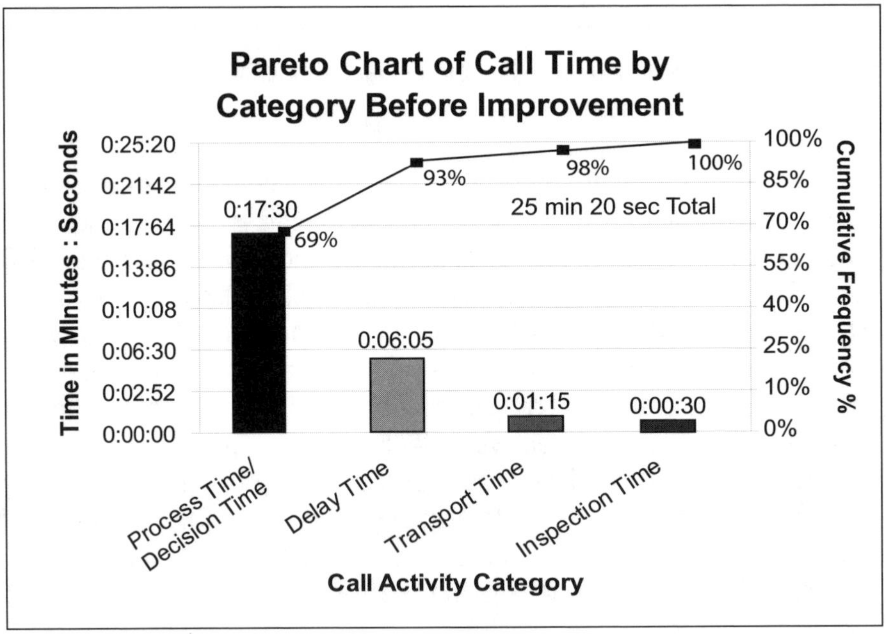

The Pareto Chart of Call Process Time "Drill Down" is shown below and indicates that the processing time item that takes the longest time is "Contact Manufacturing for LT Information."

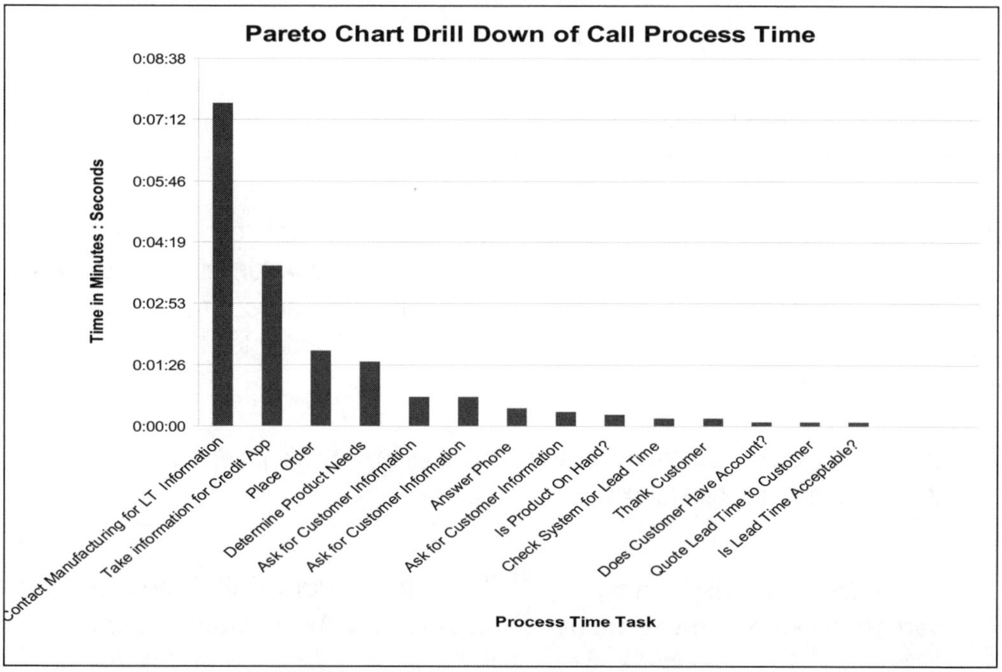

Pareto Charts are also useful to illustrate before and after improvement data. The Call Time improvement team reported the before and after improvement data with the following Pareto Charts:

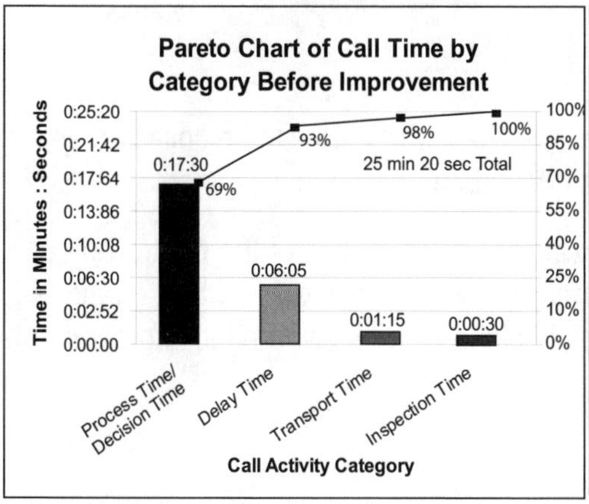

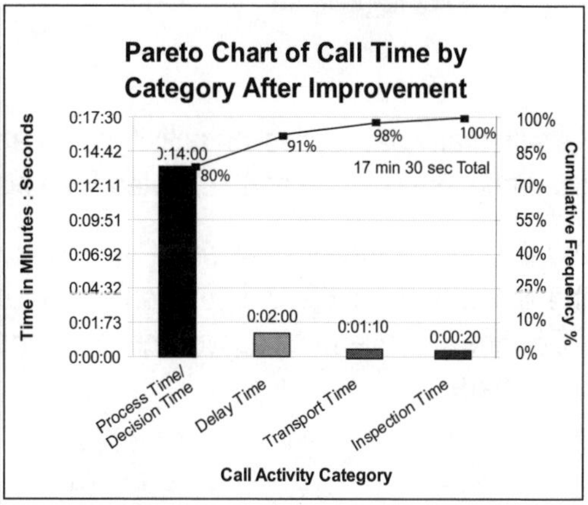

Note: These Pareto Charts display the cumulative frequency, which helps project teams more clearly show the overall impact of the improvements made.

Pie Charts

Pie Charts *are graphical representations of data in a pie shaped form where pie pieces are shown in relative size or percent of the whole.* They are similar to Pareto Charts in that they show the magnitude or relative size of different parts of the issue or opportunity and that they help improvement teams focus on the largest opportunity first. In general, they help improvement teams understand the data more clearly and prioritize the team's improvement actions to have the largest positive impact.

Pie Charts are used in a similar manner as Pareto Charts and it is largely the preference of the team regarding how they wish to represent the data. The goal for using Pareto and Pie Charts are to focus the team on the largest opportunities and issues. Improvement teams are encouraged to use the charting method that will be best understood by the majority of the team members.

The following Pie Charts illustrate the same data as shown in the previous Pareto Charts. Note the similarities and differences.

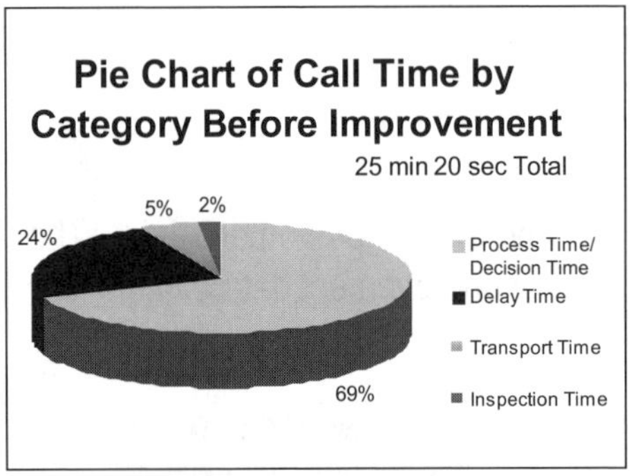

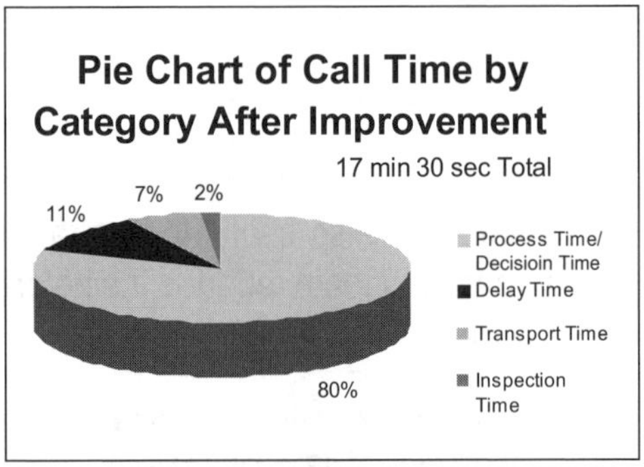

As with many data collection activities, Pareto and Pie Chart data can be collected as it is occurring, or collected and tabulated from historical data

A variation commonly seen with Pie Charts is for the relative size of the pie to represent the size of the issue. As improvements are made, the size of the Pie Chart changes to reflect the improvement, as will the size of the pie piece to reflect where the improvements were made.

Cause and Effect (or Fishbone) Diagrams

Fishbone Diagrams *allow a team to graphically display and explore, in increasing detail, all the possible causes of the problem or issue being addressed.* This will assist in determining the true root cause(s) as well as assist in determining interim containment actions. The problem or effect is identified on the head of the diagram, and brainstorming (next section) and/or other data collection techniques are used to identify and prioritize all possible causes. If done properly, the root cause(s) of the problem should be somewhere on the diagram.

To construct a Fishbone Diagram, you need to state the problem in the form of a question or state the observed outcome, problem statement, goal, or effect. The team should agree on the statement of the problem and then place this question in a box at the 'head' of the Fishbone.

Be flexible in the major "bones" or "skeleton" categories that are used. Many times the main categories are Man, Method, Machine (Information Technology), Material, and Mother Nature (Environmental Factors). There is no ideal set of categories or numbers. Make the categories relevant to your service-related problem.

The following six potential cause areas are generally thought to contain all the potential causes and cause combinations. Start the Cause and Effect Diagram with these six cause lines and use the improvement team to brainstorm or otherwise populate the Cause and Effect Diagram with potential causes. If done properly, the causes and or cause combinations will be on the diagram.

1. Manpower – How could people be causing the problem or issue, or what human resources are needed to successfully implement the goal?
2. Methods – How could the current methods be causing the problem, or what methods will we use to achieve the goal?
3. Measurements – How could our measurement technique or measuring error be causing the problem, or what measures will we use to ensure success?
4. Mother Nature – How could the environment or facilities be causing the problem, or what do we need to include in the environment or facilities to meet our goal?
5. Materials – How could the materials be causing the problem, or what materials do we need to ensure successful outcomes?
6. Machines – How can our machines or equipment be causing the problem, or what machines or equipment do we need to ensure a successful outcome?

There are many ways to populate a Cause and Effect Diagram with team ideas. Some of these methods are as follows.

- Brainstorming (structured or unstructured) with the improvement team
- Focused brainstorming around each of the 6 Ms
- Email a blank Cause and Effect Diagram to the improvement team members and ask them to populate the diagram and send it back for compiling
- Post a large Cause and Effect Diagram in a high traffic location with a note asking for everyone to list their ideas

Another form of the Cause and Effect Diagram is a simple outline form. Do not limit the team to only one right way. Be creative and obtain as many potential causes as possible.

Below is an example of a version of a Cause and Effect Diagram from a healthcare Emergency Department (ED) improvement team on why there had been an increase in the times for a patient to be admitted to the hospital from the ED.

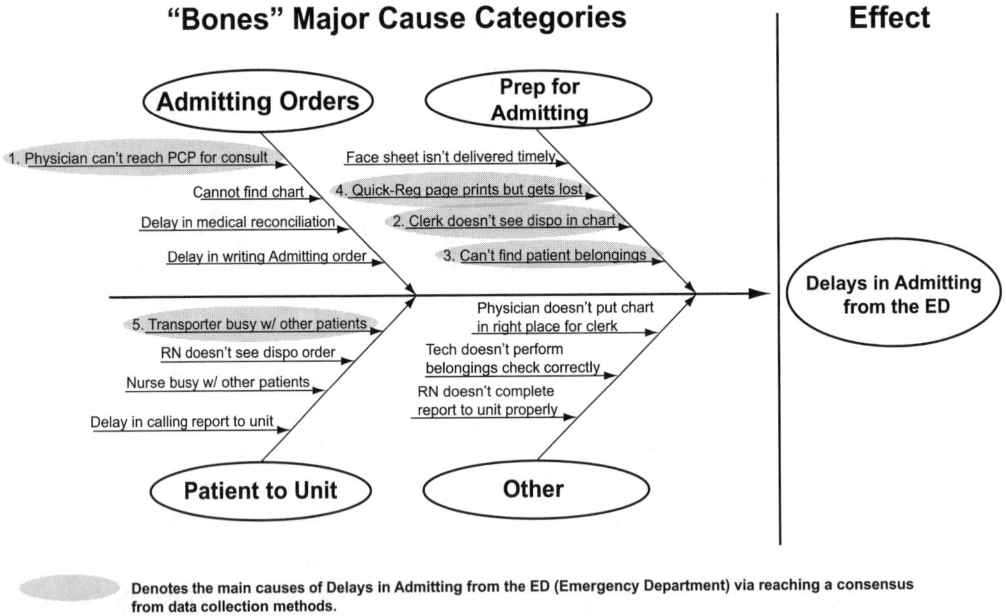

Note: As you use Lean Sigma tools, you will most likely find trends occurring (i.e., the same issues but stated a bit differently). This is normal. Continue with Brainstorming and 5 Why Analysis to consolidated like-issues through consensus building. It is good to have confirmation of why the issues or problems are occurring from these different perspectives.

Brainstorming

Brainstorming *is a technique used to generate a large number of ideas in a short period of time, typically 5 - 15 minutes, through full participation from an improvement team.*

Note: In brainstorming, there is one cardinal rule:

No idea is criticized!

There are two basic methods to brainstorming: structured and unstructured.

Structured - *A defined method in which each team member contributes his/her ideas in order until all ideas are exhausted.* This should be used if:

- The meeting will have a dominate team member
- The unstructured approach was used and numerous team members did not contribute their ideas
- The time element is critical
- The facilitator is contributing too many of the ideas in an unstructured brainstorming method

Approach a Structured brainstorming session as follows:

1. Find a quiet room with a flipchart or whiteboard (or have everyone log into the Remote Desktop Sharing application at a particular time).

2. Verbally state the problem, gain a consensus, and write it down so everyone can see it. It is critical that everyone understands the issue or problem. The facilitator should get a visual or verbal confirmation from each team member that the problem is understood. Further clarification of the problem at this stage may lend insight into potential solutions. Do not rush this step!

3. Each team member provides an idea in a round robin fashion. Round robin is receiving one idea from each person in a circular manner until everyone has stated their idea. If a team member does not have an idea for their turn, then they can pass. This rotation process encourages full participation. It may also increase some team members' anxieties about having their ideas exposed. The facilitator should acknowledge this and be helpful to any person that seems shy.

4. The team facilitator or scribe writes down each idea. Each idea should be written large enough for everyone to see. It should be exactly how the person stated the idea, without any interpretation.

5. Collect the ideas until everyone has spoken, thus indicating all ideas are exhausted. This process should take between five and fifteen minutes, depending on how well the problem was stated.

6. Review the entire list once everyone has passed. Remove any ideas that are identical in nature. If there are subtle differences keep them as separate ideas.

7. Show appreciation to everyone for their contributions. The facilitator should acknowledge that this was a very beneficial exercise for the team even though it may not have been easy for some.

Unstructured *- A method in which team members contribute their ideas as they occur (or come to mind) until all ideas are exhausted.*

There are two methods to conduct an unstructured brainstorming session. Method 1 is when the facilitator writes down any and all ideas from the team members on a whiteboard or flip chart in no specific order or fashion. Method 2 is when the facilitator provides Post-it Notes to each team member and each team member will then write their ideas on the Post-it Notes and place them on the whiteboard, flip chart, or wall. Method 2 is preferred when there is concern that some people find it difficult to speak in a public forum. Allow a maximum of 15 minutes for either method.

A brainstorming session starts with a clear question and ends with a raw list of ideas. Some ideas will be good and some will not. Once brainstorming is complete, duplicate (or similar type) ideas should be consolidated. Additional Lean tools and exercises will help to determine which of the ideas have the greatest impact on the identified problem.

Structured or unstructured brainstorming is used throughout the problem solving or improvement processes, depending on the team's knowledge of the problem and the specific tools that are being used. The principles of brainstorming are the same whether it is done in a conference room or through some type of Webinar or Remote Desktop Sharing tool with the team members. For example, PersonalBrain101 is a Web-based program that allows you to add files, Web pages, integrate Outlook and Webmail, etc. via the Internet for sharing ideas. There are many other competitive applications that do similar functions.

5 Whys

***5 Whys** is a question-asking method used to explore the cause/effect relationships underlying a particular problem, ultimately, to determine a root cause of a defect or problem.* Most often teams will observe a symptom of the problem rather than the problem itself. Always ask "Why?" while arriving at the answer with data.

Notice a few key things in the example below. First, at the second why question, and additional why question is asked. This often happens as problem solvers are investigating the problem. Look for situations where additional why questions need to be asked to clarify the situation. Secondly, notice how the 5 Why questions can actually lead to corrective actions or solutions to the problem. This too often happens during the use of the 5 why questioning technique. Lastly, notice how the number of why questions asked is not always 5. Many times problem solvers will not be able to answer more than a couple questions before more data and investigation are necessary.

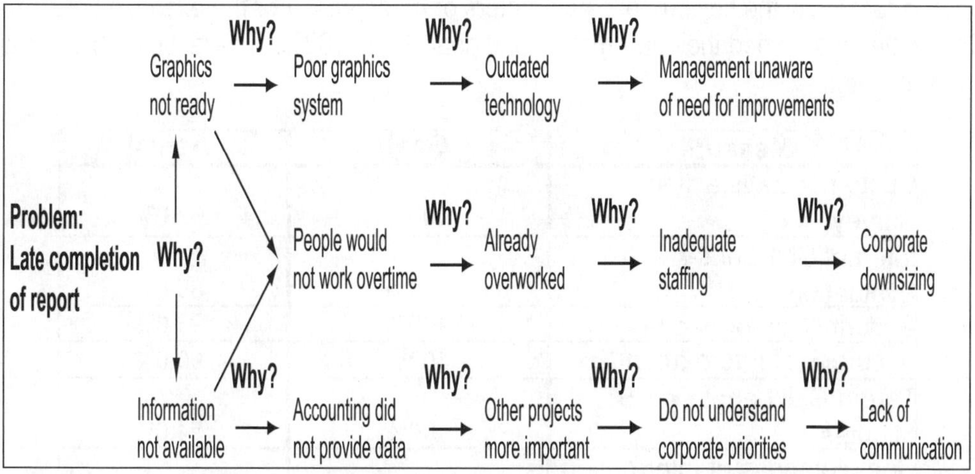

It should also be noted that if there are more than 5 Why questions asked and answered, the team has probably been taken astray with the 5 Why technique and further study should be conducted to ensure the questions are being answered with factual information. The key to remember with this technique is that is more of an inquisitive mindset and investigative or discovery process than it is a tool to deliver concrete solutions.

The 5 Why analysis can be done in a conference room or through some type of Webinar or Remote Desktop Sharing tool with the team members.

Note: The 5 Why analysis is data-driven (unlike brainstorming, which often is not).

Radar Charts

*A **Radar Chart**, also known as a Spider Chart or a Star Chart, because of its appearance, plots the values of each category along a separate axis that starts in the center of the chart and ends on the outer ring.*

Data that is arranged in columns or rows on a worksheet can be plotted in a Radar Chart. These charts compare the aggregate values of multiple data series and related data points. Each data series in the chart has a unique color or pattern and is represented in the chart legend. You can plot one or more data series in a chart. Pie Charts have only one data series.

Radar Charts are used to present between 4 - 12 data points where each measurement is targeted toward the same maximum goal. An example is a customer survey where the goal is 100% satisfaction in several different areas. The first step to constructing a Radar Chart is to identify the key process parameters or measures. For the example below, the Call Center determined their parameters and goals to be 100%. The last month's actuals are also stated.

Measure	Goal	Actual
Customer Satisfaction Survey	100%	67.0%
Internal Call Center Evaluation	100%	85.0%
Security Conformance	100%	98.0%
Accuracy of Information	100%	90.0%
Target Call Length ≤ 3.5 Minutes	100%	54.0%
Completeness of Information (Call back %)	100%	75.0%
Attendance	100%	99.6%
Safety	100%	100.0%

The following is the data presented in a Radar Chart (again, another function in MS Excel that is fairly easy to create):

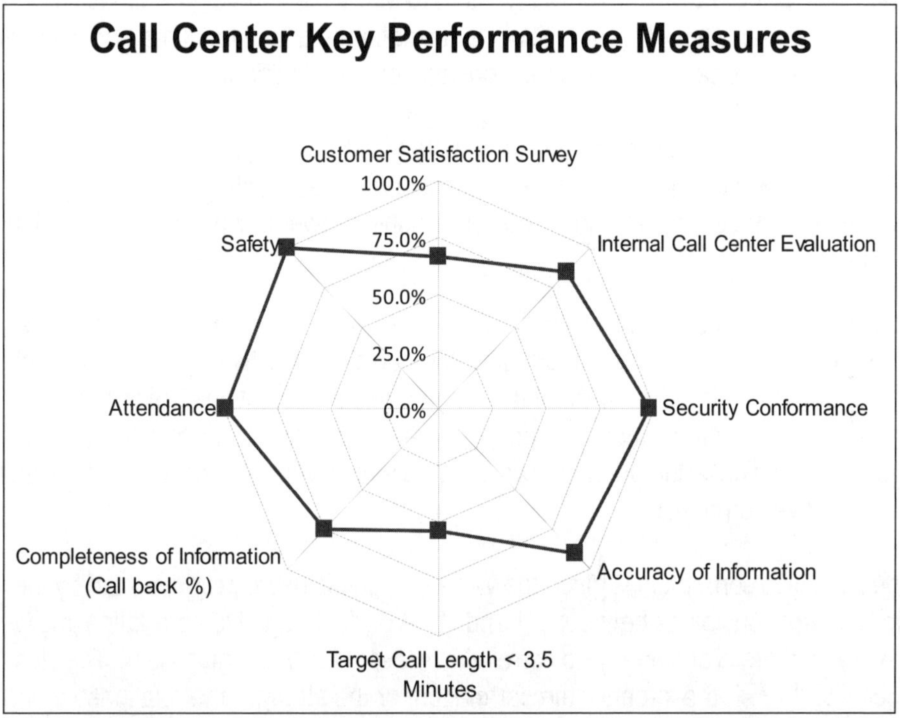

This Radar Chart clearly shows the areas of weakness for the Call Center and will help the improvement team select and prioritize improvement actions. The next step for the improvement team working on this project might be to determine why their customers are not satisfied (Customer Satisfaction Survey) and why phone calls are going over 3.5 minutes (Target Call Length $\leq$ 3.5 Minutes). A 5 Why analysis starting with the question "Why do calls go over 3.5 minutes?" might be a good starting point. Data may need to be collected, which could then be put into a Pareto Chart to illustrate the main reason for calls going over 3.5 minutes. A VA versus NVA Analysis may be of value as well. Perhaps the team would identify common reasons for calls that go over 3.5 minutes and could focus their improvement efforts on eliminating these causes.

Scatter Plots

Scatter (and Concentration) Plots *are used to study the possible relationship between one variable and another.* Through visual examination and additional mathematical analysis, problem solvers can determine relationships between variables.

Scatter Plots are similar to line graphs in that they use horizontal and vertical axes to plot data points. However, they have a very specific purpose. Scatter Plots show how much one variable is affected by another. The relationship between two variables is called their correlation.

Scatter Plots usually consist of a large body of data. The closer the data points come when plotted to making a straight line, the higher the correlation between the two variables, or the stronger the relationship. If the data points make a straight line going from the origin out to high x- and y-values, then the variables are said to have a positive correlation. If the line goes from a high-value on the y-axis down to a high-value on the x-axis, the variables have a negative correlation.

A perfect positive correlation is given the value of 1 and is usually represented by the letter r which can take on values between +1 and -1. A perfect negative correlation is given the value of -1. If there is absolutely no correlation present the value given is 0. The closer the number is to 1 or -1, the stronger the correlation, or the stronger the relationship between the variables.

In the examples that follow, actual to estimated costs are plotted against one another for labor and capital. It would be expected that if the estimates are accurate, the actual costs would be perfectly aligned or correlated with the estimated costs, and their plot would define a 45 degree line.

The Actual to Estimated Labor Cost plot below nearly defines this condition. R-squared represents the proportion of variation explained by a least squares (regression) model, and is automatically identified using the Scatter Plot feature in MS Excel. In this example the improvement team can conclude that the estimated labor costs are very accurate at predicting actual labor costs for the project due to the R^2 value of nearly 1.

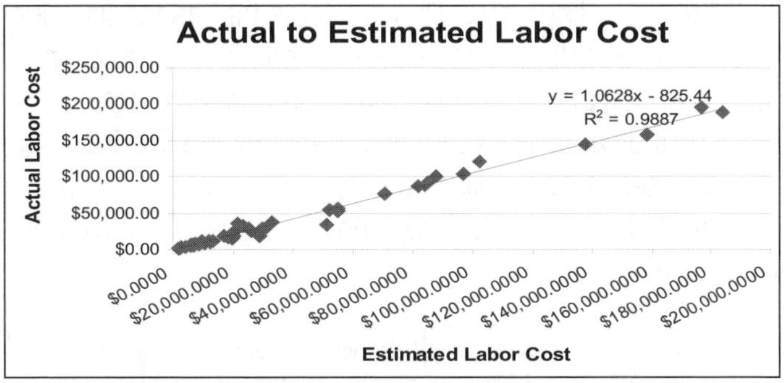

Careful analysis of the Scatter Plot below indicates several potential issues. First, the overall correlation is poor with an R^2 value of 0.4504. Either the estimated labor costs are poor estimates or the actual labor time is uncontrollable/unpredictable. This is a major concern for a service organization. If the organization cannot accurately predict their labor costs, they could either be non-competitive if their estimate is too high, or lose money if their estimate is too low. Upon closer examination, it appears that the estimated labor costs for service jobs below ~$75,000.00 estimated labor costs, have actual labor costs below the estimate, and for jobs over ~$75,000.00 estimated labor costs, there is very poor correlation or predictability. The team investigated each job and completed a Cause and Effect Diagram to understand why these conditions occurred. For improvements, the organization made adjustments in their standard labor cost estimating rates below $75,000.00 and created a standard process for estimating labor cost for jobs over $75,000.00 projected labor costs which included more detailed analysis and commitments from subcontractors.

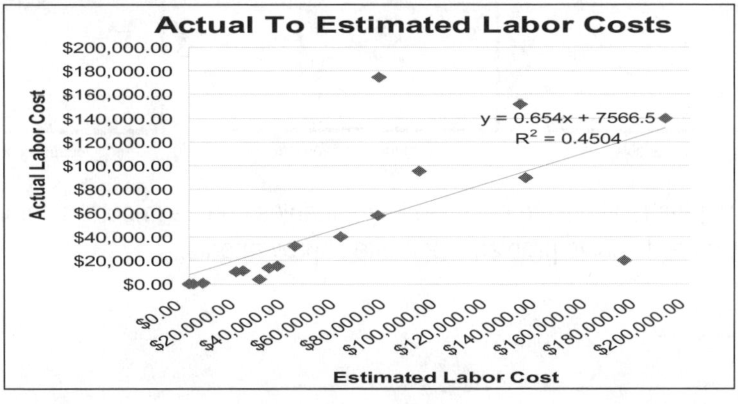

Scatter Plots indicate a correlation between two variables. Much can be learned about a process by understanding the relationship that variables have with each other. (See the various example plots below.) A Scatter Plot with points falling into the large circle of the No Correlation Scatter diagram indicates that the two variable act completely independently. Varying degrees of positive correlation are depicted in the Some Positive Correlation, and Strong Positive Correlation diagrams. This indicates that as the independent variable increases the dependant variable also increases. A negative correlation is illustrated in the Some Negative Correlation and Strong Negative Correlation diagrams. Scatter Plots with a negative correlation indicates that as the independent variable increases the dependant variable declines. Scatter Plots can also identify unique relationship patterns as illustrated in the Patterned Correlation diagram. This type of Scatter Plot indicates a changing relationship over a range of values.

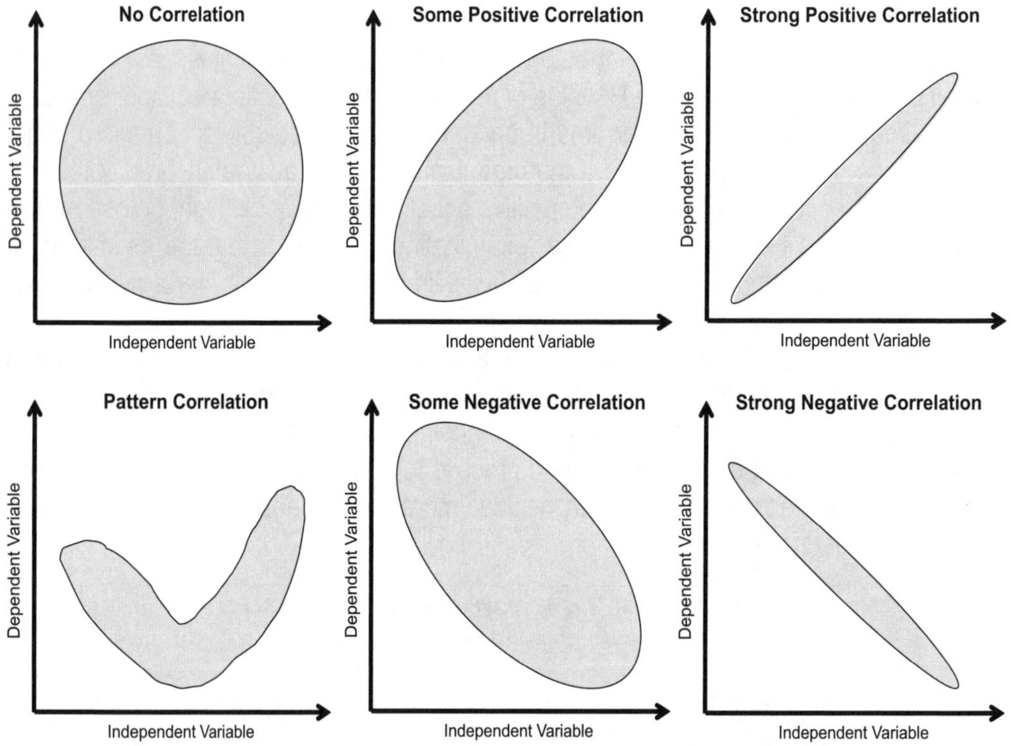

Understanding the relationship between key variables can be important for improvement teams when trying to solve problems or make improvements.

Process Capability

Process Capability *analysis is used to determine if a process, given its natural process variation in a stable state, is capable of meeting the customer's specifications or requirements.* Determining process stability is done by monitoring a process output over time, using Run Charts (Chapter 5) and or Statistical Process Control Charts (Chapter 8). True improvement in a process is achieved by balancing stability with the capability of meeting the customer's requirements, otherwise known as process capability.

To estimate process capability, simple calculations from a data sample must first be determined. The definitions and formulas for process average, range, and standard deviation are:

Process Average = Mean = X-Bar = Sum of all data points / Number of data points

Range = R = Difference between the largest and smallest data point

Standard Deviation (SD) = Root Mean Square (RMS) =
σ = [Sum of ((X- X-bar)^2 / Number of data points)]$^{1/2}$

Calculators having a "statistics" mode can simplify these calculations and complete these calculations for you after all data points have been entered. If higher level statistical computations are anticipated being used by the project team, it is recommended that the team secure a statistics capable calculator, or software application, and seek the assistance of individuals that know how to use them.

Process capabilities are calculated as follows:

Cp = Process Capability = Tolerance Range / 6σ
Cpu = Process capability to the upper tolerance limit = (Upper Tolerance Limit – Process Average) / 3σ
Cpl = Process capability to the lower tolerance limit = (Process Average- Lower Tolerenace limit) / 3σ
Cpk = the lower of Cpu or Cpl = (Closest Specification Limit to Process Average – Process Average) / 3σ

Estimates of long term process capability are best predicted by the Cpk value. Cpk considers both the process spread (σ) and the process centering to specification nominal. The standard deviation (SD) representing the process variation is proportional to the overall process spread. The SD is proportional to the process spread. A process being 6σ or 6σ capable means that ± 6σ process width falls within the specifications or tolerance limits, as illustrated in the following diagram.

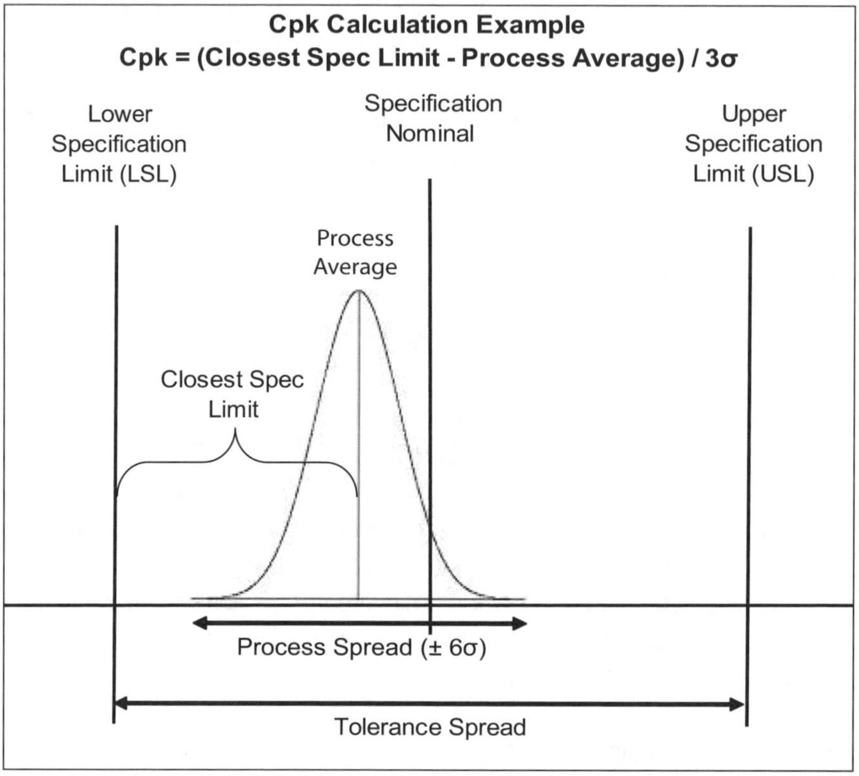

The following table shows the relationship between sigma level and Cpk (1.5 sigma long term shift included):

Cpk	Sigma Level	Process Yield	PPM Defective
0.33	1	0.6827	691,462
0.67	2	0.9545	308,538
1	3	0.9973	66,807
1.33	4	0.9999	6,210
1.67	5	1	233
2	6	1	3.4

To calculate the Cpk, collect data, calculate the data/process average and standard deviation, then complete the Cpk calculation. An example of this calculation for a simple data set is illustrated by the example from a heated self-storage service in Northern Minnesota where extremely low winter temperatures are the norm. The owner guarantees a temperature range between 35 and 55 degrees Fahrenheit (° F) during the winter to prevent freezing and has the thermostat set at 45 ° F. The following 40 measurements were taken from four different thermometers (1-4) located at various locations in the storage areas.

	A	B	C	D	E
10	DATA	1	2	3	4
11	1	38	37.9	38.9	42.8
12	2	36	38	43	40
13	3	39.3	39	41	46.8
14	4	38.8	43	36.7	38
15	5	38.9	40	42.8	39
16	6	43	42	40	43
17	7	41	37.8	45	40
18	8	36.7	38.9	38	42
19	9	42.8	39	39	37.8
20	10	40	38.8	43	38.9

	A	B	C	D	E	F	G	H	I	J	K	L	M	N
5	Nominal specification				45		Average			40.1150			Cp	1.375
6	Upper tolerance limit				55		Standard deviation			2.4248			Cpl	0.703
7	Lower tolerance limit				35								Cpu	2.046
8													Cpk	0.703

This analysis indicates that the current heating system is not statistically capable of ensuring a minimum of 35° F. The owner has a couple of options for improvement. Since the process nominal or Average of 40.115° F is below the tolerance average or Nominal specification of 45° F, the owner could increase the thermostat setting to shift the process average up to the tolerance nominal of 45° F, or the owner could modify the minimum temperature guarantee to 32° F, which would shift the Cpk to 1.116.

Generally, there are three ways to improve process capabitliy:

1. Ensure the process is centered on the process tolerances
2. Reduce variation in the process output (which narrows the +/- 3 sigma spread
3. Increase the tolerance limits

Improvement teams should review each of these areas.

The illustrations below show various levels of process capabilities and possible actions to improve process capability:

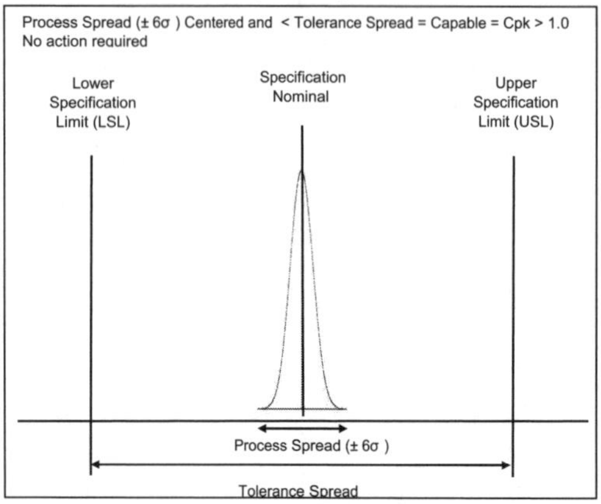

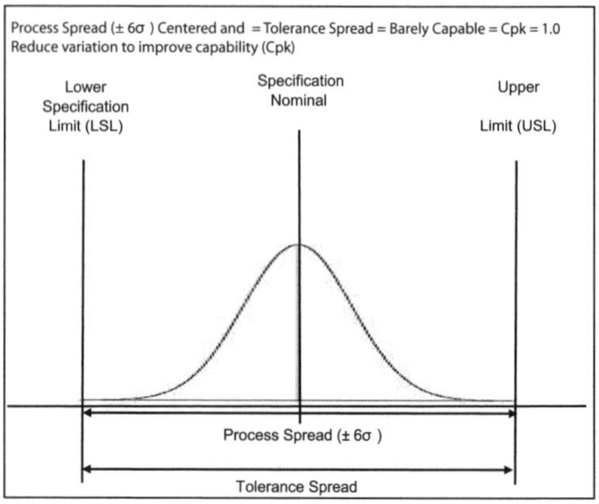

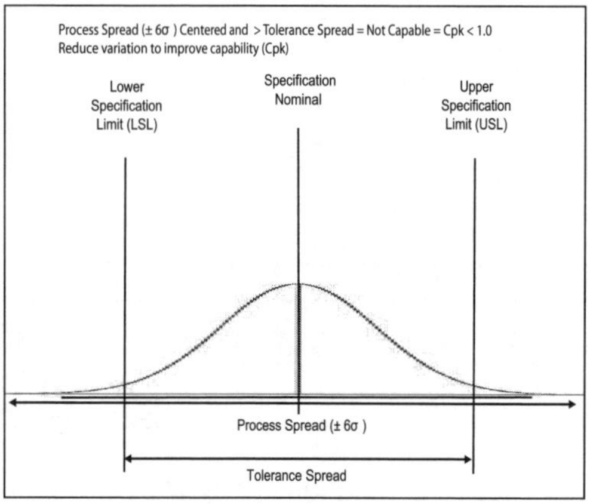

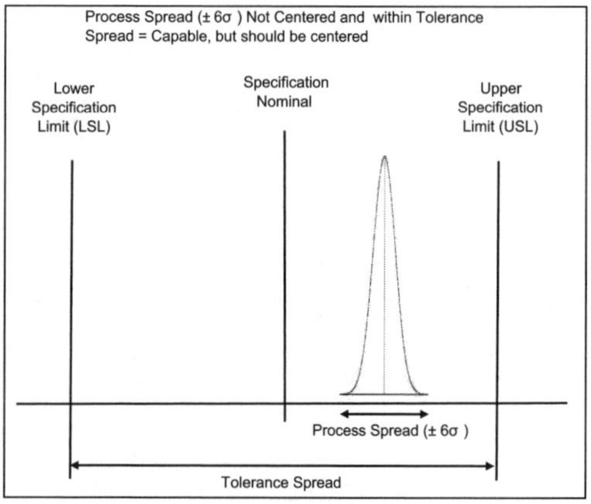

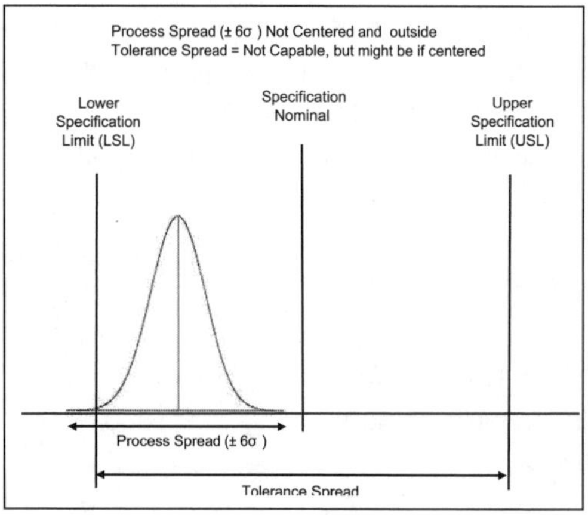

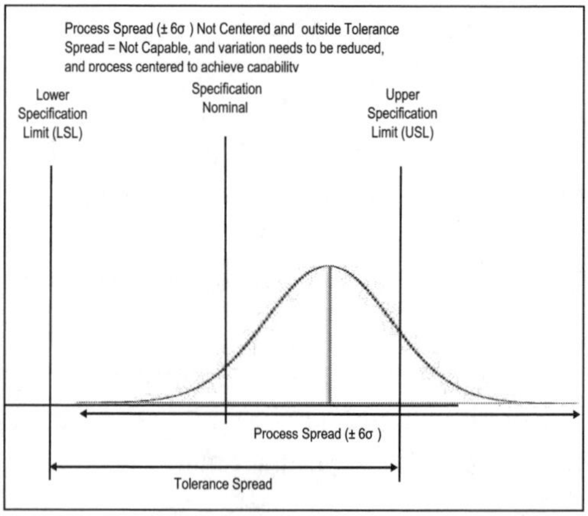

Use Process Capability analysis to better understand the long term process capability to meet customer requirements.

Force Field Analysis

***Force Field Analysis** is an extremely useful tool for understanding and illustrating the forces for and against an idea, direction, decision, or strategy.* The logic behind this technique is that when change occurs there are always two sides to change: one side is proactive and is driving the change while the other side is resistant to change and preventing change from occurring.

When using this technique, a team can carefully identify, by means of a diagram, both the positive and negative forces and then find ways to enhance the forces that are pro-change and reduce the forces that resist change. The following is an example of a Force Field Analysis for automating the guest reservation system in a hotel:

<u>Forces For Change</u>	<u>Forces Against Change</u>
Less booking errors – especially, double bookings	*Staff layoffs*
Ability to track customers	*Loss of management control*
Automatic calculations	*Uncertainty and apprehension*
More sustainable – require less paper records	*Disruption*
Accessible anytime	

Interrelationship Diagrams

***Interrelationship Diagram** is an analysis tool that allows a team to understand and identify the cause-and-effect relationships among critical issues.* Interrelationship Diagrams are used to understand and illustrate the inputs, outputs, and relationships of key processes or data. They make it easy to identify the factors in a situation that drive the observed outcomes.

Approach creating an Interrelationship Diagram as follows:

1. Develop the problem or improvement statement and ensure it is clear to all team members.
2. Develop issues around the problem or improvement statement (from brainstorming, 5 Why analysis, Issues and Opportunities Log, etc.). Write issues on Post-It Notes, white boards, fllip charts, etc. if team is physically present.
3. Arrange the issues in a circle.
4. Identify cause-and-effect relationships starting at any issue by determining if there is no cause/effect relationship, a weak cause/effect relationship, or a strong cause/effect relationship.
5. Draw arrows to indicate directions of influence. For each relationship pair identified in (4), draw an arrow with solid lines to indicate strong relationships and an arrow with dashed lines to indicate weaker relationships. Always denote by the arrow in the direction of the strong influence. Never draw two-headed arrows.
6. Total the number of arrows going in and out for each issue.
7. Identify possible root cause(s) of the problem or improvement statement by noting the higher number of incoming arrows.
8. Use the information and schedule improvement activities.

The following are guidelines for when to use an Interrelationship Diagram:

- When trying to understand links between ideas or cause-and-effect relationships, such as trying to identify an area of greatest impact for improvement
- When a complex issue is being analyzed for causes
- When a complex solution is being implemented
- After generating a Fishbone Diagram or similar analysis tool to more completely explore the relations of ideas

A customer satisfaction improvement team at a customer processing call service center determined the following factors were affecting the effective handling of a customer complaint:

- Timeliness – Did the issue get resolved quickly?
- Customer Service Representative (CSR) training
- Ability to manage customers and customer emotions
- CSR knowledge
- CSR empathy and friendliness
- CSR authority to resolve
- Cost

The following example illustrates the resulting Interrelationship Diagram developed by the improvement team.

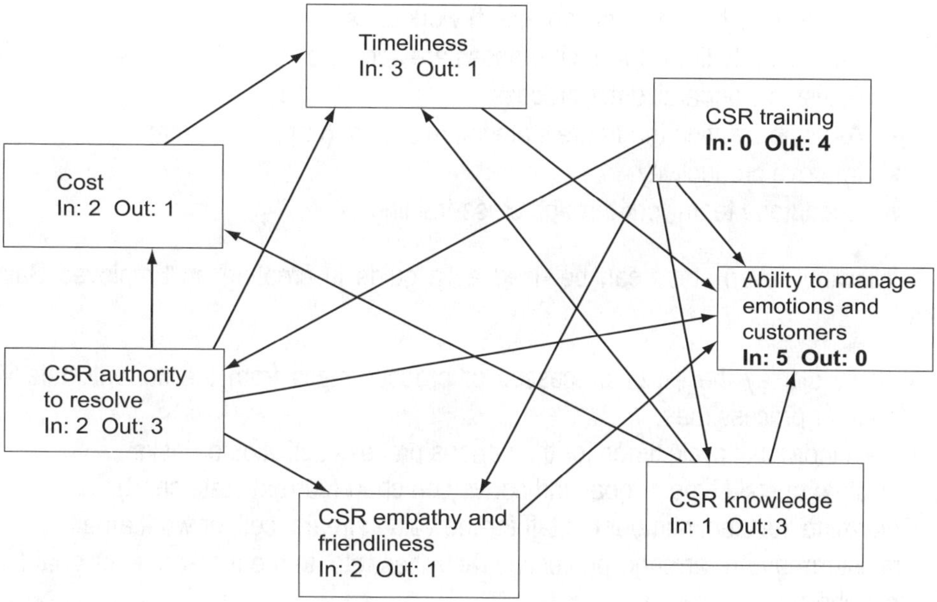

To determine the key drivers for customer satisfaction review the number of inputs and outputs from each factor. The factor with the most outputs (i.e., **CSR training In:0 Out:4**) is a key area for improvement as it affects the outcome or results of many different areas. If this area is improved, the results or outcomes will improve many areas. The area with the most inputs (i.e., **Ability to manage emotions and customers In:5 Out:0**) will be affected the most by any improvements implemented. For this example, it is clear that Customer Service Representative training is the driver for the process outcomes.

Employee Balance Charts

*The **Employee Balance Chart** is a visual display, in the form of a Bar Chart, that represents the work elements and cycle times relative to the total value stream cycle time and takt time (or pitch)* Typically there will be a current and future (or proposed) Employee Balance Chart created.

The current state Employee Balance Chart is analyzing the current state of how work relative to the value stream is allocated and ends with the future state Employee Balance Chart that represents an even and fair distribution of work, ensuring that customer demand is met with a continuous flow mentality.

Creating a current and future Employee Balance Chart will accomplish the following:

- Determine the number of staff needed for a given demand (or value stream)
- Evenly distribute (i.e., or represent) work units
- Ensure cycle times for each process are accurate
- Assist to standardize the process
- Assist in creating the future state value stream (or process) map
- Improve productivity
- Encourage teamwork through cross-training

The following seven steps can be used as a guide in creating an Employee Balance Chart:

1. Visually display the list of processes or process steps from the current state value stream or process map.
2. Obtain individual cycle times for the various process activities or tasks.
3. Calculate the takt time or goal and convey on chart (current state chart).
4. Determine the ideal number of staff for the value stream, cell, or work area.
5. Brainstorm and re-arrange processes, activities, etc. to meet takt time or goal (future state chart).
6. Determine improvement activities that will ensure (5) is completed.
7. Create standard work procedures and train staff.

The illustration on the next page shows a current and future state Employee Balance Chart of the Emergency Department Patient Dipostion to Hospital Admit value stream. Note the cycle times, takt time, process positions, and improvements (future state only). Many times balancing work loads within a department will require numerous improvements.

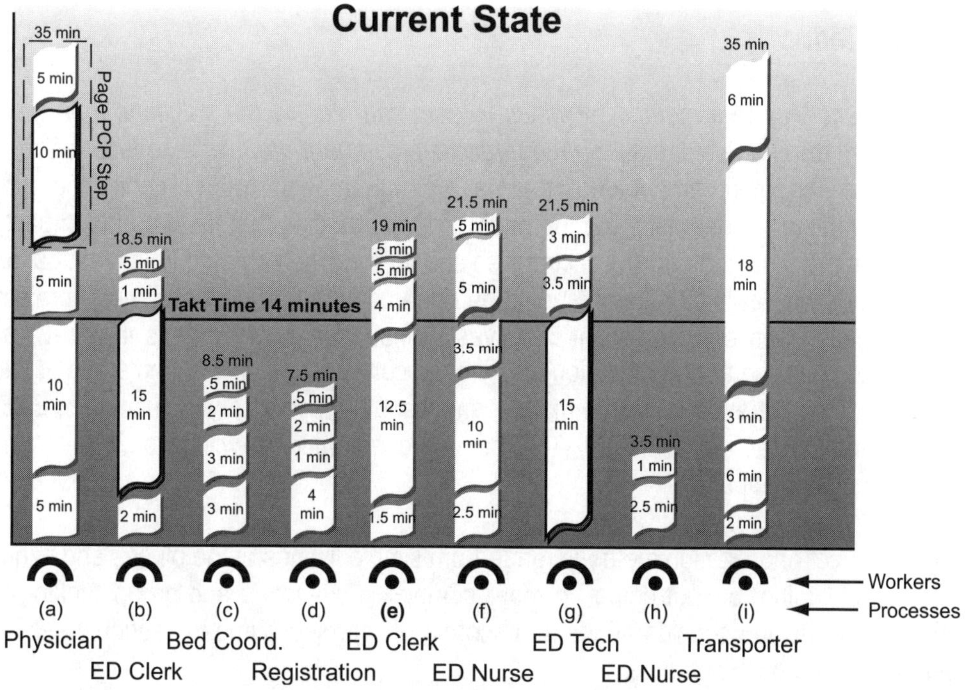
Current State
35 min
5 min
10 min
Page PCP Step
5 min
10 min
5 min
18.5 min
.5 min
1 min
15 min
2 min
Takt Time 14 minutes
8.5 min
.5 min
2 min
3 min
3 min
7.5 min
.5 min
2 min
1 min
4 min
19 min
.5 min
.5 min
4 min
12.5 min
1.5 min
21.5 min
.5 min
5 min
3.5 min
10 min
2.5 min
21.5 min
3 min
3.5 min
15 min
3.5 min
1 min
2.5 min
35 min
6 min
18 min
3 min
6 min
2 min
Workers
Processes
(a) (b) (c) (d) (e) (f) (g) (h) (i)
Physician
ED Clerk
Bed Coord.
Registration
ED Clerk
ED Nurse
ED Tech
ED Nurse
Transporter

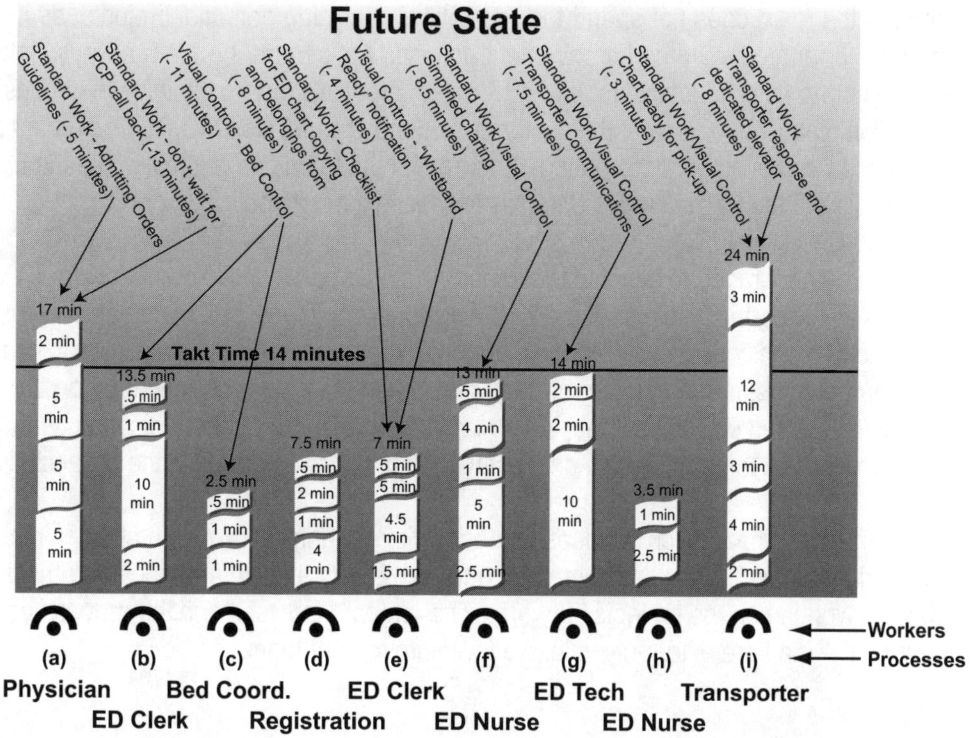
Future State
Standard Work - Admitting Orders Guidelines (- 5 minutes)
Standard Work - don't wait for PCP call back (-13 minutes)
Visual Controls - Bed Control (- 11 minutes)
Standard Work - Checklist for ED chart copying and belongings from (- 8 minutes)
Visual Controls - "Wristband Ready" notification (- 4 minutes)
Simplified charting (- 8.5 minutes)
Standard Work/Visual Control Transporter Communications (- 7.5 minutes)
Standard Work/Visual Control Chart ready for pick-up (- 3 minutes)
Standard Work/Visual Control dedicated elevator (- 8 minutes)
Standard Work Transporter response and
17 min
2 min
5 min
5 min
5 min
Takt Time 14 minutes
13.5 min
.5 min
1 min
10 min
2 min
2.5 min
.5 min
1 min
1 min
7.5 min
.5 min
2 min
1 min
4 min
7 min
.5 min
.5 min
4.5 min
1.5 min
13 min
.5 min
4 min
1 min
5 min
2.5 min
14 min
2 min
2 min
10 min
3.5 min
1 min
2.5 min
24 min
3 min
12 min
3 min
4 min
2 min
Workers
Processes
(a) (b) (c) (d) (e) (f) (g) (h) (i)
Physician
ED Clerk
Bed Coord.
Registration
ED Clerk
ED Nurse
ED Tech
ED Nurse
Transporter

Impact Maps

*The **Impact Map** is a method by which a team can identify the solutions that will most likely have the greatest impact on the target improvement area with the least effort.* Opportunities and improvement ideas that have a high impact on the organization and are easily completed should take the top priority. Opportunities that have a high impact, but will take more time and effort to accomplish should be targeted next. Ideas that have little impact, but are easily completed should be done as time permits or as "filler" projects to be completed between significant initiatives. Finally, projects or ideas that have a low potential impact on the organization and are difficult or expensive to implement could be considered at a later date. In summary, teams should reach a consensus on the EASE of implementation, as well as the IMPACT that improvement ideas will have on the organization or process output.

Other project prioritization methods range from simple listings of the pluses and minuses, or risks of "doing" or "not doing" to more complex multi-voting and group ranking techniques that include considerations and scoring of a project's impact, seriousness, risks, urgency and growth potential.

Be sure the team does not spend too much time analyzing potential projects, as it is far more important to begin the improvement actions. Make sure the team always looks for low cost or no cost solutions first and advocates "creativity before capital" when considering action plans. Also, protect the customer and the organization by minimizing the risk of a proposed improvement not working. Ensure that the team can return the situation to the current state if the improvement idea fails to meet expectations.

Teams are encouraged to develop the Impact Map in a participative manner, where everyone has the opportunity to express their thoughts and opinions, and dialog and discussion are used to reach consensus on project priorities. Team members develop a high commitment and ownership to improvement activities when they have an influence on the projects being worked on. Impact Maps also provide an excellent communication vehicle for the improvement team to explain and justify their priorities to others in the organization.

The completed Impact Map provides the team with a graphical representation of improvement priorities. With this, the team members can easily explain and show to others why they are working on the projects they are. The Impact Map itself and the process used to develop the map are extremely valuable for improvement teams.

Impact Maps provide three key things for improvement teams. First, they clearly identify improvement priorities; secondly, the participative process used to develop an Impact Map develops a high level of understanding and commitment from team members, and finally, the Impact Map documents the improvement project priorities in a manner that can easily be communicated to others in the organization. The following Impact Map is from a customer service improvement team that needed to prioritize the actions due to low customer satisfaction survey scores:

Impact Map			
IMPACT of the result (1 - Very Low to 10 - Very High) EASE of achieving (1 - Very Difficult to 10 - Very Easy)			
No.	Opportunity Log Items	EASE	IMPACT
1.	Update new fulfillment system	2	9
2.	Create new Sales update program	3	6
3.	Create IT solutions for discounts	2	10
4.	Create training plan for CSRs	10	3
5.	Create standard work and balance work loads	8	8
6.	Update fulfillment system to verify order and price discounts	7	9
7.	Create visual control for online checklist and train everyone	9	7

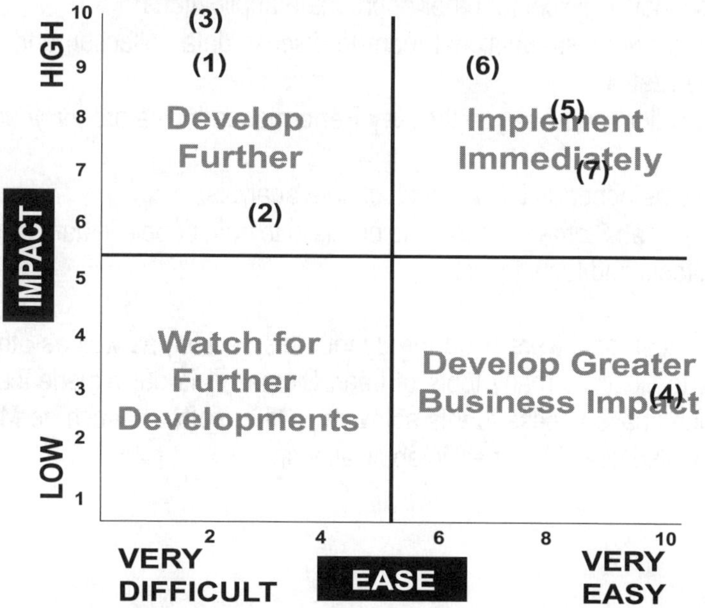

Chapter Summary

This chapter overviews the Analyze Phase of the DMAIC improvement process. Several data analytical tools are reviewed to help improvement teams break down data into logical presentations and illustrations that actually lead the team to the next phase in the DMAIC process. If done properly, the analytical tools help the data "tell a story" and provide next step direction and priorities. Improvement teams can use this chapter to provide better analysis and presentation of data, as well as to determine exactly what data to collect, and how to collect it. The Analyze Phase chapter illustrates several analytical tools for diagnosing possible root causes regarding why a process is not performing to the expected targets or goals. By using these key analysis tools, improvement teams are able to better identify and prioritize improvement activities.

Lean Sigma for Service Excellence Applications

These observations may assist in understanding how to apply the concepts and tools contained in this chapter:

- ❖ Complete a Web-search for other applications of the analytical tools listed in this chapter.
- ❖ Complete a Web-search to watch 2 - 5 minute short You-Tube videos on how-to use these tools in Excel (or other appropriate applications).
- ❖ Gather a small cross-functional team to discuss data collection and analysis at your organization.
- ❖ Begin to collect and analyze the Key Performance Indicators for your organization.
- ❖ Identify some opportunities to conduct data analysis.
- ❖ Develop a Lean Sigma tools training program to train people in data collection and analysis tools and techniques.

Note: Microsoft Excel tools were used throughout this section, as well as other parts in this book, to illustrate many tools of Lean Sigma. It is our experience that most organizations have access to this software. Other software such as Minitab (and others) are also useful for specific applications.

Analyze Phase Readiness Guide

The following Analyze Phase Readiness Guide allows you to ensure there is application of the chapter's content before proceeding to apply the Lean Sigma tools and concepts in the next chapter. If you score less than 70%, consider working on the lower scoring areas before moving on.

Analyze Phase Readiness Guide	
Use the following 5-level Likert item scale to rank each of the statements: **1 = Strongly Disagree** **2 = Disagree** **3 = Neither Agree nor Disagree** **4 = Agree** **5 = Strongly Agree**	
	Score
1. My organization does a good job of differentiating between value-added and non value-added activities.	
2. My organization does a good job of identifying constraints or bottlenecks in a process.	
3. My organizations is good at defining target improvement outcomes.	
4. My organization does a good job of using spreadsheets and tools for analyzing large volumes of data.	
5. My organization does a good job of understanding the pace of customer demand.	
6. My organization effectively uses simple tools to graphically illustrate and stratify critical data.	
7. My organization does a good job of understanding correlation between variables.	
8. My organization is effective in using 5 Why Analysis, brainstorming, Impact Maps, etc. to facilitate team decision-making.	
9. My organization has a system in place to properly analyze the data.	
10. I feel comfortable performing a Value-Added versus Non Value-Added Analysis.	
11. I feel comfortable performing Constraint or Bottleneck Analysis.	
12. I feel comfortable presenting data in different formats.	
13. I feel comfortable using demand analysis tools to understand the pace of customer demand.	
14. I feel comfortable using various tools for graphically illustrating and stratifying critical data.	
15. I feel comfortable utilizing tools for understaning relationships and interrelationships.	
16. I feel comfortable using Force Field Analysis.	
17. I feel comfortable using 5 Why Analysis, brainstorming, Impact Maps, etc. to facilitate team decision-making.	
18. I feel comfortable using brainstorming to facilitate team discussion.	
19. I see the value using the DMAIC process and tools for analyzing projects.	
20. I believe my organization should utilize and apply the concepts and tools discussed in this chapter.	
Total Score	

Case Review – Analyze Phase for Lakeview Landscaping

Lakeview Landscaping (LL) is a high-end landscaping firm targeting commercial markets and projects. They offer landscape design, construction, and maintenance services to architects, builders, property managers, and owners of commercial buildings. For new commercial buildings, they like to be involved in the early stages of the design with the architects so they are in a good position to secure the design contract. In most cases, if they can land the design work, they also get the construction and maintenance work. However, the markets are getting more competitive lately and most organizations now send each phase of the project out for competitive bids.

John has recently learned about Lean Sigma methods from his friend Bob who runs a project management firm and has decided to launch a Lean Sigma project to address his concerns. John decided to assemble the key leaders from each area to launch the Lean Sigma improvement project.

Define Phase

During the kick-off session, John outlined his two concerns to his three person team. The team included Matt, the Construction Manager, Doug, the Maintenance Manager, and himself, as the Team or Project Leader. John thought that by leading the project he would be able to learn and understand the use of the Lean Sigma DMAIC methods and tools at a higher level.

The main objectives were to eliminate the customer complaints and to improve construction project profits. On the recommendation of Bob, the team completed an initial Team Charter and agreed to focus on two key measures of construction project profit and maintenance service customer complaints. With the Team Charter complete, the team began to gather the data for the key measures.

Measure Phase

John took the assignment to gather the data on profit for the last year. Matt began his data search by gathering estimated and actual costs for all projects completed within the last two years. The data was buried in files, but with some administrative help, the data was collected and placed in simple spreadsheet format.

In the meantime, Doug gathered the data from customer complaints for the same time period. Doug's data showed the frequency and type of customer complaint.

Analyze Phase

John compiled the following spreadsheet on projected costs for analysis:

Lakeview Landscaping Construction Estimating Variance

Landscaping Installation		LABOR $					MATERIALS				EQUIPMENT				GM %		
Job Number	Job Name / Builder	Original Estimate	Actual Cost	Total Variance	Total Variance	$ Variance	Original Estimate	Actual Cost	Total Variance	$ Variance	Original Estimate	Actual Cost	Total Variance	$ Variance	Original Estimate	Final Actual	Profit
0010	Kelly	$15,837.50	$15,846.40	-0.06%	-0.06%	($8.90)	$2,134.40	$1,023.30	52.06%	$1,111.10	$2,950.00	$2,040.00	30.85%	$910.00	25.83%	35.15%	-9.32%
0011	Frazer	$687.50	$735.50	-6.98%	-6.98%	($48.00)	$190.00	$406.40	-113.89%	($216.40)	$150.00	$0.00	100.00%	$150.00	33.30%	29.32%	3.98%
0012	Frazer	$2,535.00	$2,840.80	-12.06%	-12.06%	($305.80)	$859.30	$1,149.90	-33.82%	($290.60)	$1,164.50	$1,106.20	5.01%	$58.30	42.00%	35.15%	6.85%
0013	Meyers	$5,514.50	$5,321.20	3.51%	3.51%	$193.30	$330.00	$221.10	33.00%	$108.90	$590.00	$545.70	7.51%	$44.30	29.06%	32.86%	-3.80%
0014	Mayflower	$8,385.00	$8,767.80	-4.57%	-4.57%	($382.80)	$832.00	$424.50	48.98%	$407.50	$1,405.20	$1,748.30	-24.42%	($343.10)	32.90%	32.47%	0.43%
0015	Appleton	$8,760.00	$10,066.40	-14.91%	-14.91%	($1,306.40)	$1,151.20	$1,082.40	5.98%	$68.80	$1,315.00	$1,059.30	19.44%	$255.70	31.29%	28.82%	2.47%
0016	Newcastle	$3,000.00	$2,880.00	4.00%	4.00%	$120.00	$320.00	$318.50	0.47%	$1.50	$360.00	$309.30	14.08%	$50.70	41.96%	49.07%	-7.11%
0017	Chief Brothers	$3,167.70	$3,149.10	0.59%	0.59%	$18.60	$227.10	$355.60	-56.58%	($128.50)	$670.00	$590.90	11.81%	$79.10	31.83%	41.05%	-9.22%
0018	Graphics Plus	$420.00	$400.70	4.60%	4.60%	$19.30	$496.70	$96.40	80.59%	$400.30	$135.00	$30.90	77.11%	$104.10	39.90%	33.16%	6.74%
0019	Eastman	$5,250.00	$5,520.60	-5.15%	-5.15%	($270.60)	$668.10	$648.70	2.90%	$19.40	$925.00	$475.40	48.61%	$449.60	32.00%	34.01%	-2.01%
0020	Bucksport	$9,657.20	$10,289.50	-6.55%	-6.55%	($632.30)	$1,700.30	$1,878.90	-10.50%	($178.60)	$1,917.20	$2,201.90	-14.85%	($284.70)	32.82%	34.98%	-2.16%
0021	Versa	$930.00	$897.80	3.46%	3.46%	$32.20	$62.70	$62.70	0.00%	$0.00	$107.00	$91.90	14.11%	$15.10	39.00%	44.10%	-5.10%
0022	West Point	$18,372.50	$18,829.20	-2.49%	-2.49%	($456.70)	$2,183.90	$177.50	91.87%	$2,006.40	$2,506.50	$1,851.90	26.12%	$654.60	29.51%	32.71%	-3.20%
0023	Summit	$1,185.00	$1,247.30	-5.26%	-5.26%	($62.30)	$230.00	$89.30	61.17%	$140.70	$387.80	$777.90	-100.59%	($390.10)	30.66%	50.28%	-19.62%
0024	PCA	$1,685.00	$1,801.70	-6.93%	-6.93%	($116.70)	$279.20	$207.00	25.86%	$72.20	$480.00	$465.20	3.08%	$14.80	41.68%	42.52%	-0.84%
0025	Paperworks	$2,910.00	$1,942.30	33.25%	33.25%	$967.70	$595.10	$514.30	13.58%	$80.80	$780.00	$449.00	42.44%	$331.00	28.63%	50.42%	-21.79%
0026	Blue water	$8,500.00	$9,100.30	-7.06%	-7.06%	($600.30)	$805.00	$623.50	22.55%	$181.50	$1,860.00	$1,945.40	-4.59%	($85.40)	37.52%	35.42%	2.10%
0027	Ridgewood	$620.00	$638.90	-3.05%	-3.05%	($18.90)	$263.00	$260.10	1.10%	$2.90	$50.00	$19.20	61.60%	$30.80	37.49%	38.48%	-0.99%
0028	Mead	$720.00	$683.40	5.08%	5.08%	$36.60	$120.00	$114.80	4.33%	$5.20	$196.50	$184.90	5.90%	$11.60	34.81%	36.54%	-1.73%
0029	Finch	$608.50	$685.50	-12.65%	-12.65%	($77.00)	$120.00	$114.80	4.33%	$5.20	$196.50	$184.90	5.90%	$11.60	34.81%	36.54%	-1.73%
0030	Welcher	$2,154.60	$3,502.70	-62.57%	-62.57%	($1,348.10)	$270.00	$168.40	37.63%	$101.60	$688.00	$548.10	20.33%	$139.90	35.52%	11.39%	24.13%
0031	Tampa	$278.90	$321.10	-15.13%	-15.13%	($42.20)	$44.90	$8.30	81.51%	$36.60	$82.50	$20.30	75.39%	$62.20	33.48%	42.75%	-9.27%
0032	Deikema	$2,050.80	$2,530.60	-23.40%	-23.40%	($479.80)	$182.00	$51.90	71.48%	$130.10	$255.00	$459.20	-80.08%	($204.20)	32.88%	23.74%	9.14%
0033	Windwood	$2,005.40	$1,847.20	7.89%	7.89%	$158.20	$245.00	$51.90	78.82%	$193.10	$674.50	$1,077.30	-59.72%	($402.80)	28.92%	27.40%	1.52%
0034	Windwood	$1,227.30	$967.80	21.14%	21.14%	$259.50	$309.10	$477.20	-54.38%	($168.10)	$285.00	$81.00	71.58%	$204.00	23.47%	35.88%	-12.41%
0035	Klark	$3,112.50	$3,129.80	-0.56%	-0.56%	($17.30)	$913.20	$962.50	-5.40%	($49.30)	$604.00	$314.20	47.98%	$289.80	36.83%	41.66%	-4.83%
0036	Augusta	$17,660.00	$19,633.50	-11.17%	-11.17%	($1,973.50)	$2,420.00	$921.90	61.90%	$1,498.10	$3,475.00	$5,200.00	-49.64%	($1,725.00)	26.96%	21.47%	5.49%
0037	Appleton	$2,325.20	$3,287.10	-41.37%	-41.37%	($961.90)	$340.00	$128.50	62.21%	$211.50	$610.00	$465.30	23.72%	$144.70	28.85%	25.87%	2.98%
0038	Air Force	$1,967.60	$1,445.70	26.52%	26.52%	$521.90	$86.60	$210.20	-142.73%	($123.60)	$425.00	$542.90	-27.74%	($117.90)	31.97%	39.67%	-7.70%
0039	West Point	$721.90	$623.50	13.63%	13.63%	$98.40	$50.00	$45.00	10.00%	$5.00	$25.00	$110.50	-342.00%	($85.50)	41.08%	40.35%	0.73%
0040	Summit	$5,146.00	$3,356.80	34.77%	34.77%	$1,789.20	$485.00	$595.80	-22.85%	($110.80)	$640.00	$274.10	57.17%	$365.90	31.08%	48.73%	-17.65%
0041	PCA	$5,496.00	$5,677.60	-3.30%	-3.30%	($181.60)	$760.00	$755.00	0.66%	$5.00	$650.00	$545.40	16.09%	$104.60	32.34%	32.29%	0.05%
0042	Paperworks	$3,284.20	$3,678.70	-12.01%	-12.01%	($394.50)	$925.40	$598.60	35.31%	$326.80	$914.50	$1,165.70	-27.47%	($251.20)	31.80%	27.35%	4.45%
0043	Page	$10,238.50	$12,014.30	-17.34%	-17.34%	($1,775.80)	$1,015.00	$466.60	54.03%	$548.40	$1,452.50	$5,043.30	-247.22%	($3,590.80)	20.95%	8.87%	12.08%
0044	Mead	$13,773.30	$14,399.90	-4.55%	-4.55%	($626.60)	$1,929.00	$1,610.30	16.52%	$318.70	$2,465.00	$1,650.30	33.05%	$814.70	24.55%	25.37%	-0.82%
0045	Blue water	$7,074.20	$7,665.50	-8.36%	-8.36%	($591.30)	$1,416.50	$764.20	46.05%	$652.30	$1,093.00	$799.10	26.89%	$293.90	21.15%	25.41%	-4.26%
0046	Ridgewood	$685.60	$535.50	21.89%	21.89%	$150.10	$306.30	$161.30	47.34%	$145.00	$195.10	$239.10	-22.55%	($44.00)	40.57%	53.15%	-12.58%
0047	Mead	$8,181.30	$8,688.40	-6.20%	-6.20%	($507.10)	$2,145.00	$1,081.10	49.60%	$1,063.90	$1,605.00	$1,447.60	9.81%	$157.40	29.27%	32.92%	-3.65%
0048	Finch	$960.10	$1,112.90	-15.92%	-15.92%	($152.80)	$160.00	$274.10	-71.31%	($114.10)	$255.00	$108.50	57.45%	$146.50	28.84%	33.65%	-4.81%
0049	Tampa	$2,599.60	$2,587.40	0.47%	0.47%	$12.20	$448.50	$433.00	3.46%	$15.50	$520.00	$465.20	10.54%	$54.80	40.14%	40.71%	-0.57%
0050	Deikema	$1,847.50	$1,705.50	7.69%	7.69%	$142.00	$195.00	$265.60	-36.21%	($70.60)	$100.00	$123.30	-23.30%	($23.30)	53.75%	56.93%	-3.18%
	Averages =	$4,788.40	$5,008.90				$705.36	$495.03			$879.01	$918.97					

Overall, the trend line shown in the Run Chart below indicates that profit had not been going down as John had suspected, but it was lower than he thought for all jobs. The Run Chart of profit over time indicates that they do need to make improvements in their estimating process.

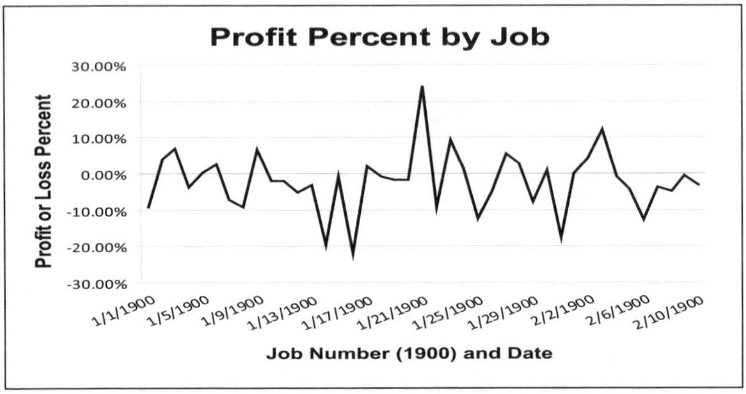

The basic estimates included labor, materials, and equipment as major cost factors. A Pie Chart of these cost elements for the average estimate is shown in the left Pie Chart below. The Pie Chart on the right shows the actual cost allocations for the installation. By analyzing these charts, John could see that the area of greatest error seems to be the materials and labor costs, but that it was unclear which element was the primary cause for the errors. Further analysis was needed. To analyze the cost estimating data the team used Scatter Plots for the comparison of the Estimated to Actual costs for labor, materials, and equipment.

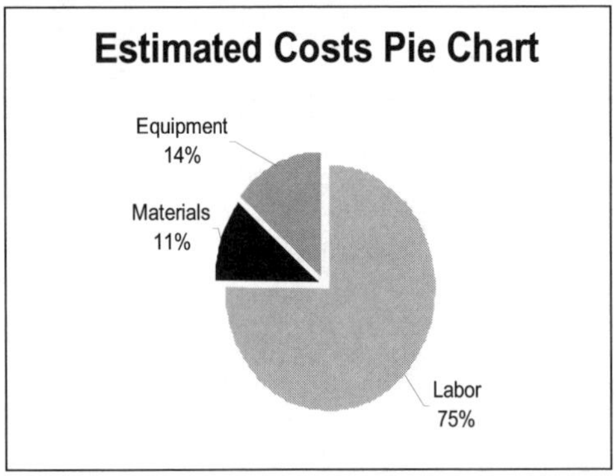

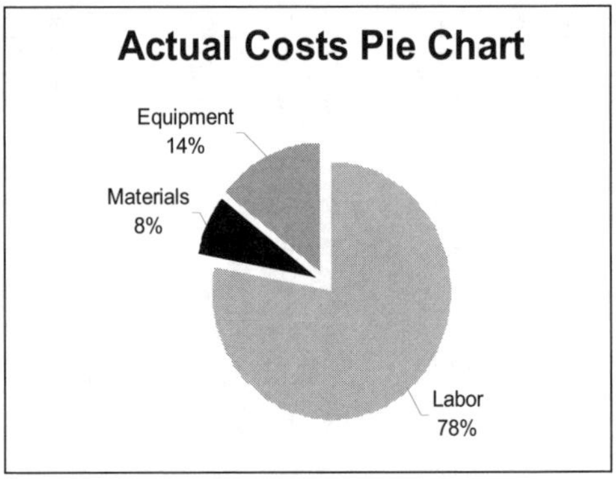

To better understand the dynamics of the cost estimates versus actual installation costs, John completed the following Scatter Plots for the estimated costs versus the actual cost for each major cost element. The Estimated to Actual Cost Scatter Plots are illustrated below:

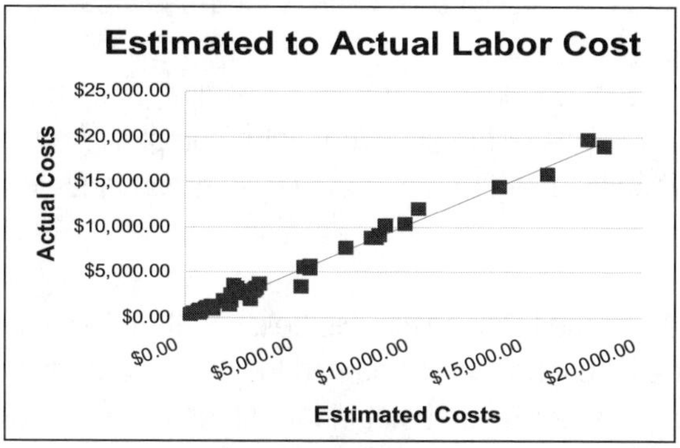

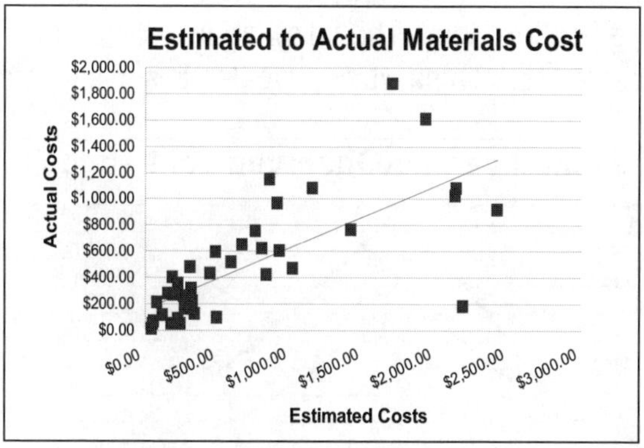

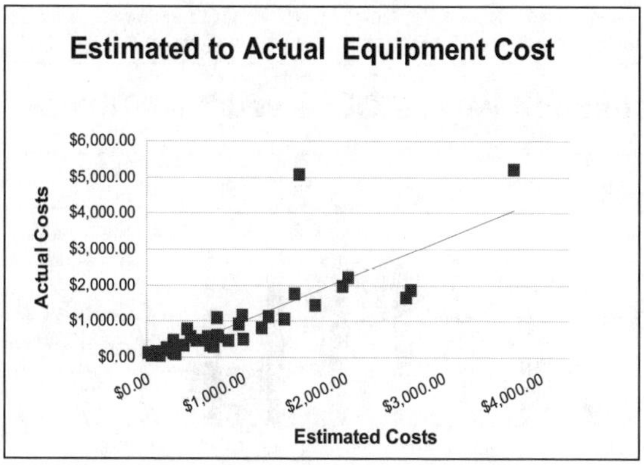

The correlation looked acceptable for the labor costs, but mostly underestimated for materials on jobs with less than $500 of materials, and overestimated for jobs between $500 and $1,500 jobs. The equipment costs appeared to be overestimated for jobs over $1,000. There were a couple of data points that were significantly off the best fit line. Upon further examination, there were clear assignable causes for these jobs.

It seemed that the material and labor errors were coming primarily from the material differences. For further analysis of the situation, John completed a future state map which included a means to identify and "firm up" material costs with suppliers before an estimate was submitted.

John was still bothered by the labor costs. He believed that they should be lower overall. John further researched the labor costs and had to go back and gather more data regarding actual time to complete tasks versus standard times use for estimating. It was determined that their labor standards were off by 5 - 7% for the longer tasks. This difference did not show up on the Scatter Plots. The following two Histograms show the estimated task times versus observed task times which revealed this misalignment:

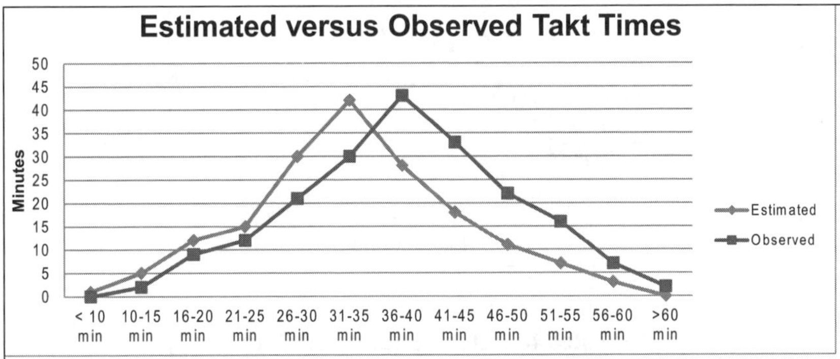

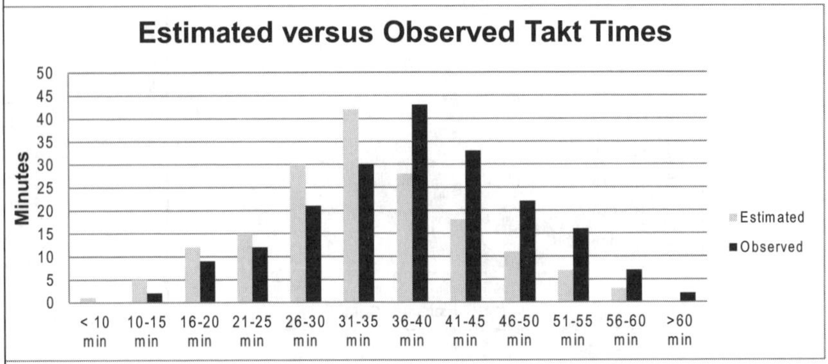

With this analysis, John was able to modify the job estimating charts to be more reflective of reality. However, he was still concerned that the standard time had increased since the estimating standards were developed and asked the team to use a Cause and Effect Diagram analysis to help understand why this may be occurring. It took two weeks, but the team sent John the following Cause and Effect Diagram:

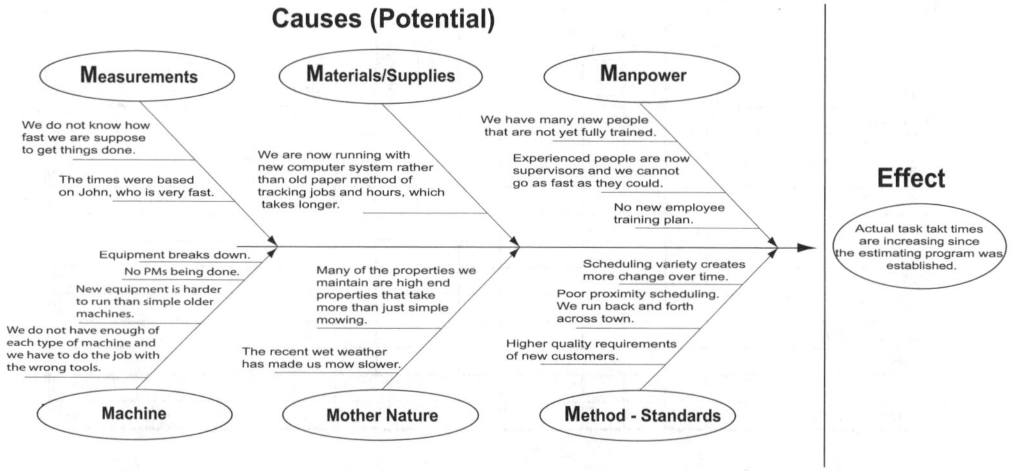

This information was very interesting to John. The Cause and Effect Diagram represented the ideas and opinions of the team, but was not specific data. With no specific data to point the right direction, John asked the team to complete an Interrelationship Diagram to help sort things out and prioritize the improvement effort. First the team identified the major factors that they felt affected job costs, then they identified the perceived relationships. The following Interrelationship Diagram was completed by the team:

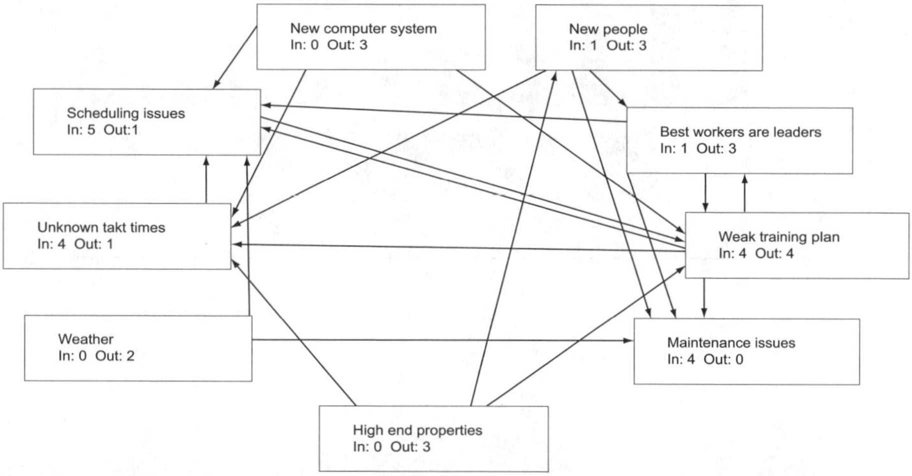

The Interrelationship Diagram indicated the weak training plan with the most inputs and outputs was a key area to address. The scheduling system also had many inputs and might be an area for opportunity.

For the customer complaint data, Doug created the following spreadsheet:

Lakeview Landscaping Customer													
Reason Codes	Jan-12	Feb-12	Mar-12	Apr-12	May-12	Jun-12	Jul-12	Aug-12	Sep-12	Oct-12	Nov-12	Dec-12	**Summary by Reason**
Too Long / Late	1		2		4	2	4	1		1			15
Too Dry					1		2	3	1	1			8
No Bark			4							1	1		6
Burn Spots				1				2	1	1			5
Clippings				1		1	2				1		5
Late Bark				3	1								4
Too Bushy		1									1		2
Wash out				1		1							2
Sprinkler Broke							1						1
Too Wet					1								1
													0
Totals by Month =	1	1	6	6	7	4	9	6	2	4	3	0	49

From the spreadsheet, Doug created a simple Pareto Chart by complaint reason code for his analysis. His graph is shown below:

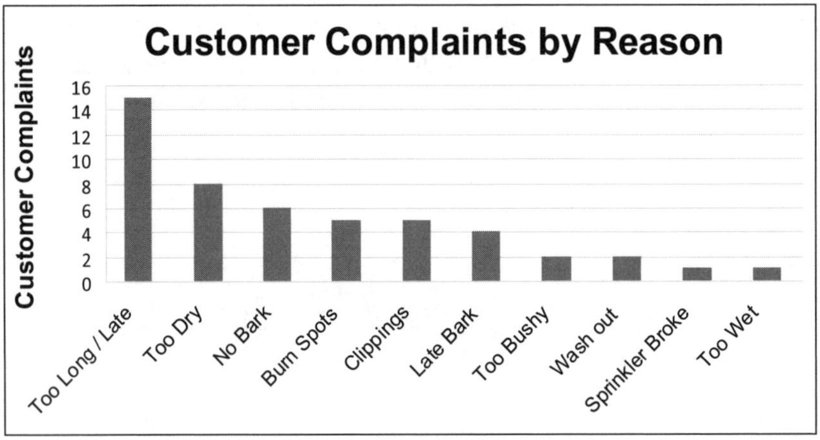

The Pareto Chart clearly illustrated that the leading reason for customer complaints were that the grass is too long or the maintenance team is late. Now the team needed to understand why they were so late.

In subsequent work sessions with the maintenance team, Doug learned that the reason the maintenance team always ran late was due to the fact that the mowing equipment was always breaking down. The reasons for the breakdowns varied, but all could be related to the lack of regular maintenance.

Improve Phase

To make the improvements in the profitability, John and Matt worked to update the estimating spreadsheets in the estimating software to reflect the current reality. If they made the appropriate updates and established a regular frequency to complete this analysis, they thought that improvements would make a difference. They were concerned that as the estimates were becoming more accurate, they might lose some installation projects due to competitive pressures. However, at least they would at least have an accurate estimate to actual.

Matt also agreed that for all jobs won, he would compile a cost to date analysis as the project progressed and complete an After Action Review (AAR) after each job concluded. They would use this information to continually update the cost estimating system. John and Matt also decided to let the team leaders help optimize the schedule and with the time they save from this, implement a more structured training program. The training program had to be addressed. Also, the workers had to know the expected takt times and be held accountable to them.

To reduce the customer complaints Doug thought it would be best to implement a Total Productive Maintenance (TPM) program, where each piece of equipment would be regularly scheduled for preventative maintenance and upgrades. To implement a TPM program with their equipment, they first identified each piece of equipment, the critical spares needed, and then the frequency and specifics with regard to what preventative maintenance tasks needed to be completed and at what frequency. To make the scheduling of the preventative maintenance simple, Doug and his subteam used a visual control board to identify when each piece of equipment was to be maintained. For the monthly tasks, the workers would simply select the days task cards and complete the tasks. When the tasks were complete, they would place the task card on the next months peg. The annual maintenance items were worked in the same manner, but on an annual basis.

Control Phase

To control and sustain the improvements, the teams began tracking key performance measures on a regular basis. Matt and the estimating group used the AAR forms to continually update the cost estimating system. The group also measured the closed profit by job reports on a monthly basis.

Doug's group utilized a couple different key measures to control their improvements. Of course they began tracking customer complaints on a monthly basis and drove problem solving to true root cause, but they also began to measure their TPM tasks completed on time. They believed that if they could keep up to date on the PMs, then the number of breakdowns would be reduced, and if the number of break downs were reduced, the overall number of customer complaints would be reduced.

The improvement team continued to meet monthly to monitor the performance measures and implement improvement initiatives. By the end of the next year, customer complaints had been reduced by 60%, and profits were up more than 12%! Clearly, the Lean Sigma process focused the team on the right areas and showed direct payback.

Chapter 7

Improve Phase

Determining What to Change and How to Do It

Chapter Overview

The Improve Phase is the core of continuous improvement efforts when using the DMAIC process or simply making independent improvements in work areas. The tools highlighted in this chapter have proven their usefulness in reducing and/or eliminating wastes in all types of service processes. By understanding the basic Improve Phase tools, and knowing when they best are applied, improvement teams can accelerate their progress in eliminating waste. This chapter provides an overview of several key Improve Phase tools and details where and when they are best applied.

Improve Phase Training and Alignment

Lean Sigma improvement techniques are designed to allow the team to take action with the opportunities identified in the previous phases of the DMAIC process. Improvement techniques are better understood if the team has studied and practiced the tools in a classroom environment, where the application and function of the tool can be studied in a simple format.

Before beginning the Improve Phase, team members should have an understanding of the following:

- Lean Sigma
- Lean Sigma 12 wastes
- DMAIC Improvement process review
- Analyze Phase tool application
- Improve Phase tool overview
- Improvement techniques and practical tool applications

Key tools to improve processes once the other three phases have been completed are covered in further detail in the Improve Phase Tool section of this chapter. These are key prerequisite skills to learn during this phase.

Improve Phase Tools

The key Improve Phase tools and their application are identified in the following table:

Phase	Lean Sigma Tool	Application Guide
IMPROVE	Rapid Improvement Events	Use Rapid Improvement Events, also known as Kaizen Events, to quickly implement improvement actions.
	Plan-Do-Check-Act (PDCA) Process	Use the PDCA process to gain support and implement improvement ideas.
	5S	Use the 5S's to clean and prepare worksites, to hold and share critical information, improve flow, and reduce waste.
	Visual Controls	Use visual control and management tools to provide key process information quickly and efficiently, eliminate errors, and implement immediate corrective actions and countermeasures.
	Mistake Proofing	Use mistake proofing tools to eliminate errors and error sources in a process.
	Standard Work	Use standardized work tools to document and define the specific steps, expectations, and responsibilities to complete work tasks.
	Process or Work Area Layout	Use process and work area layout tools to reduce the waste of motion and transportation, and improve overall flow of a process or work area.
	Mass Customization	Use mass customization tools to understand and define processes to satisfy multiple customer needs.
	Service Flow	Use continuous flow, paced flow, and scheduled flow concepts with the tools of Heijunka Leveling, Pull Systems and Kanbans, Supermarkets, and First-In First-Out Lanes to minimize or eliminate wastes of waiting and delays in service processes.
	Total Productive Maintenance (TPM)	Use TPM methods and activities to improve the machine or equipment availability and reliability times.
	Quick Changeover	Use quick changeover to improve the customer experience by reducing waiting or delay, and delivering in smaller batches.
	Cross-Training	Use cross-training to increase the knowledge and flexibility of all workers.

By using these key tools, improvement teams are able to implement improvement initiatives and report on their team's progress in an orderly fashion.

Rapid Improvement Events

***Rapid Improvement Events**, sometimes called "Kaizen Events" or "Kaizen Blitzes" are targeted events conducted by improvement teams to implement improvements quickly in a specific area.* Teams use Rapid Improvement Events (RIEs) to implement significant improvements in a relatively short time-frame. Depending on the scope of the improvement targeted, Rapid Improvement Events can last anywhere from one-to-two hours to three-to-five days.

RIEs are used instead of slower, incremental changes in the following circumstances:

- ❖ Improvement needs are urgent or at crisis levels.
- ❖ The area being addressed is continually in use by the organization and taking the area out of service can only be tolerated for a short duration.
- ❖ Only a short duration of training and facilitation can be afforded due to time or financial constraints.
- ❖ There is a very narrow area of focus.

As with any improvement event, Rapid Improvement Events take pre-planning, execution, and post event follow-up to be successful. The following can be used as a guide for planning a RIE.

A. Management Actions (at least 2 weeks before RIE)
   1. Select an area, process, or product related to the Project Charter for rapid improvement.
   2. Create an initial Team Charter and process or value stream map.
   3. Assess opportunities and needs with current state measurement and analytical Lean Sigma tools.
   4. Establish short term RIE improvement measures and goals.
   5. Select a Team Leader (who typically may be the process owner) and facilitator.
   6. Set the RIE date(s).

B. Team Leader Actions (2 weeks before the RIE)
   1. Determine and notify appropriate team members.
   2. Review Project and Team Charter.
   3. Create and distribute Meeting Agenda via email or provide hyperlink.
   4. Invite outside participants, if required.
   5. Conduct appropriate meetings prior to the dedicated days for the RIE.

C. Team Leader and Team Actions (1 week before the RIE)
   1. Create or obtain current value stream or process map.
   2. Obtain current state or baseline measurements.
   3. Communicate and obtain alignment on RIE objectives.
   4. Start a log of NVA activities (i.e., wastes) in the area to address.

D. Facilitator Actions, if assigned, otherwise Team Leader Actions (Pre-RIE)
   1. Create RIE work session detailed agendas and timelines.
   2. Arrange RIE facilities and amenities.

E. RIE Day(s)
   1. Provide Lean Sigma overview training and RIE orientation.
   2. Implement improvements using PDCA process.
   3. Document open item action plans and follow-up plan.
   4. Report out as required.

F. Facilitator (1 week after the RIE)
   1. Follow-up on open action plan items.

G. Management (1 month after RIE)
   1. Audit process improvements to goals.

An example of a 3-day RIE is as follows:

Day 1
1. Welcome
2. Review logistics of the RIE.
3. Review objectives of the RIE.
4. Conduct Lean Sigma Overview Training.
5. Review any baseline measurements and Key Performance Indicators.
6. Data collect and subsequent analysis as required.
7. Complete next day planning.

Day 2

1. Complete process and data analysis.
2. Develop proposed improvements.
3. Identify potential roadblocks to improvements.
4. Implement improvement trials.
5. Communicate with other who are affected.
6. Address potential roadblocks.
7. Complete next day planning.

Day 3

1. Run final trials.
2. Implement final improvements.
3. Develop standard work documents.
4. Conduct training as required.
5. Create open items list.
6. Identify plan for the future.
7. Prepare a management report and lessons learned wrap-up.
8. Conclude the RIE.

It is unlikely that 3 consecutive 8-hour days can be dedicated to the RIE, if this is the case, consider segmenting the activities into 4-hour increments over a 1 - 2 week period. If this is still not feasible, consider detailing each improvement initiative as a separate project. In whatever time frame is used, it is recommended that all improvement initiatives follow the PDCA process.

The Planning Phase of a RIE is the most important phase. Everyone must be aligned on the specifics of the project as well as ensuring alignment to the Balanced Scorecard or Performance Dashboard. The following schedules can be used as a guide when proceeding through this phase.

Rapid Improvement Event Preparation Schedule

The Kaizen Event Preparation Schedule should be used by the Team Leader, Black Belt, or whomever is facilitating the continuous improvement event. The success of a Kaizen Event depends on the detailed planning that is done beforehand. Place a checkmark (✔) by those items that have been completed.

3 Weeks Before Event

- ☐ 1. Select area and topic.
- ☐ 2. Meet with Sponsor (Champion), Process Owner, Financial Leader, and any other key associates to:
  - - Prioritize value streams that relate to Balanced Scorecard or Performance Dashboard
  - - Secure full time participation by team members for the event
  - - Ensure Sponsor is availalbe for the kick-off meeting and the report outs (if applicable)
  - - Discuss objectives and scope of the project
- ☐ 3. Ask these questions:
  - - Will this team improve the process/functional performance?
  - - Are the resources being focused on the right priorities?
  - - What is the business case for analyzing and improving this value stream?
- ☐ 4. When filling out a Team Charter, ensure:
  - - Facilitator is assigned
  - - Additional expertise (i.e., Black Belt, Lean Sensei, etc.) is available (if necessary)
  - - Team member roles are defined (scribe, timekeepper, etc.)
  - - Boundaries of the project are clearly defined
  - - Customers of the process are clearly identified
  - - Suppliers to the process or area are clearly identified
  - - Dates have been established and agreed to
- ☐ 5. Secure conference room for the event. The room should be:
  - - Located as close as possible to the process area that is being worked on
  - - Available for the duration of the event
  - - Large enough to conduct simulations (if required in the training)
- ☐ 6. Obtain all necessary supplies, such as:

- Post-it Notes	- Flip charts and markers	- LCD projector
- Butcher paper roll	- Acess to copy machine	- Copies of training
- Catering requirements	- Materials (pocket guides, handbooks)	- Snacks ☺

Deliverables

- ☐ 1. Team Charter created.
- ☐ 2. Metric/goal initially agreed upon.
- ☐ 3. Date(s) of the event determined.
- ☐ 4. Invititation sent to team members that includes date, location, event particulars and Team Charter.
- ☐ 5. All necessary supplies (training materials) have been ordered.

Comments/Notes:

____

____

Rapid Improvement Event Preparation Schedule

The Kaizen Event Preparation Schedule should be used by the Team Leader, Black Belt, or whomever is facilitating the continuous improvement event. The success of a Kaizen Event depends on the detailed planning that is done beforehand. Place a checkmark (✔) by those items that have been completed.

2 Weeks Before Event

❑ 1. Review the 3 Weeks Before Event list.
❑ 2. Gather data/identify sources that would be on a current state value stream map.
- Obtain financials, flowcharts, etc. of the process(es)
- Run reports of data of the current process or collect real-time data (if applicable)

❑ 3. Determine current customer steady state demand (takt time).
❑ 4. Determine key individuals needed to support the event as on an ad hoc basis (facilities, IT, HR, etc.). Communicate with them appropriately.
❑ 5. Review the Team Charter with sponsor and process owner. Discuss schedules, measurements, targets, and deliverables on the proposed event.
❑ 6. Review Lessons Learned, Sunset Reports, and Kaizen Event Evalution Forms from any previous events that may impact this event.

Deliverables

❑ 1. Team Charter completed and agreement reached on specific deliverables.
❑ 2. Sponsor scheduled for kick-off meeting and report outs.
❑ 3. Date(s) of the event determined.
❑ 4. All team members notified.
❑ 5. Data collection started.

1 Week Before Event

❑ 1. Review 3 Weeks Before Event and 2 Weeks Before Event list and resolve open issues.
❑ 2. Hold final preparation meeting with process owner.
❑ 3. Review metrics and goals with process owner for final agreement.
❑ 4. Update Team Charter, if necessary.

Deliverables

❑ 1. Team member participation verfied.
❑ 2. Team Charter released to all team members.
❑ 3. Materials acquired.
❑ 4. Room and catering verified (those snacks ☺).

Comments/Notes:

____

____

As the RIE progresses, these sessions will ensure good communications, as well as provide the opportunity to discuss issues that the team may have encountered during the days activities. The following templates are examples of reports for the daily report out, as well as a report format that can be used to track progress over time.

Rapid Improvement Event Daily Review

The Kaizen Event Daily Review allows for a team to list their accomplishments, as well as their areas of concern, that should be reviewed by the team champion on a daily basis. Many times there will be a report-out at the end of the day in which all leadership of the organization are invited to attend. This review allows for immediate communication as to the project's status.

By: Date:

Team Name or Value Stream:

Measurements	Metrics						
	# Before	Day 1	Day 2	Day 3	Day 4	Day 5	Target

Accomplishments:	Concerns:	Plans:

Rapid Improvement Event Scorecard

The Event Scorecard is meant to regularly convey the results of the improvements. In so doing, it will provide the team with the necessary data in which to make corrections if trends are negative and the improvements are not going as expected. The Scorecard will also provide management with the team's progress-to-date.

Event Name: **Site/Location:** **Date:**

Value Stream Impacted: **Process Owner(s):** **Team Members:**

Team Champion/Sponsor: **Team Leader:**

Measurements	Metrics							
	# Start of Event	# End of Event	7 Day Date: ____	14 Day Date: ____	30 Day Date: ____	60 Day Date: ____	90 Day Date: ____	Target
Overall Evaluation:			R Y G	R Y G	R Y G	R Y G	R Y G	

Key:
- Performance Meets or Exceeds Target (Green)
- Performance is Short but close to Target (within 10% of Target) (Yellow)
- Performance is Significantly Unfavorable to Target (below 10% of Target) (Red)

If a measurement is not meeting the target, use the below 3 Ws (What, Who, and When) to clearly indicate how you plan to meet or exceed target.

What	Who	When	Comments/Status

Comments/Notes:

Plan-Do-Check-Act (PDCA) Process

PDCA *is an interactive four-step problem solving and improvement process typically used to implement business process improvements.* It is also known as the Deming or Shewhart cycle. It is more than likely that numerous mini-improvements will need to be implemented to meet the deliverables as defined in the Team Charter of the Define Phase. These mini-improvements should be defined or proposed in the Analyze Phase using the tools of VA versus NVA Analysis, Histograms, 5 Why Analysis, Force Field Analysis, Impact Maps, etc. For these improvements to be implemented and verified as to their effectiveness, the use of the PDCA process may be used. The PDCA is complimentary to the DMAIC methodology as described in this book and is used to implement improvements throughout the Improve Phase.

PDCA's are sometimes referred to as an experiment or trial. The process and terms for the experiment or trial help people commit or "buy-in" to trying something new. Often getting people to try something new is one of the more challenging parts of reaching an improved state. A PDCA experiment or trial is a short term, controlled trial process used to capture data and learn about the process. This approach helps people adapt to change more easily.

The steps to the PDCA process are:

Plan – Define the improvement action plan or experiment, what will be done, who will do it, and how it will be measured; this information can be documented in the Action Item (AI) Log.

Do – Implement the improvement plan or experiment.

Check – Check that the intended improvement was realized. Measure and discuss the results of the experiment.

Act – If the improvement experiment worked and improved performance, act to standardize the new process. If the improvement experiment did not work, act to put the process back to its original condition.

Use the AI Log to document and track the progress on PDCA activities. By completing successive PDCA cycles, continuous and incremental improvement will be realized.

5S

***5S** is a process to ensure physical or electronic work areas are systematically kept clean and organized, assuring employee safety in meeting customer expectations while providing the foundation on which to build a Lean Sigma organization.* It is composed of 5 parts: Sort (or Scrap), Set-In-Order, Shine (or Scrub), Standardize, and Sustain. It is the systematic 5-step process which makes 5S unique and successful in many different industries. It is often stated, "If you can't do 5S, forget all the rest." 5S provides an opportunity to get all employees involved in the Lean Sigma process. 5S is a simple and common-sense approach in taking a first step to improving a process or work area.

In today's service environment, as well as in every industry, there are basically three main business areas that inter-relate: (1) physical elements such as work cubicles, doors, ailse ways, equipment, supplies, products, etc., (2) paper-based elements such as forms, work documents, receipts, etc., and (3) electronic documents such as reports, charts, Customer Relationship Management documents, MS Office documents in Word, Excel, Access, etc., and hyperlinks to information, Internet, 3 - 4/G communications, etc. The basic principles of 5S equally apply to all three. Throughout this section there will be examples from each of these main business areas.

5S includes the following activities:

Sort (or Scrap) involves sorting through the contents of workplace physical and electronic database areas and removing unnecessary items (papers, old manuals, out-dated files - both paper and electronic, etc.). The essence of Sort is found in the saying, "When in doubt, move it out."

Set-In-Order involves arranging necessary items for easy and efficient access and keeping them that way. The essence of Set-In-Order is found in the saying, "A place for everything and everything in its place."

Shine (or Scrub) involves cleaning everything, keeping everything clean, and using cleaning as a way to ensure all physical areas and electronic files and folders are maintained as they should be. The essence of Shine is found in the saying, "To be Lean, you must be clean."

Standardize involves creating guidelines for keeping the area and electronic files and folders organized, orderly, clean, and making the standards visual and obvious. The standards created must serve as the basis for improvement. The essence of Standardize is found in the saying, "What you don't know, you can't improve."

Sustain involves education and communication to ensure that everyone uses the applicable standards. Typical Sustain activities include process and area 5S accountability audits. The essence of Sustain is found in the saying, "Maintain the gain and forget the blame."

From its modest beginnings as a housekeeping tool, the 5S system has evolved into a method for initiating Lean Sigma projects, reducing costs, improving work flow, and most importantly, engaging all employees in participating in reducing waste. It can further engage the employee to "see" some of the early benefits of Lean Sigma that directly impact their work. Clean and organized work areas, files, electronic files and the like are key to eliminating wastes in delay caused from having to "look for things." Information or items in the right place at the right time are fundamental to the implementation of Lean Sigma methods and tools.

Note: The term "area" or "item" as mentioned in the following 5S steps can mean any of the three business entities (i.e., physical elements such as supplies, equipment, etc., paper-based work documents, or electronic documents such as Word, Excel, PowerPoint files, Outlook folders and files, etc.

The following are some general guidelines in which to implement 5S:

Step 1 - Sort (or Scrap)

This S is a weeding out of items in the target area that have not been used for a period of time or are not expected to be used. The team and/or worker should follow these steps:

a. Select an area or process to apply the 5S tool if not previously defined as an improvement activity within the Project or Team Charter. When selecting an area or process to address, ensure it is large enough to make a difference, but small enough to complete with the resources available. For example, if you only have 15 minutes at the end of the day, you might select a common lobby area, the individual's desk area, or the individual's Outlook folder.

b. Agree on the purpose of the area or process being considered. This would include agreeing on what belongs and what does not belong in the area. This may also include denoting a Red Tag staging area to remove items that do not belong in the area. Creating a group-wide Red Tag folder for any electronic documents that needed to be removed from email folders, C: drives, etc. before file standards are created. (It may also be helpful or necessary to train employees on how to effectively use Windows Explorer or some functionality with the CRM system.) The Red Tag area or folder can be used to determine further disposition of the items.

c. Take some before photos of the area and screen shots of the files/folders, if appropriate.

d. Remove all physical items or electronic documents from the area. A color-coding system can be used for an item or file: needed - but needs to move (green), not needed (red), and not sure - need additional input or approval (yellow).

e. Determine disposition of items.

Note: Many software applications can assign color-codes to track the frequency and use of electronic files to assist in this process.

Examples for Sort

Employees of a convention and visitor center for a mid-sized city completed the Sorting phase on both electronic and physical files containing restaurant and business maps. The team found that several outdated versions of maps were still in the computer and physically in the storage room. The team established an "Old Map" electronic file and agreed to place all outdated maps in this folder. In the physical storage area, the team sorted out the current maps from the obsolete maps, and reorganized and standardized the area. The obsolete maps were discarded in the recyclable paper bin.

Additional examples include such things as:

- Purging electronic customer files to delete old customers
- Deleting out-dated numbering and filing systems
- Sorting out last year's marketing information from this year's

Step 2 - Set-In-Order

This S establishes the locations where items belong, by either labeling or visual markings. The team and/or worker should follow these steps:

a. Create the appropriate visual indicators to label and identify all items in the area. This would help ensure if an item or file was removed from the area, it could "find" its way back. For electronic files, this would include bookmarks, hyperlinks to files, shared-directory file protections, etc.

b. Use visual controls as much as possible.

For example, the following color-coding system was used for physical items in a service-related organization for both their product services area as well as their administrative area:

- Yellow = General caution
- Red = Urgent items or areas
- Green = Good or on-target items
- Orange = Moveable equipment, parking spots
- Blue = Incoming orders or items
- Yellow w/Black Strip = Safety Warnings

Examples of Set-In-Order

A dentist's office instruments are cleaned and replaced in a specific location after each patient. In a fire station, set-in-place takes on an even more important role. Fire fighting tools and equipment are set back in their exact order after a call to ensure speed and readiness for the next alarm. Lives can depend on it. Speed and readiness are critical in many service environments to meet customer expectations.

Many more examples of set-in-order can be found where customers have to interact with the service process, such as shopping carts being returned to cart corrals in parking areas, then returned to a staging area inside a retail store for customer use. In these cases there are specific areas designated for return or readiness. Visual markings and signage are typically used to communicate and facilitate the process.

The following is an example of Set-In-Order for electronic files:

Client - Bed-Rock Industries (BR)
Project Name - Miller Acquisition
Document Name - Fixed Asset Valuation for Chicago Regional Headquarters
Document Type - Valuation (VAL) - This is 1 type of document from 10 different types
Revision - 1.1
Date Created - 5 Jan 09
Last Modified - 10 Jan 09
Author's Name (initials) - John William Citizen (jwc)

The previous file information can be condensed or truncated into a meaningful group of letters and/or acronyms for a file naming convention as shown in the following example:

Client: - First four characters of the customer name - "BedR" (as used in the CRM system)
Project Name: "MillerAcq"
Document Name: "FixedAssetChicago"
Document Type: "val"
Version: "1.1"
Date Created: "010509"
Author's Name (initials): "jwc"

The full naming convention may look something like:

NameOfClient_Dept or ProjectName_DocName_DocType&Version_CreateDate_Author'sName (initials)

The actual file name may look something like:
BedR_MillerAcq_FixedAssetChicago_val1.1_010509_jwc.doc

The more organized an area is with everything in its place, the less waste will be involved when locating that item or file when it is needed.

Step 3 - Shine (or Scrub)

This S is basic cleaning of the area and establishing the sequence with which the area is kept up on a regular basis. This ranges from cleaning the keyboard, to having the floor mats shampooed every month, to running a disk utilization program. The team should do the "spring cleaning," then create a standard cleaning plan. The team and/or worker should follow these steps:

a. Clean the items that will be staying in the area. Clean all gunk, grease, and dust from physical spaces; paint, polish, and restore items to a condition "like the day they were new!" This applies to offices, public spaces, and equipment or tools. This attention to detail will help you spot abnormalities and waste.

b. Ask your team why the area cannot be kept in its current condition, what it would take to keep it in good condition, why the right file can never be found in the shared directory, or why there are multiple versions of the same file. The 5S discipline is the foundation for all other continuous Improvements!

c. Use the information gathered from Step 2 for the 4th and 5th S.

d. Ensure the area is "cleaned" out on a regular basis. Regularly perusing your file system will save you time in retrieving files when they are required. This will eliminate the wastes of motion and file inventory.

Examples of Shine (or Scrub)

At a lawn service organization, lawn maintenance equipment such as mowers, weed trimmers, and clippers are hosed or rinsed off and readied each day for the next day's work. In a doctor's office, exam rooms are cleaned/prepared for the next patient. In a restaurant, equipment and cooking utensils are washed and prepped for the next day's use. In public or customer use areas, a scheduled cleaning time may be put in place and posted in the area with a note that asks customers to notify the appropriate person if the area is not up to standards or needs additional service.

Shining to standards also helps service workers spot developing or potential problems. For example, regular cleaning of a service truck may uncover a new leak or low tire pressure. Keeping an office space shined will provide customers with a sense of organization and efficiency that reflects on their overall experience and willingness to return or recommend an organization to a friend or colleague.

Step 4 - Standardize

This S involves creating guidelines or protocols for keeping an area organized, orderly, and clean (or scrubbed). This also includes making those standards visual and obvious. The team and/or worker should follow these steps:

a. Decide what the specific tasks are and where they should happen (location) and listing them on a sheet in a file. Most of this information should come out of Shine (or Scrub), Step 3.

b. Decide who will perform the tasks. Listing them in a column.

c. Decide frequency and any resources required. List them in a column.

d. Ensure everyone has access to the task list.

Examples of Standardize

Standardization of electronic files and folders naming nomenclature is an example where an organization uses standardized rules to name and update electronic files and folders. This helps reduce waste of delay and correction by having specific areas to look for files and ensuring only the most current file is in use. An example of electronic file naming protocol is noted below:

Customer name_Subject_Date_Revision level
Bilmar_Metrics_101010_RevB

Other examples of standardization in service are ensuring that there is a standard pack or contents in a travel repair or demo case. If the tools and contents are standard in any case, users can quickly and efficiently prepare for customer support and service sessions.

Standardizing and communicating regular audit or maintenance of areas is yet another example of standardizing in the 5S process. Regular schedules and specific tasks are documented and communicated to the work group to ensure that the proper activities take place on schedule.

The following is an example of Standards for a department's electronic files and folders:

Target Area	Task	Locations	Taskmaster	Frequency	Resources
Email Inbox	Extract data, attachments and takes and deletes emails from Inbox.	Outlook Inbox	User	Daily	1 User
Email Folders	Extra data, attachments and taks and delete all saved, underutilized emails.	Outlook Mail Folders	User	Weekly	1 User
Desktop	Create a folder for each project/subject and move all files into appropriate folder on your desktop. Create a folder on the network drive in the User Files folder with your name and a subfolder named "Active Files" within.	Active Desktop	User	Weekly	1 User
Hard Drive	Remove all files from My Documents/My Pictures, etc. Run the cleaning software and defragment the hard drive.	C:\	User	Monthly	1 User
Common Files	Department to review all files weekly.	Q:\Common Files\	Team Rotation	Weekly	1 Team Member
Red Tags	Every 6 months review all files and folders.	Q:\Red Tags\	Supervisor	Daily	1 Supervisor
User Files	Delete any files that are 60 days old.	Q:\User Filers\User	User	Bi-Weekly	1 User

Step 5 - Sustain

This S involves creating an audit process ensuring a long-term adherence to standards. Nearly all 5S and Lean Sigma projects have an initial enthusiasm for change; however, it is the continuation of those improvements over time that organizations require today. The team and/or worker should follow these steps:

a. Create an audit team. Audits should be performed by designated internal auditor(s) that will provide an unbiased evaluation on how 5S is working.

b. Create a 5S Audit check sheet. This will list the specific attributes that will be audited from the information derived from the 3rd and 4th S.

c. Identify the frequency of audits. Typically once a month is sufficient for the independent audit team and once per week for any individual self-assessment.

d. Use the following five-level Likert item scale for the audit possible responses to each question or statement:

1 - Strongly Disagree (or unacceptable, needs immediate improvement)
2 - Disagree (or needs improvement)
3 - Neither Agree nor Disagree (or ok, meets minimum requirements)
4 - Agree (or meets and sometimes exceeds requirements)
5 - Strongly Agree (or constantly exceeds requirements and/or use as an example of excellence)

Once an audit has been completed, it is suggested a Scoring Legend be provided to allow the total scores to be relative to a category of progression. The following is a suggested Scoring Legend (if the audit totaled up to 100 points). (Eg., you may have 20 audit-type questions or statements, each with a value of 5 points each, or 25 questions, each with a value of 4 points each, etc.)

80-100	Doing Well - Keep up the good work
60-79	Doing OK - Must make more effort
<60	Not So Good - Very little effort shown

Whatever scoring system you decide to use for your audit, remember to be as positive and supportive as possible. Low scores may indicate that the person (or group) requires more information, support, and/or training.

5. Communicate to the work group the overall success and praising those that are adhering to the process. Privately communicating to those that are not adhering to the process and addressing their concerns.

Examples of Sustain

Over the years the county courthouse had made several building additions, and residents coming in for various services found it very confusing to find their way through the maze of hallways. Not to mention different areas had become cluttered over time, as departments have moved to new locations. After completing the first 4 S's, the custodial department put into place a general standard for cleanliness, and established a weekly audit plan to "police" the building and ensure areas were well lit, labeled, and cleaned.

The first few months went well and the audit scores remained acceptable, but after a relocation of the Deeds department, several boxes were left in the hallway blocking some directional signs. The audit score dropped to unacceptable and when the report hit the building supervisor's desk, immediate corrective action was initiated. The boxes owners were identified and given a time line to rectify the situation. On the next audit, the custodial staff noticed that the boxes were removed, but the directional sign had been torn. They replaced the damaged sign and brought the audit score back into an acceptable range.

The following is an example of a Sustain audit for a department's electronic files and folders:

The Cambridge Group

5S Audit

Previous Departmental Score: 74
Current Departmental Score: 76

Audit Team Names: Sandy Silvio, Benjamin Jamies, Bashi Ramin, Kari Green, Emily Hamilton
Purpose: To sustain the personal and public file saving methods
Target Areas: Common drives and web based file share
Department: Software Development
Current Date: November 14th **Next Audit Date:** December 14th
Last Audit Score: 66 ***Current Audit Score: 72*** ***Name of person being audited: Deanna Troy***

Note: 5S Audits should be performed at a minimum of once a month by a cross-functional team.

Rank the following statements based on the employee's demonstrated use of the new 5S process by viewing the home directory and files saved by the employee as well as questioning the employee when necessary. Complete one for each employee and combine for one total score for the department.

Scoring Legend:
80 - 100 Doing Well, Keep Up the Good Work
60 - 79 Doing OK, Must Make More Effort
> 60 Not So Good, Very Little Effort Shown

Use the following five level Likert item scale for each statement:
1 - Strongly Disagree
2 - Disagree
3 - Neither Agree nor Disagree
4 - Agree
5 - Strongly Agree

1. Public files follow a standard naming convention.	1	2	3	✔	5
2. Public folders follow a standard naming convention.	1	2	✔	4	5
3. Email subject headings follow a standard naming convention.	1	2	3	4	✔
4. All files are regularly reviewed and deleted (or appropriately archived).	1	2	✔	4	5
5. Email folders follow a standard naming convention.	1	2	3	✔	5
6. Files can be located within 5 seconds on any shared drive.	1	2	3	✔	5
7. Implementing 5S has saved time.	1	2	✔	4	5
8. Implementing 5S has improved work group productivity.	1	2	3	4	✔
9. Implementing 5S has reduced errors within the work group.	1	✔	3	4	5
10. Other departments are beginning to implement 5S to their electronic files and folders.	1	2	✔	4	5
11. Relevant public files that are older than 3 months are appropriately archived.	1	2	3	✔	5
12. Public files that are less than 3 months old are saved in their appropriate directory or folder.	1	2	✔	4	5
13. Personal files are saved only to the employee's home directory.	1	2	3	✔	5
14. Files saved by the employee have been saved in the correct folders.	1	2	✔	4	5
15. Files saved by the employee in the public file share meet the required naming convention.	1	2	3	✔	5
16. The employee finds that the new public file share saves time when searching for documents.	1	2	3	✔	5
17. The employee has contributed to improving the standard.	1	2	✔	4	5
18. The employee has been trained on the new 5S process (personal and public file saving methods).	1	2	3	✔	5
19. The employee understands the new 5S process (personal and public file saving methods).	1	2	✔	4	5
20. The employee has contributed other improvement ideas based on Lean principles.	1	2	3	✔	5

Individual Total Score: 72

Visual Controls

***Visual control** is a technique employed whereby control of an activity or process is made easier or more effective by deliberate use of visual signals (signs, information displays, maps, layouts, instructions, alarms, and poka-yoke or mistake proofing devices).* These signals can be of many forms, from simple signs in a lobby area and different function keys on the keyboard, to various types of measurements relating to a problem or departmental goal, to kanbans and heijunka boxes; these signals can also be audio. A visual control will effectively communicate the information needed for decision-making.

Visual controls are one part of an overall communication system (a picture is worth a thousand words) of an organization to ensure standards are met and work is completed on time and can continue to the next process without errors. Visual controls should be used (or at least considered) at every juncture of the Lean Sigma project. It is important to note that visual controls work for internal processes or systems, as well as customer interactive processes or systems. Often customers expect a high level of visual signs and signals to help them attain a high level of service and satisfaction.

Visual controls will accomplish the following:

- Reduce opportunity for errors, omissions, and defects (i.e., customer complaints, unmet needs, omissions, non-conformances, or dissatisfied customers
- Assist in adhering to a process standards
- Improve productivity
- Improve customer satisfaction

Visual controls are used to identify conditions that may cause an error, or if an error occurs, what must be done to prevent it from becoming a defect.

The four levels of visual controls are as follows:

Level 1 - Indicators: provides information about the environment, area, or process. These are passive and people may or may not notice them or respond to them. It is the lowest form of influence on behavior. Examples of Level 1 visual controls are:

- "Allergy Alert" is highlighted in red on the patient's chart and ID bracelet
- Signs, posters, maps, arrows, etc.
- Color-coding emails or other electronic files and folders
- Bar Charts indicating disk usage
- Limit lines for entertainment queue lines (e.g., From here, approximately 15 minutes.)

Level 2 - Signals: causes a visual or auditory alarm that should grab your attention and is a warning that a mistake or error is about to occur. Signals have a higher level of influence on behavior. People still may ignore these, but they are very aware that something may be wrong. Examples of Level 2 visual controls are:

- Typing a customer's number in the CRM system and a message appears "Credit Hold"
- Door chimes when a customer arrives
- Lights indicating next check-out line is available
- Performance dashboards on Desktop screens
- Green light in front of cashier indicating that the register is open for next customer
- A sound (or chirp) from the copy machine indicating service is required or ink is low

Level 3 - Controls: physically or electronically limits or prevents something from occurring due to the negative impact it will have on the process (or area). These are more aggressive than Levels 1 and 2 and are used to guide and control or limit behaviors so that only the correct option is selected. Examples of Level 3 visual controls are:

- Mechanical wall connections (ports) specifically designed for connection to gases such as oxygen and nitrogen
- One-way turnstiles
- Locks, security codes, etc.
- Email rules and filters
- Drop-down menu selections

Level 4 - Guarantees: ensures that a correct decision is made. They are the highest level of visual control. Visual guarantees force the correct decisions to be made and are mistake proofing controls and devices (next section). Examples of Level 4 visual controls are:

- Software applications that limit program access
- Automatic portion dispensing equipment
- Automatic timed withdrawals from a checking or savings account
- Username and passwords to an account

When you create the device (i.e., a physical or electronic visual control), you will need to decide which level is most appropriate for the situation. Clearly, Levels 3 and 4 are the most comprehensive in terms of ensuring that an error or mistake does not occur, but the solution may not always be possible or cost effective. Consider information requirements and availability both upstream and downstream of the area being addressed. Once the information to share has been determined, visual controls can be selected or created and implemented. Implement visual controls in a PDCA fashion to ensure success.

The following chart summarizes the visual control levels and examples:

	Type of Device			
Attribute	**Level 1 - Indicators**	**Level 2 - Signals**	**Level 3 - Controls**	**Level 4 - Guarantees**
Power Level	Lowest Passive Only tells	Low-Medium Assertive Grabs senses	Medium-High Aggressive Narrows options	High Assured Allows only the correct response
Impact on Behavior	Influences Informs Indicates Shows Suggests	Alerts Alarms Warns Signals Prompts Announces	Directs Guides Limits Guards Restricts Restrains Hinders	Compels Forces Ensures Prohibits Inhibits Eliminates Guarantees
Road Examples	Road signs	Road lights	Road barriers	Road designs
Workplace Examples	Signs Posters Pictures Lists Maps Arrows Color-coding Bar Charts	Alarms Buzzers Horns Music Lights Counters Bells Performance Dashboards	One-way turn styles Container size File space Guarding Ropes Drop-down menus	Locks Automatic operations Rules/filters Username/ passwords

Note: The implementation devices used for each of the Visual Control Levels can be referred to as mistake proofing devices (next section), with each having different degrees of certainty in preventing an error or an opportunity for an error to occur.

Mistake Proofing

***Mistake proofing** is a system designed to ensure that it is impossible to make a mistake or error, or produce a defect.* Mistake proofing is also known as error proofing or by its Japanese name of poka-yoke. It is derived from "poka" - inadvertent mistake and "yoke" - avoid. A poka-yoke device is any physical or electronic mechanism that prevents a mistake from being made or ensures the mistake is made obvious at a glance, before it would become a defect. An example of this is the different configuration of 120v and 220v (U.S.) plugs that pevents plugging into the wrong voltage.The causes of defects lie in process errors, equipment and material errors, and worker errors and defects are the results of those errors. These mistakes will not turn into defects if these errors are discovered and eliminated beforehand. Defects occur because errors are made; the two have a cause-and-effect relationship. Many times visual controls (previous section) will play a large role in reducing the opportunity for errors to occur, thereby ensuring that no defects result from the process.

Defects vs. Errors

To be a defect:

- The process or service must have deviated from specifications or standards of service
- The process or service does not meet customer (internal or external) expectations

To be an error:

- Something must have deviated from an intended process
- All defects are created by errors, but not all errors result in defects

Mistakes or errors are a pure form of waste. Mistakes or errors not only cause a process to be repeated and corrected, they can create customer ill will. It is generally understood that a typical dissatisfied customer will tell eight to ten people about their problem. One in five will tell twenty. It takes twelve positive incidents to make up for one negative incident.

There are three critical times to apply mistake proofing methods: (1) before the process starts, (2) during the process itself, and (3) immediately after the process has been completed.

The concept of eliminating errors through mistake proofing is fundamental to Lean Sigma methods and tools. Mistake proofing devices help people avoid costly errors and customer disappointments. Mistake proofing devices limit and/or guarantee the correct behavior of a process.

Reasons for errors in service processes can be broken down into the following five categories:

1. Requests of inappropriate or unknown services, procedures, processes, or standards
2. Excessive variability in the operations and processes
3. Wrong, inaccurate, damaged or excessively variable inputs or other materials
4. Lack of proper communication of requirements and expectations
5. Simple human error – forgetting to do part of the process, doing part of the process incorrectly, or using the incorrect information or data to complete a process

Human errors are the most difficult to eliminate and occur for a variety of reasons. For the most part human errors occur because we are human, and not machines. They seem almost unavoidable. The key to mistake proofing is to develop processes where errors can be prevented, detected and/or corrected before they are passed on to downstream activities. The following example is a simple test to demonstrate the ability of humans to see information correctly and perform a simple task.

In the following paragraph, count the number of times the letter "f" is used:

The necessity of training farm hands for first class farms in the fatherly handling of farm livestock is foremost in the eyes of farm owners. Since the forefathers of farm owners trained the farm hands for first class farms in a fatherly handling of farm livestock, the farm owners feel they should carry on with family tradition of training farm hands of first class farmers in the fatherly handling of farm livestock because they believe it is the basis of good fundamental farm management.

There are 36 "f's" in the paragraph as shown in the following paragraph.

The necessity of training farm hands for first class farms in the fatherly handling of farm livestock is foremost in the eyes of farm owners. Since the forefathers of farm owners trained the farm hands for first class farms in a fatherly handling of farm livestock, the farm owners feel they should carry on with family tradition of training farm hands of first class farmers in the fatherly handling of farm livestock because they believe it is the basis of good fundamental farm management.

If you follow a standard process of counting the "f's" in a row, then adding the totals from each row, you may be more accurate.

Row 1 = 8
Row 2 = 7
Row 3 = 8
Row 4 = 6
Row 5 = 5
Row 6 = 2

Total = 36

Establishing a formal or standard process (e.g., for counting) is one way of mistake proofing a service process. Double-entry accounting is a form of this type of mistake proofing.

Other forms of service mistake proofing are redundancy checks where multiple workers will check and re-check or ask for the same information. Another popular example of mistake proofing is where surgery patients will mark the intended surgery area with a pen to ensure the surgeon works on the correct area after the patient is under anesthesia.

Mistake proofing in service can be as simple as numbering or labeling of products or files, to ensure proper sequence or use. In the case of a legal service providing documents to a labor negotiating team, folders labeled "Agreement" and "No Agreement" can be used to simplify the proper folder and actions for the team depending on the results of the session. In other cases, folders boldly labeled "STEP 1," "STEP 2," and "STEP 3" to help ensure proper order and sequence

Another mistake proofing and human error exercise is illustrated in the paragraph below.

The human mind is very powerful. What does the following passage say about mistake proofing and human error?

THE PAOMNNEMHAL PWEOR OF THE HMUAN MNID
Aoccdrnig to a rscheearch at Cmabrigde Uinervtisy, it deosn't mttaer in waht oredr the ltteers in a wrod are, the olny iprmoatnt tihng is taht the frist and lsat ltteer be in the rghit pclae. The rset can be a taotl mses and you can sitll raed it wouthit porbelm. Tihs is bcuseae the huamn mnid deos not raed ervey lteter by istlef, but the wrod as a wlohe.

These two examples of human error may be interesting and can be used to help people understand the nature of human errors. Mistake proofing is the process to prevent errors or mistakes from occurring. If we accept errors, or even 99% quality (or 10,000 errors per million events) we accept the following:

- 500 incorrect surgeries each week
- 2,000 pieces of mail lost every hour
- 20,000 wrong prescriptions filled each year
- Unsafe drinking water for 1 hour of every month
- 1,500 newborn babies dropped by doctors every year

Perfection (or zero defects) is the goal of Lean Sigma methods and tools!

Technology has provided tremendous improvement in the use of mistake proofing. Spell checks with automatic corrections, reminders to save work, drop-down menu selections in spreadsheets, auto-saving of work, and other software features help people avoid errors every day when working with computers. The basic principles of mistake proofing are:

- Eliminate the possibility of error and remove unnecessary options
- Make the work easier to perform – simplify the process to make "doing" the correct process easier than "doing" the wrong process (i.e., error)
- Detect errors before further processing - implement audit processes
- Minimize the effect of errors – reduce the impact of an error

The four steps to mistake proofing are:

1. Shift your paradigm.

Errors can be prevented! Begin looking for the source of defects, not just the defects themselves. At the same time look for opportunities to eliminate them at their source. The root cause of defects is in the process, not the people.

2. Conduct analysis.

To analyze the problem you must be able to identify and describe the defect or potential error in depth, including the rate that it may have been occurring over time. A Failure Prevention Analysis Worksheet (FPAW) can assist in this process. ***Failure Prevention Analysis*** *is a technique that allows the team to anticipate potential problems in the solution before implementing it, permitting the team to be proactive to prevent the solution(s) from going wrong.* The subsequent processes of mistake proofing would be the procedures, visual controls, alarm notifications, etc. that would prevent a mistake from being made or to ensure the mistake, if made, is obvious at a glance.

The following guidelines will assist you in using the FPAW (See example next page):

a. Create a list of potential failures for each improvement activity that has a probable cause-effect relationship with an opportunity for error.
b. Rank the potential failures by rating each by their potential and consequence for each item going wrong on a scale from 1 to 5.
c. Multiply the potential and consequence together for each of the potential failures to give the overall rating.
d. Rank each potential failure from highest to lowest (1 - XX).
e. Brainstorm with the team to modify any/all activities to lessen the likelihood of causing a problem.

There are two points in a Lean Sigma project where the FPAW may be useful. First, when developing the solutions using the tools such as brainstorming, 5 Why analysis, Fishbone, Impact Map, etc. the FPAW can help the team to determine whether any of the proposed solutions may cause unforeseen consequences. Second, after the solutions have been implemented, the FPAW can be used to determine whether some activities happen with more frequency or with more severe consequences than anticipated. In either case, the goal is to identify any/all issues that may require updated standard work procedures with appropriate visual controls and/or some type of error management.

The Failure Prevention Analysis Worksheet is most useful when there is a need to:

- Study the current process to indicate the most problematic areas of the current state and determine which problem areas would be the most important to fix
- Develop the future state to imagine what problems might occur if the process was changed
- Review the standard work after the change has been implemented to analyze the mistakes and problems that are apparent based upon observation and feedback

The following FPAW is for a college student attainment improvement initiative:

Failure Prevention Analysis Worksheet

Directions:

1. List all potential failures.
2. Assign a number from 1 to 5 for the potential and consequence on an activity going wrong.
3. Multiply the potential and consequence and rank from highest to lowest.

Potential Rating	Consequence Rating (to student)
1 - Very unlikely to occur during term	1 - Very little or no consequence
2 - Might occur rarely during term	2 - Some consequence, but easily corrected
3 - 50/50 chance to occur during term	3 - Moderate consequence, needing some action
4 - Good chance to occur at least once a day	4 - Severe consequence, requiring action
5 - Excellent chance to occur several times during term	5 - Most severe consequence requiring immediate action

Potential Failure	Potential	Consequence	Overall Rating	Ranking
A. Student drops class.	2	1	2	5
B. Student fails class.	1	3	3	4
C. Student fails exam.	3	3	9	2
D. Student fails daily work assignment.	5	2	10	1
E. Student drops out of school.	1	4	4	3

Please provide any other comments or suggestions for improvements.

A. A student dropping a class before the drop date is minimal risk to the student. The student should be encouraged to add another class at their earliest convenience.

B. A student failing a class requires that the student repeat the class to ensure graduation. Improvements may include taking the same class with a different instructor, or different time or format to improve the student's opportunity to pass the class.

C. Failing an exam requires that the student seek additional help through tutoring or meeting with the instructor to determine an improvement action plan.

D. Failing homework often only requires additional focused study time by the student. Additional improvement options may be tutoring or study sessions with the instructor. Additional structured study time methods may also improve performance.

E. A student dropping out of school represents the greatest threat to the student's success and achievement, and represents lost revenue for the school. Students considering dropping out shall be provided special counseling, and may be considered for alternative class scheduling or tutoring as needed.

All available resources will be considered to keep a student engaged.

3. Standardize the work.

Create or update the standard work instructions and train the employees to the standards. The standard can be written documentation already in existence (i.e., policy manuals, service standards, work instructions, etc.).

4. Create appropriate visual controls and/or mistake proofing devices or systems.

It may not always be possible to fully prevent mistakes from happening. Even computer systems can be over-ridden and bar codes ignored. However, the goal must be to reduce the number of defects that are likely to occur. When providing a product or service ensure the process allows for "making it easy to do the right thing and hard or impossible to do the wrong thing."

Standard Work

Standard work *establishes and controls the best way to complete a task without variation from the original intent.* These tasks are then executed consistently, without variation from the original intent, ideally to an established takt time. Standard work offers a basis for providing consistent levels of productivity, quality, and safety, while promoting a positive work attitude based on well-documented work standards. Standard work, done properly, reduces all process variation. It is the basis for all continuous improvement activities.

Standard work is meant to facilitate creativity and innovation by providing a starting point and process for implementing improvements. Standard work improves stability and reduces variation, which are key concepts in Lean Sigma improvement initiates.

The steps to creating standard work are:

1. Define the target area or process. Look for logical beginning and ending points, or repetitive tasks. Be careful not to target too large or too small a task or group of tasks. Make sure to involve the people who are doing the tasks.

2 Conduct time observations of the target tasks. Or, if actual task time data can be gathered from historical records the team may use this data. Make sure to only use actual performance data. Do not used standard or projected times. Ask the people closest to the tasks to track their time for the team if this is appropriate, and actual observation time is limited.

3. Populate a Time Observation Sheet. *A* ***Time Observation Sheet*** *is the detailed listing of each activity comprised within the process along with their start and stop times.*

Process: Computer Repair		TIME OBSERVATION SHEET							Date: Today / Time: various	OBV: Tom M. / OBV: Mary P.
Step	**Component Task**	VA	NVA	**1**	**2**	**3**	**4**	**5**	**Average TASK TIME**	**Notes**
1	Greet customer and determine issue	X		3 minutes	1 minutes	2 minutes	1 minutes	1 minutes	1.6	No problems. Customers like Holly.
2	Complete service order request online		X	2 minutes	0.5 minutes	0.5 minutes	1 minutes	0.5 minutes	0.9	
3	Establish projected completion date online	X		0.5 minutes	0.5 minutes	0.5 minutes	0.5 minutes	0.5 minutes	0.5	
4	Complete receipt for customer	X		0.25 minutes	0.25 minutes	0.25 minutes	0.25 minutes	0.25 minutes	0.25	
5	Deliver computer to repair in bound area		X	2 minutes	3 minutes	7 minutes	2 minutes	4 minutes	3.6	People can get side tracked when delivering.
6	Wait for repair		X	2 weeks	1 weeks	1 weeks	1 weeks	1 weeks	1.2	There may be opportunity to improve repair tim and reduce waste.
7	Complete repair and test	X		3 hours	5 hours	1 hours	1.5 hours	0.5 hours	2.2	This step varies depending on what is wrong w the unit.
8	Document parts and time for repair online		X	15 minutes	3 minutes	5 minutes	3 minutes	2 minutes	5.6	
9	Return repaired computer to out bound area		X	2 minutes	2 minutes	2 minutes	5 minutes	2 minutes	2.6	People can get side tracked when delivering.
10	When customer returns, collect computer from out bound area	X		2 minutes	2 minutes	2 minutes	2 minutes	2 minutes	2	This is some distance away from front desk.
11	Complete sales documents and collect fees	X		1.5 minutes	1.5 minutes	1.5 minutes	1.5 minutes	1.5 minutes	1.5	

Note: This standard work analysis covers a computer repair service. The three major steps for this process are:

A. Check-in and Drop-off repair item: Time Observation steps 1 - 5 with a task time of 4.0 minutes. Observed time = 6.85 minutes
B. Repair and Document repair: Time Observation steps 6 - 9 with a task time of 1.75 hours. Observed average time of 2.34 hours (Step 6 is a delay step due to backlog and varies with workload.)
C. Pick-up and pay: Steps 10 - 11 with a task time of 3.0 minutes. Observed time = 3.5 minutes.

Takt time for the entire organization is based on a demand of 20 units per week and a 40 hour work week. Therefore, takt time is = 40 hours / 20 units = 2 hours.

Observed process time, not counting the wait time due to backlog, is just over 2.5 hours. (6.85 minutes + 2.34 hours (or 2 hours, 20.4 minutes) + 3.5 minutes) = 2 hours, 30.75 minutes)

4. Document time observations on a Standard Work Chart as shown below. Once the Standard Work Chart has been completed, begin to review the work steps for waste and modify the work routing to reduce or eliminate waste. Use the Plan-Do-Check-Act (PDCA) process described earlier in this chapter to test, verify, and implement improvements or changes.

The following is the before Standard Work Chart:

Standard Work Chart

Area: Customer service and repair — OP N/A of ____
Process: Computer repair — PG 1 of 1
Location: Main Store — Process: Computer Repair
Takt Time: 2 hrs — Cycle Time: Variable
Updated By: Tom M — Date: 10-
Approved By: Mary P — Date: 10-
Checked By: TBD — Date: / /

Step Number	Major Operational Steps	Manual Time	Automated Time	Motion Time	Wait Time
1	Greet customer and determine issue	x			
2	Complete service order request online	x			
3	Establish projected completion date online		x		
4	Complete receipt for customer		x		
5	Deliver computer to repair in bound area			x	
6	Wait for repair				1-2 w
7	Complete repair and test	x			
8	Document parts and time for repair online	x			
9	Return repaired computer to out bound area			x	
10	When customer returns, collect computer from out bound area			x	
11	Complete sales documents and collect fees	x			

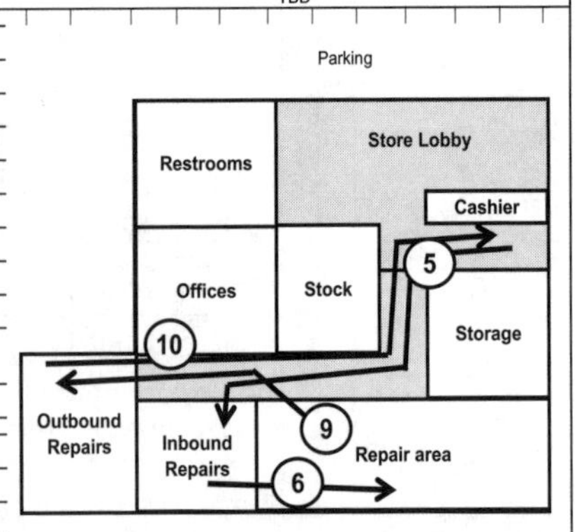

Another common charting method is the Standard Work Combination Table shown below for the same example. An advantage of this method is that it graphically displays the required takt time relative to the tasks or process steps.

Standard Work Combination Table

Part #	Various		Date	22-Nov	Demand / Shift	N/A	Operation Number	Repair	Manual = (solid bar); Walking = WWWWWWWWW; Automatic = ··········▸; Delay = DDDDDDDDDDDD
Process Name	Computer Repair		Dept.	Repair	TAKT Time	2 hours	Prepared by	Tom M.	

Step #	Description of Operation	Time in Minutes (unless specified)	Time: Manual	Auto	Walk	Wait
1	Greet customer and determine issue	1.6	X			
2	Complete service order request online	0.9		X		
3	Establish projected completion date on-line	0.5		X		
4	Complete receipt for customer	0.25	X			
5	Deliver computer ro repair in bound area	3.6			X	
6	Wait for repair	1.2 Weeks	Wait time is not shown on Gantt Chart.			X
7	Complete repair and test	2.2 Hours	X			
8	Document parts and time for repair online	5.6	X			
9	Return repaired computer to out bound area	2.6			X	
10	When customer returns, collect computer from out bound area	2	X			
11	Complete sales documents and collect fees	1.5	X			

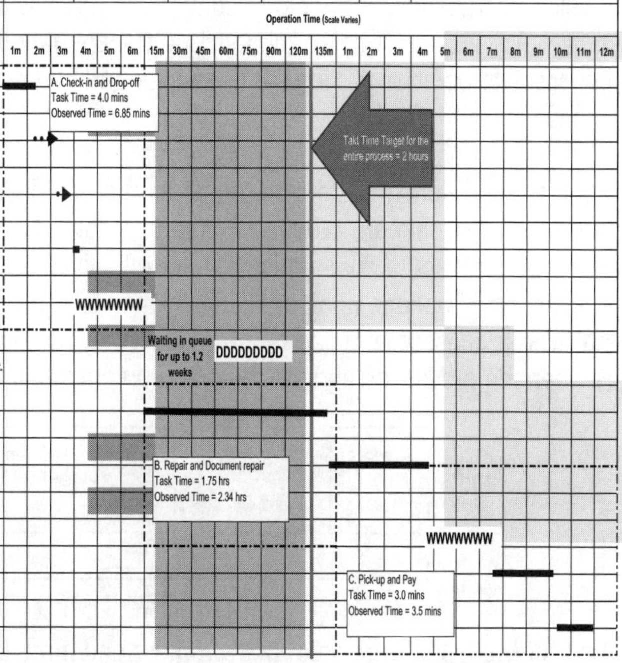

In this service repair example, the team has several opportunities for improvement to meet the takt time of 2 hours. The team decided to change the location of the in bound and out bound repair storage locations. This move alone is expected to save ~ 4 – 6 minutes. The balance of the improvement (~ 24 - 26 minutes) must come from reduction in the repair and repair documentation times (steps 7 and 8).

These charts help to create better work standards and can be easily used for training. Standard work documentation requires some time and effort, but is fundamental for the implementation of Lean Sigma methods and tools and will prove well worth the effort in the long run.

Process or Work Area Layout

Process or Work Area Layout *is the process of reducing the distance between or co-location of resources or people to ensure the product or service is delivered to the customer with minimal or no waste.* The basic concept for optimum process or work area layout/co-location is to minimize the wastes of delay, motion, and transportation (total distance traveled by materials or people to complete a process or operation), and to improve flow. To minimize wastes of delay, motion, and transportation, it is common for work areas and processes to be arranged in U or L- shapes and for key process workers and materials to be co-located.

U or L-shaped work areas allow process workers to visually see the flow and be connected directly to the upstream process to improve flow. U or L-shaped flows and co-location also allow workers to communicate more effectively as they will typically be in "eye sight and ear shot" from one another. Straight line work areas are common in many "assembly line" type processes and can be represented by the diagram below. Notice the distance between the processes and the input and output locations.

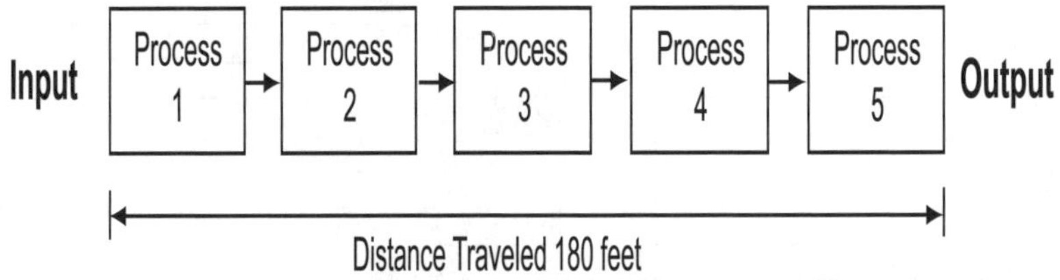

In a U or L-shaped work area, both workers and materials flow in a circular direction, and the input and output are in close proximity. This enables people to see progress, make needed adjustments, and communicate clearly any developing issues or information. A U-shaped work area is represented in the following diagram:

Layout 2

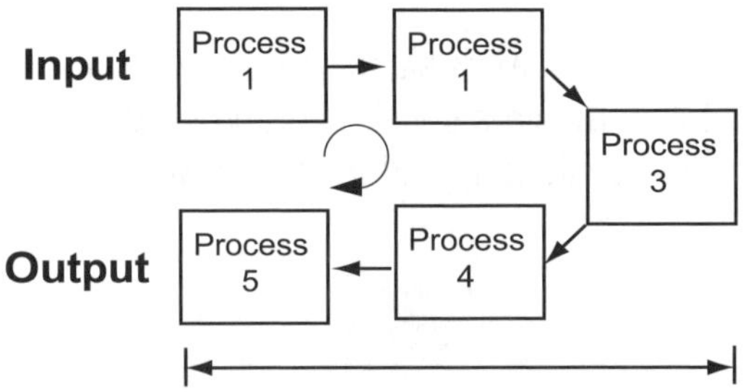

An L shape is better than a straight line, but not usually as good at reducing waste of motion as a U shaped work area.

Typically, many facilities have areas or departments separated by physical walls that may impede the efficiency of work flow. Eliminating walls may be difficult to achieve, but once people understand some of the efficiencies that can be gained, they become engaged in tackling the challenges. Many different methods can be used, such as the computer and visual controls simulating these walls coming down. It is important to realize that there are delays in many processes due to the physical separations.

The graphic below illustrates the comparison between the current physical arrangement with walls and a future Lean Sigma state designed without walls. Lean designs without walls remove any and all barriers that impact work flow, improving all types of communication and movement; no design should ever compromise safety or confidentiality.

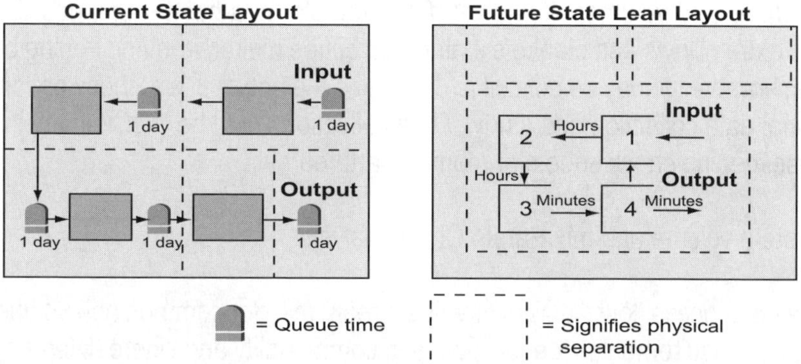

An example of layout and co-location improvement comes from a custom printing service where print requests are taken at the in-store front desk or online in customer service, and then moved to a print layout specialist for layout and cost estimating. Their office was in the back of the complex near production. After cost estimating by the print layout specialist, the request was forwarded to a sales specialist for pricing. Their office was in the store front. Once the price was determined, the information was returned to the customer service representative, located in a separate office near the customer service desk in the store, to communicate back to the customer. This process had only about 3 - 5 minutes of actual processing time, yet due to proximity of the offices, the process often took several hours to complete, and it was common for in-store customers to leave the files for a later quote from the customer service representative.

After the improvement team completed a Lean Sigma improvement project they recommended that Customer Service, Print Layout Specialists, and Sales Specialists be co-located in the front office near the customer service desk. Several issues had to be addressed before the complete transition could be completed, but once the team was in a common area, they were able to improve their speed for processing quotes by 75%!

Mass Customization

Mass customization *combines the low costs of mass production processes with the variable output required to meet individual customer needs.* Some of the best examples of mass customization are fast food restaurants. Fast food restaurants combine a variety of products with standard processes and order combinations to allow their customers to determine their choices on the spot with quick and efficient order fulfillment.

The steps to using the concept and tool of mass customization are:

1. Create a process flow diagram or value stream map noting process or service variations/options and volumes, if known. For example, in a hotel room, possible options may be extra pillows and blankets, hair dryer, coffee maker, iron and ironing board, and the like, however, it may be difficult to determine the actual use of these options without additional data collection and study. Data collection could be VOC survey information or housekeeping check sheets at room departures.

2. Complete a volume and mix Pareto Chart analysis.

3. Review the process flow diagram or value stream map for common and unique sub processes and requirements. Identify points of commonality and where differences begins to occur. For a catering service, basic meal menu combinations may be identified and offered based on past popularity.

4. Develop a plan to stage or process services to a point immediately upstream of differentiation and or develop a plan to deliver all possible options at customer demand. For fast food restaurants or catering services, this may be standard packaged meals or menus. In a hotel room, this may mean stocking each hotel room with standard items to allow guests to customize their use of the room to their satisfaction.

5. As new demand occurs, pull from staged services, create differentiation, and deliver services as required. This can also be accomplished by allowing your customers to self-serve to their specific needs such as in the hotel example discussed in step 4 above.

For example, a catering service tabulated their meal deliveries for weddings over the previous year. They determined the following breakdown of meal items:

Main Course	
Beef	75%
Chicken	20%
Fish	5%
Starch	
Potato	80%
Rice	15%
Pasta	5%
Vegetable	
Green beans	70%
Mixed	15%
Corn	5%
Other	10%
Desert	
Cake	100%
Additional Desert	
Ice cream	3%
Other	2%

From this data the caterer developed a standardized menu with options and à la carte items. Before mass customization, every meal plan was customized, and a special purchase was made for each event. With mass customization, standard meal plans were identified for clients, with the option for additional items at an up charge. The organization was able to secure reduced pricing through their suppliers as they would commit to larger purchases throughout the year. This enabled the caterer to improve their profits and sustain the high level of customization and customer satisfaction.

The following are examples of service organizations using the concept of mass customization to enhance their market position:

Computer Hardware

Customers are able to order on-line or by phone, and specify their exact hardware and software needs. Hardware providers build-to-order and ship within 2 days.

Lodging

Rooms offer alarm clocks, coffee makers, honor bars, and extra blankets and pillows to allow their guests to customize their room to their desire. These items are provided as economical standards in each room rather than trying to individually specify the needs of each guest.

Custom Home Builders

Model homes are offered with standard options and can be quickly modified to suit the customer's wishes.

Airlines

Airlines are now using pricing models based on customer needs and travel habits. Standard options are offered to suit a variety of customer needs.

Fast Foods

Restaurants offer standard menu items and combinations that allow customers to customize their orders while keeping their delivery process to an acceptable timeframe.

Event Planning

Event planners have developed standard lists of most desired options. They have standardized delivery and are prepared to deliver the options as required based on customer needs.

To develop mass customization options, organizations must first collect or gather data on customer needs, desires, and buying habits. The better an organization knows the needs of their clients, the better they will be able to design mass customization offerings.

With appropriate customer buying pattern and needs developed, analysis can be completed to determine the exact product and service offerings to bundle to satisfy the greatest customer needs. Bundling of options should be completed in such a manner so as to satisfy 80% or more of customer demands or requests.

For example, a custom tour provider finds that around 85% of their clients request ethnic restaurant maps. Their original practice was to develop a custom map for each group based on specific group requests. After their mass customization effort, they decided to develop one map that included all specialty and ethnic food choices near the city.

Now, when a tour group requests a specific ethnic food restaurant map, they get a map of all local ethnic dining options. Although this is not as "custom" as the old way of doing business, they found that the new map was perfectly acceptable to their clients. They even had some compliments on the new maps, as they provided new options that were previously not considered.

Another mass customization example is that of a law firm that specialized in last wills and testaments. They found that 90% of their basic will and testament documents were a basic format. They developed Web-based programming to capture a potential client's information in a generic format. Now, instead of a typical face-to-face meeting with the client that lasted over an hour, the attorneys are now able to achieve the same fees with only a half-hour work session.

Service Flow

There are several ways to create flow in service environments. Creating flow in service environments is important as it reduces waste and improves customer satisfaction. This section outlines service flow methods and tools used to create a smooth flow in service processes as well as service flow examples. It is important to note that in reality, many service flows are actually a combination or mixture of these flow methods and require in-depth analysis and study. This section introduces three service flow methods and four service flow tools so that improvement teams can study and apply these techniques and tools appropriately in their service flow processes. At the end of the Service Flow section, numerous examples are provided showing the various combination of the service flow methods and tools.

Service Flow Methods

The three basic service flow methods are:

1. Continuous Flow
2. Paced Flow
3. Scheduled Flow

1. Continuous Flow

Continuous flow *is when the order or demand is initiated and the process continues uninterrupted until the order or demand is satisfied.* Examples of continuous flow service processes are a make-to-order sandwich shop, a bank teller transaction, patient with heart attack symptoms at an Emergency Room, an online commodity purchase, committing resources for 911 calls, etc.

Continuous flow is most successful whenthe following conditions exist:

- Order Urgency = High
- Order Pattern = Irregular or unpredictable
- Order Fulfillment Process = Predictable or standardized

Note: The Order Fulfillment Process are the activities that eventually satisfy (or meet) a request for a good or service that is initiated by the customer, client, or patient.

2. Paced Flow

Paced flow *processing is used where order fulfillment tasks are done on a regular frequency or timed schedule or sequence.* Examples of Paced or Level flow are a security service making regular rounds at specified times throughout the day, the US Postal Service alternating between processing envelopes and boxes at a regular cadence, a laundry processing service alternating between color and white loads of laundry, delivery meals for patients at a hospital, etc. Each of these processes can be delivered in a Paced and Leveled flow format. Paced flow can be leveled by volume or process type.

Paced flow is most successful when the following conditions exist:

- Order Urgency = Medium
- Order Pattern = Regular and predictable
- Order Fulfillment Process = Predicable or standardized

3. Scheduled Flow

Scheduled flow *is where orders or demand is identified and then scheduled or reserved for fulfillment at a specific time.* For example, scheduled flow is typically used for doctor or dentist appointments, financial services and counseling, legal advice call-ins, restaurant reservations at a restaurant, etc. In these cases, clients, customers, or patients call in requesting an appointment for a specific time and date.

Scheduled flow is most successful when the following conditions exist:

- Order Urgency = Low
- Order Pattern = Irregular or unpredictable
- Order Fulfillment Process = Unpredictable or non-standard

Pitch can be used to regular workflow using any of these three flow methods. ***Pitch*** *is the adjusted takt time that establishes an optimal and smooth workflow throughout the value stream.* In other words, pitch is the adjusted takt time (or multiple of) when takt time is too short.

Service Flow Tools

Service flow tools that can be used with each service flow method to improve and/or smooth flow. Service flow tools are introduced and then shown in simple examples that follow.

The four basic service flow tools are:

1. Heijunka Leveling
2. Pull Systems and Kanbans
3. Supermarkets
4. First-In First-Out (FIFO) Lanes

1. Heijunka Leveling

***Heijunka Leveling** works to level or smooth flow by delivering goods and/or services in an alternating or patterned manner rather than large chunks of time devoted to only one service delivery.* For example, instead of only stuffing envelopes in the morning and packing boxes in the afternoon, a mail service will smooth their schedule by filling envelopes for a hour, then packing boxes for two hours, and alternate this flow sequence throughout the day. The leveling tool was implemented to eliminate running large batches of one product at a time. To be successful with this tool, quick changeovers (covered later in this chapter) from one service to another will be essential. A visual representation and example of Heijunka Leveling is as follows.

A mail order fulfillment and packing service packs the following orders through the day:

A = Small envelope orders
B = Small - Medium Box orders
C = Large Box orders

Without Heijunka Leveling:

8:00 am 10:00 am 12:00 am 2:00 pm 3:00 pm 4:00 pm 5:00 pm 6:00 pm 7:00 pm 8:00 pm 9:00 pm 10:00 pm	
AAAAAAAAAAAAAAAAAAAAAAAAAAAAAA	(30)
BBBBBBBBBBBBBBB	(15)
CCCCCCCCCCCCCCC	(15)

With Heijunka Leveling:

8:00 am	10:00 am	12:00 am	2:00 pm	3:00 pm	4:00 pm	5:00 pm	6:00 pm	7:00 pm	8:00 pm	9:00 pm	10:00 pm	
AAA	AAA	AAA		AAA	AAA		AAA	AAA	AAA	AAA	AAA	(30)
	BB	BB	BB	BB		BB	BB		BB	B		(15)
	CC	CC	CC		CC	CC	CC		CC		C	(15)

By using Heijunka Leveling the organization can deliver a variety of package sizes sooner in the day and the flow of service to the customer is smoothed. In this example, the ability to "change over" quickly from packing envelopes, to small/mid-size boxes, to large boxes is essential for Heijunka Leveling to work well.

If changeovers cannot be done fast enough, consider the following Heijunka Leveling option.

8:00 am	10:00 am	12:00 am	2:00 pm	3:00 pm	4:00 pm	5:00 pm	6:00 pm	7:00 pm	8:00 pm	9:00 pm	10:00 pm	
AAAAAAAAAA				AAAAAAAAAA					AAAAAAAAAA			(30)
		BBBBB				BBBBB				BBBBB		(15)
			CCCCC				CCCCC				CCCCC	(15)

Another practical example of Heijunka Leveling comes from Susan an insurance agent at a small, but growing insurance agency. Susan used to have her day divided neatly into the following three key segments:

(1) In the mornings, Susan would work 4 hours on new accounts and marketing trying to grow their client base.
(2) After lunch, Susan set aside 2 hours to deal with existing client issues and claims. She would work with claims adjusters and clients to ensure the issues were adequately addressed.
(3) Susan set aside the final 2 hours of her day to answer incoming emails and other written and voice-mail correspondence.

When the firm was small, this system seemed to work well for Susan. As the firm grew, she found herself working later and later into the evening. She would often miss or be delayed in responding to key email correspondence that was transmitted during the day. When she finally got to the emails, she found that she was losing a day in getting back to people and resolving issues. To improve this situation, Susan applied a Heijunka Leveling tool and modified her schedule to better address issues throughout the day. Susan shifted her schedule to incorporate this concept in the following way:

(1) In the morning, Susan would work the first 2 hours on new accounts and marketing.
(2) After those first 2 hours in morning, Susan would spend 1 hour dealing with existing client issues and claims.
(3) And then the next 1 hour, she spent catching up on current correspondence.

After the first cycle of activities (1 - 3), Susan would repeat this sequence throughout the day so that she still devoted the same amount of time a day to the three key areas. With this improved technique she was able to manage her schedule more effectively to better serve her clients and co-workers. Susan not only found that her clients were better satisfied by her more timely responses, but she was able to keep up on key issues throughout the day, and actually get home earlier! Susan's success with Heijunka Leveling reduced waste and improved customer satisfaction for her insurance agency.

2. Pull Systems and Kanbans

*A **Pull System** is a process to ensure nothing is produced upstream (i.e., supplier process) until the downstream (i.e., customer) process "signals" the need for it.* This enables the service or work to be provided without detailed schedules. The "signal" is referred to as a Kanban, Card, or Kanban Card.

***Kanbans** (pronounced Con – Bons) or "pull signals" are visual (or auditory) signals used to control flow and trigger action between processes.* Pull signals can be used to identify demand such as a door bell, service bell or alarm, or to trigger replacement of a service or service item to prevent future delay. These "pull signals" help organizations deliver goods and services with minimal waste. The general concept of Kanbans is to signal and regulate work within and between processes.

Kanbans generally fall into one of the following three categories.

1. **Withdrawal Kanban** or Move Signal (Card) - Indicates that a number of items, or electronic files or documents need to be removed or pulled from a location (i.e., supermarket) and supplied downstream. A Withdrawal Kanban or Move Signal "pulls" the required items or service from the upstream operation and puts them into use. Service organizations most often use this method to replenish consumables used at the service delivery location from a larger inventory storage area. The concept of Kanban can also be used for replenishment of information (i.e., documents, data, etc.) - also referred to as eKanban. EKanban examples include email filters and alerts notifying of impending work or responses needed, flags in various CRM or MS Office applications for notification that a document needs to be reviewed or modified, etc.

2. **Supply Kanban** or Supply Signal (Card) - Indicates the reorder point has been reached due to consumption and a service, product, electronic document, or data needs to be replenished (typically to a supermarket or outside supplier). The Supply Signal authorizes the workers using materials and services to obtain replenishment from the supplier. Service organizations most often use Supply Signals to replenish consumables used in the service delivery process. EKanban examples include signals such as bar code scans that automatically trigger a supplier to send more of a particular item or a service is required, an alert email signaling that more data needs to be processed, etc.

3. **Produce Kanban** or Deliver Signal (Card) - Indicates that services, products, electronic documents, etc. needs to be produced, processed, and/or delivered as a "batch" downstream. The number of items to be produced and supplied should replenish what was removed or pulled. Deliver Signals can be used to indicate that a customer requires a service. It is important to note that Deliver Signals are not synonymous with sales orders. Sales orders are usually unique to an order, while Deliver Signals are for a standard quantity. The Produce Kanban or Deliver Signal authorizes the upstream operation to deliver items, services, documents, or information downstream. Service organization use these to indicate that services need to be performed. EKanban examples include signals (i.e., urgent emails, text message, etc.) that all key data has been updated on a spreadsheet and a report needs to be generated, a series of applications have been received and must be reviewed, a minimum number of participants for a class has been reached and the course needed to be scheduled, etc.

Organizations will need to customize Kanbans to their specific needs. The examples previously discussed can be used as a starting point. A key factor to consider when implementing a Pull System is how many Kanbans Cards will be required. Keep in mind that these "Cards" can be electronic tallys or visual controls within various software applications. Several factors must be considered when determining how many Kanban Cards should be made regardless of what type or category they are. The key factors are:

1. Average Daily Demand (ADD): What is the daily demand and for the item of service?

2. Lead Time (LT) of replenishment of an item or service: How long will it take to get the item or service replenished?

3. Card Collection Time (CCT): How long will it take before we realize we have a pull signal?

4. Safety Stock (SS): How much safety stock shall be planned to provide protection from outages? Expressed as a percent, so to have 5% SS, use 1.05 for SS in the calculations.

5. Container Size (CS) or standard quantity: What is the quantity or size of the product to be delivered?

These factors apply directly to a formal calculation of the number of Kanban cards needed. The formal calculation for the number of Kanban Cards is as follows:

Number of Kanban Cards = (ADD * (LT + CCT) * SS) / CS

For an example of using the three types of Kanban Cards, consider providing amusement park maps to an amusement Park Information Center from their outside supplier (The Print House, Inc.) with the following parameters: (Graphically represented on page 319.)

ADD (Park Information Center 1 of 5) = 400 maps / 12 hours of operation per day
LT = 0.5 days (6 hours)
CCT = 0.5 days (6 hours)
SS = 5%
CS = 100 maps per pack

The number of Withdrawal Kanban Cards will be:

Number of Withdrawal Kanban Cards = (400 maps / day X (0.5 day + 0.5 day) X 1.05) / 100 maps per pack = 4.2 Move Cards (round up to 5 Cards and use this as a starting point for each Park Information Center)

A Withdrawal Kanban Card may appear as follows:

Move to:
Park
Information
Center 1

Withdrawal Kanban Card

Card 1 of 5

<table>
<tr><td>Item Name:</td><td>Park Maps</td><td rowspan="2"><u>Upstream Process</u>
Park Supply Center</td></tr>
<tr><td>Location:</td><td>Park Supply Center</td></tr>
<tr><td>Shelf Number:</td><td>T-3 shelf 1</td><td rowspan="2"><u>Downstream Process</u>
Park Information Center</td></tr>
<tr><td>Quantity:</td><td>1 – 100 ct pack</td></tr>
</table>

With the same example, let us consider the Supply Kanban Cards from the Park Supply Center to the map supplier (i.e., The Print House, Inc.). The Print House, Inc. takes an additional 7 days to print and deliver the map packs to the park, where there are the following parameters:

ADD (All 5 Park Information Centers) = 2,000 maps / 12 hours of operation per day
LT = 1 week or 7 days
CCT = 0.5 days (6 hours)
SS = 5%
CS = (100 maps per pack 10 packs per Box) 1,000 maps per box

The number of Supply Kanban Cards will be:

Number of Supply Kanban Cards = (2,000 maps X (7 days + 0.5 day) X 1.05) / 1000 maps per box = 15.75 Supply Cards (round up to 16 Supply Cards). If fewer Cards were desired, the supplier could be asked to supply the maps in larger standard packages.

A Supply Kanban Card may appear as follows:

Park Maps

Supply Kanban Card

Item Name:	**Park Maps**	Upstream Process The Print House, Inc. (Customer Service)
Delivery Location:	**Park Supply Center**	
Supplier	The Print House, Inc.	Downstream Process Park Supply Center
Quantity:	**1 box of 10 x 100 ct packs**	
Alternative:	Loose 100 ct packs if boxes are unavailable	Card Number : **16**

The number of Produce Kanban Cards will be:

The Print House Inc. has 5 Produce Kanban Cards to ensure they always have 5000 park maps in stock at any time. They produce 1000 maps per Kanban Card.

A Produce Kanban Card may appear as follows:

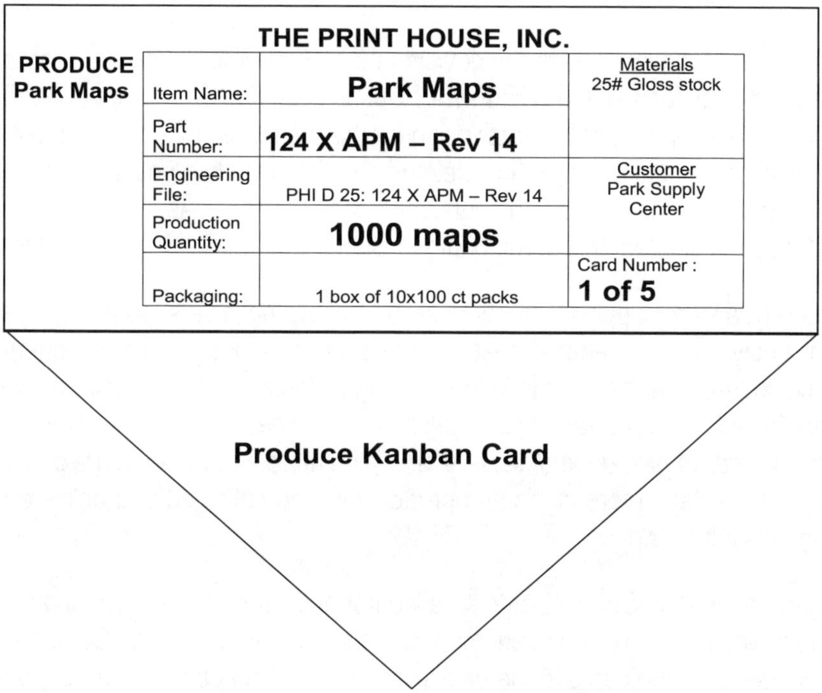

The following Kanban Pull System example is visually conveyed on the next page and is explained as follows:

To operate the Kanban Pull System at the Amusement Park, each of the 5 Park Information Centers is initially stocked with 5 packs of maps at 100 maps per pack. Each 100 count map pack has a Withdrawal Kanban Card clipped to it with a paper clip by the Park Supply Center purchasing staff.

As the maps are consumed by the park visitors (i.e., Customers) and new packs of maps are pulled and open for use, the Withdrawal Kanban Card (i.e., Move Signal Card) is pulled and placed in a Kanban Card collection bin by the Information Center staff (shown as a Kanban Post icon and at any point in time, some of the collection posts may have cards in them, and some may not, based on actual map consumption). As new packs are opened at the Information Centers the Cards begin to fill the Kanban Card collection bins.

Twice per day, a Park Supply Center worker (or runner) makes a supply and collection trip to fill previously signaled demand needs (i.e., deliver previously signaled items), and collect newly triggered Kanban Cards in the Kanban collection posts. (*A **runner** is someone that is dedicated to ensure takt time or pitch is maintained and makes service rounds at specified intervals to pick-up and deliver items.*) As more supply items are place on a pull replenishment system, more cards and products will be collected and delivered on each supply and collection trip.

Upon return to the Park Supply Center, the worker pulls from the "supermarket" map pack boxes the exact number of 100 count map packs to match the Kanban Cards as collected in their rounds, clips the cards to the packs, and readies the pack for delivery during their next scheduled rounds to the Park Information Centers.

As full boxes of maps are emptied at the Park Supply Center, the worker will pull the Supply Kanban Card and fax a copy of the card to the map supplier (i.e., The Print House, Inc.).

When the map supplier receives the faxed Supply Kanban Card, they produce and deliver a box (i.e., 1000 maps) as per the Produce Kanban Card on a FIFO system of replenishment.

During the next scheduled supply and collection trip by the Park Supply Center worker, the map packs with attached Withdrawal Kanban Cards are delivered to the specific Information Centers, and any Withdrawal Kanban Cards from the collection bin are picked up, and thus the cycle repeats itself.

This simple visual process ensures that neither the Park Information Centers nor the Park Supply Center runs out of maps during the day, which keeps the visitors happy and spending money!

The Kanban Cards in the Park Information Center Kanban posts represent consumption of maps by that Information Center. If demand is expected to increase or peak for any specific reason, temporary Kanban Cards can be added to the system to accommodate the anticipated increased demand.

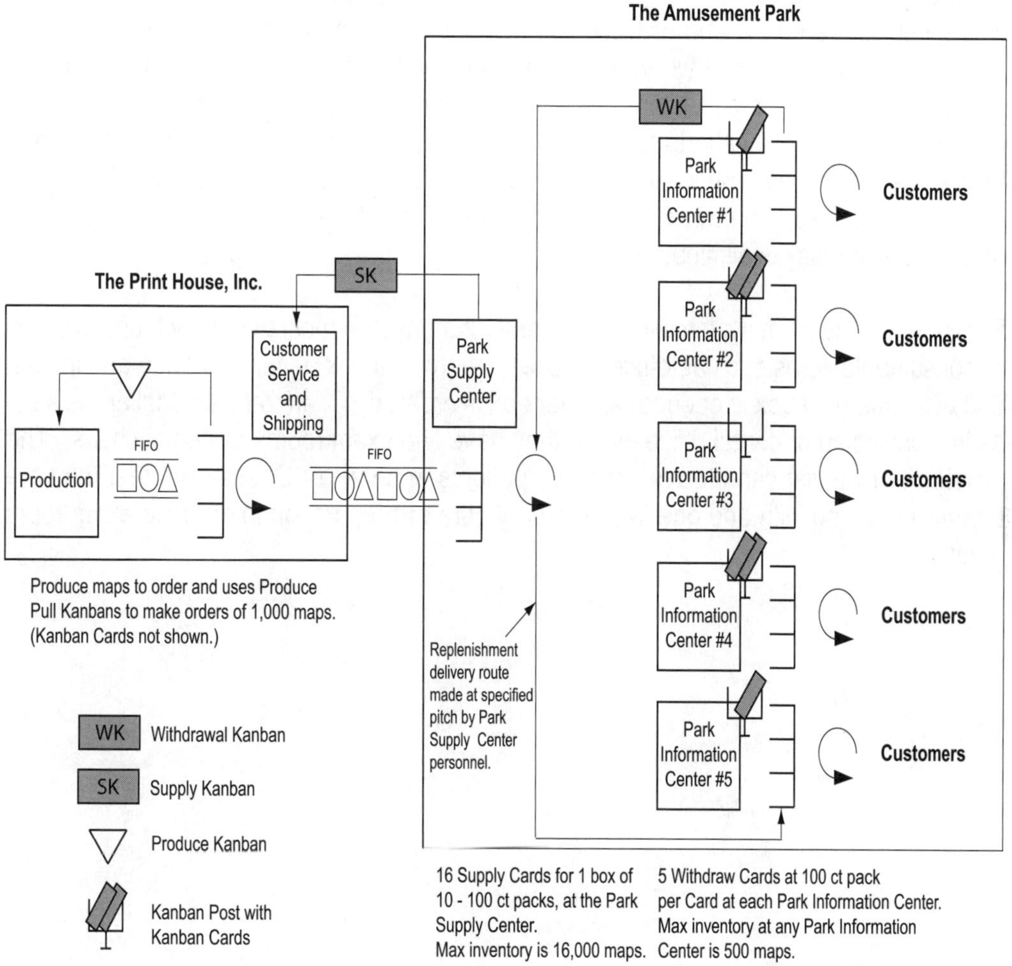

Other less mathematically driven pull signals can be much simpler. The most basic signal pull system is that for a short order cook at a small restaurant. The wait staff takes the order (i.e., Kanban Card) and places it on a rotating wheel. The cook pulls the order tickets in the order they are placed and cooks to order. When the order is ready, the cook rings a bell (auditory pull signal) to alert the wait staff that the food is ready for delivery. Consider simpler methods and trials first and then move up to more sophisticated service flow methods and tools.

Another simple and effective Pull Signal system is known as a "Two Bin" system. This is where the work area will always have two bins in circulation. Workers use parts or items from one bin (or box), and when it becomes empty, the empty bin (or box) acts as the signal to bring in another full bin (or box). This system, if done properly, should ensure that there are never any shortages or stock outs. If another full bin cannot be replenished before the next bin is empty, simply increase the size of the bin (or, add additional bins into the system) so that running out before replenishment cannot happen, and the waste of waiting and delay is eliminated.

Examples of a two-bin systems in service environments are most generally found in worker consumable items such as office supplies, where one box of items is open and in use, and when the next box is opened, another box is ordered. Or, in transactional areas such as in a physician or dental office where they have two exam rooms or dental chairs. The physician or dentist can always have two patients in service. One patient that they are currently meeting with and one in preliminary care or preparation in the next exam room or chair.

Some helpful guidelines to consider when implementing Pull Systems and Kanbans:

- The process should be standardized, stabilized, and balanced.
- Downstream or closer to the customer, processes withdraw items and services from upstream processes.
- Upstream processes only produce or deliver what is withdrawn or consumed.
- Only move 100% good or reliable goods or services.
- Kanban Cards should move with items, if appropriate, to provide visual controls and limits.
- Workers upstream pull their own goods or services.
- Nothing is made, moved, or delivered without a Kanban Card.
- The number of Kanban Cards determines the work in process inventory levels.
- Continue to try and reduce the number of signal cards in the system. A goal of Lean Sigma is to deliver goods and services to order.

These simple examples illustrate a basic manual Pull System and Kanban. As technology develops, additional means of signaling are becoming available. Simple electronic signals such as audible chimes or bells signal new mail or problems with electronic devices. Entirely electronic signal systems are already in use where signals are sent simply by clicking on a reorder symbol, which sends a reorder or replenish email or automated purchase order to the upstream supplier. Bar code scanning is also capable of sending automated signals to replenish products or services. The limitations for the application of a Pull System and Kanban is truly in the minds of the practitioners and hardware and software designers.

3. Supermarkets

Supermarket *is a term used to describe a specific inventory management process using Kanbans and specified or standard storage locations and package quantities.* A Supermarket inventory tool can be used to control service flow where make-to-order is not possible. Supermarket is a term taken directly from the inventory management/replenishment system of today's modern supermarkets. In a modern supermarket, items are provided a specific shelf space, and as items are pulled and purchased by the customers, replenishment is completed to a specified quantity or shelf space. This system ensures that the supermarket never runs out of an item and no customer ever has to wait for replenishment.

For electronic files and folders a supermarket is a work-controlled method (directory or some other Desktop icon representing work) located between two processes that contain a certain quantity of work or information "buckets" that is "pulled" by the downstream process when needed.

The following will serve as a example of how an In-process supermarket can be used with Microsoft Excel.

A district insurance sales office was recently notified that their sales volume had not met expectations for the previous two months. The office had 15 sales agents. The agents informed the Sales Manager (SM) that they were not getting their sales leads in a timely manner, which probably has contributed to the decrease in the sales volume. The SM had been purchasing an increasing amount of sales leads for the past two months, but with no increase in their Book of Business. Currently, the SM provided leads at different times throughout the month, whenever an agent requested them. The SM wanted an easier system in which everyone could benefit (i.e., leads available when they were needed, leads tracked for quality assurance, and leads ordered automatically when certain conditions were met). The solution was an In-process supermarket of sales leads provided in Excel. The In-process supermarket was set up with groups of 15 leads per worksheet with the following rules:

- Sales agents could only draw 15 leads at a time
- IT created a work group directory, with 'write' privileges only to the Status of Lead field
- The supermarket would always have 10 groups (only 4 shown in the next illustration) of 15 leads available at all times (when the supermarket got down to 5 groups of 15 leads, an automatic email was sent to the company that provided the leads for the purchase of an additional group of 75 leads)

The following illustration represents the In-process supermarket sales lead example:

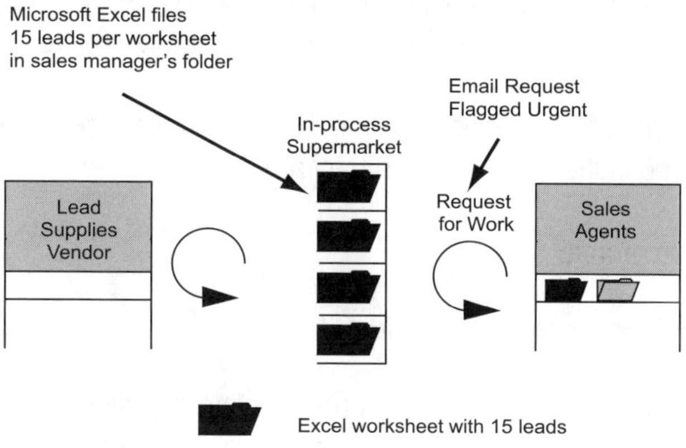

4. First-In First-Out (FIFO) Lanes

***FIFO Lanes** are a work-controlled method to ensure the oldest work (i.e., customer, electronic document, etc.) upstream (first-in) is the first to be processed downstream (first-out).* Nothing frustrates customers more than arriving first, but being assisted last.

The team can be creative in establishing the signal method which is typically referred to as a Kanban within the FIFO Lane system to indicate when the lane is full as well as when it needs to be replenished. (The Supermaket rules previously discussed also apply.) The important point is to ensure a signal (Kanban) system that will work effectively between the processes is established. When the FIFO Lane is full, the upstream worker may lend support to the downstream worker (if practical) until the work is completed or service request met. There is no point in continuing to produce upstream work when the downstream process cannot do anything with it. When this happens, it becomes an overproduction waste, which is considered the worst waste of all.

In the previous example of the SM leads, if the leads or list is time sensitive, the system of providing those leads can be modified into a FIFO Lane as shown below:

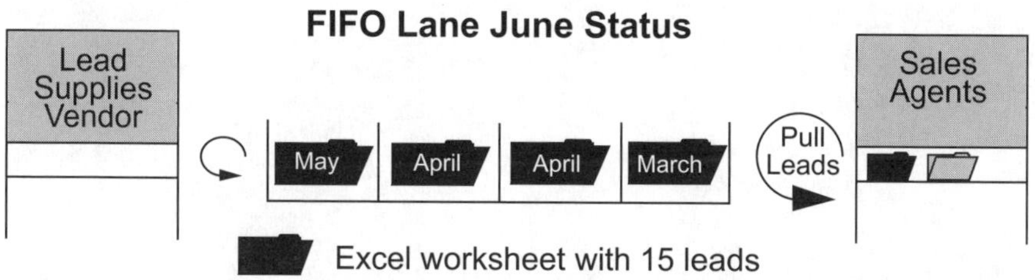

Another FIFO Lane example is that of a shuttle bus service from an airport to a remote rental car service. The first person on can select their set closest to the door thus allowing them to be first off, making them then first in line at the remote counter.

Another good example of FIFO lanes are the TSA security check lanes at US airports. People are processed in the order in which they arrive.

Service Flow Improvement Steps

The steps to creating better service flow are:

1. Define the target area or process that is not meeting a customer requirement, has a capacity issue, or is not meeting a Key Performance Indicator (KPI) goal.

2. Determine the type of service flow method that may be of value. Understand the up-stream customer's capacity and customer's requirements.

3. Determine the service flow tool that may improve the process. Understand the process' capacity.

4. Calculate the number of Kanban Cards needed and create the Cards (if appropriate).

5. Train the people who will be using the system and thoroughly explain the rules of the system.

6. Use the PDCA model and begin the trial. Remind people that the first attempt is a trial and to not become frustrated with difficulties.

7. Follow-up to determine if modifications are needed. Initially, error on the side of too many Kanban Cards to ensure the supply of goods or services is not interrupted.

Service Flow Examples

The following section outlines standard flow processes for Continuous Flow, Paced Flow, and Scheduled Flow, as well as the application of Heijunka Leveling, Pull Systems and Kanbans, Supermarkets, and FIFO Lanes in various service-related examples. These examples also illustrate how the methods and tools can be integrated in various scenarios reflecting the reality of today's service environments. These examples should provide additional insight into your overall understanding of service flow.

Continuous Flow Example

A typical standard representation of a Continuous Flow process is illustrated by a make-to-order specialty hamburger restaurant called Burger's Today!

A standard example for a Continuous Flow process for one customer order at Burger's Today! is as follows:

1. Demand identified
2. Order fulfillment process begins
3. Task 1 – make-to-order standard work task (1) for order
4. Task 2 – make-to-order standard work task (2) for order
5. Task 3 – make-to-order standard work task (3) for order
6. ...
7. ...
8. ...
9. Task (n) - – make-to-order item with (n) number of standard work tasks
10. Demand or order fulfilled and payment received
11. Ready for next demand/order (the next customer would have the same sequence of events. These are the events for one customer order.)

Typically lead time for a make-to-order hamburger is 6 minutes.

A Heijunka example for a Continuous Flow process for Today's Burgers! is as follows:

1. Demand is identified based on historical ordering patterns for a weekday lunch hour and is as follows:

   100 Regular (R) - Regular is defined as ½ pound ground sirloin, sourdough bun, special sauce, swiss cheese, fried egg, and lettuce
   50 Variation 1 (V1) - Variation 1 is defined as ½ pound ground sirloin, sourdough bun, special sauce, swiss cheese, and lettuce
   35 Variation 2 (V2) - Variation 2 is defined as ¾ pound ground sirloin, sourdough bun, special sauce, swiss cheese, fried egg, and lettuce
   25 Variation 3 (V3) - Variation 3 is defined as ¾ pound ground sirloin, sourdough bun, special sauce, swiss cheese, bacon, and lettuce
   75 Other (Specials) – Continue to build specials or make-to-order based on standard Continuous Flow methods

2. Order fulfillment process begins to pre-build hamburgers beginning at a specified time, by type and volume sequence. These hamburgers would be wrapped and placed in a warming tray. Once picked up by the server they would be unwrapped and the other items ordered (French Fries, Onion Rings, etc. supported by a different Kanban Pull System) would be placed on the plate. The Other (Specials) would be made make-to-order. Beginning at 11 am, the cook staff would use the following Heijunka or smoothed build plan:

   R-R-R-V1-V1-V2-V3-R-R-R-V1-V1-V2-V3-R-R-R-V1-V1-V2-V3-R-R-R-V1-V1-V2-V3

3. Demand or order fulfilled and payment received
4. Ready for next demand/order

Typically lead time for a make-to-order burger is 3 minutes.

Note: You may think that by wrapping the burger there is overprocessing waste as well as wastes of motion and transport; however, Today's Burgers! decided that by reducing the lead time of providing burgers from 6 minutes to 3 minutes it would increase sales and customer satisfaction which mitigated these additional wastes.

A Pull System and Kanbans example of Continuous Flow process for Today's Burgers! is as follows:

1. Demand is identified based on historical ordering patterns for a weekday lunch hour and is as follows (same as previous example):

   100 Regular (R) - Regular is defined as ½ pound ground sirloin, sourdough bun, special sauce, swiss cheese, fried egg, and lettuce
   50 Variation 1 (V1) - Variation 1 is defined as ½ pound ground sirloin, sourdough bun, special sauce, swiss cheese, and lettuce
   35 Variation 2 (V2) - Variation 2 is defined as ¾ pound ground sirloin, sourdough bun, special sauce, swiss cheese, fried egg, and lettuce
   25 Variation 3 (V3) - Variation 3 is defined as ¾ pound ground sirloin, sourdough bun, special sauce, swiss cheese, bacon, and lettuce
   75 Other (Specials) – Continue to build specials or make-to-order based on standard Continuous Flow methods

The improvement team sets the Pull Signals and Kanbans for each of the four "standard" hamburger types at the following levels:

5 Regular (R)	Lane 1 – color-coded blue
3 Variation 1 (V1)	Lane 2 – color-coded red
2 Variation 2 (V2)	Lane 3 – color-coded yellow
2 Variation 3 (V3)	Lane 4 – color-coded green

A reusable color-coded card will be used to signal when a new group of items will be requested. When the card is exposed, the counter staff will pass the card to the kitchen and the kitchen will fulfill the order quantity and type indicated on the card.

The following are examples of three of the Kanban Cards:

REGULAR **(R)**
11am Start

Item Name:	**Regular**	Upstream Process Inventory / Stock
Location:	Kitchen	
Shelf Number:	Warming tray Lane 1	Downstream Process Customer
Quantity:	**5**	
Special Instructions:	½ pound ground sirloin, sourdough bun, special sauce, swiss cheese, fried egg, and lettuce	

VARIATION 1
(V1)
11am Start

Item Name:	**Variation 1**	Upstream Process Inventory / Stock
Location:	Kitchen	
Shelf Number:	Warming tray Lane 2	Downstream Process Customer
Quantity:	**3**	
Special Instructions:	½ pound ground sirloin, sourdough bun, special sauce, swiss cheese, and lettuce	

VARIATION 2
(V2)
11am Start

Item Name:	**Variation 2**	Upstream Process Inventory / Stock
Location:	Kitchen	
Shelf Number:	Warming tray Lane 3	Downstream Process Customer
Quantity:	**3**	
Special Instructions:	¾ pound ground sirloin, sourdough bun, special sauce, swiss cheese, fried egg, and lettuce	

2. Kanban Cards are put into play at 11 am and the order fulfillment process begins. As the pre-built hamburgers are sold, the Pull Signal or Kanban Cards are moved and signal the Kitchen to make the designated hamburger and replenish the FIFO Lane. The FIFO Lane and Kanban Card application is illustrated below:

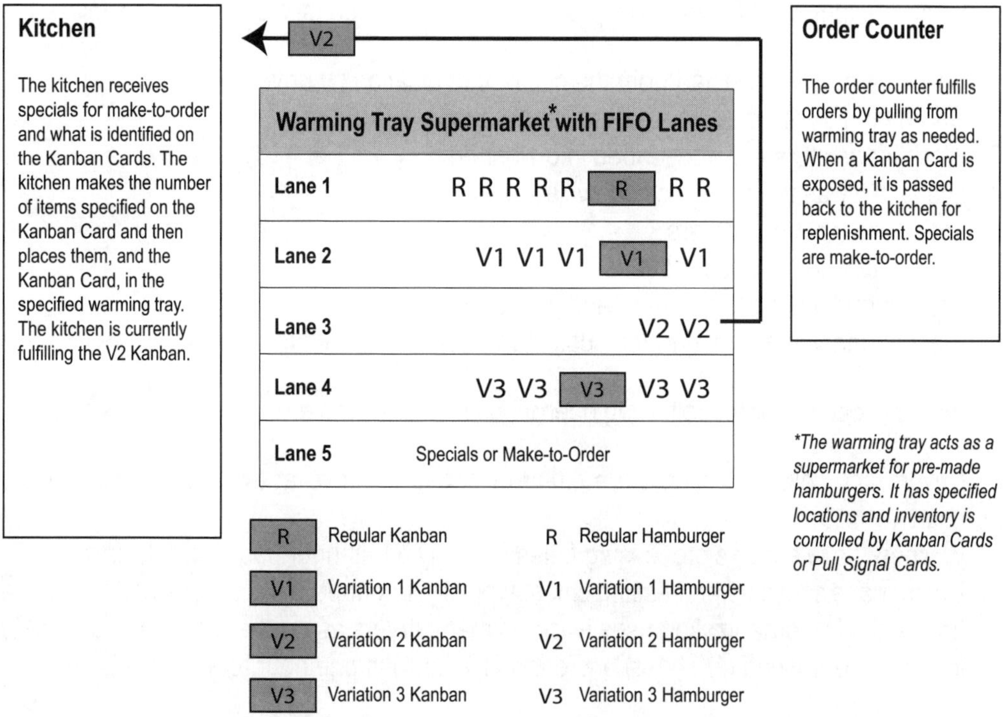

3. As the pace of demand slows, the counter staff will pull the Pull Signal Cards out of use (starting at 12:30 pm) and begin to build all hamburger variations as make-to-order, so by the end of the lunch time, 1:00 pm, all Cards will be removed and only make-to-order hamburgers will be in the system.

Typically lead time for a make-to-order hamburger is 5 minutes.

Paced Flow Example

A typical standard representation of a Paced Flow process is illustrated by a large scale laundry service called Allstar Laundry Services.

A standard example of Paced Flow process for a Allstar Laundry Services is as follows:

1. Soiled laundry is collected from the customers location by drivers
2. Soiled laundry is off loaded, sorted, and staged
3. Wash loads are sized and loaded into washers
4. Loads are washed per specified cycle
5. Loads are moved to dryers
6. Loads are dried to specifications
7. Clean laundry is sorted, folded, and packaged
8. Clean laundry is returned to the customers location by drivers

Paced Flow occurs for the following operations in this example:

1. Drivers and collection routes are timed or paced to arrive at the Allstar facility every hour.
2. Washers have specific processing times typically a half-hour pace per full load.
3. Dryers have specified processing times, typically 1 hour per full load or a half-hour for a half load. (The organization uses twice as many dryers as washers so that a complete load can be washed (1/2 hour) and dried (1/2 hour) in one hour total time.

With sorting and transportation time, the laundry service works for 24 hour turn-around time for their customers. The following is a graphical representation of Allstar's standard Paced Flow process:

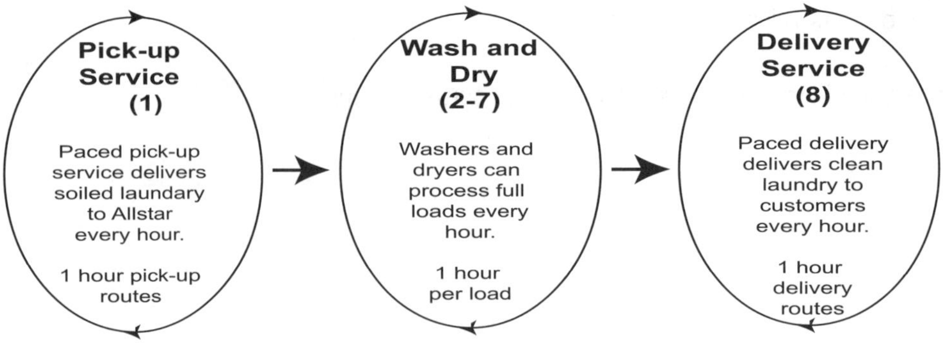

Typically lead time for processing any and all laundry is 24 hours as previously mentioned.

A Heijunka example for a Paced Flow process for Allstar Laundry Services is as follows:

1. Demand is identified based on historical processing patterns of white and color items. The historical demand pattern for laundry processing is 40 total wash and dry loads per day which takes 21 hours total (reference chart at the bottom of the page) and is comprised of the following mix:

    a. 30 color wash and dry loads per day
    b. 10 white wash and dry loads per day

2. To ensure that the workers do not save all the white loads for the end of their shift, the following Heijunka Leveling processing plan was developed:

    Color load = C = 30 per day   White load = W = 10 per day

At the start of 1st Shift, loads are processed in the following leveled order or sequence, where C = Color laundry load, and W = White laundry load.

$$CCCW_1CCCW_2CCCW_3CCCW_4CCCW_5CCCW_6CCCW_7CCCW_8CCCW_9CCCW_{10}$$

This is illustrated by the following graphical representation (only partial sequence is shown). This matrix shows wash loads in black, and dry loads in gray for the three shift operations. Open time is used to conduct improvement projects and equipment maintenance.

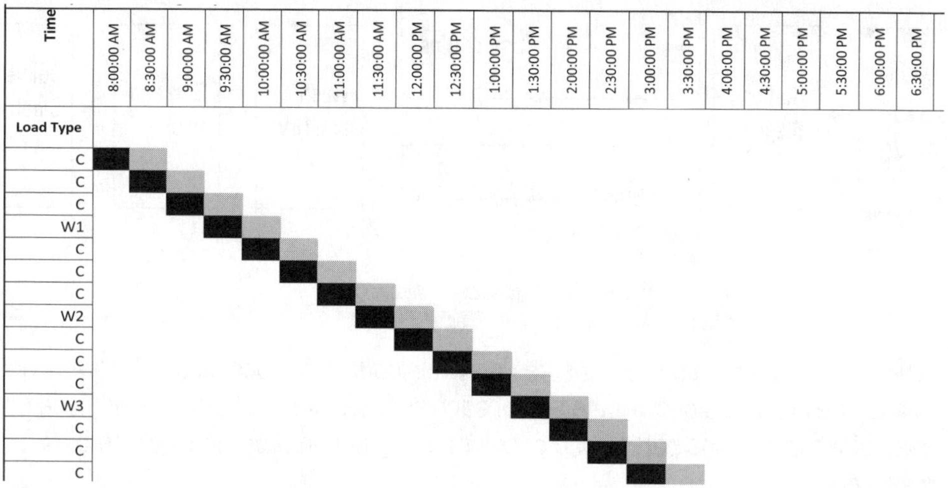

Laundry turnaround to customers is guaranteed at 24 hours or "Next Day" service as advertised. By using the Heijunka Leveling system outlined above, Allstar is able to achieve 4-hour turnarounds and promise "Same Day" service for laundry picked up before noon. This promise allowed Allstar to gain more local market share and improve their profitability.

A Pull Signal and Kanban example of a Paced Flow process for Allstar Laundry Services is as follows:

1. Demand is identified based on historical processing patterns of white and color items. The historical demand pattern for laundry processing is 40 total wash and dry loads per day which takes 21 hours total and is comprised of the following mix (same as previous example):

    a. 30 color wash and dry loads per day
    b. 10 white wash and dry loads per day

2. To ensure that the workers only process full loads, Pull Signals or Kanbans are used to control process initiation. The improvement team established a standard laundry bin size that matches the washer and dryer load sizes. The workers were instructed that a new load of wash is not to begin until a laundry bin is full. A full laundry bin acts as the "visual" Pull Signal or Kanban to initiate a full wash and dry load.

Laundry workers only wash and dry laundry when a full load is available. The incoming delivery and off-loading workers fill bins and push them to the full bin area to signal wash and dry initiation. Empty bins are returned to the off-load area. The physical process flow is illustrated below:

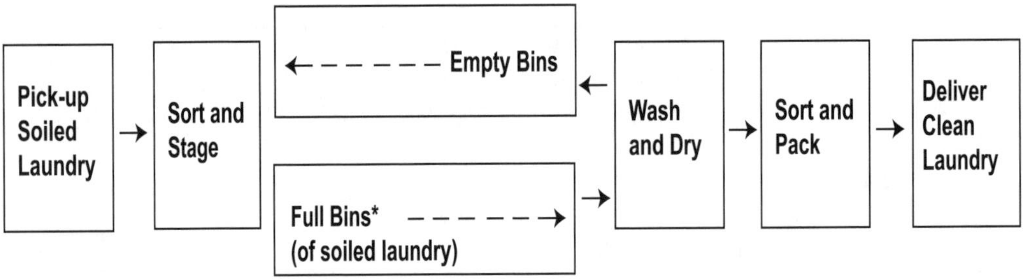

**Full bins act as a signal to initiate wash and dry cycle.*
The full bin arrangement also functions as a FIFO Lane.

3. This Kanban Signal process ensures only full loads are processed. If there is no demand, the process stops. At the end of each shift, workers will process only one partial load of white and one partial load of color as required in order to clear the bins for the next shift.

This operation now promised 4-hour turnaround on items picked up before noon and 24-hour turnaround for all others. This allowed them to gain new business. By processing only full loads Allstar was able to reduce costs of processing by over 30%! This enabled Allstar to improve their profits and add new business without adding new people or equipment.

Scheduled Flow Example

A typical standard representation of a Scheduled Flow process is illustrated by a dentist practice called The Whole Tooth (and Nothing but the Tooth). The Whole Tooth is a small practice with one dentist, 2 full-time hygienists, one part-time hygienist, and a receptionist. Scheduled flow is typically used for larger scale medical services as well.

A standard example of a Scheduled Flow process for The Whole Tooth is as follows:

1. Dentist office service demand is identified by customer call and requests for an appointment for either a specific procedure or a general cleaning (non-emergency).

2. For the appointment request, the receptionist reviews the office schedule and agrees with the customer on a mutually acceptable date and time. The appointment is then booked or scheduled.

3. In this scenario, an appointment time is scheduled for a later service fulfillment date.

4. At the time of the appointment, the desired service is delivered.

For this simple example of Scheduled Flow, appointments are scheduled for the dentist and customers (i.e., patients). The process flow is illustrated below:

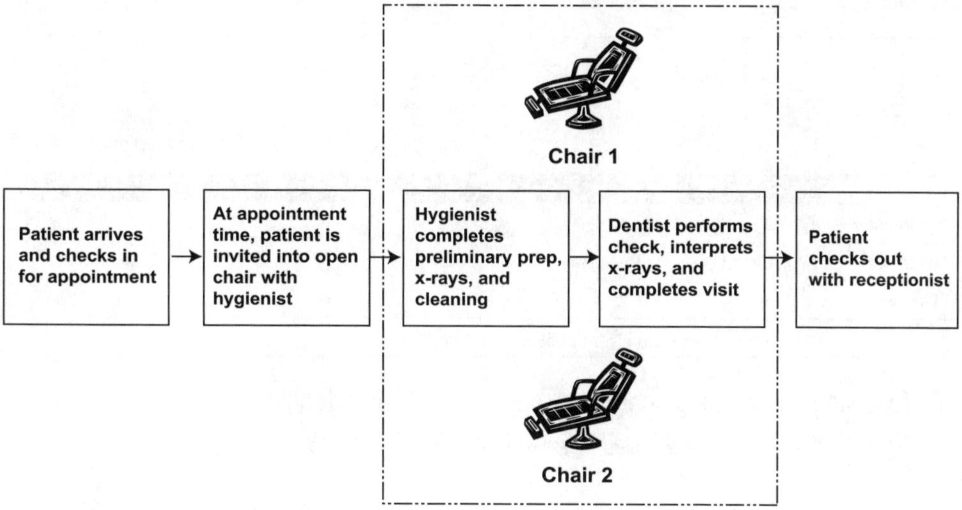

Typically lead time for scheduled flow depends on customer demand. In slow demand times there are openings in the schedule that can be filled immediately. In busier demand times, customers with non-emergency requests are scheduled into available time slots. Scheduled flow helps organizations plan and allocate resources. Once the schedule is set, customers expect to be serviced at the scheduled time, or notified in advance of any potential changes. Deviations from schedules occur for healthcare practices for many reasons. If performance to schedule is identified as a problem, cause and effect analysis should be used to identify root cause.

A Heijunka example of a Scheduled Flow process for The Whole Tooth is as follows:

1. Service demand is identified based on the following historical service patterns for hygienists and dentist.

Quantity/day	**Service**	**Who Performs**
8	General Cleaning	(Hygienist only)
8	Inspections (Checks)	(Hygienist & Dentist)
4	Procedures - 1 - 2 Surface Filing	(Assistant & Dentist)

2. To use Heijjunka leveling for a dentist's office's scheduled flow, the receptionist schedules 1 dentist and 2 hygienists to the following level flow sequence:

The Whole Tooth Load Leveling Heijunka Plan

Time	8:00:00 AM	8:30:00 AM	9:00:00 AM	9:30:00 AM	10:00:00 AM	10:30:00 AM	11:00:00 AM	11:30:00 AM	12:00:00 PM	12:30:00 PM	1:00:00 PM	1:30:00 PM	2:00:00 PM	2:30:00 PM	3:00:00 PM	3:30:00 PM	4:00:00 PM	4:30:00 PM	5:00:00 PM
Person																			
Hygienist 1	C	I		P	C	I	P	Open			C	I		P	C	I	P	Open	
Hygienist 2		C	I	C	I	Open						C	I	C	I	Open			
Dentist 1		I	I	P	I	I	P	Open				I	I	P	I	I	P	Open	

C = Cleaning I = Inspection P = Procedure

3. By following this leveling schedule, the hygienists and dentist have a comfortable pace for their day and are able to anticipate the flow of the day.

4. The improvement team established a visual signal board that replicates the daily schedule. The receptionist loads the schedule in the electronic scheduling software and the daily schedule is displayed in the commons area for the hygienist's and dentist's review. The schedule signal board changes every day and even during the day as it is updated for cancellations and emergencies. The visual signal board helps people stay on schedule and anticipate the day's workload. A typical daily schedule board is illustrated below.

The Whole Tooth Signal Schedule Board f or 10-10

Time	8:00:00 AM	8:30:00 AM	9:00:00 AM	9:30:00 AM	10:00:00 AM	10:30:00 AM	11:00:00 AM	11:30:00 AM	12:00:00 PM	12:30:00 PM	1:00:00 PM	1:30:00 PM	2:00:00 PM	2:30:00 PM	3:00:00 PM	3:30:00 PM	4:00:00 PM	4:30:00 PM	5:00:00 PM
Person																			
Hygienist 1	Open				P	P	On-line training				C	I	C	I	C	I	Open		
Hygienist 2	C	I	C	I	Open		On-line training					C	I	C	I	Open			
Dentist 1		I		I	P	P	Open					I	I	I	I	I	Open		

A more complex – high throughput case

The Whole Tooth dental practice example illustrates a simple model for scheduled and heijunka flow for a small dentist office. A more typical, and complex, example can be illustrated by expanding this example to a larger, higher volume dentist office. This higher volume office modified their delivery model to include "same visit" cleaning, check-up, and procedure completion if necessary. This is an extremely innovative concept that could only be accomplished by the support of a scheduled/heijunka flow method. Initially, the office used traditional scheduled flow techniques to schedule clients cleaning and check-up appointments. When patients arrived at the office they complete an electronic log in. The actual session triggers an open chair signal to the cleaning and check-up team. When an open exam chair occurs, the next patient is signaled or called from the waiting room to the open chair as depicted in the diagram on the next page.

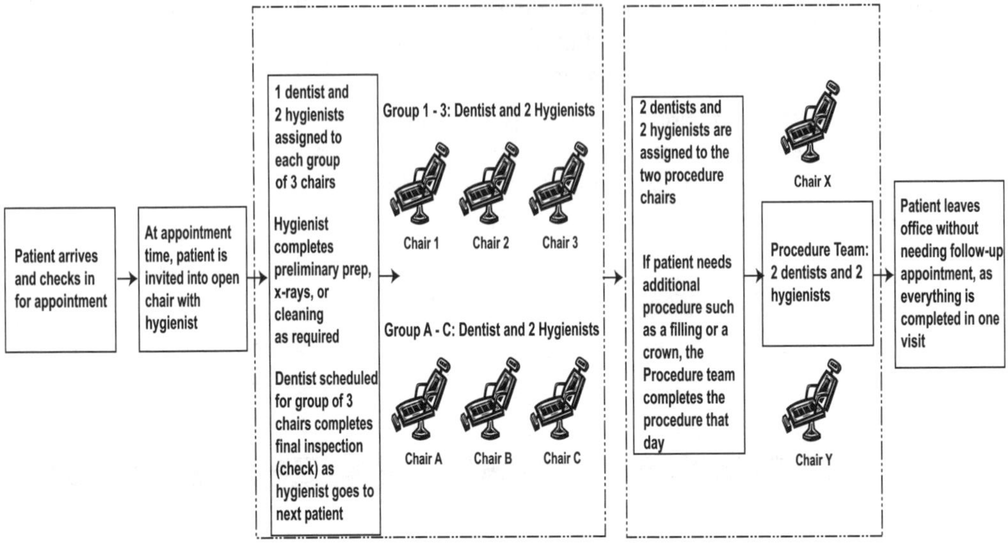

If the attending dentist discovers that a dental procedure (i.e., basic) is needed, the patient is immediately moved to the procedure chairs where attending dentists perform the standard procedure.

This high throughput scheduled/heijunka flow dentist office model employs 4 dentists, and 6 hygienists, as well as other office support people, and offers the patients "one visit" completion of services. This model may not satisfy every customer, and follow-up procedure appointments are scheduled into the X and Y procedure chairs as needed based on the patient desires. However, most of their patients appreciated this process and claim that this was the reason they switched to this office.

This high volume practice used several Lean Sigma tools to reach this level of flow. Some of the tools used are pull signals and visual controls to signal when the next chair is open and which patient is next. Standardized work for determining which procedures would be considered "standard" was a critical component of this system. Cross-training, back-up planning, and flexible work schedules are also critical to this practice. With this new method developed through the use of Lean Sigma methods, the practice was able to handle more than twice the number of patients and did not have to add chairs or people. Their profitability and return on investments also increased substantially. Most importantly, their patient survey satisfaction level increased by over 96%! Who wouldn't want to innovate something like this for their organization?

Quick Changeover (QCO)

Quick Changeover *is the ability to quickly change from delivering one product or service to delivering a completely different product or service.* Often in service delivery, providers are required to quickly switch from delivering one service to delivering a completely different service to satisfy customer needs. The goal of QCO is to improve the customer experience by reducing waiting or delay due to changeover and adjustments. The speed in which a service provider can change their delivery process is critical to the customer experience and overall satisfaction.

Consider a technical service help line provider that determines that the customer wishes to purchase a new service or device. The person providing technical assistance can quickly change from providing technical service to providing new order processing. A customer's expectations are that the change for the organization to go from technical help to order processing will be smooth, seamless, and expeditious. If the change in service requires the customer to be transferred, placed on hold, or the technical help line person requests the customer call back to the order processing line, customers will be disappointed with having to experience waste of waiting or delay.

Quick Changeovers are a foundation for many other Lean Sigma improvements. The ability to changeover quickly affects an organization's ability to achieve Just-In-Time (JIT) service deliveries, balance or level the service flows, and deliver small batches of customized services (see the Mass Customization section for additional information). QCOs are a foundation for customer satisfaction and market dominance.

QCOs in service environments are measured from the last completed service task of one process to the initiation of the first service task for the next service process being delivered. For example, changeover time is the time from taking the final order detail to initiating payment processing. Having the same person do this by simply switching computer screens and beginning the payment process is typically quicker than having to transfer the customer to a customer service accounts payable department.

QCO improvement techniques mirror standard work methods. The idea is to use standard work tools to document and improve the changeover processes. As with standard work, the first step to reducing changeover times is to document the current state. This can be done using standard work tools of direct observation and measurement, or simple mapping tools as described earlier in this book. Reference the Standard Work and Process Mapping sections for additional details on documenting the current state of a process.

With the changeover current state documented, an improvement team can analyze the process for wastes, identify and implement improvement actions. Improvement actions should be implemented in a PDCA fashion to improve the changeover process speed.

A simple example of improving changeovers is illustrated by the phone line help service call which turns into a customer order. A customer calls in to Technical Help for assistance with their computer virus protection software. The technician diagnoses and solves the problem for the customer and then recommends a product upgrade. The customer agrees, and then must be transferred to Customer Service to place the new order. If the customer's credit information is not updated, they must then be transferred to Accounting. A current state Deployment flowchart for this process is shown below:

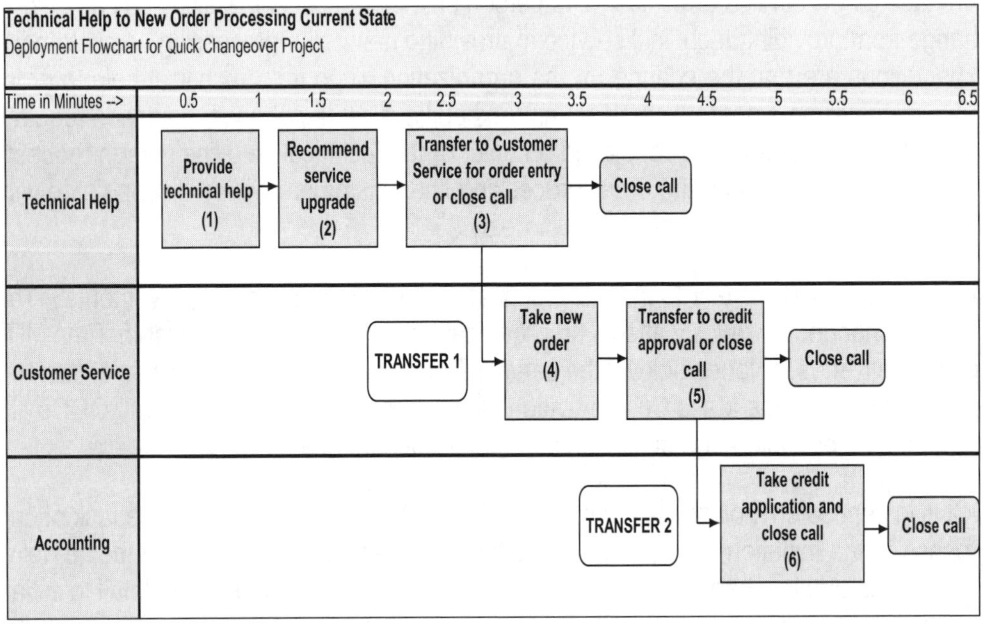

Improvement opportunities identified and placed on the Issues and Opportunities Log are:

1. Eliminating transfers by providing cross-training for the Technical Help personnel to take orders and credit application information
2. Provide multiple screens for Technical Help personnel so they can rapidly change from problem diagnosis to order entry and credit application data entry.

A future state Deployment flowchart for this process is shown below:

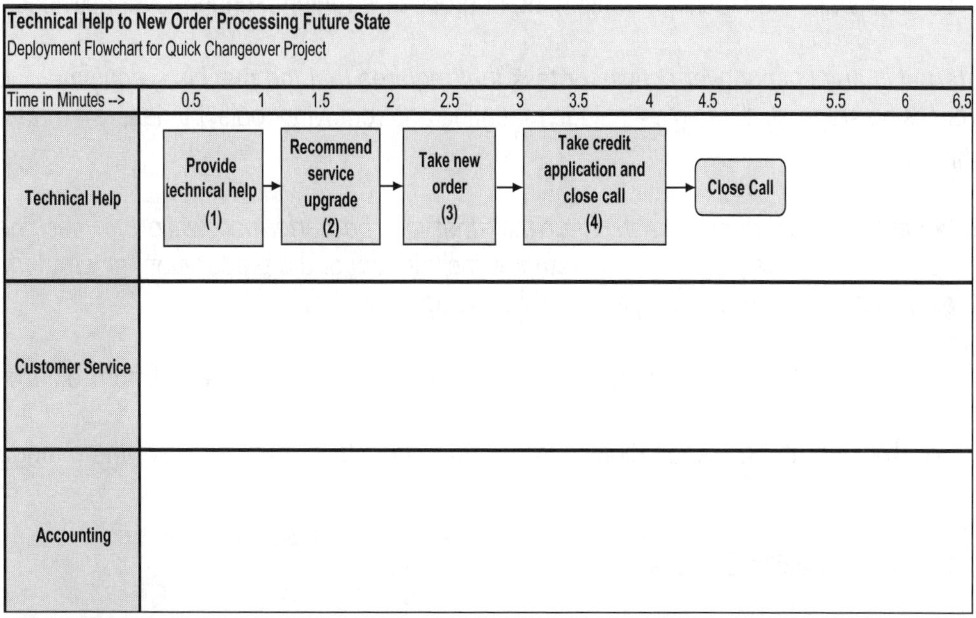

The improvements, once implemented, resulted in approximately a 1.5 minute minimum savings per call, plus service by one person, and no potentially frustrating transfers.

The future state required cross-training and quick changeover between Technical Help screens, to Customer Service (order entry) and Accounting (credit application) screens.

In service environments that operate equipment, such as printing presses, laundry equipment, ovens, mixers, saws, and the like, QCO takes on a more specific approach. For these service environments the following steps can be taken to reduce equipment delay or downtime. The steps to apply QCO to a service process where equipment is used to deliver the service are:

1. Document the current state.

    - Video an equipment changeover for future analysis.
    - Watch and study the video (laugh and/or cry).
    - Document the activities and tasks with Standard Work Charts.
    - Complete a Spaghetti Diagram for the changeover.

2. Separate Internal (need machine, equipment, or process stopped) from External (can be done while the machine, equipment, or process is running) changeover activities.

Internal *is any changeover activity or task that requires that the machine, equipment, or process be stopped.* Examples include mounting and removing tools, blades, raw materials, etc.

External *is any changeover activity or task that can be performed while the machine, equipment, or process is running.* Examples include tool or die preparation, raw material staging, paperwork preparation, assembly of setup tools, etc.

- Use check sheets and function checks to help separate internal from external activities.
- Consider the transportation of tools and materials at each stage of the changeover.

3. Convert Internal to External.

- Prepare key items and tools in advance of initiating changeover.
- Standardize functionally for tools and equipment.
- Use centering jigs and fixtures to speed adjustments.
- Use multi-purpose tools and fixtures where possible.
- Consider pre-heating or pre-staging to speed changeover process.
- Use checklists, countdowns, and visual systems to reduce wastes.

4. Streamline all aspects of setup operations.

- Use check sheets to standardize and speed the changeover process.
- Use function checks to ensure changeover is correct and working properly.
- Streamline the transportation of tools, materials, and people.

The entertainment business is where quick changeovers happen frequently. In the entertainment business it is not machine or equipment time that is being conserved, rather customer and entertainer time. It is common for some shows to require several costume, wardrobe, or set changes for one performance or engagement. To do this efficiently, these organizations must be highly organized and have specific exactness or precision in every change over task or action. For these QCO situations organizations practice several QCO concepts such as pre-staging or "kitting" of tools, equipment, devices and props, specifying and labeling of exact locations of items, and special devices, tools and equipment that speed change overs such as Velcro versus buttons on clothing, locking rollers versus fixed set pieces, cam locks on set piece connections versus nuts and bolts connections, and quick connecting single electrical connections versus numerous electrical cords to manage, to name a few.

These concepts work in many service environments beyond the entertainment business where QCOs are required. Improvement teams can use the QCO steps to discover where these concepts apply in their service environments.

The following mini case is an example of the Quick Changeover Lean Sigma tool.

Cathy's Custom Cake service is a custom cake baking and decorating service providing birthday, wedding, anniversary, and other special occasion cakes for the local community. Business was picking up and Cathy wanted to be able to produce more cakes per day without adding additional people or working longer hours. Cathy knew that one of the limiting factors (i.e., constraints) in the number of cakes made per day was the mixer. The mixer was a 5 gallon mixer she had purchased some time ago from a commercial bakery as they upgraded their equipment, and was perfect for the most popular size cakes required. Cathy figured that if she could get an additional cake or two per day from the mixer, she could keep up with demand.

Cathy formed a Quick Changeover improvement team and asked the team to look into improving the mixer changeover speed. The improvement team completed a video of the cake baking process and several additional time observations in effort to and create the Standard Work Chart (shown on next page). The Baking Process Current State Standard Work Chart includes the steps to begin an order through beginning of the baking process. The Chart includes VA and NVA mixing process as well as mixer changeover activities. The team agreed that the changeover steps begin after the last drop of batter is poured out of the mix bowl (step 10), and end when the mixer is ready to mix the next job (step 14). The changeover steps are shaded for reference.

Standard Work Chart

Location	Main Store
Process	Mixing and baking current state
Area:	Cathy's Custom Cakes — OP N/A of ____
Process:	Mixing and Baking — PG 1 of 1
Takt Time	26.25 minutes
Cycle Time	16 per day
Updated By:	Cathy — Date: 12/10/2010
Approved By :	Beth — Date: 12/10/2010
Checked By :	TBD — Date: / /
Changeover Time only =	9.50 minutes

Step Number	Major Operational Steps	Manual Time	Automated Time	Time in Minutes	Wait Time
1	Go and get next order	X		0.50	
2	Go and get recipe	X		0.50	
3	Turn on oven to recipe temperature	X	X	0.25	
4	Go and get ingredients per recipe	X		3.25	
5	Go and get baking pans per order	X		2.00	
6	Go and get measuring bowls, cups and spoons as needed	X		1.00	
7	Measure and combine to recipe	X		4.75	
8	Place measured ingredients in mixer	X		0.25	
9	Mix per recipe		X	2.00	
10	Remove mixing bowl from mixer and pour cake mix into pans	X		2.25	2.0
11*	Place pans in pre-heated ovens	X		1.25	
12	Bring all soiled mixing equipment and mix bowl to sinks	X		2.00	
13	Wash and dry all mixing equipment and mix bowl	X		3.50	
14	Replace all mixing equipment in its proper spot	X		2.50	
15	Replace the mix bowl in mixer	X		0.25	
End	Go get next order step number 1				
	* Shaded area is changeover activities.				
				Total	
				26.25	2

Parking

Note: The light line is the entire Spaghetti Diagram, the dashed heavy line is the changeover Spaghetti Diagram.

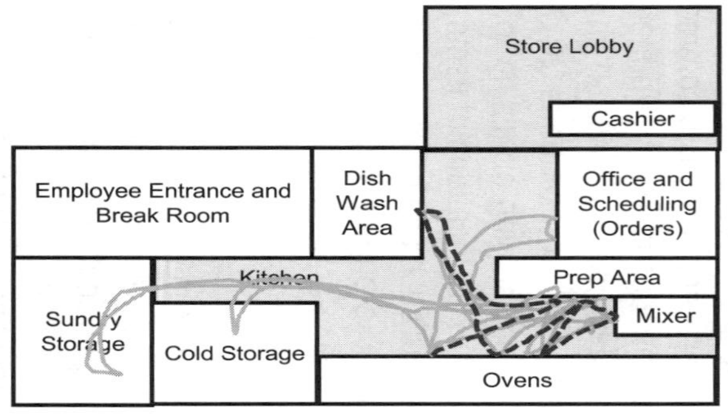

Working Sequence

Walking

Changeover only

The next step was to separate the internal changeover items from the external items. The current internal and external analysis is shown in the table below. (This can be shown on the Standard Work Chart as well, depending on the team's preference.) The team observed that in the current state, all the changeover activities were internal to the mixer, or done while the mixer was not running. In their effort to move internal items to external items, the team determined that if they purchased another mix bowl, they could move the movement and cleaning of the mix bowl to an external activity. A mixing bowl was a very low cost component of the mixer, and could easily be offset by additional business, and reduced overtime. They also determined that if they readied the mixer for mixing before they put the cake in the oven they could keep the mixer mixing more time per day.

Quick Changeover Internal and External Analysis			
Location	Main Store	Process	Mixing and baking current state
Step Number	Major Operational Steps	Internal	External
11*	Place pans in pre-heated ovens	X	
12	Bring all soiled mixing equipment and mix bowl to sinks	X	
13	Wash and dry all mixing equipment and mix bowl	X	
14	Replace all mixing equipment in its proper spot	X	
15	Replace the mix bowl in mixer	X	
	* Shaded area is changeover activities.		

Quick Changeover Internal and External Analysis			
Location	Main Store	Process	Mixing and baking future state
Step Number	Major Operational Steps	Internal	External
11*	Place pans in pre-heated ovens		X
12	Bring all soiled mixing equipment and mix bowl to sinks		X
13	Wash and dry all mixing equipment and mix bowl		X
14	Replace all mixing equipment in its proper spot	X	
15	Replace the mix bowl in mixer	X	
	* Shaded area is changeover activities.		

To streamline the process the team determined that rather than walk around the kitchen to deliver various items to various areas, they would develop and use locally placed tubs which, when full, would trigger a visual signal, and the worker scheduled to move items for the day would begin a move cycle. This reduced overall motion and extra trips per day for the workers, and allowed more orders to be mixed per day. In the end, as illustrated in the Standard Work Chart (shown on next page), the team reduced the change over times from an average of 9.5 minutes to 5.25 minutes on average. This allowed the team to make 19 cakes per day in the mixer or 3 more per day! Cathy was excited for the team and wanted the team to continue to work on the next constraint - the ovens!

Standard Work Chart

Area: Cathy's Custom Cakes — OP N/A of ____

Process: Mixing and Baking — PG 1 of 1

Takt Time 22.0 minutes — Cycle Time 19 per day

Updated By: Cathy — Date: 12/20/2010

Approved By : Beth — Date: 12/20/2010

Checked By : TBD — Date: __/__/__

Location	Main Store	Process	Mixing and baking future state

Step Number	Major Operational Steps	Manual Time	Automated Time	Time in Minutes	Wait Time
1	Go and get next order	X		0.50	
2	Go and get recipe	X		0.50	
3	Turn on oven to recipe temperature	X	X	0.25	
4	Go and get ingredients per recipe	X		3.25	
5	Go and get baking pans per order	X		2.00	
6	Go and get measuring bowls, cups, and spoons as needed	X		1.00	
7	Measure and combine to recipe	X		4.75	
8	Place measured ingredients in mixer	X		0.25	
9	Mix per recipe		X	2.00	
10	Remove mixing bowl from mixer and pour cake mix into pans	X		2.25	2.0
11*	Place pans in pre-heated ovens	X		1.25	
12	Set all soiled mixing equipment and mix bowl into wash tub	X		2.00	
13	Replace all staged mixing equipment in its proper spot	X		1.75	
14	Replace the mix bowl in mixer	X		0.25	
End	Go get next order step number 1				
	* Shaded area is changeover activities.				
				Total	
				22.0	2

Changeover Time only = 5.25 minutes

Parking

Note: The light line is the entire Spaghetti Diagram, the dashed heavy line is the changeover Spaghetti Diagram.

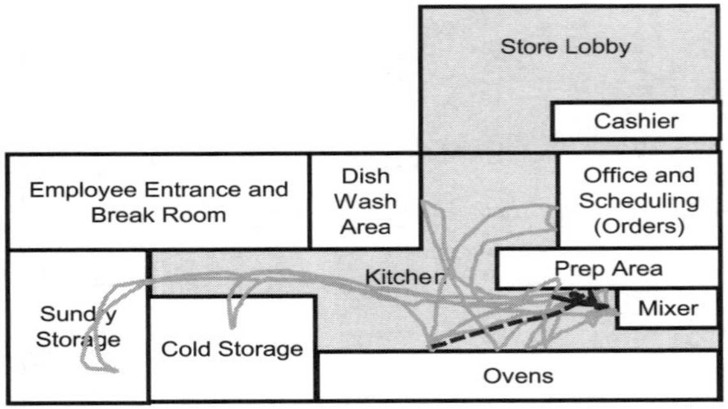

Working Sequence

Walking

Changeover only

Total Productive Maintenance (TPM)

Total Productive Maintenance (TPM) *are the tools, methods, and activities to improve the machine or equipment availability and reliability times.* Service organizations employ a variety of machines and equipment to deliver services to their customers. Landscaping services use mowers, trimmers, dozers and loaders, print shops use printers, hospitality organizations use busses, boats, and cars, and most service organizations have computers, printers, and copiers that need to work to service clients. Clearly equipment maintenance is not just for manufacturers!

By implementing TPM practices and tools, organizations can reduce waste and improve their equipment effectiveness. The overall goal of a TPM program is to reduce and eliminate equipment related productivity losses and improve overall customer satisfaction. TPM practices involve all people in an organization that plan, design, use, and maintain equipment and provide a system of comprehensive maintenance for the life-time of the equipment.

TPM activities are designed to systematically improve the effectiveness of each and every piece of equipment employed by a service organization. Every person that uses equipment must have an understanding of why this is critical to the organization's success and do their part in maintaining equipment.

To apply TPM in a service organization, teams need to first identify and complete a 5S on the critical equipment. Sources of contamination are a leading cause to equipment malfunction. Imagine if your local fire department did not take care of their equipment and it only worked 80% of the time, or if an airline's airplane only worked properly 99.99% of the time. Would this be acceptable? Absolutely not. Service organizations practicing TPM must establish standards of cleanliness and maintenance for every piece of critical equipment. People also must be trained in proper use and maintenance of the equipment.

Regular inspections and audits are also a part of a TPM plan. It is simply the PDCA process in full use. Data such as "mean time between failures" can be monitored to provide improvement standards and baselines. The goal of TPM is to reduce time losses on service equipment and machines.

Machine productivity losses can be categorized into six major areas of machine time loss. They are:

1. Breakdowns - usually unplanned
2. Setups and adjustments - often planned or scheduled
3. Idling and minor stoppages - raw material adds, changes, or breaks
4. Speed losses - running slower than standards or projections require
5. Defects - having to rework or run "extra"
6. Setup yield - having to run "warm-up" parts or allow equipment to "warm-up"

The first step in employing TPM is to document where equipment time is going. A simple equipment log sheet is the most effective way to document equipment performance.

The following example is the Total Productive Maintenance Log Sheet for mower #3 from a lawn mowing service firm:

Total Productive Maintenance Log Sheet				
Machine: Mower # 3,running 6 days a week 1 shift only				Area: North Calumet
Log Number	Date	Up Time	Down Time	Activity
1	1-May	7	1	Good day
	2-May	3	5	Oil change
	3-May	6	2	Belt broke. Quit early
	4-May	8	0	Good day
	5-May	8	0	Good day
	6-May	8	0	Good day
	7-May	0	8	Sunday
	8-May	4	4	Belt came off again
	9-May	2	6	Pulley was bent causing belt to come off. Sent to repair
	10-May	7	1	Good day
	11-May	7	1	Good day
	12-May	9	-1	Good day
	13-May	9	-1	Good day
	14-May	0	8	Sunday
	15-May	6	2	Good day
	16-May	8	0	Good day
	17-May	7	1	Good day
	18-May	10	-2	Good day
	19-May	3	5	In shop for running rough
	20-May	8	0	Good day
	21-May	0	8	Sunday
	22-May	3	5	Oil change
	23-May	1	7	Broke down. Oil plug misaligned and leaking
	24-May	8	0	Good day
	25-May	9	-1	Good day
	26-May	8	0	Good day
	27-May	9	-1	Good day
	28-May	0	8	Sunday
	29-May	7	1	Good day
	30-May	8	0	Good day
	31-May	9	-1	Good day
May Total =		182	66	
Macro Up Time %		64%		Considering we only run one shift
Planned Up Time		84%		Planned up time

Further analysis using a Pareto Chart of the TPM Log Sheet is shown below. The data shows that the key to increase mower #3 uptime is to minimize the time for oil changes. Since oil changes cannot be eliminated, the team agreed to begin to monitor total engine hours to determine oil changes rather than their pervious method of twice per month. They also lost a significant number of hours due to an oil plug problem which is related to poor maintenance service quality. This needed to be addressed with the maintenance team.

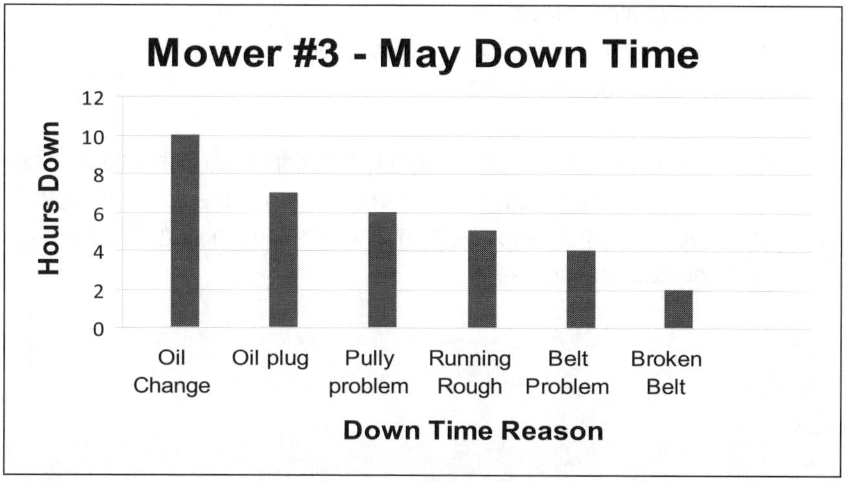

By attacking equipment down time in a Total Productive Maintenance manner, service organizations can improve their service to their clients.

Cross-Training

Cross-training applies to nearly every area of Lean Sigma implementations. The simplest way to manage cross-training is to complete a training matrix for the organization. There are three levels of training for every member of the organization. The training levels are:

1. Job description responsibility level
2. Improvement and problem solving tools training level
3. Next level job growth preparation level

To complete the cross-training matrix, first identify individual job description, Knowledge, Skill, and Ability (KS&A) requirements, and document them in the Job Description section of the training matrix form. Identify improvement and problem solving KS&A requirements. Consider the following core training areas:

Business KS&A
Technical KS&A
People KS&A

Document these in the Improvement and Problem Solving section of the training matrix. Then, identify the next level or promotion KS&As needed and document them in the "Next Level" section of the training matrix. For each member of the organization, identify the areas of the matrix where training and proficiency have occurred by completing each section of the matrix.

A cross-training matrix example is shown on the next page that shows specific job descriptions for each employee in what they have been trained in as well as their level of proficiency.

Employee	Job Description							
	Job Title	Position Specific Technical Skill and Overall Safety	Phone Skills	Data Entry	Office Word	Office Excel	Interpersonal Relationships	Email Procedures
3423	44	1	2	1	3	3	3	4
3456	33	3	1	3	1	3	3	3
3954	44	2	2	3	1	4	3	3
1896	44	3	3	4	4	4	4	3
4389	33	2	3	3	3	3	1	3
4574	44	3	3	3	1	3	3	3

Legend: 1 = Initial training
2 = Developing
3 = Proficient
4 = Trainer

Chapter Summary

This chapter defines several Lean Sigma improvement tools used to identify and reduce waste in service processes. Lean Sigma tools and application examples are used to illustrate how the Lean Sigma tools drive improvements. A key to the Improve Phase is for the Lean Sigma practitioner to understand when and why to use each of the improvement tools and techniques using the PDCA process. This will improve through use and practice with the tools. By using these key Improve Phase tools, teams are able to implement improvement initiatives.

Lean Sigma for Service Excellence Applications

These observations may assist in understanding how to apply the concepts and tools contained in this chapter:

- Develop a list of where each Lean Sigma tool might apply in your organization.
- Provide a brief training session on 5S and apply this tool to a common area in your organization such as a lunch or break room, copier room, or some desktop files and folders.
- Identify additional resources to learn more about Lean Sigma tools and techniques.
- Complete a cross-training matrix for your organization.
- Develop a comprehensive training program to train people in business, teaming, and technical skills.

Improve Phase Readiness Guide

The following Improve Phase Readiness Guide allows you to ensure there is application of the chapter's content before proceeding to apply the Lean Sigma tools and concepts in the next chapter. If you score less than 70%, consider working on the lower scoring areas before moving on.

Improve Phase Readiness Guide

Use the following 5-level Likert item scale to rank each of the statements:

1 = Strongly Disagree
2 = Disagree
3 = Neither Agree nor Disagree
4 = Agree
5 = Strongly Agree

	Score
1. My organization does a good job of using the PDCA process for implementing improvements.	
2. My organization does of collecting and sharing critical information to improve flow and reduce waste.	
3. My organization utilizes visual and management tools to provide and act on key process information.	
4. My organization does a good job of understanding and defining processes to satisfy multiple customer needs.	
5. My organization does a good job of eliminating errors and error sources in a process.	
6. My organization effectively uses cross-training techniques to develop worker flexibility.	
7. My organization does a good job of identifying and eliminating waste.	
8. My organization is effective in improving overall flow of a process or work area.	
9. My organization has a system in place to document and encourage improvements.	
10. I feel comfortable using the PDCA process for implementing incremental improvements.	
11. I feel comfortable applying 5S in my area.	
12. I feel comfortable applying the implementing visual controls to help reduce waste, share information, and reduce errors.	
13. I feel comfortable participating in continuous improvement activities.	
14. I feel comfortable developing and applying mass customization options.	
15. I feel comfortable using the kanban/pull signal system.	
16. I feel comfortable applying performance metrics and scoreboards to a process.	
17. I feel comfortable using Lean Sigma tools to eliminate different types of waste.	
18. I feel comfortable using mistake proofing tools to eliminate errors and improve processes.	
19. I see the value in using the DMAIC process and tools for improvement projects.	
20. I believe my organization should utilize and apply the concepts and tools discussed in this chapter.	
Total Score	

Case Review – Improve Phase for Medical Practice

In Dr. Andrew McNeal's office, every day is a mystery. On some days his waiting room is filled with unsatisfied patients waiting for their appointments. On other days, it seems his physicians and staff workers have time to play solitaire on their computers. The feast or famine approach to scheduling the team of doctors was tearing the practice apart. Everyone thought they had the solution. Everyone thought their problems were driving the inconsistency. Everyone was right!

Dr. McNeal's medical practice includes a team of five physicians, three physician assistants, and four administrative specialists. The physicians are internists operating a basic family-focused general practice. Each physician has a significant number of patients. Many of the patients have a Health Maintenance Organization (HMO) which requires referrals from a primary care physician to a specialist for certain procedures and ailments. Others patients simply visit the office for a variety of services from basic physicals, to prescription requests and diagnostics to early cancer detection and counseling. Overall, Dr. McNeal's practice covers a wide range of services.

As the practice has grown, so too have the problems. The biggest issue lately is the frustration of the patients, doctors, and staff regarding the extreme fluctuation of work loads. Dr. McNeal has had to take action. One of Dr. McNeal's patients was a Lean Sigma specialist, who had just waited over an hour over his scheduled appointment time. While discussing the chaos and delay in the waiting room with this patient, Dr. McNeal requested his patient send him some information about the Lean Sigma improvement process.

Upon reviewing the Lean Sigma material that arrived a few days later as well as reading numerous articles regarding improvements using Lean and Six Sigma in healthcare, Dr. McNeal decided to convene a small cross-section of his office personnel and begin the DMAIC improvement process.

Define Phase

Dr. McNeal chaired the informal work session and began with an overview of the situation. Everyone understood the situation very clearly and wanted improvement. Dr. McNeal then provided a brief overview of the basics of the DMAIC process with the team. He provided everyone with *The Lean Sigma Pocket Guide* (www.theleanstore.com) so they had some type of reference material. He explained that as they go through the steps, the tools will be thoroughly explained and then the right tool will be chosen. The team unanimously agreed to begin the improvement process.

Their mission was to reduce the general frustration that everyone was feeling, from the patients to the physicians and staff. The extreme fluctuation and imbalance in work load was driving the group crazy and threatened to drive patients away to other physician practices.

Together the team roughed out a Team Charter and created a value stream map of the appointment process from the patient's initial call through subsequent visits. These parameters were not currently being measured but the measurements or KPIs for success were patient wait time, schedule attainment, and accuracy. The team believed that if these parameters were measured and improved upon, the chaos and frustration would be greatly reduced. The team determined that the process definition and goals were appropriate to move forward to the Measure Phase.

Measure Phase

To measure the process, the team determined that they must put some data into the value stream map that was developed in the Define Phase. Some of the data was readily available and some was not. They began to use basic data gathering tools such as Check Sheets and Frequency Charts to collect actual times and other critical process data. Approximately half the data was available from their Electronic Medical Records database. They divided up the work and collected data for the following items:

1. Types of procedures and services performed
2. Estimated times to conduct standard procedures
3. Actual patient wait time in lobby
4. Appointments per day
5. Actual time for appointment by procedure
6. Actual cycle times to complete administrative tasks

Data collection lasted several weeks and the team updated their Project Planner to show the data collection time. After significant data was collected, the team scheduled another work session. The group was amazed at how much they had learned about the process just by collecting data. This type of "discovery" is very common in the Measure Phase. With the data in hand, the team moved to the Analyze Phase.

Analyze Phase

At initial review of the data, Dr. McNeal's team identified up to 45 minute variations in visit times from doctor-to-doctor, and from patient-to-patient for the same procedure. This concerned the team and they felt that as long as there was so much variation, they could never determine the appropriate takt time for procedures and make the necessary improvements to gain control.

The team populated several spreadsheets with data and used the Pivot Table tool in Microsoft Excel to help sort the data into more manageable segments. From the data analysis, the team could see general time groupings based on doctor, patient, and procedure. Some procedures took longer than others, some doctors took longer with each procedure than others and some patients took longer no matter what doctor they visited!

The team also used a Cause and Effect Diagram and an Affinity Diagram to help them analyze why these variances may be occurring, and if they could reduce the observed variation. They brainstormed for all possible reasons for the chaos and poor schedule attainment occurring in their office. The team decided to use these findings and the data collection information to construct an Interrelationship Diagram to determine which variables had the largest impact on schedule attainment, wait time, and delay in the office.

The Interrelationship Diagram indicated that the top three key variables to schedule attainment were as follows:

1. Category or Type of Procedure – Certain procedures just took longer, and certain procedures had greater variation in time to deliver.
2. Individual Patient needs – Some patients needed more explanation and comforting than others.
3. Physician preference and bias for speed – Certain physicians worked faster than others. Some physicians took more time with patients than others.

With the analysis, about 70% complete the team felt they could move on to the Improve Phase of the DMAIC process.

Improve Phase

As the team began to discuss their project with other doctors, they received significant resistance. Concepts such as standard work, takt times, and variation reduction did not fit well with their personal styles of operation. However, as they were science-based people, they did appreciate the Plan-Do-Check-Act process, as it mirrored the scientific method. Dr. McNeal had to have a special alignment session with the team of physicians to keep the improvement work on track. He discussed with the other physicians how this work would be in everyone's best interest, and would make their work less stressful and more rewarding. His persuasive leadership worked, and cleared the way for the team to begin making improvements.

Throughout the Analyze Phase the team came up with several ideas for improvements. They documented these ideas in the Issues and Opportunities (IO) Log and when it came time to identify improvements they had a great list to start with. The preliminary list of items is as follows:

1. Schedule less appointments per day
2. Add staff and physicians
3. Begin scheduling by procedure or type of appointment
4. Reduce the number of patients served
5. Get a bigger office

The team studied additional Improve Phase tools and used this small list of IO Log notes to initiate additional brainstorming and discussion. Some new ideas were identified and documented on the IO Log. The enhanced list was prioritized and specific tasks assigned to sub groups for PDCA improvement activities. The enhanced list and updated Issues and Opportunity Log is found on the next page.

Issues and Opportunities Log - Dr. McNeal's Stress Reduction Team

Objective: Record and track Opportunities (O), Ideas (I), Roadblocks (RB), and Parking Lot (PL) items. **Revision Date:** Aug 15

Medium shading or green color signifies moved to Action Item Log.

	Opportunity (O), Idea (I), Roadblock (RB), or Parking Log (PL)	Category (O/I/RB/PL)	Benefit	Action Summary	Date Logged	Date Closed
1	Schedule less appointments per day.	I	This would control the chaos, but not allow us to grow.	No action - hold.	15 Aug	
2	Add staff and physicians.	I	This would control the chaos, but add costs.	No action - hold.	15 Aug	
3	Begin scheduling by procedure or type of appointment.	I	This would be difficult to do, but would control flow.	Moved to AI Log and assigned to sub team.	15 Aug	
4	Reduce the number of patients.	I	Same as #1.	No action - hold.	15 Aug	
5	Clean up and standardize exam rooms.	I	This would make exams go smoother and reduce motion and waiting waste.	Moved to AI Log and assigned to sub team.	15 Aug	
6	Develop standard times for procedures.	I	This would give us targets to shoot for and gain control of the schedule.	Moved to AI Log and assigned to sub team.	15 Aug	
7	Hold people accountable to work standards.	RB	This will help maintain the schedule and standardize the work.	Assigned to Dr. McNeal and closed.	15 Aug	15 Aug
8	Get a bigger office.	PL	We would move around better.	No action - hold.	15 Aug	
9	Place a schedule board in the waiting room so patients can see where they are on the schedule.	I	This would allow patients to see where they are on the schedule and see how many are in front of them.	Moved to AI Log and assigned to sub team.	15 Aug	
10	Have appointment sceduling work more closely with check-in so critical data is more accessible.	I	This would better align the schedule to actual performance.	Moved to AI Log and assigned to sub team.	15 Aug	
11	Reduce the errors and communication problems from check-in to exam rooms.	I	This would make things go smoother and reduce defect waste.	Moved to AI Log and assigned to sub team.	15 Aug	
12	Physicians will be relunctant to do this at first.	RB	No benefit to resist. Physicians may claim improved???? quality, but must consider this.	Assigned to Dr. McNeal and closed.	15 Aug	15 Aug

The following table summarizes the team's Improve Phase action plan and Lean Sigma method and tool application:

Issues and Opportunities Log Summary		
Idea / Opportunity	**Action**	**Proposed Lean Sigma Method & Tool Use**
1. Schedule less appointments per day	No action - Hold	N/A
2. Add staff and physicians	No action - Hold	N/A
3. Begin scheduling by procedure or type of appointment	Assigned to sub group for PDCA	Standard work, demand flow scheduling/ Continuous flow, and PDCA
4. Reduce the number of patients served	No action - Hold	N/A
5. Clean up and standardize the exam rooms	Assigned to sub group for PDCA	5S, standard work, visual controls, Kanban, mass customization, PDCA, and RIE
6. Develop standard times for procedures	Assigned to sub group for PDCA	Standard work, and PDCA
7. Hold people accountable to work to standards	Assigned to Dr McNeal	Performance management
8. Get a bigger office	No action - Hold	N/A
9. Place a schedule board in the waiting room so the patients can see where they are in the schedule	Assigned to sub group for PDCA	Visual controls, standard work, and PDCA
10. Have appointment scheduling work closer with check-in so the critical data is more accessible	Assigned to sub group for PDCA	Cell design, flow layout, PDCA & RIE
11. Reduce the errors and communication problems from check-in to exam rooms	Assigned to sub group for PDCA	5S, standard work, visual controls, PDCA, and RIE
12. Physicians will be reluctant to do this at first.	Assigned to Dr McNeal	Performance management, involvement, training, and PDCA

Begin Scheduling by Procedure or Type of Appointment (Opportunity Log #3)

The team found a great deal more opportunity in this area once they embarked on their improvement plan. An unintended outcome was that they were able to gain access to a nationwide patient database to eliminate repetitive data entry. This saved a significant amount of time for administration during the check-in process and reduced the wait time for patients, as they did not have to arrive 15 minutes early for their appointment to complete and/or check and revise their personal data.

The team also found that just scheduling by procedure was not good enough. They also had to accommodate for slight differences in doctors and patients. They established a method to categorize patients by their typical needs; a patient categorized as an "A" needs a below average time with the physician as their appointment time is driven by the physician and the procedure only. Patients categorized as a "B" needs the average amount of time with the physician. Patients categorized as a "C" needs above average or "extra" time with the physician. The team believed by using this method, drastic improvements would be made in the schedule.

In a similar way, some of the physicians were just consistently faster with patients than others. Some people liked this brief "bedside manner," some did not, but it was clear through the data collection that this too should be considered in the scheduling improvement planning. The sub group rated the physicians in a similar way as what was just described for the patients. Interestingly enough, the physicians actually took pride in this rating system and chided each other over whose method was better.

The team developed and implemented the following tables of procedure, patient, and physician categories to build the appointment schedule around:

Standard Work Schedule Multiplier Grid				Patients A: Faster Than Average (1, 2, 3)	Patients B: Average (4, •, •)	Patients C: Slower Than Average (•, •, n)
Physicians	A	Faster Than Average	1, 2, 3	10 % Faster than Average	5% Faster than Average	Average
Physicians	B	Average	4, •, •	5% Faster than Average	Average	5% Slower Than Average
Physicians	C	Slower Than Average	•, •, n	Average	5% Slower Than Average	10% Slower than Average

National Averages/Standards		
Categories		Procedures
A	10-15 Minutes	1, 2, 3
B	15-20 Minutes	4, •, •
C	20-30+ Minutes	•, •, n

Standard Work Schedule Multiplier Grid				Patients A: Faster Than Average (1, 2, 3)	Patients B: Average (4, •, •)	Patients C: Slower Than Average (•, •, n)
Physicians	A	Faster Than Average	1, 2, 3	0.9	0.95	1
Physicians	B	Average	4, •, •	0.95	1	1.05
Physicians	C	Slower Than Average	•, •, n	1	1.05	1.1

National Averages/Standards		
Categories		Procedures
A	10-15 Minutes	1, 2, 3
B	15-20 Minutes	4, •, •
C	20-30+ Minutes	•, •, n

To build the standard time for scheduling, the scheduler would simply look-up the procedure's average time from the national database, find the combination of physician and patient category on the grid, and then multiply the standard time by the multiplier to determine how to build the appointment schedule.

The team conducted several PDCA experiments and collected data to ensure the scheduling method reflected reality. When they got within +/- 5% accuracy, they standardized the scheduling matrix and technique.

Clean up and Standardize the Exam Rooms (Opportunity Log #5)

The sub group working on the exam room 5S RIE conducted their pre-REI activities as described below.

Dr. McNeal's Clean Team - Rapid Improvement Event (RIE) Planning and Execution:

A. 1 - 2 weeks before Exam Room 5S RIE

1. The team selected exam room 1 and notified Dr. McNeal and requested scheduling to block out the day for exam room 1. The team worked with scheduling to plan the event during a slower period to avoid major conflicts.
2. A floor plan was sketched out, and storage locations and drawers identified.
3. A baseline assessment was done and pictures were taken to document the current state condition. The area appeared messy and several critical items were found to be missing.
4. The goal was established to not only clean and organize exam room 1, but to develop a standard list of items for each exam room, and create a checklist to follow for future monitoring and control.
5. The 5S day agenda was set to follow the 5S steps for exam room 1 and report out to Dr. McNeal at day's end.
6. The team checked to make sure the proper cleaning supplies were on hand.

B. The day of the 5S RIE

1. A brief overview of Lean Sigma methods and tools was provided by Dr. McNeal and then the team began implementing 5S.
2. The team sorted out and scrapped many of the old magazines that had accumulated in the exam room. They went through every drawer, and with the assistance of Dr. McNeal, determined which items were needed and which items were not needed. They cleaned all work surfaces and made notes regarding how often they felt areas should be cleaned. When things were cleaned, they carefully identified the location for items to be placed and labeled every drawer and countertop space with visual parking spots for specific items. Once things were in their place, the team documented the standard list of items, their location, and the practices (audit process) expected to keep things in this order.

During the 5S, the team discovered an opportunity for using the Lean Sigma Kanban tool for exam room consumables such as gloves, tissue, and swabs. By having one container on the counter and in use, and another full container in the drawers, the exam rooms should never run out of consumables. When the new container is opened and placed in the countertop containers, the empty container will serve as the Kanban or signal to restock the exam room. Whoever opens the new container is responsible to restock the item. Physicians included!

Also during the 5S RIE, the team noticed the opportunity to use the mass customization tool by outfitting and stocking each exam room with each item that may be used for the various types of exams and procedures performed by the practice. The team had to purchase a few smaller expense items to do this, but the practice of mass customization eliminated scheduling conflicts for procedure specific exam rooms.

They reviewed the standard work item location list and standard work list with Dr. McNeal, and developed a weekly audit plan to monitor the 5S status. The Standard Work Item Location and Audit List is as follows:

Exam Room - 5S Standard Work Item Location and Audit List

Number	Item	Location	Quantity	Kanban (Yes or No)	Weekly Audit Check
1	Exam table	Room	1	N	
2	Exam table paper	On exam table	1 roll	Y	
3	Patient chairs	Room	2	N	
4	Physician stool	Room	1	N	
5	X-ray display system	Room	1	N	
6	Magazine rack	Room	1	N	
7	Magazine(s)	Magazine rack	4 max	N	
8	Wall Picture	Wall	1	N	
9	Wall Charts	Wall	2	N	
10	Wall Diploma	Wall	1	N	
11	Blood pressure instrument	Wall	1	N	
12	Gloves	Countertop	1 box	Y	
13	Swabs		1 container	Y	
14	Paper towels		1 roll	Y	
15	Tissues		1 box	Y	
16	Gloves	Drawers	1 box	Y	
17	Swabs		1 container	Y	
18	Paper towels		1 roll	Y	
19	Tissues		1 box	Y	
20	•				
21	•				
22	•				

The Weekly 5S Standard Work List is as follows:

Exam Room - Weekly 5S Standard Work List			
Number	Task	Responsible	Weekly Audit Check
1	Wipe down exam table	Nurse Staff	
2	Restock exam table paper	Nurse Staff	
3	Wipe down patient chairs	Nurse Staff	
4	Wipe down physician stool	Nurse Staff	
5	Clean X-ray display surface	Nurse Staff	
6	Wipe down and bring to standard the magazine rack	Nurse Staff	
7	Magazine(s)	Nurse Staff	
8	Straighten and clean if needed all wall hangings and wall picture	Nurse Staff	
9		Nurse Staff	
10		Nurse Staff	
11	Wipe down and straighten blood pressure instrument	Nurse Staff	
12	Check all Kanbans and countertops	Nurse Staff	
13	Swabs	Nurse Staff	
14	•		
15	•		

After the 5S improvements, the doctors and nurses found that there were able to reduce their delays due to not having items in the exam room from around 10 times per day to zero!

Develop Standard Times for Procedures (Op Log #6)

The sub group team had located published data for typical procedure times in a national database. This was a good first step, but the more critical second step was getting the physicians and nurses to agree on these standards and to work to them. This is where more pushback or resistance was encountered by Dr. McNeal and the improvement team. One doctor was heard to say, "We are healing people, not making parts!"

(Clearly, one of the biggest challenges improvement teams will have is getting highly skilled people to follow standard work practices. The best way to deal with resistance is to address it directly and try to understand why it is occurring. In this case, highly skilled and trained professionals do not want to be told how long a procedure should take. After all, they have invested a good portion of their lives learning their profession which requires careful observation, study, and diagnosis, and thoughtful action planning and control. How can this creative and thoughtful process be standardized?

The facts are that people are standardizing creative and thoughtful practices and tasks every day and the organization that can best harness standardization practices will benefit greatly in the marketplace and the bottom-line. It is true that some creative processes are easier to standardize than others, as some creative processes can be broken down into smaller, more regular parts which can easily be standardized. Imagine an author trying to create a chapter a week or an artist creating a painting a month. In general, the facts are, deadlines and standards add a positive target for improved efficiency and effectiveness.)

Dr. McNeal needed to navigate this situation with care for his team, the physicians, and nurses. He spoke with small groups of physicians, nurses, and individuals urging them to try the Lean Sigma ways. Again, the reception was mixed, but Dr. McNeal felt the team had an excellent plan for this to be successful. All that the team proposed was to validate the national standards. This meant that data would need to be collected for actual times for their practice, and compared to the national standards.

The team asked the physicians and nurses to document the events of their day, including the timing and outcomes of patient visits on a simple standard work Time Observation Sheet as illustrated on the next page. The physicians agreed to document these collection activities as a PDCA event, but only agreed to collect data for two weeks.

Name:		TIME OBSERVATION SHEET		
Date:				
Time	Component Task	VA	NVA	Procedure or Activity Notes
7:00 AM 7:30 AM				
8:00 AM 8:30 AM				
9:00 AM 9:30 AM				
10:00 AM 10:30 AM				
11:00 AM 11:30 AM				
12:00 PM 12:30 PM				
1:00 PM 1:30 PM				
2:00 PM 2:30 PM				
3:00 PM 3:30 PM				
4:00 PM 4:30 PM				
5:00 PM 5:30 PM				
6:00 PM				
Other Time:				

After the two weeks of data collection, the physicians and nurses felt much better about the standard work procedure times, as their actual times seemed to be slightly lower than the projected national standards. The physicians and nurses even came up with a more efficient way to collect the data for the team and agreed to try to stay within the projected standards. Their preference was actually to develop their own standards through the data collection process. This is true continuous improvement! A Plan-Do-Check-Act to IMPROVE!

Dr. McNeal made certain to thank each physician and nurse for their effort and continued support.

Place a Schedule Board in the Waiting Room (Op Log #9)

The visual schedule board was perhaps the most significant improvement for the patients, the physicians, nurses, and the support staff at the office. A computer screen connected to their server was initially placed in the lobby to provide information to/for the patients on how the day's schedule was progressing and what their wait time might be (patients identified by their last four digits of their phone number). It was amazing to see the transformation in the mood of the patients just by keeping them better informed. When the professional staff saw the impact of the visual display, they requested one in their area as well.

The design of the visual display was simple. The visual schedule detailed every half hour increments for each exam room and doctor/nurse team for the day. Color-coding was used to indicate if the exam room and team were on schedule (green) or falling behind (red). Other visual signals such as additional colors, and flashing numbers or fields could also be used as the display became further refined and improved. The displays were similar to flight scheduling monitors in an airport. The display was updated as patients arrived at the office and concluded their visit.

As patients arrived at the office, they could immediately see where they were scheduled and how their doctor/nurse team was adhering to their schedule. If they were behind, the new projected times were also shown. The arriving patients now knew what to expect and could plan their wait accordingly.

From the staffs' perspective, the visual displays provided a visual reminder of their day's commitments and provided them the initiative to move things along on schedule. They did not want to rush patients through, but the patients also knew how the schedule was going and would be quicker to ask the needed questions and minimize the small talk. Not only were people less stressed, the displays also worked to help doctors keep things on schedule.

A representation of the visual display board is illustrated below (color-coded not shown):

Please the desk to confirm your arrival, and then make note of the current status below regarding your appointment.								
Date:	**Doctor and Exam room schedule**							
	McNeal		**Kieff**		**Coopmans**		**Herdon**	
Time	Patent	Room		Room		Room		Room
7:00 AM	2234	A1						
7:30 AM								
8:00 AM	3345	A3	4435	A2	8657	B1	7970	B2
8:30 AM	7763	A1						
9:00 AM					5275	B3	45	B1
9:30 AM	3746	A1	5786	A3				
10:00 AM					5732	B2	5547	B3
10:30 AM	3167	A2	5564	A1				
11:00 AM								
11:30 AM	3436	A2	2494	A3				
12:00 PM								
12:30 PM								
1:00 PM					4678	B1	8684	B2
1:30 PM								
2:00 PM					4845	B3	5544	B1
2:30 PM	6653	A1	5543	A2				
3:00 PM					9907	B2	5673	B3
3:30 PM	9647	A3						
4:00 PM								
4:30 PM								
5:00 PM								
5:30 PM								
6:00 PM								

Appointment Scheduling Work with Check-in for better critical data access (Op Log #10)

To ensure the success of the scheduling visual display board, the check-in process needed to be coordinated with the check-out process. The current state locations of these activities were in different locations within the office environment as shown in the following illustration:

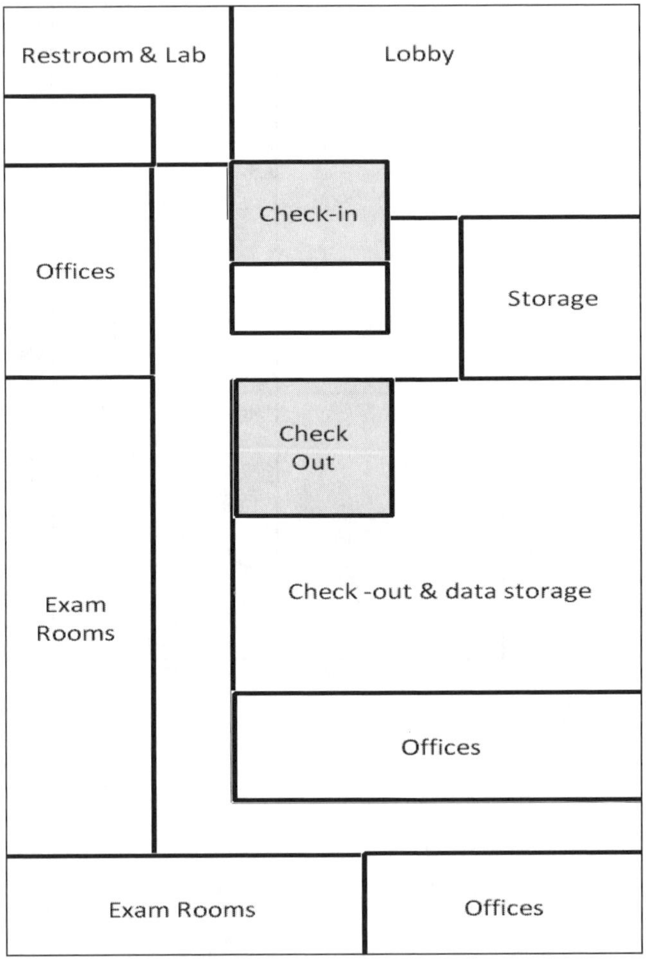

The team agreed on a co-location or “bull pen” type office arrangement to improve communication and take a shared roll in schedule board maintenance. Standard work rules were developed regarding primary and secondary, or back-up, responsibilities for the visual display board maintenance. The two groups trained together on the software for the visual display board and implemented the plan. The current state locations of these activities were in different locations within the office environment as shown in the following illustration:

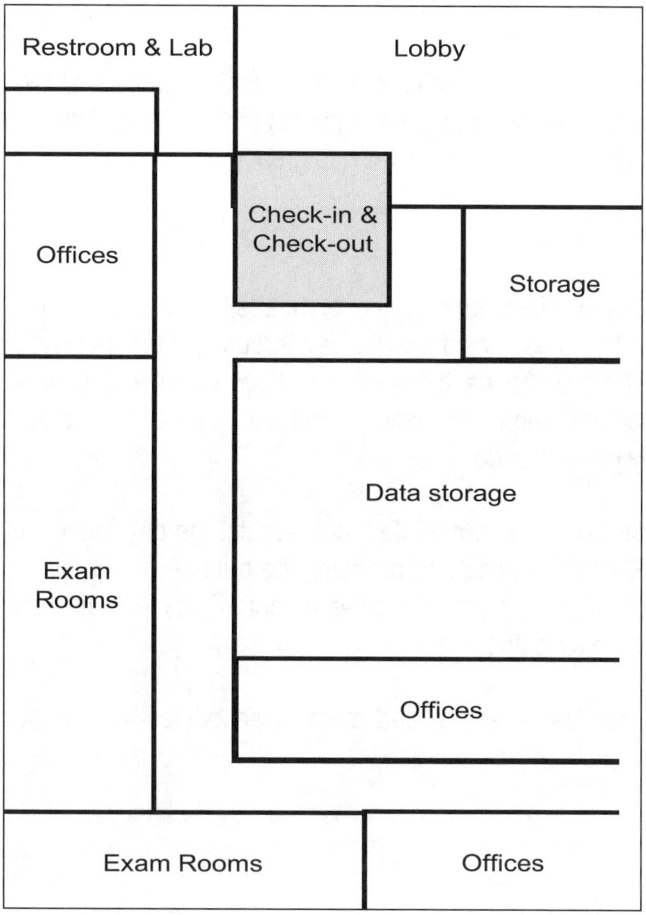

Reduce Errors and communication problems from check-in to exam rooms (Op Log #11)

The visual display schedule boards also reduced a great deal of the communication required between the front office staff and the professional staff. Many of the previous communication problems arose from not knowing how the day's activities were progressing, or which appointments were being cancelled. With the visual display screen, the need to have the face-to-face communications diminished, and the speed and accuracy of the information improved.

Additionally, the co-location of the check-in and check-out process allowed the team members to quickly resolve issues and get things right the first time. The errors improved to 6 sigma levels, and the overall stress level was greatly reduced for everyone involved.

Improve Phase Summary

Things were far from perfect, but clearly everyone felt the improvement in the flow of their day. They were able to balance the work load throughout the day and smooth things out over the week. The "pace" of each day was more consistent and planned. The physicians were able to give their time to the patients that needed it and to do the deeper research they occasionally needed to do.

As the patient classifications came into the schedule, the physicians noticed another improvement. Instead of hurrying and dreading the patient with greater needs, they could anticipate their questions and provide better support. They felt better prepared and anticipated the flow of the sessions.

The team was now less stressed and meeting schedules, and work began to be fun again!

Control Phase

The Control Phase was fairly easy for the Midwest Healthcare Alliance. The "heavy lifting" was done during the Analyze and Improve Phases. Once the new scheduling system and visual display boards were in place, the schedule practically managed itself. As the practice improved, they grew and offered more services and/or procedures, and the team of physicians and nurses had to establish new standard times. As the practice gained new patients, they continually spot-monitored their times and subsequently updated the standards list.

The team determined several operational KPIs to monitor and control performance. The following operational KPIs 30 days after the improvements were made were as follows:

KPI	Initial State	Improved State	Percent Improvement	Sigma Level
Patient Wait Time (average)	25 minutes	5 minutes	80%	N/A
Schedule Attainment or Accuracy	76%	99%	30%	3.83
On-time to Schedule	76%	99%	30%	3.83
Performance to standards by physician	65%	90%	38%	2.78
Performance to standards by nurse	80%	95%	19%	3.14
Number of patents served per day	32	50	56%	N/A
Number of patents served per month	640	1000	56%	N/A
Number of patents served per practice	3453	5456	58%	N/A
Billing Errors Per Million Opportunities (EPMO)	36	2	94%	6.11

Chapter 8

Control Phase

Sustaining the Gains

Chapter Overview

The Control Phase is arguably the most critical phase of the DMAIC process. The Control Phase is the final step and works to sustain the gains made in the previous phases. If the Control Phase is not executed well, organizations can fall back to the previously inefficient and wasteful business practices. In this chapter several key Control Phase tools are reviewed and demonstrated. The Control Phase describes basic project management tools as well as other tools that help leaders communicate the progress of the PDCA initiatives from the Improve Phase. Performance management and accountability tools are also covered. This chapter is designed to help leaders and managers sustain the gains made during the previous four phases.

Control Phase Training and Alignment

There are multiple levels of training and education needed during the Control Phase. Senior-level leaders, mid-level leaders (i.e., managers), first-level leaders (i.e., supervisors), and worker-level employees need to develop an understanding on the use of Control Phase tools. Truly everyone, at every level has an active role in sustaining improvements; if any one level fails the entire system is at risk of failure. Training is one clear way to generate understanding and creating a commitment of sustaining improvements in the Lean Sigma transformation.

For best results, training should be linked to actual application and follow the PDCA process. Some organizations may have already provided training on specific tools of the Control Phase. While this is good, it is recommended that a comprehensive training plan be a critical part of any Lean Sigma transformation.

Before beginning the Control Phase, team members should have an understanding of the following:

- Lean Sigma
- Lean Sigma 12 wastes
- DMAIC Improvement process review
- Improve Phase tool application
- Control Phase tool overview
- Improvement techniques and practical tool applications

Key tools to improve processes once the other four phases have been completed are covered in further detail in the Control Phase Tools section of this chapter. These are key prerequisite skills to learn during this phase.

Control Phase Success through Key Measures

The key to the Control Phase is results-focused accountability and follow through. The Control Phase Accountability Cycle (shown below) also follows the DMAIC process and should be used at all levels of an organization. The Policy Deployment tool described in Chapter 3 (pages 74 - 80) should be used to link or align the goals and measures throughout all the various levels within an organization.

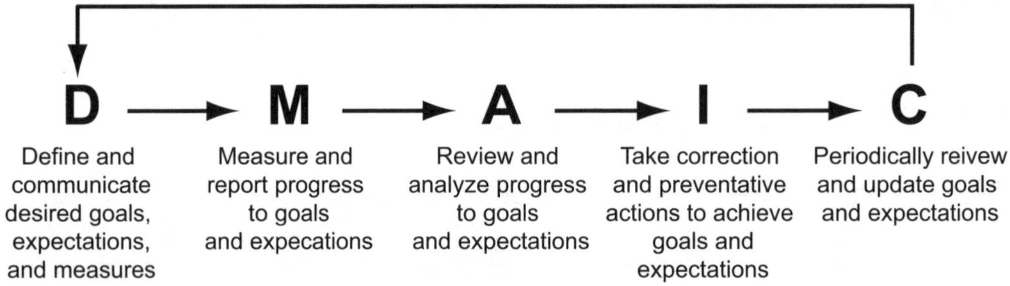

Many organizations struggle with the steps of the Control Phase. The discipline to define and communicate specific, aligned, and measurable goals and expectations is typically not completed to a sufficient degree. Even organizations that do have specific and measureable goals often do a poor job at holding teams and individuals accountable. It really is a matter of leadership, discipline, and effective communication of those goals that become a key function of management. The tools in this chapter will help leaders and teams develop the discipline and effectively communicate improvement initiatives to control the gains made.

Control Phase Tools

The key Control Phase tools and their application are identified in the following table:

Phase	Lean Sigma Tool	Application Guide
CONTROL	Project Management	Use project management tools to facilitate improvement activities for individuals, groups, or teams.
	Statistical Process Control (SPC)	Use SPC tools to monitor and control processes.
	Visual Management	Use visual management tools to provide key organizational information quickly and efficiently, to eliminate errors, and to take immediate corrective actions or counter measures.
	Standard Work for Leaders	Use standard work for leader tools to provide systematic and consistent principled leadership for an organization or team.
	Performance Management	Use performance management to guide desired performance outcomes or goals.
	Problem Solving – Corrective and Preventative Actions	Use problem solving tools to systematically identify and eliminate root causes for problems.
	Layered Process Audits (LPAs)	Use Layered Process Audits to monitor key process characteristics and verify key process conformance on multiple levels of workers, supervisors, and managers.

Control Phase tools cover three areas of control which are as follows:

1. Feed Forward Controls – planning tools used before the project begins to control inputs and ensure success. These are tools such as the Project Charter, Team Charter, etc. (as described earlier in Chapter 4 - Define Phase), and the Project Management and Policy Deployment tools described in Chapter 5 - Define Phase. Feed Forward Controls can be considered good planning techniques and are reviewed, updated, or modified in the Control Phase.

2. Concurrent Controls - are monitoring tools used to monitor progress or throughputs, as they are occurring. These are tools such as the Action Item Log described in the Define Phase, the PDCA process in the Improve Phase and SPC, Visual Management, and Standard Work for Leaders tools described in this chapter. Concurrent Controls can be considered good implementation techniques.

3. Feed Back Controls - are tools that provide post project review, feedback, or outputs on the success of the project or initiative. These tools are the Performance Management and Problem Solving - Corrective and Preventative Actions tools described in this chapter. Feed Back Controls can be considered good follow-up, closure, and lessons learned techniques.

These three areas of control need to be present throughout the DMAIC process. Understanding these areas of control ensures a link between the inputs, throughputs, and outputs of a project. This would help ensure the project does not stray from its original intention.

Project Management

Project management *is the process of establishing, prioritizing, and carrying out tasks to complete specific objectives.* This involves identifying and prioritizing tasks, identifying and assigning resources, in-process performance management of progress-to-outcomes, and taking actions to ensure success. This follows the classic PDCA process.

Program management is a broader topic and involves the process of managing multiple projects simultaneously in an on-going manner. Service organizations may be simultaneously involved in program management of their Lean Sigma transformation and project management of several Lean Sigma improvement projects or initiatives.

Lean Sigma improvement projects are initiated from gaps identified in the assessment and gap analysis, gaps in performance metrics actual performance to targeted requirements or expectations, improvement opportunities identified through value mapping activities, or market or regulatory driven projects to address customer needs and desires. It is critical to manage the resources needed to complete this work effectively. Organizations that initiate more projects than they can effectively support will find it difficult to succeed on a consistent basis. Resource management is a critical part of project management.

There are several popular project management tools. The most predominant tool for project and program management is the Project Planner chart, as described in the Define Chapter. This chart is commonly referred to as a Gantt Chart and can easily be created in Excel. There are also many project management applications available online. If you currently are working with a Customer Relationship Management (CRM) application, that application may have a module for project management with Gantt Chart or similar charting options.

The following is a Gantt Chart for a 3-month project for Timberland Tree Services:

PROJECT PLANNER

Timberland Tree Services Gantt Chart

Objective: Record and track the key events and milestones to complete the initiative.

Revision Date: 15-May

Project Planner (PP)
3 Month Plan

Shading or green color signifies completed implementation activities.

Shading or red color signifies behind target on implementation activities.

Shading or yellow color signifies on target for implementation activities.

Project Planner Objective: Identify major activities by deliverable and time frames to complete

% Comp: 0% (not started), 25% (underway), 50% (half complete), 75% (nearly done), 100% (complete)

	Week #	% Comp	May 1	May 2	May 3	May 4	June 1	June 2	June 3	June 4	July 1	July 2	July 3	July 4
Define Phase														
1	**Project Charter**	**100%**												
2	**Team Charter**	**100%**												
3	Meet with each team in the field	**35%**												
Measure Phase														
1	**Baseline Data Collection and Value Stream Mapping**	**25%**												
2	Field data collection at various sites	**50%**												
Analyze Phase														
1	**Critical Review of Data**	**0%**												
2	**Identify High Potential Improvement Actions**	**0%**												
3	Discuss analysis with field personnel	**0%**												
Improve Phase														
1	**Develop Improvement Implementation Plan**	**0%**												
2	**Implement Improvements**	**0%**												
3	Work with field personnel to get ideas	**0%**												
4	Work with field personnel to implement PDCAs	**0%**												
Control Phase														
1	**Establish Measures and Audit Plan to Sustain the Improvements**	**0%**												
2	**Follow-up with Field Teams**	**0%**												

Once the project Gantt Chart has been created, the team leader or project/program manager must follow the Control Phase Accountability Cycle described earlier in this chapter to control and ensure progress towards goals is being made. It is this discipline that many organizations find most difficult. Regular work sessions (meetings) may be required to follow-up on activities. Many improvement teams find that a weekly session with regular reporting and updates helps to keep the team on track.

Progress is documented on the Gantt Chart by indicating the completed tasks in some fashion. Improvement teams will also find that concurrent updates on the Action Item Log will lead them to success in project management.

Proper project management requires a balancing between Quality, Costs (Resources), and Timeliness or due dates represented by the following equilateral triangle below:

If any of these items becomes out of balance unexpected consequences can occur. For example, if resources are pulled away from projects, due dates will be missed. Once due dates are missed, it may take extra resources to catch the project up to the original target dates. If resources are reallocated, target due dates should be reconsidered. Conversely, to move up target due dates, additional resources may be required.

Project management is an extensive field of study that reaches far beyond the scope or need for successful DMAIC improvement projects. Managing projects can range from the very simple to extremely complicated; however, the basic steps are the same. Use the following project management steps to guide teams in proper project management techniques:

1. Describe the project in terms of overall objectives, measurements and activities, tasks, or events. Equally important is defining what is not included in the scope of the project. At this point, list the major pieces or steps of the project.

2. Assemble the project team and gain alignment in what was defined in (1).

3. Identify resources that will lead to successful project completion.

4. Construct a Gantt Chart or Project Planner showing the relationship/priorities between tasks and resources. At this point, list the minor or detailed steps (i.e., tasks) of the project.

5. Develop a timeline and estimate due dates or targets and resources for each task.

6. Shift resources and assign responsibilities as needed to meet the timeline and quality objectives. There seems to never be enough time, money, or expertise assigned to projects. Work with management early on to identify and commit proper resources and to establish priorities to ensure the overall success of the project.

7. Document and monitor progress on a regular basis relative to schedule, budget, and objectives. Make corrective actions as necessary.

Use the Project Planner (PP) worksheet and Action Item (AI) Log to help teams get started. These tools are reviewed in detail in Chapter 4. Project closure is yet another critical time for project management. To properly close a project all open items should be resolved and/or assigned to individuals for closure. It may also be helpful for the organization if the project team completes a Lessons Learned report or an After Action Review (AAR) so key learnings can be documented,and used in other areas of the organization as needed. This too is an opportune time for leaders of the organization to thank the people for their diligent and thoughtful Lean Sigma work.

Statistical Process Control (SPC)

***Statistical Process Control** is a group of tools used to monitor and control process outputs.* The idea behind SPC is to monitor processes to determine if they are in control, are developing trends, and/or when they go out of control. Processes are said to be in control if only natural or common cause variation is occurring. SPC Charts, also simply referred to as Control or Shewhart Charts, will clearly identify when special cause variation has crept into the process. They are used to predict the future performance of a process. If special cause variation has crept into the process, additional actions are required to contain the process output and regain control. SPC methods can be very powerful in assuring control in the Control Phase.

Control Chart attributes are:

- Points representing measurements of a quality characteristic in samples are taken from the process at different times
- A center line, drawn at the process characteristic mean, is calculated from the data
- Upper and lower 3 sigma control limits, sometimes called natural process limits, that indicate the threshold at which the process output is considered statistically 'unlikely'
- Upper and lower warning limits, drawn as separate lines, typically two standard deviations above and below the center line (3 sigma control limits are the most common, 2 sigma limits would be used when the cost of investigating a false signal is much lower than the cost of missing a true signal - which often occurs in healthcare) (you get many more false signals with 2 sigma control limits)
- Division into zones, with the addition of rules governing frequencies of observations in each zone (optional)
- Annotation with events of interest, as determined by the improvement team members, Black Belt, or Lean Sensei that is in charge of the improvement project

The purpose of Control Charts are to allow simple detection of events that are indicative of actual process change. This simple decision can be difficult where the process characteristic is continuously varying; the Control Chart provides statistically objective criteria of change. When change is detected and considered good, its cause should be identified and possibly become the new standard of working, where the change is considered bad, its cause should be identified and eliminated.

There are several types of Control Charts designed for specific types of data and sampling ability. SPC Charts work with two types of data: variable data and attribute data. ***Variable data*** *is data such as length, time, weight, etc. that is measured along a continuous scale of some type.* ***Attribute Data*** *is qualitative in nature, and is defined by counting defects, number of defects per part / transaction or process, or percent defective, depending on the control charting method being used.*

The following SPC Charting techniques are used for the data types and sampling abilities specified:

Types of Variable Data Charts

- Run Chart: Numerous applications (covered in detail in Chapter 5 - Measure Phase)
- X and Moving Range Chart: Where the sample size is 1, such as a daily sales chart
- X-Bar and Range Chart: Where the sample size is 3 - 7, evaluating the cycle time of a service process (e.g., delivering fast food, taking order from a customer, answering a phone call, etc.)
- X-Bar and S Chart: Where the sample size is > 10, such as when measuring the time of each transaction completed during a day's activities

Types of Attribute Data Charts

- P Chart (Percent Error Rate or non-conforming): When measuring the number of transactions with errors versus total transactions processed
- C Chart (Defects per unit): When measuring the number of errors on specific transactions

Note: Examples of these charts are provided later in this section.

Control Charts for variables, such as X and Moving Range, X-Bar and R Charts, and X-Bar and S Charts are developed by taking a number of samples (usually 25 - 30 samples) of a certain size (usually 3 - 10 items per sample) from a process that is thought to be in statistical control and calculating the sample means and ranges. Using standard statistical methods, the grand mean (or mean of the sample means) and average range (R-Bar) are calculated and used as centerlines for the segments of the X-Bar and R Charts.

Based on these values, and calculated parameters for control limits, the control limits for the sample X-Bar and R values are established. Then the sample values are plotted on their respective charts. Any values or groups of values are deemed to be out of control if any of the following conditions occur:

- ❖ One point above the Upper Control Limit (UCL)
- ❖ One point below the Lower Control Limit (LCL)
- ❖ Any increasing run or trend of 7 consecutive points
- ❖ Any decreasing run or trend of 7 consecutive points
- ❖ 7 consecutive points above the X-bar
- ❖ 7 consecutive points below the X-bar
- ❖ Any point outside the range control limits
- ❖ Two out of three consecutive points in the outer one-third region of the control limits
- ❖ Four out of five points in the outer two-thirds region of the control limits

Assignable causes must be determined for any out of control condition, the out-of-control samples (if applicable) must be discarded, and the Control Chart characteristics must be re-calculated. Additional tools such as brainstorming, 5 Why Analysis, etc. can be used to determine the out-of-control condition and what must be done to correct it. Control Charts are created and reviewed to ensure processes remain in control. Assignable causes may be traced to one-time events such as calculating error, power surges, new workers, inspectors, machine settings, day versus night shifts, or seasonal effects. Trends can be caused by such things as worker fatigue, improving worker skills, or seasonal effects. The idea is to quickly understand the process conditions and act to sustain the desired outcomes.

3 Standard Deviations (3 SD or 3 sigma) gives a "confidence level" which encompasses 99.73% of all events or 99.73% of ALL events will fall within +/- 3 SD. X-Bar plus 3 SD, referred to as the UCL, is the + 3 SD marker and X-Bar minus 3 SD, referred to as the LCL, is the -3 SD marker. This is used to recognize what is "normal" and what is "abnormal." Basically, as long as the individual plots are between the UCL and the LCL, the process is exhibiting "NORMAL" variation. However, 99.73% of events means that 0.27% of the points on the Control Chart would be outside the +/-3 SD control limits when the process is operating in control, and these would be false signals.

For very critical processes, it is recommended to use +/- 1SD. This most likely would result in many false signals, but there would also be very few missed signals. This would provide increased protection against the process producing an error.

Note: For more technical information on Control Charts and how they can be used to detect when a process is out-of-control, it is suggested you consult a statistical methods book or conduct further research online. An excellent reference is *Essentials of Quality* by Victor E. Sower, Ph.D.

The following examples are developed to aid understanding of how simple charts can be used to control and sustain process improvements. In the example below, the charting technique allows the revenue to be monitored, controlled, and diagnosed on a daily basis. For more "real-time" information, plot the sales revenue on an hour-by-hour basis; or through proper reporting, make sales figures available in real-time. An example of real-time reporting might be the data provided by a stock exchange. Changes in stock values are continually updated throughout the day in real-time.

The following is an example of a daily sales data collection table:

Observation Number	Date	Day	Daily Sales
1	16-Jul	Friday	$ 2,390.00
2	17-Jul	Saturday	$ 2,765.00
3	18-Jul	Sunday	$ 2,245.00
4	19-Jul	Monday	$ 1,234.00
5	20-Jul	Tuesday	$ 2,345.00
6	21-Jul	Wednesday	$ 1,457.00
7	22-Jul	Thursday	$ 1,328.00
8	23-Jul	Friday	$ 2,122.00
9	24-Jul	Saturday	$ 3,300.00
10	25-Jul	Sunday	$ 2,543.00
11	26-Jul	Monday	$ 1,190.00
12	27-Jul	Tuesday	$ 2,456.00
13	28-Jul	Wednesday	$ 2,566.00
14	29-Jul	Thursday	$ 2,344.00
15	30-Jul	Friday	$ 2,899.00
16	31-Jul	Saturday	$ 2,900.00
17	1-Aug	Sunday	$ 2,267.00

The following is an example of a Run Chart of the above daily sales data collection table:

The following is an example of a Moving Range Chart of the previous daily sales data collection table:

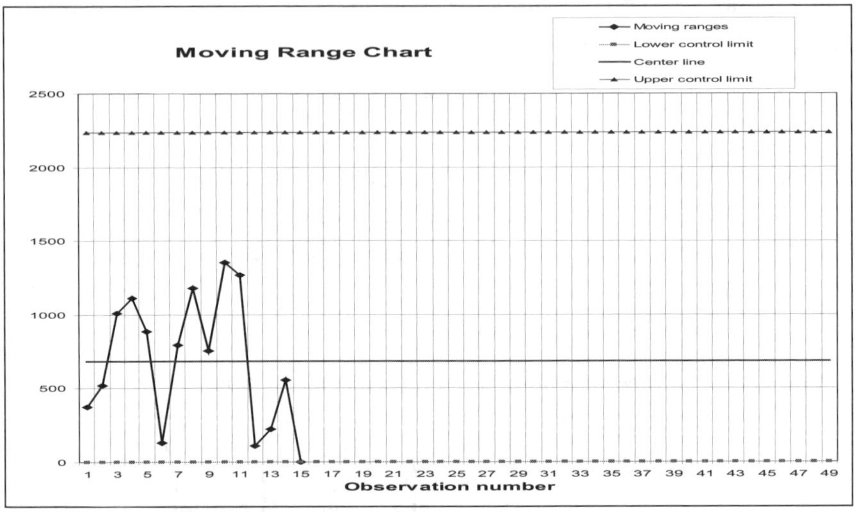

Perhaps an even more revealing way to plot this daily sales data may be with a trend line added to the X Chart as shown in the following example. With the trend line, progress (or trouble) can quickly and easily be seen. Trend lines can be added very simply using Excel.

The following is an example of a P Chart, which tracks the percent error rate or percent non-conforming, such as errors during a check-in process at a hospital, hotel, or airline, or bank transaction. This Chart addresses the question, "Of all the transactions completed, how many had errors?"

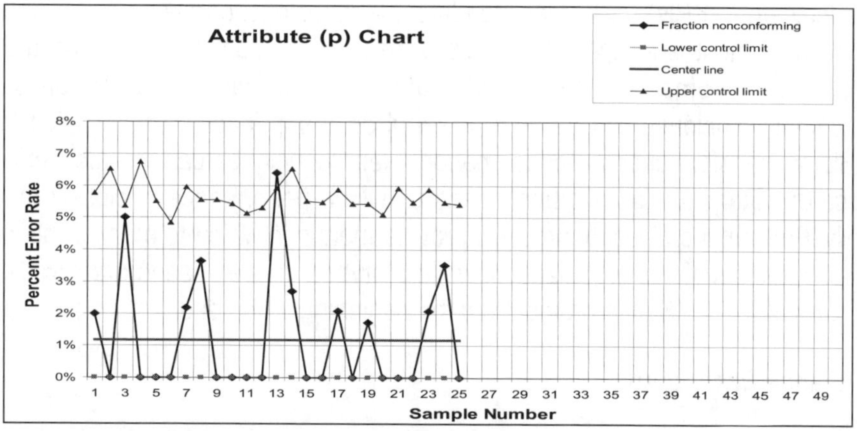

To maintain control, assignable cause(s) and corrective actions would need to be determined for sample number 13.

The following is an example of an Attribute C Chart, which tracks the number of defects or errors per unit or event, such as the number of errors during a check-in process or bank transaction. This chart addresses the question, "On the transactions with errors, how many errors were on each?"

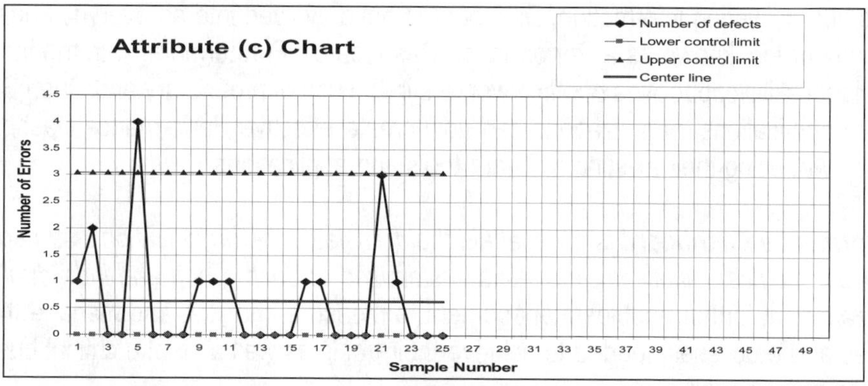

In this example, sample numbers 5 and 21 require further study for assignable cause and corrective actions for control.

This discussion and these charts are provided for example purposes only. Further study and use of SPC techniques is recommended for organizations seriously considering a Lean Sigma transformation.

Visual Management

Visual Management *is the use of visual techniques that graphically display relevant business performance data.* The relevant business performance data can be Key Performance Indicators (KPIs), customer mandates, legal or environmental compliances, etc. Visual Management is a higher level approach to visual controls that is used to monitor and control an organization's, a work team's, or an individual's performance. Visual management techniques can be very powerful drivers in leading organizations through Lean Sigma transformations. Visual management techniques can include Performance Dashboards, Storyboards, or other means by which performance is closely monitored. Typically, Performance Dashboards will provide means in which to monitor the Key Performance Indictors of any organization, while Storyboards are used to graphically convey major parts of a Lean Sigma project from the beginning to the end.

Performance Dashboards

Dashboards have long been a fixture in automobiles and other vehicles and only in the last 20 years or so have organizations adopted their usage to monitor and control performance. In business, these Dashboards initially started out as Executive Information Systems (EIS), but they never gained a foothold through an organization because they were geared to so few people in each company and were cumbersome to change due to Information Technology dependencies. Since Information Technology has advanced at such a rapid pace, supplanted by the Web as the preeminent platform for running applications and delivering information, Dashboards have evolved into an everyday business improvement tool known as a Performance Dashboard. Furthermore, with the increase in individual skills/capabilities of office workers in the use of proprietary and Open Source software applications, organizations can now create effective Performance Dashboards on their own, using their existing software tools and applications.

A ***Performance Dashboard*** *is a visual aid that translates the organization's strategy into objectives, metrics, initiatives, and tasks customized to each group and individual in an organization.* It further enables management to measure, monitor, and manage the key activities and processes needed to achieve their goals as well as make critical business decisions more quickly.

Performance Dashboards are used effectively when the following conditions exist:

- Critical business processes and activities are monitored to alert the appropriate person when a potential problem arises
- Root causes of problems have had thorough investigation and detail to identify and eliminate issues
- People and processes have improved decision-making skills to optimize performance and steer the organization in the right direction

Dashboards may or may not be balanced. The three areas of 'balance' to consider are metric-to-metric balance, leading and lagging balance, and area-to-area balance. There is said to be metric-to-metric balance to Performance Dashboards if the performance measures provide protection from optimization of one performance goal at the expense of another. For example, an organization could improve their customer wait time by adding several people to serve clients. This may be good for the customer wait time, but bad for profitability. A measure of total employees or customer wait time per employee would need to be tracked to "balance" the measures.

Another concept of 'balance' is to have leading and lagging performance measures. A leading indicator to customer satisfaction may be employee attendance. If employees are not showing up at work when required, customer satisfaction (a lagging or after the service measure) may suffer. Typically, good people performance leads to good operational performance, which leads to good customer satisfaction performance, which leads to good financial performance. There is a causal relationship between people, operations, customer satisfaction, and financial performance, and it is important to have balance in measures in these areas.

The last area of balance to consider is area-to-area within an organization. Since work flows horizontally through organizations, it is critical to seek balance by measuring indicators in each area of an organization. For example, only measuring the performance of final sales dollars will not provide an organization the critical information needed to improve operational areas. Organizations should seek balanced Performance Dashboards in the key areas of operations (productivity, quality, and delivery), sales, and innovation or new product or service offerings.

Note: Performance Dashboards are also used at a departmental or work group level, which would have more specific departmental or process level measurements that are linked to the organizational measurements.

Performance Dashboards provide a competitive advantage by empowering employees to work pro-actively and make better decisions by giving them relevant, actionable information real-time. There are different levels of information that can be represented on a Performance Dashboard.

There are numerous commercial Performance Dashboard applications available, with many offering a 30-day free trial. It what you require is not too complicated or involved, consider using Microsoft Excel or other applications within your current Operating Platform to relay the information you require.

The following are the benefits that can be obtained by using a Performance Dashboard:

- Communicates much needed information about a process to the right people
- Instills the message, "what gets measured, gets done"
- Allows for a single vision of what is required
- Empowers employees by giving them self-service access to information
- Delivers actionable information to the right people in a timely fashion that allows action to be taken
- Increases coordination between departments allowing for robust dialogue about performance
- Allows managers to make decisions more accurately and efficiently
- Allows workers to take ownership of their performance-to-target and allows managers to avoid the need to 'micro-manage' staff

The following are some Performance Dashboard examples:

1. Fast food restaurants track speed of delivery by shift and team on a scoreboard behind the service counter
2. Call centers track the speed and wait time of their call center individuals and teams
3. Financial service organizations post the stock market exchange on a real-time basis
4. The Department of Motor Vehicles (DMV) posts current wait times
5. Leader boards at golf tournaments
6. On-time arrivals and departure information at airports
7. Customer number being "currently processed" at a service counter
8. Place, humidity, temperature, and radar view from a weather channel or site

The key to using Performance Dashboards is posting the key information in an area where it can easily be seen, and then reacting to the data to make improvements and or adjustments to keep the process in control and performing at peak levels. This takes discipline and accountability.

Once Key Performance Indicators (KPIs) and goals have been established, a means of measuring and reporting will need to be established by leadership. It is usually best to make clear assignments regarding who will update the Performance Dashboard, at what frequency it will be updated, how often and by whom it will be reviewed, as well as who has ownership for each KPI. There should also be a reaction plan available to guide the owner or management team for measurements under performing.

Note: Performance Dashboards will most likely be reviewed in the Define Phase to assist with determining the measurements (goals, KPIs, etc.) required for the Project or Team Charter and will be the main driver for all continuous improvement efforts.

The following is an example of a Performance Dashboard for a hospital:

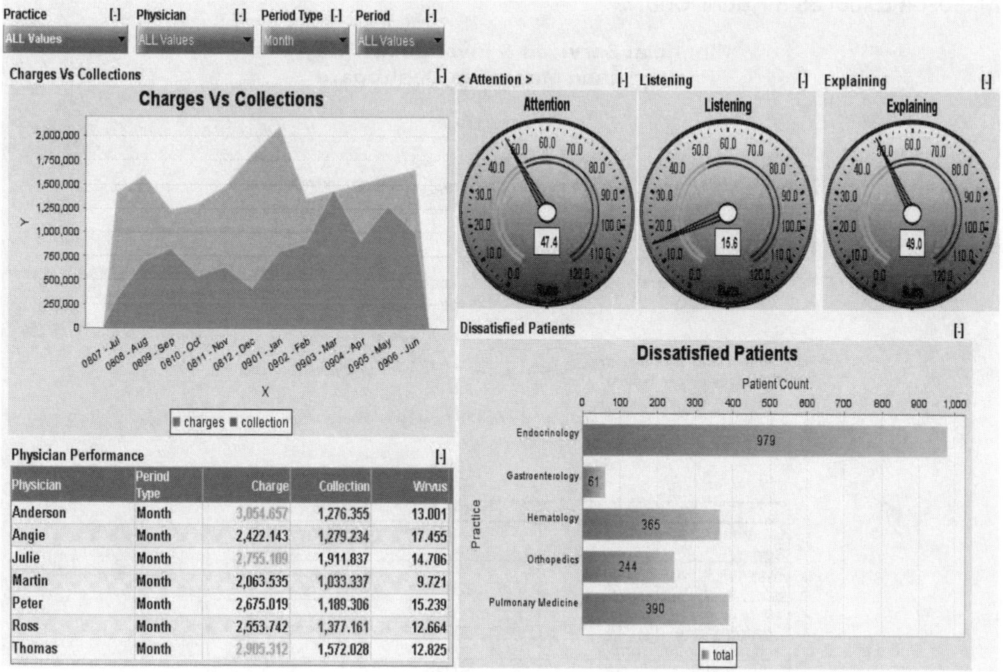

Physician	Period Type	Charge	Collection	Wrvus
Anderson	Month	3,054.657	1,276.355	13.001
Angie	Month	2,422.143	1,279.234	17.455
Julie	Month	2,755.109	1,911.837	14.706
Martin	Month	2,063.535	1,033.337	9.721
Peter	Month	2,675.019	1,189.306	15.239
Ross	Month	2,553.742	1,377.161	12.664
Thomas	Month	2,905.312	1,572.028	12.825

The following is a Performance Dashboard for a restaurant/gift shop in resort area:

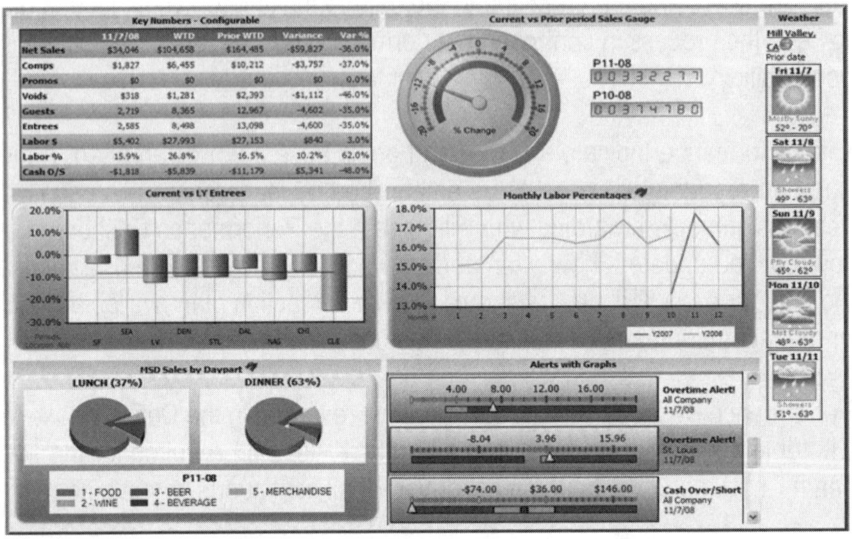

The following is a Performance Dashboard for a financial advising firm that was created in Microsoft Excel as a Radar Chart:

Measure	Goal	Actual
Customer Satisfaction Survey	100%	98.0%
Average Internal Audit Scores	100%	92.8%
Security & Exchange Conformance	100%	100.0%
Accuracy of Information	100%	90.0%
New Customers to Goal	100%	76.0%
Completeness of Information (100% equals no call backs)	100%	95.0%
Attendance	100%	100.0%
Account Growth to Targets	100%	82.0%

Storyboard

*The **Storyboard** is a poster-size or larger framework for displaying all the key information from the Lean Sigma project.* It can be created in Excel, Visio, or some other application that is available. The Storyboard is very similar to an A3 report (representing the 11" x 17" paper size) and is a visual aid for communicating the progression of a continuous improvement project. The Storyboard is organized into various areas that can be represented by a graph, illustration, and/or a simple sentence or two. The information is then displayed on a format that is graphically rich and engaging. The Storyboard will contain many of the tools used throughout the project.

The Storyboard segments may include some, if not all, of the following categories:

- Reason for Selecting the Project (Problem Statement)
- Data Chart of Present Condition (Pareto Chart, Fishbone, etc.)
- Target Goal
- Plan of Action (portion of Gantt Chart)
- Results (New Standards, Metrics, etc.)
- Team Recognition
- Next Target

The Storyboard should be posted in the area where the continuous improvement activities are occurring and should be updated frequently as new information is obtained. Storyboards should be fun in design, many times taking on a graphical theme (e.g., an Emergency department in a hospital may display the various sections in comparison to an ambulance, an Operating Room comparison to an operating table, a financial services organization comparison to various currency denominations, etc.). Team members who are responsible for creating the Storyboard should make it engaging by using color, themes, etc.

The following is an example of a Storyboard for a hospital's Emergency Department patient arrival to that patient receiving an inpatient bed:

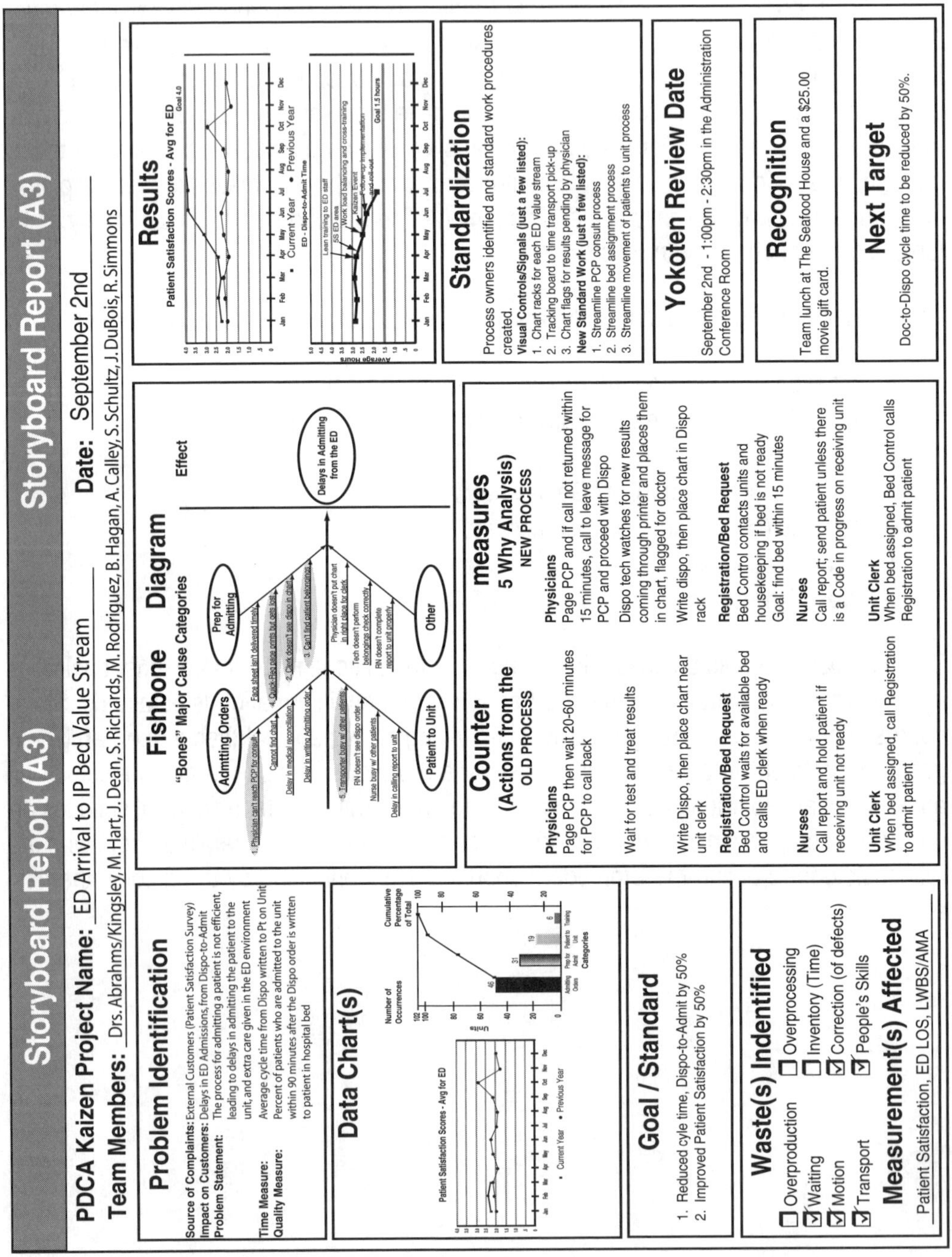

Storyboard Report (A3)

PDCA Kaizen Project Name: ED Arrival to IP Bed Value Stream **Date:** September 2nd

Team Members: Drs. Abrahms/Kingsley, M. Hart, J. Dean, S. Richards, M. Rodriguez, B. Hagan, A. Calley, S. Schultz, J. DuBois, R. Simmons

Problem Identification

Source of Complaints: External Customers (Patient Satisfaction Survey)
Impact on Customers: Delays in ED Admissions, from Dispo-to-Admit
Problem Statement: The process for admitting a patient is not efficient, leading to delays in admitting the patient to the unit, and extra care given in the ED environment
Time Measure: Average cycle time from Dispo written to Pt on Unit
Quality Measure: Percent of patients who are admitted to the unit within 90 minutes after the Dispo order is written to patient in hospital bed

Data Chart(s)

Goal / Standard

1. Reduced cyle time, Dispo-to-Admit by 50%
2. Improved Patient Satisfaction by 50%

Waste(s) Indentified

- ☐ Overproduction
- ☑ Waiting
- ☑ Motion
- ☑ Transport
- ☐ Overprocessing
- ☐ Inventory (Time)
- ☑ Correction (of defects)
- ☑ People's Skills

Measurement(s) Affected

Patient Satisfaction, ED LOS, LWBS/AMA

Fishbone Diagram

"Bones" Major Cause Categories

Counter measures (Actions from the 5 Why Analysis)

OLD PROCESS	NEW PROCESS
Physicians Page PCP then wait 20-60 minutes for PCP to call back	**Physicians** Page PCP and if call not returned within 15 minutes, call to leave message for PCP and proceed with Dispo
Wait for test and treat results	Dispo tech watches for new results coming through printer and places them in chart, flagged for doctor
Write Dispo, then place chart near unit clerk	Write dispo, then place chart in Dispo rack
Registration/Bed Request Bed Control waits for available bed and calls ED clerk when ready	**Registration/Bed Request** Bed Control contacts units and housekeeping if bed is not ready Goal: find bed within 15 minutes
Nurses Call report and hold patient if receiving unit not ready	**Nurses** Call report; send patient unless there is a Code in progress on receiving unit
Unit Clerk When bed assigned, call Registration to admit patient	**Unit Clerk** When bed assigned, Bed Control calls Registration to admit patient

Results

Standardization

Process owners identified and standard work procedures created.

Visual Controls/Signals (just a few listed):

1. Chart racks for each ED value stream
2. Tracking board to time transport pick-up
3. Chart flags for results pending by physician

New Standard Work (just a few listed):

1. Streamline PCP consult process
2. Streamline bed assignment process
3. Streamline movement of patients to unit process

Yokoten Review Date

September 2nd - 1:00pm - 2:30pm in the Administration Conference Room

Recognition

Team lunch at The Seafood House and a $25.00 movie gift card.

Next Target

Doc-to-Dispo cycle time to be reduced by 50%.

In today's fast paced global market place, Storyboarding techniques are becoming more virtual, meaning that rather than a large board physically displayed in a specific area, Lean Sigma improvement teams are creating Storyboards that can be accessed around the globe. If the project is large enough, Web pages are created to illustrate and track progress. Below is an intranet page for a financial institution that contains open and closed Lean Sigma improvement project's documentation:

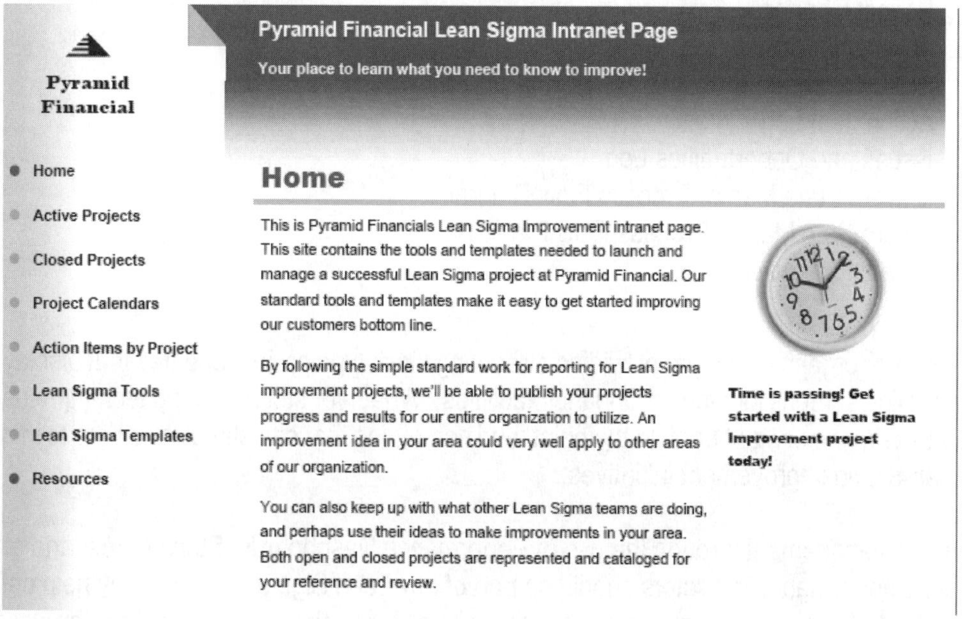

Other progressive organizations are storing Storyboard information in public folders so that people with access can review project status, and possibly learn from previous projects. Typically organizations will have standard naming and content requirements or templates to use to document projects. Spreadsheet templates or files usually contain the following items or tabs:

1. Project Charter
2. Team Charter
3. Project Planner
4. Action Item Log
5. Issues and Opportunities Log
6. Current State Map or Process Flow Diagram
7. Future Sate Map or Process Flow Diagram
8. Data and Analysis

Still other organizations are providing streaming kiosk type project updates that display on television screens located around their facilities. Whatever storyboarding technique used, try to keep the content brief, to the point, and something that can stimulate others to initiate Lean Sigma improvement initiatives.

Visual management through the use of Performance Dashboards, Storyboards, and other visual performance indicators should be part of any Lean Sigma project. They help define the limits for processes and measure as well as define the action plan if the processes and measures are not performing to expectations (reference the Control Phase Accountability Cycle described earlier in this chapter). The process to manage using Performance Dashboards is also discussed in the next section, Standard Work for Leaders.

Standard Work for Leaders

Standard work for leaders is a concept derived from general standard work practices. ***Standard Work for leaders*** *prescribes specific tasks, actions, and time frames for completion of work for a manager or supervisor.* Every position in every organization should have standard work processes to follow.

Standard work for leaders is critical on several levels. First, standard work is the basic building block for continuous improvement. Without standard work for everyone, there is no baseline for improvement efforts, and improvements cannot be properly documented and measured. Leaders need to be responsible and accountable to continually improve their personal effectiveness. Standard work for leaders, a basic predictable approach to leading, is an essential first step.

Secondly, standard work for leaders assists leaders to understand how the organization, teams, and individuals are performing and to address areas of abnormalities and waste with countermeasures (and improvements), or to say "Thank you" where appropriate. Much of the standard work for leaders involves monitoring the KPIs of the organization or department and taking corrective and preventative action as required. This is critical to an organization's sustained success.

Additionally, as improvement teams see leaders performing standard work they will better understand that standard work for their positions is here to stay. The best way to show people that the organization is serious about implementing Lean Sigma methods and tools is for the leaders to practice the methods and tools themselves. By "walking the talk," leaders will also build trust with workers, and trust is another key ingredient for sustained Lean Sigma success. This is what truly transforms the organization to a Lean Sigma environment or culture.

Standard work for leaders defines for every level leader a systematic approach to setting the direction for the organization and deploying the tactical plan to achieve the goals. This includes defining Key Performance Indicators and targets, identifying improvement target areas, team building, teaching, communicating, etc. Standard work for leaders defines a systematic approach to running a world class service organization.

The table on the next two pages describes typical standard work for leaders at various levels in an organization. It provides a general guideline on what is expected at each level. Use this as a guide when establishing standard work for leaders within your organization.

Activity and Frequency

Level	Daily	Weekly
Corporate Leader	Follow appropriate work instructions, procedures, and complete Job Description activities. Lead by example!	Establish rolling weekly agendas and conduct weekly meetings with each departmental manager. Use the DMAIC, process and project management format. Meeting should focus on KPIs and on-going improvement initiatives
	Complete and analyze required corporate productivity reports. Meet with appropriate departmental managers to review reports. Acknowledge success.	Track requirements from what was discussed and expected at weekly meetings.
	Focus on reports that show a negative trend. Gather data and conduct appropriate meetings. Communicate once per day to all direct reports demonstrating engagement and involvement.	Continue to monitor KPIs that show a negative trend. Continue to work to support improvement efforts.
Departmental Manager or Supervisor	Follow appropriate work instructions, procedures, and complete Job Description activities. Lead by example!	Establish and conduct weekly meetings with supervisors and team leads.
	Complete and analyze departmental productivity reports. Meet with appropriate leads to review reports. Acknowledge success.	Be available for direct reports for contact.
	Establish pro-active actions to address any and all negative trends. Initiate Lean Sigma teams for appropriate issues. Look for other continuous improvement activities.	Monitor all performance measurements and follow-up with teams or individuals that have responsibility to address negative trends.
Work Team Lead	Follow appropriate work instructions, procedures, and complete Job Description activities. Lead by example!	Establish and conduct weekly meetings for continuous improvement efforts.
	Complete daily tasks, encourage improvement initiatives, support departmental initiatives, and acknowledge workers that contribute ideas for improvement.	Be attentive to employee's concerns (and ideas for improvement).

Activity and Frequency

Monthly	Semi-Annually	Annually
Complete and submit monthly highlights to owners, stockholders, board of directors, etc.	Review all organizational level KPIs, goals, and individual subordinate performance measurements. Check for alignment with organizational strategy. Modify as needed.	Review all organizational level KPIs, goals, and individual subordinate performance measurements. Check for alignment with organizational strategy. Modify as needed.
Establish rolling monthly agenda and conduct monthly meetings with departmental managers.	Provide mini-performance feedback sessions for each direct report. Assign appropriate improvement plans to ensure employee development and KPIs are met, as applicable.	Conduct performance appraisals for each direct report. Assign appropriate improvement plans to ensure employee development and KPIs are met, as applicable.
		Review strategic direction, adjust to market conditions, and develop alignment with new or revised KPIs.
Review monthly departmental goals or KPIs with leads and employees, if appropriate.	Communicate the organizations priorities including customer satisfaction.	Create and implement an innovative communication plan to clearly define to organization members the vision and mission that includes customer satisfaction.
Continue to support continuous improvement and problem solving teams.	Communicate progress to date to all employees. Continue to support continuous improvement efforts.	Continue to address departmental areas of concern and allocate appropriate resources to ensure success.
		Learn and communicate any and all new or revised improvement methodologies to leads and employees.
Review monthly goals with employees, if appropriate.	Communicate the organizations priorities including customer satisfaction to all employees.	Create and implement an innovative communication plan to clearly define to organization members the vision and mission that includes customer satisfaction.
Continue to demonstrate support and enthusiasm for continuous improvement efforts.	Provide employees with specific improvement initiatives that have contributed to improving departmental measures and/or KPIs.	Continue to work to develop employees.

Performance Management

***Performance Management** is the process of establishing desired performance outcomes or goals, monitoring progress to goals through measurements, and then taking action to ensure success.* The key to managing human performance is to follow a consistent system or process. The following diagram illustrates the process or steps to managing human performance. This follows the classic Plan–Do–Check–Act cycle. The Control Phase Accountability Cycle can also be used as a performance management process.

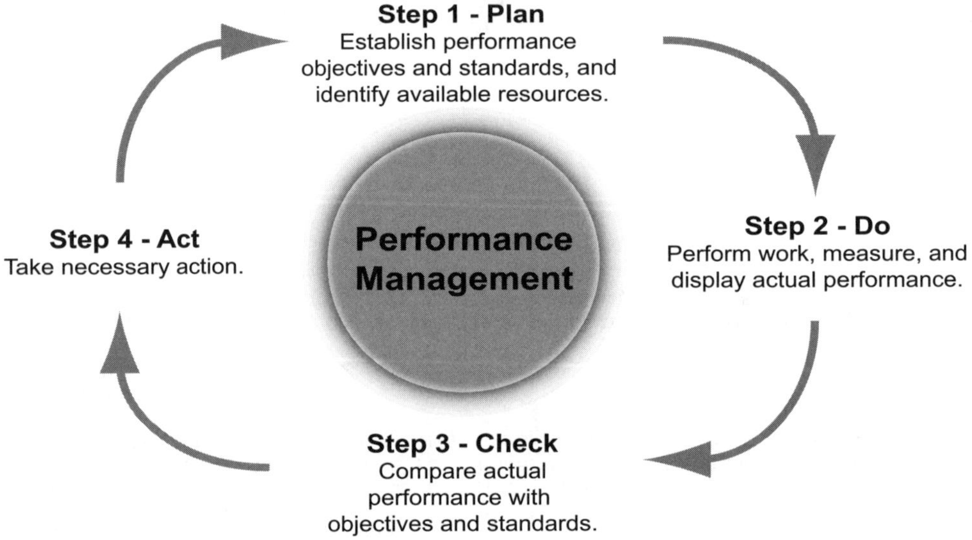

One of the most important steps to performance management is creating clearly defined expectations and goals. Goals and expectations should meet the following SMART criteria. (SMART stands for Specific, Measurable, Assigned, Realistic, and Time-bounded). Use this checklist to help establish SMART goals for yourself and others. (Briefly discussed in Chapter 3, pages 74 - 75.)

If people do not clearly know the expectations, odds are they will not meet them. The SMART Goals Worksheet can be used as a guide to start setting SMART goals. This is also a useful tool for delegating tasks. Establishing SMART goals is more difficult than it may seem. Leaders and managers are typically not used to setting goals that meet the SMART criteria.

Clearly one of the following statements better fits the SMART goal criteria:

Goal Statement 1: Increase productivity in the sales area.

Goal Statement 2: The sales team, led by Sarah, will increase productivity in the sales area by 15% (by the end of this calendar year) by implementing Lean Sigma methods.

The following will serve as a mini-case study for performance management:

After years of lack luster productivity at the Happy Cookie Company, Kris the team leader, was ready to give up. When Kris spoke with employees they seemed to not care that their productivity was low. They pointed fingers at management and other employees for the performance problems. They said "I get paid the same for making rate or not, why should I break my back working harder when the next person doesn't and makes the same?" and "It just doesn't matter."

Kris knew that they had some good points. She knew that the work environment set no positive rewards for success and often rewarded failure or mediocrity the same. She knew she needed to do something. She decided to implement some goals for the team and individuals.

Kris reviewed the daily expectations for batches, scrap pounds, schedule attainment, accidents, and attendance. She documented these expectations for herself on the SMART Goals Worksheet on the next page. She then shared these goals with her team. The team basically said "So what?" When Kris asked why the team did not meet the goals she once again got many "excuses." Some of the reasons were legitimate assignable causes (e.g., the mixer is running at a reduced rate because a blade is broken, Beth had not been trained on the oven setup, Pat had just come in late for work, etc.).

Kris started to post a daily scorecard. She also developed a similar SMART Goals Worksheet for each team member. Once the goals were established, Kris led a weekly meeting to identify the assignable causes for not meeting the goals. From these meetings, action items were developed. Each day action items were assigned and subsequently reviewed the next day. Other items, such as developing a method to keep the product flow going smooth from area to area, were for the team to address. Over time, the performance measures started to improve. When they did, Kris made sure to celebrate somehow. The celebrations were small and simple and matched the achievement. One time she brought in candy bars for everyone and just said "Thank-you." to each team member.

Kris also conducted regular performance feedback sessions with each team member and gave them data supported feedback on their individual as well as team performance. As the company's productivity increased, so did the rewards.

The following is the initial SMART Goals Worksheet for Kris:

Specific Task	Measurement of Success (How will we know the goal is achieved?)	Who is Responsible	Time Frame for Completion (Follow-up dates)	Comments
1. Attend Lean Sigma training session	Completion certificate	Kris will sign up and secure funds from the training budget	Within the next 6 months	I need to use this method to make improvements.
2. Start a daily scorecard	If we have one or not	Kris	End of the month	N/A
3. Complete 12 batches every shift	Daily scorecard measure	Kris and the shift production teams	12 batches per shift by next month, 14 batches per shift by year end	N/A
4. No more than 50 pounds of scrap per shift	Daily scorecard measure	Kris and the shift production teams	Today	This needs to be more closely measured.
5. Attain schedule 100%	Daily scorecard measure	Kris and the shift production teams	By next month	We need to get the schedule out to the team.
6. Zero injuries	Daily scorecard measure	Kris and the shift production teams	Immediately	We have had no injuries this year. Complete daily reminders.
7. Zero unexcused absences	Daily scorecard measure	Kris and the shift production teams	Immediately	Many people have had unexcused absences. This may be due to poor morale.

Problem Solving - Corrective and Preventative Actions

Problem solving *is an improvement approach that involves objectively identifying the causes of a problem and proposing potential, often creative, solutions to the problem, which will be agreeable to multiple parties or individuals.* People solve problems every day. Most problems identified can be solved relatively quickly with little formal process or documentation. As problems become more complex, additional study and documentation may be required to sufficiently solve the problem. For these instances, a standardized problem solving process can be used to improve our natural problem solving ability, allow teams of problem solvers to work effectively together, and to properly document the solution to a problem. Standard tools and methods are used to create a common language and methodology for a systematic approach to problem solving. Standard tools and methods provide the following:

- Helps teams define the reason(s) for the problem
- Prevents problems from returning
- Creates better standards
- Encourages team work
- Allows for solving problems permanently

The 7-step problem solving methodology described in this section provides several advantages:

- It is simple.
- Both groups and individuals can use it.
- It can be used at all levels of the organization.
- It can focus teams on the issue at hand with minimal training.

The 7-step problem solving methodology is as follows:

1. Describe and define the problem.
2. Implement containment actions to prevent the problem from spreading.
3. Determine potential root causes of the problem.
4. Test and determine the actual root cause or causes of the problem.
5. Analyze and determine potential solutions to the problem.
6. Implement solutions to eliminate the problem.
7. Verify effectiveness of solutions and prevent the problem from occurring again.

1. Describe and define the problem.

This is a critical step that many problem solvers take for granted or complete haphazardly. If done properly, this step can lead directly to root cause identification. A poor or incomplete problem definition can lead to more confusion and problems. To complete this step, first write a statement describing the problem as it is observed. This initial statement may be only an observed symptom of the true problem, as a headache is a symptom of poor blood flow to the brain. A good problem statement describes the situation in terms of your own experience and in measurable terms. The statement should be:

> Specific - What is the observed problem and what is not the problem? How broad is the problem? Is the problem increasing, decreasing, or unchanging?
> Time-bounded - When did the problem or symptom first appear? How was the problem or symptom first identified? What other events occurred at or near the same time?
> Current Direction - What is the present trend?

The clearer and more precise the data is the better opportunity will exist for determining cause and subequent improvement.

Note: Microsoft Excel has excellent functionality to analyze and chart data in the problem solving process, however, there are also many applications on the market that may be of value. It is suggested that you use the functionality of Excel, and, then if and when more advanced features are needed, consider additional commercial applications. These commercial applications combine charts, graphs, and advanced data visualizations in an easy-to-use reporting tool for further understanding and representation of your Excel spreadsheets.

***The Is/Is Not Analysis** can be used to help define the scope of the problem before any resources are committed.* The Is/Is Not Analysis on the next page is for a situation where the hotel management has observed a decline in their customer satisfaction rating due to housekeeping.

Note: This hotel case study situation will be used throughout the problem solving section to illustrate several tools and the problem solving steps.

Is/Is Not Analysis

Symptom: Customer complaints

Date Opened: 9/1

Problem Description: Declining Customer Satisfaction rating over the last month due to declining scores in Housekeeping and Facilities areas.

Is/Is Not Questions		Is	Is Not	Deductions About Facts and Other Information		Direction/Priority Setting
				Differences	Changes and Dates	Most Likely Causes and Proposed Next Steps
What	Object?	Declining Facilities score, and poor scores in the Housekeeping and Room Check in/out scores	Declining dining, front desk, room, or shuttle scores	Housekeeping is a separate department from the other areas.	None, have always been organized this way.	
	Defect?	Declining survey scores	Direct complaint from guests	If customers are really upset, they complain directly; so this problem is believed to be an irritant or nuisance complaint or concern.	None, this is typical for survey scorfing.	
Where	On object?	Our facility	Other facilities in the city owned by the same company	Location, equipment, staff	Laundry equipment break down last month for a couple of days, June 15 -18.	It is possible that the 3 day slow down in laundry processing caused several guests to rate our service lower. Determine if the laundry days caused poor ratings.
	Geographically?	Our facility	Other facilities in the city owned by the same company	Location, equipment, staff, water supply, detergents		
When	First seen?	This month's survey scores	Last month's scores, last year's scores	Time is different.	None.	
	Else seen?	Last year when we remodeled the lobby	Never had a problem with Housekeeping	Last time this occurred we were remodeling the lobby, this time we are remodeling the pool area. Pool area versus lobby area - all guests use the lobby area, only some use the pool area.	No changes in this.	
	In process seen?	On customer surveys	Direct complaints	Customer surveys are a less aggressive way to express dissatisfaction.	No changes in this.	
How	Many objects have defects?	One month's survey scores	Multiple month trend	No trends yet.	No changes in this.	
	Many defects per object?	Only poor scores on Room Check in/out, Housekeeping and Facilities; multiple days have low scores	One disgruntled customer	One complaining guest versus a general drop in satisfaction. Everyone noticed a drop in Housekeeping service.	No changes in this.	
What	Is the trend?	Trend in facilities scores since the pool improvement project started in mid-month. Room Check in/out was a few bad days below goal.	Trend for several months, good or bad.	Trend means we have been steadily getting better or worst. We were good up until last month.	Pool remodel and laundry equipment break down.	It is possible that the pool remodeling has caused a few guests to rate our Housekeeping lower. Did any quests who rated us poorly leave their contact information, and can we contact the guests to ask them specific questions about their scores?

2. Implement containment actions to prevent the problem from spreading.

This step is about taking the necessary actions to ensure the customer does not experience any of the effects and the problem does not spread to other areas or grow out of control. It is often a temporary or "stop-gap" measure until a permanent solution can be applied. Containment actions for this case study included the following:

- Setting up alternate check-in area
- Using backup computer or manual process
- Bringing in extra ice to the lobby area so guests will not be inconvenienced
- Moving guests to alternate rooms, arranging rooms for outplaced guests in another local hotel
- Providing guests with coupons to local restaurants, implementing an additional audit of housekeeping activities
- Contacting guests shortly after arrival to their rooms to ask if everything is in place and acceptable

3. Determine potential root causes of the problem

Once the problem has been identified, and temporary containment is in place, it is time to analyze the problem more carefully to determine the root cause. The systematic approach to problem solving is more of an investigation to discover cause as it is a rush to fix the problem. To determine potential root causes, data must be gathered about the problem. There are three powerful tools that help problem solving teams determine potential causes such as the Cause and Effect (or Fishbone) Diagram, brainstorming, and the 5 Why questioning that were all thoroughly discussed in Chapter 6 - Analyze Phase.

The following is the initial Fishbone Diagram for this case study:

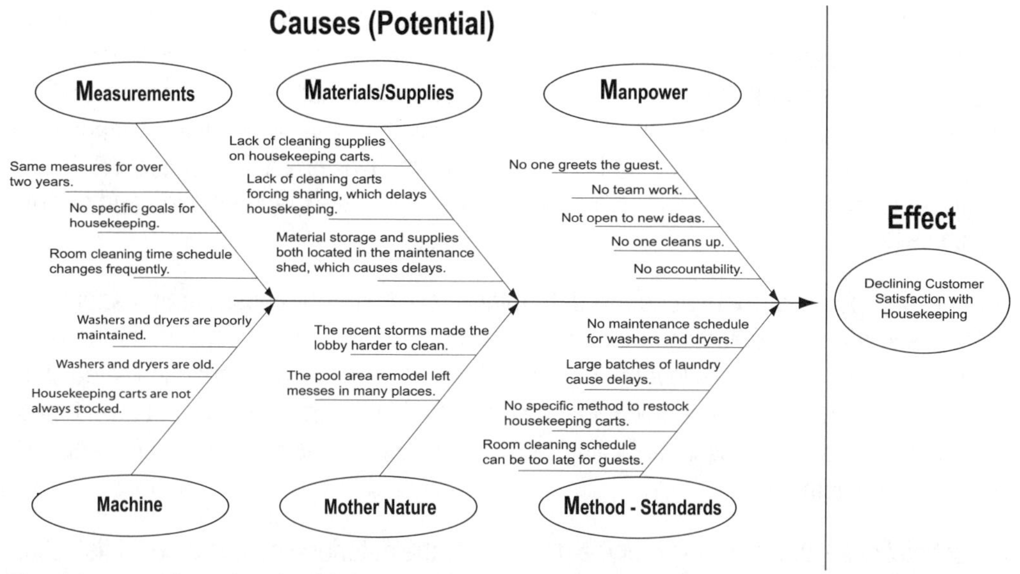

The team continued to brainstorm and created the following future state Fishbone Diagram:

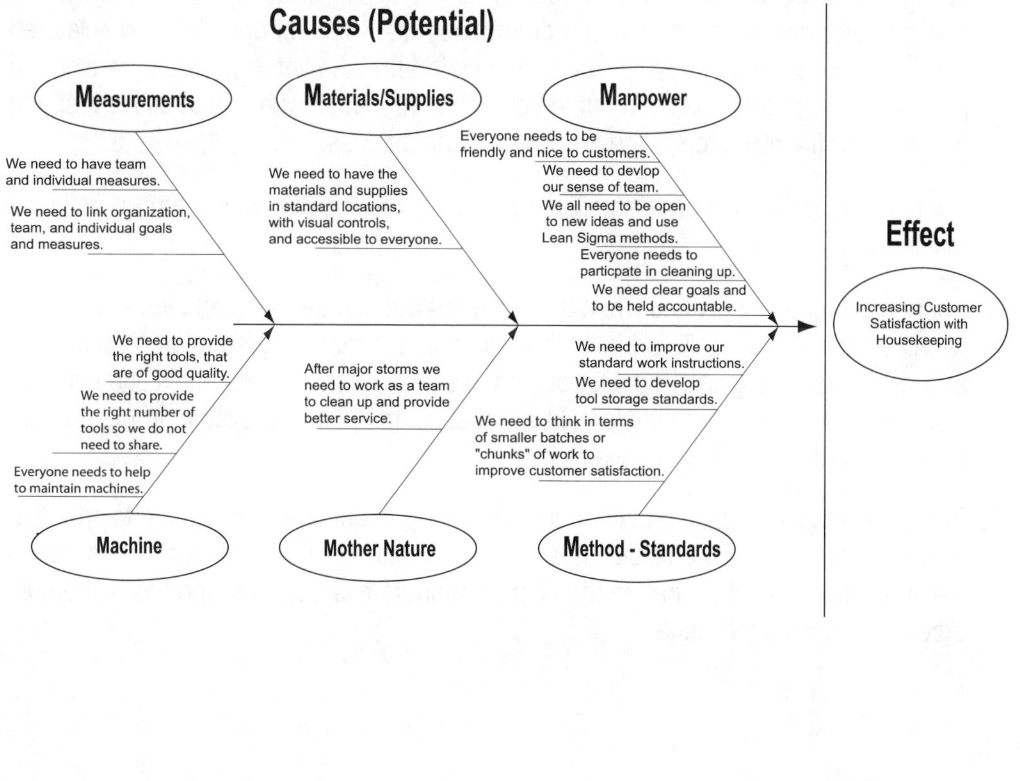

4. Test and determine the actual root cause or causes of the problem.

Once potential root causes have been identified, each potential root cause must be tested to determine which potential root cause is the actual root cause. In today's complex world, it is common to have several root causes occurring together or in succession that actually cause the problem at hand to occur. Look for these relationships in root cause testing. To properly complete the root cause testing, it is likely that several "what if" scenarios will have to be considered through a series of experiments. Design Of Experiments (DOE) is a popular term and systematic method used to describe this experimentation and discovery process.

After testing potential root causes to determine the actual root cause, teams should be able to recreate the problem in a controlled environment and essentially turn the problem on and off at will. Often this level of testing will not be practical or economically feasible, and problem solving teams should use good judgment in determining to what level to test to. For some problems this level testing may never be completed, yet improvements will need to be implemented.

In our hotel case, the root cause for the problem for the deteriorating customer satisfaction scores is determined to be in part due to the following:

A. Dryers overheating because the dryer lint traps were not cleaned properly. To verify this the team did not want to overheat the dryer again, so they reviewed the dryer manufacturer maintenance plan and determined that the lint traps should be cleaned after every load. The current process only stated that the lint trap should be cleaned periodically. The team decided not to verify the root cause with a destructive test and moved on to the next step in the problem solving process.

B. Remodeling of the pool area and since the project is completed, not further action is required.

C. Poor housekeeping services when the team ran out of materials and supplies, or had to share cleaning tools. To address this situation, the team requested additional tools so that each cleaning cart had a full set of tools. Regarding the materials and supplies issue, the team decided to implement a visual control pull card system to ensure that they do not run out of key supplies.

D. Finally the team recognized that the overall management program needed to improve. This was thought to be outside the scope and control of the team, so a recommendation was submitted to their leadership to address this situation and the leadership agreed to address the issues.

5. Analyze and determine potential solutions to the problem

Once the most likely causes have been determined, teams will need to develop improvement actions to eliminate the problem and prevent recurrence. It is important to gain consensus of the action plan for the implementation of the solutions. Ensure key decision-makers approve the course of action. Plan the implementation, when it will start, who will be doing what, and what type of measurement is needed.

Clarify what constraints might apply to a proposed solution (approvals required, timing, impact on other departments, etc.). The following questions may be useful in determining root cause:

- Is there a better way to do things?
- Will the proposed solution eliminate the problem entirely?
- Can the root cause be eliminated entirely?
- Can drawbacks to improvements be minimized?
- Can the proposed solution be simplified?
- Have all possible scenarios been explored?

To address cause A from the previous page, the improvement team for the hotel example brainstormed the following potential solutions to ensure the lint traps are cleaned at the appropriate times:

1. Modify the procedure to indicate that the lint traps need to be cleaned after every load which is the manufacture's recommendation.
2. Install an alarm to make sure that the lint trap is pulled and cleaned after each load.
3. Have a sensor not let the next load start unless the lint trap was cleaned.
4. Install a temperature sensor to shut the dryer down before it overheats and causes major delays and repairs.
5. Install an air flow sensor to ensure the lint trap has been cleaned. Have the air flow sensor shut down the dryer if there is insufficient air flow.

The team decided to select and implement items 1 and 5.

6. Implement solutions to eliminate the problem.

Use the Project Planner and Action Item Log to identify and document improvement action items to implement solutions. Once implementation has begun, ensure the correct measurements are in place tracking each solution relative to the problem description. If the problem has been eliminated, update the work standards or documentation.

The team's AI Log was updated to reflect who and when these actions would be addressed and appeared as follows:

Action Item # 1 - Modify the procedure to indicate that the lint traps need to be cleaned after every load which is the manufacture's recommendation.
Action Item # 5 - Install an air flow sensor to ensure the lint trap has been cleaned. Have the air flow sensor shut down the dryer if there is insufficient air flow.

7. Verify effectiveness of solutions and prevent the problem from occurring again.

This stage of the problem solving effort is where previously implemented solutions are audited to ensure they worked effectively over time in preventing recurrence of the problem. Follow-up audits should be planned before a problem solving team has disbanded and should occur after sufficient time has passed to determine if the implemented solution has been effective. It is best to place the initial follow-up audit on the Action Item Log, then to establish a regular audit or metric to control the issue in the future.

In conclusion, the hotel team was able to quickly discover and implement several improvement ideas to improve customer satisfaction. On subsequent customer satisfaction surveys, the team was please to have their actions validated by customer satisfaction scores improving by slightly over 15% over the next two month period. The team was rewarded with a pizza party to celebrate their success and use of the Lean Sigma problem solving methods and tools. This helped build trust and additional sense of team for the group.

Note: It is recommended that the details of the entire problem solving effort be saved in an Excel file with multiple tabs that represent the Is/Is Not Analysis, Cause and Effect Diagram, 5 Whys, Project Planner, Action Item Log, etc.

Layered Process Audits (LPAs)

Layered Process Audits (LPAs) *are a system of process audits performed by multiple levels of workers, supervisors, and managers to monitor key process characteristics and verify process conformance on an ongoing basis.* LPAs ensure that standard work is being used and that processes are performing as expected to desired outcomes or measures.

Typically a Layered Process Auditing system is comprised of a series of process audits on critical or high risk processes, multiple layers of audits by workers, supervision and management from different areas, and a system of reporting and follow-up that ensures conformance and corrective actions are implemented. Layered Process Audits provide an excellent tool for minimizing variation and sustaining improvements in processes. LPAs help organizations error-proof their processes/systems and making significant progress toward achieving perfection.

Historically, audits in service organizations have been both documented and undocumented. The most effective audits are documented and reviewed for corrective and preventative actions if required. LPAs that find conformance to standards and that the desired outcomes are being achieved are an opportunity to reinforce positive behaviors, thank the work team for their performance and to encourage continued improvement and success.

To get the most out a LPA system it is best to perform audits as close to real-time as possible. An audit performed on last week's work may be revealing, but will not provide the opportunity for avoiding problems, only fixing them in hindsight. An audit performed as a task is being completed affords the worker the opportunity to correct undesirable behaviors as they go.

The frequencies of LPAs are usually based on the volume or level of risk associated with the process or action. Real-time audits are often used in the healthcare area where a patient may be asked several times to confirm who they are, the issue or area of the pending surgery or procedure, etc. This type of repetitive real-time audit is sometimes called a redundancy check if the LPA is not documented. Redundancy checks are often helpful where there is a great deal of human interaction in the process, and there is a great potential risk if the process is done wrong. Another area where redundancy checks are commonly used is in the cockpit of airplanes before the flight begins. The pilot and co-pilot may complete redundancy checks on the operating systems of the aircraft, as well as function checks of other issues concerning the flight.

LPAs are more assuring than redundancy checks because they require documentation of the audit process. LPAs should be conducted for service transactions or operations where there is a high level of human interaction and a high risk if the transactions or operations are completed incorrectly. Examples of these service transactions and operations are public transportation, healthcare, and financial transactions, to name a few.

The four elements of a layered process auditing system are:

1. A Collection or Series of Audits - Audits are simply an organized group of questions designed to examine equipment, supplies, or a process. Audits in an LPA system should focus on areas where errors represent a high-risk for customers and organizations.

2. Layers of Auditors - In an LPA system, your collection of audits is performed on a scheduled basis, at a predetermined frequency, by multiple layers of management from across the organization.

3. Prevention and Containment - For a Layered Process Audit system to be truly effective, it must integrate analysis, action, and improvements. If an auditor finds a non-conformance while performing an audit, that auditor should not only record their finding, but also take immediate initial corrective action to ensure customers are not affected by the potential error.

4. Reporting and Follow-up - Information about the finding should be recorded and readily available to management for later analysis. A regular system of LPA reviews should be put in place to ensure the effectiveness of the entire LPA system

There are numerous types of LPAs. The following list differentiate between different types of audits. Each type of audit can be performed to a set and published schedule, or conducted by surprise.

- Simple audit – This is a simple yes or no question and answer format to determine if the process is working properly and may be performed concurrent or after the process is delivered.
- Concurrent audit – This LPA is completed as the process is being delivered to ensure completeness, accuracy, customer satisfaction and/or perfection.
- Layered audit - This is an audit by a different level of leadership to ensure the LPAs are being performed to plan.

- ❖ Self-audit – This is an audit completed by the worker delivering the service. This audit is basically a checklist to ensure the process is complete and accurate, and that the customer is satisfied.
- ❖ Co-worker Audit – This is similar to a Self-audit, but it is completed by a co-worker or peer.

An example of an LPA for a fast food drive-thru window service is shown below and on the next page:

Drive-Thru Window Co-Worker level LPA example: Once per shift

Co-worker Drive-Thru Window Order Process **Audit Date:** Observe the process once per shift and complete the audit form below. Post results on the dashboard.	
Greeting - Review items below for completeness and accuracy:	**Results**
Is the customer pleasantly welcomed to the store, and asked if their order could be taken?	Yes☐ No☐
Is the customer offered the daily special promotion?	Yes☐ No☐
Notes:	Correction Action Issued? Yes☐ No☐
Take Order - Verify process completeness and accuracy:	**Results**
Is the order taken in a simple and effective manner?	Yes☐ No☐
Are the customer's questions and needs met in an effective manner?	Yes☐ No☐
Is the order and cost confirmed with the customer?	Yes☐ No☐
Notes:	Correction Action Issued? Yes☐ No☐
Collect Payment - Verify process completeness and accuracy:	**Results**
Is the cost stated to the customer?	Yes☐ No☐
Is the transaction completed in an effective manner without delay?	Yes☐ No☐
Is the customer asked if they require condiments? If so, were they provided in a timely manner?	Yes☐ No☐
Notes:	Correction Action Issued? Yes☐ No☐
Deliver Order - Verify process completeness and accuracy:	**Results**
Is the order delivered in less than the target time?	Yes☐ No☐
Is the order correct?	Yes☐ No☐
Is the customer thanked?	Yes☐ No☐
Notes:	Correction Action Issued? Yes☐ No☐
Audit Score = [(11 – (Number of "No" results)) / 11] * 100 (Do not include "No" results for "Corrective Action Issued?" questions.)	**Audit Score:** %

Drive-Thru Window Shift Supervisor level LPA example: Once per day

Shift Supervisor Drive-Thru Window Order Process **Audit Date:** Observe dashboard daily, and complete the audit form below. Post the results on the dashboard.	
Co-worker Audit - Review items below for completeness and accuracy:	**Results**
Is the Co-worker audit being performed once per shift?	Yes☐ No☐
Are the Co-worker audit results being posted on the dashboard?	Yes☐ No☐
Notes:	Correction Action Issued? Yes☐ No☐
Corrective Actions - Verify process completeness and accuracy:	**Results**
Are the Co-worker audits Corrective Actions being identified on the dashboard?	Yes☐ No☐
Are the Co-worker audits Corrective Actions being addressed appropriately?	Yes☐ No☐
Are the Co-worker audits Corrective Actions being closed in a timely manner?	Yes☐ No☐
Notes:	Correction Action Issued? Yes☐ No☐
Audit Score = [(5 – (Number of "No" results)) / 5] * 100 (Do not include "No" results for "Corrective Action Issued?" questions.)	**Audit Score:** %

Drive-Thru Window Store Manger level LPA example: Once per week

Store Manager Drive-Thru Window Order Process **Audit Date:** Observe dashboard weekly and complete the audit form below. Post the results on the dashboard.	
Shift Supervisor Audit - Review items below for completeness and accuracy:	**Results**
Is the Shift Supervisor audit being performed once per day?	Yes☐ No☐
Are the Shift Supervisor audit results being posted on the dashboard?	Yes☐ No☐
Notes:	Correction Action Issued? Yes☐ No☐
Corrective Actions - Verify process completeness and accuracy:	**Results**
Are the Shift Supervisor audits Corrective Actions being identified on the dashboard?	Yes☐ No☐
Are the Shift Supervisor audits Corrective Actions being addressed appropriately?	Yes☐ No☐
Are the Shift Supervisor audits Corrective Actions being closed in a timely manner?	Yes☐ No☐
Notes:	Correction Action Issued? Yes☐ No☐
Audit Score = [(5 – (Number of "No" results)) / 5] * 100 (Do not include "No" results for "Corrective Action Issued?" questions.)	**Audit Score:** %

Through implementing this LPA audit system this store's drive-thru food service window was able to reduce the errors and complaints by 16% and 32% respectively over a two month period. Improving customer satisfaction is key for all service organizations. LPAs can help service organizations do this by providing critical review of actual process performance, and driving corrective and improvement actions.

Chapter Summary

The Control Phase of the DMAIC process is critical to long-term success of an improvement initiative. Control Phase tools are designed to monitor improvement actions to ensure improvements are sustained over time. This chapter identifies key activities and tools used during the Control Phase. Many of the Control Phase tools are fundamental management tools required to plan, lead, organize and control an organization's performance.

The Control Phase methods and tools are not only critical for improvement initiatives, they also apply directly to overall organization performance management. By using these key Control Phase tools, teams are able to sustain improvement initiatives.

Lean Sigma for Service Excellence Applications

These observations may assist in understanding how to apply the concepts and tools contained in this chapter:

- Gather a small cross-functional team to discuss current Control Phase tools in use at your organization. Discuss new applications that require Control Phase tools to ensure performance improvement.
- Identify a current project that is in process at your organization and begin to use the Project Management tools to document and track progress.
- Identify an appropriate processes or activities to track using SPC methods and begin monitoring
- Establish KPIs for a specific area within your responsibility, and begin tracking the KPIs using visual management and Policy Deployment techniques.
- Identify a current problem that your organization is facing and use the problem solving tools and methods to discover a permanent resolution.

Control Phase Readiness Guide

The following Control Phase Readiness Guide allows you to ensure there is application of the chapter's content before proceeding to apply the Lean Sigma tools and concepts in the next chapter. If you score less than 70%, consider working on the lower scoring areas before moving on.

Control Phase Readiness Guide	
Use the following 5-level Likert item scale to rank each of the statements: **1 = Strongly Disagree** **2 = Disagree** **3 = Neither Agree nor Disagree** **4 = Agree** **5 = Strongly Agree**	
	Score
1. My organization does a good job of defining and communicating desired goals and expectations.	
2. My organization does a good job of measuring progress to goals and expectations.	
3. My organizations is good at reviewing progress to goals and expectations.	
4. My organization takes necessary corrective and preventive actions to achieve goals.	
5. My organization periodically reviews and updates goals and expectations.	
6. My organization effectively uses visual management tools to provide key information efficiently.	
7. My organization uses Lean Sigma tools to identify and eliminate root causes for problems and errors.	
8. My organization utilizes lean sigma tools to systematically solve complex and chronic problems.	
9. My organization has a system in place to monitor and improve individual, group, or team performance.	
10. I feel comfortable in using SPC to monitor and control processes.	
11. I feel comfortable in applying visual management and performance dashboards.	
12. I feel comfotable using the 5 Whys to discover root causes to errors and non-performances.	
13. I feel comfortable using the Is-Is Not Analysis tool to solve complex and chronic problems.	
14. I feel comfortable in the understanding of Performance Dashboards.	
15. I feel comfortable using the corrective and preventive action tools for effective problem solving.	
16. I feel comfortable using the standard work for leaders tool.	
17. I feel comfortable using project management tools to facilitate improvement activities	
18. I feel comfortable using the Storyboarding tool to report progress to leaders, customers, etc.	
19. I see the value in using the DMAIC process and tools for controlling projects.	
20. I believe my organization should utilize and apply the concepts and tools discussed in this chapter.	
Total Score	

Case Review – Control Phase for Reinventing Government

In any large city, crime is an issue of great concern. Crime rates reflect personal safety, and personal safety, real or perceived, influences investment, tourism, and housing decisions. These factors in turn influence the very viability or survival of the city's neighborhoods. A dying or shrinking neighborhood leads to more crime, mass exodus by home owners and investors, and further degradation. It is a terrible negative spiral that many large cities have faced.

In this particular large city the newly elected Mayor had inherited a crime problem, as well as major budget deficit. The Mayor had been elected for many reasons, but many believed her crime reduction pledge is what won her the election. Clearly it was time for Mayor Marion Hines to make a difference.

The statistics were daunting; every FBI report from the previous decade had the city ranked in the top ten in each of the following major crime areas ranked:

- Murder
- Rape
- Robbery
- Felonious assault
- Burglary
- Grand Larceny
- Grand Larceny Auto

The Mayor needed a new approach to government responsibility and accountability. She needed to reinvent how government worked. From her campaign experience, it seemed that many in the private sector seemed to have a better system to handle accountability when running a large organization. Private sector organizations were clearly responsible to their shareholders and were measured regularly to validate their performance. Through her many fund raising events, Mayor Hines had talked with many local business people who were using the Lean Sigma approach to improve their business processes and results. She thought that the Lean Sigma systematic approach to improvement and control would apply to city government as well.

Mayor Hines assembled a team of key leaders, as well as local business leaders who were well-versed in the Lean Sigma approach. The team went to work with the DMAIC improvement process.

Define

The mission was clear. Mayor Hines needed to make good on her election pledge to reduce crime. Reducing crime was the only way to build a safer city. A city where neighborhoods would grow, where people would invest and stay, where people could walk the streets with a sense of safety and security, and where people would feel safe to live and work.

The team developed a Project and Team Charter that identified very aggressive goals for crime reduction and accountability. The team believed that it was their responsibility to make a significant difference, and that responsibility and accountability is a key. The benefits were their very survival.

The team's initial measurements were the key FBI statistics, but they felt that these reports were much too old by the time they were reported. This and the fact that the FBI statistics were not predictive of crime drove the team to establish other key measures.

Currently the key measures from the Police Department were the number of arrests and response time to 911 calls. Once again, these measures were not predictive enough to prevent future crimes. Also, the timeliness of this data was too slow to be useful.

Instead, the team determined a new set of metrics to be used at the precinct level that could be reported daily, used in a proactive manner to actually see patterns, and to prevent future crimes. The new key daily measures included things like:

- Number of Complaint Calls (CC)
- CC exact location in the city
- CC time
- CC category by issue or crime

The Mayor, on the other hand, would measure on a monthly basis other more social metrics regarding the city such as home purchases, business investments, and school attendance, as a way to monitor the overall progress of the effort.

Measure

The city's Police Department had the basics in place to compile the data on a reasonable time frame, but daily processing would be a challenge. Even with the electronic reporting format being used, they had to create new reports to pull and compile the data on a daily basis. It took several weeks and the use of some key resources to develop a system that could deliver the information they needed for improvement.

It became a priority for each of the major three districts to report and roll up the data from simple reports delivered once per day to each of the three Police Chiefs. A larger version of the report, which included the statistics from each of the three districts, would go to the Police Commissioner, as well as the Mayor's office, on a weekly basis.

Analyze

Timeliness of the data was critical; just as a speedometer does little good to help avoid speeding tickets if it is on an hour delay, good crime data two days old is of little use for crime prevention. Daily analysis and review was critical to the success of the improvement effort.

Initially, each Police Chief was uncertain on how to use the daily reports. The reports seemed to be just another thing for them to do. However, after a few weeks of reviewing the reports, they began to see trends and got excited when they could actually predict something that was about to happen. Once understanding the power of timely data, most chiefs began to share the reports throughout the ranks. The Police Chiefs that shared the information realized immediate improvement in the numbers.

To better analyze the daily reports, trend plots were also published to allow each district chief to see their progress. The data was presented in a variety of time frames. Certainly, the daily numbers received attention and drove action; however, it was other time statistics that allowed leaders to take preventative actions. Data was presented in month-to-date (MTD) and year-to-date (YTD) time frames to allow leaders to analyze trends and ask the right questions.

The data was also presented in a manner to show comparisons from prior year's performance, showing percent change, up or down. The data had to be accurate to be useful, so the team implemented an audit system of sorts by analyzing the data for statistical abnormalities, good or bad. The team made it very clear that if any data falsification was done, disciplinary action would be immediate. This was serious business and data integrity was critical.

Improve

With the key data available on a daily basis, Police Chiefs began to see trends and patterns in their districts. Their proactive directions and questions to their work force could now be put to test to prevent future crimes. Initially, some of their directions were met with some skepticism, but they were instructed to press forward. Their briefings with their officers began to get more specific and targeted to crime prevention.

Standard work was developed for daily briefings at the precinct level, weekly accountability sessions with the mayor, and monthly all Chiefs sessions conducted with the Mayor and her staff, other political figures, such as the Chiefs and their support teams from each of the three districts. The standard work rhythm of the work sessions was daily, weekly, and monthly.

As the data began to flow and the reports hit the Police Chief's desks, they could clearly see there were issues to address. They found that patterns such as a series of 2 am break-ins across the city could now be anticipated. Prior to the daily reports, a savvy Police Officer might make the connection if they were reviewing the daily briefings, but this was hit and miss, and there was no way to connect their thoughts with officer deployment across the city. Even if a Police Officer did communicate a concern to their leaders, they had no way of anticipating where the next break-in might occur, and there was no incentive to communicate across district lines.

With the daily reports from each district being shared with all chiefs, they could better anticipate issues and redeploy resources to meet and question suspicious persons before crimes occur, rather than hoping that the 911 call comes in soon enough to allow them to apprehend the suspicious person(s) fleeing the crime scene. Much of the improved communication methods were standardized by making the data more visible through real-time visual performance scoreboards.

Certainly not every crime could be anticipated, but it was clear that standardized practices, improved briefings, and deployment of resources was preventing crimes from occurring. A key finding was that if given the right data, the entire police force became better at crime prevention.

Control

The Control Phase of the improvement activities was Mayor Hines' crowning jewel. The Control Phase is where the accountability piece was executed with perfection. The overall plan was to conduct the standard work accountability sessions and dig into the data. Beginning shortly after the daily reports became available, the Mayor began conducting the standard work weekly sessions with each of the three district Police Chiefs. Each week, key government officials and the Police Chief from one of the three districts would meet to review the numbers. This is a basic Statistical Process Control (SPC) methodology. The data spoke louder than words!

Every week each district Police Chief would attend the work session to explain and defend their performance numbers. Accountability came in the form of questions such as "Why are car thefts down 20% in every other district, but up 5% in your district?" or "Can you explain why break-ins were down for three straight months but have started to rise in the last two months?" The Police Chiefs quickly understood that they had better come to the meetings prepared and have legitimate answers to the questions. The best way to handle the questions was to get the numbers going in the right direction. The best way to do this was to cooperate with other Police Chiefs and get their people involved, engaged, and committed. The method of control actually led to additional improvement ideas and actions.

Accountability came in other forms as well. Leaders would bring items such as photographs of problem areas and issues so that the Police Chiefs could not claim that there were no problems. After several months of sessions with the Police Chiefs, police district staff workers were also invited to the work sessions to encourage further accountability. With staff workers in attendance, the Chiefs could no longer pass the blame to lower level staffers. Accountability started with the Chiefs and cascaded through the ranks. For the most, part people appreciated the new accountability. The one's who did not were dealt with on an individual basis, on their performance review, and/or through employee union communications.

The Mayor and her staff also came under scrutiny. The Mayor had her own key measures that were reviewed periodically. This review would help assure alignment between what was being measured on a daily basis and what the mayor had promised to deliver during the past election campaign. The measures reviewed by the mayor and her staff were home purchases and values, business investments, school attendance, and tax revenue for the city.

When things were going in the wrong direction, the Mayor would assign the Chiefs special improvement projects to determine cause and corrective action for the declining metric. Problem solving and mistake proofing tools would be employed where applicable.

The data collection matrix, data spreadsheets, and data charts are shown below and on the next few pages. The idea behind the cascading or multi-level, linked KPIs at various levels is that improvements in the lower level District KPIs will lead to improvements in the City Crime KPIs which will ultimately lead to improvements in the City Macro KPIs which of course will lead to re-election for the Mayor! This represents the classical Policy Deployment technique for "control" of a process and organization.

Data Collection Matrix:

Key Performance Indicator (KPI)	Data Location	Control Points	Leader	Data Reporting Frequency	Report Review Frequency
City Macro KPIs	-	-	-	-	-
Home sales total count	Reality Board	Districts	Mayor	Daily	Quarterly
Business investment dollars	Chamber	Districts	Mayor	Daily	Quarterly
School attendance percent	School Superintendant	Districts	Mayor	Daily	Quarterly
City Crime KPIs					
Murder	Precinct	Districts	Commish.	Daily	Weekly
Rape	Precinct	Districts	Commish.	Daily	Weekly
Robbery	Precinct	Districts	Commish.	Daily	Weekly
Felonious assault	Precinct	Districts	Commish.	Daily	Weekly
Burglary	Precinct	Districts	Commish.	Daily	Weekly
Grand Larceny	Precinct	Districts	Commish.	Daily	Weekly
Grand Larceny Auto	Precinct	Districts	Commish.	Daily	Weekly
District Daily KPIs					
Total Staff	Accounting	Precincts	Chief	Daily	Daily
Operating Costs	Accounting	Precincts	Chief	Daily	Daily
Attendance percent	Human Resources	Precincts	Chief	Daily	Daily
Safety (Injuries)	Human Resources	Precincts	Chief	Daily	Daily
Arrests	Precincts	Precincts	Chief	Daily	Daily
911 call response time	Precincts	Precincts	Chief	Daily	Daily
Complaint calls total	Precincts	Precincts	Chief	Daily	Daily
Complaint call location	Precincts	Precincts	Chief	Daily	Daily
Complaint call time	Precincts	Precincts	Chief	Daily	Daily

Data Spreadsheets:

ALL Districts Daily KPIs

ALL Districts Daily KPIs	1-Jan	2-Jan	3-Jan	4-Jan	5-Jan	6-Jan	7-Jan	8-Jan	9-Jan	10-Jan	MTD Actual	MTD Target	YTD
Total Staff	101	101	101	101	101	101	101	101	101	101	101	100	101
Operating Costs	$ 40,440	$ 41,477	$ 42,568	$ 40,728	$ 40,048	$ 42,684	$ 41,324	$ 40,384	$ 41,808	$ 40,462	$ 887,343	$ 935,000	$ 887,343
People Absent	2	3	1	1	3	1	0	0	2	1	1	0	1
Safety (Injuries)	0	0	0	1	0	0	2	0	0	0	0	0	0
Arrests	40	50	35	36	24	27	40	41	34	30	28	20	28
911 call response time	6	7	7	8	5	8	6	7	6	5	6	5	6
Complaint calls total	190	101	111	143	111	206	235	111	133	76	123	100	123

District 1 Daily KPIs

District 1 Daily KPIs	1-Jan	2-Jan	3-Jan	4-Jan	5-Jan	6-Jan	7-Jan	8-Jan	9-Jan	10-Jan	MTD Actual	MTD Target	YTD
Total Staff	30	30	30	30	30	30	30	30	30	30	30	30	30
Operating Costs	$ 12,000	$ 12,364	$ 12,894	$ 11,998	$ 12,098	$ 13,209	$ 12,263	$ 12,364	$ 12,784	$ 12,012	$ 266,906	$ 330,000	266906
People Absent	0	0	0	1	2	0	0	0	0	1	0	0	0
Safety (Injuries)	0	0	0	0	0	0	0	0	0	0	0	0	0
Arrests	10	12	7	9	2	5	2	6	7	2	106	100	106
911 call response time	5	10	10	10	5	10	5	10	5	5	6	5	6
Complaint calls total	60	32	35	45	35	65	74	35	42	24	39	30	39
Complaint call location	1	2	4	2	3	1	2	3	3	3	N/A	N/A	N/A

District 2 Daily KPIs

District 2 Daily KPIs	1-Jan	2-Jan	3-Jan	4-Jan	5-Jan	6-Jan	7-Jan	8-Jan	9-Jan	10-Jan	MTD Actual	MTD Target	YTD
Total Staff	45	45	45	45	45	45	45	45	45	45	45	45	45
Operating Costs	$ 18,000	$ 18,356	$ 18,456	$ 18,292	$ 17,425	$ 17,983	$ 18,392	$ 17,263	$ 17,902	$ 18,000	$ 388,229	$ 440,000	388229
People Absent	2	3	1	0	0	1	0	0	0	0	1	0	1
Safety (Injuries)	0	0	0	1	0	0	2	0	0	0	0	0	0
Arrests	18	23	17	16	13	13	23	21	16	17	358	300	358
911 call response time	10	10	10	10	10	10	10	10	10	10	9	5	9
Complaint calls total	78	42	46	59	46	85	96	46	55	31	50	60	50
Complaint call location	3	2	3	3	3	1	2	1	2	4	N/A	N/A	N/A

District 3 Daily KPIs

District 3 Daily KPIs	1-Jan	2-Jan	3-Jan	4-Jan	5-Jan	6-Jan	7-Jan	8-Jan	9-Jan	10-Jan	MTD Actual	MTD Target	YTD
Total Staff	26	26	26	26	26	26	26	26	26	26	26	25	26
Operating Costs	$ 10,440	$ 10,757	$ 11,218	$ 10,438	$ 10,525	$ 11,492	$ 10,669	$ 10,757	$ 11,122	$ 10,450	$ 232,208	$ 165,000	232208
People Absent	0	0	0	0	1	0	0	0	2	0	0	0	0
Safety (Injuries)	0	0	0	0	0	0	0	0	0	0	0	0	0
Arrests	12	15	11	11	9	9	15	14	11	11	148	130	148
911 call response time	3	1	2	3	1	3	2	1	3	1	2	5	2
Complaint calls total	52	28	30	39	30	57	64	30	37	21	34	25	34
Complaint call location	3	2	4	1	2	2	1	2	4	3	N/A	N/A	N/A

MONTHLY PERFORMANCE	Year 1										
Key Performance Indicator (KPI)	1	2	3	4	5	6	7	8	9	Yr 2 Summary	Improvement from Yr 1 to Yr 2
	1-Jan	1-Feb	1-Mar	1-Apr	1-May	1-Jun	1-Jul	1-Aug	1-Sep		
City Macro KPIs											
Home sales total count	15	14	12	13	14	11	26	11	14	216	37
Business investment dollars	$ 319,105	$ 432,943	$ 374,902	$ 546,932	$ 564,294	$ 584,539	$ 639,123	$ 364,823	$ 493,001	$ 7,646,794	$ 1,719,304
School attendance percent	72%	74%	82%	74%	80%	81%	78%	83%	79%	89%	10%
City Crime KPIs											Crime Reductions
Murder	2	1	3	0	0	2	1	0	0	6	6
Rape	4	6	5	4	5	3	2	5	3	25	25
Robbery	19	14	27	26	23	21	17	21	18	209	45
Felonious assault	27	21	42	32	45	46	41	32	21	293	95
Burglary	99	85	89	96	120	156	176	113	123	1130	360
Grand Larceny	325	267	279	384	324	390	387	367	345	2762	1088
Grand Larceny Auto	30	28	21	46	38	51	48	34	28	266	116
ALL District Daily KPIs											KPI Improvements
Total Staff	110	110	110	110	110	105	105	105	105	1211	101
Operating Costs	$ 123,987	$ 123,954	$ 124,083	$ 124,629	$ 128,390	$ 128,092	$ 127,304	$ 129,374	$ 125,789	$ 1,465,464	$ 48,590
Attendance percent	99%	99%	97%	99%	100%	97%	98%	99%	100%	100%	1%
Safety (Injuries)	10	0	0	0	1	0	0	1	0	2	1
Arrests	150	134	145	154	143	134	165	154	145	127	17
911 call response time (min)	12	13	15	12	11	12	10	10	8	7.67	4
Complaint calls total	190	176	187	165	190	183	175	165	156	141	-29

City Level - These graphs would be reviewed monthly by the Mayor and other government officials. They would identify improvement opportunities and action plans.

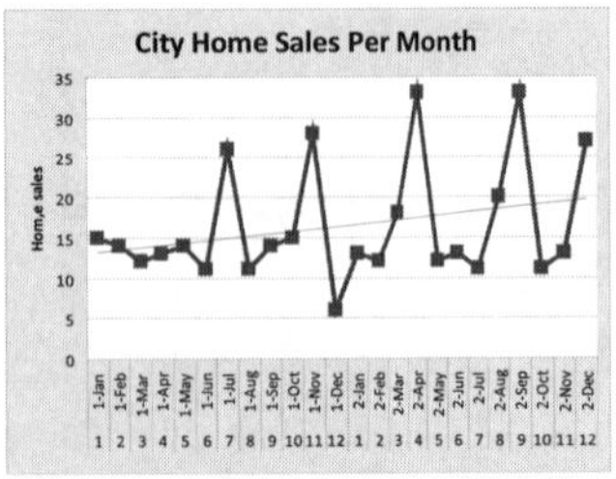

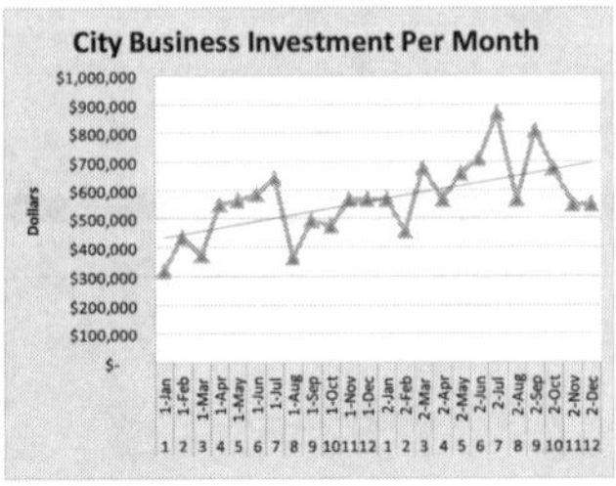

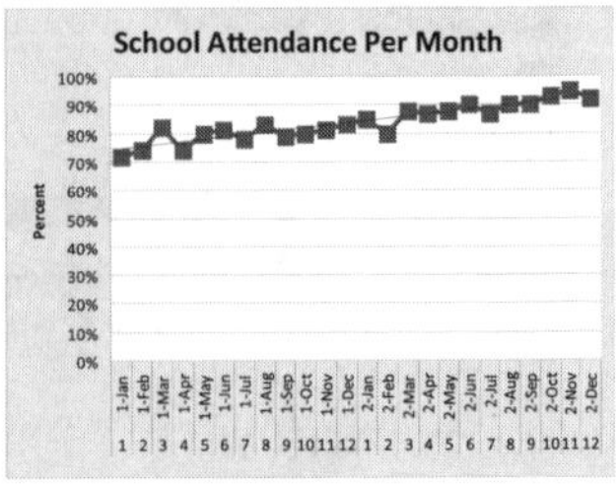

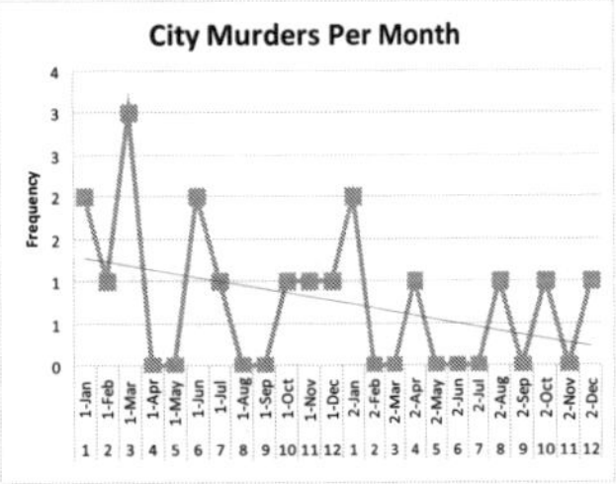

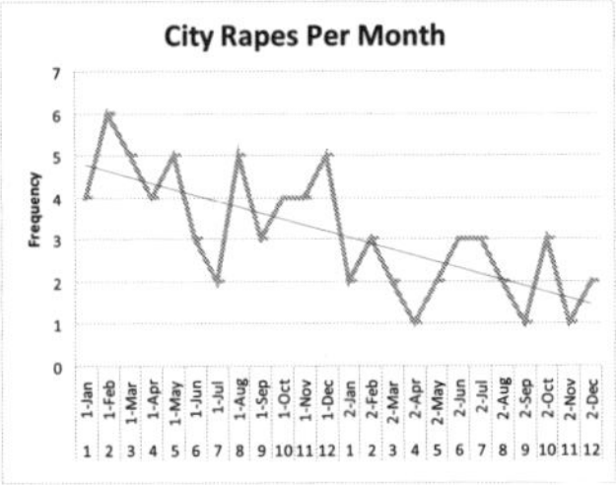

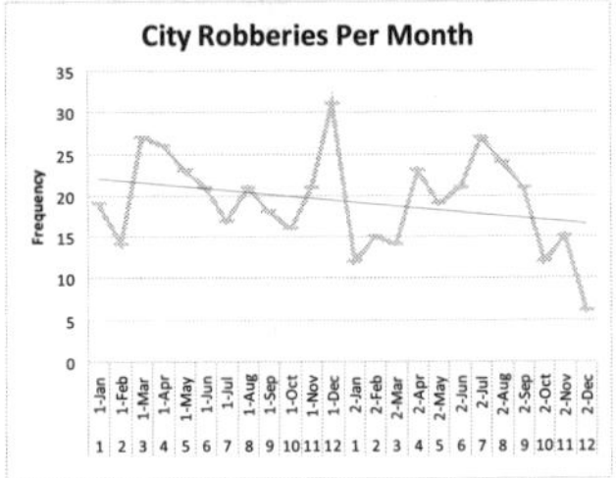

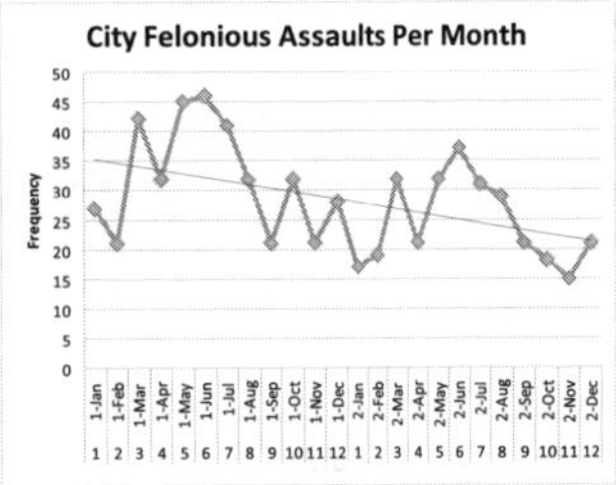

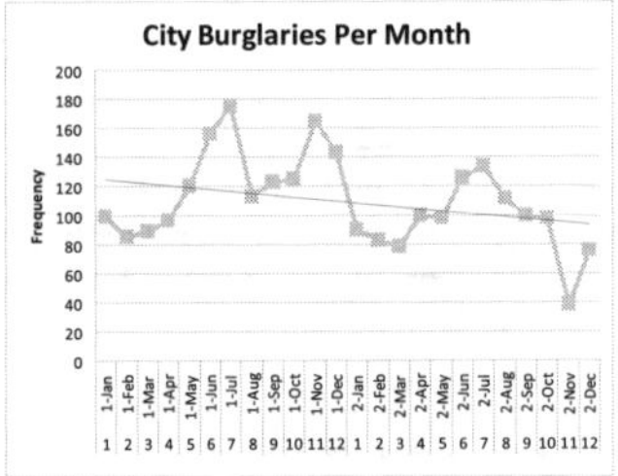

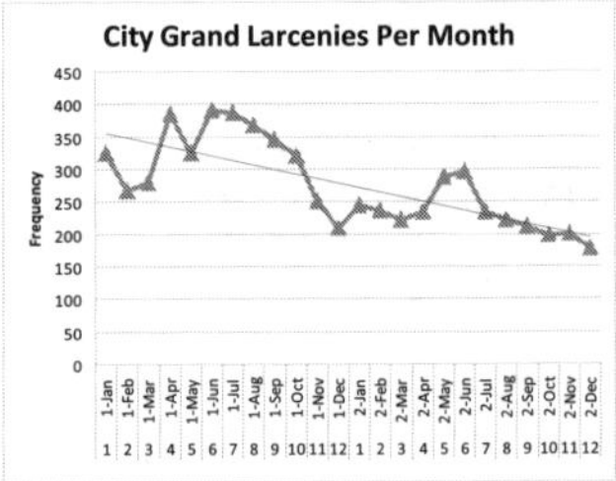

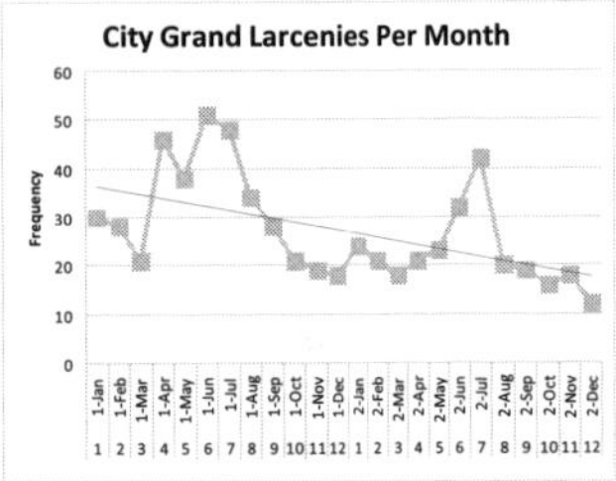

District Level - The Mayor, Police Commissioner, and three Police Chiefs would review these graphs weekly, and identify cause and effects, and preventative measures.

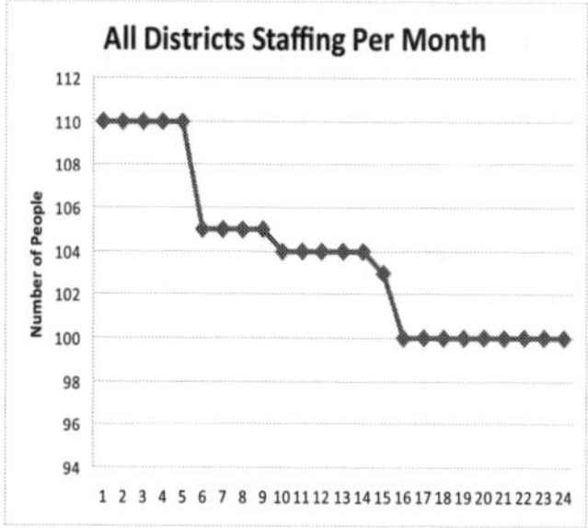

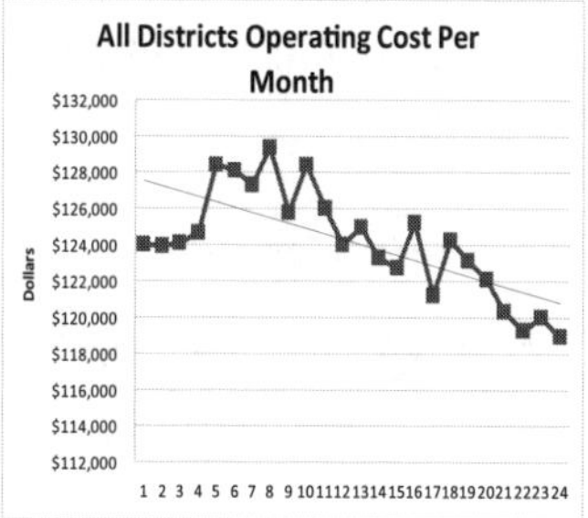

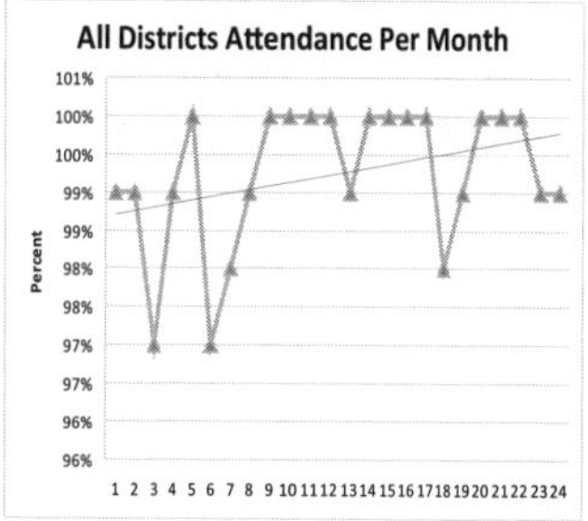

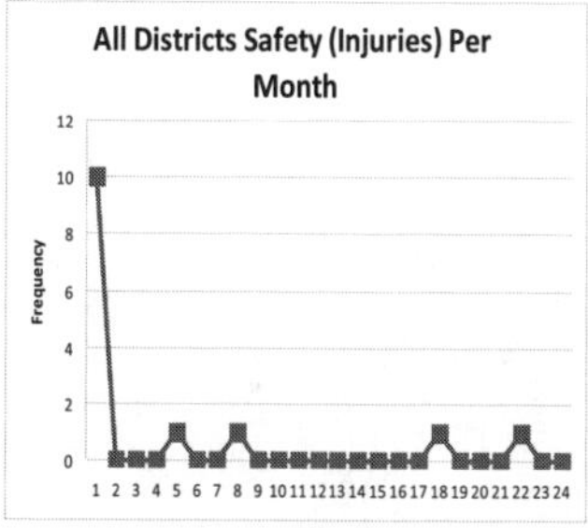

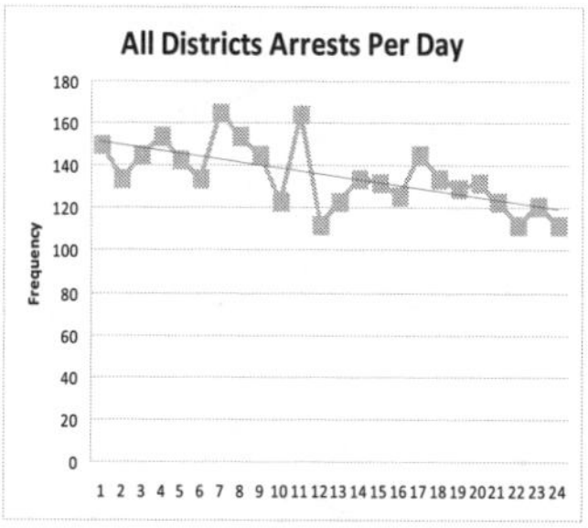

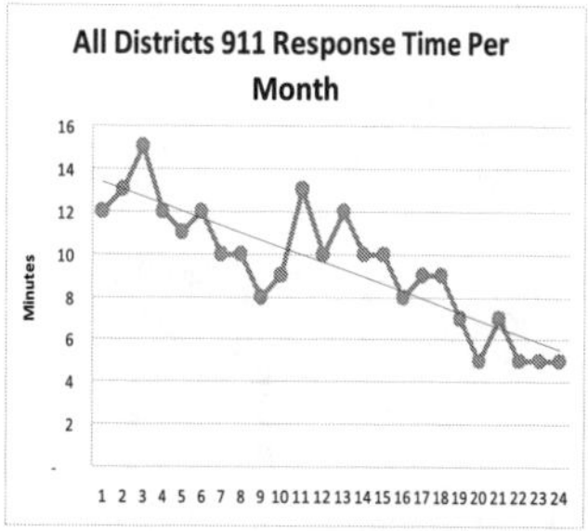

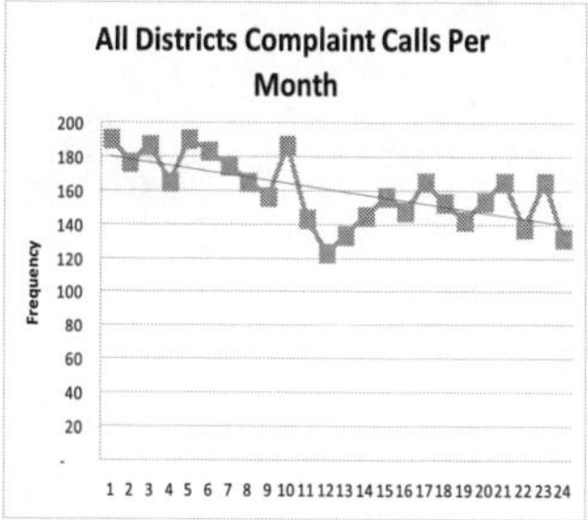

Data Charts (Scoreboard Graphs):

Precinct Level - Each precinct would post the following graphs in their briefing rooms. The precinct staff would review these graphs daily. They would discuss trends and identify ways to prevent crimes from occurring.

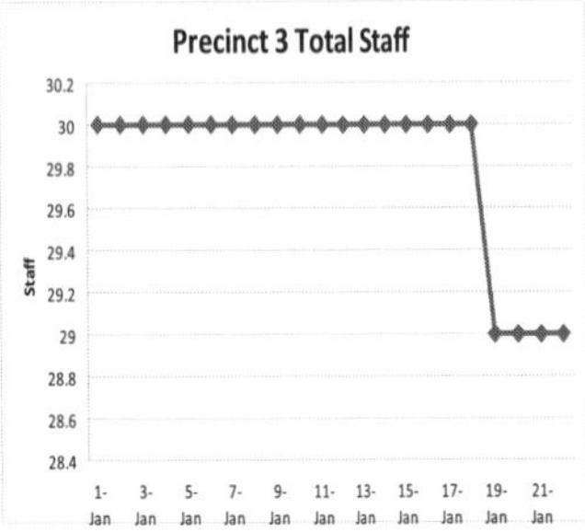

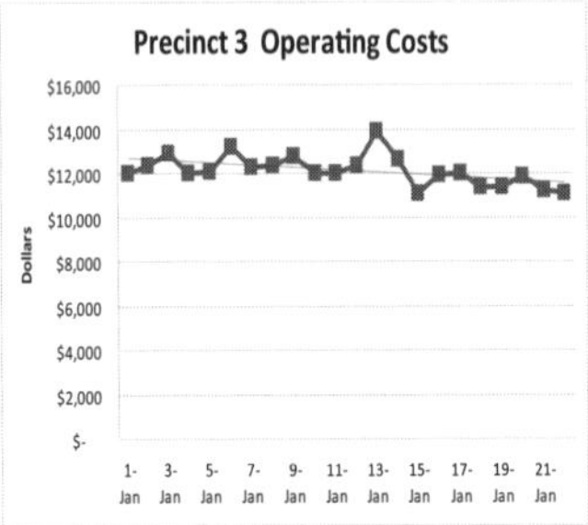

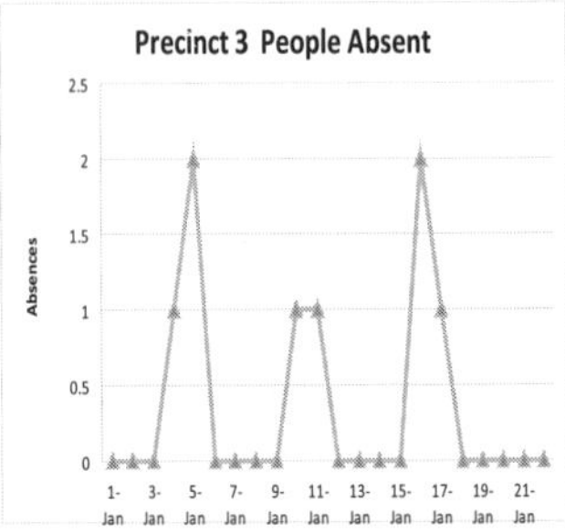

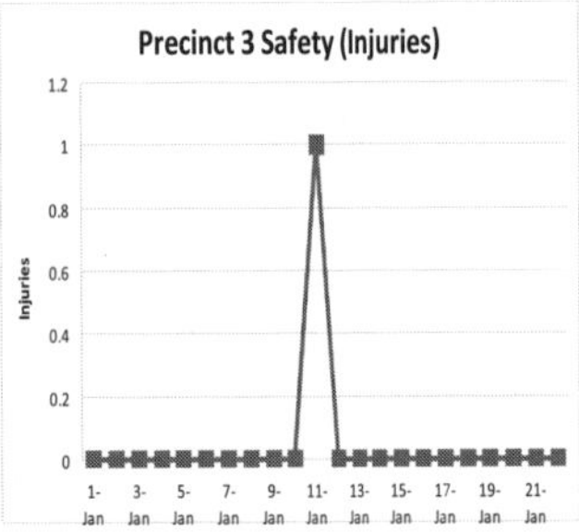

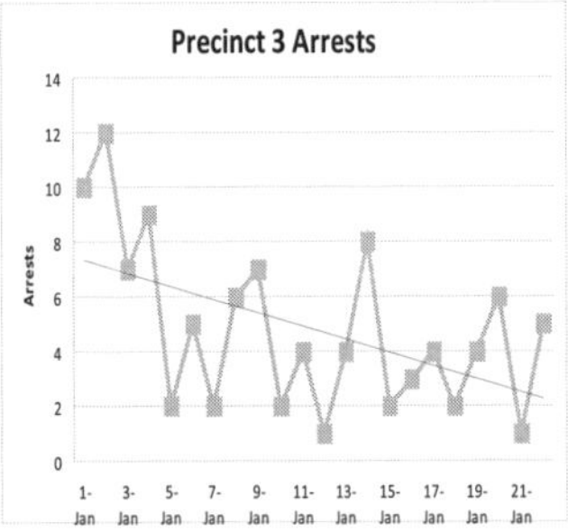

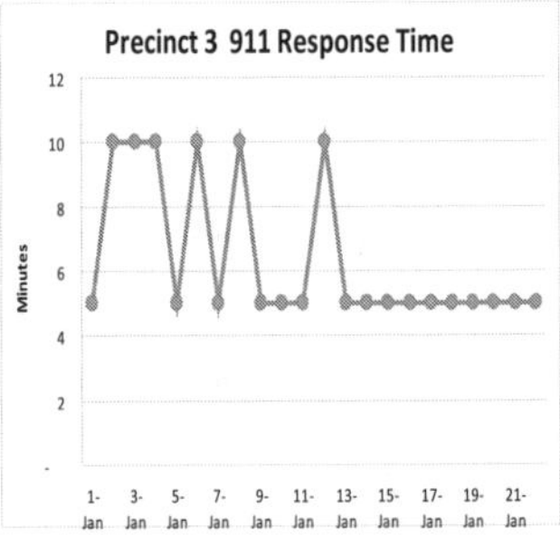

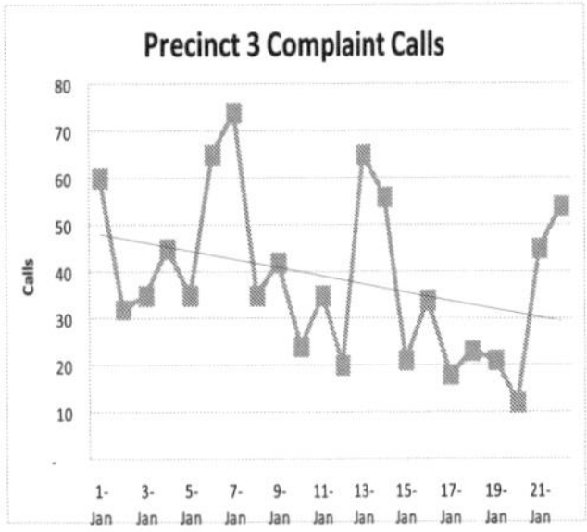

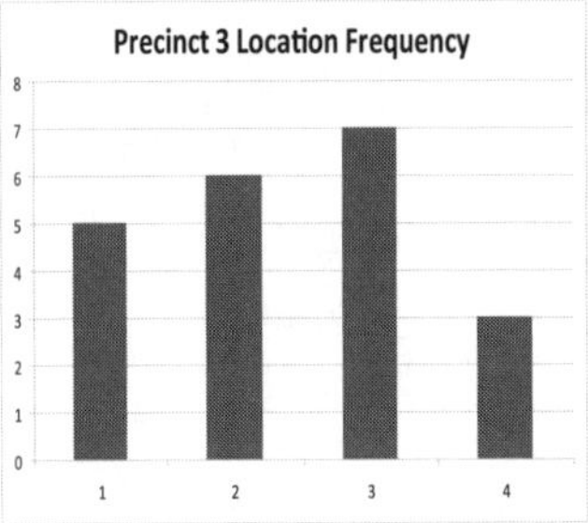

The standardized agendas for the work sessions are found below. In general, the work sessions became the standard work for leadership in the city.

Mayor Hines' Weekly Accountability Work Session Standard Agenda
Attendance: Mayor, mayor staff, District Police Chief and staff (every Friday)

7:00 am	Call to Order
	Welcome and Introductions
7:10-7:30 am	Old Business
	Follow-up on previous Action Items and Responsibilities
	Additional Next Steps
7:30-8:00 am	New Business
	District Key Data Trend Review and Discussion
	1. Number of Complaint Calls (CCs)
	2. CC exact location in the city (Map/GPS review)
	3. CC time
	4. CC category by issue or crime
	Action Planning
8:00-8:30 am	Special Issues
8:30 am	Adjourn

Mayor Hines' Monthly Accountability Work Session Standard Agenda
Attendance: Mayor, mayor staff, Police Commissioner, District Police Chiefs and staff (first Monday of each month)

7:00 am	Call to Order
	Welcome and Introductions
7:10-7:30 am	Old Business
	Follow-up on previous Action Items and Responsibilities
	Additional next steps
7:30-8:30 am	New Business
	City Level Key Data Trend Review and Discussion
	1. Home purchases
	2. Business investments
	3. School attendance
	4. City level crime data and graphs
	Action Planning
8:30-9:00	Special Issues
9:00 am	Adjourn

Through this methodical and persistent method of implementing the Control Phase of the DMAIC process, the Mayor, Police Commissioner, District Police Chiefs, and staff all became tremendously successful and were able to maintain the improvements at desired levels. The real winners were the people of the city!

The before and after improvement table is shown below. The results are unquestionably positive for the city and the everyone involved in the improvement process.

FBI Crime Measures	Before Improvements (Incidents per Month)	National Rank	After Improvement (Incidents per Month)	National Rank	Percent Improvement
Murder	2	Worst 10%	1	Best 25%	50%
Rape	4	Worst 10%	2	Best 25%	50%
Robbery	19	Worst 10%	6	Best 25%	68%
Felonious assault	27	Worst 10%	21	Best 25%	22%
Burglary	99	Worst 10%	75	Best 25%	24%
Grand Larceny	325	Worst 10%	176	Best 25%	46%
Grand Larceny Auto	30	Worst 10%	12	Best 25%	60%

Perhaps most important, a PDCA methodology driven by objective data is used to drive improvements in the entire organization's performance. True sustainable improvement cannot be made just by using as many Lean Sigma tools as possible. The key is to identify and use the key Lean Sigma tools and methods that best fit the needs of the organization.

Pursuing Perfect Service

Part Four.

Putting It All Together to Achieve and Sustain Lean Sigma for Service Excellence

Chapter 9

Sustainability (or Becoming Green)

Becoming "Green" with Lean Sigma

Chapter Overview

Lean Sigma and sustainability are closely linked. Lean Sigma foundations are in the elimination of waste and the conservation of resources. Sustainability is the conservation of resources to ensure a sustainable, enduring business model into the future. Organizations have taken or are currently undertaking a variety of actions to address green or sustainable business issues. This chapter provides an overview of sustainability and demonstrates how the Lean Sigma methods and tools can be applied to improve an organization's sustainability.

"Sustainability" and "green," or "greening," are buzzwords that are often used these days. Though they are very different, they tend to be used interchangeably. Sustainability is a broader term and denotes the economic, ecological, and social improvements made by (service) organizations for improving efficiencies. On the other hand, "green" or "greening" means specific applications for short-term benefits. For example, a service organization promoting "greening" may focus only on recycling or waste minimization. A service organization that is promoting "sustainability" would focus on the entire eco-system to create long-term value.

Sustainability

The fundamental principles on which both Lean and sustainability are built upon include waste elimination, conservation of resources, customer focus, employee empowerment, sharing of knowledge, reducing risks, and continuous improvement. The main difference between these two techniques is that historically, Lean has focused more on the customer or the value-added economics of the customer-supplier relationship. The decision criteria under sustainability is broad and encompasses environmental and social responsibility as well. A manager that works for an organization that is committed to sustainability will focus on **social**, **economic**, and **environmental** issues when making decisions. The impact on measurements in these areas is considered the Triple Bottom Line (TBL) of sustainability.

Other common representations of the social, economic, and environmental areas of sustainability are the three "P's" of:

1. Planet
2. Profits
3. People

Or, the three "E's" of:

1. Environment
2. Economic
3. Equity (Social)

Sustainability *is defined by organizations demonstrating social responsibility and cooperation, environmental responsibility and stewardship, and economic value-added products and services.*

These three key elements are further defined by the following issues or characteristics:

Environmental (Planet)

- Waste of resources
- Pollution
- Resource overconsumption
- Land use
- Energy use
- Climate impact
- Water consumption
- The three “R’s” of resource conservation: Reduce, Re-use, and Recycle

Economic (Profits)

- Living wages
- Job and wealth creation
- Local economic development
- Green purchasing
- Accountability and stewardship
- Governance
- Shareholder value
- Value-added

Equity (Social) (People)

- Fair trade
- Poverty
- Literacy and education
- Discrimination
- Nutrition
- Health and safety
- Working conditions
- Human rights
- Social value and self-worth
- Social networking mediums (Facebook, Twitter, etc.)

Incorporating sustainability goals during a Lean Sigma improvement initiative can include:

- Improving process flow
- Reducing lead times
- Lowering material costs and consumption
- Lowering waste removal costs
- Lowering regulatory non-compliance risks
- Meeting customer expectations more consistently
- Improving environmental quality
- Improving employee morale and commitment

By incorporating sustainability principles along with Lean Sigma principles, service organizations can deliver products and services with stronger environmental, social, and economic impact, thus achieving significant competitive advantage, provided sacrifices in time, quality, or cost are not incurred. Service organizations that incorporate sustainability elements into their business improvement model (i.e., Lean Sigma program) can also hope to attract new customers and more easily retain existing customers. Management of these service organizations should strive to maximize the use of different types of capital and should partner with internal and external constituents to enhance long-term value and profitability through sustainability integration. The ultimate goal of these service organizations should be to improve the TBL.

Sustainability Tools

Sustainability tools are critical for conservation of and the stewardship of resources for an organization. Sustainability tools are for all levels of an organization and can be passed along to a service organization's clients. An example of this might be hotel chains that are now asking their guests to conserve resources by using their bath towels a second or third time between washes.

As with most Lean Sigma initiatives, the sustainability effort must be driven by senior leadership in order to be fully beneficial. The key to reducing resource consumption is first being able to identify where resources are consumed. Sustainability tools help organizations to do this, and to reduce, re-use, and recycle critical resources to improve an organization's sustainability.

The key Sustainability tools and their application are identified in the following table:

Phase	Lean Sigma Tool	Application Guide
SUSTAINABILITY	**Resource Treasure Hunt**	The Resource Treasure Hunt is designed to help people understand and see the areas of resource consumption. Once visible, teams have an opportunity to reduce consumption.
	Resource Flow Map	The Resource Flow Map tracks all incoming resources through to disposal. The map helps teams to identify areas for improvements.
	Going Green Metrics	Sustainability or Going Green Metrics help organizations align and measure their efforts in reducing resource consumption as well as for computing eco-efficiency ratios and developing appropriate measures.

Note: The (Resource) Flow Map and Metrics have been discussed earlier in this book and require only a slight modification. The Resource Treasure Hunt will be discussed in detail as it is an entirely new tool.

Resource Treasure Hunt

*The **Resource Treasure Hunt** is used to help people recognize and identify sources of resource consumption in their organization.* The Resource Treasure Hunt (RTH) template is taken to various areas and completed by the project team members to the best of their ability. The "treasure" in the treasure hunt is identifying wasted resources and then conserving them ensuring that the same level of service is provided. The Treasure Hunt allows employees to look closely at the process or area and to think like a crime scene investigator in regards to environmental, social, and economic waste (i.e., the TBL).

Use the Resource Treasure Hunt form and format to search out and identify resource consumption in various areas of an organization. The following guidelines will assist you in conducting a Resource Treasure Hunt:

1. Gather a small team and provide a brief training discussion regarding Sustainability and the TBL of economic, environmental, and social wastes.

2. Introduce and distribute blank RTH forms to participants.

3. Select an area or several areas to visit to observe resource wastes. Suggestions are to define an area small enough so the improvement team can observe the process or area together and openly discuss their findings.

4. Visit the area and observe and look for economic, environmental, or social wastes. Examples of each type of waste are:
    a. Economic
        i. Paying for services such as housekeeping that are not being performed
        ii. Specifying a high-end paper when a lower cost paper would work
        iii. Poor return or non-performing bonus programs
    b. Environmental
        i. Electricity used to light an area that is not being used
        ii. Continuously running water
        iii. Electricity used to run a large refrigerator, when a small refrigerator would be sufficient
        iv. Paper in a garbage can
        v. Printed material that uses a great deal of ink
    c. Social
        i. Investing in training that is not used
        ii. Investments in charities that are not being appropriately distributed, properly managed, or not having any impact

5. Document the team findings on the RTH form.

6. Reconvene to discuss findings and brainstorm possible opportunities for improvement. Document these opportunities on an Issues and Opportunities Log.

7. Prioritize and select opportunities for improvement and develop a PDCA improvement plan to implement.

8. Implement the PDCA improvement, and track the progress with the standard DMAIC process forms and Storyboards.

The following example of a RTH form was completed by an improvement team in a Law Office. It took about an hour to complete the process for the areas observed, and the team developed several excellent improvement activities and ideas to reduce the wastes of TBL resources.

Resource Treasure Hunt

Area	Resources Used	Inputs	Outputs	Suggested Improvements
Lobby	*Electricity:*	Lights Computers	Heat & light Heat & information	Reduce lighting. Use low wattage lights.
	Fuel (Gas, etc.):	Heat		
	Water:	Water fountain	Excess water goes to drain	Eliminate water fountain and use bottled water.
	Chemicals:			
	Materials:	Visitor badges	Badges get thrown away	Do not use badges.
		Brochures	Brochures get thrown away in favor of on-line	Offer smaller on-line cards that direct people to website.
	Other wastes:			
Area	**Resources Used**	**Inputs**	**Outputs**	**Suggested Improvements**
Offices	*Electricity:*	Lights Computers	Heat & light Heat & information	Reduce lighting or use low energy bulbs. Set computers to sleep sooner.
		Heaters	Heat	Set plant heaters to work properly and declare no personal heaters.
	Fuel (Gas, etc.):	Heat		
	Water:			
	Chemicals:			
	Materials:	Paper	Trash	Set new standards for what should be printed. Hold people accountable.
		Calendars	Trash	Only use electronic calendars.
	Other wastes:	Excess furnishings	Take up space	Reduce office space and remove excess furnishings.
Area	**Resources Used**	**Inputs**	**Outputs**	**Suggested Improvements**
Break area	*Electricity:*	Lights Vending machines Microwave Refrigerator	Heat & light Heat & light Heat & processing Heat, light & cold	Reduce lighting and use low energy bulbs. Turn lights off in vending machines. Purchase energy efficient microwave. Purchase energy efficient refrigerator.
	Fuel (Gas, etc.):	Heat		
	Water:	Sink		Post signs indicating water cost per gallon.
		Dishwasher	Excess water	Hand wash dishes only.
	Chemicals:	Cleaning materials	Chemical pollutants	Look for low impact cleaning materials. Use washable rags versus paper towels.
	Materials:	Bulletin board posting	Information	Keep postings to a minimum. Use online versions.
		Food waste Aluminum cans Glass bottles	Garbage Empty cans Empty bottles	Compost food waste. Recycle cans. Recycle bottles.
		Paper plates	Garbage	Use real dishes and wash them. Hold people accountable.
	Other wastes:			

Resource Flow Map

A ***Resource Flow Map*** *is a value stream or process map that includes resource flows.* To complete a resource flow map, first complete a value stream or process map and then use the Resource Treasure Hunt form to document the resource consumption and flow for each value-added process.

The following icons can be used to represent economic, environmental, or social wastes:

Fire or Heat - Excessive heat loss is represented by a simple flame. This can range from ovens that run continuously throughout the day, to computer rooms that generate potentially useable heat, to entry areas that lose heat rapidly. Improvement ideas can range from revolving doors in entry areas, to reusing heat from computer rooms, to putting ovens on timers.

Electricity - Excessive electricity consumption is represented by a simple light bulb. Excessive electricity consumption can be observed in many areas of an organization where lighting is left on when people are not in the area or equipment is left "on" during non-business hours, or non-essential lighting is used. Improvement ideas can range from motion-sensing lighting, to automatically shutting off circuits, to taking light bulbs out of non-essential areas such as soda machine panels.

Water - Excessive water consumption is represented by a simple clear drop symbol. Excessive water consumption can be observed in many areas in service organizations such as faucets that leak, non-recycling systems, and partial loading of equipment. Improvement ideas can range from minimal water restroom equipment, to recycling the processing water in secondary loops, to variable use controls on water valve.

Sewage - Excessive waste water is represented by a shaded drop symbol. Excessive waste water disposal can come from excessive cleaning techniques to continuously running processes. Improvement ideas can range from water reclaim processors, to reduced flow or consumption ideas.

Paper - Excessive paper use is represented by this paper symbol. Excessive use of paper includes the printing of reports that are not read and/or proposals that are not delivered. Improvement ideas are to establish standard rules regarding the use of paper and the distribution of reports for the organization and implementing recycling programs.

Recycling - The recycling symbol is used to identify areas where recycling may be appropriate. Recycling can be done for many different types of materials such as aluminum cans, glass bottles, steel, paper, cardboard, and the like.

Ink - Excessive use of ink is represented by an ink cartridge symbol. Printer ink, at $8,000 - $20,000 per gallon, is the most expensive fluid on the planet! Excessive use of ink for such things as the printing of reports or the use of heavy ink fonts can be identified by the ink cartridge symbol. Improvement ideas such as establishing standard rules for printing and fonts to use can save organizations considerable funds over time.

Gas - Excessive gas consumption is represented by a simple gas nozzle symbol. Excessive use of gas could come from boilers working around the clock when only periodic use is needed, excessive driving, or transportation or motion of gas-using vehicles. Improvement ideas may be the reduction or improved scheduling of operating times for boilers or reduced travel or motion for gas-using vehicles.

$$$

Spending - Excessive spending is represented by simple dollar signs. Excessive spending on items can be observed in many areas of an organization. Improvement teams can use this symbol to indicate that there may be improvement opportunities in an area to reduce spending by buying more economic quantities, using a less expensive, but equivalent item, or conducting competitive bidding on a process item or service.

Overspecified - Overspecification is represented by a handheld magnifying glass symbol. Overspecifying items or requirements for items such as 24 lb paper where 20 lb paper will do, or a high thread count material where a medium or low thread count material will do, are numerous in service environments. Somehow people believe that overspecifying will better satisfy the customer. Improvement ideas are to conduct PDCA experiments to determine acceptability of a new specification or simply asking customers to better define their needs and perceptions of quality.

Social - Social waste is the waste of human resources in terms of unfocused energy, strength, and brainpower. Or, simply not using people and social networks to their full ability. This waste can be caused by leadership constraints or by people not working to their potential (e.g., employee spends too much time texting or “surfing the web”). Further investigation for cause is usually needed to eliminate this waste.

The illustration shown below is from the Hotel Check-In Current State Value Stream Map (Chapter 5) with additional sustainability value stream mapping symbols being used:

Hotel Check-In Current State Value Stream Map

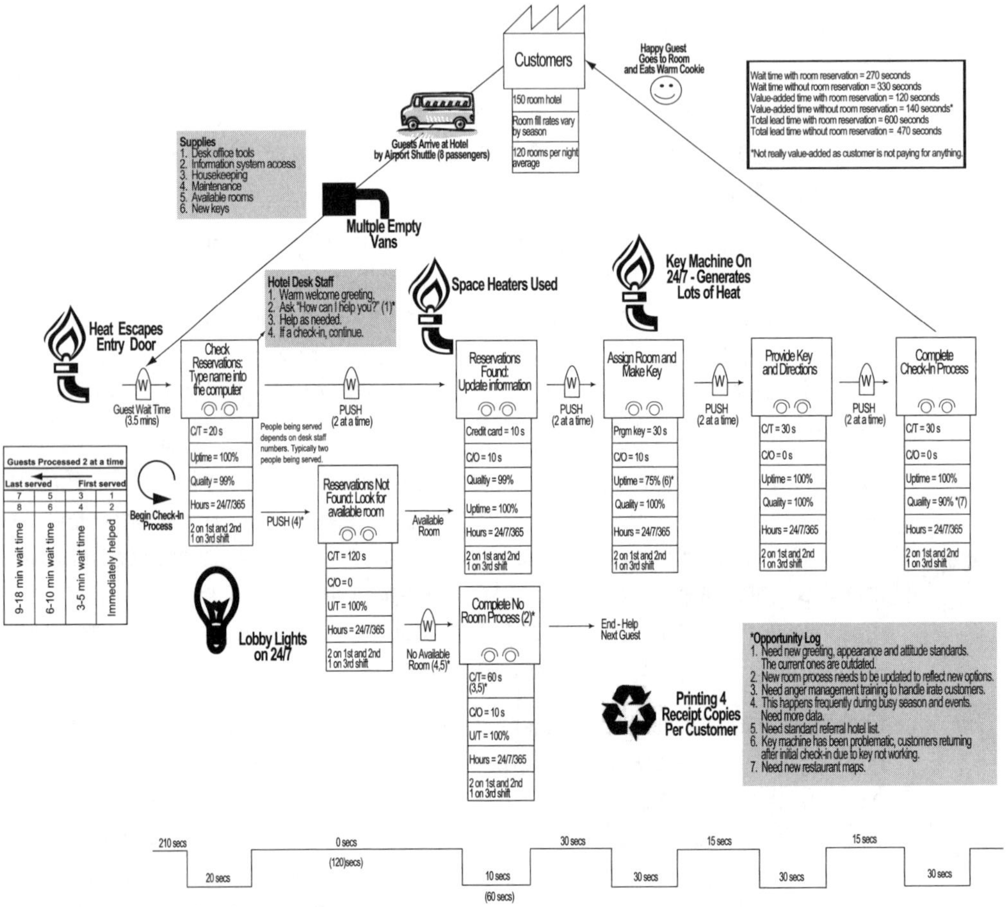

Note: The symbols or icons can also be located on a process flow map.

Going Green Metrics

Going Green (or Sustainability) Metrics *help organizations identify, align, and focus on sustainability issues.* Sustainability metrics include the following areas:

Energy use	Materials use	Chemical use
Water use	Waste water discharge	Scrap food weight
Hazardous waste generation	Solid waste generation	Air emissions
Paper waste or trash weight		

Use Sustainability Metrics to track an organizations progress to sustainability. Develop a few key metrics for the team to monitor and post or publish the results in a common area for everyone to have access to. The very presence of Sustainability Metrics will get people thinking more about this key issue.

The following will serve as a mini-case study for Sustainability Metrics at the Three Palms Hotel.

The new owners of Three Palms Hotel, a family-owned hotel in Florida, decided to use sustainable principles and practices to improve the efficiency of their hotel and to distinguish themselves from competitors. A project team of seven key individuals from different departments was created. The first task of the team was to identify the critical success factors and to develop a Scorecard (or Performance Dashboard) based on existing and new sustainability metrics and indicators. After a brief brainstorming session the team designed an initial TBL Scorecard and decided to focus on improving efficiencies in the following three areas: (1) paper reduction, (2) energy conservation, and (3) human resource development. The first two areas were geared to improving environmental efficiencies while the third was geared to improving the social environment. The team was convinced that all three areas would help improve the organizational financial bottom-line and enhance economic efficiencies. The team decided that they would form three smaller teams to study and examine these issues and use the PDCA cycle to initiate new ideas and improvement trials.

The following measurements would be used for their project and represents their TBL Performance Dashboard (or Scorecard). One team would address paper wastes, another energy consumption, and the third, customer complaints.

Economic	Environmental	Social
Customers/Guests % New customers % Returning customers % Internal vacancies filled % Satisfied customers **Employees** % Employee turnover % Employee absenteeism % Employee satisfaction **Owners** $ Net profit % Revenue from room sales % Food/beverage profit	$ Waste reduction $ Energy $ Recycling $ Renewable energy	$ Investment in employees $ Investment in community

In order to address the paper reduction issue, the paper waste team decided to first identify the total paper consumption and also identify the inefficiencies and/or wastes. After talking to key people in each department and looking at past orders/consumption, it was determined that approximately 250 rims of paper were consumed per month, on average, by employees and guests of the hotel. The employees were also quick to identify that waste occurred on account of single-sided printing, printing of multiple copies, and printing of unnecessary documents and reports. In order to improve the situation, the team agreed to do the following:

1. Reduce paper consumption by 70% in the next three years.
2. Photocopy and print paper documents double-sided, whenever possible.
3. Eliminate multiple copying.
4. Create agendas, minutes, and reports to be sent electronically.
5. Reduce, reuse, and recycle paper, plastics, food scraps, etc.

A team member emailed each department the progress and savings made on a monthly basis.

The team in charge of energy consumption decided that they would reduce energy consumption by roughly 5% each year for the next 5 years. The team decided to use the following strategies to achieve this goal:

1. Identify and remove all unnecessary electric outlets and fixtures.
2. Replace fluorescent light bulbs with energy efficient light bulbs.
3. Install timers throughout the hotel to reduce electric consumption.
4. Replace outdated air conditioners and equipment with new energy star products.
5. Invest in renewable and alternative energy sources.
6. Develop a system to encourage and reward guests that reuse towels.

In recent years, customer complaints had increased and the team decided that it was critical to invest in Lean Sigma training for their people in order to fix this problem. After the Lean Sigma basic training, they decided to form a small team to address increasing customer complaints. The first thing the team decided to do was to identify why customers were unhappy. After careful examination of complaints, the team concluded that there were two major customer concerns:

1. Waiting lines and service took too long
2. Employees were slow in responding, impolite, and not knowledgeable

After further investigating the complaints, the team realized that the following causes could be attributed to the problem:

1. Short staffed
2. 25% of the employees were new and not properly trained
3. Lack of experienced supervisors
4. Employees not empowered to make decisions and fix complaints
5. Low employee morale and lack of motivation

The team recommended the following be done to improve the situation:

1. Create a working environment that creates empowerment, caring, and retention of employees.
2. Invest money in appropriate training of supervisors and employees.
3. Create procedures and documents of best practices that employees can refer to when communicating with customers.
4. Conduct regular supervisor and employee meetings.

5. Work to enhance wages, benefits, and reward programs.

As the teams implemented the PDCA improvement initiatives, they began to see an impact of their efforts on the TBL measures. After only 6 months of addressing sustainability wastes, the teams were able to realize the following improvements in their TBL Scorecard as shown below:

Three Palms Hotel TBL 6 Month Improvement Results			
Economic	**Initial State**	**After Six Months of Improvement PDCA's**	**Improvement**
Customer/Guests			
% New customers	12%	24%	12%
% Returning customers	55%	68%	13%
% Internal vacancies filled	6%	10%	4%
% Satisfied customers	87%	96%	9%
Employees			
% Employee turnover	7%	4%	3%
% Employee absenteeism	5%	2%	3%
% Employee satisfaction	76%	87%	11%
Owners			
$ Net profit	$998.00	$1,345.00	$347.00
% Revenue from room sales	85.0%	80%	- 5% *
% Food/beverage profit	15.0%	20%	5%
Environmental			
$ Waste reduction	0	$3,270.00	$3,270.00
$ Energy	0	$4,500.00	$4,500.00
$ Recycling	$55.00	$650.00	$595.00
$ Renewable energy	0	$750	$750
Social			
$ Investment in employees	$40.00	$400.00	$360.00
$ Investment in community	$1,000.00	$3,500.00	$2,500.00

Chapter Summary

The identification, control, and conservation of consumable resources is critical to an organization's short and long-term success. This chapter outlines what is meant by Sustainability or "Becoming Green" and illustrates several tools and techniques to help organizations make the move to sustainability for the future. This chapter also discusses how sustainability and Lean Sigma methods and tools complement one another when practiced simultaneously.

Sustainable service organizations may also develop additional clients by showing responsibility and stewardship for social, environmental, and economic issues. Customers want to work with organizations that are pursuing these sustainable or "green" goals.

Lean Sigma for Service Excellence Applications

These observations may assist in understanding how to apply the concepts and tools contained in this chapter:

- Complete a web search for sustainable or "green" business practices.
- Gather a small cross-functional and cross-level team to discuss the conservation of resources at your organization.
- Complete a Resource Treasure Hunt with a small group of people.
- Begin to define the Sustainability Metrics for your organization.
- Identify some opportunities or value streams to begin your organization's sustainability effort.
- Investigate other methods for sustainability.

Sustainability Readiness Guide

The following Sustainability Readiness Guide allows you to ensure there is application of the chapter's content before proceeding to apply the Lean Sigma tools and concepts in this book. If you score less than 70%, consider working on the lower scoring areas before moving on.

Sustainability Readiness Guide	
Use the following 5-level Likert item scale to rank each of the statements: **1 = Strongly Disagree** **2 = Disagree** **3 = Niether Agree nor Disagree** **4 = Agree** **5 = Strongly Agree**	
	Score
1. My organization is committed to sustainability.	
2. My organization does a good job of conserving and balancing critical resources.	
3. My organizations uses the TBL reporting system.	
4. My organization is committed to saving the planet/environment.	
5. My organization is a good corporate citizen.	
6. My organization is committed to conserving resources.	
7. My organization does a good job of maximizing the use of different types of capital.	
8. My organization is effective in partnering with internal and external constituents to enhance long-term value and profitability through economic, environmental, and social efficiencies.	
9. My organization has a system in place to encourage and reward employees for sustainable improvements.	
10. I feel comfortable using the PDCA process for sustainable projects.	
11. I feel the management of my organization is committed to sustainability.	
12. I can see how Lean Sigma and sustainability complement each other and why my organization needs to implement both.	
13. I am confident that my organization will generate new customers if they focus on sustainability.	
14. I feel comfortable developing a Resource Treasure Hunt	
15. I feel comfortable developing Resource Flow Maps.	
16. I feel comfortable applying sustainability metrics and scoreboards to a process or area.	
17. I feel comfortable designing a TBL Balanced Scorecard.	
18. I feel comfortable using performance/gap analysis for computing efficiencies.	
19. I see the value in using the process and tools for making my organization more sustainable.	
20. I believe my organization should utilize and apply the concepts and tools discussed in this chapter.	
Total Score	

Chapter 10

Transformation Case Study

Getting the Big Picture

Chapter Overview

Organizations wishing to improve their bottom line by implementing Lean Sigma methods and tools often find it useful to follow an example of an organization that has made the transformation. This chapter chronicles the transformation journey of the Treasure Bay Resort & Marina (TBR&M). This chapter will help leaders and practitioners understand the difference between simple Lean Sigma tool implementation versus a comprehensive Lean Sigma transformation.

From the humble beginnings of reading a Lean Sigma for service article in an industry journal, to the cultural shift to continuous improvement and empowered problem solving, this chapter illustrates one organization's trials and tribulations to achieve service excellence. Readers will experience how Treasure Bay Resort & Marina leveraged the four enablers to ensure Lean Sigma success, used the DMAIC process for several projects in various areas, and then "saw" the results of a balanced and focused approach to their Lean Sigma journey.

This chapter is designed to aid leaders and managers in Lean Sigma transformations by letting them know what to expect and illustrate how one successful organization completed the passage.

Note: The details of this case study are based on an actual Lean Sigma transfomation and any names referenced are purely coincidental.

Background – The Treasure Bay Resort & Marina

The Treasure Bay Resort & Marina is a privately owned resort hotel and marina located on Treasure Bay. They operate and maintain a 150 room hotel, a 50 slip marina, and several restaurants, bars, and retail outlets selling souvenirs, rental items, and adventure outings. They experience seasonal fluctuations in bookings depending on the local events, festivals, and vacation or holiday schedules. Their organizational structure covers various areas and is illustrated below:

Treasure Bay Resort & Marina Organizational Chart

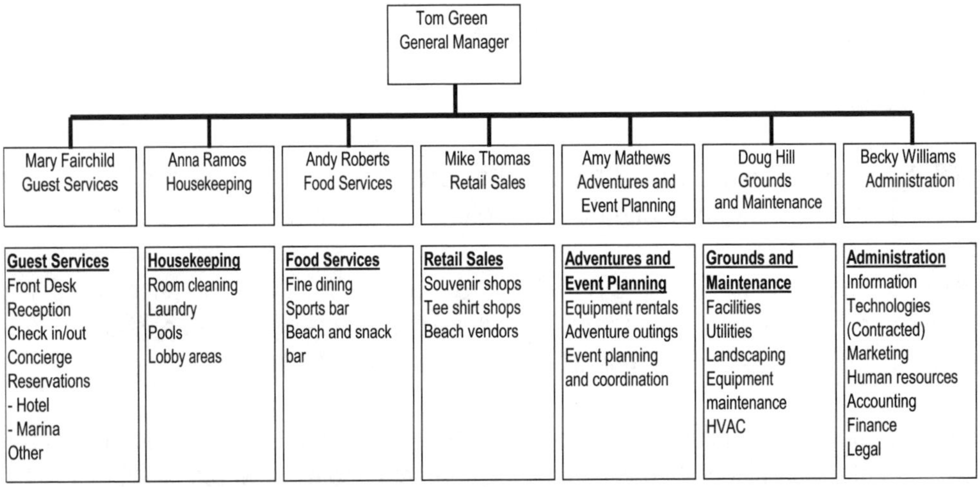

Each area leader has a staff to manage, which consists of workers ranging from entry level to skilled trades people depending on the area. Total employment is 100 people. It is a very diverse mix of people in terms of skills and education/training levels. The General Manager, Tom Green, keeps a relatively flat organizational structure and is actively involved in many activities throughout the business. The Leadership team is made up of Tom's direct reports listed above.

Over the past several years, the resort has come under competitive pressures from newer resorts being built in the area. The staff has become comfortable with operations, yet Tom has seen the revenue on a steady decline. Tom was looking for a way to reinvent the "Good ol' days" when the resort was bustling with people and events, and the financial kitties were overflowing.

While waiting for a flight, Tom read an article about Lean Sigma in a hospitality and travel magazine. Tom was intrigued by the concept, and upon his return, purchased a copy of the first edition of this book for each of his team members. Tom distributed the books to his leadership team and asked them to read the first three chapters by the next team work session and to be prepared to discuss their improvement ideas and any current efforts.

Getting Started

At the work session Tom explained the current business environment to the team. Tom did not pull any punches. He told them the brutal truth, in that, if they did not improve they may have to close or sell the resort. Throughout the years, the Hilton and Marriot hotel chains had shown interest, however, that would most likely come with significant management and personnel change. They all understood the situation and felt the same as Tom did, but they did not know what to do about it. They all felt they were doing their best. Tom mentioned that he is not dissatisfied with any of the team members' performances, just the organization as a whole.

Basically, Tom felt that they were underachieving and he wanted to do something about it. This Pursuing Perfect Service book that he passed along seemed to be a step in the right direction. The book outlined four enablers as prerequisites for hospitality management wishing to pursue a Lean Sigma Transformation. The enablers are as follows:

Enabler #1 Principled Leadership: Demonstrating Management Commitment and Effective Leadership
Enabler #2 People Focus: Ensuring Employee Engagement
Enabler #3 Policy Deployment: Creating Goal Alignment, Ownership, and Accountability
Enabler #4 Practical Lean Sigma Tool Application: Using the Right Tool for the Job

The team discussed where they felt they stood on each enabler. For Principled Leadership, they felt they did a good job at communicating the daily issues and needs to their employees. They all felt committed to the organizations success. They had a mission statement but no stated vision or values. They felt that as a team, they were aligned on the vision and values, but that it would be a good idea to document these. They formed a sub team of Mary, Anna, and Andy to update the mission and document the vision and values for team review at the next session.

Regarding the People Focus, again they felt they did a good job engaging their workers. In a hospitality and service environment, people had to be connected with the customers and guests. The team felt that if they pursued a Lean Sigma transformation, much more training would be needed.

Policy Deployment was a new term for the team. They knew Tom had financial measures that he looked at, and they each had their own way of knowing how things were going in their areas, but there was no comprehensive program to connect the items. The team members did not really know of a specific strategy that Tom was using or how they impacted it. The team welcomed the concept of having goals and measures, but was nervous that too many measurements would weigh them down. They thought that Tom should lead this process by documenting what key measures and goals he considered to be most critical to achieving the organization's strategy. Tom agreed to work with Becky to document what they believed were the critical measures and goals to achieve success.

The last enabler, Practical Lean Sigma Tool Application, was something that they agreed they would all have to learn together as they progressed.

The book also had a flow diagram for a Lean Sigma transformation as shown below:

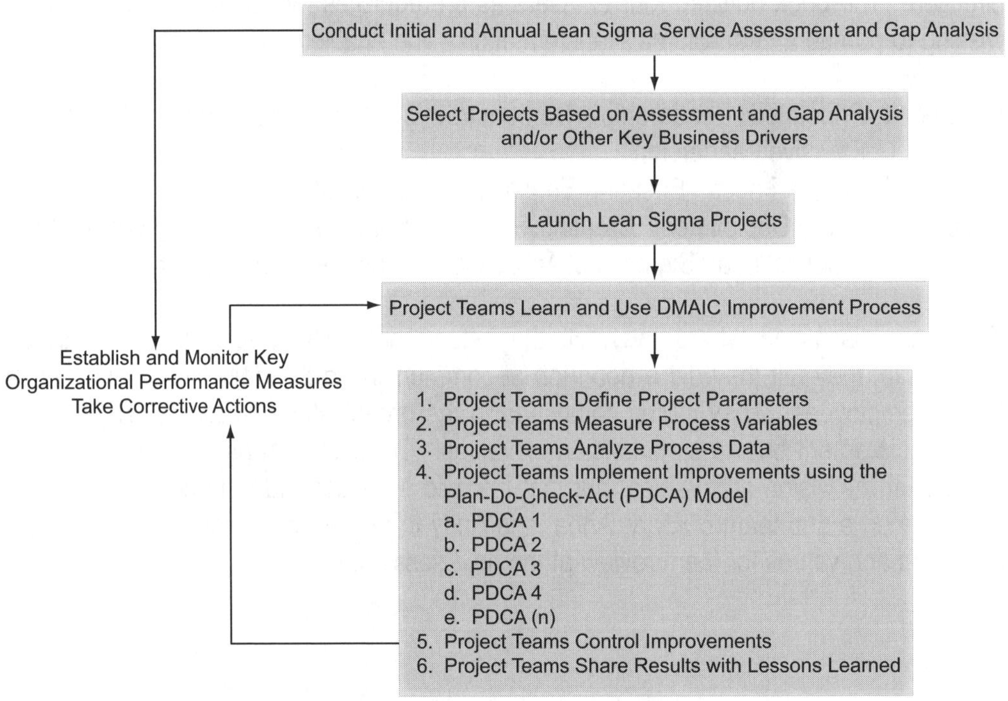

The Lean Transformation flow diagram indicated that an initial Lean Sigma for Service Excellence Assessment and Gap Analysis would be required to document their current state situation. The team felt this was a good idea and agreed to each complete the Lean Sigma for Service Excellence Assessment and Gap Analysis provided in this Appendix and forward their scores to Becky for compiling into one assessment.

This was plenty of work for the leadership team after their first session. The team set the date for the next work session and adjourned.

The Action Items from the first session were as follows:

1. The sub team of Mary, Anna, and Andy to update the mission and document the vision and values for team review at the next session.

2. Tom and Becky to work together to document the key measures for the organization.

3. The team members to complete the Lean Sigma for Service Excellence Assessment and Gap Analysis provided and forward their scores to Becky for compiling into one assessment.

Initial Assessment and Gap Analysis

The results from the initial Action Items are the foundation elements for initiating a Lean Sigma transformation, and are identified in the new few pages.

1. The mission, vision, and values sub team met and developed the following document for review by the Leadership team:

LEAN SIGMA MISSION STATEMENT
TREASURE BAY RESORT & MARINA

Vision: The vision of the Treasure Bay Resort & Marina is to be the resort and marina destination of choice. We will provide a positive and memorable vacation, holiday, or event experience for our guests. We strive to provide superior service and value in effort to meet our guest's needs in every way possible, and to be a preferred resort and marina destination.

Mission: The Treasure Bay Resort & Marina exists to provide a safe and pleasant resort and marina environment, where our guests and employees feel that they are truly valued, and our shareholders receive better than average return.

Values: We value:

Our Customers and Guests – They are who we serve and why we exist.

Our Employees – They are our greatest asset and the key to continuous improvement.

Meeting Our Commitments – Our customers and co-workers expect us to make commitments and stick to them.

Being Flexible and Creative – We need to be flexible to the changing needs of our guests and creative in finding ways to achieve our mission.

Integrity - Acting with honest intent

Quality - Striving for excellence which results in customer satisfaction

Respect - Recognizing the worth, quality, and importance of others regardless of position and/or background

2. The key measures were discussed by Tom and Becky, and documented in the following table (for review by the Leadership team):

Treasure Bay Resort & Marina Key Measures	
Category	**Measure**
Customer Focus	Customer Satisfaction Survey Response Rate Customer Satisfaction Survey Scores New Offerings per quarter
Financial Focus	Sales Revenue Profit Return On Investment EBITA Performance to Budget
Productivity Focus	Sales Revenue per Employee Sales Revenue per Operating Costs
Quality Focus	Customer Complaints Repeat Visits Percent Fill Rate - Resort & Marina
Delivery Focus	Commitments met per schedule or plan
People Focus	Absenteeism per day Injuries Training Hours Internal Promotions

3. The last Action Item from the work session is the Lean Sigma for Service Excellence Assessment and Gap Analysis. Each team member completed the assessment for their work areas and forwarded their scores to Becky for compiling. Becky compiled the data in a spreadsheet shown below and on the next two pages:

Lean Sigma for Service Excellence Assessment and Gap Analysis

Assessor Becky - Summary Analysis

Section 1 Leadership

		Score (1-5)
Vision	Leadership has defined and communicated a clear vision and is committed to promoting service excellence.	3.4
Planning	Service excellence is regularly discussed at our strategic planning meetings.	1.0
Resources	Adequate resources are continuously assigned for achieving service excellence.	3.0
Objectives	We have a good balance of attainable and stretch goals.	1.8
Accountability	We have process owners that are held accountable for performance measurements.	1.0
Average		**2.0**

Section 2 Customer Focus

		Score (1-5)
Listening	My organization does a good job of listening and involving its customers.	4.3
Measures	Customer satisfaction measurements capture actionable information needed for improvement.	1.0
Benchmarking	My organization obtains and uses customer service information relative to competition and/or benchmarks.	3.9
Expectations	Customer satisfaction takes top priority at my organization.	4.5
Flexibility	My organization remains flexible to changing customer needs and expectations.	4.0
Equity	We practice fair and equitable business practices for our customers, shareholders, and employees.	2.3
Average		**3.3**

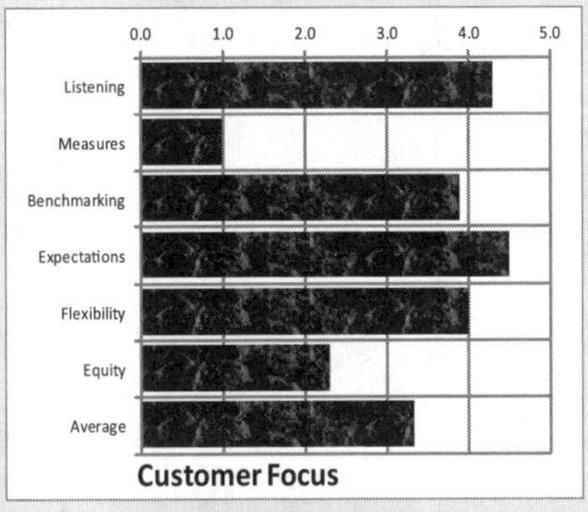

Section 3 Process Management

		Score (1-5)
Process Focus	My organization identifies its key service and delivery processes to achieve improved performance.	2.5
Measures	Performance measures are used for the control and improvement of service and delivery processes.	1.5
Efficiency	The processes that we use are smooth and work well.	2.9
Influence	Input from internal and external customers are incorporated into process improvement efforts.	2.9
Information	All necessary resources and information are available to do the work properly.	3.6
Variation	Process variation is understood and monitored at my organization.	1.0
Average		**2.4**

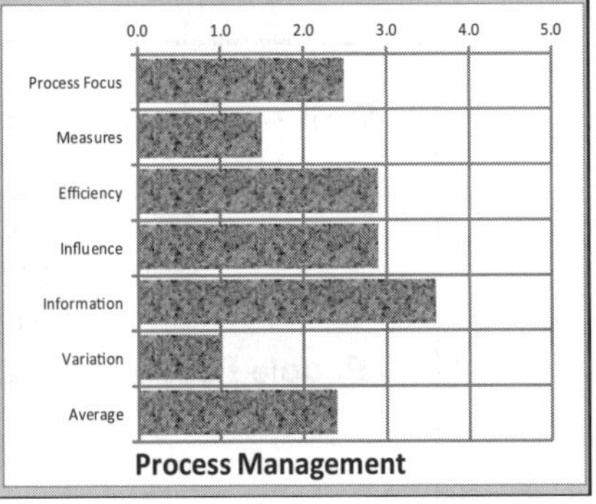

Section 4 People Management		Score (1-5)
Safety	Leaders demonstrate that the safety of people is of paramount importance.	4.1
Training	People's training and development needs are openly discussed and followed through on.	1.3
Development	Leadership creates an encouraging and motivating environment and helps people reach their full potential.	3.0
Obstacles	People can openly identify obstacles/problems and seek help in finding solutions.	2.9
Accountability	Our performance management system supports and rewards high performance.	2.6
Being Valued	People are treated as valued employees, where short and long term needs are met.	3.3
Average		**2.9**

Section 5 Information and Analysis		Score (1-5)
Information	My organization makes every effort to ensure data and information is appropriate, accurate, and reliable.	4.3
Monitoring	There is a system in place to monitor organizational progress against set objectives or goals.	1.4
Visibility	The monitoring system is clear and visible to all of the organization (e.g., scoreboards).	1.0
Decisions	It is clear to people how we use organizational level analysis to improve decision-making.	1.3
Challenge	People are responsible for questioning and/or challenging the status quo.	4.0
Improvement	There is an effective process to incorporate positive improvement ideas into the business plan.	3.0
Average		**2.5**

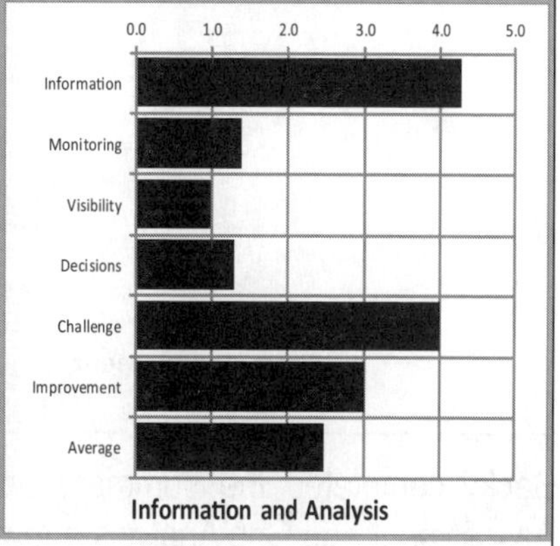

Summary	Average Score
Leadership	2.0
Customer Focus	3.3
Process Management	2.4
People Management	2.9
Information and Analysis	2.5

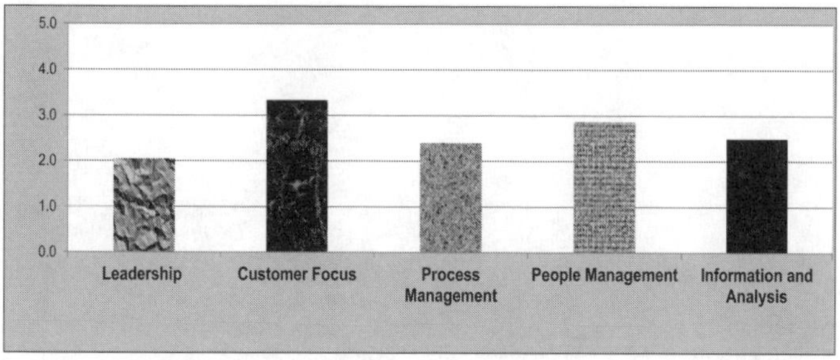

Note: The Bar Charts and Radar Chart (next page) have the minimum value of "0" for readability. The responses will be 1, 2, 3, 4, or 5.

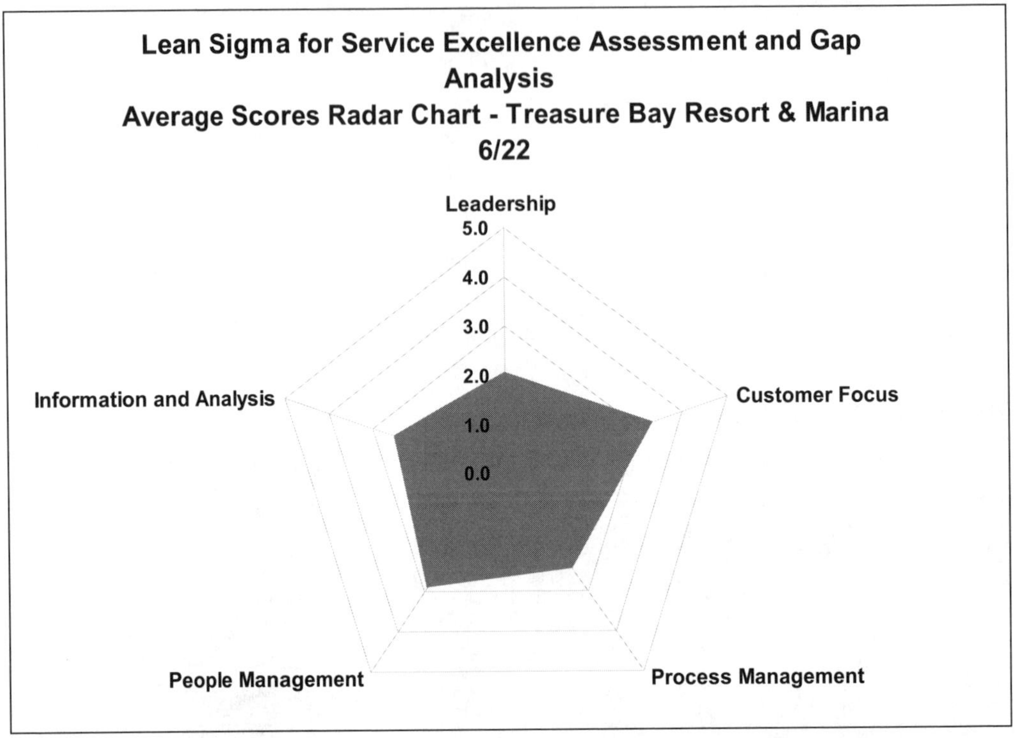

Becky completed the summary analysis of the Lean Sigma for Service Excellence Assessment and Gap Analysis a few different ways. First, the Radar Chart shown above indicates that the Leadership area was the lowest scoring category for the team, yet every indicator except Customer Focus was below 3.0, which showed room for improvement in many areas.

Becky also looked at the lowest scores in each category. This review indicated that the following questions were the lowest in each category. Becky prepared the following table for discussion at the next Leadership team work session.

Assessor:	Becky - Summary Analysis	
Section 1 Leadership		**Score (1-5)**
Planning	Service excellence is regularly discussed at our strategic planning meetings.	1.0
Accountability	We have process owners that are held accountable for performance measurements.	1.0
Section 2 Customer Focus		
Measures	Customer satisfaction measurements capture actionable information needed for improvement.	1.0
Section 3 Process Management		
Variation	Process variation is understood and monitored at my organization.	1.0
Section 4 People Management		
Training	People's training and development needs are openly discussed and followed through on.	1.3
Section 5 Information and Analysis		
Visibility	The monitoring system is clear and visible to all of the organization (e.g. scoreboards).	1.0

Becky also looked at areas where the team was the most misaligned, and to see if there was any one person that caused extreme bias on the assessment. The average score by person (i.e., department) is documented in the following table:

Person	Average Scores
TG	3.1
MF	2.4
AR	2.1
AR	3
MT	2.6
AM	2.8
DH	2
BW	3.1

Tom and Becky's area scores tended to be a bit higher than the rest of the team and Doug and Anna had the lowest average scores. The scoring averages would be compared to future scores to determine if a trend or other special cause issues were in effect.

The Transformation Action Plan

At the next work session, the team discussed the three action items from the previous session. The team first reviewed the updated mission, vision, and values document developed by the sub team, and agreed with it. They wondered how any organization could work without such a document, as it represented their basic identity as an organization.

They then reviewed Tom's key measure list. Many of the team members had no idea that Tom looked at this information, what it meant, or even how anything that they did could possibly affect these numbers. Since some of these issues were also highlighted on the assessment, the team agreed to move on to discuss the Lean Sigma for Service Excellence Assessment and Gap Analysis report.

Becky presented the data from the assessment. When they got to the lowest scores analysis, they discussed what might be causing some of the areas to score low. Their discussion and action ideas are documented in the following table:

Lean Sigma for Service Excellence Assessment and Gap Analysis			
Lowest score in each category analysis		Discussion	Possible Action Items
Section 1 Leadership			
Planning	Service excellence is regularly discussed at our strategic planning meetings.	We do not have strategic planning meetings.	Develop a strategic plan and conduct communications and discussions around service excellence.
Accountability	We have process owners that are held accountable for performance measurements.	We have department or area leaders, but there are few performance measures to be held accountable to.	Develop performance measures for each area and hold people accountable.
Section 2 Customer Focus			
Measures	Customer satisfaction measurements capture actionable information needed for improvement.	We conduct customer surveys, but the data comes too late to do anything positive. We are more reactive to customer surveys and usually just try to explain why the scores might have been low. (Bad weather, demanding guests, etc.)	Develop a more real-time customer feedback system that can be used to improve a guests' experience during their visit. Also, look at the current customer survey data to determine if we should start a Lean Sigma improvement project.
Section 3 Process Management			
Variation	Process variation is understood and monitored at my organization.	We do not do this at all. The concept of "process variation" is foreign to us.	Develop a few Lean Sigma projects in each area to begin to learn about process variation and improvement.
Section 4 People Management			
Training	People's training and development needs are openly discussed and followed through on.	We have training plans, but we usually look at them during our performance review process which happens only once per year.	Consider developing more comprehensive training plans for every employee. Include Lean Sigma training.
Section 5 Information and Analysis			
Visibility	The monitoring system is clear and visible to all of the organization (e.g. scoreboards).	We (the Leadership team) are just learning about what Tom measures and reviews. We have no scoreboards.	Consider formalizing the key measures and cascading them through all areas of the organization. Also, develop area scoreboards that will show everyone how we are doing.

From this discussion, the Leadership team developed and agreed to the following Initial Transformation Action Plan, set the schedule for the next work session, and adjourned:

Lean Sigma for Service Excellence Assessment and Gap Analysis			
Number	Action Item	Responsible	Target
1	Develop a strategic plan and conduct communications and discussions around service excellence.	Tom	6 months
2	Develop performance measures for each area and hold people accountable. Each area leader will develop and begin measuring key measures in their area.	Tom & Leadership team	1 month to initiate with regular updates
3	Develop a more real-time customer feedback system that can be used to improve a guests' experience during their visit. Also, look at the current customer survey data to determine if we should start a Lean Sigma improvement project.	No action at this time	N/A
4	Develop a Lean Sigma project in each area to begin to learn about process variation and improvement. Each area leader will begin a Lean Sigma improvement project in their area. The overall goal will be to identify and reduce wastes. Report outs to the Leadership team will be conducted monthly.	Each area leader	1 month to initiate with monthly updates
5	Consider developing more comprehensive training plans for every employee. Include Lean Sigma training. Becky will investigate bringing in additional Lean Sigma training sources.	Becky	2 months
6	Formalize organization level key measures and cascade them through all areas of the organization. Also, develop area scoreboards that will show everyone how we are doing.	Tom & Leadership team	1 month to initiate with regular updates

The team felt that this was quite an aggressive plan, to take on organization key measures (Numbers 2 and 6) and Lean Sigma improvement projects (Number 4). They decided to hold off on doing any work at this time on the customer survey and/or to assign Tom and Becky other individual activities.

Working the Plan

Tom decided to practice the Lean Sigma methods himself and completed a Project Charter for the entire Lean Sigma transformation. Tom completed this as best he could and sent it to the area leaders for use in developing their Lean Sigma Team Charters. Tom's overall Project Charter is shown below:

Project Charter - TBR&M

Company Name:
Treasure Bay Resort & Marina (TBR&M)

Proposed Team Members:

TG	MF	AR	MT
AM	DH	BW	

Leadership Sponsor:
Tom Green

High Level Objective:
1. Initate a Lean Sigma for ServiceExcellence (LSSE) Organizational Transformation!
2. Grow revenue.
3. Reduce costs.
4. Improve service and customer satisfaction.
5. Improve employee knowledge, skills, and abilities.
6. Employ a systematic approach to leadership and improvement.

Why is this important to our organization?
TBR&M needs to reinvent itself to remain competitive as newer, more modern competitors come into our area of operation. We are viewed as the "old resort" by many and need to refresh out image to gain business.

Boundary Conditions (Process Scope and Organizational Scope):
The Lean Sigma forService Excellence Transformation will involve all areas of the organization. The Leadership will lead by example.

Project Budget:
To be determined.

Expected Deliverables and Outcomes:
1. A trial of a systematic approach to management and continuous improvement.
2. Improvement projects completed in every area.
3. Learning about LSSE methods and tools.

Goal/Target Action (this supports):

Metrics	Current Condition	Target Condition
Productivity/Cost		
Sales Revenue per Employee	$20K	$32K
Sales Revenue per Operating Costs	2	>5
Quality		
Customer Complaints	6/week	<5/week
Repeat Visits	1/week	>3/week
Percent Fill Rate	64%	>75%
Delivery		
Commitments met per schedule or plan	90%	>95%

Metrics	Current Condition	Target Condition
People		
Aberteeism per day	3%	<1%
Injuries		
Training Hours	~1 hr/mo	~4 hrs/mo
Internal Promotions	100%	75%
Customer		
Customer Satisfaction Survey Response Rate	60%	>70%
Customer Satisfaction Survey Scores	76%	>80%
New Offerings	2	>10
Financial		
Sales Revenue	$225K/mo	$321K/mo
Profit	10%	>25%
Return On Investment	8%	>20%
EBITA	4%	>15%
Performance to Budget	-5%	+/-10%

Projected Project Completion Date:
3 month project duration

Tom also put together a draft Project Planner (Define Phase) time line shown below, for the beginning of the transformation projects and forwarded both documents to the area leaders:

Project Planner - TBR&M

Objective: Record and track the key events and milestones to complete the initiative. **Revision Date:** 6/6

Project Planner (PP)
3 Month Working Plan

Project Planner Objective: Identify major activities by deliverable and time frame to complete.

% Complete: 0% (not started) 25% (underway) 50% (half complete) 75% (nearly done) 100% (complete)

Medium shading or green color signifies completed implementation activities.
Dark shading or red color signifies behind target for implementaion activities.
Light shading or yellow color signifies on target for implementation activities.

	Phase / Activity	% Comp	Month 1				Month 2				Month 3			
			1	2	3	4	1	2	3	4	1	2	3	4
	Define Phase	% Comp												
1	**Project Charter - LSEE transformation**	100%												
2	**Team Charter for all areas**	0%												
3	**Project Planner for all areas**	0%												
	Measure Phase	% Comp												
1	**Baseline Data Collection and Process Mapping**	0%												
2	Additional data collection and flow mapping	0%												
3	Develop the current state map	0%												
4	Collect process flow data	0%												
5	Collect Key Performance Indicators (KPIs)	0%												
	Analyze Phase	% Comp												
1	**Critical Review of Data**	0%												
2	Review current state map for process and flow	0%												
3	Review other data	0%												
4	**Identify High Potential Improvement Actions**	0%												
5	Document process and opporunities	0%												
	Improve Phase	% Comp												
1	**Develop Improvement Implementation Plan**	0%												
2	Complete a future state map	0%												
3	Develop the detailed improvement plan for PDCAs	0%												
4	**Implement Improvements**	0%												
	Control Phase	% Comp												
1	**Establish Measures and Audit Plan to Sustain Improvements**	0%												
2	Provide ongoing weekly scoreboard reports	0%												

The plan of attack was for each area leader to meet with their team to discuss the Lean Sigma for Service Excellence transformation background and Project Charter. Each area leader, with their team, would then develop a Team Charter (Define Phase) and begin the Measure Phase with a value stream or flow map of a key process in their area. This was a bit challenging at first as the leaders had never worked like this before and many of the Lean Sigma tools were new to them. After all, they were used to just going to work and reacting, and this was more of a systematic approach to leading. Tom asked that the area Team Charters, process maps, and draft Project Planners be complete for next month's report-out sessions.

The area leaders and teams went to work. A few of the leaders requested additional training materials and/or help in getting started. Becky provided a variety of training and material options for the leaders. Becky provided refresher classes and a check sheet for basic team building and meeting leading. Tom and Becky knew that it is at this point that many organizations also engage an expert Lean Sigma coach or facilitator to assist with the training and mentoring of key staff leaders (typically for their first project). Large organizations may simply hire a full time Lean Sigma Champion. Tom and Becky decided to allow the area leaders to start the process on their own and see how things went. Tom was not completely opposed to bringing in help but wanted to give the teams a chance on their own first.

Area Work Sessions

Standardized objectives and agendas were set by the Leadership team for the first area Lean Sigma work sessions. The objective of the first area team work sessions is to provide a brief update on the business conditions and competitive realities, provide a brief overview of Lean Sigma for service industries, review the Project Charter initiated by Tom and the Leadership team, begin developing the Team Charter to support the Project Charter, and provide the plan for the next steps. The following is the standard agenda for the objectives for the area teams:

1. Provide a brief update on the business conditions and competitive realities.
2. Provide a brief overview of Lean Sigma for service organizations.
3. Review the Project Charter initiated by the Leadership team.
4. Develop an area Team Charter to support the Project Charter.
5. Establish the path forward, expectations, and the next steps.

The Lean Sigma overview is to be conducted by each area leader. By doing this, the area leaders will have to further study the Lean Sigma material in chapter 2 and be prepared to teach their teams about Lean Sigma methods and tools. A brief written statement from Tom regarding the business update and competitive realities will be provided to the area leaders, as will copies of the original Lean Sigma article that Tom had read, so that it can be used as a training aid. This training effort supports the employee training and engagement enabler as well.

The work sessions went well, and for the most part, the teams understood the common objectives of the Lean Sigma DMAIC projects and journey that was to begin. Most employees could see what was happening to the TBR&M in the market place and wanted to make improvements. Some people were skeptical that this new approach would not be any better than the last new approach; regardless, the leaders pressed forward. Since the Leadership team had standardized the approach, the teams had many things in common when developing their Team Charters. The Team Charter elements listed below were thought to be common for all teams:

1. Mission or Purpose of the Project: Since this is the initial or launch project for each area, the primary purpose is to establish key measures and implement some key improvements using the Lean Sigma tools. A secondary purpose is to learn and use Lean Sigma methods and tools.

2. Deliverables or Expected Outcomes: Expected outcomes are: 1) Measurable improvements in every area and 2) Practice and learn using Lean Sigma methods and tools.

3. Benefits of Expected Outcomes: Benefits are: 1) Begin the Lean Sigma Transformation journey, which can revitalize the business, 2) Work should become easier to perform, and 3) Guests and customers will have an improved experience which can lead to repeat business.

4. Expected Approach and Activities: Each area team will use the Lean Sigma DMAIC process to initiate and manage their projects.

5. Time Frame: (Start date, end date, and major milestone target dates) Project will be on-going for the next 6 months, with monthly report-out sessions with the Leadership team.

The area teams spent much of their time discussing the following remaining elements of the Team Charter:

Measures – Productivity, Quality, Delivery, People, Customer, and Financial
Key Customers/Outputs and Suppliers/Inputs
Assumptions
Current Issues to Address or Solve
Risks to Consider

The following outlines the discussions at each area work session on these topics:

Guest Services - Define Phase
Mary led this work session and documented the following Team Charter elements:

Measures – Productivity, Quality, Delivery, People, Customer, and Financial
The key measures for the Guest Services team were room fill rates and average room price for the night. The team looked at this data regularly as it had a direct impact on their workload and was a measure of their ability to hold their pricing on room rates. The team also included the customer survey feedback.

Key Customers/Outputs and Suppliers/Inputs
The team decided to improve the Check-In process. The key suppliers to this process are the Reservations group, who supplies the bookings and the Information Technology group, who provides the computer systems and the key card equipment. The process will be documented with a flow chart as a next step. Outputs and Customers are the guests, who receive a smooth check-in and the correct room key and room assignment, Accounting, who receives detailed billing information for each guest, and Marketing, who uses certain guest information to develop future marketing plans.

Assumptions
The team assumed that they would spend no money to improve the check-in process. They would look for low cost/no cost improvement ideas.

Current Issues to Address or Solve
The team was unsure how they could affect the room fill rates directly as many of the bookings are made weeks in advance. They did feel that they could affect the average room prices, but were concerned about upsetting guests by holding full rate pricing. The team also felt they could have a direct impact on the customer survey.

Risks to Consider
The main risk the Guest Services team identified was that if they try too hard to hold full rate pricing, they may get lower scores on their customer feedback surveys.

Next Steps
The next steps for the team were to process map the Check-In process and determine a better way to capture the Voice of the Customer (VOC) on a more frequent and current time frame. The team made the assignments to sub groups of 2 - 5 people, set the expectations and schedule for the next work session, and adjourned.

Housekeeping - Define Phase

Anna led this work session and documented the following Team Charter elements:

Measures – Productivity, Quality, Delivery, People, Customer, and Financial

The key measures for the Housekeeping team were customer complaints and having each day's work complete by 3:00 pm. Their key objective was to have each room cleaned and serviced every day by 3:00 pm. Complaints came on occasion and were dealt with on an individual basis. The team occasionally looked at customer survey feedback as well, so they included it as a key measure to improve.

Key Customers/Outputs and Suppliers/Inputs

The process team decided to improve the Daily Room Cleaning process. This included the rooms where guests were remaining, as well as the guests that were checking out. The key suppliers to this process are Laundry, who supply clean linens and various cleaning materials, and supplies suppliers. The process will be documented with a flow chart as a next step. Outputs and Customers are the guests, who receive a clean and serviced room and Guest Services who receives information regarding room readiness.

Assumptions

The team assumed that they would spend no money to improve the room cleaning and prep process. They would look for low cost/no cost improvement ideas.

Current Issues to Address or Solve

The team knew what the keys were for their success, but it was not clear on a daily basis if they met the goal or not. There was little sense of team and accomplishment, as most people worked individually and were never sure how Housekeeping was doing. Due to the lack of team work, the team had recently lost a couple key people to the other resorts. The team also felt that there had been a problem with suppliers as it seemed that their service carts were always empty of key service materials or cleansers.

Risks to Consider

The main risk the Housekeeping team identified was that if they do not improve teamwork they will lose more good people.

Next Steps

The next steps for the team were to process map the room cleaning process and begin measuring and displaying the actual success rates for the team. The team required everyone to begin documenting the completion times and number of occurrences of when the service carts were lacking a key material or cleanser. They set the schedule for the next work session and adjourned.

Food Services - Define Phase

Andy led this work session and documented the following Team Charter elements:

Measures – Productivity, Quality, Delivery, People, Customer, and Financial

The key measures for the Food Services were daily sales receipts and customer complaints. Andy looked at the sales data every day and was often on the front line receiving customer complaints. Complaints were not tracked formally but when Andy got complaints, he shared them with the team. The team also included the customer survey feedback as a key measure to improve.

Key Customers/Outputs and Suppliers/Inputs

The process team decided to improve overall Food Service for all dining areas. This was a big area to address, but they had representation from each area on the team, and felt that if they split up the work, they could accomplish improvements in the overall process. The key suppliers to this process are food and supplies suppliers. The actual process of food receiving, order taking, preparation and delivery to the customer to final cleaning is the process to be mapped. Outputs and Customers are the guests, who receive meals to order. The ultimate output is a satisfied customer who feels they received a good meal for a good value.

Assumptions

The team assumed that they could change anything they needed to change. This included menus, offerings, and hours of operations.

Current Issues to Address or Solve

Most of the complaints centered around running out a daily special item or not being able to get exactly what was wanted due to the ridged menu and service location schedules established by Andy. It was felt that if they could better serve the customer's needs, they might be able to increase sales receipts.

Risks to Consider

The main risk the Food Services team identified was that if they make changes, they might actually reduce sales. They were very concerned about making too many changes too fast.

Next Steps

The next steps for the team were to process map the Food Service process and determine a root cause for their major customer complaint of running out of the daily special. The team split the work up between each dining area, set the schedule for the next session and adjourned.

Retail Sales - Define Phase
Mike led this work session and documented the following Team Charter elements:

Measures – Productivity, Quality, Delivery, People, Customer, and Financial
The key measures for the Retail Sales group were net daily sales receipts.

Key Customers/Outputs and Suppliers/Inputs
The process the team decided to improve was the Product Ordering through Sales process. The key suppliers to this process are the various suppliers of the items offered for sale in the stores, the Information Technology group who supplies the sales data, and the Marketing group who provides new designs and product ideas. The process will be documented with a value stream map as a next step. The Outputs and Customers are the customer purchasing the items from the stores. The outputs from the retail sales process are cash receipts and profit.

Assumptions
The team assumed that they would spend no money to improve the retail sales process. They would look for low cost/no cost improvement ideas.

Current Issues to Address or Solve
The team knew that their biggest concern was that they would regularly run out of high selling items and not be able to get replacements in time to capitalize on the customer demand. It seemed when large groups came to the resort, they would have a run on sales of certain items and run out of the item entirely. This was seen as lost sales and the team wanted to improve this situation.

Risks to Consider
The main risk the Retail Sales group identified was that if they did not do something, they would continue to lose sales and not achieve their potential.

Next Steps
The next steps for the team was to process map the Product Ordering through Sales process. The team made the assignments to each store to begin tracking when product "stock-outs" occurred and for what product it occurred. The team set the expectations and schedule for the next work session and adjourned.

Adventures and Event Planning - Define Phase

Amy led this work session and documented the following Team Charter elements:

Measures – Productivity, Quality, Delivery, People, Customer, and Financial

The key measures for the Adventures and Event Planning group were the number of people using adventure offerings, daily sales receipts, and from the Event Planning area, the key measure was the total number of room bookings. The Event Planning room bookings were looked at every month, but the Adventures numbers were reviewed daily by Amy. The team is a small group that mainly works to facilitate or flow work to local vendors.

Key Customers/Outputs and Suppliers/Inputs

The process team decided to improve the Adventures Planning and Booking process. The key suppliers and inputs to this process are local adventure providers and their marketing materials. The process will be documented with a value stream map as a next step. Outputs and Customers are the guests, who receive an exciting and memorable adventure and memory, and an overall positive customer experience.

Assumptions

The team assumed that they would spend little or no money to improve the Adventure Booking and Delivery process. They would look for low cost/no cost improvement ideas.

Current Issues to Address or Solve

The biggest current issue was the capacity of the rental equipment and local adventure suppliers during the busy times. During busy times, it was not uncommon for customers to have to wait for rental equipment. Customers were often told estimates of when equipment would be available, but these estimates were not very accurate, and customers often became upset or angry if the equipment was not available when they were told it would be. The team felt that this led to loss sales and frustrated customers.

Risks to Consider

The main risk the team identified was that if they did nothing, they could not be competitive with the other local resorts and they would lose business.

Next Steps

The next step for the team was to process map the Adventure Planning and Booking process, which included the rental equipment. The team also agreed to begin to track the number of times and circumstances where shortages occurred. The data would help them develop an improvement plan. The team documented the plan, made the assignments to individuals, set the next session schedule and adjourned.

Grounds and Maintenance - Define Phase

Doug led this work session and documented the following Team Charter elements:

Measures – Productivity, Quality, Delivery, People, Customer, and Financial

The key measures for the Grounds and Maintenance team were almost non-existent. They tried to keep a regular grounds maintenance schedule, but the weather often caused the team to fall behind. When this happened they just continued to work to the schedule as the conditions permitted. They basically worked to the "squeaky wheel" schedule, that is, the most vocal customer or area got their work done first. It was a very chaotic environment. The closest thing they had to a measure is customer complaints or calls per day.

Key Customers/Outputs and Suppliers/Inputs

The team decided to improve the Customer Support and Repairs process. The key suppliers to this process are various local parts and supplies suppliers, as well as other local skilled trades sub-contractors. Outputs and Customers are the guest and resort employees who receive repaired and or maintained rooms and facilities.

Assumptions

The team assumed that they would have little time to work on this project as there were so many crises to deal with.

Current Issues to Address or Solve

They team was always in crisis mode. It was felt that this was the major reason for Doug's low scores on the Lean Sigma Assessment. Doug felt like they did not have the resources to get the right things done and wanted some way to prevent the crises from occurring in the first place.

Risks to Consider

The main risk identified by the Grounds and Maintenance group was that if they could not make improvements, they may lose key people to the other local resorts. The other risk identified was that there was no time to work on this project. If they work on the improvements, the crises will not get fixed quickly enough.

Next Steps

The next steps for the team were to process map the Customer Support and Repairs process and determine an improved way to prevent a crisis from occurring. The team felt that a maintenance calls per day chart, and some type of measurement and analysis of what types of maintenance calls they were receiving would help them to understand the situation. Doug agreed to do the mapping work for the team and asked Becky for some help in the daily data collection process. Doug set the schedule for the next session and let his team get back to work.

Administration - Define Phase

Becky led this work session and documented the following Team Charter elements:

Measures – Productivity, Quality, Delivery, People, Customer, and Financial

Becky had several teams that interacted together. They agreed to address the Accounting and Purchasing area, in particular, the Purchase Requisition to Payment process. The measures for this process are speed and accuracy of procurement and the number of delays and errors/corrections in the process. Although they currently were not measuring these parameters, they felt that some type of measurement was needed for improvement.

Key Customers/Outputs and Suppliers/Inputs

The process team decided to improve the Purchase Requisition to Payment process. The key suppliers to this process are various areas of the organization submitting purchase requisitions. These range from food, retail, maintenance, capital, and other supply items. Outputs from this process are purchase orders, fulfilled orders to schedule, and paid bills. The Customers of this process are internal resort employees and key suppliers.

Assumptions

The team assumed that they would make improvement by working cross-functionally to reduce the time and efficiency of the Purchase Requisition to Payment process.

Current Issues to Address or Solve

The team felt that the order fulfillment process was slow, and that this cost the resort lost sales on several occasions. The team also felt that their error rate could be improved. In the past few weeks, they have had to modify or correct several invoices for minor errors in quantities or pricing. The errors and corrections also causes delays the order fulfillment process, as well as extra work for the team members.

Risks to Consider

The main risk the Purchasing and Accounting groups identified was that they need to be careful not to pay bills prematurely unless there is appropriate incentive to do so.

Next Steps

The next steps for the cross-functional team were to process map the Purchase Requisition to Payment process and determine a streamlined way to eliminate waste and errors. The team made the assignments to sub groups of 2 - 5 people, set the schedule for the next work session and adjourned.

After each area team had documented and submitted their Team Charter drafts, Becky developed a Team Charter Matrix Summary table in Excel and noted the following:

1. All initial Team Charter's objectives were very similar in nature.
2. Area specific issues were well-noted on the Team Charters.
3. Not every team's time line progressed at the same rate.
4. Major objectives for many of the teams were to establish key measures.
5. All teams submitted their Team Charters on time and were beginning the improvement process.
6. Each team noted the importance of the report out to the Leadership team each month.

The Project Planner that Tom developed was placed as a template on the shared network drive for each team to modify with more details for each of their projects.

The next step for the teams was to shift to the Measure Phase of the DMAIC process and develop a map or flow of their key processes. This included creating the structure or process in which to collect the key data which would identify and illuminate wasteful practices. Once completed, this would lead the way to Lean Sigma tool applications through the PDCA improvement cycle.

Key Measures

While the area teams were working on following the DMAIC process, Tom compiled the key measures from each Team Charter and documented them in the following table:

Treasure Bay Resort & Marina Key Measures

Category	Measure	Goal	Initial State (Before)
Customer Focus	Customer Satisfaction Survey Response Rate	> 70%	60%
	Customer Satisfaction Survey Scores	> 80%	76%
	New Offerings	> 10 items	2
	Number of people using equipment & facilities	Increasing	Decreasing
Financial Focus	Sales Revenue - by area	$321K per Mo	$225K
	Profit	> 25%	10%
	Return On Investment	> 20%	8%
	EBITA	> 10%	4%
	Performance to Budget	At or below budget	5% over
	Average room sell price	> $200	$185
	Expenses		
	Room bookings for events	> 30 per Mo	25
Productivity Focus	Sales Revenue per Employee	$32K/Emp.	$20K
	Sales Revenue per Operating Costs	> 2 times	2
	Room Fill Rates	> 70%	62%
	Cleaned by 3pm	100%	95%
	Repair Work Orders per week	< 5 per day	10 per day
	Days per purchase requisition to purchase order	< 3 days	5-7 days unless rushed
Quality Focus	Customer Complaints	< 5 per week	6 per week
	Repeat Visits	> 3 per week	1 per week
	Percent Fill Rate - Resort & Marina	> 75%	64%
	Errors and Corrections per week	Minimal	Not Counted
Delivery Focus	Commitments met per schedule or plan	> 95%	90%
	Dining schedule of operation	By plan	Rigid
	Product availability	No goal	10+ stock-outs per month
	Time to complete work order	No goal	3-5 days, unless emergency
People Focus	Absenteeism per day	< 1%	3%
	Injuries	0	0
	Training Hours	4 / Emp./ Mo	~ 1 hr/Mo
	Internal Promotions	75%	100%
	Teamwork	No goal	No measure
	Improved Planning	No goal	No measure
	Frustration Level - Absenteeism	No goal	No measure

These measures would be the starting point for their Policy Deployment efforts. For the Policy Deployment work, Tom and the Leadership team would establish goals for each KPI and begin to track and display actual performance measures in a visual scoreboard fashion in each area. Many KPIs were posted in each area every day. Some of the financial data was only reported once a month. The area managers would use the KPI scoreboards to conduct visual management efforts for performance monitoring and improvement.

Team DMAIC Progress Matrix/Summary

Over the next several months, each team conducted weekly one-hour work sessions in effort to follow the DMAIC process for Lean Sigma improvement. Each month, the improvement teams reported out their progress to the Leadership team. The Leadership team challenged and guided the area teams through the improvement process phases. The Leadership team also worked to eliminate barriers, such as lack of data and resources and departmental "turf issues," and provide additional training to various teams. Perhaps the most important thing that the Leadership team did was to ensure each team followed the DMAIC process.

The improvement teams identified several opportunities and key findings during each DMAIC Phase of the improvement process. The teams identified tools and improvement methods that required several PDCA trials for learning and implementation. The following table documents the progression of each team through the DMAIC Phases as well as the main Lean Sigma tools applied throughout the improvement process.

The Leadership team noted several similarities from one team to the next during the movement through the DMAIC phases. The most notable differences were in the actual Lean Sigma tools applications. Overall the teams were glad to see the commonality and believed that this consistency would allow them to move more quickly as an organization along their Lean Sigma journey.

Treasure Bay Resort & Marina Lean Sigma DMA								
	Define			Measure			Analyze	
Area	Lean Sigma Tools Used	Findings	Next Steps	Lean Sigma Tools Used	Findings	Next Steps	Lean Sigma Tools Used	Findings
Guest Services	Team Charter, Project Planner, AI Log, IO Log	The Define Phase tools worked well to define the improvement needs. There are not many measures in any area.	Map the main process flow and collect data from the customer regarding their perceptions.	Process Mapping, Key Metric Data Profiles, VOC, QFD, Check Sheets	Data collection is time consuming but very revealing.	Complete the analysis of data in the Analyze Phase.	Demand Analysis, Cause and Effect Diagram	Customers want improved sense of urgency and speed. "Island Time" speed for services is unacceptable.
Housekeeping	Team Charter, Project Planner, AI Log, IO Log	The Define Phase tools worked well to define the improvement needs. There are not many measures in any area.	Map the main process flow and document issues and opportunities.	Process Mapping, Key Metric Data Profiles, SIPOC, Frequency Charts	Data collection is time consuming but very revealing.	Complete the analysis of data in the Analyze Phase.	VA versus NVA Analysis, Pareto Chart, Cause and Effect Diagram	Lack of organization causes delays in room processing. A great deal of laundry costs are from hot water washing.
Food Services	Team Charter, Project Planner, AI Log, IO Log	The Define Phase tools worked well to define the improvement needs. There are not many measures in any area.	Map the main process flow and collect data from the customer regarding their perceptions.	Process Mapping, Key Metric Data Profiles, VOC, QFD, Run Charts, Takt time	Data collection is time consuming but very revealing.	Complete the analysis of data in the Analyze Phase.	Demand Analysis, Cause and Effect Diagram, Speadsheets, Pivot Tables	Lack of flexibility in menu causes shortages and frustated customers. A great deal of food products are thrown in the garbage and sent to the landfill.
Retail Sales	Team Charter, Project Planner, AI Log, IO Log	The Define Phase tools worked well to define the improvement needs. There are not many measures in any area.	Map the main process flow and collect data from the customer regarding their perceptions.	Process Mapping, Key Metric Data Profiles, VOC, QFD, Run Charts, Takt time	Data collection is time consuming but very revealing.	Complete the analysis of data in the Analyze Phase.	Demand Analysis, Takt time, Pitch, Cause and Effect Diagram, Spreadsheets, Pivot Tables	Lack of systematic reordering process causes shortages in best selling products.

IC Project Summaries

	Improve			Control		
Next Steps	Lean Sigma Tools Used	Findings	Next Steps	Lean Sigma Tools Used	Findings	Next Steps
Develop an improvement plan using Lean Sigma tools to eliminate or reduce customer frustration and waste.	PDCA, Standard Work, Sustainability, Cross-training	PDCA process does a great job in documenting improvement efforts and keeps teams on track. Standard work helps change the culture of the organization.	Use Control techniques to maintain the gains in the Improve Phase. Email receipts instead of printing to save ink and paper.	Visual Management	Visual Management techniques are simple and drive the right questions to be asked.	Establish a more real-time measure to monitor progress.
Develop an improvement plan using Lean Sigma tools to eliminate or reduce customer frustration and waste. Develop a plan to use less hot water washes	PDCA, Sustainability, 5S	5S is simple and easy to implement and can improve an organizational's culture.	Use Control techniques to maintain the gains in the Improve Phase.	Visual Management	Visual Management techniques are simple and drive the right questions to be asked.	Establish a more real-time measure to monitor progress.
Develop an improvement plan using Lean Sigma tools to eliminate or reduce customer frustration and waste.	PDCA, Sustainability	Mass customization is a flexible way to meet customer needs and improve sales revenues. Compost all food waste.	Use Control techniques to maintain the gains in the Improve Phase.	Visual Management, SPC	Visual Management techniques are simple and drive the right questions to be asked.	Establish a more real-time measure to monitor progress.
Develop an improvement plan using Lean Sigma tools to eliminate or reduce customer frustration and waste.	PDCA, Service Flow	Service Flow Kanban signals help to make sure we never run out of products and improve sales revenue. Kanban system take regular attention to implement properly.	Use Control techniques to maintain the gains in the Improve Phase.	Visual Management, SPC	Visual Management techniques are simple and drive the right questions to be asked.	Establish a more real-time measure to monitor progress.

Treasure Bay Resort & Marina Lean Sigma DMA								
	Define			Measure			Analyze	
Area	Lean Sigma Tools Used	Findings	Next Steps	Lean Sigma Tools Used	Findings	Next Steps	Lean Sigma Tools Used	Findings
Adventures and Event Planning	Team Charter, Project Planner, AI Log, IO Log	The Define Phase tools worked well to define the improvement needs. There are not many measures in any area.	Map the main process flow and collect data from the customer regarding their perceptions.	Process Mapping, Key Metric Data Profiles, Frequency Charts	Data collection is time consuming but very revealing.	Complete the analysis of data in the Analyze Phase.	Demand Analysis, Cause and Effect Diagram, Spreadsheets, Pivot Tables	Lack of systematic approach to booking process causes confusion and frustrated customers.
Grounds and Maintenance	Team Charter, Project Planner, AI Log, IO Log	The Define Phase tools worked well to define the improvement needs. There are not many measures in any area.	Map the main process flow and document issues and opportunities.	Process Mapping, Key Metric Data Profiles, SIPOC, Frequency Charts	Data collection is time consuming but very revealing.	Complete the analysis of data in the Analyze Phase.	VA versus NVA Analysis, Pareto Chart, Cause and Effect Diagram	Lack of preventative maintenance program causes "crisis management" and frustated customers.
Administration - Accounting	Team Charter, Project Planner, AI Log, IO Log	The Define Phase tools worked well to define the improvement needs. There are not many measures in any area.	Map the main process flow and collect data from the customer regarding their perceptions.	Process Mapping, SIPOC, Frequency Charts	Data collection is time consuming but very revealing.	Complete the analysis of data in the Analyze Phase.	Demand Analysis, Cause and Effect Diagram, Speadsheets, Pivot Tables	Distance and process barriers cause delay in customer processing and frustated customers.
Administration - Purchasiing	Team Charter, Project Planner, AI Log, IO Log	The Define Phase tools worked well to define the improvement needs. There are not many measures in any area.	Map the main process flow and collect data from the customer regarding their perceptions.	Process Mapping, SIPOC, Frequency Charts	Data collection is time consuming but very revealing.	Complete the analysis of data in the Analyze Phase.	Demand Analysis, Takt time, Pitch, Cause and Effect Diagram, Spreadsheets, Pivot Tables	Lack of quality system causes excess errors and delays which frustrates customers and suppliers.

IC Project Summaries

	Improve			Control		
Next Steps	Lean Sigma Tools Used	Findings	Next Steps	Lean Sigma Tools Used	Findings	Next Steps
Develop an improvement plan using Lean Sigma tools to eliminate or reduce customer frustration and waste.	PDCA, Service Flow	Service Flow Kanban signals help smooth the flow and keep customers happy and informed.	Use Control techniques to maintain the gains in the Improve Phase. Email receipts instead of printing to save ink and paper.	Visual Management, SPC	Visual Management techniques are simple and drive the right questions to be asked.	Establish a more real-time measure to monitor progress.
Develop an improvement plan using Lean Sigma tools to eliminate or reduce customer frustration and waste. Develop a plan to use less hot water washes.	PDCA, 5S, Visual Controls, TPM	Preventative maintenance activities reduce the "crisis management" and unscheduled breakdowns to enable us to keep more customers happy, more consistently.	Use Control techniques to maintain the gains in the Improve Phase.	Visual Management, SPC, Problem Solving	Visual Management techniques are simple and drive the right questions to be asked.	Establish a more real-time measure to monitor progress.
Develop an improvement plan using Lean Sigma tools to eliminate or reduce customer frustration and waste.	PDCA, Mistake Proofing, Physical Layout, Sustainability, Cross-training	Mistake proofing reduces reworks and credits. Emailing customers reduces paper and ink consumption.	Use Control techniques to maintain the gains in the Improve Phase.	Visual Management, Standard Work for Leaders	Visual Management techniques are simple and drive the right questions to be asked.	Establish a more real-time measure to monitor progress.
Develop an improvement plan using Lean Sigma tools to eliminate or reduce customer frustration and waste.	PDCA, Mistake Proofing, Physical Layout, Continuous Flow, Cross-training	Cell layout streamlines workflow when multiple approvals are required.	Use Control techniques to maintain the gains in the Improve Phase.	Visual Management, SPC	Visual Management techniques are simple and drive the right questions to be asked.	Establish a more real-time measure to monitor progress.

Team Outcome Summary

The following outlines the main Lean Sigma tools used throughout the improvement project for each area:

Guest Services

The Guest Service team discovered through the VOC measurement and analysis that customers wanted improved sense of urgency and speed. When customers came to the resort they were on an "exotic" vacation and wanted to be pampered – their entire time at the resort. The workers had to understand that it was a holiday for their customers 365 days a year. The quaint and once treasured concept of slow service affectionately known as "Island Time" was no longer was acceptable and the new resorts knew this.

To address this shift in customer needs, the Guest Services team developed standard work procedures, practices and standards that ranged from dress codes, to greetings, to speed of services and timeliness (i.e., takt time targets). Training classes were developed and delivered for all levels of Guest Service workers. Measurements were put into place to monitor these changes. As a result, customer survey scores began to improve.

The team also implemented a sustainability or Green measure by inquiring if guest receipts could be emailed rather than printed. Around 80% of the guests allowed their receipts to be emailed, reducing the use of paper and ink by 80%!

Housekeeping

Housekeeping's frustration with poor teamwork and things not being in the right places was dealt with at a couple levels. To deal with the poor teamwork, Anna, the area leader, established a daily scoreboard and began posting the daily results. Anna established team based rewards and developed standard work with takt times to encourage and support a team approach to hitting the daily goals.

Anna's team was also able to reduce the use of hot water by utilizing warm water washing with an improved detergent designed for warm water. The water heating bill was reduced by $1.25 per load.

Anna also led the team through a 5S event on their standard cleaning carts, supplies, and tools. Rules were established and enforced to ensure that the carts and other 5S areas were maintained. Anna established an audit team and they conducted weekly audits and held people accountable. Visual control and management techniques enabled Anna to lead her team to improved performance and teamwork. The biggest impact from Anna's perspective was that they reduced their customer complaints to less that 3 per week and the tips for the Housekeeping staff nearly doubled!

Food Services

The Food Services team learned through problem solving that there was no systematic approach to meal planning. They began to track data regarding daily special outages and quantities compared to booking or fill rates. They found a direct correlation between the Resort's fill rates and food service requirements. The team established standard work practices to purchase food requirements based on resort fill levels. Their daily special outages did not go away completely, but they were greatly reduced.

The Food Services team also implemented a waste food compost rather than sending the waste food items to the landfill. Although this took considerable coordination and new standard practices, the team was able to reduce their landfill waste hauling costs by approximately 10%!

To increase revenue, the Food Service team used VOC information to determine that customers no longer liked special meal night, but would prefer more options throughout the day. Through mass customization concepts, the team developed a menu variety that could be served any time during the day and delivered to any local location on or near the resort. The results of this improvement were documented by a 25% improvement in customer survey scores for food services!

Retail Sales

The Retail Sales team found that their reaction time to increasing sales of a particular item was too slow to allow them to recover and prevent stock-outs. They worked with a local supplier to establish a signaling (or Kanban) system to ensure there would be a reduced incident of stock-outs of popular items. Slow moving and specialty items were not addressed with the Kanban system at this time. The team had to conduct several PDCA experiments to get the system to function properly, but once the team found the correct levels of inventory to maintain with Kanban signals, stock-outs were virtually eliminated. As a side benefit, with a better established ordering system, purchasing was able to reduce the costs on the per item basis by an average of 7%!

The Retail Sales team also began to use daily scoreboards and other visual management techniques to display their real-time performance in each store. They were able to increase sales by engaging potential customers to help them achieve their daily goals by buying products with more special offering and close-out sales. This added another level of excitement and accomplishment for both the customer and the employee.

Adventures and Event Planning

The Adventures and Event Planning team greatly improved their customer satisfaction levels by providing better, more accurate communications to their customers. Instead of having customers continually check-in to determine the status of the rental equipment, the team established a visual control board to graphically display the current and expected equipment availability. The team also worked to establish a color-coded board to identify the schedule for use. Customers, once given a color to watch, could tell at a glance when it was their turn with the equipment.

This was well received by the customers. By sticking to the visual board schedule, the team also found that the equipment got returned closer to on-time than ever before. By increasing the turns per day, the team raised the daily sales revenue targets.

The team also began to work closer with their local adventure outfitters. It was felt that if they standardized their processes around the resort schedules and fill rates, they could increase their sales and improve the overall experience for the resort guests. By developing a standardized scheduling process, the team was able to increase sales revenue by over 15%!

Grounds and Maintenance

The Grounds and Maintenance team had perhaps the greatest opportunity for improvement; however, they resisted the Lean Sigma improvement initiative at first, claiming that they were too busy. (Being too busy to improve is not acceptable in a Lean Sigma transformation.) With management support, encouragement, and a bit of pressure, Doug was able to get to the improvement items needed. Doug and the Grounds and Maintenance team used the Lean Sigma tool of Total Productive Maintenance to initiate improvements in their area. The first step for their team was to collect failure data and analyze why the failures were occurring and on what pieces of equipment in order to understand the pattern. They established Frequency and Check Sheets to collect data, and then presented the data in Pareto Chart format to determine their biggest problems and priorities.

The team used the data and analysis to prioritize improvement action items. They prioritized critical business items first and customer-related items second. They began to implement a preventative maintenance program that called for proactive maintenance activities such as periodic inspections and check-ups on critical items such as guest room equipment (e.g., televisions and remote controls, coffee makers, bathroom fixtures, etc.). This took a while to implement and was very difficult to do as they were continuing to fight fires. Doug lobbied for and received additional temporary resources to keep the plan moving forward.

The team continues to make improvements and has greatly reduced their crisis management mode of operation. They now feel more in control of the maintenance process. The guests have noticed the impact as well, as indicated on the customer survey feedback scores and customer complaints. Customer complaints due to maintenance issues have been reduced by 80%!

Administration

The Accounting and Purchasing team took on the process of Purchase Requisition through Payment process and found a great deal of opportunity and waste. They found several occasions where multiple and redundant approvals were required, with no specific criteria. This was confusing to the workers and created several stops and starts in the process. The approval process was streamlined and the team was able to cut the average time from requisition to order by 50%! One of the tools used to do this was the Lean Sigma tool of cell design and co-location of resources.

The team also worked with their suppliers to reduce the paperwork required for order processing. When possible, orders were emailed to reduce the use of paper and ink. This was done at essentially no cost to anyone, yet saved TBR&M over $85 per month.

Perhaps the greatest improvement for this team came through co-location and cell design. By co-locating the buyers with accounts payable, the coordination of requisition and order approvals cut several redundant steps from the process. Additionally, the co-location allowed better communication for discount options. The negotiations for discounts improved as the cell team worked on buying and payment issues together. The co-location and cell design also reduced their errors in the process to 6 sigma levels!

Transformation Summary and Next Steps

After six months of Lean Sigma efforts, Tom and the Leadership team had realized some significant improvements, and learned a lot about their processes and the impact that Lean Sigma methods and tools can have on organizational performance. Tom and Becky had also provided many learning opportunities for all employees, such as lunch-and-learns, Ten-Minute training sessions, day seminars and workshops, in-house success story telling, and Lean Sigma reading materials, so as to increase the awareness and knowledge of Lean Sigma methods and tools throughout the organization.

As Tom and the team continued to study Lean Sigma transformations, they knew that the work never ended and that their next step was to start at the beginning again with conducting the Lean Sigma for Service Excellent Assessment and Gap Analysis and compare it to the previous one. Tom expected that there would be improvements in the assessment scores, but he also knew there would be a lowest score area or gap to work on.

At this point, Tom and the Leadership team were initiating new Lean Sigma projects based on the monthly review of the KPIs. This was now a standard procedure for the Leadership team. Tom knew too that after the next Lean Sigma Assessment, they would probably kick-off a project or two to address the gaps. Tom felt in control and confident that continuous improvement would be a way of work at Treasure Bay Resort & Marina. Tom no longer longed for the "Good ol' days," as he knew the future Lean Sigma ways would far exceed his expectations.

The scoreboard results on the next page are from the six month launch of the Lean Sigma projects and yielded the following improvements.

Treasure Bay Resort & Marina Key Measures					
Category	**Measure**	**Goal**	**Initial State (Before)**	**After Improvement Projects**	**Area**
Customer Focus	Customer Satisfaction Survey Response Rate	> 70%	60%	74%	Tom Green
	Customer Satisfaction Survey Scores	> 80%	76%	92%	Tom Green
	New Offerings	> 10 items	2	25	Tom Green
	Number of people using equipment & facilities	Increasing	Decreasing		All areas
Financial Focus	Sales Revenue - by area	$321K per Mo	$225K	$250K	Tom Green
	Profit	> 25%	10%	10%	Tom Green
	Return On Investment	> 20%	8%	10%	Tom Green
	EBITA	> 10%	4%	6%	Tom Green
	Performance to Budget	At or below budget	5% over	At budget	Tom Green
	Average room sell price	> $200	$185	$210	Guest Services
	Expenses				All areas
	Room bookings for events	> 30 per Mo	25	28	Adventures and Event planning
Productivity Focus	Sales Revenue per Employee	$32K/Emp.	$20K	$22K	Tom Green
	Sales Revenue per Operating Costs	> 2 times	2	2.3	Tom Green
	Room Fill Rates	> 70%	62%	75%	Guest Services
	Cleaned by 3pm	100%	95%	100%	Housekeeping
	Repair Work Orders per week	< 5 per day	10 per day	8 per day, plus 5 PMs per day	Grounds and Maintenance
	Days per purchase requisition to purchase order	< 3 days	5-7 days unless rushed	2.2 days	Accounting & Purchasing
Quality Focus	Customer Complaints	< 5 per week	6 per week	4 per week	Tom Green and all areas
	Repeat Visits	> 3 per week	1 per week	1 per week. Too early to tell	Tom Green
	Percent Fill Rate - Resort & Marina	> 75%	64%	70%	Tom Green
	Errors and Corrections per week	Minimal	Not Counted	3 per week	Accounting and Purchasing
Delivery Focus	Commitments met per schedule or plan	> 95%	90%	95%	Tom Green
	Dining schedule of operation	By plan	Rigid	Flexible	Food Service
	Product availability	No goal	10+ stock-outs per month	2 stock-outs per month	Retail Sales
	Time to complete work order	No goal	3-5 days, unless emergency	Same day	Grounds and Maintenance
People Focus	Absenteeism per day	< 1%	3%	1%	Tom Green
	Injuries	0	0	0	Tom Green
	Training Hours	4 / Emp./ Mo	~ 1 hr/Mo	4/ Emp./ Mo	Tom Green
	Internal Promotions	75%	100%	98%	Tom Green
	Teamwork	No goal	No measure	Improving	All areas
	Improved Planning	No goal	No measure	Improving	Grounds and Maintenance
	Frustration Level - Absenteeism	No goal	No measure	Improving	All areas

Chapter Summary

This chapter chronicles how the Treasure Bay Resort & Marina (TBR&M) progressed through a Lean Sigma transformation. From the initial learning of the term Lean Sigma in an article, Tom Green, the General Manager at the TBR&M, leads his team through the steps of a Lean Transformation. Key milestones discussed in this chapter are the initial Lean Sigma for Service Excellence Assessment and Gap Analysis, Lean Sigma project launches, Policy Deployment, and completing the first DMAIC improvement cycle for multiple improvement teams. Finally, this chapter outlines several keys to Lean Sigma transformations.

This chapter is designed as an example and guide for leaders of service organizations to follow in their pursuit of transforming their organizations to a Lean Sigma focus.

Lean Sigma for Service Excellence Applications

These applications may assist in understanding how to apply the concepts and tools contained in this chapter:

- Update your organization's vision, mission, and values, if you have them, if not, create them.
- Consider the best way to create leadership interest in Lean Sigma transformation, methods, and tools, and then begin the learning process.
- Gather a small team and document the perceived barriers to initiating a Lean Sigma transformation. Consider how to reduce or eliminate the barriers.
- Define the Key Performance Indicators for your organization, area, or department. Consider how these KPIs link upward to higher level KPIs.
- Identify training materials to use in your organization's Lean Sigma learning.
- Identify what critical resources would be needed to launch a Lean Sigma transformation in your organization.
- Gather a small team and discuss how your organization demonstrates their total system, process, and result focus. Consider what would be needed to improve the organization's total system, process, and result focus.
- Gather a small team to discuss how to improve employee involvement at your organization.
- Investigate more formal methods for Policy Deployment.

Pursuing Perfect Service

Appendix

Appendix

Lean Sigma for Service Excellence Assessment and Gap Analysis

Background

This assessment is based on a Plan, Do, Check, Act (PDCA) Improvement cycle. The questions are based on The Malcolm Baldrige Award Criteria and are the key ingredients to ensure your organization is enabled to deliver service excellence. It should also be used for discussion to more narrowly focus improvement efforts. It is recommended you create a similar-type assessment in Microsoft Excel. It is also available as a customizable worksheet at http://theleanstore.com/elean-etools.php and contains all the information that is presented in this example assessment contained on the next few pages.

Completing the Assessment

The leader and team members should complete the assessment individually or as a team. Rate each statement according to the five-level Likert scoring scale below.

1 Strongly Disagree
2 Disagree
3 Neither Agree nor Disagree
4 Agree
5 Strongly Agree

Review and Action

Compile averages, document comments and determine common themes/issues. Use brainstorming, 5 Why Analysis, Cause and Effect Diagram, etc. for further investigation into the lower scoring categories and statements. Develop an Action Plan to address any areas that require attention to improve the overall performance culture.

Scoring Guidelines

An average score of < 2 indicates that the organization is weak in this area and steps need to be taken immediately to improve performance.
An average score between 2 and 3 indicates that the organization is making some progress in these categories but more work needs to be done.
An average score of between 3 and 4 indicates that the organization is making good progress in these areas and should continue to improve.
An average score between 4 and 5 indicates that the organization is performing well in these areas and should be encouraged to continue to do so.

Section 1 Leadership		**Score (1-5)**
Vision	Leadership has defined and communicated a clear vision and is committed to promoting service excellence.	2
Planning	Service excellence is regularly discussed at our strategic planning meetings.	1
Resources	Adequate resources are continuously assigned for achieving service excellence.	2
Objectives	We have a good balance of attainable and stretch goals.	1
Accountability	We have process owners that are held accountable for performance measurements.	1
Average		**1.4**

Your Team's Score >>>>	1 Strongly Disagree	2 Disagree
		To get to the next level in Leadership,
Vision	Participatively define and document the vision for the organization or team, and then communicate the results to all organization or team members. Review Chapter 3 to understand why a vision is critical for success.	Participatively review and update the vision as needed, then develop a communications plan to clearly communicate the vision to every member of the organization.
Planning	Add an Agenda Item for service excellence discussions. Develop an innovative way to communicate to and reward all organization members for items or activities that bring the organization closer to service excellence.	Add an Agenda Item for service excellence discussions. Regularly discuss items or activities that bring the organization closer to service excellence, and items and actions that take the organization further away from service excellence.
Resources	Consider the organization or teams resource allocation planning methods. Develop a systematic method if one does not exist. Discuss openly realistic resource plans. Use historical data to help reach agreements.	Use historical data to help reach agreements. Communicate the method to all levels of the organization, and develop measures to monitor the success of the methods. Work for continuous improvement in predictability and accuracy.
Objectives	Participatively develop and communicate regular and stretch goals for all members and levels of the organization.	Participatively develop and communicate regular and stretch goals for all members and levels of the organization. If balance is the issue, develop additional attainable and stretch goals to stimulate improvements.
Accountability	Participatively assign process owners and develop a method of accountability.	Participatively review process owner assignments and responsibilities. Establish a means to consistently hold process owners accountable.

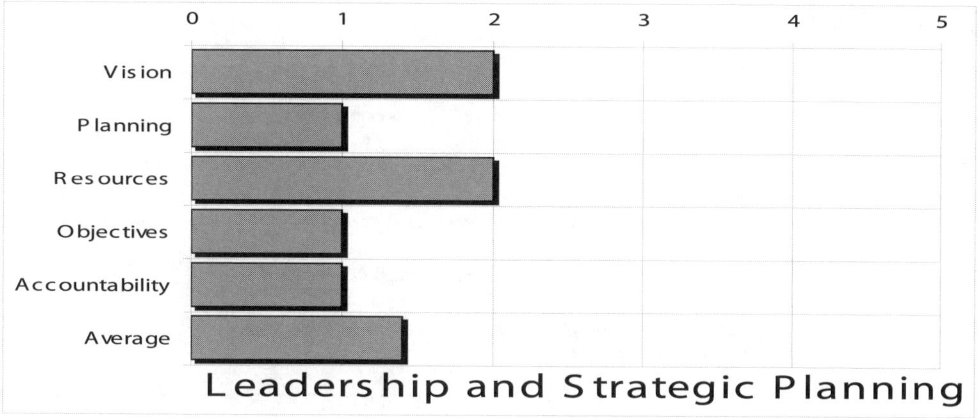

3 Neither Agree nor Disagree	4 Agree	5 Strongly Agree
consider doing the following.		
Participatively review and update the vision as needed, then develop a communications plan to clearly communicate the vision to every member of the organization.	Participatively review and update the vision as needed, then develop an innovative plan to help every member of the organization bring the vision into their everyday work.	Participatively review and update the vision as needed, then develop an innovative action plan to help every member of the organization bring the vision into their everyday work.
Add an Agenda Item for discussions. Develop an innovative way to communicate to and reward all organization members for items or activities that bring the organization closer to service excellence.	Add an Agenda Item for discussions. Develop an innovative way to communicate to and reward all organization members for items or activities that bring the organization closer to service excellence.	Develop an innovative way to communicate and reward all organization members for items or activities that bring the organization closer to service excellence. Challenge each employee to improve every minute of every day!
Communicate the method to all levels of the organization, and develop measures to monitor the success of the methods. Work for continuous improvement in predictability and accuracy.	Develop feed forward systems to continually review and improve resource allocation and performance. Visually communicate the plan and results to all members of the organization through visual performance management scoreboards.	Visually communicate the plan and results to all members of the organization through visual performance management scoreboards. Strive to reduce resource requirements through new and innovative ways.
Develop a performance management program to monitor and hold people accountable for working to goals. If balance is the issue, develop additional attainable and stretch goals to stimulate improvements.	Develop a visual performance management program to monitor and hold people accountable for working to goals. If balance is the issue, develop additional attainable and stretch goals to stimulate improvements.	Develop a visual performance management program and work to self-monitoring, improvement and accountability for achieving goals. Participatively develop additional stretch goals in all areas of the organization.
Establish and deploy innovative rewards for success and action plans for under performance. Establish a means to consistently hold process owners accountable.	Regularly review process owner assignments and responsibilities and adjust as needed. Communicate clearly and make visible through performance scoreboards, the process owner assignments and accountability methods.	Establish and deploy innovative rewards for success, and aggressive action plans for under performance. Establish a means to stimulate an ongoing culture of responsibility, self-discipline and accountability.

Section 2 Customer Focus		Score (1-5)
Listening	My organization does a good job of listening and involving its customers.	3
Measures	Customer satisfaction measurements capture actionable information needed for improvement.	3
Benchmarking	My organization obtains and uses customer service information relative to competition and/or benchmarks.	2
Expectations	Customer satisfaction takes top priority at my organization.	5
Flexibility	My organization remains flexible to changing customer needs and expectations.	1
Equity	We practice fair and equitable business practices for our customers, shareholders, and employees.	1
Average		**2.5**

Your Team's Score >>>>	1 Strongly Disagree	2 Disagree
	To get to the next level in Customer Focus,	
Listening	Develop and implement methods to collect the voice of the customer input. Begin collecting and communicating customer feedback to all members of the organization.	Develop and implement more formalized methods to collect the voice of the customer input. Begin collecting and monitoring trends in customer feedback to all members of the organization.
Measures	Identify and begin to collect data regarding customer experience and preferences. If the current data is not in actionable forms, redevelop the customer measures so that they drive improvement.	If the current data is not in actionable forms, redevelop the customer measures so that they drive improvement.
Benchmarking	Develop an organizational plan to benchmark customer service measures against best in class customer service measures. Identify best in class benchmark data sources.	Begin to develop plans for improved customer service measures to achieve best in class levels of service.
Expectations	Reconsider the organizations priorities. Create and communicate to organization members, a new vision and mission statement that includes customer satisfaction and focus.	Define the organizations priorities to include customer satisfaction, and hold people accountable for their actions.
Flexibility	Reconsider the organizations priorities. Create and communicate to organization members, an expectation to be flexible to customer needs and expectations.	Develop flexibility options for team members to employ.
Equity	Discuss the needs and expectations of the customer, the employees, and the shareholders of the organization. Ask how each can receive a fair return for their investment.	If there are not fair or balanced benefits for each entity, ask why, and brainstorm for ways to improve an equitable balance of mutual benefits.

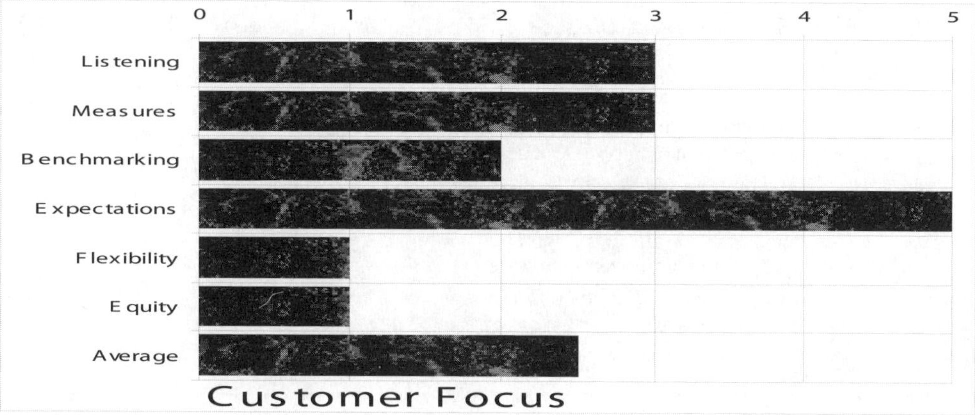

3 Neither Agree nor Disagree	4 Agree	5 Strongly Agree
consider doing the following.		
Develop a means for teams to use the voice of the customer feedback into improvement planning. Visually display voice of the customer data in key locations.	Develop improvement teams around improving voice of the customer feedback.	Create internal "fun" competitions for improvements. Focus on using the voice of the customer information to develop service excellence..
Implement a program or plan to have each organization member or team develop plans for improving customer related measures.	Implement a program or plan to have each organization member or team develop plans for improving customer related measures.	Create internal "fun" competitions for improvements. Focus on using the voice of the customer information to develop service excellence.
Consider improving communications plans for the use of benchmarking activities.	Consider improving communications plans for the use of benchmarking internal customer service information and activities.	Develop, communicate, and employ innovative ways to improve internal and external customer service performance.
Define the organizations priorities to include customer satisfaction, and hold people accountable for their actions.	Communicate the organizations priorities including customer satisfaction. Explain to people how they will be held accountable.	Create and implement an innovative communication plan to clearly define to organization members, the vision and mission that includes customer satisfaction.
Develop flexibility options for team members to employ.	Develop additional flexibility options for team members to employ.	Develop creative and innovative ways flexibility options for team members to employ.
Establish measures for each entity and communicate regularly the balance,	Develop and share key measure data and information regarding fair and equitable benefits for the customer, the employee, and the shareholder. .	Develop and implement innovative friendly competitions to improve and expand the benefits for all.

Section 3 Process Management		Score (1-5)
Process Focus	My organization identifies its key service and delivery processes to achieve improved performance.	2
Measures	Performance measures are used for the control and improvement of service and delivery processes.	1
Efficiency	The processes that we use are smooth and work well.	2
Influence	Input from internal and external customers are incorporated into process improvement efforts.	1
Information	All necessary resources and information are available to do the work properly.	1
Variation	Process variation is understood and monitored at my organization.	1
Average		**1.3**

Your Team's Score >>>>	1 Strongly Disagree	2 Disagree
		To get to the next level in Process Management,
Process Focus	Discuss and identify the key service and delivery processes. Document and communicate the key processes in a standardized fashion to all employees.	Create visual flow or value stream maps to help communicate key processes.
Measures	Participatively define key measures for key business processes, and begin collecting performance data.	Consider posting key performance data in a scoreboard fashion in all work areas. Use statistical process control techniques to monitor and control performance measurements.
Efficiency	Use key process performance measures to track the efficiency of key processes.	Use key process performance measures to track the efficiency of key processes. Consider improved communications plans for performance measures and problem solving and improvements.
Influence	Develop a means to collect internal and external customer input regarding process performance and improvement needs.	Report internal and external customer feedback on scoreboards for everyone to observe and understand.
Information	Begin a process to identify required resources for key business processes.	Begin a process to identify required resources for key business processes. Define, document and communicate the required resources for key business processes to all employees.
Variation	Consider training and education sessions on process variation and statistical process control.	Consider training and education sessions on process variation and statistical process control. Implement statistical process control techniques in key areas of the organization.

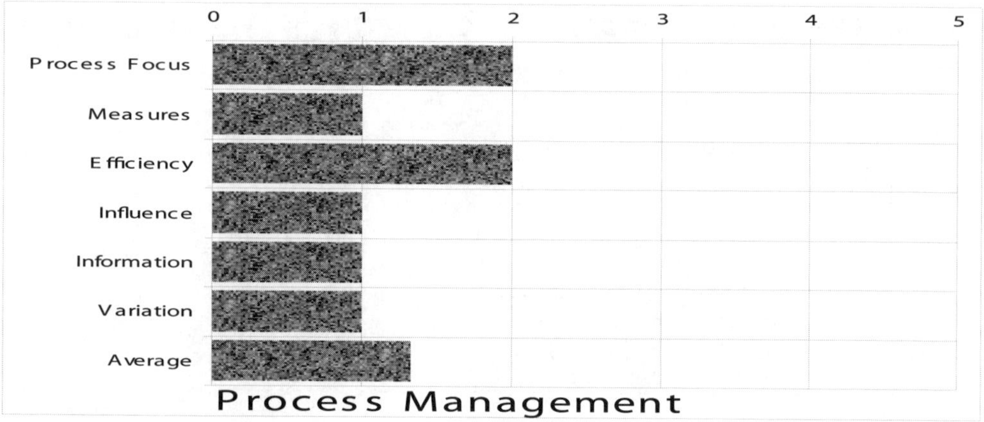

3 Neither Agree nor Disagree	4 Agree	5 Strongly Agree
consider doing the following.		
Create visual or value stream flow maps to help communicate key processes. Consider other creative means to communicate the key business processes.	Sponsor a friendly competitive process to define and document key processes in more areas.	Consider other creative means to communicate the key business processes.
Conduct regular work sessions to review performance measures and results.	Conduct regular work sessions to review performance measures and results.	Assign individuals or teams to each performance measure, and conduct problem solving and improvement initiatives to provide continuous improvement
Consider improved communications plans for performance measures and problem solving and improvements. Use problem solving teams to address under performing processes.	Use problem solving teams to address under performing processes. Use story boards and public scoreboards to show progress and improvements.	Use Storyboards and public scoreboards to show progress and improvements. Standardize the approach to monitoring and improvement of key processes.
Assign individuals or teams to respond to internal and external customer feedback.	Assign individuals or teams to respond to internal and external customer feedback. Initiate improvement teams to improve internal and external customer satisfaction.	Communicate improvements and try to share them across organizational areas. Develop an appropriate reward program for improvements.
Define, document and communicate the required resources for key business processes to all employees. Ensure required resources are provided.	Ensure required resources are provided. Consider establishing a measurement to illuminate when key resources are not available.	Consider using Lean Sigma methods and tools to ensure seamless resources replenishment.
Implement statistical process control techniques in key areas of the organization. Conduct regular process variation review sessions.	Assign individuals or teams to specific process control charts, and hold them accountable for improvements, and the education of other teams.	Consider Storyboarding performance measures and improvements.

Section 4 People Management		Score (1-5)
Safety	Leaders demonstrate that the safety of people is of paramount importance.	3
Training	People's training and development needs are openly discussed and followed through on.	2
Development	Leadership creates an encouraging and motivating environment and helps people reach their full potential.	3
Obstacles	People can openly identify obstacles/problems and seek help in finding solutions.	3
Accountability	Our performance management system supports and rewards high performance.	2
Being Valued	People are treated as valued employees, where short and long term needs are met.	2
Average		**2.5**

Your Team's Score >>>>	1 Strongly Disagree	2 Disagree
	To get to the next level in People Management,	
Safety	Develop and understanding through education and training regarding safety implications in the workplace. .	Developed improved communication plans to reinforce the importance of safety in the work place.
Training	Participatively develop and document a training and development plan for each employee. If this is complete, begin devoting the resources to implement the training plan.	Consider tracking progress and improvement in a training matrix.
Development	Define the current state environment and document potential improvements. Discuss specific actions leadership could implement to create a encouraging environment.	Discuss specific actions leadership could implement to create a encouraging environment. Develop an improvement plan and begin implementation.
Obstacles	If employees are intimidated or fear bringing up bad news, leadership must reexamine their view of problems or barriers.	Examine why the score is low in this category, and develop appropriate action plans. Communicate and educate all employees regarding how to identify problems and how to seek help.
Accountability	If a performance management system does not exist, develop and implement one. If the rewards are counter productive, participatively develop an improved reward system.	Communicate clearly the performance management system to all employees.
Being Valued	Develop and understanding through education and training regarding developing mutual respect. Consider revisiting the organizational values, and hold leaders accountable.	Determine specific activities and behaviors that will demonstrate treating people with respect and appreciating their value.

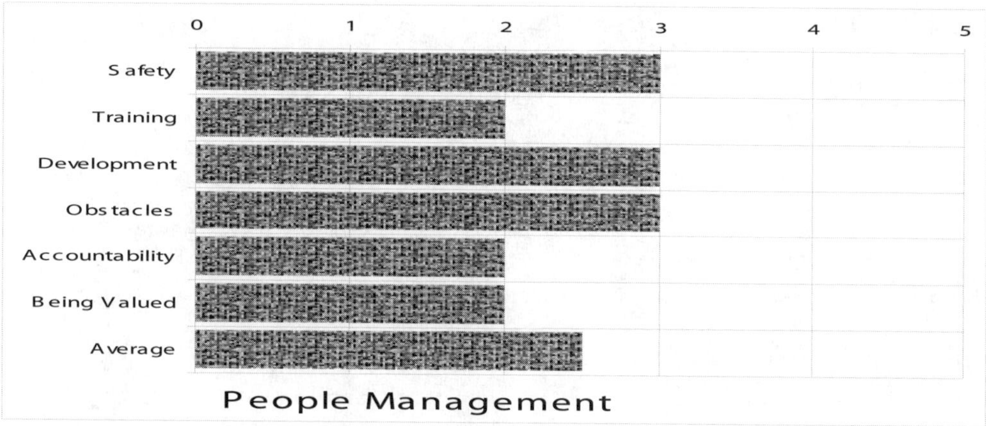

3 Neither Agree nor Disagree	4 Agree	5 Strongly Agree
consider doing the following.		
Assign teams of workers to educate and communicate all employees regarding the importance of safety in the work place.	Conduct regular safety reviews and monitor safety performance measurements.	Consider increasing safe working rewards and benefits to stress importance of safety in the work place.
Consider sharing or communicating the training matrix publicly, and continue to work to implement the training and development plans.	Consider additional reward programs to support training and development improvements as the new skill, knowledge or ability is employed at work.	Consider additional reward programs to support training and development improvements as the new skill, knowledge or ability is employed at work.
Develop an improvement plan and begin implementation. Develop a communications plan, and a means to get constructive feedback from employees.	Develop a communications plan, and a means to get constructive feedback from employees. Develop development plans for each employee, and help everyone make improvements.	Implement improved incentive programs to stimulate improvement and involvement.
Communicate and educate all employees regarding how to identify problems and how to seek help. Develop a systematic approach to problem identification.	Document and educate everyone on the systematic approach to problem identification and improvement.	Track or monitor problems and improvement initiatives to stimulate ideas in other areas.
Communicate clearly the performance management system to all employees. Ensure the performance management system is fair an balanced, and based on data, not opinion.	Develop an improvement team to evaluate and make improvements to the performance reward systems. .	Establish a regular review of the performance reward systems. Make this part of standard work processes.
Implement specific action plans to improve this area. Measure progress.	Support improvement with an appropriate reward system. Conduct events to show appreciation and value.	Say thank you to people for a job well done. Teach others these values.

Section 5 Information and Analysis		**Score (1-5)**
Information	My organization makes every effort to ensure data and information are appropriate, accurate, and reliable.	2
Monitoring	There is a system in place to monitor organizational progress against set objectives or goals.	1
Visibility	The monitoring system is clear and visible to all of the organization (e.g., scoreboards).	3
Decisions	It is clear to people how we use organizational level analysis to improve decision-making.	1
Challenge	People are responsible to question and/or challenge the status quo.	3
Improvement	There is an effective process to incorporate positive improvement ideas into the business plan.	2
Average		**2.0**

Your Team's Score >>>>	**1 Strongly Disagree**	**2 Disagree**
		To get to the next level in Information and Analysis
Information	Discuss specific data and information that is suspect or subjective, and develop plans to improve data collection and representation.	Determine areas to improve the communication of where and how data and information is collected and/or presented. Discuss how to improve the integrity of the information at the organization.
Monitoring	Participatively establish Key Performance Indicators for specific areas of the organization.	Ensure people know how their work impacts the Key Performance Measures.
Visibility	Discuss how to make the key performance measures visible and available to all. Seek to understand why people do not believe the information is available.	Implement standard methods in all areas for monitoring the key measures.
Decisions	If organizational data is used in decision-making, but it is not clear to people how this is done, initiate an in house training program or class to illustrate how this is done in the organization.	Define several case examples where organizational level analysis is used to improve decision-making, and present this information to employees.
Challenge	Develop and understanding regarding why this is not currently the case. Ask for specific examples to better understand the issues. Most importantly, leaders must be seen challenging the status quo.	Discuss and develop plans and means for people to challenge the status quo. Communicate the plans and means to all employees.
Improvement	Participatively develop a method for improvement ideas to be incorporated into the business plan.	Implement the business plan, and review the results on a regular basis. Train people on how to use the system for improvement ideas.

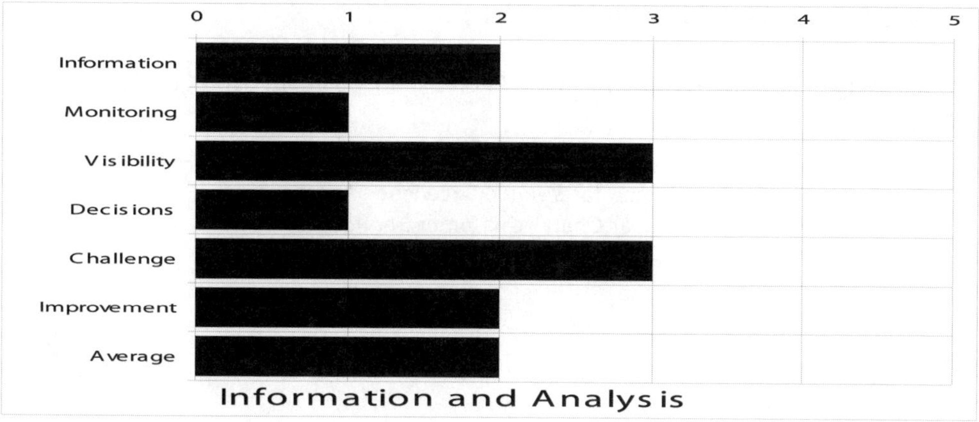

3 Neither Agree nor Disagree	4 Agree	5 Strongly Agree
consider doing the following.		
Develop an orientation class for the organization that teaches people to understand the company data and information. Do not assume people understand.	Get employees involved in teaching other employees.	Get employees involved in teaching other employees. Reward and support rigorous data collection and information sharing.
Assign individuals or teams to be responsible and \accountable to each Key Performance Indicator.	Monitor on a regular basis the Key Performance Indicators. Develop countermeasures for under performing areas, and rewards for achievement.	Develop countermeasures for under performing areas, and rewards for achievement.
Have experienced employees present and teach less experienced employees about the monitoring system.	Develop standard methods of reporting key measures such as area scoreboards.	Standardize scoreboards in all areas. Hold people accountable for improving performance results.
Continue to educate people as to how organizational level analysis is used to improve decision-making.	Develop a means to make the organizational decision-making process transparent and obvious at all levels of the organization. Consider developing standard decision matrixes.	Develop a means to make the organizational decision-making process transparent and obvious at all levels of the organization.
Develop a reward system for successful improvement initiatives developed by challenging the status quo. Communicate success stories and examples to all employees.	Establish and monitor key measures for new ideas.	Develop standard work methods for after action reviews and improvement initiatives. Hold individuals and groups accountable. Reward accordingly.
Train people on how to use the system for improvement ideas. Implement a reward system for approved and implemented improvement ideas.	Hold people responsible and accountable for participating in the program.	Build the improvement idea system into the regular individual and team performance review system. Hold people accountable for improvement results.

Example Assessment Radar and Bar Chart

The following Radar Chart represents the example assessment average scores for each category.

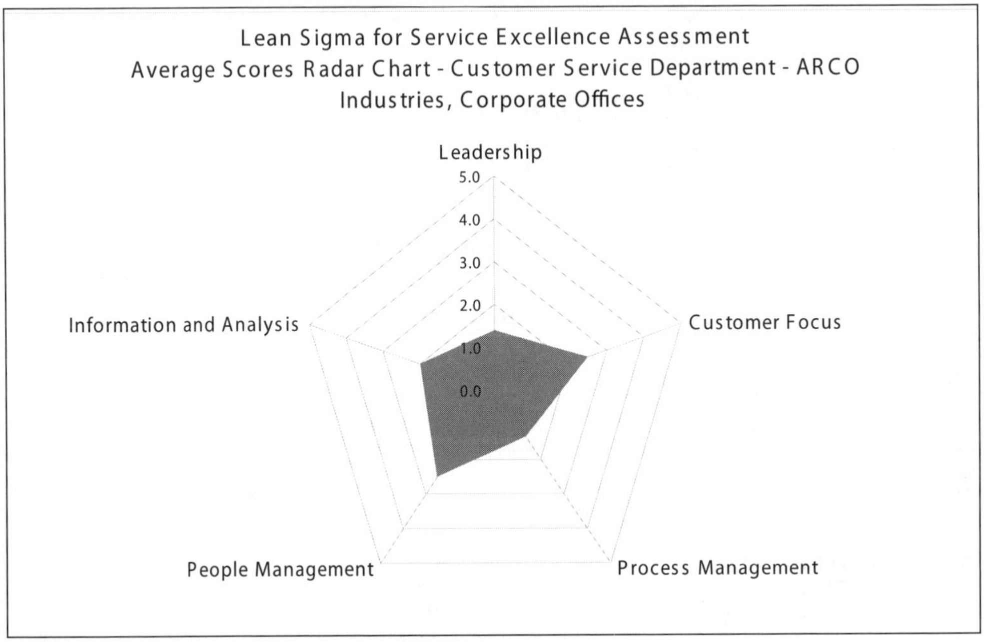

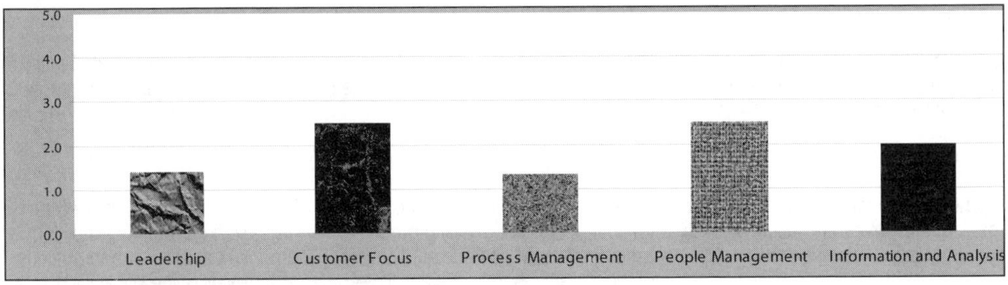

Summary	Average Score
Leadership	1.4
Customer Focus	2.5
Process Management	1.3
People Management	2.5
Information and Analysis	2.0

Example Assessment Subsequent Analysis

This example assessment denotes that Leadership at 1.4 and Process Management at 1.3 being the lower scoring categories, which would require a more detailed look at the specific statements of:

Leadership: with scores of 1

Service excellence is regularly discussed at our strategic planning meetings.
We have a good balance of attainable and stretch goals.
We have process owners that are held accountable for performance measurements.

Process Management: with scores of 1

Performance measures are used for the control and improvement of service and delivery processes.
Input from internal and external customers are incorporated into process improvement efforts.
All necessary resources and information are available to do the work properly.
Process variation is understood and monitored at my organization.

Subsequent discussion with the team and using the Improvement Guide, as well as knowing other business factors, would then have the team determine specific actions to address those lower scoring areas.

Glossary

5S - is a process to ensure physical or electronic work areas are systematically kept clean and organized, assuring employee safety in meeting customer expectations while providing the foundation on which to build a Lean Sigma organization.

Act - the standardization of the improvements after the Check step of the PDCA improvement cycle.

Action Item (AI) Log - used by the team to assign and follow-up on specific actions items agreed to during the project.

Attribute data - a numerical quality that assumes only two values: good or bad, pass or fail, etc. and is measured by counting the frequency of items matching the condition.

Baby Boomer Generation - the second oldest generation in the workforce and these people were born between 1946 and 1964.

Basic process maps (macro level) - identifies all the major steps in a process - usually no more than six steps. They are mostly used for the 30,000 foot view for management review.

Basic process maps (micro level) - examines the process in detail and indicates all the steps or activities that would include the decision points, waiting periods, tasks that frequently must be redone (rework), and any feedback loops.

Bin numbers - numerical values used to represent the intervals in the Histogram tool to use for measuring the input data.

Brainstorming - a technique used to generate a high volume of ideas with team members' full participation that is free of criticism within a 5 - 15 minute time period.

Cause and Effect Diagram - a graphical display of all the possible causes of the problem. Also known as a Fishbone Diagram.

Check - the verification of the Do implementation step of the PDCA improvement cycle.

Check Sheets - a method in which to collect, organize, prioritize, and analyze data.

Constraint or Bottleneck analysis - the identification of the slowest process step in the product or service being provided.

Continuous flow - the movement of work or a service between processes with minimal or no queue time.

Control Chart - a tool used to determine whether a process is in a state of statistical control or not. Also referred to as a Statistical Process Control Chart, Shewhart Chart, or Process-Behavior Chart.

Cyber Generation - the newest generation to be coming in the workforce, born after 1999.

Defect waste - refers to all processing required in creating a defect and the additional work required to correct a defect.
Define Phase - the initial determination of purpose of the improvement, resources required, and a plan.
Demand Analysis techniques - methods used to understand the pace of customer demand.
Deployment process maps - the visual representation of a process in terms of who is doing the steps. It is conveyed in the form of a matrix, showing the various participants and the flow of steps among these participants.
DMAIC (Define - Measure - Analyze - Improve – Control) - a five step statistical-based problem solving and improvement methodology commonly referred to as the DMAIC Phase (or process).
Do - the implementation step of the PDCA improvement cycle.

Effective meetings - the efficient and timely organizational communication for a group of people for issues to be discussed, priorities to be set, and decisions to be made.
Environmental waste - any output of a process that negatively impacts the environment.

Facilitator - a person that ensures that everyone attending the meeting stays on task and participates.
Failure Prevention Analysis - a technique that allows the team to anticipate potential problems in the solution before implementing it, permitting the team to be proactive to prevent the solution(s) from going wrong.
Frequency Charts - a method by which to collect, organize, prioritize, and analyze data.

Gantt Chart - a graphical representation of project tasks, sequence, relationships, and time required.
Generation Xers - the people born between 1965 and 1980.
Generation Y (Millenials) - the youngest working generation in the workforce; born between 1981 and 1999.

Histograms - a method by which to display the spread and shape of the distribution of data.

Impact Map - a method by which a team can identify the solutions that will most likely have the greatest impact on the problem with the least effort.
Interrelationship Diagram - an analysis tool that allows a team to understand and identify the cause-and-effect relationships among critical issues.
Inventory waste - excessive piles of paperwork, computer files, supplies and time spent searching for a document.
Is/Is Not analysis - a method to help define the scope of the problem before any resources are committed.
Issues and Opportunities (IO) Log - a log developed by improvement teams to identify and document opportunities, ideas, issues, concerns, obstacles, roadblocks, and/or other items that the team is not quite sure what to do about.

Kanban - a card or visual indicator that serves as a means of communicating to an upstream process precisely what is required at the specified time.
Key Metric and Data Profile tool - a method to assist the team to consider and determine the key data that will need to be collected.

Lean - the tools and concepts derived from the Toyota Production System that minimizes and eliminates waste using Total Employee Involvement (TEI) and a common-sense approach.
Lean Sigma for Service Excellence Assessment and Gap Analysis - a list of statements within five categories that will help assure alignment, open communications regarding issues and problems, and provide a perspective on where the organization needs to focus resources.
Lean Sigma - the combination of the customer-focused efforts of Lean and waste elimination with the quantitative methodology of Six Sigma.
Leveling flow - a concept that enables service organizations to smooth and balance the flow of tasks to better serve their clients.

Mass customization - a concept that combines the low costs of mass production processes with the variable output required to meet individual client needs.
Matures (Traditionalist, Veterans, and Silent) Generation - the oldest generation in the workforce and these people were born between 1925 and 1945.
Measure Phase - a full and thorough documentation of the customer needs or market demand for the process being improved as a continuation of the Define Phase.
Mission Statement - a basic statement of the identity of an organization and its purpose or mission.

Mistake proofing - a concept, device, and/or system designed to ensure that it is impossible to make a mistake or produce a defect.
Motion waste - any movement of people, paper, and/or electronic exchanges that does not add value.

Opportunity process maps - the visual representation of the activities that comprise the process and lists differences between value-added and non value-added activities.
Overburdening (or overloading) waste - the unknown capacity or non-productive scheduling of a process.
Overprocessing waste - putting more work or effort into the work required by internal or external customers.
Overproduction waste - producing some type of work prior to it being required.

Paced Flow (or Heijunka) processing - used where customer demand requests are done on a regular or timed schedule or sequence.
Pareto Chart - a bar chart format that represents the Pareto principle.
Pareto principle - refers to 20% of the sources cause 80% of the problems.
Performance Dashboard (or Balanced Scorecard) - a visual aid that translates the organization's strategy into objectives, metrics, initiatives, and tasks customized to each group and individual in an organization.
Performance Management - the process of establishing desired performance outcomes or goals, monitoring progress to goals through measurements, and then taking action to ensure success.
Pitch - the adjusted takt time that establishes an optimal and smooth workflow throughout the value stream.
Pivot Table - a generic term used for a specific type of spreadsheet function where key data is compared and 'pivoted" to a new table for analysis.
Plan - the define step of the PDCA improvement cycle that determines what will be done, who will do it, and how it will be measured.
Plan-Do-Check-Act (PDCA) - an iterative four-step problem-solving process typically used in business process improvement.
Policy Deployment - a methodology to consistently establish, align, communicate, and measure the progress of an organization in achieving their strategic objectives and mission.
Process map (or flowchart) - a visual representation of a series of operations (tasks, activities) consisting of people, work duties, and transactions that occur in the delivery of a product or service.
Project Charter - a document that defines the high level objectives and expectations for an improvement project team.

Project management - the process of establishing, prioritizing, and carrying out tasks to complete specific objectives.
Project Planner (PP) - a project planning, tracking, and management tool used by improvement teams to identify and track the steps to complete the improvement project.

Qualify Function Deployment (QFD) - a tool that takes the Voice of the Customer information and turns it into specific and measurable quality requirements that can be used to design improved service processes.

Radar Chart - a graphical representation of the values for each listed category along a separate axis that starts in the center of the chart and ends on the outer ring. Also known as a Spider Chart or a Star Chart because of its appearance.
Rapid Improvement Events (RIEs) - targeted events conducted by improvement teams to implement improvements quickly in a specific area. Also referred to as Kaizen Events or Kaizen Blitzes.
Resource Flow Map - a value stream or process map that includes resource flows.
Resource Treasure Hunt - used to help people recognize and identify sources of resource consumption in their organization.
Run Chart - a graphical representation of serial data points over time.
Runner - someone that is dedicated to ensure takt time or pitch is maintained and makes service rounds at specified intervals to pick-up and deliver items.

Scatter (and Concentration) Plots - a graphical representation to study the possible relationship between one variable and another.
Scheduled flow - the method by which orders or demand is identified, and then scheduled for fulfillment at a specific time.
Scribe - the person who records the notes of the meeting; and/or the person who captures the group's thoughts on flip charts, white boards, or the laptop that is being projected on the wall or screen, etc.
Service - work performed for someone else's benefit or pleasure.
Set-In-Order - the part of the 5S step that involves arranging necessary items for easy and efficient access and keeping them that way.
Shine (or Scrub) - the part of the 5S step that involves cleaning everything, keeping everything clean, and using cleaning as a way to ensure all physical areas and electronic files and folders are maintained as they should be.
Sigma (σ) - the representation and mathematical symbol that defines the variation or "spread" of a process.
SIPOC Diagram - a tool used by a team to identify all relevant elements of a process improvement project or identified value stream to help ensure all aspects of the process are taken into consideration and that no key components are missing.

Six Sigma (as a business tool) - a structured, quantitative, five-phase approach to continuous improvement and problem solving.
SMART - an acronym related to goal setting that stands for S= Specific, M= Measurable, A= Assigned, R= Realistic, and T= Time-bounded.
Social waste - the excess time, energy, and resources used that contributes to poverty, injury, malnutrition, etc. as well as non-value added time spent on account of social media networking.
Sort - the part of the 5S step that involves sorting through the contents of workplace physical and electronic database areas and removing unnecessary items (papers, old manuals, out-dated files - both paper and electronic, etc.).
Spaghetti diagram process maps - a continuous line to trace the path of a part, document, person, or service that is being provided through all its phases.
Standard work - a method that establishes and controls the best way to complete a task without variation from the original intent.
Standard Work for leaders - the guide that prescribes specifics tasks, actions, and time frames for completion of work for a manager or supervisor.
Standardize - the part of the 5S step that involves creating guidelines for keeping the area and electronic files and folders organized, orderly, and clean, and making the standards visual and obvious.
Statistical Process Control - a group of tools used to control and monitor process outputs.
Storyboard - a poster-size framework for displaying all the key information from the Lean Sigma project.
Structured Brainstorming - a defined method in which each team member contributes his/her ideas in order until all ideas are exhausted.
Sustain - the part of the 5S step that involves education and communication to ensure that everyone uses the applicable standards.
Sustainability Metrics - measurements that help organizations identify, align, and focus on sustainability issues.

Takt time (or Service Rate) - defines the pace of repetitive customer demand.
Team champion - the person who has the authority to commit the necessary resources for the team.
Team Charter - the document that details the team structure, membership, overall objectives, measures, and resources required to be successful.
Team leader - the person responsible for the day-to-day or week-to-week running of the team.

Team member - the person who is responsible for keeping an open mind, being receptive to change, and contributing their ideas in a respectful manner.
Teaming - a group of individuals working together for a common cause or objective.
Technical representative (tech rep) - the person from IT (or someone with advanced computer application skills) who provides insights into technology tools available and/or makes the team aware of upcoming technology that may impact the team's mission.
Timekeeper - the person responsible for ensuring the scheduled times (start, stop, topics, etc.) are followed.
Total Productive Maintenance (TPM) - the tools, methods, and activities used to improve the machine or equipment availability time.
Transport waste - the excess movement of work to the next process.

Underutilization of people waste - the result of not placing people where they can (and will) use their knowledge, skills, and abilities to their fullest potential.
Unevenness waste - the lack of a consistent flow of inputs/information/scheduled work from upstream processes.
Unstructured Brainstorming - a method in which team members contribute their ideas as they occur (or come to mind) until all ideas are exhausted.

Value stream map - a visual representation of the material, work, and information flow, as well as the queue times between processes for a specific customer demand.
Variable data - data such as length, time, weight, etc. that is measured along a continuous scale of some type.
Vision Statements - the specific attributes and qualities that define the future identity of the organization.
Visual control - a technique employed whereby control of an activity or process is made easier or more effective by deliberate use of visual signals (signs, information displays, maps, layouts, instructions, alarms, and poka-yoke or mistake proofing devices).
Visual Management - a use of visual techniques that graphically displays relevant business performance data.
Voice of the Customer (VOC) - is a term and method used in business and Information Technology to describe the in-depth process of capturing a customer's expectations, preferences, and aversions.

Waiting waste - the time delay in expecting or delivering some type of work.
Waste - anything that does not add value.
Waste Walk - an activity when project team members visit a process area that is being considered for improvement, ask questions, and then identify the wastes on the current state value stream or process map.

Index

F

G

H

I

Notes

Notes

Notes

Notes

Notes

Notes

Notes

Best Selling Books from The Lean Store

Visit www.theleanstore.com to see these and other best selling books to assist you in your continuous improvement activities:

iLean - *21st Century Lean - Today's Improvement Methodologies for Increasing Office Productivity*
Lean Office Demystified II - *Using the Power of the Toyota Production System in Your Administrative, Desktop and Networking Environments*
The 5S Desktop (PC) Pocket Handbook - *Using the Power of the Toyota Production System (Lean) to Organize and Control Your Electronic Files and Folders*
The 5S for the Office User's Guide
The Lean Pocket Handbook for Kaizen Events - *Any Industry - Any Time*
The Lean Six Sigma Pocket Guide XL - *Combining the Best of Both Worlds Together to Eliminate Waste!*
The New Lean Healthcare Pocket Guide - *Tools for the Elimination of Waste in Hospitals, Clinics, and Other Healthcare Facilities*
The New Lean Healthcare Pocket Guide XL - *Tools for the Elimination of Waste in Hospitals, Clinics and Other Healthcare Facilities*
The New Lean Office Pocket Guide - *Tools for the Elimination of Waste in Paper-Based and Electronic Workflow Environments*
The NEW Lean Pocket Guide - *Tools for the Elimination of Waste*
The New Lean Pocket Guide (Spanish Edition) La Nueva Lean de Bolsillo (Produccion Lean)
The New Lean Pocket Guide XL - *Tools for the Elimination of Waste*
The Simply Lean Pocket Guide - *Making Great Organizations Better Through PLAN-DO-CHECK-ACT (PDCA) Kaizen Activities*
Today's Lean! *Learning About and Identifying Waste*
Today's Lean! *Using 5S to Organize and Standardize Areas and Files*
Value Stream Management for Lean Healthcare - *Four Steps to Planning, Mapping, Implementing, and Controlling Improvements in All Types of Healthcare Environments*

...plus many types of Lean training sets, games, eforms, and books in Spanish and Chinese!